GEOGRAPHY OF HEALTH

Also available

District Planning : A Handbook/ **R.P. Misra**
Environmental Ethics : A Dialogue of Cultures/ **R.P. Misra** (Ed.)
Fundamentals of Cartography/ **R.P. Misra** and **A. Ramesh**
Habitat Asia : Issues and Response **(Vol.1 : India)/ B.S. Bhooshan** and **R.P. Misra**
International Divisions of Labour and Regional Development/ **R.P. Misra** (Ed.)
Micro-Level Rural Planning : Principles, Methods and Case Studies/ **R.P. Misra** and **R.N. Achyutha**
Regional Planning: Concepts, Techniques, Policies and Case Studies/ **R.P. Misra**
Research Methodology : A Handbook/ **R. P. Misra**
Rural Development : Capitalist and Socialist Paths **(In 5 Vols.)/ R.P. Misra** (Ed.)
Conflict Resolution Through Non-Violence : Role of the Universities **(In Two Vols.) K.D. Gangrade** and **R. P. Misra**
Gandhian Alternative (In 5 Volumes)/ **General Editors Prof. R. P. Misra and Prof. K. D. Gangrade**
Gandhian Model of Development and World Peace/ **R.P. Misra** (Ed.)
Rediscovering Gandhi, Volume I—Hind Swaraj/ **R.P. Misra**

About the Author

Prof. R.P. Misra (*b.* 1930) is a geographer planner, institution builder and Gandhian scholar of great repute. Apart from being the chairman of the post-graduate department of Geography since 1965, he founded the Institute of Development Studies, University of Mysore in 1971 and remained its director until 1979. Moving over to the UN Centre for Regional Development, Nagoya Japan (1979-84), he brought the well-known ten-volume series on Regional Development. As Vice-Chancellor of the University of Allahabad, (1984-87), he made the University sit up again. After a 9-year tenure (1988-95) as Professor of Regional Planning at the Delhi School of Economics, Delhi University, he has been devoting his time to Gandhian studies. Most recently (2002-04), he was Mahatma Gandhi National Fellow of Gandhi Smriti & Darshan Samiti, New Delhi.

Professor Misra began his academic life as a social geographer; then he moved to the field of Development Planning and finally arrived at Gandhian Studies. Editor of Anasakti Darshan, an International Journal of Nonviolence-In-Action, he has authored and edited over 100 seminal books, contributed over 300 papers to reputed journals, worked as UN expert in over fifteen countries of Asia, Africa and Latin America, and continues to be in advisory panels of many government and non-government organizations

GEOGRAPHY OF HEALTH

A Treatise on Geography of Life and Death in India

R.P. MISRA

CONCEPT PUBLISHING COMPANY, NEW DELHI-110059

Cataloging in Publication Data—DK
Courtesy: D.K. Agencies (P) Ltd. <docinfo@dkagencies.com>

Misra, R. P.
Geography of health : a treatise on geography of life and death in India/ R.P. Misra.
p. cm.
Includes bibliographical references.
Includes index.

ISBN 8180693864 (P.B.)

1. Medical geography—India. 2. Public health —India.
I. Title.

DDC 614.425 4 22

ISBN 81-8069-385-6 (H.B.)
ISBN 81-8069-386-4 (P.B.)

First Published 2007

Published and Printed by

Concept Publishing Company
A/15-16, Commercial Block, Mohan Garden
New Delhi-110059 (INDIA)

Phones : 25351460, 25351794
Fax : 091-11-25357103
Email : publishing@conceptpub.com

Preface

My interest in The Geography of Health otherwise known as medical geography is old and abiding. My first major venture in this field was *Medical Geography of India* published by the National Book Trust, New Delhi in 1970. It was addressed to all those interested in health and its relationship with the physical, biological environment in which man lived. It was a general publication based on data pertaining to nineteen sixties. The book, however, received overwhelming response from public in general and geographers, medical professionals and social scientist in particular. It laid the foundation for a systematic study of geography of health in India. its shortcom8ings notwithstanding.

It is now almost thirty-five years since the publication of the first edition of Medical Geography of India. Since then, I have tried to revise and update it several times without much success. I took up this task again in 2001 and here is what I have been able to produce. The book, as its title indicates, is not the second edition of Medical Geography of India. It is a new book with a new ideas, new perspectives, new objectives and new data. Since the publication of Medical Geography of India in 1970, the health scenario in India has changed enormously; health information system has improved and general interest in health has grown. It is now possible to undertake more thorough and penetrating study in geographic dimensions of life and death.

Geography of Health is now being taught in most Indian universities and colleges at both graduate and post-graduate levels. It is also known as Geography of Health. In fact, its second title is more appropriate for the term 'medical' gives a restricted notion of diseases and their treatment. Health, on the other hand, connotes a much broader meaning. It is neutral term: it covers both good health and ill health. However, the two terms have been used interchangabley.

Geography of Health is a sub-field at the junction of Human Geography and Biogeography. Environmental Medicine taught in medical schools is a branch of Geography of Health and so is Social and Preventive Medicine. A fairly good number of students opt for doctoral research on problems related to spatial and environmental dimensions of health. These students and researchers have to depend on a very limited and discrete literature spread over many books and magazines for guidance. Many of them never get into the heart of the discipline; they conduct research on a limited problem without understanding the broader framework that might have given rise to the problem under investigation.

There is a definite need of a book that is comprehensive and incisive enough to meet the needs of the graduate students of geography on the one hand and researchers in such fields like social welfare, medical sociology, medical anthropology, health economics, environmental medicine and human development on the other. Their concerns and problems are linked to the issues and problems that fall within the domain of geography of health. This book is meant to serve this purpose.

There is another reason behind the publication of this book. As stated earlier, the health scenario has undergone phenomenal changes during the last three decades: both positively and negatively. Mortality rates have secularly declined; some of the dreaded diseases like smallpox have disappeared; health services, even if inefficient, have reached every nook and corner of the country; and the people are prepared to invest in health more than ever before. Infant and child mortality rates have come down rather drastically. Life expectancy at birth has doubled from 32 years in 1951 to 64 years in 2001. Food production in the country has gone up by more than four times since 1950. And hence the deficiency diseases, so common in the past, are no longer our chief concerns. Medical science has made great advances; it is now possible to transplant kidney and heart. Vaccines have strengthened preventive medicine. It is now possible to control and even eradicate the diseases, which once took millions of lives. And genetic research has opened up new frontiers in the understanding of human body and mind.

These welcome changes have, however, been accompanied by a series of negative developments forcing the national governments and international agencies to redouble their efforts to improve further the health scenario the world over. Rapid increase in population (from 300 million in 1951 to over 1000 million in 2001) has placed unbearable pressure on our resources, natural as well as man made. Fertility rates have remained much higher than mortality rates. Environment degradation has made life and living hazardous; pollution of soil, water, and air has given rise to a number of infectious and chronic diseases. Unprecedented urbanization and accompanying growth of slums has made living conditions stressful and precarious. Many of the great killers like malaria and tuberculosis, which appeared to be on the way out are on their come back trail. There is a lurking fear that even plague and smallpox may return with a bang. Deficiency diseases like anaemia are still common among the poorer sections of the society, especially among the women. Respiratory and water borne diseases are on the increase and so are the cardiovascular diseases, cancers, psychosomatic disorders and sexually transmitted diseases. Among the systemic disorders hypertension, diabetes, and mental derangements are posing serious problems for health planners. AIDS (Acquired Immuno Deficiency-Syndrome) is the latest in the list of new diseases. It is an outcome of growing sexual permissiveness in our society.

The concept of health too has changed enormously. It has come out of the orbit of bio-medical disciplines; its cultural, environmental and economic dimensions are no longer peripheral. The growing realization that augmenting health care facilities and more potent medicines alone would not help, has forced medical scientists to look beyond their narrow disciplines and venture in geographical and social disciplines too for the causes and remedies of diseases and ill-health; nor do better diagnostic methods and tools solve the problems of health. Health has to be seen holistically and it must become a part of life style. People must behave responsibly; they must treat their body and mind as biological phenomena rather than inanimate machines, which can be reproduced, repaired and replaced. It is not enough to find cures for diseases as and when they attack human body. Conditions that keep human body healthy; that make it immune from germs; and that prolong healthful longevity are the real answers. It is possible to live long and unhealthy. But if unhealthy longevity of life is going to be a norm, it will be counterproductive and would place unbearable economic and psychological burden on the individual and the society.

Health is thus inextricably linked with the quality of life and human development index. The United Nations Development Program (UNDP) brings out an annual report on the level of human development in the world. Health receives special attention in this exercise. Child mortality rate, life expectancy, availability of hospital beds, physicians, etc. constitute important components of human development indices. The World Development Report, 1997 was completely devoted to the health aspects of human development. And the World Health Organization brings out an annual report devoted to health and assists national governments in improving the health scenario in member countries. UNICEF in its own annual reports and other publications offers information on the welfare of mothers and children and directly participates in immunization and other programs launched globally. There are other global agencies, which devote resources on human development and health.

While the developed countries of the world have consistently improved the health situation with respect to classical major killers, most of the developing countries continue to lag behind. They face serious problems not only because of considerable backlog of the work to be done and huge population base but also because they are passing through a critical phase of epidemiological transition. They are still fighting the menace of communicable diseases, infant mortality, and lack of basic health facilities in rural areas. As the morbidity and mortality data and the vulnerability of women, children, aged, disabled and poor suggest, countries like India have to go a long way before they can win over some of the old scourges. At the same time, diseases symptomatic of developed societies have come with a bang.

Wide and at times growing regional disparities in the quantity and quality of medical services deny a large section of the people not only specialized services but also the most basic health facilities. While the major cities have much of what the developed parts of the world possess, the rural parts, where a majority of people live, are yet to get basic services. India formulated a National Health Policy in 1983 to correct the imbalances in health care. It focused on women and children living in rural areas and urban slums. As a follow up, a chain of primary health centers were established all over the country. A number of special programs for women and children were launched to immunize children of meningitis, tetanus, chicken pox, polio, etc. Lack of information, unwillingness of the medical professionals to go to remote rural areas, and the inability of the poorer sections of the society to use whatever services exist, have proved to be major stumbling blocks in the success of these programs. Nevertheless, their overall impacts have been positive. To fill the remaining gaps, the country has just promulgated a new Health Policy-2002 and a Health Mission in 2005.

Geography could not remain untouched and unconcerned with these developments. Geographers found clear correlation between environment and health. This growing concern gave rise to a body of geographic knowledge, which through time evolved into medical geography or geography of health. The roots of discipline go deep in the past. Bio-geographic knowledge has always helped man keep himself healthy All ancient systems of medicine treated man in relation to his natural environment. Diseases were considered as products of disharmony among man and vital environment on the one hand and between certain natural forces within the human body on the other.

Geography of Health tries to answer questions like: What is the state of health in different parts of the world? Who is sick of what, where and why? Why diseases are more common in some parts of the world than in other parts? What environmental factors (both natural and cultural) cause/promote various kinds of diseases? Do people have access to health facilities in adequate quantity and quality of health. If not, then how to locate them spatially to optimize access? Until very recently, geography I did not aim at finding causal relationship between environment and health; it stopped at correlation analysis pointing to the factors that might be responsible for ill health and diseases. Research on causal relationship is, however, no longer outside its purview. It has just begun: there is a vast vista before it to explore.

To use its potentials in full, geography of health must widen its scope further. It must enter the applied field and evolve its own system of medicine. A well-trained geographer should not only be able to contribute to the knowledge of spatial structure of health situation globally, nationally and locally but should also be able to directly participate in the campaign to ensure health for all. If the neglect or misuse of geographic factors can cause ill health, then their proper use and living in conformity with the laws of nature can also promote good health. I do not know why the geographers so far did not cultivate the applied side of of their discipline.

Human body is a biological product; its functioning is greatly influenced by the natural laws that govern the whole creation. *Yatha pinde tatha brahmande*. The body and mind of man can be healthy only so long as they are in tune with these laws of nature, which give us the science and art of living. Further, all living things depend on five basic natural phenomena or substances: earth, water, air, energy (sunlight) and ether (open space), so says the Ayurveda, the Indian science of medicine. All the five contain great therapeutic values and have been used by naturopaths for centuries to cure patients suffering from various diseases. They regulate the internal functioning and external relations of the body. Impurity in these substances has adverse implications for health. The violation of biological laws that govern human body and the pollution of the environment, which supports life on planet earth, are important causes of ill health. The stage appears to have come for medical geography to develop a sister discipline called *Geographic Medicine.*

Modern medical science comes into the picture only when man is sick. It pays less attention, if at all to the maintenance of good health by appropriate life style changes; changes in diet, natural and cultural environment; practice of meditation and Yoga and use of organic medicines derived from herbs and natural minerals. Geographic medicine should be based on the scientific laws of biogeography as applied to human body. It should be holistic in nature and include naturopathy, herbal medicine, yoga, acupressure, magnetic therapy and Ayurveda. It should focus on the maintenance of good health so that the disease burden is reduced and people can lead a healthful long life. Geographic Medicine is not an alternative to allopathic medicine otherwise known as modern medicine. Geographic medicine and allopathic medicine should complement and supplement each other. Both are needed.

This book does not cover the subject matter of Geographic Medicine. It centers on geography of health. It tells who lives and dies where and why? Those interested in Geographic Medicine should consult a companion volume by the author entitled *Geographic Medicine: Theory and Practice of Science and Art of Healthy Life.*

Geography of Health: A Treatise on Geography of Life and Death in India would hopefully be useful not only to geographers, and medical professionals but also to all other academics and professionals interested and involved in social work, social welfare, sociology, anthropology, economics and human development. I am confident that the book will fill an important gap in literature on health and will help many a student carry out further research on relationship between environment and health; on spatial distribution of health and ill-health; and on health policy, planning and programming. The book is based on the information available from WHO, Ministry of Health and Family Welfare, Government of India, Central Bureau of Health Intelligence, Census of India, and other governmental and private organizations and publications.

No book can be perfect. This applies to Geography of Health too. Despite my very sincere efforts to get latest information on various aspects of health, diseases and medicines discussed in this volume, I succeeded only partly. Some times the information used is old and dated. The most important drawback of the book emanates from the use of state level data on diseases, medical facilities and health institutions. Some of the states of India are larger than most of the countries of the world. Ideal situation will be one in which district level data were used. Unfortunately, such data with regard to diseases and several other aspects of health are not available and if they are available, they are not reliable. Lastly, the book is not based on research on correlates of health. The research in this field is scares, statistically weak and dated.

It is only hoped that these weaknesses will be taken care of in the next edition of the book as and when it is published. I hope the book would be useful to all those who are interested in the health and medicine as also to those who consider human welfare their major concern.

The first draft of the book was completed in December 2002. I requested Professors D.K. Nigam, Professor of Medicine; Professor V.N. Mishra, Professor of Ophthalmology; Professor O.P. Gupta, Professor of Medicine and Director Ganga Memorial Hospital (all of them associated with MLN Medical College, Allahabad); and Professor P.C. Mishra, Professor in Paediatrics (Children's Hospital, Allahabad) for their comments. I am grateful to them for sparing time to go through the manuscript and suggest a number of changes to improve the text. Dr. Mohan and Ms. Sameena Mukhija, National Informatics Center, Delhi, have been very helpful in computer mapping. But for their help the cartographic work would have been incomplete. While expressing my gratitude to them, let me add that responsibility for any flaw left in the text or maps lies with me.

I am thankful to Sri Ashok Kumar Mittal, Concept Publishing Company, New Delhi for bringing the book out so beautifully.

New Delhi
March 1, 2006

R.P. Misra

Contents

List of Tables

List of Figures

1

Introduction

Health is a major determinant of happiness. A sick person can never be happy, no matter how well off he may otherwise be. High standard of living is important but we know that money cannot buy everything; it does not ensure happiness. A bed-ridden person with a huge bank balance and all the comforts and luxuries of life will remain unhappy. The tragic part of the story is that wealth in modern days has become one of the most important causes of ill-health. Wealthy persons, who can afford to eat whatever they want, are not necessarily healthy. Many of them are unhealthy and the percentage of wealthy being unhealthy is on the increase.

At the other extreme, the poor, who cannot afford to meet their two ends, are also unhealthy and unhappy. Poverty and poor health are interrelated. Poverty leads to under- and mal-nutrition, which in turn leads to attack of diseases. A sick person cannot work hard, so his income declines; and low income means that the person in question cannot get medical attention nor can he get good food. His health further deteriorates. Poverty-low purchasing power-malnutrition-attack of diseases-low working capacity-still lower income constitute a circular chain reaction without any beginning or end, otherwise known as vicious circle (Fig. 1.1). It applies not only to individuals but also to communities and nations. It is, therefore, not surprising that less developed countries of the world have less healthy people.

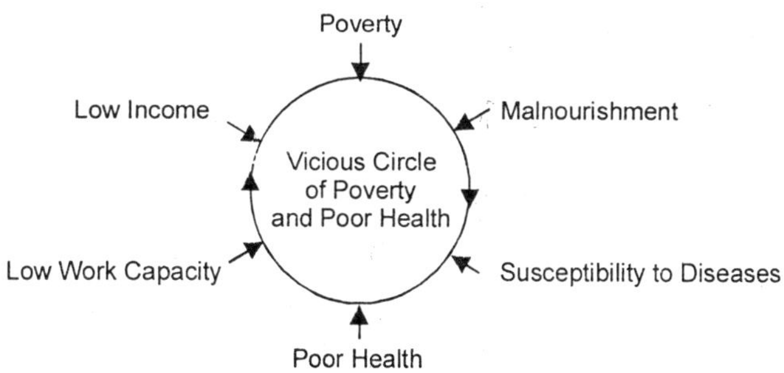

Fig. 1.1: Vicious Circle of Poverty and Poor Health

'Health is wealth.' This is what we have learnt from our elders since early childhood. This aphorism has been derived from the experiences of several millennia passed on and enriched from generation to generation. A person with poor health is often a liability to his family and society. A society burdened with unhealthy people cannot be prosperous. Health is really the wealth. Healthy people use their wealth most judiciously.

In spite of the paramount importance of health and diseases in the life of individuals and societies, neither of these terms has been defined precisely and comprehensively. Who is a healthy person? What is a disease? Does absence of disease means good health? These and other related questions appear to be simple but they have no readymade answers.

In this chapter we propose to answer these questions. We will discuss how different societies from ancient times to this day have looked at health and diseases and what has been the implication of their varying perspectives on the systems of medicine they evolved.

CONCEPT OF HEALTH

Health is often equated with 'absence of disease'. We, however, know that many unhealthy persons do not exhibit symptoms of diseases. A person may be unhealthy because he does not get enough food to eat or because the food he gets is not nutritive enough to keep his body in optimal working condition. He looks weak and tired; he cannot work hard; he loses interest in himself and the world around him. Sooner or later he may become a victim of one or several of diseases. But to begin with, he is just unhealthy. His problem is nutritional deficiency and diminished immunity.

Then there are those who overeat and therefore suffer from constipation and obesity. They are slow, docile and prone to many diseases of modern civilization. One also comes across people with sound physique and mental calibre, but prone to violence and crimes against themselves and the humanity at large. The root cause of mental derangement of the people is often traced back to certain hereditary traits, drug abuse, economic and social pressures, or bad education and company. Such people also fall in the category of sick, even if they do not suffer from conventionally known diseases.

The World Health Organization (WHO) has defined health rather broadly ever since its establishment in 1946. "Health is a state of complete physical, mental and social well-being and not merely the absence of disease or infirmity." Later, it was amplified to include "socially and economically productive life." This definition has been adopted by all member states of the WHO for health policy, planning, and programming. It has, however, been criticized on a number of counts. Some consider it too broad as it declares almost everyone to be unhealthy as no one is perfect. Others consider it too narrow as it excludes spiritual dimensions of life. Still others claim that health is not a state; it is process of continuous adjustment to changing demands of life and the meaning we give to our existence.

The above definition has been elaborated by a WHO study group for operational purposes. It identifies two orders or dimensions of health: broad and narrow. Broadly speaking, health can be seen as a condition or the quality of the human organism in a given genetic and environmental condition. In a narrow sense, it means a state where there is no evidence of any disease and the person concerned is functioning within normal limits of variation to health standards generally set for a particular age, sex, time, place and community.

Although the WHO definition does not go far enough to include moral or spiritual dimensions, it is much better than defining health as mere absence of diseases. A truly healthy person is not only physically and mentally sound; he is also overflowing with love, compassion, fellow feeling; he is agile and active in creative and constructive work; and he follows a style of life, which energizes the body and mind and takes him to a righteous path. He follows the dictum of *Vasudhaiva Kutumbakam*, which the Indian Rishis perfected, practised and propagated over three millennia ago. This definition takes health out of the narrow confines of diseases and confers on it a more realistic and broader scope and meaning.

We can now conclude that health has several dimensions; each of these dimensions is important but its relative importance *vis-à-vis* other dimensions depends on the circumstances in which an individual or community exists and functions. Among these dimensions are:

1. Physical,
2. Mental (stability, knowledge, cognition, etc.),
3. Nutritional,
4. Environmental,
5. Educational,
6. Socio-cultural,
7. Economic,
8. Spiritual and emotional,
9. Preventive, and
10. Curative.

Taking all the above dimensions into account, a new meaning of health has evolved in recent years. It is based on seven broad perspectives:

1. *Biological*: a state of the body in which every cell and organ functions optimally;
2. *Psychological*: a state in which the individuals feel a sense of perfect well-being and fully integrated in environment;
3. *Humanistic*: a state in which none is denied the opportunity to enjoy it;
4. Social: a state in which individual's participation in the social system is optimum; and in which it is a major social goal;
5. *Developmental*: a state in which health is an inseparable part of the development process;
6. *Qualitative*: a state in which health is a major determinant of quality of life; and.
7. *Multi-sectoral*: a state in which health is a concern of all—individuals, communities, medical professionals, pharmaceutical companies, governments and international agencies.

The WHO's definition of health has now been accepted by almost all member states of the United Nations. It calls for complete well-being of people. Given the current world development scenario, it is, however, not possible to implement it in its entirety anywhere in the world and more so in the developing parts of the world. Moreover, acceptable quantitative measures of 'complete well-being' of people are yet to be worked out. People differ widely in terms of age, sex, occupation, socio-cultural background, and natural and cultural environments. The fact is that even among the healthy people some are healthier than others. Further, a person may be healthy at one time and unhealthy at another or at one place than at another.

To allow for individual and environmental differences in opportunities for acquiring good health, Irwin has defined optimum health as "a state of the highest possible level of physical, mental and emotional fitness and efficiency commensurate with individual capacity." This means that a person, in the state of optimum health, functions at or near his peak capacity without excessive fatigue or emotional upset. Those who do not possess optimum health are partially or fully unhealthy. It is also clear that those who do not have positive, creative and tolerant approach to life do not enjoy optimum health. Thus, there is always scope for improving health. It must be a sustained and conscious life long endeavour.

Human body is a live organic system. It is not an inanimate machine that runs on borrowed power. Like an engine, it is an assemblage of so many small and big parts whose number may run into billions (if we go to the level of the cells), but unlike a mechanical engine, each part of it has evolved in conjunction with other parts, not independent of the whole. Each part is inextricably linked with the rest; each one is self-controlled, self-directed and self-managed. Each conforms to the needs of the larger system above it and lower sub-systems below it. This is how it remains in a healthy state. Any malfunctioning of even a single cell has its implications for the whole body system instantaneously and simultaneously. What the mind images has its impact on the body and the emotions and what the body does has its impact on the mind. The feelings towards oneself or the outer world affect both body and mind.

Let us, however, keep in view that each man is unique; no two persons, even twins, are replica of each other. The outer environment, therefore, affects each man differently. Man is healthy so long as his body, mind and emotions cooperate with each other. And this is possible only if there are no inherited deficiencies, and man lives in an environment that promotes complete integration of feeling, thought, speech and action. The relationship between environment and man is mediated by culture, which differs from individual to individual, community to community and society to society. It is culture, which determines the style of life – the way people live. That is the reason why in the same natural environmental setting, one can find both very healthy and very unhealthy people (Figure 1.2).

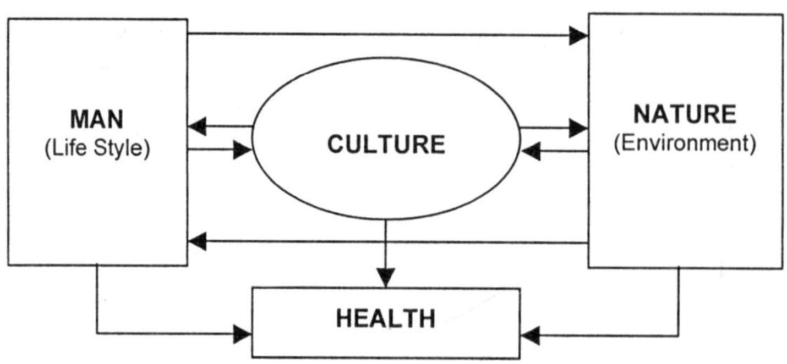

Fig. 1.2: Man-Nature-Culture Nexus and Health

The factors, which influence health, are:

1. Heredity,
2. Physical environment,
3. Socio-cultural milieu,
4. Style of life, and
5. Worldview concerning health.

Man has no control over what he inherits from his parents and grandparents, but he can very much minimize the health hazards resulting from hereditary susceptibilities by positively manipulating the natural and cultural environments and adopting a style of life that does not stress body, mind and emotions beyond their threshold limits. They not only keep him in good health but also lessen the chances of his progenies inheriting diseases he inherited from his predecessors. Thanks to genetics, it is now possible to know the potentials of each individual. What is needed is an environment in which the potentials are fully harnessed and the education and training that can support and hasten their cultivation.

Physical environment includes both natural and man-made surroundings. The air we breathe, the water we drink, the food we eat, and the work we do have their implications for our health. The main reason for our concern about environmental pollution is the adverse effect it has on our health. The social system in which we live also has its impact on health. A conflict-ridden society cannot produce healthy people. Social pollution is a major hazard for health in modern times. Over-population and under-population also have adverse effects on health. The style of life we follow has serious implications for our health. A sedentary man is less likely to be healthy: a society of self-centred individuals cannot be peaceful. And finally, the worldview of the people, the standards against which they evaluate everything, has its own implications for health. Hitler believed in the superiority of German race. He landed the whole world into a war that killed millions of people, far more than the diseases would have ever killed within a span of just five years.

Unfortunately, the culture of violence has gripped the minds of a fairly good section of the population to such an extent that humanity is on the verge of dehumanization. They terrorise, loot and kill people to secure personal or ideological objectives; they even kill people for pecuniary benefits on contract. Such people have no faith in freedom, democracy, human rights, and human duties and values. Overshadowing these perpetrators of violence are the religious fundamentalists called Islamic *Jehadis* who consider other faiths as heretic and are so overtaken by the 'love' of their religion that they want to eliminate all those who do not subscribe to their faith. They are indoctrinated to kill. Until recently, they were active at the local level in many countries: in Afghanistan, India, Philippines, Turkey, Russia, etc. Now they have spread their tentacles to practically the whole world and become a menace for the civilized world. They have now acquired power, organization, knowhow and skills to attack even the most powerful nation of the world, the USA, as they did on September 11, 2001 when they destroyed the twin towers of the WTC in New York and part of the Pentagon building in Washington DC. And later, on December 13, they attacked, even though unsuccessfully, the Parliament building of India. Unfortunately, religious intolerance, which is the very antithesis of all religions including Islam, is gaining ground in all religions of the world for one reason or the other.

Fanatics have a sick mind; they have no religion, nor do they believe in reverence for life. They prefer to rule over the cemeteries of dead than to live in love and harmony with living human beings. The germs of *Jehad* are far more dangerous than the biological germs that cause epidemics and pandemics. The tragedy is that such germs have infected even the most liberal societies like that of India during the last few decades.

Ideally speaking then a healthy person is one who:

1. has a positive attitude towards life, is full of hope, is self-confident, and ever engaged in creative thinking and work;
2. has an integrated personality so that the body, mind, feeling, speech and action are in harmony with each other;
3. has subdued fear, anger, jealousy, hatred and over attachment to creature comforts;
4. is full of energy and enthusiasm;
5. is compassionate;
6. is ever-ready to help others;
7. is as close to the status of *sthitapragya* (who maintains equanimity in pleasure and pain) as possible;
8. takes balanced diet and eats to live, not lives to eat;
9. has no diseases and if the diseases do come, he is able to overcome them through natural processes or moderate medications having no side effects; and
10. knows how to die peacefully.

In nutshell, we can say that a man is healthy if he gets adequate nutritious food to eat, is able to keep his body clean of things that do not suit the biology of man and is able to keep his mind clear of thoughts that disturb peace or prompt him to indulge in violence, revenge and similar other negative deeds. Body is polluted when we eat and drink things that do not conform to the natural metabolism or when we lead a style of life that does not conform to the physical, chemical and biological requirements of the body. The mind gets polluted when we harbour thoughts that generate anger, hatred, greed and lust for power.

Many modern foods contain toxic materials that cannot be eliminated through normal metabolic processes. Unfortunately, even ground water is polluted by toxins and is unsuitable for drinking without purification. Some persons over eat; some do not get enough to eat. The so-called modern style of life perpetrates violence against both one's own body and mind, apart from hurting the nature and civil society. Nature tries to bring the biological system back to normalcy by expelling out the unwanted matters and thoughts through various ailments and diseases. But once the body's threshold to cleanse the system is overstepped, systemic imbalances having no cures set in. Fever, for example, is the nature's initial effort to cleanse the body. When such warnings are ignored or responded by medicines that suppress the symptoms, systemic disorders like hypertension, diabetes, arthritis, etc. take over the command.

The parameters of good health given above are idealistic; they constitute the standards or norms, which only the rare souls can accomplish. For ordinary men and women, they cannot be adhered to in full. Nevertheless, they are indispensable. No society can prosper without ideals. Ideals provide the perspectives towards which one has to advance. They thus chart the route to be followed. They ask people to move in a particular direction, and make a sincere effort to step forward. If all individuals, communities and societies try to follow the ideals, people would be much healthier than they are today. Unfortunately, in this age of consumerism and extra care for external look, healthy life and living is not a priority goal. Health is no longer a life long process; it has become a state, which can be achieved through medicines. This is the reason why health policies the world over centre on treatment, elimination and eradication of diseases. Multiplicity of hospitals and physicians has now become indicator of development. Should it not be the other way round?

PERSPECTIVES ON HEALTH

As stated earlier, different disciplines look at health from the perspectives of their own specialization and thrust. These approaches do not do full justice to health in its broadest sense, but they are not unwanted. It is necessary to examine parts in order to understand the whole, so long as we keep in view that the parts do not represent the whole. It would be pertinent for medical geographers to know the perspectives of all relevant disciplines so that they can communicate with all those who aim at making people healthy, no matter what their disciplinary background might be.

In the pre-industrial society, keeping the body healthy was the primary responsibility of each individual. In fact, health was so much integrated with the whole culture of life and living that people did not have to make efforts to keep themselves healthy. Nutritious food, physical exercise and a healthy style of life were essential ingredients of day-to-day life. Good physique and mental alertness were valued traits. Health was the responsibility of the individuals for it was in their hands. If a disease did come, the remedy was sought in the immediate nature. Through the experiences and experiments of centuries, people had discovered that practically all plants and minerals had some medicinal properties. The roots, barks, stems, leaves, flowers and fruits of plants independently or together with various minerals in raw or treated forms, were used for curing ailments. Ayurveda in India, for example, developed into a very advanced system of medicine. Similar was the case with Chinese and Greek medicines. Each individual was a medicine man; only when the problem appeared unusual, a physician was consulted.

Biomedical Approach

With the advent of industrial revolution, scientific investigations in the causes of human and animal diseases were intensified in Europe to begin with. By the middle of the nineteenth century, the etiology of diseases converged on a single factor i.e. germ. It was widely accepted that when microbes invaded human body, they disturbed the normal functioning of the system causing various kinds of diseases. Robert Koch and Louis Pasteur were among the pioneers of this discovery. Modern medicine with its antibiotics, sterilization kits, chemotherapy and sophisticated techniques of surgery represents further improvement, expansion and application of this theory.

Credit for the eradication of many of the major killers like plague, smallpox, cholera, etc. can be solely attributed to the germ theory of diseases. It has saved millions of lives. But it has done some harm too. As discussed earlier, germs do not invade all humans with equal ferocity. Germs succeed only if the host is vulnerable. There can, therefore, be two approaches to keeping human body disease free: one, to strengthen the immunity of the body so that the germs fail in their mission, and two, to kill the germs as and when they attack human body. In fact, a two-pronged approach would be ideal. Unfortunately, the first approach was given a good bye and medical profession solely relied on the second approach. It had very adverse implications for health. With this approach, the responsibility for health shifted from the individual and community to the physicians, surgeons and hospitals.

There is increasing evidence that people have become callous about their health; they place excessive reliance on hospitals, doctors and insurance companies. As such, people may now live long but unhealthy. Further, all diseases are not caused by germs. Germs cause communicable diseases. There are many diseases, which have nothing to do with germs such as mental disorders, cancer, hypertension, diabetes, genetic deformities, deficiency diseases, asthma, alcoholism, drug abuses, violence, etc. These and several other diseases have something to do with the way people live: the food and drinks they consume, the environment in which they live, the work they do, the attention they pay to their health, etc. Far more people than ever before are suffering from systemic diseases for which there are no cures.

The germ theory suffers from another drawback. If each human body is unique in details, there cannot be a single approach to curing it. A particular medicine need not work equally for all even if the symptoms are the same. Each body reacts differently to a given stimulus. Commonly applied etiology of diseases puts all the people in one basket and treats them as if they are mechanical devices with same nuts and bolts. In the long run, it proves counter-productive. Modern allopathic medicines contain toxins that cannot be ingested by human body. They remain lodged in the blood vessels, muscles and bones to cause unsuspected and unexpected side effects on the body and mind. They affect the reproductive processes leading to genetic disorders. We are not quite sure of the long-term consequences of these medicines even if they have been tested on humans and animals for a long time. The side effects of many of these medicines may show up in discernible form only after one or more generations.

These questions about the germ theory of diseases are genuine and pertinent. They must engage our attention. Nothing should be done which may jeopardize our health and the health of the future generations. This does not, however, mean that the germ theory is useless and should be discarded. Prevention and cure are important dimension of health. They are meant to provide immediate relief to those suffering from diseases, which were difficult to control until very recently. Germ theory is particularly helpful in controlling and eradicating contagious and communicable diseases, which are in plenty even today in the developing parts of the world. What is important is to know its strong points as well as its limitations and ill-effects. It can cure only some but not all diseases. Moreover, it cannot ensure a healthy life after the disease is gone. It is essentially curative, to some extent preventive, but it cannot keep people healthy.

New advances in biotechnology, particularly in gene therapy, have opened new vistas in medical science. But there are inherent pitfalls too. Unless man becomes morally strong and follows certain human values, he is likely to misuse these technologies as he has done in the past with respect to his other achievements. He may move from germ warfare to cloning men and women who are giants and rogues capable of destroying all that man has created so far. Alternatively, he may produce people with good physical, mental and emotional health to bring peace on planet earth. These questions apart, should man indulge in his own reproduction—discarding natural processes, which have evolved through many millennia, and adopting artificial means, with all the potentials of creating conditions in which human survival is jeopardized.

Psychological Approach

The psychological perspective on health has two dimensions: one, mental health, which has become now a major concern; and two, the approach of patients and their families towards health and disease. The interaction of individuals with each other and the society at large produces a variety of stresses and strains. Some persons can cope with these but many others succumb and get mentally disturbed. If the emotional imbalances continue for a long period of time, structural changes in many organs like endocrine, autonomic and motor systems can take place. Among the diseases, which are associated with psychological factors, are asthma, ulcer, coronary heart diseases, hypertension, mental disorders and deviant behaviours.

But diseases apart, psychological factors have great bearings on the overall health and feeling of being healthy or unhealthy. A good number of people feel sick, without being sick. They look at the world very negatively; everything appears to be wrong and going wrong. They feel threatened and insecure. Many of them lose their mental balance and go crazy. Unfortunately, the number of such cases in India is on the increase, especially among the youth and the elderly.

Sociological Approach

According to Rene Dubos (1964), "health and disease cannot be defined in terms of anatomical, physiological or mental attributes alone. Their real measure is the ability of the individual to function in a manner acceptable to himself and to the group of which he is a part." Elsewhere (1965), he defined health and disease as state of continuum. "Health and disease cannot be seen in dichotomy; rather a continuum from health to disease and into health." Park (1989) introduced spectral concept of health i.e. the health of an individual is not static. It fluctuates within a given range. It cannot, therefore, be attained once for all. It has to be renewed from time to time.

In general, the sociological approach takes health as a human construct, which exists without someone describing or recognizing it. It does not deny the scientific basis of disease but interprets it in the light of the social realities as exhibited by religion, community, gender, natural environment, etc.

Health can thus be considered to be a process with several stages ranging from complete health (ideal) to death (no health).

Good Health

Complete health
Positive health
Better health
Freedom from ill-health

Average Health

Poor Health

Unrecognized sickness
Mild sickness
Severe sickness
Death

Medical sociology is a branch of sociology, which deals with the impact of social factors on health, society's approach to health and diseases, and social sanctions for various kinds of medications and treatment procedures.

Economic Approach

Economics is deeply interested in the health of the manpower that produces wealth. Medical economics also known as health economics has emerged as a separate speciality. It treats health as a commodity people should possess because it gives them satisfaction; it enables them to work to their optimum capacity and produces goods and services. Health can be purchased in the market from doctors, hospitals and medical stores. All that is needed is to have enough resources. The price one pays for the factors of health-hospitals, doctors, medicines, etc. are determined by the market forces of demand and supply. Poor health proves costly to society due to man-days lost. And so do the factors that generate ill-health. Investment in health is essential because it increases productivity and income. Relationship between investment in health services and income and wages of the people, economic models of physician and hospital behaviour, cost-effectiveness and cost-benefit analysis, competition, regulation, health marketing, health insurance, financing, economics of medical education, etc. constitute some of the major concerns of medical economists.

The key variables of health are food including drinking water, clothing, housing, air, education, environment, information and health-care. As income rises investment in these in general increases. Increasing costs and advancing age tend to lower the stock of health. As the patients get more protected through insurance or subsidy, demand for medical care increases. This leads to higher prices and greater surplus for further investment of capital in medical services. Higher investment in turn escalates costs making insurance an essential part of life.

The economic approach has been criticized on several counts. Health is a basic need that must be met irrespective of the presence or absence of demand. People living below the poverty line may not have effective demand for costly medical care. Those who are ignorant about modern health care may also not demand such facilities. But the basic needs of the people have to be met. It is part of their human rights.

Geographic Approach

Geography studies health from the spatial and environmental perspectives. Its main focus is geography of health and health-care. A number of geographic factors influence and at times even determine the status of health of humans, animals and other life forms. The natural environment and its constituent elements like land, water, air, vegetation, animals including microorganism and human beings themselves make certain places more livable and healthy than others. Physical, human and biogeography are the branches which study these elements.

The amount and quality of food produced and available for human consumption is a major determinant of health. Food deficiency leads to under- and mal-nutrition. Adequate income is necessary to meet basic needs like food. Most people in the developing countries do not have access to the basic needs. The status of their health is invariably low. Economic geography studies the availability and distribution of income and food.

Culture plays a very significant role in health. Race, religion, ethnic background, caste and community influence the choice of health delivery system and medicines. Human geography studies these aspects.

Spatial analysis is the point of departure for the science of geography. It uses this analysis to answer questions like who lives where and in what state of health? Spatial network analysis has been effectively used to plan health delivery systems and thus to reach the maximum number of people with minimum cost. Simulation models have been used to study the origin and spread of a number of diseases, particularly the communicable ones.

Geography considers health "as a harmonious equilibrium between man and his environment and disease as a maladjustment of human organism to his total environment." Jacques May, an American physician turned medical geographer, considers disease as a product of interaction among the agent, host and environment. The agent and the host mutually interact and both concurrently interact with the complex matrix called the environment, which is both physical and cultural (Figure 1.3).

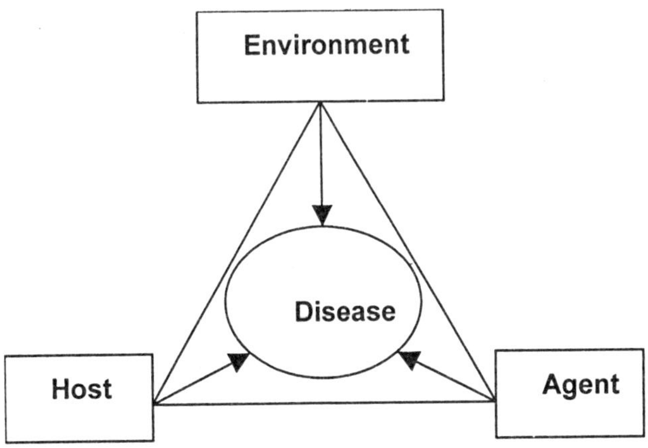

Fig. 1.3: Environment-Host-Agent Nexus and Diseases

Disease being the product of interaction among the host, agent and environment, it falls within the scope of geography. Since all the three inter-actors are space rooted, one cannot but agree with Hunter that geography is ideally suited for the study of health and diseases. May called the agent as pathogen and the environment as geo-gene. Geo-genes include both the physical and man-made environmental elements while the pathogens include all the organisms that cause diseases.

Griggs (1977) identified three components that distinguished medical geography from other sister disciplines. Medical geography studies spatial patterns of ill-health, spatial patterning of the physical and human environmental characteristics, which induces good or bad health, and spatial patterning and use of health care delivery systems to fight diseases and hazards to health. Pyle (1977) and Phillips (1981) further elaborated them for different spatial scales. Important among them are diffusion of diseases, modeling and behavioural attributes at the global, national, regional, local, household and individual levels.

In fact, in a classic study undertaken by John Snow in 1954, the utility of mapping disease outbreaks to identify the source of cholera epidemic to a water pump was demonstrated in the Soho district of London suburb. That there was a close relationship between place and disease was known from ancient most times. As geography became a specialized discipline in the nineteenth century, it was only a matter of time before geographers too started systematically studying the geographic aspects of health and healthcare.

Closely related to and often overlapping geographical approach is the ecological approach. According to Rene Dubos, "health implies the relative absence of pain and discomfort and a continuous adaptation and adjustment to the environment to ensure optimal function." In this approach man and his cultural heritage are taken together. Environment includes all external forces: natural, cultural and social.

The geographic perspective is essentially holistic in nature. Holism includes the spiritual dimensions too. According to this approach, health depends on a combined effect of all the factors discussed above plus spiritual. Man lives in a complex environmental setting; which factor will affect when and in what quantity will depend on the other factors interacting with each other. Faith is an important component of the inner environment. The belief that health is improving energizes the body and mind. Just the opposite happens, when one feels sick. And hence our approach to health improvement too has to be holistic.

CONCEPT OF DISEASE

Everyone appears to know the diseases because none is spared of it, but no single definition of disease is comprehensive enough to be acceptable to all. Webster dictionary defines it as "a condition in which body health is impaired, a departure from a state of health, an alteration of the human body interrupting the performance of vital functions." Oxford English dictionary defines disease as "a condition of the body or some part or organ of the body in which its functions are disrupted or deranged." We can say that disease is opposite of health: any deviation from normal functioning or state of complete physical or mental well-being; health and disease are mutually exclusive; they cannot go together.

The main problem surrounding definition of disease is inherent to its very nature. Disease is identified by the symptoms it produces. But the symptoms do not tell the whole truth; rather they tell only the visible part of the reality. There is lot behind a disease that is not visible. That is why, it has been compared to an iceberg. The vast submerged portion of the iceberg represents the hidden and undiagnosed part of the disease (Figure. 1.4).

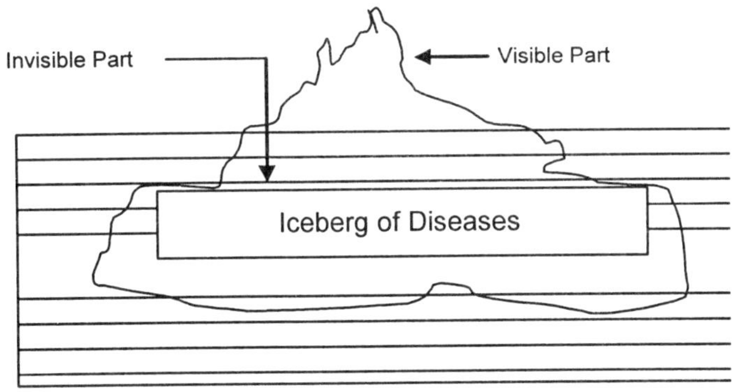

Fig. 1.4: Iceberg of Diseases

Diseases must have been a major concern of man from earliest times. Different places and regions gave rise to different diseases and different ways of overcoming them. Evidences of spatial distribution of diseases and way of curing them can give a reliable picture of the society of the time. Unfortunately, we do not have dependable information on diseases prevalent in ancient times. Nor do we have information on how the diseases were treated. We nevertheless can speculate that diseases are as old as life itself. A disease, according to Virchow, is nothing but life under changed circumstances. Man must have suffered injuries and the body's innate healing power must have worked to overcome the lesions and to restore the injured part to working condition (Virchow, R).

Man is able to live in widely different environmental settings: from snow covered Himalayas to the desert region of Rajasthan. Human body, however, must have a threshold of adaptability. Once the threshold is crossed, the reaction of the body to the stimuli is no longer physiological. It becomes pathological i.e. a symptom of disease. It is also clear that the phenomenon of parasitism must be an old one and some parasites invading human body to cause diseases cannot be ruled out.

HISTORY OF DISEASES

When did man know of diseases? Perhaps, ever since he became aware of himself and his body. All ancient cultures had developed medical systems of their own to treat diseases. Our present day industrial civilization has got its own system.

There are three sources of information, which point to a very long history of disease: paleopathology, historical records, and scientific discoveries and inventions.

Paleopathology

Fossil bones of animals as well as humans are the major sources of information. Paleopathology is the science of diseases, which can be demonstrated in the human and animal remains of ancient times. Efforts were made as early as sixteenth century to study fossil bones but with little success. In 1761, Geovanni Battista Margagani laid the foundation of pathological anatomy. Since then the fossil bones showing pathological changes were described more frequently in the bones of bears and lions found in caves. During the mid-nineteenth century, Virchow, a pathologist-cum-anthropologist, put paleopathology on sound foundations. It relies on the remains of bones and teeth because they are preserved in relatively large numbers, from far remote periods and from various parts of the earth. With the use of microscope, the research results have considerably improved.

Paleopathological research received a shot in the arm with the discovery of Egyptian mummies and burial grounds in many parts of the world. R. Fouquet, G. Elliot Smith and F. Wood Jones undertook the examination of the skeletal remains of Nubian mummies for pathological lesion at the end of nineteenth century. They found many evidences of diseases in the bones of the mummies. Similar studies were conducted on the skeletal remains of early man found in the cave of Europe, South America and Africa.

These studies have proved that diseases existed in olden times in practically the same form they are found today and in all places where the environment favoured. Some of the illnesses were universal such as the bone dislocations and fractures; some were rare such as rickets, which is a disease of vitamin D deficiency. Not a single mummy found in Egypt had signs of this disease. The diseases for which there are paleopathological evidences are osteomyelitis, arthiritis, tuberculosis, syphilis, tumors, pyorrhea and several minor ones. All of them are associated with bones.

The evidence for diseases related to other organs of the body are scanty and conjectural. They only prove their existence; no further details can be derived because other organs after death do not last for long.

Historical Records

One gets more reliable information from religious and literary works, which mention the diseases prevalent at the time they were written or compiled. Chinese, Indian and Greek literatures mention a number of diseases like leprosy, tuberculosis, intestinal diseases and injuries. Details of the diseases are not given but one has better knowledge of their nature and typology.

By 1000 BC, human knowledge of diseases had grown rather enormously in the then developed parts of world: India, China, Greece, Egypt, etc. Diagnosis of the diseases had also progressed so that the causative factors were better, if not fully, known. This gave rise to different systems of medicine. The Indian system is known as Ayurveda. We would return to the history of medicine in the next chapter. Here suffice it to say that man has consistently tried to understand diseases, which he suffered from and tried to discover cures.

Scientific Discoveries and Inventions

With the advancement of science and technology, the diagnosis of diseases is no longer based on symptoms and what the patient tells. The agents of diseases are identified by various scientific tests and diseases are named and classified on the basis of the agents causing them or other conditions promoting them.

Pollution of body by foreign matter i.e. the matter that is not supposed to be in the body for its normal functioning is one of the main causes of ill-health. If our body is unable to remove this matter through its normal metabolic and circulatory processes, the body gets polluted and becomes a victim of various agents that cause diseases. Disease is thus a symptom of something fundamentally wrong with the body, mind and emotions included. It is a warning signal; it should, therefore, be welcome. Attempt to suppress the symptoms or to ignore them produces serious implications for health.

Modern medical science does not reject the above explanation but it does not subscribe to the view that suppressing the symptoms is injurious because, leaving aside illnesses caused by injuries and heredity, most other diseases are caused by germs (viruses, bacteria and other micro-organisms). If the germs are not eliminated, the disease will win over the body and the patient will die. It is based on the germ theory of disease.

The germ theory of diseases, however, does not tell the whole truth. Germs may cause diseases, but what causes the germs to multiply and attack the body? Diseases come because the body's immune system has failed giving opportunity to the germs to overpower it. And why has the immune system failed? It may be because of under- or mal-nutrition; it may be because of over-nutrition; it may be because of unhealthy style of life; or it may be because of the poisoning of body by toxic materials taken with foods, drinks, drugs, medicines, etc. Causes may be many but unless the internal environment of the body is favourable, germs would not survive, nor would they grow and cause diseases.

The immediate and most apparent cause of many diseases may be the germs, but the primary cause is the violation of the laws of nature, which regulate the human body. The violation generates imbalances and impurities, which may appear as diseases in the whole or part of the body, and at different seasons and situations. Medical geography considers environment as an important determinant of health. Here environment is treated broadly to include both external (in which man lives) and internal (inside the body) environments.

No matter how sincere we are about our health, we cannot avoid being sick sometimes or the other. Nature shows the way to cure practically all diseases except the ones having genetic origin. The environment that causes ailments also provides the ante-dotes to stop them from attacking or to cure them if already in the body. Let me relate here an experience I had recently. During one of my visits to Shimla, I inadvertently touched a plant. I felt as if a scorpion had stung; I sat down with acute pain. One of the friends accompanying me realized what had happened. He plucked a few leaves of another plant and rubbed them over the place I was stung. Within seconds the pain disappeared. I was told that the two plants grew side by side. One injures and the other cures. Nature has ante-dotes for all ailments.

With the passage of time, man has developed many chemical medicines to cure diseases. These medicines have now become an important part of our life. There is, however, a difference between natural and man-made medicines. Both give relief, but the former conforms to the biology of human body; it cures slowly and restores the immune system of the body to enable it to fight the disease. The latter cures fast by suppressing the disease; it not only forces the body to find some other avenue to evacuate the toxins that give rise to the disease, but also adds some more impurities, thus further weakening the immune system of the body.

Before we end this section, let us be clear that disease, illness and sickness are not the same thing although they are often used inter-changeably. Sickness is a social dysfunction; it is the role one assumes when ill. One can be sick of anything including a disease. It is more of a mental disease. Illness is a subjective state of a person who feels aware of not being well. He does not know the disease from which he suffers. It is the general feeling of not being physiologically well. Disease is a physiological dysfunction of the whole or part of the body. It is painful, can be identified, and has a name.

NATURAL HISTORY OF DISEASES

We discussed earlier that in the causation of most of the diseases at least three major factors are involved: agent, host and environment. Some diseases, however, do not involve agents like pathogens such as diabetes, heart attack, hypertension, cancer, etc. In these cases the agent is replaced by risk factors such as smoking, sedentary life style, drug addiction, etc.

Diseases do not come all of a sudden although some of them appear to be so. They pass through three phases: pre-pathogenesis phase, pathogenesis phase and post-pathogenesis phase. The pre-pathogenesis phase is marked by all the conditions both internal and external that favour the entry of pathogens in the body. This phase is the product of interaction between the agent, the host and the environment. The favourable conditions for a particular disease are found at the junction of the three factors (Fig. 1.3). In the case of non-infectious diseases like cancer and diabetes, in the pre-pathogenesis phase, the role of the agent is taken over by risk factors like smoking, drug addiction, malnutrition, etc.

The pathogenesis phase begins with the entry of the agent in the susceptible human host. This is called incubation period. The disease agent, once in side the host, multiplies and induces physiological changes to give rise to early pathogenesis. When the agent has done its job fully, the disease reaches its late pathogenesis stage. The pathogenesis phase can be modified by external intervention measures. Finally, the patient either recovers because he has enough strength to get over the disease or he becomes disable or dies. In the chronic diseases like diabetes, coronary heart diseases, arthritis, etc. the early pathogenesis phase is not dramatic. The patient is often unaware of the disease unless it has reached the pathogenesis stage.

The agent, host and environment factors involved in pathogenesis are given below:

Agents

1. Biological agents (viruses, rickettsiae, fungi, bacteria, protozoa and metazoa);
2. Nutrient agents (proteins, fats, carbohydrates, vitamins, minerals and water);
3. Physical agents (climatic elements, electricity, sound etc.);
4. Chemical agents (endogenously created like urea, serum bilirubin, uric acid, etc. and exogenous agents like allergens, metals, gases, insecticides, fumes, etc.);
5. Mechanical agents (dislocation, crushing, tearing, sprains, etc.);
6. Shortage or excess of a factor necessary for health (any or all of the above);
7. Social agents (smoking, drugs, parental deprivation, anomy, unhealthy life styles, etc.);
8. Risk factor (in cases of chronic and systemic diseases).

Human Host

The human host functions like soil and the disease agent as seed. The host factors may be classified as:

1. demographic factors (age, sex, ethnicity, etc.);
2. biological factors (genetic factors, functioning of various organs, blood group, immuniological factors, etc.);
3. socio-economic characteristics (poverty, education, occupation, etc.); and
4. life style factors (smoking, drinking, drug addiction, etc.).

Environment

1. physical environment;
2. biological environment; and
3. psychological environment (man is the agent of his own disease).

CONTROL OF DISEASES

Control of diseases implies actions to reduce the:

1. incidence of diseases;
2. duration of diseases;
3. effects of infection; and
4. financial and institutional burden on the community.

It would be useful to understand the meaning of various terms used in controlling diseases such as disease surveillance, disease control, disease elimination, and disease eradication. Disease surveillance means 'continuous scrutiny of the factors that determine the occurrence and distribution of disease(s) and other conditions of poor health'. In case of disease control, the agent causing the disease is allowed to remain in the community at a level where it ceases to be a public health hazard. Disease elimination connotes a step forward beyond disease control; the agent is not allowed to spread further in the locality or region concerned. That is to say that the transmission of the disease has been locally or regionally halted. For example, polio has been eliminated from some countries. It may also be called regional elimination. Eradication literally means to root out. Diseases, which are rooted out from the whole world, fall in this category. Plague and smallpox have been eradicated from the world.

The idea behind prevention is to intercept the agent or cause and halt its progress. Prevention depends upon the adequate and correct understanding of the cause of the disease, dynamics of its transmission, risk factors involved, availability of early detection techniques and treatment measures, an institutional infrastructure to apply the measures, and continuous evaluation. Prevention is possible at four levels:

1. primordial,
2. primary;
3. secondary; and
4. tertiary.

Primordial prevention applies mainly to chronic diseases or systemic disorders. Change in the style of life, diet and thinking are designed to discourage children and youth growing up with unhealthy habits. It may be called most primary of primary preventions.

Primary prevention consists of 'action taken prior to the onset of disease, which removes the possibility that a disease will ever occur.' It can be achieved by promoting general health and well being so as to improve the level of immunity. It can be applied on a mass scale or on those who are at risk. In this connection it should be noted that the present day developed countries were able to get rid of many of the diseases by raising the standard of living of their populations, improving diet, hygiene and general environmental conditions.

The secondary prevention includes actions, which halt the progress of the disease. It includes screening tests and adequate treatment. It is largely in the domain of clinical medicine. In an ideal situation, secondary intervention should be rare. Primary intervention is the answer. Unfortunately, most of the governmental programmes fall in the category of secondary intervention

The tertiary intervention becomes necessary when the disease has reached an advanced stage or late pathogenic stage. It is designed to minimize suffering, disabilities and deaths. It includes rehabilitation.

CHANGING PATTERN OF DISEASES

Diseases tend to change their character in response to the external and internal environments in which they grow. Both these environments have changed enormously during the last two centuries. As such the character of the diseases has also changed. These changes are generalized in what is known as epidemiological stages.

In the early epidemiological stages, number of people were few and the diseases also not many. As population grew, the deficiency diseases emerged as important causes of morbidity as well as mortality. And then came the infectious diseases like plague and smallpox, which killed millions of people. Industrialization changed the environmental setting so drastically that it gave rise to a number of new diseases not known earlier or if they were known, they were not major killers. Infectious diseases grew in number as well as in intensity. Over crowding, poor hygiene and poorer sanitation were the main causes of these diseases. And now in the post-industrial era, new diseases like AIDS have the potentials of wiping out far more people than any war could do. The tragedy is that some of the modern diseases are not diseases in the real sense. They are systemic disorders. There may be no medicines for them.

This changing pattern of diseases is well reflected in the US data given in Table 1.1. A similar trend is noticeable in India too (Table 1.2). We do not have dependable historical data to be sure as to how and when these trends set in. But they are there to see and experience.

CLASSIFICATION OF DISEASES

Each country adopts its own criterion for diagnosis of diseases. It makes international comparison of prevalence of diseases almost impossible. Several efforts were made by individuals and groups to classify diseases during the last two centuries. Nothing, however, could be universally accepted even in Europe until the WHO worked out its own International Classification of Diseases (ICD). The ICD is revised every ten years; the last revision was carried out in 1993.

The ICD is arranged in 21 major chapters. The first character of the ICD-10 code is a letter and each letter is associated with a particular chapter. There are a few exceptions to this rule. For example, letter D is used in chapters II and III and letter H in chapters VII and VIII. Chapters I, II, XIX and XX use more than one letters in the first position of their codes.

Table 1.1: Leading Causes of Death in the USA (per cent of deaths from all causes)

Causes of Death	*USA*	
	1900	*1994*
Pneumonia and influenza	11.80	3.60
TB	11.30	–
Diarrhoea and enteritis	8.30	–
Heart disease	8.00	32.10
Cerebrovascular disease	6.20	6.80
Chronic nephritis	4.70	-
Accidents	4.20	3.90
Cancer	3.70	23.50
Diseases of infancy	3.60	–
Diptheria	2.30	–
Chronic obstructive pulmonary	–	4.50
Diabetes	–	2.40
Suicides	–	1.40
Chronic level diseases	–	1.10
HIV infection	–	1.80
All other causes	35.90	18.90

Note: Less than 1 per cent is not given.
Source: Times of India, April 21, 1996.

Each chapter has three-character categories to cover its contents. Most of these are sub-divided by adding a fourth numeric character (ranging from 1 to 10) after decimal point. Where the fourth character is not filled, letter 'x' is placed to indicate the vacancy. Where a disease has uncertain etiology, 'U' code is assigned to indicate 'unusual'.

The 21 major chapters of the ICD-10 are as follows:

1. Certain infections and parasite diseases (A00 –B99);
2. Neoplasm (C00 – D48);
3. Diseases of the blood and blood forming organs and certain disorders involving immune mechanism (D50 – D89);
4. Endocrine, nutritional and metabolic diseases (E00 – E90);
5. Mental and behavioral disorders (F00 –F99);
6. Diseases of the nervous system (G00 –G99);
7. Diseases of the eye and adnexa (H00 –H59);

8. Diseases of the ear and mastoid process (H60 –H95);
9. Diseases of the circulatory system (I00 –I99);
10. Diseases of the respiratory system (J00 –J99);
11. Diseases of the digestive system (K00 –K93);
12. Diseases of the skin and subcutaneous tissue (L00 –L99);
13. Diseases of the musculoskeletal system and connective tissue (M00 –M99);
14. Diseases of the genitourinary system (N00 –N99);
15. Pregnancy, child birth and puerperium (O00 to O99);
16. Certain conditions originating in perinatal conditions (P00 P96);
17. Congenital malformations, deformations and chromosomal abnormalities (Q00 – Q99);
18. Symptoms and signs not covered elsewhere (R00 – R99);
19. Injury, poisoning, etc. (S00 –T98);
20. External causes of morbidity and mortality (V01 –Y98); and
21. Factors influencing health status and contact with health services (Z00 –Z99).

As mentioned earlier, a fourth numerical character is added after decimal to give further details. For example in chapter XXI

Z72. Problems related to life styles,
Z72.0 Tobacco use,
Z72.1 Alcohol use,
Z72.2 Drug use,
Z72.3 Lack of exercise,
Z72.4 Inappropriate diet and eating habits, and
Z72.5 High risk sexual behavior.

Table 1.2: Leading Causes of Death in India (per cent of total deaths)

Major Causes	*1986*	*1987*	*1988*	*1989*	*1990*	*1991*	*1992*	*1993*	*1994*	*1995*
Accidents/Injuries	7.00	6.50	6.50	7.40	8.50	8.50	8.70	8.40	8.80	10.30
Maternal Deaths	1.00	1.00	0.80	0.90	1.00	1.00	1.00	1.30	1.10	0.90
Fevers	10.40	9.40	8.00	7.40	7.30	7.30	7.70	6.70	7.30	7.30
Digestive Disorders	7.70	7.20	6.50	6.60	6.20	6.40	6.20	6.80	6.20	6.30
Respiratory System Disorders	19.70	20.00	20.30	20.20	18.80	18.90	19.60	19.20	19.30	20.70
Central Nervous Disorders	3.70	3.90	4.60	4.80	4.30	4.40	4.50	4.20	5.00	4.80
Circulatory System Diseases	9.00	9.50	10.00	10.90	11.10	11.10	10.80	10.60	11.20	12.50
Other Symptoms	8.60	9.30	8.80	8.20	8.50	8.30	8.40	8.90	10.30	12,50
Diseases of Infancy	10.50	10.20	9.80	9.80	9.80	10.20	9.60	11.00	9.60	9.80
Senility	22.40	23.00	24,70	23.80	24.40	23.80	23.30	22.90	21.20	14.90

Source: Registrar General of India, Survey of Causes of Death (Rural), 1997.

REFERENCES

1. Adams, Francis (translator). *The Genuine Works of Hippocrates*, Baltimore, Williams and Williams, 1939.
2. Bruhnes, Jean. *Human Geography, An Attempt at a Positive Classification, Principles, and Examples*, translated by T. C Le Compte and edited by Isiah Bowman and Richard Elwood Dodge, New York: 1922.
3. Dubos, Rene. *Man, Medicine and Environment*, London, Pall Mall Press, 1968. also see his *The Mirage of Health.*
4. Esper, E.J.C., *Ausfuhrliche Nachrichten von neuentdeckten, Zoolithen unbekannter vierfussinger Thiere*, Nuremberg, 1774; cited in H.E. Siegerist.
5. Huntington, Ellsworth., *Principles of Human Geography*, New York: New American Library, 1943.
6. Irwin, L.W., *Health for Better Living*, Columbus, Ohio: Charles E. Merrill Books, 1964.
7. Kawata, K., *Environmental Sanitation in India,* Ludhiana: Christian Medical College, 1963, pp. 9-10.
8. Lee, D.H.K. Climate and Economic Development of the Tropics, *Malayan Medical Journal*, Vol. II, 1930. Also see his Physiology and Tropics, *Malayan Medical Journal*, 11, 1930, pp. 105-8.
9. Markhouse, S.F., *Climate and the Energy of Nations*, London: Oxford, 1942.
10. May, Jacques M., *Ecology of Diseases*, New York: American Geographical Society, 1958. See also his *The Ecology of Human Disease*, New York: Academy of Sciences, 1960.
11. Moodie, Roy Lee (1880-1934)., *Antiquity of Disease,* Chicago: University of Chicago Press, 1923.
12. ———, *Paleopathology, An Introduction to the Study of Evidences of Diseases*, Urbana: University of Illinois Press, 1923; Park, K., *Preventive and Social Medicine*, Jabalpur: Bhanot Publications, 2000.
13. Payyapilly, Celline., "What is Holistic Health": *Health for the Millions*, Vol. 18, No. 4, Aug. 1992.
14. Platter, Felix (1536-1614). professor at Basle and author of De carporis humani structura et usu libri III, Basle, 1583, cited in *History of Medicine*, by Henry E. Siegerist, Vol. I.
15. Ratzel, Friedrich. *Anthropogeographie* (2 vols.), Stutgart: J Inglehorn, 1882, 1891.
16. Registrar General of India. Survey of *Causes of Death (Rural): Annual Report, 1997.*
17. Siegerist, H.E. *A History of Medicine, Vol I: Primitive and Archaic Medicine*, New York: Oxford University Press, 1951.
18. Scheuchzer, J.J. (1672-1733), *Homo diluviitestis*, Zurich, 1726, cited in H.E. Siegerist, *op. cit.*
19. Smith, G. Elliot. The Unrapping of Pharoh, *British Medical Journal*, 1908. Part 1. *The Royal Mummies*, Cairo: 1912.
20. Siegrist. Henry E. 'Problems of Historical-Geographical Pathology', *Bulletin of History of Medicine*, 1933, vol. 1, pp. 10-18; see also his 'The Historical Aspects of Art and Medicine', *Bulletin of Institute of History of Medicine,* 1936, vol. 47.
21. *Times of India*, April 21, 1996.
22. USDA. *Climate and Man*, Washington DC, 1941.
23. Vidal de la Blache, P. *Principle de geographie humaine*, Paris: 1922.
24. Virchow, Rudolf. cited in Siegerist, *op. cit.*
25. William, H.U. 'Human Paleopathology', in *Archaeological Pathology*, 1929, Vol. 7.
26. World Health Organization. *Our Planet, Our Health*, Geneva: WHO, 1992.
27. ———, *International Statistical Classification of Diseases and Related Health Problems,* Tenth Revision, 1993.

Wood, Jones. *Report on Human Remains*, The Archaelogical Survey of Nubia, Report for 1908-8, Cairo: 1910.

2

History of Medicine

For several millennia, a human like beast lived in the forests and caves. Generations after generations, he lived and died unmindful of himself and his environment. He had no memory power to accumulate experience and knowledge. When his brain developed further to improve upon the brain of the chimpanzee, he became alive of himself and started making Eolithic (stone) tools to do what animals do with their hands. These tools were small so that they could be handled by hand. It took several millennia before man improved upon these simple tools to make drills, knives, scrapers, and spearheads of flint and needles, javelin points, harpoons, etc. of bones. He used animal fir to protect himself from cold and he learned to use fire.

The Stone Age man was hunter and gatherer. He drew sketches on stones, bones and limestone representing animals, women and other things of importance to him. He buried the dead and believing the departed one would return one day, he put besides the dead body all that the departed person would need until then. Those who died of bone injuries etc. had visible marks on the skeletons found in burial grounds and mummies of Egypt and Peru. The Palaeolithic man had some inkling of diseases, which produced pains and sufferings; he must have tried to find reasons for their onset and also cures. What these primordial medicines were is still shrouded in mystery. But if present is key to the past, he must have secured them from experiential knowledge about the way he lived and about the natural environment around him.

The Palaeolithic man lived some 30,000 years ago. And New Stone Age set in Europe about 7000 to 10,000 years BC and in Asia a bit earlier. During the intervening 20,000 years, man advanced from hunting and food gathering stage to ploughing the land and growing crops of food grains; he started domestication of animals and living in self made huts and villages; tree trunks were hallowed to make boats, stones were polished and tools became sharper. He started covering himself with skins, barks, and even textiles.

The newly evolving civilization must have given man increasing experience and knowledge about diseases and how to handle them when they did come. May be, he used the herbs that we use today or he used mineral geysers for hydrotherapy to treat skin diseases. Neolithic man was quite skillful. Did he indulge in some sort of surgery to drain out the boils and to reset the fractured bones? There are evidences to prove that he did perform surgery of even the skulls of those who suffered from brain tumour or similar other disease.

Perhaps the initial reaction of man towards disease was just instinctive with a mixture of awe and reverence. The system of mutual aid perhaps emerged from the inability of individuals to cope with diseases and death. The Palaeolithic man helped his fellow beings is evident from burial customs. Not understanding the possible causes of diseases and death, he attributed them to some supernatural forces: departed souls, witches, ghosts, gods and goddesses. He must have come to the conclusion that the forces, which brought disease and pain would also be able to cure them. And thus emerged the practice of witchcraft and a wide variety of techniques of spiritual healing. Most of these practices continue to this day in most societies in one form or the other. As the limitations of modern medicine become more obvious, they appear to be returning in a variety of sophisticated forms like *Pranic* healing, *Reiki, hypnotism,* etc.

Minor ailments caused by overwork, over-eating, injuries, etc. were treated in the normal course by digestive and antiseptic herbs. But in matters of serious illnesses, our primitive ancestors resorted to sorcery backed by religious rites and some medications. For them, there was no difference between sorcery and medicine; they formed an integral part of the methodology adopted and went together. For example, the Egyptian society consisted of not only the living human beings but also the gods and the dead. In addition to these three elements, there were spirits, demons and evil forces. And they were all interlinked and inseparable. The common man felt secure if he were at peace with them all.

As our ancestors entered a more enlightened state of life, they evolved newer approaches and methods to maintain their health and deal with ailments, which visited them from time to time. Experiences accumulated and in due course of time, methods of diagnosing and treating diseases with the help of herbs, salts, minerals and massages together with *mantras* and *tantras* were codified to form various systems of medicine. Each system conformed to the natural conditions prevailing in the region, availability of plants and animals needed in the treatment, the beliefs and faiths and the experiential knowledge they accumulated.

To sum up, we cannot but agree with Lovelock that, "early in history, medical wisdom accumulated by shrewd observation and trial and error. The discovery of the curative value of drugs like quinine was not in some brightly lit laboratory. Rather, it was in the early experiments and observations of a village genius, who realized that there were real benefits to be had from chewing that bitter bark of the cinchona tree or real comfort implicit in the dried latex of the poppy head" i.e. opium. Even in the early part of the twentieth century, "the practice of medicine was only largely a matter of administering symptomatic relief and trying to ensure that the environment of the patient was most favourable for the powerful natural processes of healing that we all possess."

In this chapter, we propose to discuss some of the systems of medicine our ancestors, living in different geographical and cultural environments, developed (Fig. 2.1). The medical systems that we have at present are rooted in the history of civilizations. Some of the older systems still survive. Ayurveda and Chinese medicine can be cited as examples. Some other like the Greek system disappeared from the place of its origin but has survived to this day as Unani system of medicine in a vast region covering West Asia and South Asia. Then there are others like the Egyptian system of medicine or the Aztec and Maya systems of medicine, which died as the respective civilizations died. As information about these dead and alive systems becomes available, we realize that in some respects these older systems were much advanced than our present (allopathic) system of medicine. There is a lot that we can learn from them. Who knows, they may provide the base for future developments in the field of medicine.

The medical systems we propose to discuss in this chapter are Egyptian, Mesopotamian, Greek, Persian, Chinese and Ayurvedic (Indian) and, of course, what we call modern allopathic system. Many other civilizations of Africa and South America had their own systems of medicine. But we do not have enough information about them. One thing that was common among all the older civilizations in matters health was that they all practiced holistic medicine. Medicine was not outside the day-to-day life of the people.

The location and extent of these civilizations is given in Figure 2.1.

EGYPTIAN MEDICINE

The Egyptian civilization is the oldest known so far if we take archaeological evidences alone into account. In ancient Egypt, prevention and cure of diseases consisted in the wearing of amulets, reciting of incantations, and performing of certain rites, all intended to keep off or drive off the evil spirits. The texts of incantations and descriptions of other magic procedures are encountered scattered all over the Egyptian literature of sixteenth century BC. The sorcerer used many ways of driving away the evil spirits. The simplest way was to order him out: *'Get thee hence, thou female breaker of bones, thou crusher of stones, who enters into the vessels.'* Here is another incantation threatening the ghost: *'O ghost, male or female, thou hidden, thou concealed one, who dwelleth in this my flesh, in these my limbs – get thee hence from this my flesh, from these my limbs. Lo, I brought three excrements to devour! Beware, hidden one, be on your guard, concealed one, escapel.'*

Egyptians, apart from indulging in magical-cum-religious medicines, had also developed empirical-cum-rational approach to treatment of diseases. A number of Papyri (manuscripts written on a particular kind of paper in ancient Egypt) have been discovered which deal with the treatment of diseases but very few of them have been found intact. Veterinary and Gynaecological Papyri of Kahun offers interesting details about treatment of animals and women. The Papyri are named after their discoverers and the place of discovery. The Smith Papyri were discovered by Edwin Smith and hence they are known as Smith Papyri. They were found at Kahun, a place in Egypt, so they are known as Edwin Smith Papyri of Kahun. The papyri pertain to nineteenth century BC.

The *Smith Papyri* reveal that Egyptians had a well-organized health service. Physicians had four major ranks: General Physician, Chief Physician, Inspector Physician, and Superintending Physician. The head of the medical corps was called the Greatest Physician of Lower and Upper Egypt. The best physicians of Egypt were attached to the court.

Egyptian physicians were keen observers. They looked at the body especially face, eyes, nostrils, belly; temperature and pulse; enquired about the nature of the pain; asked the patient to move the limbs in pain, etc. They did almost everything that a modern physician does, barring, of course, the laboratory tests. The Papyri mentions of several remedies for both external and internal use. According to Papyrus Ebers, a dislocation in the hinder part should

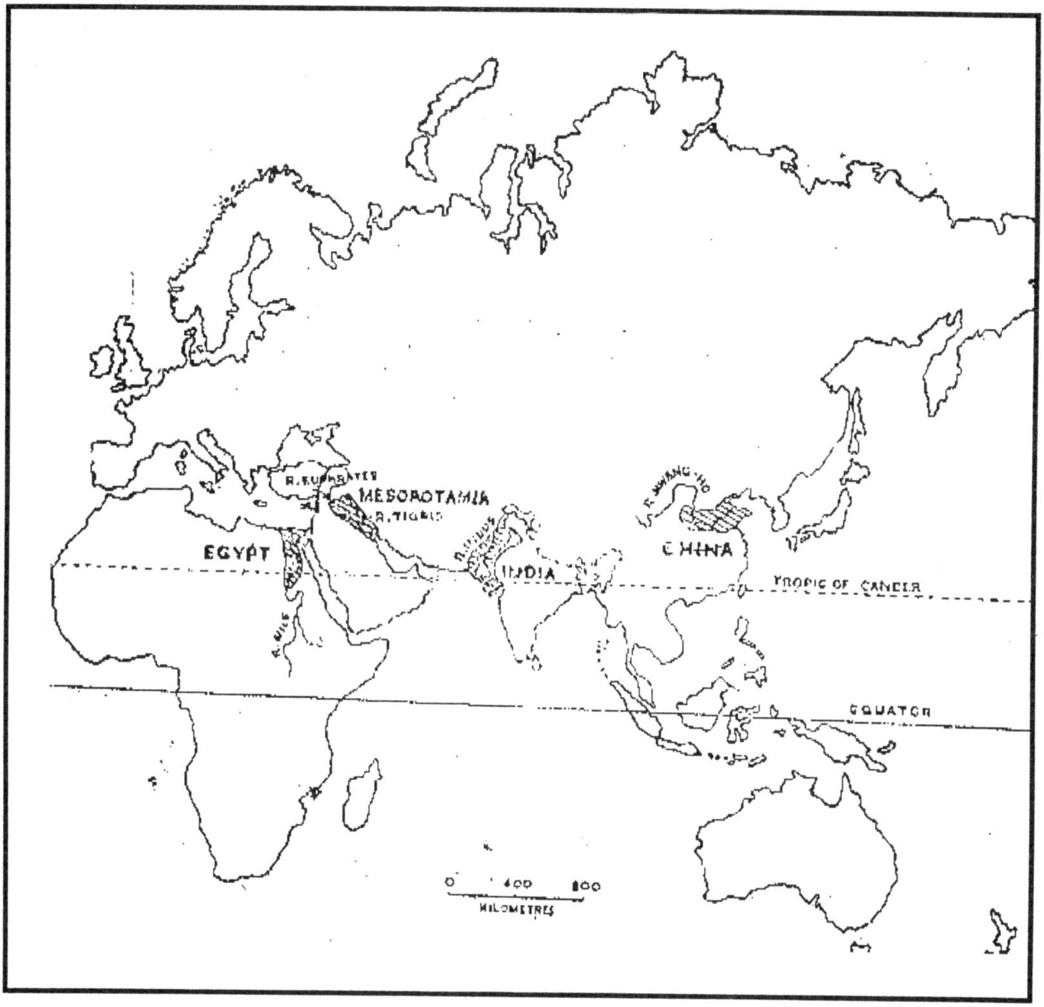

Fig. 2.1: The Great Civilizations of the World

be treated in following ways: *myrrh, frankincense, rush-nut from the garden, mhtt from the shore, celery, coriander, oil, salt are boiled together, applied in seed wool and put in the hinder part.* There are several other prescriptions for different diseases and ailments.

It is interesting to note that some of the medicines, Egyptian physicians prescribed, are still in use. Apparently, the experiential knowledge they had was not unscientific. Look at what the Papyrus Ebers says about the efficacy of castor oil. *If its peel is brayed in water and applied to a head that suffers, it will be cured immediately as though it had never suffered. If a few of its seeds are chewed by a person who is constipated it will expel the feces from the body of that person. The hair of woman will be made to grow by means of its seeds. Bray, mixed into one mass, and apply with grease. Let the woman anoint her head with it.* Its oil when applied on sores with foul discharge for ten days in the morning, the sore would disappear. A number of plants and animal parts were used in the treatment of diseases. Castor was just one of them.

Egyptians were aware that vessels go from heart to every limb of the body carrying blood. Major organs of the body were known and had names and it was believed that they all were connected with each other, either directly or via the heart. The heart was considered to be the central organ; the nose was also considered important as it carried the air inside. These speculations were important because they heralded the beginning of medical science in those early years of Egyptian civilization.

The Egyptian culture declined during the first millennium BC but Egyptian medicine continued its onward march. It exerted considerable influence far beyond its geographic borders. Many Egyptian physicians were loaned to other countries including Persia. The Greeks too learnt a lot from them.

MESOPOTAMIAN MEDICINE

Mesopotamian medicine was very much influenced by religion. The gods created man for their service—to cultivate the land, build temples, breed animals, etc. Service of the gods was the principal duty of man. Leading a pure life, observation of various religious taboos, prayer, sacrifice, and use of magic, amulets, solemn incantation were the methods employed. Magic was a perfectly legitimate science and man's chief means of protection.

Detailed knowledge of the religious and magical practices in Mesopotamia is, however, hard to get. Unlike Egypt, the Mesopotamians did not produce anything like Papirus. Nor did they leave behind mummies, which could become sources of medical information. They have, however, left a large number of tablets, which contain lot of medical information. Unfortunately, what we learn from these tablets is names of the demons that caused diseases, and incantations (mantras), which could tame them. K. Tallquist (1894), David W. Myhrman (1902), and R. Campbell (1903-4) have published some of these incantations. The tablets also give information about diseases and their symptoms, the incantations and herbs used to treat them.

'May Shamash and Marduk give thee health' was usual part of Babylonian greeting. The Assyrians said 'May Ninib and Gula give the king my lord happiness and health'. Health was thus a prized state of life and everyone wanted to possess it. Mesopotamians believed that a disease was a sort of punishment given to people for their or their kinsmen's bad deeds or sins. Such beliefs continue to this day in one form or the other all over the world. It was difficult for the Babylonians to understand why good people suffered from diseases.

Babylonians also believed in poetic justice. If "a man has destroyed the eye of a patrician, his own eye shall be destroyed,' prescribes the code of Hammurabi. Similar rules prevailed in Assyria also. The Hittites were, however, very humane; they punished offenders only monetarily.

Mesopotamian medicine consisted of incantations, magic and witchcraft, apart from herbal treatments, hydrotherapy and heat therapy to remove the demon responsible for diseases. Man could become sick not only because he did something sinful or he annoyed the demon, but also because some sorcerer transferred diseases from other person or place.

GREEK MEDICINE

The Greek tribes, which in the course of time populated the islands that now form a part of Greece, Cyprus and Turkey, came down in waves from 2000 BC onwards. The Achaeans were the first to arrive; then came the Dorians in 1200 BC. The northern territories of the eastern Mediterranean basin was settled by the Aeolians, whose language was immortalized by the poems of Sappho; the central part by Ionian who gave Greek science and medicine; and the south was settled by Dorians whose Dorian language was the *lingua franca* of Sparta. Hippocrates, the father of western medicine, was an Ionian.

Like Egypt, Greece was a small country. One wonders how small countries like Egypt and Greece produced cultures, which produced global ripples. River Nile opened Egypt to outside world; and mountains, seas and islands gave Greece the character of an outward looking society. Its location at the junction of East and West has been its greatest asset. The 5th century BC was the golden age of Greek civilization; it was the time that formulated ideas and ideals, and set the style for centuries. Athens, a city-state, had no more than 300,000 population, one third of them being slaves, and one fifth of the remaining being resident aliens (metics). Pericles made the city one of the most beautiful one in the world. Greece had the privilege to produce Thucydides – a great historian, and Socrates – a great philosopher. Earlier, it had given to the world Hippocrates – one of the greatest physicians of the world. Greece invented a new way of territorial governance, the city based republics. It was a great departure from the kingdoms of Egypt, and the states of Mesopotamia. People were highly politicised and a citizen's time was almost entirely spent in the service of his polis.

Much of the information about Greek medicine comes from Hippocratic Collections (*Corpus Hippocraticum*). Hippocrates was a great physician of fourth century BC. He is supposed to have written extensively on health, diseases and medicine. Hippocratic Collections contain material supposed to have been written by him but it is now proved that it is not so. Hippocrates in Greek medical tradition was something like Vyasa in Indian literary tradition of ancient times. So many people wrote in the name of Vyasa. Now we do not know as to which treatise was authored by the real Vyasa. Similarly, anything written on medical issues in ancient Greece was attributed to Hippocrates. And all such writings were later compiled to form *Hippocratic Collections.*

These collections date from fifth to fourth century B.C. It contains all the medical literature available at the time in Alexandria. There are treatises, which are as short as one page or as long as a big book. Some of the treatises bear titles, which do not match with the contents. Among the treatises are those On Anatomy, On the Nature of Bones, On Flesh, On Glands, On Ancient Medicine, On Breaths, On the Nature of Man, On Diseases, On Humors, On Crisis, On Critical Days, On Epidemics, On Airs, Waters and Places, On the Use of Liquids, On Diet, On Fractures, On Wounds in the Head, On the Nature of Child, On the Diseases of the Maidens, On the Sacred Diseases, etc. etc.

For the Greeks, education of the youth was not complete unless they had a full exposure to physical education. They had clean habits and took bath regularly. They built gymnasia for bodybuilding. The Olympic games were founded in the eighth century BC. How health conscious were the Greeks is clear from the prescriptions of Oribasius for the gentlemen about morning routine.

"The cultivation of health begins with the moment a man wakes up. This should as a rule, be when the food he ate the previous day, has already moved from stomach to the bowels. A young or middle-aged man should take a walk of about 10 stadia just before sunrise, in summer, however, he should walk only five, and older men will take a shorter walk in winter as well as summer. After awakening one should not rise at once but should wait until the heaviness and torpor of sleep have gone. After arising one should rub one's neck and head thoroughly in order to overcome the stiffness caused by the pillow. Then rub the whole body with some oil. ...Thereafter one shall every day wash face and eyes with the hands using pure water. One shall rub the gums in order to strengthen the teeth or simply rub the teeth inside and outside with the fingers using some fine peppermint powder and cleaning the teeth of remnants of food. One shall anoint nose and ears inside preferably with well-perfumed oil. ... One shall rub and anoint the head everyday but wash it and comb it at intervals...."

For the common people who could not afford to follow the above routine and "drink and eat what they happen to get, and who are obliged to work, and to travel by land and sea in order to make a living, who are exposed to unwholesome heat and unwholesome cold, and who otherwise lead an irregular life", there was a Hippocratic book On Diet. It is the best early Greek treatise on diet. Book I deals with the nature of man and Book II with nature of foods. Man was supposed to have been constituted by two elementary qualities hot and dry, cold and moist. Centuries later, Galen wrote a treatise On the Faculties of Foods in three volumes wherein he gave detailed instructions on the effects and uses of practically everything we eat and drink.

Hippocratic Collections contain another treatise entitled On Sound Diet. Cited below is one of its very modernistic prescriptions on obesity for the rich. "Fat people and all those who wish to reduce must do all hard work on an empty stomach, and then begin eating while they are still out of breath from exertion and without having refreshed themselves having only had some diluted and not very cold wine. Their food should be prepared with sesame, sweet spices and similar substances, and should be rich, for thus they will feel satiated with minimum of food. Furthermore, one should have only one meal a day, should not bathe and should sleep on a hard couch. One should walk nude as much as possible. Those who wish to gain weight should do the contrary." The book also has a chapter on vomiting and the taking of enema as a matter of hygiene. One of the Hippocratic collections 'Airs, Waters, Places' clearly shows that the Greeks paid special attention to environmental setting of dwelling places.

Greeks believed that human body possessed a large number of humors having elementary qualities. So long as their blend was perfect, body was healthy; when the balance among them was upset, diseases set in. Later the number of humors was brought down to four: two pairs with opposite qualities. The humors were phlegm, blood, bile and water. They enter the semen, male or female, from which the embryo was supposed to have been formed. This explained the inheritance of parent's qualities by children. By first century BC, the centre of civilization shifted to Rome. Roman borrowed their medicine from Greece, which they had conquered. Romans, being more practical minded, laid emphasis on sanitation, drainage, water supply, sewage system and established hospitals to combat malaria and other diseases, which had become common by that time.

Galen (130-205 AD) was a great Roman medical teacher. He was physician to the Roman emperor. He was of the view that health was more important than disease and hence its preservation should get greater and prior attention. Disease should receive relatively less attention than health. He attributed three reasons for diseases: predisposing, exciting and environment. He was thus very modern. He wrote over 500 treatises on medical subjects. He, along with Hippocrates, ruled the medical world for over 1400 years.

UNANI MEDICINE

The Unani System of medicine owes its origin, as its name suggests, to Greece (Yunan). From Greece it travelled to Arabia and then to Persia and India imbibing the best from Persian and Indian systems of medicine. The present day Unani system of medicine is, therefore, an amalgam of Greek-Arab-Persian-Indian systems of medicine.

In between Greece and India, the two regions where Unani medicine reached great heights, lies the plateau of Persia where existed a great empire in the sixth century BC. Cyrus was its greatest king; his kingdom extended from Aegean Sea to Indus river and from Black Sea to the Arabian Sea. Persia was a menace to both Greece and Egypt. The Persians were empire builders but not builders of civilization as the Greeks, Egyptians and Indians were. They borrowed from everywhere and tried to create a Persian symbiosis; they did not succeed fully though. After the death of Cyrus the empire collapsed. Persian religious beliefs were similar to those held by other Indo-European immigrants. They believed in animal sacrifice to propitiate gods like Mithra; they did not burry their dead, they were left to be devoured by eagles and dogs. The idea was to be useful to others even after death.

In sixth century BC Zarathrusta or Zoroaster preached a purified monotheistic religion and did away with the lesser gods. The new religion declared Ahura Mazda as the God Almighty. The new religion spread fast when Darius, a great Persian king, embraced it. The tenets of the religion were codified in Avesta, the sacred book of the Persians of the time. His teachings are known as Gatha.

The Persians were great synthesizers. They borrowed liberally from Greek and Indian systems of medicine and developed their own science and art of healing. They identified three types of healers: those who healed with a knife, those who healed with herbs and those who healed with holy water.

Persian medicine took a new turn when the Arabs occupied Persia and converted Zoroastrians to Islam. Arabs were in frequent contact with Greece as well as India. They adopted the Greek medicine and adapted it to their local conditions. Their contact with India enriched it further. And thus they evolved, what is now known as, the Unani system of medicine. The Persians blended this system with their own and enriched it further. The Unani system of medicine is very close to India's Ayurvedic system. India recognizes it as one of the indigenous systems of medicine.

The theoretical base of the Unani system of medicine is derived from the teachings of Hippocrates. Arab and Persian physicians borrowed from the Greek writing especially of Galen (131-210 AD) during the ninth and tenth centuries. It treats disease as a natural process and its symptoms are responses of the body to the disease. The chief function of the physician is to strengthen the natural forces of the body so that diseases fail to overpower it.

The Unani system is based on the Humoral theory. Humors are the body fluids of four types: the Dam (blood), Balgham (phlegm), Safra (yellow bile) and Sauda (black bile). Each of these is linked to its own temperament. Blood is hot and moist, phlegm is cold and moist, yellow bile is hot and dry and black bile is cold and dry.

In India the Unani system of medicine was introduced around tenth century AD by the Arabs and later by the Persians. It received patronage from Delhi Sultans, particularly the Khiljis and Tughlaqs and later, the Moghal emperors. The Unani medical practitioners called Hakims were appointed as court physicians. The system got good response from the public as it was very close to Ayurveda, the Indian system of medicine.

The Unani system suffered during the British Raj as did the other indigenous systems but it remained popular among sections of the people especially in Punjab. Among the famous Indian Hakims of the nineteenth century were: Hakim Ajmal Khan of Delhi, Hakim Ahmed Hussain Usmani of Allahabad, and Hakim Abdul Aziz of Lucknow. The Nizam of Hyderabad gave patronage to this system in the South.

After Independence of the country, the Unani system of medicine was officially recognized as one of the Indian systems of medicine and steps were taken to develop it further and to popularise among the people.

AYURVEDIC (INDIAN) SYSTEM OF MEDICINE

India has had a well-developed system of medicine from ancient times, known as Ayurveda i.e. Science of Life or Longevity. Ayurveda is an integral part of the Vedas, which makes it at least 5000 years old. Around 1000 BC, Charak, the father of Indian system of medicine, compiled a treatise called *Charak Samhita* giving the philosophy and principles of health and medicine. About the same time, Sushruta, a great surgeon compiled *Sushruta Samhita* giving the principles and methods of surgical operations. According to Ayurveda, the ultimate goal of man is to achieve Nirvana, that is self-realization. But being a social being and creator of his own culture and civilization, he has other goals to achieve. These are: *dharma* (performance of one's duty towards others including nature and other life forms); *artha* (to earn livelihood and create a sound economic base for future generations); *kama* (to reproduce and live a satisfying life) and *moksha* to realize one's spiritual potentials to merge in the Almighty God. To achieve these goals, man must live long and possess a healthy body and mind. Ayurveda, therefore, takes a very integrated view of health. It does not mean just absence of disease; nor does it mean just physical and mental health in conventional sense. It means sound physique, alert and cool mind, and compassionate and loving attitude towards all that is living. Thus, the Indian concept of health has four dimensions: physiological, mental, social and spiritual.

According to Ayurveda, each human being is a sum total of five basic gross elements (*pancha mahabhootas*), seven body tissues (*sapta dhatus*) and five senses (*panchendriyas*) along with mind (*manas*), which performs the sensory and motor functions, intellect (*buddhi*) and soul (*atma*). The *panch mahabhootas* are: lithosphere (solid earth), hydrosphere (water in various forms), atmosphere (air), sunlight (fire or energy), and ether (space). They join together to create three humors in human body called *tridoshas*. So long as these *doshas* are in balance, body is healthy. Imbalance among the *doshas* appears in the form of various kinds of diseases.

Air+Ether produce *Vata;* Water +Earth produce *Kapha*, and Fire gives rise to *Pitta*. The mental and spiritual aspects of health are depicted by three temperaments (*prakriti*) or personality traits: *Satva, Rajas* and *Tamas.*

Ayurveda tries to keep each of these functional and structural entities in a functional state of equilibrium. This is called good health (*Swasthya*) in this system of medicine. Imbalance among them for reasons internal or external, produces diseases. The task of Ayurveda is to restore the equilibrium using various medicines, techniques, procedures, regimens and foods.

Ayurveda considers man to be a replica of the whole universe. The laws that govern the universe also govern man and each cell within man (*Yatha Pinde tatha Bhhmande*). Human body is a complex biological system; it should not be considered in isolation. While treating it, one has to consider the body and temperament (*prakriti*); sex, age, and metabolic system; style of life–work, rest, sleep patterns, etc and the environment in which one lives. Ayurveda approaches health from two perspectives: preventive consisting of *Swastha-vritt* (personal hygiene, regular daily routine, and *aachar* i.e. appropriate social behaviour) and *Rasayan Sevana* (use of rejuvenative foods, and medicines) and curative measures using *Aushadhi* (drugs), *Anna* (diet), *Vihar* (relaxation).

Ayurveda has several specialized branches. During the Samhita period (1000 BC), main specialities were: Internal Medicine (*Kaya Chiktsa*); Padiatrics (*Kaumar Baritya*), Psychiatry (*Graha Chikitsa*), ENT (*Shalkya*), Surgery (*Shalya Tantra*); Toxicology (*Vish Tantra*); Geriatrics (*Rasayana*); and Science of Virility (*Vajikarna*). During the last few decades, several new specializations have developed. These are: Principles of Ayurveda (*Ayurveda Siddhanta*); Ayurveda Samhita; Anatomy (*Rachna Sharira*); Physiology (*Kriya Sharira*); Materia Medica and Pharmacology (*Dravya Guna Vigyan*); *Ras Shastra*; Pharmaceuticals (*Bhaishajya Kalpana*); Ganecology and Obstetrics (Prasuti-Tantra); Social and Preventive Medicine (*Swasth-Vritla*); Pathology (*Rog Nidan*); and Rejuvenation Methods (*Panchakarma*). The diagnosis of diseases is carried out by questioning, inference and examination of pulse, urine, feces, tongue, eye and visual/sensual appearances.

Originally, Ayurveda was not a separate composition. It formed part of the four main Vedas: Rik, Sama, Yajur and Atharva. Later, the health related topics were culled out and put together as Ayurveda. It is, therefore, considered to be an auxiliary branch of the Vedas called Upveda.

As time passed and more knowledge was accumulated, Ayurveda developed eight specific branches of medicine and two main schools: School of Physicians and the School of Surgeons, the former headed by sage Atreya; and the latter by sage Dhanvantari. These schools made Ayurveda a scientifically verifiable and classifiable medical system. Through research and testing, they dispelled the doubts and removed the aura of mystery that surrounded the concept of divine revelation. Ayurveda thus emerged as a respected and widely used system of healing. People from different countries of the world came to India to learn Ayurveda. It was taught in all universities and seminaries. That may explain many similarities between Ayurveda and other older systems of medicine discussed in this chapter.

Ayurveda was reorganized sometimes during the seventh and eighth centuries by two great specialists: Charaka and Sushruta. They compiled the latest knowledge in the field of medicine and surgery into two Samhitas. Charaka Samhita deals with medicine, while the Sushruta Samhita deals with surgery. A combined version of the two Samhitas called Ashtanga Hridaya

Samhita was also prepared by Vegabhata. These three Samhitas constitute the basic books of Ayurveda and its three author sages are something like three Hippocrates of India. According to sage Bharadwaja, the sages, concerned about increasing number of diseases, initiated the following inquiry: *Health is the supreme foundation of virtue, wealth and enjoyment and salvation. Now the diseases are the destroyers of health, of the good of life, and even of life itself. Thus has arisen the great impediment in the progress of humanity. What shall be the means of remedying it? Having observed thus they sat into meditation.*

Charak belonged to the Atreya School of Physicians. The Charak Samhita deals with physiology, anatomy, etiology, pathogenesis, symptoms and signs and symptoms of diseases; methodology of diagnosis, treatment and prescription of patients, prevention of diseases and longevity. According to Charak, the primary cause of ill health is loss of faith in God-belief that each individual is part of the universe and is bound by the laws of nature. The next in importance are climate, diet and style of life. There are separate sections on herbs, diet and reversing the aging process. Charak has given month to month details of the development of foetus in mother's womb.

Sushruta, on the other hand, belonged to the Dhanvantari School of Surgeons. His samhita gives details of surgical equipments, typology of abscesses, burns, fractures and rectal surgery. Human anatomy focusing on the bones, joints, nerves, heart blood vessels, and circulatory system forms part of the Samhita. He also gives the theory and practice of massage using marma points or vital points in the body, which parallel Chinese system of acupuncture.

The tridosh theory of diseases was formulated in the middle of the first millennium BC. The period extending from 600 B.C. to 1000 AD is considered to be the creative period of Indian medicine. During this period Taxila and Varanasi developed as great centers of medical education and research. Several treatises on medicine and surgery were written during this period to add, elaborate and modify the knowledge contained in Ayurveda. It was during this period that Susruta, the surgeon wrote Salyatantra, a treatise on surgery. Atreya at Taxila trained a large number students drawn from all over the then known world and declared that "all suffering whether of the body or mind, has for its basis ignorance; all happiness has its foundation in pure scientific knowledge."

Susruta recognized three causes of diseases: physical i.e. hereditary, congenital or derangement of dosas (humors); environmental and natural (divine). Diseases were considered as mere symptoms of certain internal disequilibria among dosas (humors) and dhatus (minerals) in the system. Medicines were designed to bring about the balance, and thus to cure the diseases indirectly. With the destruction of many of the centers of education and research and burning of libraries in medieval times, systematic research in Ayurveda ceased. It remained confined to what the pioneers wrote in days bygone. Its decline also produced a curious amalgam of experiential knowledge of grandmother's folk medicine and propitiation of super natural powers like ghosts and witches through tantras and other dubious practices.

SIDDHA SYSTEM

The Siddha system is based on the principle of free flow of pranic energy (life) all through the body all the time. When this flow clogged or stopped diseases take their roots. Restoring the free flow of energy is restores the health of the patient. No medicines are needed for this. It can be done by meditation and yoga.

Chakras are the seven vital centers in the body staring from the lowest point of the central chord to the top of the head. The clogging of the charkas and sushumnas occurs partly because of heredity and partly because of environment, both internal and external, in which a newly born grows up into an adult and becomes a mature individual. Modern behavioural sciences postulate that man is the product of heredity and environment. This is what the theory of Karma also says. Heredity is determined by the Karma of the mother, Karma of the father and the Karma of one's own accumulated Karmas from the previous lives. According to the Diddha system of medicine, the charkas and sushumna of the newly born are already clogged to some extent. And further clogging takes place because of unfavourable environment. The blockages stop the free flow of life sustaining energy in certain parts of the body. This is what appears as a diseases.

While growing up, every impression, feeling and thought is stored in the chakra, sushumnas and the subconscious mind. Every second, we are storing experiences even if unconsciously. Some of these we able to recall but many others we cannot. Siddha say, "you are anant anand" (infinite and eternal bliss) but the load that we accumulate and carry cuts off our access to divine power and ultimately governs and modifies our thoughts and actions.

The impurities clogging the charkas reduce life energy flow to some endoctrine glands and body tissues and organs. They also accumulate in certain amount in some organs which start malfunctioning. All diseases are caused by the distotion of energy grid in the body by wrong thoughts and beliefs. Psychics who can see and photograph auras around can discern the nature of the diseases by the colour of the aura.

A Siddha physician can find the reasons underlying diseases. Suppressed anger, appears as fever; suppressed crying as cold; suppressed speech as cough; bitterness as gal bladder stone; lack of sweetness in life as diabetes; refusal to see what needs to be seen or to see what ought not be seen as eyesight problem; stiff and inflexible attitude as arthritis; irritation of mind as itching; mental disturbances as phobias, guilt, depression, arrogance, lack of self-confidence. Each disease is a message that our body gives that we are getting into the unbalanced thought patterns.

The blockages can be removed or very much tempered by meditation, Yoga and related practices.

CHINESE SYSTEM OF MEDICINE

The Chinese system of medicine is one of the oldest and is least influenced from outside. According to legend, it commenced with Fu His in the last century of 3rd millennium (2953) BC. Emperors Shen Nung (2838 BC) and Huang T (2698-2598 BC) developed it further. The latter popularly known as Yellow Emperor, is credited to have composed Nei Ching (The Cannon of Internal Medicine) although some claim that it is not older than 3rd century BC. There are two more compilations, which deserve mention here: Mo Ching (Pulse Classic) written in 3rd century BC, and Golden Mirror, prepared in 17the century AD. The latter title is a collection of medical writings of the Han dynasty. The European medicine entered China in the nineteenth century but the indigenous system continues to be quite popular with the masses.

Chinese medicine recognizes only two vital forces-*Chi* and *Yin*. Diseases are caused by imbalances among them. The balance can be brought about through the administration of herbal, mineral and other medicines, and by acupuncture.

The religious teachings prohibit the mutilation of dead body. And hence the system is week in anatomy. The blood vessels are supposed to contain blood and air in proportions varying with those of the *yang* and *yin*. They circulate in the 12 channels and thus control the pulse.

Materia medica of Chinese medicine is very extensive consisting of vegetable matter, animal products and minerals. About 1000 of the herbs were compiled in 52 volumes of Pen-Ts'ao Kang Mu (the Great Herbal) in 1552-78 by Li-Sheh-chen. The drugs are related to five organs, five planets, five colours, etc. Several of the drugs of Chinese origin are being used by other systems. Hydrotherapy has an important place in Chinese medicine. The inoculation of smallpox was practised in China from ancient times.

Acupuncture consists of insertion in the skin and underlying tissues of a metal needle, hot or cold. The theory is that the needle will affect the distribution of yang and yin. Surgery did not get recognition because it amounted to interference with the body. Castration was the only practice common in China.

MODERN (ALLOPATHIC) MEDICINE

The period following 1500 AD was marked by a variety of changes in practically all aspects of life in Europe. 1453-1600 was the period of individual scientific achievements. Swiss born Peracelsus (1493-1541) publicly burnt the works of Galen and Avicena and made the medicine a scientific practice. Fracustorius (1483-1553), an Italian physician, advanced the theory of infection. Andhreas Vasalius (1514-1564) of Brussels debunked Galen's ideas and established anatomy on scientific basis. Similarly, surgery was given a scientific base by Ambroise Pare (1510-1590), a French army surgeon. The seventeenth and eighteenth centuries were marked by still more exciting discoveries. Microscope helped identify viruses and bacteria; Jenner's vaccination stopped further expansion of smallpox, and new awareness about hygiene and sanitation gave rise to the concept of public health. French bacteriologist, Louis Pasteur, came with germ theory of diseases in 1873; Robert Koch (1843-1910) demonstrated that anthrax was caused by a bacterium. By the end of the nineteenth century, several disease-causing microbes were discovered. Bruce, an army surgeon, traced the cause of sleeping sickness in Africa to tsetse fly in 1896, and Ross in 1998, demonstrated that malaria was caused by anopheles mosquitoes. Walter Reed and his colleagues proved that Aedes mosquito was the cause of yellow fever.

Cholera, which is often called 'father of public health', devastated the western world during the nineteenth century. An English epidemiologist, John Snow, studied the epidemiology of cholera in London from 1848 to 1854 and established the role of polluted water drawn from a water pump. Similarly, William Budd established that typhoid was also caused by polluted water. This led to the enactment of Public Health Act of 1875 in England. Similar measures were adopted in other European countries and across the Atlantic in America. Along with public health, preventive medicine got a firm foundation and search for drugs and vaccines, which could prevent diseases, became a major preoccupation of the scientific community.

The beginning of the twentieth century saw the eradication of many of major killers in the west. At the same time, the pattern of disease started changing and the so-called diseases of modern civilization emerged as major health hazards. These new diseases could not be explained by germ theory. It was realized that other factors – genetic, environmental, social, psychological and economic – were also important. Along with the germ theory, multi-factorial causation theory was also mooted to explain the occurrence of diseases. And thus were born a number of new branches or new thrusts to old branches of medicine.

Curative Medicine

Curative medicine aims at removing diseases from patients. It involves treatment by administering anti-bacterial and antibiotic drugs, which produce a reaction that neutralizes the disease. It is as old as medicine itself but in the twentieth century it acquired unprecedented scientific knowledge about diseases, medicines and ways of administering the medicines. With the growth of medical sciences, specialization based on skills such as surgery, radiology, and anaesthesia; on parts of the body such as E-N-T and cardiology; on sex such as gynaecology and obstetrics; and on age such as paediatrics and geriatrics developed. Specialization raised the standards of medical care but the cost of the medical services increased many-fold. Today it is difficult for a poor person to secure medical services at a price he can afford.

Preventive Medicine

Preventive medicine is applied to healthy persons in groups. That is, it focuses on populations rather than individuals. It received a shot in the arm when vaccines and anti-sera were discovered for dreaded diseases like diphtheria, tetanus and typhoid fever. The anti-viral polio vaccine came in the market during 1955-60. The last case of smallpox in India was recorded in 1977. Search for newer and better drugs and vaccines for malaria, leprosy, syphilis and other parasitic diseases has produced good results and many developing countries afflicted by infectious diseases can now hope to eradicate these diseases in the foreseeable future.

Nutrition is another field in which preventive medicine has played very important role. Nutritional blindness and iodine deficiency disorders have been reduced substantially. Discovery of vitamins, minerals, proteins and other nutritional requirements of a healthy body has prevented the onset of many diseases. Nutritious diet not only prevents deficiency diseases but also prepares the body to face other diseases, specially the infectious diseases which are so common in the developing parts of the world.

Added to the progress on the nutritional front, was the introduction of sulfa drugs and multi-drug therapy. Antibiotics against some of the dreaded diseases like malaria, tuberculosis and leprosy, and mass drug treatment made modern treatment within the reach of the common man. The concept of disease eradication was also the product of changed medical scenario. Use of screening in the diagnosis of diseases in their pre-symptomatic stages is also the gift of the twentieth century medicine. X-ray proved to be a great boon especially for those who suffered from chest diseases like T.B. and broken bones resulting from increasing number of accidents. Population control through fertility control and contraceptives is the latest addition to the responsibilities of preventive medicine. Search for a vaccine that can be administered to males to check pregnancy is in its final stage. It will add another feather in the cap of the preventive medicine.

Modern preventive medicine has been defined as the art and science of health promotion, disease prevention, disability limitation and rehabilitation. It operates at three levels. At the primary level, it aims at keeping healthy persons immune from diseases; at the secondary level, it treats those who have the disease; and at the tertiary level, it tries to lower the impact of the disease on those who have it.

Social Medicine

Social medicine is the epidemiological study of people and communities in their total environmental setting. It looks at social causes, social consequences and social therapies in the etiology of diseases. Its focus is on community, rather than individuals. That social factors impact human health was known earlier too. Neumann in 1847 and R. Virchow in 1848 had clearly indicated this dimension of medicine in the nineteenth century. As we saw in earlier sections on ancient medical traditions, social factors were always considered significant in the treatment of diseases.

Credit for the revival of social medicine as an important branch of modern medicine goes to Alfred Grotjahn of Berlin (1869-1931); he called it social pathology. In India, it is still an academic discipline something like medical geography. Medical science and medical profession are yet to recognize its importance, role and potentials.

Public Health

Public health is no longer confined to cleanliness, sanitation, water, sewage system, etc. It is a major component of the global programme of Health-For-All (HFA). Its emergence to the present state can be traced in four phases: disease control, health promotion, social engineering and Health-For-All. The disease control phase began in later part of the nineteenth century and ended with the first quarter of the twentieth century (1880-1920). During this phase number of legislative measures were taken in the west to improve sanitation and living environment. All activities were related to specific diseases like cholera, and smallpox.

In the second phase (1920-1960), apart from control of diseases, health promotion became an important activity. CEA Winslow, one of the leading figures in public health, defined it as 'the science and art of preventing disease, prolonging life and promoting health and efficiency through organized community effort'. Public health became the responsibility of the government all over the world. The idea of primary health centres in rural areas where the majority of people of developing countries lived was the products of this phase.

During the social engineering phase (1960-1980), social and behavioural dimensions of health got new attention. It was in response to emergence of systemic disorders like diabetes, cancers, heart problems and arthritis, which were related to smoking, drug abuse, intoxication, obesity, sedentary life style, and other behavioural traits. Controlling the risk factors became one of its major preoccupations. The goals of public health and preventive medicine almost merged to form what is now know as community medicine.

The last phase (since 1980) of public health focused its attention to the poor and deprived people of the world. It was found that most of the diseases people in the developing countries suffered from were related to public health. Hence, a global programme was chalked out under the auspices of the WHO to eradicate infectious diseases by providing clean drinking water, better housing, basic health facilities and mass scale administration of vaccines and drugs to eradicate infectious diseases like polio and tuberculosis.

Family and Community Health

Francis Peabody, Professor of Medicine at Harvard University, commented in 1923 that specialization in medicine had gone too far; he called for the return to general practice. The Millis Commission in UK (1966) and Willard Committee in the USA also expressed the same view. Thus was born the concept of Family and Community Medicine, which in essence means the rediscovery of social, cultural and human aspects of medicine and recognition of family and community as the focal point of healthcare. WHO recommends that each community should have its own health care facility charged with the responsibility of promoting health and preventing diseases. Community health assesses the health requirements of the whole community; makes provisions to meet its health needs; to carry out research in community health; and to organize health education for the people.

The Health-For-All (HFA) Plan jointly prepared by WHO and UNICEF and approved at Alma-Ata in 1978, focuses on community medicine. It has eight basic elements:

1. Education about the prevailing health problems and the ways of preventing and controlling them;
2. Food security with a view to improve nutritional status of the people;
3. Safe drinking water and sanitation for all;
4. Maternal and child care as part of the family planning programme;
5. Immunization against infectious diseases;
6. Prevention and control of endemic diseases;
7. Appropriate treatment of common diseases and injuries; and
8. Provision of essential drugs.

The plan gives priority to socialization of the primary health services and education with a view to remove the prevailing impression that they were something beyond the purview and understanding of the common man and to making them accessible to all by well trained commoners and lay workers. In olden days, the common health problems were handled locally by medicine men possessing experiential knowledge. That system needs to be revived with the proviso that such commoners are trained and certified for specific jobs. This will spare people from unnecessary calls to the physicians; it will save money too.

Surgery

One of the major contributions of modern medicine is advancement in surgery. It has made the treatment of many diseases, which were earlier untreatable, possible. Surgery is not a new thing; it was practiced even in ancient times, so the records say. But those were rare and simple cases. With the improvement in knowledge of human anatomy, and better instruments and equipments it is now possible to conduct surgery of even the brain. With the introduction of anaesthesia, it has become a painless treatement.

Let us, however, keep in view that it is one thing to be able to treat even untreatable diseases but quite another the check the diseases from taking hold of human body and mind. If we can give as much emphasis on good health from the day a baby in conceived and create social conditions in which man feels happy and blissful, the advances in modern medicine and surgery can make far greater contributions to human welfare.

EPILOGUE

At the threshold of the twentieth century, modern medicine uncovered the genetic code to modify and even control the capacities of man by direct intervention into and manipulation of their bodies and minds, otherwise known as genetic counselling, genetic engineering, prenatal diagnosis of diseases, in *vitro* fertilization, and even cloning. It is now possible to transplant many organs of the body; to transfer the functioning of the heart and kidney to the machines, and to energize people who are old and weak.

All these and many others are outstanding achievements of modern medicine but there is something amiss. The very purpose of medicine appears to be losing ground. It is being criticized and questioned on the ground that the more it develops the less it is accessible to the common man. It has become elitist; only a few can afford it. It has failed to counter the threats posed by many diseases like malaria. New strains of the disease emerge the moment the old strains are controlled. Longevity of life continues to be low in most of the developing countries; and child and maternal mortality has remained high. Further, the spatial distribution of health services continues to be uneven both in terms of quantity and quality.

The high technology medicine seems to be getting out of hand. It is moving from health promotion for many to expensive treatment of a privileged few. It appears the impact of modern medicine has reached its limits. There is real failure behind apparent success. R. Virchow said as early as 1849, 'medicine is a social science and politics is the medicine on large scale.' Medicine must come out of its scientific and technological shell and venture in the social field to be really effective as an instrument of health promoting discipline.

REFERENCES

1. Ahmed and Coelho, *Towards a New Definition of Health*, New York: Pleum, 1979.
2. Calcutta University, *Bheda Samhita*, 1921 (Sanskrit Text).
3. Childe, V.C., *The Aryans, New York, 1926.*
4. Elgood, C., *A Medical History of Persia*, Cambridge, 1951.
5. Edelstein, L., 'Hippocrates' in *The Oxford Classical Dictionary.*
6. Fichtner, H., *Die medizin im Avesta*, Liepzig: 1924. Zimmer, H.R. *Hindu Medicine,* Baltimore, 1948.
7. Fillenboaum, *The Wel-being of the Elderly*, WHO Pub. No. 84,1985.

8. Finke, Leonard Ludwig, 'On Different Kinds of Geographies, but Chiefly on Medical Topographies and How to Compose Them' (translated by George Rosen), in *Bulletin of History of Medicine*, 1946.
9. ——, *A Medical Geography by a Rural Practitioner*, 1792-95.
10. Government of India, *Health Information of India – 1997 and 1998*, New Delhi: Central Bureau of Health Intelligence. 2000.
11. Hoermie, A.F.R. *Studies in the Medicine of Ancient India*, 1907.
12. Hoffmann, Friedrich *A Dissertation on Endemical Diseases or Those Disorders which Arise from Particular Climates, Situations and Methods of Living*, London, 1746.
13. Howald, E. *Die Kulture der Antike*, Zurich, 1948.
14. Hume, E.H., *The Chinese Way in Medicine*, 1940.
15. ICSSR & ICMR, *Health For All: An Alternative Strategy*, New Delhi: Voluntary Health Association of India, 1981.
16. Lovelock, James., *The Ages of Gaia: A Biography of Our Living Planet*, New York: Oxford University Press, 1988, p. 154.
17. Kaviraj Kunjalal Bhishagratna (trans), *The Susruta Samhita*, Calcutta, 1907.
18. Moodie, Roy Lee, *The Antiquity of Disease*, University of Chicago Press, 1923.
19. Morse, W. R*Chinese Medicine*, 1934.
20. Mukhopadhyaya, G. *History of Indian Medicine* (3 volumes), 1923-29; also see his *Surgical Instruments of Hindus* (2 volumes), 1913-14.
21. Shree Gokulchand Ayurvedic Society, *Charak Samhita*, Jamnagar, 1949.
22. Smith, Elliot & Dawson, W.R. *Egyptian Mummies*, New York, 1924.
23. Thompson, Campbell, 'Assyrian Medical Texts', *Proceedings of the Royal Society, Medical History Section, 1924*. One can get reports on Babylonia and other ancient cultures also in these proceedings.
24. Smith, Edwin, *Papirus*.
25. Sigarist H.E., 'Sphere of Life and Death in Early Manuscripts', *Bulletin of the Institute of History of Medicine*, 1942, no. 11.
26. Singh, Bhagvat, *History of Hindu Medical Science*, New Delhi: Logos, 1995.
27. ——, 'Problems of Historical-Geographical Pathology', *Bulletin of the Institute of History of Medicine*, 1933.
28. ——, Medical and Human Welfare, New Haven: Yale University Press.
29. ——, Medical and Human Welfare, New Haven: Yale University Press.
30. Schumacher, J. 'Der Physic-Begriff Empedodles' in *Sudhoffs Arch. Gesch. Med.*, 1941, no. 34.
31. UNDP, *Human Development Report, 1999*.
32. Vakil, R.J. *Our Glorious Heritage*, Bombay: Times of India Press, 1968.
33. WHO, *World Health Report, 2001 and 2002*.
34. Wong, K.C. and Wu Lien-The. *History of Chinese Medicine*, 1936.
35. Wood, J.S., *Yoga System of Patanjali*, Harvard Oriental Series 17, Cambridge, Mass., 1914.
36. Zimmer, H.R., *Hindu Medicine*, Baltimore, 1948.

3

Evolution of Medical Geography

Medical geography is not a new subject of study. The idea that place, location, climate and culture influence health, has been known to physicians and commoners alike from times immemorial. Many diseases are environment specific; there are others, which are culture specific. Change in the climate and use of locally produced herbs and plants for curative purposes is a time-honoured practice. The experiential knowledge thus gained was codified into medical treatises from time to time. Each civilization thus has a system of medicine, which is unique and directly influenced by its natural and cultural environment.

When geography branched off as an independent discipline in the nineteenth century, it was only a matter of time for geographers to concern themselves with the relationship among space, geographic environment in particular, and health. They tried to answer five main questions:

1. Why do diseases attack some people but not others?
2. Why are certain diseases more common in some places than in others?
3. Why are certain diseases more prevalent in some cultures than in others?
4. How and why diseases spread from place to place?
5. How can the knowledge of geography help individuals and communities maintain good health?

Geographer's interest in the study of man-environment nexus through the medium of culture on the one hand and the general welfare of the people on the other, has produced a body of knowledge on the impact of environment on health, spatial distribution of diseases, location and distribution of medical facilities and health services, globally as well as nationally, which is of vital importance for health planning today. To begin with, this concern was clubbed with human geography and biography but as information on and about health and diseases increased, particularly in the nineteenth and twentieth centuries, a new branch of the discipline known as medical geography took a definite shape.

This chapter is devoted to the study of the evolution of medical geography globally with special reference to India.

DEFINITION AND SCOPE

Definition

Medical geography can be defined as a branch of geography that studies the relationship between environment and health, life style and health and spatial differences in health status and healthcare. It is also known as geography of health. It aims at understanding the geographic factors, both natural and socio-economic, which affect health favourably or unfavourably and the spatial patterns emerging from them. Among its sister social science disciplines are medical sociology, medical anthropology, medical psychology, demography, medical cartography and medical economics. The physical and biological disciplines, which feed it with raw data and information, are biophysics, chemistry, botany, zoology, nutrition, biochemistry and medicine.

In this volume we would not make any distinction between medical geography and geography of health. But the reader must know that there is a subtle difference between the two. Medical geography is related to the profession of medicine, which focuses on the diagnosis of diseases and their treatment with the help of chemical, biological formulations called medicines or with the help of surgery. Medicine is thus curative; it takes charge of the human body once it is sick i.e. gripped by diseases. Health geography on the other hand is much broader in scope. How to maintain good health; what natural, social and life style factors influence and affect health; and what should be done to remain healthy; what type of medicines or treatments should be used to get over diseases and ill health? These are some of the questions that fall within the purview of health geography.

Health geography thus has a much wider scope than medical geography. It studies not only the spatial aspects of bad health (diseases) and the curative measures and services thereof but also, and more importantly, the preservative, generative and preventive aspects of good health. Thus, it goes beyond diseases and factors that cause them; it also covers aspects, which keep a person healthy. The scope of medical geography has grown to include all those physical, cultural, social, economic and other relevant dimensions of life and living, which influence health directly or indirectly. In the recent past, medical geography has been increasingly focusing on health rather than diseases. Thus the term Geography of Health has gained currency among geographers interested in the field. The medical professionals, however, find themselves more comfortable with the term-medical. Hence, the two terms (medical geography and health geography) are now used interchangeably.

The idea that geography influences health is old, rather ancient, indeed. As we noted in chapter two, the medical systems of most of the ancient civilizations were based on the belief derived experientially that violation of the natural laws was the reason for the onset and attack of diseases. And hence our forefathers tried to identify naturally occurring products as cures. Further, they modified their styles of life to suit the requirements of natural living. The most important medicines were derived from different parts of plants, naturally occurring salts, treated minerals, etc. A general belief that supernatural powers too caused diseases, led to formulation of a number of *mantras* and *tantras* to propitiate those powers. Human body being biological, every effort was made to treat it biologically. This is being realized by modern medicine too.

G.M. Howe, a British medical geographer, defined medical geography as "*an interdisciplinary field of study concerned with spatial variations of disease incidence as expressed by mortality or morbidity indices and with the demonstration of possible cause-effect relationship with elements of physical, biological and socio-cultural environment in space. It assists in answering the question 'who has what and where?' but it does not presume to answer the question why except in a limited sense. Medical geography may offer pointers to possible answers but not the proof. That must remain the function of the medical men. Where relationships have been demonstrated and apparently adequate hypothesis advanced, the data of medical geography are such that they cannot be regarded as having proved its truth. Correlation in space can be as misleading as correlation in time, and the data provided by medical geography are usually of this character. Proof of causation in the ordinary sense of the phrase required detailed evidence of conjunction of cause and effect in the individual as well as in the community.*" Thus medical geography is a branch of knowledge that studies the relationship between environment, both natural and cultural, and health; that maps the spatial distribution of health status, events, happenings, or developments to form health regions; that finds out the space specific factors and processes operative in different regions, areas, or ecological complexes giving rise to specific health scenarios; and that applies the knowledge so gained to improve national health policy, health services and health delivery systems. Medical geography is more concerned with the well-being of the society as a whole than with the well-being of individual patients. The later is the task of various systems of medicine.

In general, medical geography a discipline, which analyses the human-environmental relationship of disease, nutrition and medical care system in order to elucidate it relationship in space. Several other definitions of medical geography are in currency but none has been able to catch all the existing and emerging nuances of the discipline. Its scope is widening so fast that some geographers prefer to call it geography of health. Dudley Stamp, a noted British geographer, titled his book on the subject as *Geography of Life and Death*, which is the second title of the present volumes too. In my opinion medical geography is too narrow a title to cover all concerns geography in matters health. Geography of health is indeed a better title. No academic discipline can, however, be bound by a definition given at a particular time and no discipline has remained within the bounds of the definition it was given in its infancy. As such it is not necessary to change the name of a discipline with the change in its scope. As such it should not be necessary to do away with 'Medical Geography' as a term so commonly and widely used by geographers and sister disciplines. It is better to incorporate in its scope its new vistas and nuances. This is the approach of the author of this volume. The traditional title of the book has been retained but many new areas not covered earlier have been incorporated. To indicate its focus on India, the main title is followed by a second title i.e. 'A Treatise on Geography of Lif and Death in India'.

Scope

Medical geography is concerned with four aspects of health. First, it studies the spatial patterns of health and ill-health at all possible levels: global to local. Second, it studies the intensity and frequency of the problems encountered: degree of morbidity and mortality; periodicity of occurrence; the characteristics of the population affected: age, sex, rural, urban, agricultural, industrial; and the natural as well the physical environmental settings of the regions affected. Third, it studies the determinants of health and ill-health by testing etiological hypotheses to identify underlying causes or risk factors. And fourth, it provides models for policy analysis, planning and programming of health services.

Griggs identified three components that distinguished medical geography from other sister disciplines. Medical geography studies spatial patterns of ill-health, spatial patterning of the physical and human environmental characteristics, which induce good or bad health, and spatial patterning and use of health-care delivery systems developed to fight diseases and hazards to health. Elaborating further Pyle and Phillips included diffusion of diseases, modeling, and behavioural attributes at the global, national, regional, local, household and individual levels.

Medical geography is ecological and holistic in perspectives. It recognizes that diseases are produced by the disequilibria between nature's laws and human behaviour on the one hand and exposure of the people to certain disease causing agents and conditions on the other. To eradicate the diseases, the lost equilibrium must be re-established, and the conditions causing the disease must be altered. In this context, the study of environmental conditions, which promote health or give rise to diseases, becomes important. Today when so many of the pandemic and epidemic diseases have been brought under control, doctors are puzzled by the multiplicity of newer diseases, particularly the systemic ones, which have no cures. Unless we create a natural, cultural and social environmental milieu in which man can take full responsibility for the maintenance of his health, we shall fail to ensure health for all. Science and technology are neutral to their use; they can only support individuals and societies tide over their problems; they cannot ensure their judicious and right use. Since medical geography concerns itself with this complex of environmental milieu that differs so widely from place to place, it can play a significant complementary role in the implementation of 'Health-For-All (HFA)' project.

Modern medicine has done a lot of good for man. But it is now becoming a mixed blessing. While old diseases are being eradicated, the new ones, more deadly and powerful, are emerging. The tragedy is that some of them have been caused by the over and indiscriminate use of medicines. Added to the problem is the return of the diseases supposed to have been controlled, in more virulent forms. The pathogens have the tendency to become immune to the antibodies that destroy them. Thus, the germ theory does not appear to help in the long run. New and more powerful germs require new and more potent medicines. And thus a vicious circle is generated that threatens the very survival and development of man.

As stated earlier, the term medical geography no longer gives full expression to the concerns of geography in matters of health. At present its scope is far wider than what even modern medical geographers tend to think. In my view, it tries to answer the following questions.

1. How to keep healthy?
2. Who gets sick of what, where and why?

3. Why are certain diseases more common in some places and regions than in others?
4. How do diseases spread from place to place?
5. How accessible are the health services: hospitals, physicians, and paramedical personnel, to people?
6. What principles should be adopted to locate health services more equitably?
7. What is the relationship between culture and health?
8. How to correlate environment, culture and health?
9. How to treat diseases naturally?
10. How to map diseases and health related data?

Medical geography, along with other biological and social sciences, is engaged in a continuing debate on what constitutes good health. But it does something that no other discipline does. First, it studies the spatial pattern of health and ill-health caused by heredity, style of life, nutritional deficiency, micro-organism, etc. in relation to the natural and cultural environment. Second, it analyses the processes of spatial spread of diseases with a view to locate their origins and to predict their further expansion. And third, it examines the spatial distribution of health-care facilities with a view to suggesting policies, programmes, and methodologies for locating them optimally and in conformity with the current and future needs.

In my view, medical geography can grow and prosper only if it expands its scope and becomes an applied discipline. If environmental factors can induce and even cause ill-health, the same factors can also remove ill-health and improve health. This amounts to scientific application of geographic phenomenon (soil, water, air, open space, diet, plant and animal products, minerals etc.) for strengthening health and improving immunity from diseases. I prefer to call this aspect of medical geography as geographic medicine. It is very close to naturopathy but is not limited to it. It is far more holistic and eco-sensitive.

Geographic medicine lays emphasis on healthy life, instead of curing diseases as and when they come. It uses natural products and natural laws to maintain health as also to restore health. It is based on the principle that ill-health is caused by the accumulation of foreign matter in the body. Nature has its own ways to clean up the body. But when it fails to do so either because of excessive accumulation or continuing addition of toxins, diseases of various kinds emerge. Geo-medicine can be relied upon to clean the system and thereby to cure diseases. It uses modern clinical methods of diagnosis along with the symptomatic method. Its focus is individual and the environment in which he lives. It does not offer panacea; nor does it give quick and immediate relief. It is most suited to systemic ailments like hypertension, arthritis, asthma, heart diseases, as also to common ailments like fever, stomach disorders, headache, etc. It is inexpensive, practically non-toxic, and accessible to all. It does not require constant attention of specialists and hospitals. It can be carried to the doors of the patients. It gives as much attention to treatment of the sick as to the health of education of the healthy so that they do not fall sick. Geographic medicine can thus become a very powerful complimentary and supplementary medical system most suited to the developing countries of the world.

ELEMENTS OF MEDICAL GEOGRAPHY

Spatial Distribution of Health and Ill-Health

Much of the medical geographic literature centres on spatial distribution of diseases of both humans and animals and its environmental correlates. Cartographic techniques have been used effectively to portray differing intensities of diseases. Three major areas of concern in this regard are: distribution of diseases, distribution of health promoting and retarding factors and distribution of agents and hosts of micro-organisms causing diseases.

Spatial distribution of diseases and their spread through time and space have been studied in cross-environmental and cross-cultural settings to demonstrate that there is something special in the area and its people, which could be responsible for the onset and spread of the disease under study.

Geographers have also studied the possible factors responsible for diseases of various kinds. The frequent occurrence of lung cancer in Andhra Pradesh was traced by medical geographers to widespread consumption of tobacco in one form or the other by the common people, specially the farmers. Heart ailments in Punjab and Haryana are related to use of non-vegetarian foods and too fast lifestyle.

Among the health promoting factors are medical services of various kinds. Medical geographers have made some important contributions on the optimum location of medical facilities. Such studies produce models for locating facilities at points most convenient to largest number of people. This becomes specially important in countries like India where distribution of population is very uneven, In a state like Rajasthan, one may not get even 100 persons in a an area of let us say 25 sq. km. Elsewhere, within this area there could be 10,000 people. Yet, even these 100 people have to be provided with basic health facilities.

Certain diseases are linked to agents, which grow in certain host animals. For example, the host for the plague flea to develop and grow is the mice. Distribution of mice population, is linked to the chances of plague occurring once the disease is set in somewhere in the neighbourhood. Rabies is likely to occur where street dogs are more in number. Relationship between mosquitoes and malaria and filarial is well known. There are many other diseases, which have origin in their hosts. Geographic studies can and have proved very useful in combating those diseases.

Correlation Between Environment and Health

Geography is the study of dynamic interaction between man and nature through the medium of culture. Health is thus closely related to the natural environment in which man lives. Medical geographers have carried out many studies on the impact of environment on health and the impact of man on environment. Here we propose to take up just two aspects: climate and health and living environment and health.

The relationship between climate and diseases is well known. Some diseases are typical to warm climate, some to wet climates and some to cold climates. It is often noted that a particular disease like arthritis, for example, is more painful in winters than in summers. Heat strokes are more common in hot and dry climatic conditions.

Medical geographers have been studying the relationship of health and climate for centuries. But depth analysis has been lacking because, they have not taken medical geography as a science requiring the knowledge of both climate and human physiology. This is an area where geographers can make signal contribution, provided that they become more rigorously scientific in approach.

Living conditions or habitat, consist of the home and the outer environment in which the home is situated. Living conditions range from urban slums to posh colonies with all modern facilities. In a country like India, majority of people live in rural areas where houses are no longer as good as they used to be earlier and basic amenities are terribly lacking. This is one of the major reasons why the health scenario of rural India is highly depressing.

Indian cities are full of slums. A large number of people live in shelters that cannot be called houses. The air, water and land pollution is so great that even the healthy persons become easy victims of diseases. Geographers have studied these unhealthy conditions and correlated them with different kinds of diseases.

Bio-geographic Factors and Health

Among the biographic factors influencing health, plants, animals and foods people take have been taken note of by medical geographers. Plants are biological phenomena; they create an environment conducive to healthy and happy life. How plants release oxygen without which no human or animal life is possible is well known to discuss here. Plants provide the foods for both.

We have already discussed the role of animals both domesticated and wild, including the micro organisms in the production and propagation of diseases of various kinds. Suffice it to restate that plant and animal lives have much to do with the health of the people both positively and negatively.

Anthropo-geographic Factors and Health

Two anthropo-geographic factors have been consistently studies by medical geographers as health promoting and retarding factors. These are culture and lifestyle. Culture, as discussed elsewhere in this book, is a term that conveys a very broad and comprehensive meaning of life style as dictated by the value system inherited and observed by a society or individuals. This includes the attitude towards health, medicines and treatment.

Health of the people depends, to a great extent, on the cultural background of a society. On the religion, language, food habits and paradigm of thinking.

Demographic Factors and Health

A number of demographic factors have serious implications for health. The birth rate, death rate, sex and age ratio, occupational structure and mobility, are clear indicators of general health of the people. All these aspects are discussed in appropriate chapter in this book. Suffice it to mention here that the demographic factors have been studied by medical geographers, all over the world, as indicators as well as factors of health.

Socio-economic Factors and Health

Medical geography pays special attention to the relationship between socio-economic factors specially income, expenditure on nutrition and health services and health.

Health Services and Health

Access to health services, both governmental and private, impact health of the people significantly. Medical geography studies the location of these services and determines its optimality to render the quantity and quality of service the people of a particular region need.

METHODS AND TECHNIQUES

Descriptive Methods

Until very recently, medical geography was basically a descriptive science. In fact, it started as a descriptive discipline and continues to be so even if with respectable exceptions. Main thrust of the discipline lies in the spatial distribution of diseases and general correlation between natural and social environments, on the one hand, and health, on the other.

Quantitative Methods

During the last few decades, specially after the quantitative revolution in geography triggered during the 1960s and 1970s, medical geography moved from descriptive to quantitative analysis. It started using a number of statistical and mathematical methods and tools to offer more precise answers to the questions relating to the relationship between natural and socio-cultural environment, on the one hand, and ill-health and diseases, on the other.

Among the statistical methods used by medical geographers are deviation, correlation and factor analysis, apart from means of various types. Deviation has been used to show variations in distribution from national or international average; correlation to demonstrate relationship between environmental factors and diseases and their intensities. And factor analysis has been used to identify the relative importance of various factors responsible for diseases and ill-health.

Mathematical methods have also been increasingly used by medical geographers in studying the diffusion of diseases from place to place, and network analysis to offer the optimum location and distribution of health services. GIS and GPS are the information technology tools used by medical geographers to work out most efficient routings of mobile medical services.

Cartographic Methods

Apart from the qualitative and quantitative methods used by medical geographers, cartographic methods have also been used rather extensively not only to give the distribution of various diseases but also of different health services. Cartographic methods have been so widely used by medical geographers that medical cartography has emerged as a sub-branch of cartography.

Several atlases have been published, particularly in Germany and the USA, which offer a general picture of health scenario in different parts of the world. In this connection, the work of Dr. J.M. May deserves special attention. In India, the Registrar General of India and the Ministry of Health publishes maps showing the distribution of diseases, disease control activities and health services. The NATMO at Calcutta too has published many useful maps.

HISTORICAL BACKGROUND

Birth of Medical Geography

Dependable evidences on geography of diseases are scanty. Main source of evidence lies in the dead bodies but it is not easy to find them well preserved for anatomical analyses. In most counties, the dead were cremated; elsewhere they were buried without any treatment. Except those buried in caves and other naturally protected places, very few skeletons have survived the ravages of time. Only those places and civilizations, which embalmed the dead bodies before burial, provide some reliable source of information.

It was observed very early that some diseases were more common in certain places and countries than elsewhere. But information on paleopathology being sketchy, it was not possible to map out the distribution of diseases. Egypt is rich source of information on human diseases, thanks to the preserved mummies; France is a good source of information about Neolithic period; North America is rich in fossil bones of early vertebrates; the mummies of Peru also give reliable information; but for the rest of the world we have very little to depend on. In India, the great physicians and surgeons laid special emphasis on natural principles of health. Speculations about the relationship between geography and diseases have been there from ancient times.

The Greeks studied the influence of topography, climate and other elements of natural environment on health. Hippocrates explored this relationship in his famous treatise *Air, Water and Places* as early as 400 B.C. The book was designed to help the itinerant physicians who visited unknown places and people suffering from various kinds of diseases. Book I and III of *Epidemics* by Hippocrates offer very good medico-geographic raw material particularly with respect to relationship between weather and diseases. The theory that epidemics were caused by some cosmic or telluric influences and that a certain genius foci was essential for the genesis of an epidemic, led to a very extensive investigation of geographical conditions promoting diseases.

During the renaissance in Europe (14th to 16th centuries), Peracelsus wandered around many countries and said "diseases wander hither and thither throughout the breadth of the world, and stay not in one place. If a man wishes to recognize many diseases, let him travel; if he travels far, his experience will be great and he will learn to recognize many things...How can a good Cosmographus grow in the chimney corner, or a Geographus?" He tells physicians to be "Cosmographus: not to describe how the countries wear their trousers, but to attack more bravely what diseases they have." (Paracelsus in Defensiones).

The Colonial Era

In Europe knowledge about newly discovered lands in the fifteenth and sixteenth centuries brought geography and health together once again. The expeditions, which the Europeans undertook to discover for themselves the lands they did not know before, brought for them not only immense riches but also knowledge about new lands. And thus began the era of exchange of diseases like plague, cholera, smallpox, tuberculosis, sexually transmitted diseases, etc. They were no longer confined to certain localities, countries and continents. As people and goods moved from one continent to another, the communicable diseases also followed the shipping routes and soon spread over to the whole world. Not many us know that Columbus, the first European to touch American soil, even if accidentally, carried to Europe not only new knowledge about the land which he thought was India but also syphilis, a sexually transmitted disease, which spread to the whole world in due course of time.

It would not be out of place to mention that the revival of medical geography to some extent owes to environmental determinists like Semple and E. Huntington, who emphasized the control of environment over human behaviour. A sort of neo-environmentalism developed in medical geography during the world wars when war zone disease atlases were prepared by the European colonizers to depict the spread of tropical diseases in colonial countries. It was perhaps overdone to prove that tropical diseases were caused by the environmental factors alone. And so the colonial governments had no control over it

The most important factor, which triggered European interest in diseases of the foreign lands, was economic. When they extended their frontiers overseas and colonized much of Americas, Africa and Asia, they did not know the local geographic and cultural conditions, nor did they know the diseases prevalent over there. The pioneers who went there were, therefore, exposed to unknown diseases. Some of them carried with them the diseases prevalent in their motherlands but absent in the new colonies. And since the voyages of discovery and creation of colonial empires took place during sixteenth to nineteenth centuries, globalisation of diseases, which were earlier confined to certain pockets of the world, became clear and obvious. It was during this period that the concern about diseases shifted from local to global sphere. Scientific studies on diseases prevalent in other parts of the world, particularly the newly discovered colonies, became common. Thus emerged medical geography as an useful branch of geography.

As the European countries reached the tropics and immigration of people increased, studies on geography of diseases increased by leaps and bounds. A Dutch physician, who lived in Indonesia, wrote *De Medicina Indorum* in 1642 and Daniel Drake explored the medical topography of the Mississippi valley in 1850. Any country interested in going to the tropics had to take note of these studies. Institutions to study tropical diseases were set up in many countries of Europe.

Tropical Medicine

Efforts to control diseases and to prevent the spread of epidemics from country to country represent another line of development in geographic studies. The beginning was made with the plague pandemic of 1348-49 when port authorities quarantined vessels, which passed through plague-infested countries. When the Suez canal was opened in 1869, it was made a filter for diseases that threatened European countries. And finally, a number of international agencies were created for the purpose.

Studies in tropical medicine, medical intelligence and related activities now constitute important aspects of medical geography. But it was not so during the eighteenth and nineteenth centuries. German scholars were, however, an exception. Germany was then divided into 30 states, yet the feeling of universalism pervaded the Germans. Germany produced the greatest geographer of early nineteenth century: Alexander von Humboldt. A small town physician, Leonard Ludwig Finke, brought out *Versuch einer allgemeinen medicinisch-practischen Geographie, worin der historische Theil der einheimischen Volker-und Staaten-Arzeney-kunde vorgetragen wird*. Leonard compiled the book from available materials rather indiscriminately: he never ventured out of Germany and hence had no experience of his own to cross check. He was very much influenced by Johanen Peter Frank, the greatest hygienist of the time who in his *System einer vollstandigen medicinischen Polizey* studied the life of a man from conception to death in relation to the physical and social environment. In this book he discussed the diseases people suffered from in countries like Germany, Italy and China, the physical and social conditions responsible for them and the treatment given and conditions of medical practice. The book suffered from inaccuracies traceable to the source materials he used. But it did demonstrate the importance of medical geography as a bridge between social sciences and medicine.

Finke wrote another book entitled *A Medical Geography by a Rural Practitioner* (1792-95). In 1792, L.L. Frank, a German physician and professor of medicine, published his classical work: *General Medical-Practical Geography* wherein he not only examined the role of physical geography in matters health, but also explained the geographic basis of customary and indigenous medicines and medical practices. His contributions to the discipline remained confined to the German-speaking world as the book was not translated into English or French until very recently. By far the most popular book of the kind published during the mid-nineteenth century was written by August Hirsch under the title *Handbuch der historisch-geographischen Pathologie*. First published in two volumes in 1860 and 1864, it was revised and republished in three volumes between 1881-1886. The English translation was done by Charles Creighton and published in three volumes in 1883-86. According to H.E. Sigerist, "Hirsch's book is remarkable not only for the overwhelming amount of information and literary references it contains, which make it unsurpassed even today, but also for the fact that it combines the history and geography of disease—in other words it traces a disease entity in time and space."

In the second half of the nineteenth century, a number comprehensive books on medical geography and geographical pathology came in the market. Every book on history of diseases, particularly of epidemic diseases, had to have geographic data for diseases did not occur in a vacuum and epidemics moved along the highways of traffic. Hirsch very judiciously combined the historical and geographic approaches to the study of diseases. Following his footsteps, the two brothers, Heinrich and Gerhard Rohlfs, both physicians and one of them geographer also, launched a journal called *Deutsches Archiv fur Geschichte der Medicin und medicinischen Geographie* (German Archives for History of Medicine and Medical Geography) in 1878. The journal was discontinued in 1885 but a new journal entitled *Janus, Archives Internationales pourl'histoire de la medicine et pour geographie medicale* was launched in Netherlands.

John Snow, a British physician, used spot mapping as a cartographic technique to locate the source of cholera epidemic in Soho, London during an epidemic in 1854. He mapped the cholera cases and discovered that the highest density of cases occurred in household, which used the public pump on Broad Street as their water source. Based on these findings he hypothesized that cholera was a water-borne disease, long before the birth of bacteriology. Similarly, Maxcy in 1920 prepared spot maps showing places of employment and hypothesized that a rodent reservoir was responsible for typhus fever. More recently, the case clustering of sex contacts and blood products gave the clue that AIDS was an infectious disease.

Thus the geographic variations in the occurrence of diseases became important dimension of descriptive as well as analytical study of epidemiology. Classic examples of place-related diseases include yellow fever, schistosomiasis, sleeping sickness and endemic goitre. Cancer, asthma, cardiovascular diseases, blood group and abnormal haemoglobins have also been related to geographic location. All diseases have definite spatial patterns. Further researches are needed to match these patterns: geographic, environmental and socio-cultural.

Impact of the Germ Theory

After a period of great spurt in the nineteenth century, medico-geographic studies declined in importance. The germ theory, postulated by Louis Pasteur in 1861, overwhelmed medical geographers and thus the work they were doing had a setback. The study of relationship between environment and health was no longer a popular subject. To understand and cure diseases all one had to do was to identify the relevant germs and administer medicines that killed them. Etiology of disease became the dominant concern in medical sciences and bacteriology developed as an important discipline in the life sciences. And the old ideas about cosmic-atmospheric-telluric influences were discarded.

Another reason why medico-geographic studies became unpopular is their tenuous theoretical and empirical rigor. The analysis and syntheses carried out were highly generalized and often based on undependable data. Professor Stokvis, in preface to the first edition of *Janus,* had lamented thus: "Medicine is in a period of development of which we the contemporaries cannot grasp the full significance but one thing is obvious, namely, that what we lack is no longer facts, observations, experiments, new treatments; it is rather the philosophy of medicine that is gone astray. It is all too apparent that carried away we too much neglect the lessons of medicine of all times and peoples, that in the great family of medical sciences the history of medicine and medical geography are no longer considered full members with an authoritative voice but rather ladies in attendance who merely serve to add glamour on festive occasions."

In 1880, the great American sanitarian, John Billings, said: "In Medical topography as a science there has been little advance for a thousand years, and so long as present methods are pursued, no great addition to our knowledge in this direction can be expected. Vague generalities and opinions must be replaced by specific information and from square miles we must come down to square feet. The results, which we now have, can best be compared to those obtained by the young chemist who made an analysis of a rat-putting the entire animal into his crucible."

So at the beginning of the twentieth century, systematic studies in medical geography were at rather low ebb. There were exceptions such as Clemow's book on Geography of Disease published in 1903 by the University of Cambridge. Some of the best books on human geography do not even mention the geography of disease or they mention it just cursorily. This was the period of the railways and the First World War. People were on the move as colonizers, soldiers, businessmen or just ordinary travellers. Unaware of the health situation in the places they went, many of them died. Malaria took a heavy toll of life of Europeans in West Asia; Indian soldiers in Europe suffered from tuberculosis. Soon after the war, epidemics broke out all over the world. This led to the rekindling of interest in medical geography, but lot of damage was already done.

German School of Geo-medicine

Much broader in its approach and far more forceful than medical geography was geo-medicine in Nazi Germany. Geo-medicine as conceived then was a branch of geopolitics, a science that goes back to the German geographer F. Ratzel, although the term was first used by the Swedish political scientist R. Kjellen. According to Ratzel, political geography studied the spatial distribution of political power over the surface of the earth as determined by geography. Kjellen took the Ratzelian concepts and adapted them to political science. He coined the term geopolitics while studying the frontiers of Sweden and postulated state as a living organism. General Houschofer and his co-workers converted geopolitics into applied political geography or the science of geographic determination of political processes.

Once geopolitics was accepted, other disciplines became conscious of geography and began to play with maps. Medicine with its long tradition of geographical studies could not stay behind. And thus was born the discipline of geomedicine. The father of geomedicine in Germany was Heinz Zeiss. Zeiss was a hygienist who had travelled widely and was loaned to the Soviet Union by the University of Hamburg. He was given an important chair in the University of Berlin when Hitler came to power.

According to Zeiss, geomedicine was much more than geography of diseases or geographical pathology because it was concerned not only with geography but also medicine that is the maintenance and restoration of health and the prevention of disease in various areas. He distinguished it from medical geography, which was a branch of geography, and which investigated and explained the effects of geographical space of the earth and its vital manifestations on man, animal and plant. Geomedicine, said Zeiss, was not geography; it was medicine. "While geopolitics puts into the hands of the statesmen, the weapon required for the present and future security of the state, geo-medicine will enable the physicians to draw the attention of the statesmen to momentary and still threatening health hazards, the combating of which represents a political measure that is significant in internal as well as foreign policy."

He outlined the scope of the geomedicine in following terms:

1. creation of geographic and cartographic means of communication as geo-medical method. Preparation of geo-medical and medico-geographic maps to replace the earlier ones;
2. promotion of cooperation between physicians, veterinarians and botanists, on the one hand, and geographers, meteorologists, agronomists, entomologists and geologists, on the other side to elucidate the connection between natural environment and diseases; and
3. development of geomedicine as a science of prognosis, since it was as dynamic as geopolitics. While geographical medicine and medical geography were static, geo-medicine was dynamic.

The above objectives were quite appealing to many persons even outside Germany. Fielding H. Garrison in America hailed it as a 'new science in gestation'. It took some time and the horrors of the war before the true character of the discipline as conceived by the Nazis became apparent. To be fair, we must, however, recognize that the fault did not lie with geomedicine as a discipline; it lay with the Nazis who used it for ulterior purposes. Like geopolitics, geomedicine was so thoroughly integrated in Nazi's theory of *lebensraum* that in the post-war era they became untouchable by the intellectual circles in general and geographers in particular.

Second Half of the Twentieth Century

Studies in medical geography, specially the spatial incidence of diseases, got a new a shot in the arm in the second half of the twentieth century. A. Askanazy, professor of pathology at the University of Geneva, had founded the International Society of Geographical Pathology in 1929. Askanazy was from Koenigsberg in East Prussia where he had seen people, brought from outside, suffer from leprosy and scleroma and other parasitic diseases that were endemic as a result of the local custom of eating raw fish. When he came to Switzerland he noticed a large number of cases of goitre and cirrhosis. That is how he became interested in geography of diseases. Askanazy wanted to study diseases in relation to climate, soil, food, customs, general civilization, economic status and hygiene. The membership of the society was, however, confined to professors of pathology and pathological anatomy and hence the geography part was neglected. Only an interdisciplinary team could have done this job. The society could not achieve much due to its very narrow approach and breaking out of the Second World War.

The Division of Medical Sciences of the National Research Council of the USA appointed a committee on Survey of Tropical Diseases in early thirties. Earl Baldwin Mckinley was the director of the studies. In 1935, he produced a very disappointing book entitled *A Geography of Diseases*. It covered all diseases; he got them listed, and gave whatever information he could lay his hands on. No follow up action was taken. In fact, there was very little interest in the USA in tropical diseases and that too limited to the Army and US Public Health Service. Only after Japan overran Manchuria in 1931 and started challenging the European and American interests elsewhere, it was realized that knowledge of geographical pathology was necessary.

In the meantime, it was being increasingly realized that the factors that caused diseases were far more complex than the germ theory postulated. The germs did not come from nowhere; they originated and grew only in specific localities and regions. Further, they did not attack each and every person equally and with equal vehemence. Genetics can make many individuals immune or susceptible to certain diseases. Cultural practices, level of nutrition and individual attitudes and behaviours played important roles in health status. Moreover, a great number and variety of germs existed in human body. Most of them were necessary for body's immune system. Some of them grew in one habitat while others grew in other habitats. A germ could overpower the body when the immunity was weakened. Hence a proper study of health must include, among others, a study of the relationship between the pathological factors that gave rise to diseases and the environment, both external and internal, which induced these factors to cause diseases. J.M. May called the pathological factors as Pathogens and the environmental factors as Geogens.

The global character of the World War II forced all countries to engage in studies of geographic medicine and the medical divisions of the armed forces took active interest in it and produced a large number of reports, monographs and health guides.

The post-War period saw the publication of a number of books, which promoted the cause of medical geography. Some of these are: *Climate and Energy of Nations* by S.F. Markham (1942), *Climate in Everyday Life* by C.E.P. Brooks (1950), *Climate Makes the Man* by Clearance Mill (1957), *Climate and Economic Development in the Tropics* by D.H.K. Lee (1957), and *Climate and Man* by U.S. Department of Agriculture (1949).

The period between 1950 and 1970 saw the publication of a number of atlases of health and diseases. American Geographical Society published the *Atlas of Diseases* in three volumes under the pioneering leadership of Dr. Jacques M. May. The volumes were: *Ecology of Disease* (1958); *Studies in Disease Ecology* (1961); and *Ecology of Malnutrition in Far and Near East* (1961). In Germany, *The World Atlas of Epidemic Diseases* was edited by E. Roden Waldt in 1952-56. The Royal Geographical Society of U.K. published the *National Atlas of Disease Mortality* in 1963 under the editorship of G. Melvin Howe. Dudley Stamp wrote the *Geography of Life and Death* in 1965. These publications proved beyond doubt that defining health was a complex matter; it was not a linear function of presence or absence of certain disease causing organisms. A number of other factors played their roles. In 1972, L.L. Park, a German physician and professor of medicine, revitalized medical geography by publishing his classic work *General Medical–Practical Geography*. He examined the role of place as it affected health and diseases. He used medical geographic approach to explain indigenous and customary methods of medicine. His focus was on medical geography rather than on geographical medicine.

MEDICAL GEOGRAPHY IN INDIA

In India, A.T.A. Learmonth along with L.S. Bhat did pioneering work in Mysore state in the 1950s. Some of their researches were published in the *Papers of the Institute of British Geographers* in 1957 and in *Geographical Journal* in 1961. The first comprehensive, even if very general, book was written by R.P. Misra (the present author), in 1970 and was titled *Medical Geography of India*. Published by the National Book Trust of India, it was meant for the general reader and highlighted the role of geographic factors in health and incidence of diseases.

The chapter headings of the book were:

1. Introduction,
2. Heredity and Health,
3. Natural Environment and Health,
4. Cultural Environment and Health,
5. Some Vital Facts about Our People,
6. Infant Morality in India,
7. Major Diseases of India–I
8. Major Diseases of India–II
9. Major Diseases of India–III

10. Hunger and Malnutrition in India,
11. Food for the Future, and
12. Medical Facilities in India.

The book inspired and induced many a young geographer to conduct research on spatial aspects of health and diseases. Several university departments of geography introduced courses in medical geography and number of students enrolled for doctoral research increased phenomenally. Misra's work was followed by significant research work by Rais Akhtar at Srinagar, Jayshree De at Baroda, Gopalkrishnan at Madurai, Jayanti Hazara at Calcutta, A. Ramesh at Madras, A.K. Dutt (USA) and several others in different parts of India. The National Atlas and Thematic Mapping Organization, Calcutta brought out some useful maps on health particularly on the distribution of health facilities. The quantity and quality of health information also improved particularly during the 1981–2001 decades.

These welcome developments notwithstanding, medical geography in India is yet to realize its potentials. After Misra's *Medical Geography in India*, no systematic and comprehensive work has come out. Research papers dealing with the spatial distribution of diseases in certain states and districts of India have been published in several journals both in India and abroad and some very useful edited books containing such papers have also been published. Geographical Aspects of Health and Disease in India by Rais Akhtar and ATA Learmonth, published in 1985, can be cited as an example.

Medical cartography, a sub-branch of medical geography, did, however, make some good contributions. As stated earlier, the National Atlas and Thematic Mapping Organization, Calcutta published a number of maps showing the distribution of health facilities, with district as the basic unit. The National Institute of Nutrition at Hyderabad has been publishing Nutrition Atlas of India from time to time. They also publish maps showing areas where certain deficiency diseases are more prevalent. The Ministry of Health, government of India brings out selected maps and graphs showing the distribution of diseases and health facilities in the country. Census of India is the major source of information and also maps related to birth and death rates and other demographic features of Indian population relevant to medical geography. Then there are a number of government departments and NGO involved in the eradication of various diseases. They too publish maps showing the intensity of selected diseases.

Medical geography has yet to receive the legitimacy it deserves. It is partly because the contributions, the medical geographers of India have made so far, fall short of scientific rigour and depth, and partly because the medical profession in India is so conservative, traditional and self-protective that it does not countenance anything outside the main stream of curative medicine. It has yet to shift its attention from cure of diseases to making the people of India healthy through better nutrition, positive style of life, environmental improvement and stress management. It is so exclusive that even Ayurveda, homeopathy, naturopathy and other systems of medicine received attention only when they were widely accepted in the west as the medical systems of the future. Integrated approach to medicine remains most disintegrated.

Notable exceptions apart, much of the medical geographic work done in India lacked depth and scientific rigour. It has also been highly traditional seeking spatial patterns without much knowledge of the phenomena that form the patterns. Geography is an interdisciplinary field with its own methods and techniques of analysis and synthesis. Just as knowledge of geology is a must for a landform geographer or geomorphologist, or of economics for economic geographer, knowledge of ecology and biology is essential for the medical geographer. Higher education in India is so archaic and rigid that students do not have the opportunities to study what they like most; they cannot change their field of interest as they progress in their studies. Geography in India is generally clubbed with social sciences. There is no opportunity to study biology, geology, nutrition and other relevant disciplines taught in the faculty of science. Medical geography is handicapped by this rigid structure. Yet, it is making steady progress because of its crucial role in identifying areas and regions, which need attention and in optimal and most efficient health services planning.

Modern medicine has become a huge industrial and business enterprise involving international organizations, multinational pharmaceutical companies, hospitals, physicians, paramedical personnel, governments, and wholesale and retail traders. It is one of the fastest growing industries, next only to information technology. Its goal is to increase production and invest in R&D to further improve and innovate. The growth is so fast, that it cannot see what is wrong with it. But it is now becoming clearer than before that modern medicine and healthcare systems are only a short-term palliatives. It is not a panacea for health problems the world is facing today or is likely to face in future. Unless health is seen in holistic perspective, there can be no solution to the problems of ill-health.

Mahatma Gandhi was an applied medical geographer par excellence. He promoted nature cure system in India. This system is very close to geography and ecology. That is why most of the ancient systems of medicine such as Ayurveda and Unani medicine give due importance to nature cure. Mahatma Gandhi called it nature cure. He applied certain biological principles and life styles to maintain good health and five natural elements that form the biosphere to cure diseases. It is very close to what I would like to call geo-medicine. According to this system, human body is made of five complex elements (panchamahabhootas): land, water, air, energy, and ether. Gandhi once said, "I believe that man has little need to drug himself. 999 cases out of a thousand can be brought round by means of a well-regulated diet, water, earth treatment and similar household remedies. He who runs to the doctor, vaidya or hakim for every little ailment and swallows all kinds of vegetable and mineral drugs, not only curtails his life, but, by becoming the slave of his body instead of remaining its master, loses self-control and ceases to be a man." Given the present state of health, the Mahatma appears to have proved right.

REFERENCES

1. Ackerknecht, Erwin H. 'Malaria in the Upper Mississippi Valley, 1760-1900' in *Bull. Hist. Med.*, 1945.
2. Akhtar, R. Goitre Zonation in the Kumaon Region: A Geo-medical Study, *Social Science and Medicine*, Volume 12, 1978, pp. 157-163.
3. ——. Geography of Cancer in India, *Medicine Biologie Environment*, Vol. 6, 1978, pp. 20-30
4. Askanazy, M. *Comptes rendus de la premiere de pathologee geographique*, Geneva, Oct. 1931
5. Banerjee, B. and Hazra, J. Geo-ecology of Leprosy with Special Reference to West Bengal, *Geographia Medica*, Vol 12, 1982, pp. 26-58.

6. Barkhuus, Arne. *Medical Geographies*, Ciba Symposium, 1945. Also see his Geomedicine and Geopolitics discussed in the same symposium. Brooks, C.E.R. *Climate in Everyday Life*, 1950
7. Brunhes, Jean. *Human Geography, An Attempt at a Positive Classification: Principles and*
8. *Examples*, Chicago: 1920. This book mentions the geography of diseases and says that such a science exists.
9. Calcutta University, *Bheda Samhita*, 1921 (Sanskrit Text).
10. Chevers, N. *Diseases of India*, London: J & A Churchill, 1886
11. Childe, V.C. *The Aryans*, New York, 1926.
12. ——, 'Sphere of Life and Death in Early Manuscripts', *Bulletin of the Institute of History of Medicine*, 1942, no. 11.
13. ——, 'Problems of Historical-Geographical Pathology', *Bulletin of the Institute of History of Medicine*, 1933.
14. Choubey, K. Diseases of Sagar City in the Light of Environmental and Nutritional Deficiency Factors: A Case Study in Medical Geography, *Geographical Review of India*, Vol. 33, 1971. pp. 88-100.
15. Clemow Frank G. *The Geography of Disease*, Cambridge, 1903.
16. Cliff A. and P. Haggett, 'Island Epidemics', Scientific American, 250, 1984, pp. 110-17.
17. Cromley, E. and S. McLafferty, *GIS and Public Health*, New York: Guilford.
18. ——, and Rosenburg M. 'Locating Ambulatory Medical Care Facilities for the Elderly' Health Services Research, 21, 1986.
19. Drake, Daniel. *Medical Geography of the Mississippi Valley*, 1850-59.
20. Dubey, S.C. *India's Villages*, London: Oxford, 1946.
21. Dutta, M.K. The Diffusion and Ecology of Cholera in India, *Geographical Review of India*, Vol. 35, 1973, pp. 243-262.
22. Dyek, I. Putting Chronic Illness in Place: Women Immigrants' Accounts of Their Health Care' Geogorum, 26, 1995, pp. 247-260.
23. ——, Using Qualitative Methods in Medical Geography: Deconstructive Moments in a Sb-discipline', Professional Geographer,51(2),1999, pp. 243-53.
24. Edelstein, L. 'Hippocrates' in *The Oxford Classical Dictionary.*
25. Elgood, C. *A Medical History of Persia*, Cambridge, 1951.
26. Fayer, J. *Climate and Fevers of India*, London: J&A Churchill, 1882.
27. Finke, Leonard Ludwig 'On Different Kinds of Geographies, but Chiefly on Medical Topographies and How to Compose Them' (translated by George Rosen), in *Bulletin of History of Medicine*, 1946.
28. ——, *A Medical Geography by a Rural Practitioner*, 1792-95.
29. Gandhi, M.K. *Nature Cure*, Ahmedadabad: Nav Jivan Trust. See also his *My Experiments with Truth*, pp. 330-333.
30. Garrison, Fielding H. Geomedicine: A Science in Gestation, *Bulletin of the Institute of History of Medicine*, 1933.
31. Gober, P. and Rosenberg, M., Looking Back, Looking Around and Looking Forward: A Woman's Right to Choose' in I. Dyck, N. Lewis and S. McLafferty, eds. Geographies of Women's health, New York: Routldge, 2001, pp. 88-103.
32. Gould, Peter, 'The Slow Plague: Geography of the AIDS Pandemic' Cambridge: Blackwell.
33. Hirsch, August *Handbuch der Historisch-geographischen Pathologie, 1860-64* (*Handbook of Geographical and Historical Pathology* (three volumes), New York: The New Syderham Society, 1883-8).

34. Hoermie, A.F.R. *Studies in the Medicine of Ancient India*, 1907.
35. Hoffmann, Friedrich *A Dissertation on Endemical Diseases or Those Disorders which Arise from Particular Climates, Situations and Methods of Living,* London, 1746.
36. Howe, G. Melvyn 'Some Aspects of the Medical Geography of the United Kingdom' *Paper read in the Meeting of the Commission on Medical Geography, 21st. International Geographical Congress,* New Delhi, 1968. Also see his *National Atlas of Disease Mortality,* published by the Royal Geographical Society, 1963.
37. Hume, E.H. *The Chinese Way in Medicine*, 1940.
38. Huntington, Ellsworth. *Principles of Human Geography*, New York: 1943. The book discusses the spatial spread of diseases. Also see his *Civilization and Climate* and *Mainsprings of Civilization,* New York: New American Library, 1945.
39. Irwin, L.W. *Health for Better Living*, Columbus, Ohio: Charles E. Merril Books, 1964.
40. Joseph, A. and Phillips, D. Accessibility and Utilization: Geographical Perspectives on Health Care Delivery, New York: Harper and Row, 1984
41. Kaviraj Kunjalal Bhishagratna (trans), *The Susruta Samhita*, Calcutta, 1907.
42. Kawata, K. *Environmental Sanitation in India*, Ludhiana: Christian Medical College, 1963.
43. Kearns, R. 'Place and Health: Towards a Reformed Medical Geography', *Professional Geographer,* 45, 1993.
44. Learmonth, A.T.A. see his articles in *Geographical Journal*, 1961 and *Papers of the Institute of British Geographers,* 1957.
45. Lee, D.H.K. *Climate and Economic Development in the Tropics*, New York: Harper, 1957. Also see his 'Physiology and Tropics' in *Malayan Medical Journal*, vol. 11, 1930 p. 37.
46. Lowe, J. and Sen, 'A. Gravity Model Application in health Planning Analysis of an Urban Hospital Market' Journal of Regional Science, 29, 1996, pp. 629-651.
47. Macnamara, F.N. *Climate and Medical Topography in the Relation to the Disease Distribution of the Himalayan and Sub-Himalayan Disticts of British India: with Reasons for Assigning a Malarious Origin to Goitre and Some Other Diseases*, London: Longman, 1880.
48. Markham, S.F. *Climate and the Energy of Nations*, London: Oxford university Press, 1942.
49. May, Jacques M. *An Atlas of Diseases*, New York: American Geographical Society 1944.
50. ——, *Ecology of Diseases*, 1958; *Studies in Disease Ecology*, 1961; and *The Ecology of Malnutrition in the Far and Near East*, 1961, all published by the American Geographical Society.
51. Mayer, J. 'Medical Geography: Some Unresolved Problems' *Professional Geographer*, 1982.
52. ——, 'Geography, Ecology and Emerging Infectious Diseases, *Social Science and Medicine*, 50, 2000, pp. 937-952.
53. Mill, Clarence *Climate Makes the Man*, 1957.
54. Misra, R.P. Medical Geography of India, New Delhi: National Book Trust, 1970.
55. Moodie, Roy Lee *The Antiquity of Disease,* University of Chicago Press, 1923.
56. Moore, W. *Tropical Climates and Indian Diseases,* London: J & A Churchill, 1880.
57. Morse, W.R. *Chinese Medicine*, 1934.
58. Mukerjee, A.B. Disease Ecology of a Small Cul de Sac: Chandigarh Dun, *Social Science and Medicine*, Vol. 14, 1980, pp. 331-336.
59. Mukhopadhyaya, G. *History of Indian Medicine* (3 volumes), 1923-29; also see his *Surgical Instruments of Hindus* (2 volumes), 1913-14.
60. Rodenwalt, E. *World Atlas of Epidemic Diseases (Welt-Senchen Atlas), 1952-56.* Ruston G., Improving the Geographical asis of Health Surveillance Using GIS', in A. Gatrell and M. Loytonen, *GIS and Health*, pp. 63-80, Philadelphia: Taylor & Francis, 1998.

61. Robert, E. 'Neighborhood Social Environment and the Distribution of Lowweight in Chicago' American Journal of Public Health, 87, 1997, pp. 597-603.
62. Ross, N. *et al.*, 'Relation between Income Inequality and Mortality in Canada and in the US', British Medical Journal, 320, 2000. pp. 898-902.
63. Schumacher, J. 'Der Physic-Begriff Empedodles' in *Sudhoffs Arch. Gesch. Med.*, 1941, no. 34.
64. Shree Gokulchand Ayurvedic Society, *Charak Samhita*, Jamnagar, 1949.
65. Sigerist, H.E. 'The Social Sciences in the Medical School', *The University the Crossroads,* New York, 1946.
66. Singh B.P. and Singh, R.P.B. Spatial Pattern of Thyroid Disorder (Goitre) in Eastern Uttar Pradesh, India: A Geo-medical Analysis, *Geographia Medica*, Vol. 10, 1980, pp. 61-85.
67. Smith, Elliot & Dawson, W.R. *Egyptian Mummies*, New York, 1924.
68. Stamp, L. Dudley *Geography of Life and Death,* 1965.
69. Thompson, Campbell 'Assyrian Medical Texts', *Proceedings of the Royal Society, Medical History Section, 1924.* One can get reports on Babylonia and other ancient cultures also in these proceedings.
70. UNO, Department of Social Affairs, *Preliminary Report on the World Social Situation with Reference to Standard of Living,* New York, 1952.
71. U.S. Army, *Global Epidemiology: A Geography of Diseases and Sanitation Covering India and Far East*, London, 1944.
72. U.S.D.A., *Climate and Man*, Washington D.C., 1941.
73. Vakil, R.J. *Our Glorious Heritage*, Bombay: Times of India Press, 1968.
74. Vidal de la Blache, P. *Principles de geographie humane*, Paris, 1922. This book does not mention medical geography as a branch of Human Geography.
75. Voigt, Gerhard *Die medizinischen Topographien in Deutchland bis zum Ende de 18Jahrhunderts,* Diss. Berlin, 1939.
76. Wallace, D. and Wallace, R. A lague on Your Houses: The War on the Urban Poor, New York: Verso, 1998.
77. WHO, *Constitution of the World Health Organization, Geneva,* 1964.
78. Wilton, R. 'Diminished Worlds? The Geography of Everyday Life with HIV/AIDS', *Health and Place,2,* 1996, pp. 69-84.
79. Wong K.C. and Lien-The, Wu. *History of Chinese Medicine*, 1936.
80. Wood, J.S. *Yoga System of Patanjali*, Harvard Oriental Series 17, Cambridge, Mass., 1914.
81. Zeiss, H. *Geomedizin (Geographische Medizin) oder medicinisch Geographie*, Munchen, med. Wscher, 1931.
82. Zimmer, H.R. *Hindu Medicine,* Baltimore, 1948.

4

Heredity and Health

Heredity means the transmission of certain traits from parents to offsprings in all life forms: micro organism to human beings. With the decoding of the genes, it is now clear that there is continuity in the evolution of species and individuals and communities. All cultures believe in heredity but only now they know how it is passed on from one generation to the other. Many customs pertaining to marriage, lineage, family, community etc. prevalent in various cultural traditions are rooted in the experiential knowledge about heredity.

Scientific study of heredity is a relatively recent phenomenon although one can trace it back to the works of Galen and Mendel in the nineteenth century. It is only during the last few years that science of genetics has made rapid progress. The discovery of the role of nucleic acids in biological systems is taking biology in a totally new direction. And its impact on medical sciences is indeed phenomenal. Already over 2300 hereditary diseases have been identified and more are added to the list every year. It is estimated that between 25 to 40 per cent of all diseases have something to do with heredity.

Heredity explains both likeness and differences between parents and offsprings. According to Encyclopaedia Britannica, it "may be defined as the study of all those aspects of living organisms which are specifically governed by certain determining elements derived from the parents but not from the external environment. As a consequence of the activity of these determinants of heredity characters, which are called genes, an individual plant, animal or microbe resembles its parents in a great many ways characteristic of its race, and species. Sometimes an individual is like its grandparents or other more remote relations in characters not evident in the parents, because genes may be present in an organism without necessarily having an effect on its appearance."

What determines the personality of an individual? Is it only what the genes of his forefathers have transmitted? The question is still being debated but one thing is now clear. What an individual turns out to be depends partly on his physical heredity (genetic constitution) and partly on his environment (cultural heredity).

Our hereditary background goes back to thousands of years, although we rarely remember even the names of our great grand parents. The basis of our hereditary traits and characteristics such as physique, intelligence, temperament, sex, blood type, eye, skin colour, facial structure and health lies in our genes. But there is something else that has a modifying influence, i.e. environment – physical as well as cultural. Let us see what genes are and how they determine or influence our health.

WHAT ARE GENES?

Just fifty years ago we did not know what genes were, although we knew that certain traits, both biophysical and behavioural, were transmitted from grand parents and parents to children. How these characteristics were transmitted from one generation to another was not known. In 1953, James Watson and Francis Crick at the Cavendish Laboratory in Cambridge, USA, unveiled the structure of deoxyribo-nucleic acid or DNA, the materials from which genes are made. The discovery paved the way for virtually everything that constitutes modern genetics. Later in 1990s, Watson headed the Human Genome Project aimed at blue printing every human gene, from those that determine eye colour or the skin pigment to those that cause diseases. We can now define gene as the ultimate biological unit of heredity; the part of or place (locus) on the chromosome that determines physical inheritance and constitution. It is a functional piece of DNA, which in turn is the basic functional unit of heredity. Genome is the one set of the basic DNA complement (1n where n= number of chromosomes).

According to Irwin, "The DNA (deoxyribo-nucleic acid) molecules transmit hereditary information through another nucleic acid, ribonucleic acid or RNA, which moves out of the cell nucleus into the cytoplasm where it determines the specificity of protein structure and the rate of protein production. Hence by controlling the blue print for protein manufacture, DNA becomes the chief architect and administrator of all body structure and function."

DNA is coiled double-chain made of four inter-linked elements called base pairs, arranged in a specific sequence. Normal human body has 46 chromosomes in each cell: 22 pairs of autosomes and one pair of sex chromosomes, XX in females and XY in males. Autosomes are numbered according to their length: the first pair being longest and the last one being shortest. Sex chromosomes are not numbered. They are termed X and Y. DNA has two properties: replication and flow of information. Replication takes place through reproduction → inheritance → carrier of genetic information; and flow of information via DNA → RNA → Proteins. It thus contains information to build the organs. Figure 4.1 gives the genome view of Homo sapiens and a mouse. It is clear from the figure that Homo sapiens have 46 pairs of chromosomes while the mice have only 42.

There are over 10 trillion cells in human body. Each cell has a nucleus, the life centre of the cell; it contains all the 46 chromosomes that contain thousands of genes. The chromosomes are lined up in 23 pairs but those in the sex cells are not paired. Each of the male sperm cell and female ovum contains 23 single chromosomes. When the two unite, half of the child's genes are derives from the mother and the other half from the father. The presence of one or more extra chromosomes results in congenital deformities. If genes in the sex chromosomes undergo mutations resulting from such environmental factors like cosmic rays, ultraviolet rays, temperature, etc., the mutations are passed on to the offsprings. But the mutations occurring in other cells are not passed on to the children.

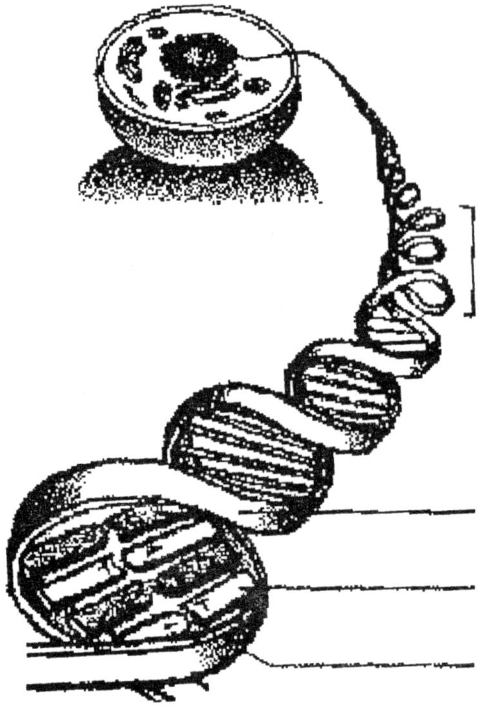

Fig. 4.1: Structure of the DNA

Autosomes are classified into 7 groups according to their length and characteristics:

Group A 1 to 3 pairs
Group B 4 and 5 pairs
Group C 6 to 12 pairs (including X chromosomes)
Group D 13 to 15 pairs
Group E 16 to 18 pairs
Group F 19 and 20 pairs
Group G 21 and 22 pairs (including Y chromosomes).

As the cell divides, each chromosome also divides lengthwise into two sister chromosomes called chromatids. One chromatid joins one daughter cell, while the other joins the other cell. Thus each daughter cell inherits the same number and kind of sister chromosomes.

Chromosomes are caterpillar-shaped bodies less than 2.5 millionths of a centimeter long. They are visible in the nucleus of the cell only during its division. They are in pairs: one from the mother and the other from the father. They are made of DNA (deoxyribo nucleic). DNA consists of genes arranged like beads of a necklace. Number of chromosomes in each species is fixed. With some exceptions, all individuals of the same species have same number of chromosomes. Thus the number of chromosomes in humans is 46; in fruit fly just 8; in garden peas 14; and in potatoes 48.

GENES AND HEALTH

Genes are units of heredity. They contain the heredity information encoded in their chemical structure for transmission from generation to generation. They direct the growth and evolution of human body. Since each of the genes is formed by millions of base pairs, the relationship between the genes and human body is complex indeed. The body is so finely tuned that lethal disorders can arise from the mix-up in just one base pair. A single defective gene can cause cystic fibrosis. Heart diseases, cancers and other major disorders can be triggered by defects involving two, three or more genes. This explains why such seemingly nonhereditary illnesses run in families.

Human body has 100,000 genes packed into 46 chromosomes: 50,000 of them are inherited from father and other 50,000 from mother. A full set is found in the nucleus of virtually each human cell. They occupy a very specific position in human chromosome; they also occur in pairs. Genes are generally stable, but at times, normal genes are converted into abnormal genes. This change is called mutation. Mutation is a regular phenomenon in nature. The natural mutation rate is increased by exposure to mutagenes such as ultraviolet rays, radiation, or chemical carcinogens. Genes by themselves cause only a few diseases, but they make human body susceptible to many diseases. The diseases may appear when certain environmental factors trigger them off. So a person predisposed to lung cancer may not get this disease unless he smokes. Other diseases, which are known to be related to 'disease' genes are colon and breast cancers, Alzheimer's disease, coronary heart disease, emphysema, multiple sclerosis and diabetes, and fragile X syndrome (mental retardation). Some scientists believe that virtually all diseases have a genetic component.

Recent researches indicate that the outer layer of the genes called cytoplasm also exerts some influence on inheritance of physical and mental traits. Although the genes direct and govern all developments including the relations of the tissues of our body, they do permit the tissues to respond to outside stresses and challenges with a certain degree of plasticity. Thus the genes produce two types of characteristics-fixed and plastic. The fixed characteristics are called genotype; the plastic are called the phenotype. According to J.S. May, "The two types can be best compared with a pellet of clay. Any given pellet of clay has definite weight, density, volume and chemical composition but the artist's fingers, i.e. the environmental pressure, can make the clay into a horse, a woman, a dagger or anything else. Though the appearance of the pellet of the clay changes with the pressure applied, it will always retain the same weight, density, volume, and chemical composition. There are, therefore, an infinite number of possibilities within a finite set of basic characteristics."

The mutations occurring in the sex cells are transmitted to the offspring; they do not affect the individuals whose cells undergo mutations. But the phenotypic changes become visible in the individuals themselves during their life times. Let us take the example of scar created by a wound. The scar so created is not transmitted to the offspring but the tendencies that govern its formation are. The formation of the scar is governed by the genotype but it is a part of the phenotype. When a microbe attacks a person, a defense process is initiated in his tissues. Depending upon the success or failure of the defense mechanism, a scar of positive or negative immunization is left in the tissues. As new experiences in the form of scars get stored in the individual, he continues to undergo transformation. The number of scars so created depends upon the degree and frequency of environmental stresses.

As discussed earlier, some diseases are hereditary but they may not become clinical unless environmental factors are favourable. The genetically determined bio-chemical make-up and the multiple environmental factors interact to produce these diseases. Thus, there are certain constitutional conditions that make certain individuals more susceptible to diseases like arteriosclerosis, hypertension, rheumatic fever, rheumatoid arthritis, diabetes, some skin diseases, gout, allergies, pernicious anemia, goitre, cancers and peptic ulcers. Favourable environmental conditions are, how era, needed for the disease to take hold of the individual. "If a large number of hereditary factors producing susceptibility to a given disease is present, one may get that diseases even under moderate environmental stresses. As against this, very strong environmental stresses are needed to generate diseases in persons who are free from or have very few of such hereditary traits." (Irwin)

Mendel in nineteenth century formulated the law of inheritance. He crossed two races of peas: one tall and the other short. The first generation (F) consisted of entirely tall ones. When the F_1 generation was inbred, it produced a mixed generation (F_2) of tall and short in the ratio of 3:1. All short plants of the F_2 generation produced only short plants, but the tall ones gave a mixture of tall and short in the same ratio (3:1). Thus the F_2 generation had 25 per cent tall, 50 per cent mixed, and 25 per cent short. This is called Mendel's law of inheritance.

Genetics has opened new vistas for medical sciences. Mapping the genes can help detect those genes, which cause certain diseases. For example, if in a family people have been dying of heart attack from generation to generation, it should now be possible to identify the heart attack causing gene and take it off so that the tendency of heart attack in future generations is no longer there. Further, if a person suffers from a particular disease not because of heredity but because of some mutant gene, his mutant gene can be removed.

The above examples indicate a very positive contribution of knowledge about gene and gene therapy. Let us, however, hope that this new technique would not be used for destructive purposes as has been the case with many other scientific inventions and discoveries.

GEOGRAPHY AND GENETICS

With the understanding of DNA molecules that enclose the structure and process of life, the science of genetics has expanded the knowledge of how genetic information is stored, transmitted and activated at appropriate times.

Genetic disorders show that the geography of genes and human genetic patterns are currently interactive with various features of environment, or were so historically. For example, the density of skin pigments may be interactive with latitudinal belts of incoming ultraviolet solar radiation. In low latitudes density of skin pigments protects against skin cancer whereas the de-pigmentation in high latitudes minimizes the biosynthesis of scarce vitamin D essential for bone formation. Lactose intolerance, an inability to metabolise milk products, is caused by chronic deficiency of lactase enzyme in the stomach. A map of lactose intolerance in Africa reveals a human genetic frontier that is closely coextensive with the biological realm of tsetse fly.

Prof. Hunter has done an interesting study on lactose intolerance among few world communities where he tries to establish this intolerance through geography. Genetic predisposition or otherwise of certain communities and groups of people to certain foods or diseases might have something to do with long exposure to certain physical and cultural environmental regimes. Take the case of lactose intolerance (milk allergy or glactosemia). It is caused by inborn error of metabolism, an autosomal recessive trait. Normally the ingested milk sugars (lactose) get hydrolyzed into glucose but in case of lactase enzyme deficiency in the small intestine, it is not absorbed. In extreme cases, the non-absorbed lactose is deposited in lever and spleen, ultimately giving rise to cataracts in the eye, protein losses through the urine or even mental retardation in infancy. The enzyme deficiency is, however, rarely complete and the effect of intolerance is limited to gastrointestinal problems after 30 to 40 minutes of milk consumption.

The lactase intolerance and lactase deficiency is not a random phenomenon. Certain groups of people are highly prone to it. Seventy to eighty per cent of the Black Americans have some lactase deficiency as compared to only 5 to 19 per cent of the Whites. In India, lactase mal-absorption is in the order of 80 per cent. Comparative figures for various communities are given in Table 4.1.

Table 4.1: Lactase Mal-absorption in Different Communities

	Community	*Per cent Mal-absorption*
1.	Chinese	90
2.	Eskimos	88
3.	Black Americans	70-80
4.	Indians (South Asia)	
	Northern	60
	Southern	85
5.	Africans	
	Wet West Africa	85
	Savanna Africa	70
6.	American (Oriental)	67
7.	American Indians	67
8.	Europeans	12

Note: Percentages *are* based *on limited inquiries and hence should be treated as indicative only.*

Source: Simoons, Frederick J. 'Primary Adult Lactose Intolerance and the Milking Habit: A Problem in Biological and Cultural Interrelation'. *American Journal of Digestive Diseases*, Vol. 14, 1969.

The causes for lactase deficiency are genetic. But how do we explain it? If we divide human society in two: milking and non-milking, we find that the level of intolerance is higher in the latter. It is found that milk tolerance improves after several generations.

Domestication of cattle began in West and Central Asia around 4000 BC. It spread to India and Europe through the Aryans sometimes between 2000 to1500 BC. Later, the Hindus and Buddhists carried it to South East Asia; and Mongols to China. Tropical Africa and Americas were the last to domesticate animals. Studies show that longer a society has been using milk, greater the lactase tolerance it has. It is also noticed that milk tolerance increases after adoption over several generations.

The pastoral societies learnt to preserve milk in the form of yogurt, cheese, butter, ghee, etc. These are the products in which lactase is broken down. Cow's milk has five per cent lactose but yogurt has less than two per cent. Civilizations of different societies and regions have, therefore, something to do with the genetic disposition of people for certain diseases, metabolic functioning, procreation, etc.

Is alcoholism hereditary? It is a question that deserves investigation. Europeans, particularly the Russians, have a very high tolerance for alcohol, while Chinese, Jews, and Indians have lower tolerance. Is it because of climate or because of the role alcohol is assigned in different cultures? The question is whether low or high tolerance for alcohol is the cause or effect of genetics. There exists some evidence of heredity in alcoholic behaviour. Children of alcoholic parents often turn out to be alcoholic. There is some linkage between culture, genetics and environment. And, therefore, heredity can be described as the inherent tendency of an individual to react to his environment in a particular way. Environment cannot alter hereditary characteristics.

Some of the diseases, which are clearly genetic, are Kleinefelter's Syndrome (eunuchoid man) having XXY or XXXY chromosomes; XYY Syndrome (antisocial behaviour, aggressiveness, criminal tendencies); Turners's Syndrome (females with underdeveloped sex glands and only 45 chromosomes of XO in stead of XX.). O = zero; Super Females (females with 3 to 5 X chromosomes; they suffer from mental retardation and undeveloped genitalia; Down's Syndrome (Mangolism) caused by an extra chromosome in 21st pair.

Blood group is also determined by gene. Some diseases are associated with blood groups. It is noted that duodenal and gastric ulcers are associated with O group. Pernicious anaemia is associated with A group; rheumatic heart disease is common with those having O group and Thrombosis with A group.

Of the 14 blood groups identified in humans, the most commonly found groups in Indian population are given in Table 4.2.

Table 4.2: Frequency of Blood Groups in Indian Population

Genotype	*Phenotype*	*Per cent*
OO	O	40
AA, AO	A	22
BB, BO	B	33
AB	AB	5

GENETICS AND HEALTH-CARE

Having discussed the relationship between heredity, health and environment, we realize that there are many questions that need further research. Are moral traits inheritable? Quite often people tend to ascribe to heredity even such traits, which one acquires in childhood from the family and community environment. Childhood cataract may not be because of heredity. It may be because of mother's illness during pregnancy. Similar is the case with congenital syphilis. Many psychosomatic diseases such as stomach ulcer in the early childhood are due to absence of mother's care or emotional disturbances. The belief that some diseases run in the family is also not correct. It may be because of cultural heredity rather than physical heredity.

With new advances in biotechnology and genetic mapping, it might be possible to answer the above questions more definitively. The fact, however, remains that the environment in which one is born and brought up has a great influence on hereditary characteristics. If some hereditary traits are influenced by factors outside the genes, genetics and heredity are no longer synonymous. Environment appears to influence heredity through phenotypic mutations. What would happen to each succeeding generation of humans if the environmental stresses continue to increase? In our own country, many people are exposed to the stresses of under-and malnutrition and they suffer from a number of communicable and other diseases. The cultural environment too is becoming stressful. The food habits, living conditions, sex life and ideals as practiced are far from satisfactory. The rural life is particularly depressing but the urban one is not far better, especially for those who live in slums and squatter settlements.

India is a land of over 1000 million people, almost one-sixth of humanity. Half of the people of the country live a life not worth living. We want India to be a great nation. Greatness cannot, however, be achieved by arming ourselves and detonating atom and hydrogen bombs. While these might be necessary for the protection of the country from enemies beyond our borders, they have no relevance for the enemy within. The enemy within is the poor quality of life of the people. India will achieve greatness the moment it is able to upgrade the living standards of the people both in material and spiritual senses. India cannot be great so long as its people are unhealthy-physically, mentally and spiritually. Practically all the great men of India laid emphasis on healthy life and living. If the present scenario of health in India does not change soon, we may become one of the weakest nations of the world. An island kingdom like Britain subjugated a vast nation like India because the quality of our life had deteriorated. Mahatma Gandhi, in our own lifetime, laid great emphasis on good health, creative education, right thinking, and good character because he knew that a healthy and morally strong people alone can win and retain their freedom. Whatever we think and do has its impact on our lives through the mutation of our genes.

I am not trying to exaggerate the dangers ahead nor am I overemphasizing the role of heredity in health policy and planning. We have no intention to become a martial race to subjugate or threaten others. We only want to ensure that India is not subjected to all those tragedies that it has gone through for many centuries. A great majority of our people has lived miserably. No wonder then that Ghories, Ghaznavis and the British just walked across our borders without any matching resistance. The philosophical heights our forefathers reached has not been matched by organizational and managerial capabilities to maintain peace and harmony, on the one hand, and national unity and integrity, on the other.

The time is ripe for us to ponder over the current health scenario in the country. This nation of over one billion people has immense untapped potentials. We should move fast and systematically to improve the health of our people. We should also seriously ponder over our behaviour and the way of life and living, and the implications they may have for future generations. We must protect our natural and cultural heritage from the onslaughts of 'modernity'. Each culture creates its own modernity by blending the heritage of the past with the new aspirations of the future. We too should do this blending, not just copy the west. Only then we shall be able to overcome the crisis generated by deteriorating health standards and health environment in India.

It is not to suggest that hereditary diseases and infirmities are likely to be our major concerns in future. There is, however, no doubt that by slow doses of phenotypic changes, we may head towards a biological stalemate from which there may be no return. Once we are gripped by systemic disorders, we may live long but remain bed-ridden for much of our life span. We should take remedial steps while the time is still there. We should so plan our life individually as well as collectively that the possible dangers we face today do not become a reality in future.

REFERENCES

1. Amery, A.E.H. *Elements of Medical Genetics*, London: Livingston, 1974.
2. Corwin, E.H.L. *Ecology of Health*, New York: Commonwealth Fund, 1949.
3. *Encyclopaedia Britannica*, 1961 edition, Vol. II, pp. 484-85.
4. Indian Council of Medical Research, *Genetics and Our Health*, New Delhi: ICMR, 1972.
5. Hunter, John M. 'Geography, Genetics and Culture History: The Case of Lactose Intolerance', *The Geographical Review*, Vl. LXI, No. 4, October, 1971.
6. Irwin, L.W., *et al. Health for Better Living*, Columbus, Ohio: Charles E. Merrit Books, 1964.
7. Keller, P.C. *Chromosomes and Genes*, Edinburgh: Oliver & Boyd, 1968.
8. May, J.M. *The Ecology of Human Diseases*, New York: M.D. Publications, 1958.

   Simoons, Frederick J. 'Primary Adult Lactose Intolerance and the Milking Habit: A Problem in Biological and Cultural Interrelation'. *American Journal of Digestive Diseases*, Vol. 14, 1969, pp. 819-36; and Vol. 15, 1970, pp. 695-710.

5

Natural Environmental and Health

"The Microbe is Nothing: the Terrain Everything"

— L. Pasteur, on his death-bed

We noted earlier that the genotypic characteristics of humans are inborn and given, whereas the phenotypic characteristics are subject to change in response to environmental stresses, on the one hand, and the genotypic characteristics of individuals concerned, on the other. Genes determine the genotype; the environment in its broader senses determines the phenotype. Since the genotype and phenotype together determine the health of an individual, study of environment and its relation to health is a must for health planner and manager. Environmental Pathology is the diagnosis of health and health problems in different natural or ecological regions and settings.

Environment means different things to different people. For traditional geographers environment means natural environment; sociologists stress on social environment; while anthropologists see environment in cultural terms. In economics, environment means the economic conditions in which man lives and works. Each discipline defines environment in its own way. Medical geography treats environment as a composite milieu within which human beings live and work. It includes the natural as well as the social, cultural and economic environment. In this chapter, we propose to discuss the natural environment and its relation to health.

Natural environment includes factors like relief, soils, climate, flora and fauna in all their details. We can group them into two composite factors: organic and inorganic. The latter covers temperature, humidity, air, light, water and the trace elements present in them. Factors like radiation, magnetic field, cosmic rays, static electricity, etc. are also important. The organic elements consist of plants, animal life and micro-organisms.

It would be pertinent to note that the organic and inorganic factors are not exclusive of each other. There exists a symbiotic relationship between the two. Various organisms exist only in relation to each other in a given habitat. For example, the climatic and vegetation regions are identical and overlapping. So are the climatic, vegetation and soil regions. Animal life is closely linked to the landforms, climate and vegetation. Different species of plants and animals are also interdependent. If one goes deeper into the functioning of life and its support system on planet earth, one can see the intractable vertical as well as horizontal relationship between the physical and biological evolutionary processes.

Man-environment relationship has always been a major concern of geography and geographers. In the eighteenth and nineteenth centuries, a large number of monographs were brought out giving details of human activities in various natural regions of the world. They were based on visible and apparent relationship between man and environment: causal analysis on scientific lines was rare, if not absent. Environmental determinists did produce considerable amount of literature based on the information supplied by the explorers and traders but the conclusions they derived there from were not based on scientific analysis of the data so gathers. They misconstrued the simple correlation and association between natural environment and flora and fauna, on the one hand and human behaviour, on the other, as causal relationship. They did not realize that in different historical and technological settings, the results could be totally different even if the environmental setting remained the same. The tropics were invariably undeveloped in the nineteenth century. It was, therefore, concluded that the tropical environment was not conducive to development.

Apparently, the natural environment alone does not determine the development potentials of a place or region; other factors, both geographic and non-geographic, played their own respective roles. The environmental determinists were right in laying emphasis on man's inextricable links with the earth he inhabits and the influences the earth exerts on his thinking and working behaviour. All life forms function within the frameworks of the laws of nature. Man can manoeuvre these laws to his advantage but he cannot ignore or break these laws without paying penalty for it. This applies to development as much as to health.

The environmental determinists of the early part of the twentieth century were not all that wrong. Despite their wrong premises, some of their conclusions were right, and the same have been validated in recent years. What went wrong with them was the assertion that man's role *vis-à-vis* the natural environment was at best passive and the basic behaviour patterns in different natural settings were already set forever. As such the tropical regions with year round heavy rainfall and uncomfortable weather conditions were condemned to remain poor and unhealthy. As against this, the people of the temperate regions were destined to be energetic and intelligent. They could not foresee the potential human capabilities to transform the natural environment to the best advantage of man.

The theory of environmental determinism was the product of a paradigm of thinking which had its roots in the scientific revolution of the eighteenth and nineteenth centuries. Darwin postulated the theory of evolution of the species; Freud postulated the theory of sex as the driving force in human relations; Adam Smith and Marx identified the desire to satisfy material wants as the driving force that made human beings work; and Ratzel, Semple and Huntington saw the natural environment as the determinant of human behaviour and civilization. All these concepts and theories were prefixed by conditionality of 'other things remaining the same.' But we all know that in a changing world, other things never remain the same.

While other disciplines improved upon their deterministic theories, geographers threw out environmental determinism as an intellectual plague. They forgot that theories did not tell the truth; they only led to the truth; and that all theories are partial and time-space specific; the premises underlying them may be flawed and therefore subject to correction. A long drawn research throwing up various hypotheses must precede even a partial theory. The successors of Ratzel became defensive and tried to introduce concepts like possiblism, probablism, etc. without going deep into the nature of the environment they were concerned with and the nature of man they were trying to correlate with.

Unable to substantiate environmentalism, geographers dumped environmental determinism to the dustbin of academic history. Geography too accepted the supremacy of man over nature: man became the measure of everything. The consequences of this turnaround are now apparent to us. Geography lost the theoretical base and remained a descriptive discipline. On the practical side, the gap in the knowledge about environment-man relationship led to the slow poisoning of the earth and the ecological and environmental disasters we face today.

The need of the hour was to reject environmental determinism while at the same time rejecting the thesis that man, as the chosen species, had right to exploit the nature the way he liked. They ought to have built new theories on man-environment relationship, both inductively and deductively, which centred on nature-man symbiosis. Case studies of progress different societies made in different environmental settings through time would have provided enough data to prove that tropics were once the most developed parts of the earth. Unfortunately, they were so Euro-centric that they could not go beyond the present and that too beyond what was visible physically.

INORGANIC ENVIRONMENT

Tectonic Movements

The earth we inhabit is about 5.6 billion years old. It is almost spheroid with equatorial and polar radii of 6377 km and 6357 km respectively. It consists of inorganic as well as organic materials. Among the inorganic elements of the natural environment that influence human life, the forces generated within the interior of the earth hold considerable significance. These forces are responsible for earthquakes, which take away thousands of lives and destroy properties built in centuries. It would be out of place to give details of these forces and the way they act to change the surface of the earth. Some broad features of the same are given here.

The earth's interior consists of three major segments: the upper layer is called 'crust' (0-40 km); the middle layer is called mantle (40-2897 km), and the central layer is called 'core' (2897-6373 km). The core is solid, the mantle is plastic and the crust is hard. The crust floats on the mantle; it is not an unbroken sheet sitting on the viscous mantle. It is broken into several pieces called plates, which move in different directions. These plates are drifting apart for the last several million years and would not perhaps rest until the seven continents of the earth become one again. When two plates meet, unstable conditions develop leading to mountain building activities, earthquakes and volcanic eruptions.

Earthquakes and volcanic eruptions constitute two major natural disasters. They affect adversely the health scenario in the regions of their occurrence. Many lives are lost and many more become homeless and physically handicapped. And the atmospheric pollution they generate lasts for years to adversely affect the health of the people.

As stated earlier, the earthquakes are caused by the movement of the tectonic plates of the earth in certain set directions (Fig. 5.1). When two plates collide, one of them either slips under the other or breaks down to disturb the equilibrium. It leads to tremors releasing shock waves all around. India had had a number of severe earthquakes during the last few decades. The recent one occurred in Bhuj, Gujarat in 2002 AD.

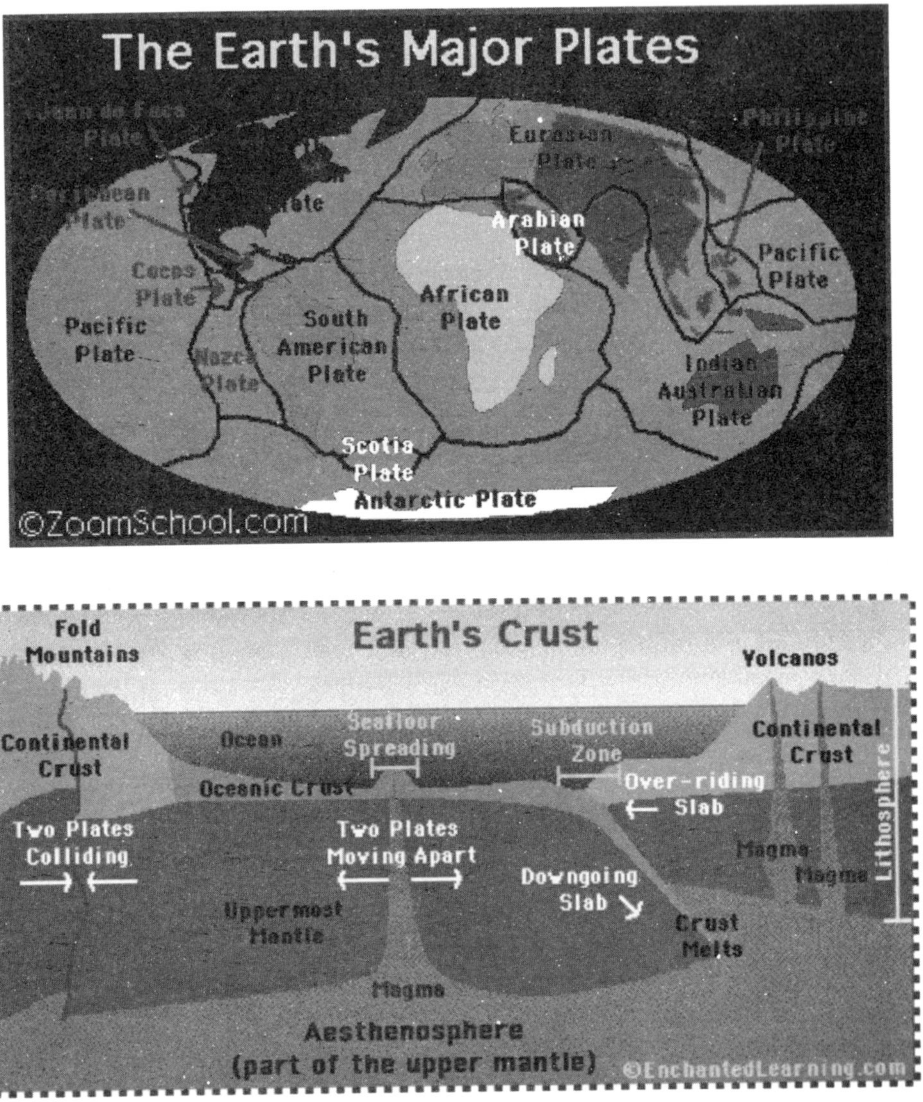

Fig. 5.1: Earth's Major Plates

Source: http://www/enchantedlearning.com/subjects/astronomy/planets/earth/continents.shtml

Topography

Topography includes all those surface characteristics that give a piece of land its individuality in terms of relief, slope, rocks, soils, minerals and water bodies, together with man-made features like railways, roads, canals, houses, tanks, dams, etc. In this section we propose to discuss only natural features.

Topography has a great influence on land use and land productivity. It also influences the presence and survival of other life forms including the organisms that cause diseases and hosts through which they reach the human body. During the agricultural era, the great river valleys of Nile, Indus, Yangtze, Tigris and Euphrates, endowed as they were with fertile soits, were the most developed parts of the world. Leaving aside the Mayan and Aztec civilizations of South America, it was in these river plains that the great civilizations of the past emerged. If our current experience is any indicator, it is only a healthy people who can build great cultures and civilizations.

Food is the basic need of all living things, man included. We know that much of our food comes from the plain areas of the world, of course, with favourable climatic conditions. It is for this reason that the density of population is invariably high in fertile plains of the world. Even industries have location preferences for plains. The density of people as well as that of the means of production has great impact on the health through access to food and income. In underdeveloped economies, too many people huddle together in the plains to make the man-land ratio highly unfavourable. As we will see in following chapters, most of the sick people as also the diseases are concentrated in these densely populated plains of the developing countries.

Certain well recognized physiological effects on human body are directly related to altitude. Because of the low oxygen content (hypoxia), high altitude accelerates respiration increases the number of red blood cells and metabolic rate. High mountain areas are, therefore, not conducive to people suffering from heart and blood vessel diseases. Moderate altitudes, however, offer very healthy and invigorating environment. At these altitudes the air is clean, temperatures low and sunshine abundant. That is the reason why T.B. sanitariums are sought to be located on mountains.

Altitude also has great influence on the weather and climate. Higher the elevation, lower the temperatures, is the general rule. Many of the disease generating microbes thrive only in warm and moist climatic conditions. High altitudes are, therefore, less suitable for their growth and hence are less frequented by many of the warm climate diseases. Malaria can be cited as an example. It has been conspicuously absent from the Himalayan zone.

Elevation has adverse effect on blood pressure. Those suffering from high blood pressure are worse off in mountain areas and those from low blood pressure are better off.

Relief has a bearing on the onset and end of several communicable diseases. Slope determines the drainage system of an area. Gentle gradient is conducive to water logging and hence favourable for the breeding of microbes, mosquitoes and various kinds of insects that produce diseases like malaria, filaria, dysentery, etc. Cholera epidemic is known to end with the onset of rains in well-drained areas. Malaria is more common in low-lying areas marked by water logging. It is also common in urban slums where water remains stagnant for days and weeks.

Climate

Climate is defined as the average weather reckoned in months, years and decades. It can also be defined as the combined effect of mutual interaction between sun's radiation, atmosphere, oceans, and the lithosphere on the biotic phenomenon including man. Its chief elements are temperature, air pressure, winds, humidity and precipitation. It runs in latitudinal bands following the inclination of the sun rays to the surface of the earth but can be modified by local conditions such as relief, altitude, distribution of land and water, oceanic currents, cyclonic storms, etc.

Climate has a great impact on human activities, the style of life and the capacity to work. It is the main determinant of plant coverage and animal life. Despite great strides made in artificial irrigation, food production is still controlled by the climatic conditions. In this discussion climate includes weather, which is the day-to-day occurrence of the climatic elements.

Atmospheric Pressure

Atmosphere consists of air, which is a mechanical mixture of various gases, water vapour and a number of suspended materials. Natural air contains:

1. Nitrogen, 78 per cent,
2. Oxygen, 20.93 per cent,
3. Carbon dioxide, 0.03 per cent, and
4. Minute quantities of Argon, Neon, Krypton, Xenon and helium

Close to the sea level, atmospheric pressure measures 760 mm of Hg, which is known as 1 atmospheric pressure. Man is adapted to this atmospheric pressure. Any thing more or less than this causes discomfort and diseases. At a height of let us say 100,000 ft a.s.l. the atmospheric pressure is 10 mm Hg. As we go down, it increases at the rate of 1 mm Hg per 10 meters of descent. Man cannot survive at an altitude of 25,000 ft without supporting breathing equipment.

Low atmospheric pressure causes increase in breathing, increase in concentration of haemoglobin, and increase in cardiac output. Acute mountain sickness and high altitude pulmonary oedema, cough, mental confusion, hallucination, seizures and even coma are the other symptoms.

Pressure is measured with the help of a barometer. The Indian Meteorological Department uses Kew Pattern Station Barometer. Barographs give continuous record of pressure.

Air Temperature

Air temperature is measured with the help of thermometers. Thermometers are usually tubes filled with mercury or alcohol, which expand with increase in temperature. Dry bulb thermometer is an ordinary thermometer covered with Stevenson's screen fixed 1.20 to

1,80 meters above the ground. Wet bulb thermometer is kept wet by a muslin cloth itself kept wet by a wick attached to a water bottle. Its temperature reading is lower than that of dry bulb thermometer. When the air is completely saturated dry and wet temperatures are equal. Globe thermometer is used to measure mean radiant temperatures of the surroundings directly.

High temperatures generate heat stresses. Beyond certain limits, living things cannot tolerate heat stress. For human beings a heat stress index has been prepared which varies from 0 to 100.

0	No thermal stress
10-30	Moderate to mild heat strain
40-60	Severe heat strain
70-90	Very severe heat strain
100	Upper limit of heat tolerance

Heat strains produce a number of health problems. *Heat Syndrome* is the most common occurrence. Body temperature may not increase, but because of sudden or constant exposure to heat and lack of water, person may collapse because of pooling of the blood in the lower limbs of the body. *Heat Cramps* occur when a person engages in manual work in high temperature. It happens because of loss of sodium chloride in the blood. *Heat Exhaustion* occurs when there is shortage of water and salt in the blood and the body temperature has increased to 39° C. *Heat Hyperpyrexia* results from impaired heat regulatory mechanism. When body temperature reaches 44° C it can lead to *heat stroke*. *Heat Stroke* is caused when the heat regulatory mechanism of the body fails and the temperature goes up to even 43° C. The person suffering from heat stroke should be kept in ice cool water till rectal temperature is down to 38° C. This should be done under a physician's supervision. There is always a danger of over cooling (hyperthermia).

Thermal comfort in a room is not dependent on temperature alone. Humidity and cooling power of the air are the most important factors. Humidity is absolute or relative. Humidity is measured with the help of dry bulb hygrometer (DBT), and wet bulb hygrometer (WBT). Relative humidity is measured with the help of psychrometer.

A special thermometer called Kata was used to measure the comfort level in residential buildings and work places. A dry Kata of 6+ and a wet Kata of 20+ were regarded as comfortable. The Kata measure was not found very practical because it was based on temperature and humidity alone, and hence in 1923, Houghton and Yaglou gave the concept of effective temperature (ET), which took into account the velocity of air movement also. An ET value of 30° C indicated saturated atmosphere of 30° C with no air movement. Further improvement was effected by the introduction of the concept of Corrected Effective Temperature (CET). Instead of dry bulb temperature, CET uses globe temperature to allow for radiant heat. CET scale thus deals with all the four factors, which determine comfort level: air temperature, wind velocity, humidity and mean radiant heat.

For India, the comfort zones on CET scale are as follows:

Comfort Zones	CET Values in Degree Celsius
Pleasant and Cool	<20 degrees
Comfortable and Cool	20-25 degrees
Comfortable	25-27 degrees
Hot and Uncomfortable	27-28 degrees
Extremely Hot	>28 degrees
Intolerable	>30 degrees

Sweat rate is also used to find out comfort zone. It is calculated for a period of four hours and expressed as P_4SR: it connotes the amount of sweating in four hours. P_4 SR for comfortable zone is 1-3 litres; for just tolerable, 3-4.5 litres; and for intolerable zone, >4.5 litres.

Climate and Health

There is close relationship between climate and diseases. Certain diseases are seasonal. Dehydration and cholera are common during hot summers; malarial fever during rainy season; and cough, cold, and bronchitis during winters. Of the other season-specific diseases, the most common ones are infantile paralysis, dysentery, chickenpox, common cold and heat stroke. When humidity in the air is low, the delicate membranes of the nose, throat and other respiratory tracts are adversely affected making people fall easy prey to common cold. Arthritis, rheumatism and gout patients suffer more in winters and rainy seasons (Figure 5.2).

General climates apart, even microclimates have considerable impact on the health of the people. Air and water pollution, particularly in urban areas, gives rise to a number of diseases that were so rare in the past. Asthma is no longer confined to aged persons, it is becoming common among the children. Mental cases are also on the increase and so are the cases of hepatitis and lung infection of various kinds.

Close relationship between climate and health can be felt by one and all but the degree of causality is debatable. Does climate impact human body to such an extent that man loses his biological stamina and some of his ability to control the environment? Whether the kinds, numbers and varieties of external aggressors upon his organism are greater in the tropics than in the temperate climates? These and other questions are of such a complicated nature that they cannot be answered satisfactorily without deeper and cross-cultural studies. Our knowledge is still very limited, says Dr. May. "When we find tropical man living with three million red cells per cubic millimeter (normal = five and a half million) supporting ascarids and hookworms, and having at one time or the other suffered from malarial infections to the point where the scars still exist in his reticuloendothelial system, it is quite impossible to state which of those causes is dominant, which influent, and how they combine to produce, among others, this physiological feature of low red cell count. No comparison with white man living in the tropics is valid, for the white man brings with him a control over the environment, which makes him less vulnerable to outside attacks than the natives. There are some indications that, if placed in similar conditions, he will acquire the same disease-fostering parasites, with the same harmful

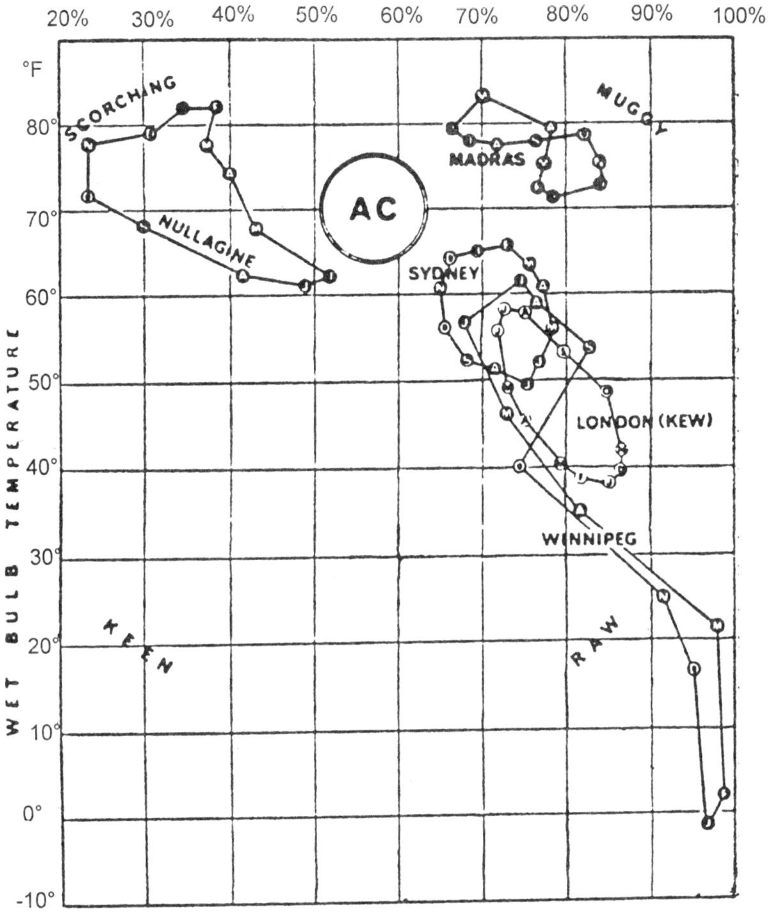

Fig. 5.2: Humidity and Health

effects upon his physiology. No experimentation artificially induced has so far reproduced all the causes found in nature, which can be blamed for impaired physiology, so that the problem is without a solution. Yet it can be assumed that the low oxygen-carrying capacity of tropical population as a whole is important in governing their physical and mental development. Their tissues are submitted to a permanent semi-anoxia. Their culture has provided them with ways whereby they can survive as a group, but it has not developed in the direction where the individual's survival should be long and pleasant, which is characteristic of our culture. As long as the species reproduces itself in increasing numbers, the mysterious requirements of natural laws seem to be satisfied, there being no provision in these laws for pleasantness and duration of individual life.... Those diseases which affect large numbers... have different ways of lowering man's aggressiveness towards his environment. Blood tissues and organ infections such as malaria, filariasis, schistosomiasis, permanent fungal infections and many others act upon human physiology in different ways. Most of these various parasites affect blood, tissues, and organs at various stages of their life cycles.

As stated by May, "The tropical man can thus be viewed as constantly subjected to the spoliating or toxic action of millions of larval or adult forms of exogenous life. At the same time, he is starving. The point before us is to decide where these factors are the dominant ones in creating the type of ecological adaptation which is common in the tropical world, and which results in the state of affairs we want to modify for our benefit and theirs."

Dr. May's conclusions raise a number of questions. Diseases are not necessarily endemic to tropical climates. Many communicable diseases were present in the temperate climates too and millions of people did die of those diseases in Europe. In fact, some of them appear to have come to the tropics from temperate zones. Moreover, is it really important to know whether climate is a causative or only a conditioning factor in disease ecology? According to D.H.K. Lee, "the widespread incidence of debilitating, incapacitating, and life shortening disease must seriously reduce both the desire for work and the efficiency of performance, and that these effects will in turn increase the likelihood of malnutrition and decrease the efficacy of preventive measures in a self perpetuating cycle of poverty and disease."

Climate and Human Physiology

The influence of climate on human physiology is enormous. Part of it is direct in terms of comfort and discomfort we feel in different climatic regimes and in terms of resources that we spend to ward off its unwanted consequences. Several studies point to a close relationship between climate and physical and mental agility. The environmental determinists relied very heavily on the apparent evidence of people living in the warm and humid climates being slow and less energetic. Markham noted energy differences between the races living in temperate and warm climates, which could not be explained by differences in diet and mode of living alone. According to him, "the man in the tropics has lower oxygen consumption, lower blood pressure and a lower capacity to meet emergencies than the inhabitants of the temperate zones." Some psychologists assert that each climatic zone is marked by a mental make up of its own and hence the behaviour of the people is different in different zones.

The conclusions of the type mentioned above may not be based on cross-climatic and cross-cultural observations and studies as such they may not conclusively prove as to which of the several climatic elements really influence health, in what circumstances, how and in what measure. But the fact that working capacity of man is greatly influenced by temperature and humidity in particular cannot be denied. Humid climates of the tropics do reduce man's capacity for both physical and mental work. Those of us who have visited or lived in coastal cities of Kolkata, Chennai and Mumbai know how trying it is to live there during summer months. In these cities diseases of the respiratory system are very common. True, it is now possible to create artificial climates inside the room by air conditioning, but one cannot avoid being influenced by the general atmospheric conditions altogether. Further, it is not possible to use air conditioning on a mass scale in developing countries where electricity is yet to reach every home. High temperatures above 40° C cause heat strokes and force people to remain inside for much of the day. Low temperatures also restrict human activity. One can easily see the effect of very high and very low temperatures on density of population. Very few people live in hot and cold deserts.

Lee (1941) developed a climatic strain chart for predicting the influence of climate on the efficiency of a person in summer clothing doing moderate work. Figure 5.3 shows this chart superimposed on climogram to give a comparative idea of the net climatic strain. A similar chart devised by Taylor, is also given in the figure. Although these charts are based on the reaction of people exposed to different climatic conditions only temporarily, they do provide important leads for further research.

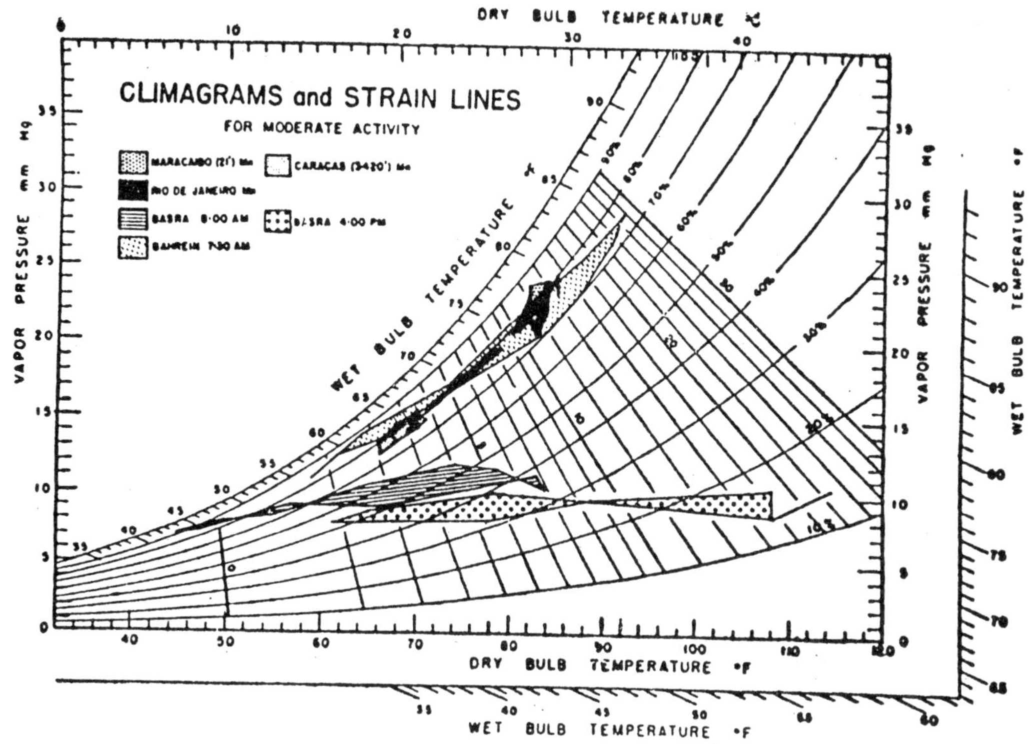

Fig. 5.3: Climatic Strain Charts

The best climates appear to be those, which are marked by a good balance between heat loss and heat gain by human body. Too hot and too cold climates are, therefore, not considered to be comfortable. Human body, however, can adjust to such differences to a great extent. Man has always used his technological resources to counterbalance climatic extremes. Look at the way the Eskimos have adapted themselves to climatic vagaries of the Tundra, or the way the people of hot deserts have fashioned their life. "The process of acclimatization to heat consists largely in learning to sweat more volume with less salt in it, and this must be accompanied by taking more water and more salt" (USDA). Hot climates restrict heat loss, while the cold ones force the body to lose heat. The fact that these extremes of climates are not very good for the young, the old and the sick cannot be denied. Some details of seasonal physiology are given in Table 5.1.

Table 5.1: Seasonal Physiology

Physiological Processes	*Observed Seasonal Changes*
1. Blood	
Total protein	Often more than 8.5 gm 100 cc serum in winter; less than 7.5 gm in summer
Hemoglobin	Lower in summer than in winter: minimum in June
Calcium	Minimum in February-March; Maximum in August
Blood volume	Lower in winter than in summer
Oxygen capacity	Higher in children below 6 years in Jan.-May and children above 6 years in Feb.-August.
CO capacity	Maximum around 21 December and minimum around 21 June.
Phosphate	Due to increased vitamin D synthesis in the skin, minimum in February and maximum in summer and autumn
2. General metabolism	In children: maximum during autumn; sharply decreasing during winter. In rickets patients: decreases during winter due to Vitamin D shortage. Human amino-acid-excretion: max. in winter (Feb.-March)
3. Blood pressure	High in winter; low in summer
4. Gastro-acidity	Hyper acidity high in winter; low in summer
5. Growth and weight of children	Slow growth in winter, rapidly increasing in spring; increase in height maximum in March-May and Nov.-Jan. Weight increases in Sept.-October. Babies born in June-July have higher weight; those born in Dec.-March have lower weight.
6. Birth frequency	Highest number of conceptions take place in May-June. The frequency of stillborn is more in January
7. Mortality	In Western Europe, it is highest in Dec.-January and lowest in July
8. Acclimatization	Acclimatization to cold stress is more difficult in summer than in winter

Source: Contributed by Prof. SK Agrawal, Delhi School of Economics.

"In tropical climates, there seems to be a lowering of blood pressure; the volume of blood presumably increases, but it is more diluted; sweating takes a toll of plasma, fluid, and salts which must be made up. There is a decrease in gastric secretions accompanied by constipation and impaired appetite and digestion; there is also reduced energy for work, but this may often be only a sign of malnutrition or some other trouble. Those who have a higher energy production because of the overactive thyroid are likely to become neurasthenic in the tropics. There is less oxygen per cubic foot in hot than in cold air, and this may reduce the effectiveness of all bodily functions unless the body becomes adjusted to it. ...Constant sweating and the increase of blood flow to the capillaries induced by warmth have a harmful effect in blood chemistry and tone of internal organs lowering resistance to infection" (USDA). Excessive heat can exhaust people and lead to heat strokes that are so common in tropical countries in summer months (for seasonal pathology, see Table 5.2).

The Best climates for cattle rearing are those where temperatures range between 5° and 32°C and rainfall varies from 50 to 100 cm per annum. Even hot climates approaching semi-desert conditions with good irrigation facilities and modern dairy management techniques are good for cattle rearing. Wet climatic conditions, particularly in the tropics are not conducive to animal health. While fodder availability is copious, these climates are breeding grounds for infectious diseases.

Table 5.2: Seasonal Pathology

Pathological Processes	*Observed Seasonal Changes*
I. Pseudo-seasonal Phenomena	
Non-infectious Diseases	
Bronchitis	Maximum in winter
Bronchial asthma	Maximum in winter
Appendicitis	More common in summers
Glaucoma	High in winter
Retinal detachment	Less in winter; more in June-July
Rheumatic diseases	More common during cold and humid seasons
Diabetes	More common in December –March
Goitre (simple)	Maximum in winter
Mental diseases	Maximum unrest in November-January
Infectious Diseases	
Tuberculosis	High mortality in Spring; High sensitivity to TB tests in March April; low sensitivity in autumn.
Diphtheria	Incresing from Sept.-March; maximum in November and December
Common cold	Increasing from Sept.-March; maximum in February-march.
Influenza	Max. in December-February
Pneumonia	Maximum in December-February
II. Truly Seasonal Phenomena	
Non-infectious Diseases	
Hey fever	Usually in may-June
Rickets	Most frequent in winter due to Vitamin D deficiency
Infectious Diseases	
Cholera	Increases from May. Maximum in July-August
Typhoid fever	Increasing from May; maximum in August-September.
Poliomyelitis	
Bacillary dysentery	Maximum in summer

Source: Contributed by Prof. S.K. Agrawal, Delhi School of Economics.

Climate and Nutrition

In predominantly agricultural countries like India, food intake is determined by what is locally and regionally produced and what is produced is very much dependent on climatic conditions. If the rains are good, people have access to more and greater variety of foods. When drought and floods come, people suffer from shortage of food; many of have been able to get over this problem by import of food from surplus countries. Agricultural societies being economically underdeveloped have to depend on their own resources. Some people die of hunger and many others suffer from deficiency and other diseases. Climate plays a very significant role in food production, particularly in countries like India where agriculture is still 'a gamble in monsoon'. Climate has both indirect and direct effects on agriculture. It is a major factor in soil formation, distribution of flora and fauna, domestication of plants and animals, and agricultural management in general. Areas with heavy rainfall are subjected to soil erosion, flooding and leaching. These are also the areas where plant and animal pests and diseases abound. In moist climates the quality of animals is poor while the cost of maintaining them is high. The yield of milk per animal is low. There is a general shortage of animal proteins in the diet.

Tropical grass and forage are very luxuriant but lack nutritive elements. Low productivity of cattle is, to a great extent, because of the nutritional deficiency they suffers from. High temperatures and precipitation combine to leach the soil of soluble minerals and compounds so essential for proper nourishment of animals. The bulk of this vegetation is composed of water and fiber. The former is abundantly found in the body of the animals and the latter is hard to digest and is heat producing. Proteins and carbohydrates are generally lacking or in short supply. Minerals like calcium and phosphates, and trace elements like cobalt, manganese and iodine, are also limited. As a result, animals in hot moist climates suffer from bone maladies, anaemia, goitre and several other diseases. During summers without rains or in years of droughts, the situation further deteriorates leading to very high rate of morbidity and mortality among animals. To withstand the heat, animals have to resort to heavy breathing that has adverse effects on their health and productivity.

The factors, which militate against the health of animals, are conducive to the growth of viruses that cause diseases. Diseases like anaplasmosis, piroplesmosis, ngana, surra, liver fluke, hydatid fly strike, helminithiasis, etc. caused by these viruses are found abundantly in most hot climates. One has to agree with Lee that "the ecological pattern of the humid tropics is that of a multiplicity of species, constant competition and continuous evolutionary experiment. In such a milieu, every opportunity is given for the emergence of some inimical agent whenever a new species or strain of domestic animals introduced. Man has achieved some notable victories in his campaign against tropical diseases, but the guerrilla tactics of nature in the tropics are not easily overcome, and victory in one phase may be largely upset by new disease developments in another."

The cattle, subjected to such environmental stresses without matching veterinary services, do not grow in stature, nor do they produce good quality and quantity of milk. In the face of keen competition for scarce nutrients, only smaller animals that need a lower daily requirement of food survive. This explains the poor quality of animals in tropics. In India, the quality of animals in the eastern states like West Bengal, Assam, Orissa and Bihar is not satisfactory. This situation adversely affects the nutritional status of the people. In India, most of the people are vegetarians partly because of cultural and partly economic reasons. Milk and milk products are thus the only main sources of animal proteins.

ORGANIC ENVIRONMENT

Organic environment has three basic components, which deserve our attention. The first component is the plant life; second, the animals including the micro organisms; and third, the human beings themselves. In this section, we propose to deal with the first two: plant and animal life.

Plant Life

Plants play a very crucial role in human survival and development; they keep the atmospheric gases and heat in balance. But for them, there will be no soil formation and hence no organic life. Plants, in their most primitive forms, the moss, were the first life forms to emerge on the earth surface. Today the most obvious representative of plant life is the tree. Let us, therefore, examine what a tree is?

From the seed that falls to the ground and is covered with leaves and soil comes a tree. As the soil gets warm in summer, and moisture is abundant in the monsoon season, deep changes take place in the dormant seed and the embryo tree awakens from its slumber. What causes this to happen is not yet fully known. The growth hormone is activated; the enzymes become active. The fats and starch stored in the seed break down to soluble sugars, mainly dextrose. The enzymes break down into 20 soluble compounds called amino acids.

Both dextrose and amino acids are rushed to all the growth points of the baby tree. Proteins are formed from the amino acids. The dextrose is used up to build the body of the tree; part of it is burnt up to provide necessary energy to keep the process of growth operational. Soon the seed shell splits open and newly born tree emerges above the ground. It forms roots, which go down, and shoots which go up. Then onwards, the tree has to get its nutrients from the place it is born or transplanted later. In nature, the newly born tree remains there for the whole of its life and grows in company with other plants, as has been the case with its predecessors from time immemorial.

As the tree emerges from the ground, it starts developing a cambium layer between the bark and the wood. Cambium layer is a single layer of cells, which divide themselves for the whole life of the tree. It produces both the bark and the wood. When removed, the tree dies. The formation of the wood in them takes place annually so that all grow in rings from which one can guess their age.

Almost two thirds (about 60 per cent) of the wood of a tree is cellulose, which is also a form of sugar. Much of it is used in papermaking. The remaining one third consists of lignin, a binding material composed of carbon, oxygen and hydrogen. Small quantities of fats, starch, sugar, resins and tannins are also found in the wood. About 10 per cent of the wood mass is found underground in the form of roots. Function of the root is to provide water and minerals to the tree and to anchor it securely to the ground. Any violence to roots has its immediate adverse effect on the tree.

Trees are similar to animals in matters of respiration and digestion of fats; but they differ from animals in some very significant ways. Trees take their nutrition and minerals from the soil; animals take them from plants. Plants are the only producers of organic matter; all others are consumers.

The process by which plants produce the organic matter is called photosynthesis that is, building with the energy of light. Organic matter is formed literally from water and air. Air contains minute amounts of carbon dioxide (0.03 per cent). The air penetrates the leaves through millions of pores or stomata in the leaves and gives up about 10 per cent of its carbon dioxide. Leaf cells have small particles called chloroplasts containing green substances called chlorophyll, which for all practical purposes function as hemoglobin of the blood. The carbon dioxide unites with the chlorophyll and in combination with oxygen and hydrogen of water and with the regulatory action of the enzymes, produces sugar. The excess of oxygen in the process is released in the atmosphere. The energy needed for the purpose of converting carbon dioxide and water into organic substance (dextrose) is supplied by sunlight. Only one per cent of the solar energy falling on the leaves is used for photosynthesis. Dextrose is converted into other sugars; it may also be combined with nitrogen to form the amino acids, which form the building blocks of proteins on which all life depends. Part of the dextrose goes in the formation of fats, starch and other substances.

Mild temperatures 20° to 25° C with diffused and moderate light constitute the most ideal conditions for photosynthesis. In summer months, efficiency of photosynthesis goes down. Fertility of the soil also determines the health of the plant: soil supplies the minerals. Respiration is another important life process. Plants too respire by oxidizing dextrose sugar. It is just the opposite of photosynthesis in terms of chemical reaction. In case of photosynthesis carbon dioxide + water + energy are expended to produce dextrose + oxygen, while in the case of respiration dextrose + oxygen release carbon dioxide + water + energy. During the day both the processes-photosynthesis and respiration-go together.

Oxygen liberated in photosynthesis is used for respiration; and carbon dioxide exhaled by the tree is used in photosynthesis. Since photosynthesis is more intensive a process than respiration, a tree releases more oxygen and uses more carbon dioxide. If because of some reasons the process gets reversed, the tree starts losing its weight. In respiration oxygen is taken in and carbon dioxide is released. Thus respiration is continuous process in all life forms and every cell of each living thing. Photosynthesis, on the other hand, is related to water supply to the roots also; it stops in the night and is lowered in hot seasons and practically stops during droughts. Trees are damaged in intense heat because photosynthesis stops but respiration continues.

Trees use the nitrogen to produce proteins. Proteins are necessary for the growth and division of cells. That is why, an abundance of nitrogen promotes vegetative growth. The atmosphere has lot of nitrogen but the trees cannot use this nitrogen directly. It has to first process it into ammonia or nitrates. Some plants develop nitrogen-fixing nodules in their roots to collect nitrogen from the atmosphere and soil, but most plants do not have this facility. Another source is fallen leaves. But they contain only one per cent of nitrogen. The most important source is the animal waste. Plants are very frugal in nitrate use; they use it again and again. All that is needed is to let nature work for itself. Alternatively, fertilizers should be used in measured quantities. Excess fertilization is harmful to the crops as well as to the soil. Apart from nitrogen, trees need oxygen, hydrogen and carbon. All these are available in the atmosphere and soil

Among the mineral elements, potassium, phosphorus and calcium are needed in relatively larger quantities. Iron, sulfur and magnesium are needed in smaller quantities. Trace elements like zinc, manganese, copper, boron and molybdenum are necessary only in minute quantities. The total amount of all minerals in dry wood is just 0.5 per cent. Trace elements are rarely absent in any soil. Thus minerals do not constitute a major hurdle in the growth of trees. Wherever, there is a shortage, chemical fertilizers in measured quantities can be used to supplement the natural supply.

Water is contained in all the tissues of a tree, dead or alive. It is an indispensable substance for plant life. Trees collect water through their roots; push it up to the leaves through the trunk using the energy supplied by the sun. The openings in the leaf called stomata suck carbon dioxide from the air; they also transpire water to the atmospheres. These pores open early in the morning; start shrinking by noon and by sunset they are fully closed. This is how trees maintain a balance between water supply and transpiration, on the one hand, and photosynthesis (intake of carbon dioxide) during the day and exhalation of oxygen in the night, on the other.

Plants and Health

What the plants do for human beings is now clear to us. They keep our atmosphere in balance. None of the gases naturally increase or decrease except while in a closed space. It is estimated that the leaves of the plants give to the earth each year something like 200,000 million tons of organic matter and 100,000 tons of oxygen to keep the grand cycle of the biosphere in balance. In addition to these, they supply adequate amount of minerals and trace elements. If man uses the plant life judiciously and scientifically, there would be no environmental pollution. Unfortunately, he does not care for nature. He treats nature as a resource for exploitation. And in this self-destroying thinking, it is the plants, which become the first target of attack.

In this way the atmospheric constituents remain in balance and there is no increase in temperature. At least one third of the land of the earth must remain under forest. Each country must keep at least 33 per cent of its land under forest. Of course, the percentage will be higher in mountainous areas and lower in those of plains.

Plants should not be seen only as necessary ingredient of the biosphere. They also provide the raw materials for many of the medicines man uses or may use in future to maintain good health and cure diseases. They are not only source of nutrition; they are also the precursors of various life forms. It is the primordial moss from which everything living was born. Plants also provide the necessary biological environment for happy life and living.

Animals and Health

Domestication of animals heralded the first great revolutionary change in human civilization. We now call it agricultural revolution. Modern civilization is no less dependent on animals. Nutritional requirements apart, animals are significant contributors to ecological balance, which appears to be in jeopardy. The role of microorganisms in human health is well known to us all. Advances in the prevention of infectious diseases became possible only after the germ theory of diseases was put forth.

According to Felix Marti-Ibanez, human health can be taken as a product of the "convergence in time and space within the person of the patient an environmental stimuli, organic, inorganic or socio-cultural. These stimuli constitute a challenge, which induces a cellular response, that is disease (communicable, degenerative or behavioural), which in its turn eventually results in ecologic adaptation and survival or in total maladjustment or death." (Felix Marti-Ibanez) Disease is thus "the alteration of the living tissues which jeopardizes survival in the environment and which results from an accidental collision between two or more forms of life, each pursuing its own destiny"

The causative factors of diseases can be seen at three different levels. At the primary level stand the primary causes, which include heredity, environmental stresses and style of life one chooses. From these primary factors emerge the secondary factors, such as bacteria and viruses, which are grouped as germs. The germs invade the body weakened by under-or malnutrition, intake of intoxicants and polluted water and food. Thinking that diseases are temporary interruptions in the normal functioning of the body, we use medicines to control them. The germs get used to medicines. They become immune from it. In the meantime, the systemic balance of the body is lost, and man gets diseases, which have no cures. The systemic disorders constitute the tertiary causes of diseases.

There is no major difference in three levels of comprehension of diseases. Germs are the agents that produce diseases. Most germs do not enter the human body directly but some do. They originate and grow in certain foods, rodents and animals and from there they come to man. These foods and animals function as vectors. And then finally we have reservoirs where agents wait until favourable environmental conditions develop for them to expand. It is clear that the agent, the host, the vector and the reservoir constitute part and parcel of the environment in which man lives. J.M. May has rightly pointed out that "All plants and animals establish themselves in societies by elimination of weaker competitors for food or shelter that the environment can supply. As long as they are established in a balance, they are in a pattern of mutual tolerance. Any upsetting factor, such as change of temperature, or humidity, can favour a barely existing form and change the dominance among competitors, establishing a new social pattern.".

The disease organisms also form patterns and compete with other organisms to survive and grow. When they overpower the organisms that build and protect the human body, diseases set in. Usually, it happens when the body is weakened and the organisms keeping it in optimum running condition are either decimated or reduced in number. Diseases are thus symptoms, not causes of ill-health. It is the germ theory that proclaimed disease to be a cause.

All plants and animals are bound together by interdependence. They cannot lead a mutually exclusive existence. They exist and grow within the overall natural and cultural patterns. Change in the natural or cultural environment without counterbalancing or compensatory inputs, disturbs all living organisms. It was also the conclusion of J.M. May. "This concept, basic in plant and animal ecology, does not usually enter the physician's thinking when he is discussing a human disease. However, this social pattern exists everywhere in nature. It affects the internal environment of every living thing where the parasitic load is concerned. It plays a direct role in the epidemiology of transmissible diseases and an indirect one in the epidemiology of other maladjustments"

The disease agents being living organisms, that coexist with other organisms, all of them are not found everywhere in the world. As a consequence the diseases are also not equally distributed all over the world. At times, the organism, which creates a particular disease, has a fierce enemy in its habitat. As soon as the virus enters that habitat, it is either subdued or destroyed, and hence fails to cause the disease. Some agents spend their early part of life in hosts other than human beings. These hosts too live only in given environmental setting. The bladder worm responsible for causing schistosomiasis cannot complete its life cycle without a snail. The snails are not found everywhere as they can live only in moist climatic conditions. The poliomyelitis virus is most active during summer and severe winters. Various species of anopheline mosquitoes require very specific environmental conditions for breeding. Anopheles crucians breed in all types of waters; anopheles barberi prefer waters collected in tree holes; while anopheles gabiae usually breed in sunlit shallow pools. Anopheles hyrcanus causes malaria in East Asian and ASEAN countries like Indonesia, Malaysia and China, but not in India.

Two forms of life, that collide with each other to create human diseases, are human beings and minute organisms like viruses. These organisms after entering the human body, function in an environment, which is determined by heredity and external stresses. Before entering the human body they have to breed, survive and grow in a different set of environmental conditions. The organisms will succeed in jeopardizing the health of a person only when both the external environment (geographical and socio-cultural) in which it originates and internal environment (the human body) in which it grows offer favourable conditions for multiplication.

The disease generating organisms belong to different species and types. Some of them are too small to be seen even with the help of microscope, while many others can be seen with naked eyes. On the basis of their size and function, they are classified as viruses, rickettias, spirochets, bacteria, fungi, protozoa and metazoa (May).

Viruses are those pathogenic organisms which can survive only in the living cells and which exhibit a high degree of parasitism. Their size varies from 230 to 8 milli microns. They are responsible for causing diseases like poliomyelitis, measles, trachoma, and yellow fever, among others. Rickettias are a little larger than viruses in size. They are also parasitic and hence cannot exist outside the human cells. Often they begin their life history in ticks, lice and fleas. They cause diseases like typhus.

Spirochets vary in characteristics from bacteria to protozoa. They can be found almost everywhere and are associated with ticks, lice and rodents. They are passed on to human body either by bite or through water or food contaminated with the urine of the infected animals. Some of them enter the human body directly. Agents that cause syphilis and yaws enter human blood stream directly. Bacteria are a vegetable group of organisms found all over the world. They are also the oldest organisms to survive to this day. They are responsible for such diseases as enteric fevers, pneumonia, etc.

Protozoa are unicellular organisms. They are responsible for some of the prevalent tropical diseases like malaria whose causative agent, plasmodium, is transmitted to man through mosquitoes. Metazoa have a pluricellular structure. They are visible to the naked eyes and their growth and survival are very much dependent on external environment.

Anthropoids that Cause Diseases

The anthropoids that cause diseases are of three types: insecta, arachnida and crustacea. Given below is a list of the anthropoids and the diseases they are associated with.

Class of Anthropods	*Associated Diseases*
1. Insects	
(a) Mosquito (i) anaphelenes (ii) culicenes	Malaria, filaria, viral incephalitis (JE), viral fevers like Dengue, west Nile, viral haemorrhagic fever
(b) Flies (i) house fly	Typhoid, diarrhoea, dysentery, cholera, gastroenteritis, amoebiasis

(*Contd.*)

(*Contd.*)

Class of Anthropods	*Associated Diseases*
	helminthic infestations, polio-myelitis, conjunctivitis, trachoma, anthrax and yaws
(ii) sand fly	Kala Azar, sandfly fever, oriental sore, oraya fever
(iii) tsetse fly	sleeping sickness
(iv) black fly	onchocersiasis
(c) Human lice	
(i) head lice	
(ii) crab lice	
2. Arachnida	
(a) Ticks	
(i) hard	Tick typhus, viral J.E., viral fevers, viral haemorrhagic fevers, Kyasanur Forest Disease, tularemia, tick paralysis, humano babesiosis
(ii) soft	Q fever, relapsing fever
(b) Mites	
(i) leptotrombidium and	trombiculid mites Scrub typhus, ickettsialpox
(ii) itch mites Scabies	
3. Crustacea	
(a) Cyclops	Guinea worm disease, fish tape worm
(b) Cochroches Enteric pathogens	

Anthropods transmit diseases in three ways: direct, mechanical and biological. Scabies are transmitted directly. Diarrhea is transmitted mechanically. Plague, malaria and filarial are transmitted biologically. The plague transmission is propagative, that of malaria, cyclo-propagative and of filarial cyclo-developmental.

A number of diseases have animals as reservoir hosts. A partial list of such diseases and the animal hosts associated with them is given below.

Bacterial Infections

1. Anthrax	Pigs, herbivores
2. Brucellosis	Cattle, sheep, goats, camels, pigs, dogs, horses, buffaloes
3. Ornihosts	Wild and domestic birds
4. Q fever	Cattle, sheep, goats, wild animals
5. Leptospirosis	Rodents, mammals
6. Tuberculosis	Cattle, sheep, goats, pigs, cats and dogs
7. Plague	Rodents

Viral Infections

1.	Cowpox	Cattle
2.	Monkeypox	Monkeys and rodents
3.	Eastern equinine encephalitis	Horses, rodents
4.	Ross river fever	Horses, cattle, goats, sheep, dogs, rats, bats, pigs
5.	Yellow fever	Monkeys
6.	Japanese encephalitis	Wild birds
7.	Rabies	Dogs, fox, mongoose, bats, jackals

Protozoan Infections

1.	Leish maniasis	Dogs, cats. Swines
2.	Toxoplasmosis	Cats, mammals, birds
3.	Trypanosomiasis	Game animals, cattle
4.	Babesiosis	Cattle

Helminthic Infections

1.	Clonor Chiasis	Dogs, cats, swines, wild animals, fish
2.	Fasciolopsiasis	Dogs and swines
3.	Schistosomiasis	Rodents
4.	Echinococcosis	Dogs, angulates, wild carnivores
5.	Taeniasis	Cattle
6.	Trichinellosis	Rodents, swines, wild carnivores, marine mammals

ENVIRONMENTAL POLLUTION AND HEALTH

Air Pollution

Presence in the ambient atmosphere of gases, chemicals and particulate matters in excess of what human body :an tolerate or which is injurious to animals and vegetation, directly or indirectly, is called air pollution. More than one hundred air pollutants have been identified. Important among them are: carbon dioxide; hydrogen sulfate; fluorine compounds, organic compounds such as hydrocarbons, aldehydes, ketones, organic acids; metallic contaminants such as arsenic, zinc, lead, and iron; and radio-active compounds.

The chief sources of air pollution are: automobiles, industries, domestic activities, tobacco smoking and miscellaneous activities like pesticide sprays and natural sources. Meteorological factors too influence the level of pollution. The lower most 30 km of atmosphere holds the major portion of the atmospheric gases. Man is concerned with only 8-10 km of it. The level of atmospheric pollution depends on topography, air movement and climatic conditions in general. Vertical movement of pollutants depends on the temperature gradient. Cooling at lower levels traps the pollutants from escaping to the upper atmosphere.

For fresh air, the living quarters should be well ventilated. Ventilation connotes movement of air. According to De Chaumont, a person needs 3000 c. ft. of air per hour to lead a healthy life. This requirement is easily met if the rooms in which we live or work are well ventilated allowing the air to move in and out. When we breathe out, the respiration does not rise towards the ceiling; it remains in the lower parts of the air space. As such high ceilings (more than 12 ft.) do not ensure good ventilation. A room of 50 to 100 sq. ft. is adequate provided that it is well ventilated.

Natural ventilation is ideal. Open windows serve the purpose well. Alternatively, mechanical devices can be fixed. Exhaust fans can be used to take the air out of the room; plenums can be fixed to blow in the fresh air; and air conditioners can be fixed to do many things simultaneously. It controls temperature, humidity, air movement, dust, bacteria, odor and toxic gases.

The rooms should be well lighted. Day light should be allowed to get into the room at least for some time. Day light has effects on biological rhythm of body temperature, physical activity, stimulation of melanin synthesis, activation of precursors of vitamin D, adrenocortical secretions and food consumption. It is being used as a therapeutic measure in premature infants with hyperbite rubinemia.

Light in the living or workroom should be sufficient, well distributed, steady, without glare and sharp shadows. Brightness would depend on the colour of the walls, etc.

Water Pollution

There are more diseases because of water than any other climatic element. It is for this reason that 1980-90 decade was declared as the decade of Drinking Water Supply and Sanitation. Safe drinking water constitutes a basic component in the HFA 2000.

Water requirements are multiple. First and foremost is the physiological requirement, which amounts to about 2 liters per head per day depending, of course, on the climate and occupation. Apart from the quantity, the quality of water makes a lot of difference. Most of the diseases are caused not because of the quantitative shortage of water but because of its poor quality. The drinking water must be safe and wholesome. Safe water is:

1. free from pathogens,
2. free from harmful chemicals,
3. free from colour or odour and pleasant to taste, and
4. suitable for domestic purposes also.

In addition to these two uses, water is also needed for industrial purposes, for power generation and for washing of the wastes.

We get water from three main sources.

1. Rain
2. Surface Run off
    - Natural lakes
    - Artificial reservoirs
    - Rivers
    - Tanks
    - Canals.

3. Ground Water
    Shallow wells
    Deep wells
    Natural springs.

Rainwater contains dissolved solids (0.0005 per cent); it is soft and collects impurities (dust, soot, micro-organisms, gaseous sulfur and nitrogen oxides) as it passes through the atmosphere. Surface water contained in lakes, reservoirs, rivers and tanks is not safe for drinking purposes without treatment. The main source of surface water is rain. As it flows along the slope to various water bodies, it collects both soluble and solid impurities and deposits the same in rivers and reservoirs. Seawater is saline to the extent of 3.5 per cent. Off shore ocean-water contains about 30g salt per litre of water. The main dissolved constituents of per litre of seawater are: chloride, 1.99g; sodium, 1.06g; and magnesium, 1.27g. It gives a total of 4.32g. Seawater can be purified for domestic purposes but, being an energy intensive proposition, it is scarcely resorted to.

There is no pure water (H_2O) in nature. It consists of a number of dissolved gases such as nitrogen, carbon dioxide, hydrogen sulfate and various salts mentioned earlier. Most of these impurities are, however, not harmful to human life. But the impurities caused by human activities such as sewage, industrial effluents, fertilizers and pesticides used in agriculture, and heat and radioactive substances released in water are the ones that are harmful to all life forms.

Water is considered to be polluted if it contains certain substances in excess of what is considered to be accepted norm. Pollution is indicated by the presence of one or all of the following substances in water in suspension or solution:

1. total suspended solids,
2. bio-chemical oxygen demand (BOD) at 20° C temperature, and
3. concentration of chlorides, nitrogen and phosphorus, and absence of dissolved oxygen.

WHO and UNEP have jointly created a global network for water and air quality monitoring in more than 60 countries of the world. The quality of surface and ground water is being monitored in over 350 cities of the world. Table 5.3 gives the status of various countries of Southeast Asia with regard to availability of safe drinking water and sanitation.

Table 5.3: People Having Access to Safe Drinking Water and Sanitation in South and Southeast Asia: 1997 (in per cent)

Country	*Safe Drink-ing Water*	*Sanitation*
India	85	29
Bangladesh	80	30
Bhutan	21	22
Indonesia	63	51
Myanmar	39	42
Nepal	48	22
Srilanka	57	66
Thailand	70	74
Maldives	83	40

Source: WHO, Regional Health Report (South and South-East Asia), 1997.

Noise Pollution

Noise means unwanted sound. Noise pollution means wrong sound made in a wrong place and at a wrong time. Sound is measured in decibels (dB), which means the pressure above the smallest indistinguishable noise, also known as reference sound pressure i.e. 0.0002 microbars or dynes/cm^2. The scale varies from 0 to 200. 85 dB is the recommended maximum beyond which the noise affects the ear drums or mental state. On this scale, the whispering sound is at 20 dB level. At 160 dB, mechanical damage of the ear can take place. Normal conversation takes place at 60 dB level; motor horn sound measures 120 dB.

The human ear responds variably to perceived sound-pressure levels. A weight-age curve called Curve A has been constructed to take care of the subjective effects. Sound pressure levels are, therefore, measured in dB(A). The acceptable noise levels in dB(A) for various requirements have been standardized to enable environmentalists to measure noise pollution. Some of these are given in Table 5.4.

Table 5.4: Acceptable Noise Levels

Places/Locations	*Acceptable Noise Levels in dB(A)*
1. Residential	
Bedroom	25
Living room	40
2. Hospital (wards)	20-35
3. Educational	
Library	30-40
Classroom	35-40
4. Commercial	
Office	*35-45*
Conference	40-45
Restaurant	40-60
5. Industrial	
Workshop	*40-60*
Laboratory	40-50

Noise pollution affects human beings in three ways. The most direct effect is auditory leading to hearing loss; it also generates fatigue and headache. Among the physiological effects are hypertension and sleeplessness.

Radiation

Radiation is caused by radioactive substances natural or man made. Among the natural substances are cosmic rays which come from outer space; thorium, uranium, radium, carbon, and radon and thoron gases, which are terrestrial and atmospheric; and potassium 40 and carbon14, which are internal in the sense that they are generated within the body. Among the man-made radiation sources are medical X-rays, occupational exposure to radiation, nuclear radioactive fall out and a number of household goods like TV, radioactive dial watch, isotope tagged products, luminous markers, etc.

Radiation is of two types: electromagnetic (X-rays and gamma rays) and corpuscular (alpha particles, beta particles and protons). Alpha particles are ten times more harmful than X-rays, beta particles or gamma rays, but they have very little penetrating force. X-rays, beta particles and gamma rays are deep penetrating.

Radiation is measured in becquerel (Bq). 1 Bq = 1 disintegration per second. The potency of radiation is measured in Roentgen, Rad or Rem. Roentegen measures the radiation absorbed in the air at a given point: number of ions produced in 1 ml of air. Rad measures the amount of radiation absorbed per gram of tissue or any material. Rem measures the degree of potential danger to health from radiation.

Radiation has several effects on health: both somatic and genetic. Somatic effects are of two types: immediate and delayed. Radiation sickness and acute radiation syndrome are the two most important immediate effects. Delayed effects show up in the form of leukaemia, carcinogenesis, fetal abnormalities and shortening of life. Among the genetic effects, chromosome mutation and point mutation are most common.

CONCLUDING REMARKS

In real life, we cannot expect everyone to follow all the laws of healthy living. People do break the rules of the game and subject their body to various kinds of stresses and strains. It is more so in modern times of mad rush for success in life by fair or foul means. Further, we are living in a society which is highly iniquitous in terms of income and wealth distribution and access to life supporting resources at all territorial levels: international, national, sub-national and local. These disparities are not regional alone: they extend to sexes, races, communities, castes and places of origin. In such an in-equitous society, some people will always remain at the socio-economic margin unable to lead a healthy life. A third factor, that militates against the health of the people and over which individuals have no or little control, is ecological degradation and environmental pollution. Even if one tries to lead a very healthy life style, the polluted air he breathes, the contaminated water he drinks, the unhealthy food he eats, and the severe stresses under which he functions, adversely impact his physical as well as mental health. This being the situation, human society has not only to try to tackle the primary cause of ill-health but also the secondary and tertiary causes. The immediate task is to develop vaccines and medicines that can kill the germs attacking human body. This, of course, is not the final and lasting solution. Unless we tackle the primary cause of ill-health, while at the same time tackle the secondary and tertiary causes appearing as diseases, we cannot build a healthy society. The programme of 'Health-For-All' would not reach its goal even in 2025 AD if over reliance on medicines continues and we do not adopt a health promoting style of life and fail to follow the biological laws of nature.

REFERENCES

1. Boyd, J.T. 'Climate, Air Pollution and Mortality', *British Journal of Social and Preventive Medicine*, Vol. 14, 1960, pp. 267-271.

2. Diamant, R.M.E. *The International Environment of Dwellings*, London.
3. Hunter, John M., 'The Challenge of Medical Geography', in Geography of Health and Disease, Papers of the First Calolina Geographical Symposium, University of North Carolina at Chapelhill, Department of Geography, 1974.
4. Huntington, Ellsworth. *Principles of Human Geography*, New York: New American Library, 1943.
5. Lee, D.H.K. 'Physiology of the Tropics', *Malayan Medical Journal, Vol. 11, 1930. pp. 105-08.* See also his *Climate and Economic Development in the Tropics*, New York: Harper, 1957.
6. Markham, S.F. *Climate and Energy of Nations*, London: Oxford, 1942.
7. Marti-Ibanez, Felix. Foreword to the *Ecology of Human Diseases* by J.M. May.
8. May, J.M. *Ecology of Diseases*, New York: American Geographical Society, 1958; also see his *Ecology of Human Diseases*, New York: Academy of Sciences, 1960.
9. ——, Medical Geography: Its Methods and Objectives, Geographical Review, Vol. 40, 1950, pp. 9-41.
10. Ministry of Health, 'Mortality and Morbidity During London Fog of December, 1962', *Quarterly Journal, Royal Meteorological Society*, Vol. 89, 1954, pp. 267-271.
11. Payapilly, Celine, 'What is Holistic Health?' in Health for the Millions, Vol. 18, No. 4, Aug. 1992.
12. Ratzel, Feiedrich, *Anthropgeographie,* Studgart: J. Inglehorn, 1891.
13. U.S. Department of Agriculture, *Trees,* Yearbook, 1949, Washigton D.C.; also see *Climate and Man.* Yearbook, 1941.
14. WHO, Our Planet Our Health, Report of the WHO commission on Health and Environment, 1992.
15. P.K. Zuttsi, *Science Today*, Oct. 1970.

6

Natural Environment of India

SIZE AND EXTENT

India is one of the largest countries of the world, both in terms of area and population. It exhibits a great variety in its natural environment. That is why, it is known as Indian subcontinent. The separation of Pakistan and Bangladesh from India has made very little difference in its environmental complexities.

The surface area of India extends to 3.29 million sq. km; it stands seventh among the large countries of the world. Even though it is seventh in terms of total area, it holds second position in the world in total arable land, the USA being the first. As such it has tremendous potentials for agricultural development. High pressure of population has, however, weakened this advantage: per capita availability of arable land is too low to make average size of farms economically viable (Table 6.1).

Table 6.1: Land Resources of Selected Countries

Country	*Area in '000 sq. km.*	*Arable Land in '000 sq. km*	*Arable Land as % of Total Land*	*Population per unit of Arable Land*
Russian Federation	17,075	7.0	1286	113
USA	9,167	18.5	1732	144
South Africa	1,228	7.0	1280	123
China	9,532	9.8	916	1217
Indonesia	1,905	9.9	186	850
Brazil	8,512	4.9	417	373
Australia	7,682	6.0	464	37
Bangladesh	144	65.8	94	1200
Nigeria	924	32.3	298	332
India	3,228	50.5	1650	502
World	132,858	10.0	13266	384

Source: www.Rockford-india.com/irrigation-arableland.htm

Further, land-man ratio is not the same all over the country. Pressure of population on land is very high in the river basins; it is relatively lower in other parts of the country. Due to inheritance laws, the farm sizes are becoming smaller and smaller. About half of all operational land holdings are marginal i.e. less than one ha each. They account for only 20 per cent of total arable land.

Large holdings are common only in semi-arid and arid areas. In terms of productivity, they give no special advantage to the farmer. We will discuss the question of land use in greater details in chapter XV on nutrition and health.

PHYSICAL FEATURES

India is a unique physiographic entity. It has a great variety of landforms, relief, river systems and soil types. We cannot discuss all the physical features that make India unique in this chapter. A brief sketch with particular reference to health is therefore attempted here.

India can be divided into three broad tectonic divisions. Variation in relief, landforms and rock structure within each of these divisions is so great that we can get only a generalized picture of the physical configurations of the country. These regions are: (1) Himalayan mountains in the North, (2) The Indus-Ganga-Brahmaputra river basin in the middle, and (3) the Peninsular plateau in the South. The narrow coastal plains and the islands are often treated as fourth and fifth physical regions of India (Fig. 6.1).

The Himalayan Mountains

The Himalayas form a vast arc of mountains curving southwards. With deep gorges, steep cascades, and ordinary channels running along as well as across the mountain ranges carved out by the headwaters of Indus, Ganga, Brahmaputra and their innumerable snow-fed tributaries, they are the youngest mountains of the world still rising and evolving. According to plate tectonic theory, Himalayas were formed by the collision of the north-north-eastward moving Indo-Australian Plate against the stable Euroasian Plate of which the Tibetan plateau is a part. The resulting folding, faulting, and uplifting of the sedimentary deposits of the Sea of Tetheys constitute the present day Himalaya. The Indus-Ganga-Brahmaputra basin forms the remainder part of the sea which has been filled up by the rivers flowing southward from the rising Himalaya. (See Fig. 6.1).

The Sea of Tethys divided the Eurasian continent into two halves and extended all the way from the present day Mediterranean Sea to the Pacific Ocean. As the pressure increased, the frontal portions of the Indo-Australain Plate warped and slid under the Eurasian Plate pushing the fractured Precambrian rocks up. Much of the Himalayas are formed by plutonic rock of pre-Miocene age such as gneisses and schists. The marine sediments of Palaeozoic and Mesozoic times deposited in the Sea of Tethys do not constitute bulk of the Himalayas.

The rise of the Himalayas from the Sea of Tethys was not a single event. It occurred in millions of years. Broadly speaking, it happened in three distinct phases and each phase was marked by a different amalgam of rocks. The earliest phase was post-Eocene. It is evident in the Great Himalayas bordering the Tibet Plateau and ranging in height from 3660 to 4300

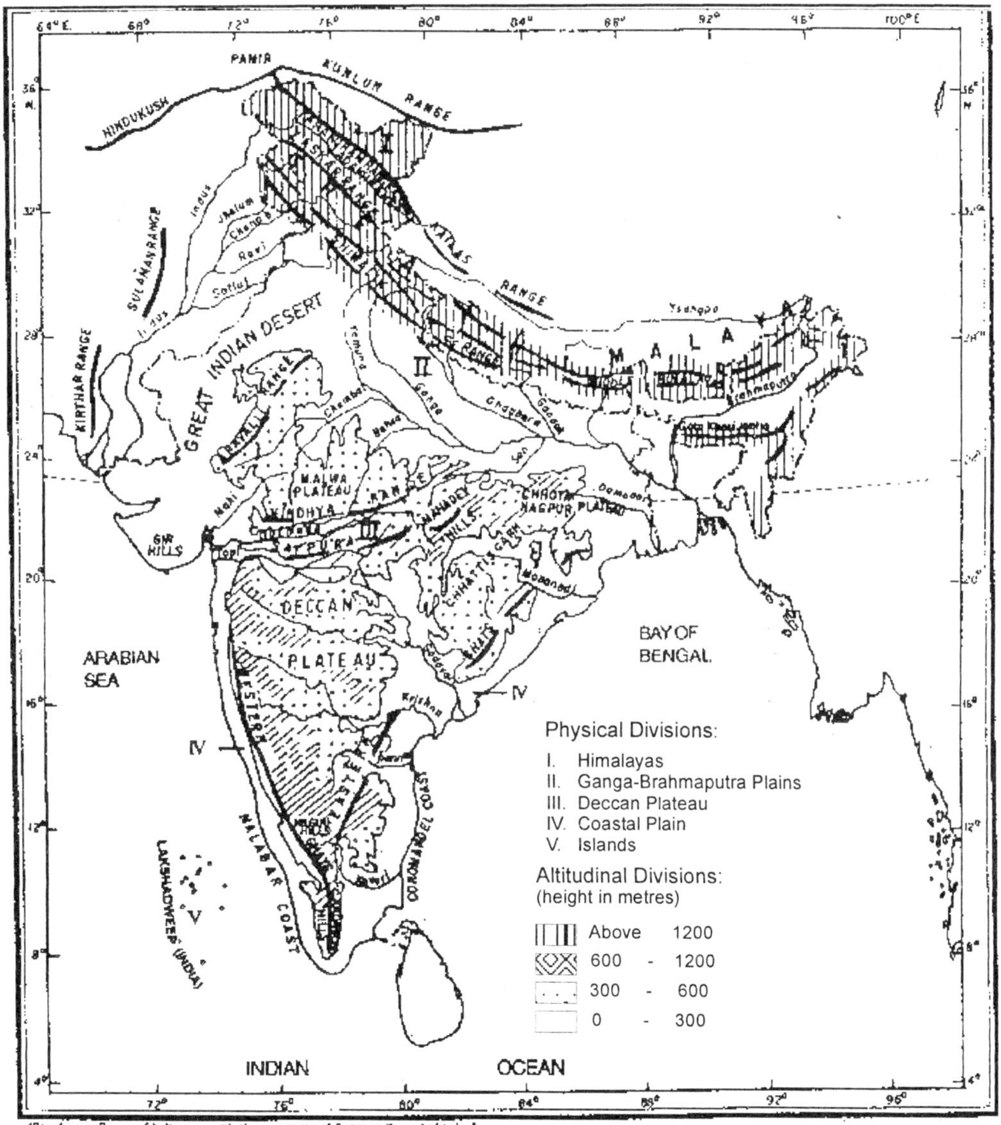

Fig. 6.1: India: Major Physical Divisions

meters. They contain some of the highest peaks of the world such as Everest (8848 m), K2 (8611m), Kanchenjunga (8598 m), Makalu (8481 m), Dhaulagiri (8172 m), and Nanga Parbat (8126 m). Most of them are in Nepal. The second movement took place at the end of the Miocene epoch. It produced the Middle or Lesser Himalayas. And the last movement occurred very recently at the end of the Tertiary to form the outer Himalayas or the Shiwaliks.

The Himalayas are not a single continuous range of mountains. They are usually divided into three parts: Western Himalayas, Central Himalayas and Eastern Himalayas. They consist of several parallel ranges intersected by enormous valleys and separated by plateaus of various sizes. These ranges vary from 160 to 400 km in width. Lengthwise they are as much as 2500 km long from west to east. As one enters the Himalayan region from the Great Plains of India, one comes across four distinct belts of mountains with different characteristics. The first belt consists of the Outer Himalayas or the Shiwaliks, which are the youngest mountains of the system. Middle or Lesser Himalayas come next. The third belt contains Great or Inner Himalayas and the last one the Trans-or Tibetan Himalayas.

The Himalayas have made much of India what it is today. Without them the Great Plains of India would be snow covered in winter and drier in summer. There would be no great rivers to irrigate the land. They have become a part of the Indian psyche. Due to their great heights, the Himalayas are cool and offer respite for those who can afford to spend their summer months in its valleys and less inhospitable ridges. The whole region is still natural and least polluted. If developed properly, it can become one of the most attractive regions of the country. It has tremendous potentials for small-scale electronic industries, tourism and horticulture. The people of the region are very hard working, gentle and cultured. Poverty forces them to move down to the plains. Deforestation has inflicted lot of damage to the environment in the region. Environmental pollution caused by urbanization and tourism insensitive to nature, ecology and natural environment has started posing problems that may get further aggravated, if not tacked in time.

The Great Plains

The Indus-Ganga-Brahmaputra plain is a vast fertile land stretching from the upper reaches of Indus and its tributaries in the west to the Brahmaputra valley in the east. The plains constitute thick deposits of sediment brought by Indus, Ganga and Brahmaputra and their tributaries. Elevation of the plains ranges from 150 to 300 metres above the sea level. The basin is marked with high fertility of land, high density of population, and low standard of living. Man-land ratio is so adverse that per capita availability of arable land does not exceed half an acre in much of the basin. Problems generated by subsistence agriculture are further compounded by low level of industrialization and poor social services.

Poverty is the major problem of this region of great economic and cultural potentials. Often visited by floods and droughts, the ill-governance of the states of the basin, particularly those of Bihar and Uttar Pradesh, has made the health scenario rather discouraging. People are frequent victims of diseases like cholera, tuberculosis, goiter, Kala-Azar, leprosy, menengitis, dysentery and many other diseases. When the mercury crosses 40°C, cholera, sunstroke and fevers of various kinds claim many lives. And in winters when the continental climate lowers temperatures down to even 0° C, diseases like common cold, arthritis, and asthma are aggravated. The rainy season is the worst, for it is the time when water gets contaminated and intestinal diseases and malaria break out.

The Peninsular Plateau

Peninsular India, a remnant of the Gondwanaland and once connected with southern part of Africa, stretches as far north as Delhi in the form of Aravali hills. Its northern boundary follows the course of Yamuna and Ganga. With an average elevation of 300 to 1800 meters, the peninsula slopes to the east. To the west are the Sahyadri mountains formed by the subsistence of a landmass to the west that now lies buried under the Arabean Sea. The east flowing peninsular rivers are almost graded and senile.

Much of the peninsular India consists of plateaus with extensive rolling plains at altitudes ranging from 300 to 1000 metres above the sea level. Malwa and Vindhyan plateaus in Central India slope down to the north from the Vindhyan mountains, the rocky lands of Eastern Rajasthan and Madhya Pradesh are degraded former highlands, the Maharashtra plateau is formed entirely of basalt of volcanic origin, and the plateaus of Karnataka and Tamil Nadu are essentially composed of Archaen geneses. Undulating topography of the plateaus provides ample opportunities for water harvesting and prosperous agriculture in the broad valleys that separate the gently sloping ridges.

Peninsular India is less densely populated except, of course, the fertile coastal plains, which, due to high humidity, provide favourable environment for disease causing microorganisms. Diseases of the respiratory system are quite common in coastal cities like Mumbai. Along the Malabar coast in Kerala and further up in Mangalore in Karnataka, filariasis is a common disease. In tobacco growing areas of Andhra Pradesh a large number of people suffer from cancer of mouth and throat.

The Coastal Plains and Islands

Coastal plains stretch in a narrow belt all the way from the Rann of Kuch in Gujarat to the Delta of Ganga in West Bengal girdling the whole peninsula. They constitute one of the most fertile and beautiful lands of India and are rich in agriculture, coconuts and fisheries, and port towns.

Andaman and Nicobar Islands and Lakshdweep and Minicoy Islands constitute two very important centrally administered Union Territories of India. Fisheries and coconuts gardening are the two main activities of these islands. Andaman and Nicobar Islands have great strategic importance for the country.

THE RIVERS

The river systems of India can be divided into two: the Himalayan and the Peninsular. Most of the Himalayan rivers flow eastward to discharge themselves in the Bay of Bengal but those of the Indus system flow southwestward and discharge in the Arabian Sea. The peninsula slopes to the east and hence most of the rivers flow from west to east. Those flowing from east to west are small riverlets originating in the Western Ghats except Narmada and Tapti, which flow through two rift valleys of the Vindhya and Satpura mountains.

The drainage system of the Himalayas is of complex nature. Many of the rivers, which appear to have originated after the Himalayan orogeny started, is not correct. Even before these mountains came into being, they flowed southward from the Tibetan plateau to the Sea of Tethys. These rivers are thus older than the Himalayas. During the prolonged and slow process of mountain building, these rivers kept to their own channels although acting at an accelerated rate. Thus the processes of mountain building and river valley formation took place simultaneously. Some of the rivers drain not only the southern slopes of the mountains but also the northern slopes of the Tibetan plateau. Some of the rivers like Sind, Sutlej and Brahmaputra flow through the longitudinal valleys and then all of a sudden turn to the south right across the southern ridge to drain in the Sea of Tethys to form the Great Plains of India. Some of transverse gorges of the Himalayas are as deep as 5000 metres.

The snowline on the southern slopes of the Himalayas facing the plains of India, varies from 4300 metres in the east and 5800 meters in the west. On the Tibetan side the snow line is 900 metres higher as the Himalayas obstruct the moisture bearing winds to reach there. The Great Himalayan range is the gathering ground of snow, nourishing a multitude of glaciers some of which are among the largest in the world outside the Polar Circles. Most of the glaciers are relatively small-less than five kilometers. Some of them are, however, longer than 30 kilometers.

THE CLIMATE

Climate has a major influence on the health of human beings and practically all life forms. Climate is the product of the general circulation of the air on the surface of the earth. Climatic typology is, therefore, influenced by global as well as local factors. This being the case, climatic patterns would be different from the physical patterns discussed earlier.

India can be divided into six major climatic regions. These are:

1. Tropical wet (along the western coast),
2. Tropical wet and dry (covering much of the peninsula),
3. Humid sub-tropical (extending to much of the Ganga valley and the Vindhyas),
4. Semi-arid (forming a north-south belt from central Maharashtra to Kanyakumari and through the middle of the peninsula; a semi circular belt covering southern Punjab, east Rajasthan and Kathiawad),
5. Arid Rajasthan, and
6. The Himalayan mountains extending from Kashmir to Arunachal Pradesh (Fig. 6.2).

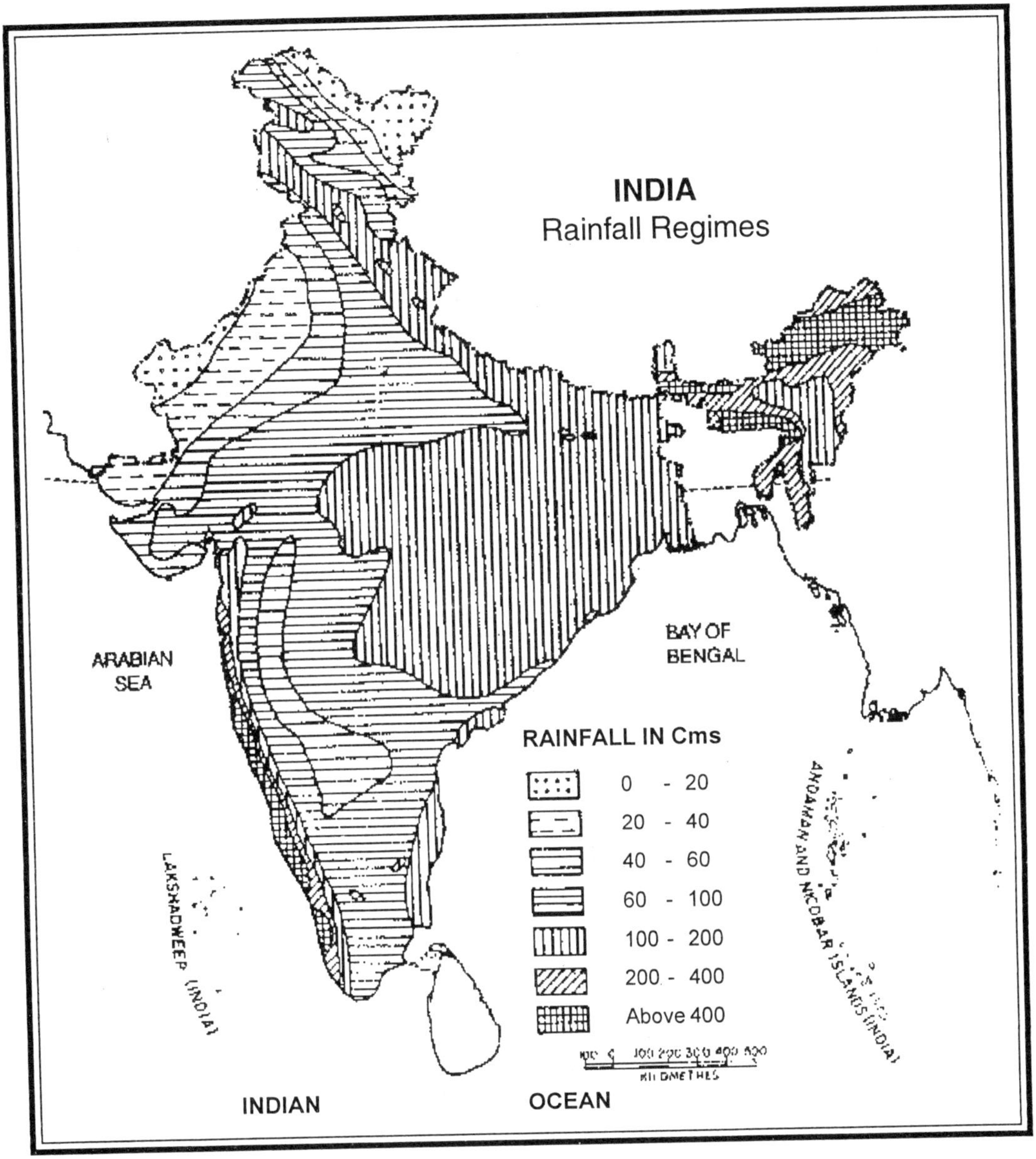

Fig. 6.2: Rainfall Regimes

For each climatic zone, the disease ecology is different. For example, the arid and semi-arid zones are marked by deficiency and various kinds of eye ailments, apart from sunstrokes and dehydration. The humid areas have many cases of intestinal and certain kinds of deficiency diseases apart from the communicable diseases, which cut across all climatic boundaries.

Two elements of climate that have great impact on health are temperature and rainfall. We would, therefore, discuss them in some detail.

Temperature

Much of India between 15° N and 35° N latitudes has practically uniform average temperature ranging from 25.5° C and 29° C. Such high temperatures are very favourable for the growth and survival of the microorganisms that are linked to various diseases. The difference between the highest and lowest diurnal temperature has its own impact on health. Such differences are most pronounced in Rajasthan. Next comes Vidarbha region of Maharashtra.

During the winters, temperatures are low in the North (less than 10° C along the foothills of the Himalayas) and high in the South (25° C near Kanyakumari) because of meridianal flow of atmospheric circulation from north to south. The hot weather from March to June marks a steady movement of the area of high temperatures northwards. In March, the Deccan plateau with nearly 38° C day temperature is the hottest area. In April, the heat zone with 38°-43° C temperature lies in MP and Gujarat, in May-June, it shifts to Rajasthan and from there spreads to the Indo-Gangetic plain as the hot wind called Loo moving from west to east make people run for shade and water. July is the hottest month although the early monsoons often temper the heat to bearable level. And from then on the season of communicable diseases sets in.

Humidity and Rainfall

The humid areas are those that are marked by high percentage of humidity in the air. In general, relative humidity is lowest in Punjab and increases in all directions. During the monsoons the air is almost saturated and that is why despite low temperatures the environment is very comforting.

Rainfall is the most significant climatic element in India and is unevenly distributed in the country. The range is rather wide, the two extremes being 150 mm annual rainfall at Leh in Ladakh and 1600 mm at Mahabaleswar and Chirrapunjee. On the basis of rainfall, India can be divided into eight rainfall zones: very wet, wet, moderately wet, sub-dry, dry, hot desert and cold desert. These eight zones can be regrouped into four regions: humid, sub-humid, semi-arid and arid. Humid areas experience over 100 cm of rainfall per annum; the sub-humid areas get 50 to 100 cm annual rain; the semi-arid areas get between 25 and 50 cm annual rain; and the arid areas get less than 25 cm average annual rain.

Water Resources

Rainfall in India is copious if we consider the total amount of water we get each year. Much of this, however, flows down the river channels to the sea. It is estimated that 167,500 million cubic meters of water flows to the sea through Indian rivers. Of this, only 55,500 million cubic metres can be utilized for agricultural, industrial and domestic uses. Withdrawal from Indian rivers has exceeded 80 per cent. The demand from agriculture, given the present irrigation technology, may be more than 4.5 to 6 million ha m of surface water and 21 million ha m of ground water. Other consumers of water are: households, 2 to 2.5 million ha m; manufacturing, 1.7 to 3.9 million ha m; and power generation, 3.6 to 9.3 million ha m.

India has a vast reservoir of ground water which is safe from evaporation and seepage. It is, therefore, easy to conserve. Ground water reserves of India up to a depth of 300 metres is estimated at 3700 million ha m with an annual recharge of about 67 m ha m. Even the peninsular rocks contain huge amount of ground water. Of this huge potential only about 42 m ha m can be drawn. With the present withdrawal of only 10 m ha m, only one-fourth of the potential is being utilized for domestic and irrigation purposes.

Since the ground water is more evenly distributed, India should have a special plan to recharge ground water resources, and make greater use of it, particularly in areas that cannot be served by canals. Water harvesting during rainy season and channeling the accumulated water to known aquifers is the need of the hour. In this regard, the efficacy of watershed management deserves special attention

To meet the ever-growing demand for water, India needs a water resource development policy that include

1. declaration of rivers and water bodies as national property;
2. long term planning;
3. integrated development with stress on water harvesting, conservation and management;
4. fullest utilization of water resources without adversely affecting the ecological balance; and
5. application of latest scientific knowhow and technology to expand irrigated area and provide safe drinking water to all.

India must change over from flow irrigation to sprinkler and drip irrigation. Pricing of water should be such that people desist from misusing it. The country is not short of water. Currently, only 10 per cent of the total annual flow and 25 per cent of the usable flow is being used. It is short of managerial skills to use it. But the demand pattern is changing fast. With increasing urbanization, domestic requirements are on the increase. Large cities cannot be self-sufficient in water. They have to get it from rivers and lakes. It is, however, a costly proposition. As such, most cities are short of water and they are able to provide drinking water for only an hour or two every day. Further, they do not have the capacity to treat all the water they supply for domestic use.

Clean water is essential for healthy life. In India, it is becoming scarce. Our shortsighted policies have led to massive pollution of water resources, both surface and ground resources. The rivers are polluted, the lakes are polluted, the ground water is polluted; even the oceans are getting polluted. With increasing pace of urbanization, the problem of pollution of water is likely to get more serious. Cities are not able to recycle their liquid and solid wastes. Much of it accumulates in the low lying areas or nearby rivers polluting the underground as well as surface water.

Until very recently, pollution was confined to the cities. It has now invaded the rural areas too. Chemical fertilizers and pesticides used by farmers to increase production of crops flow down to the rivers with the rain-water. Many agriculture based factories like sugar and paper located in rural areas are also major pollutants of rivers.

Many communicable diseases are water-borne. With growing scarcity of potable water, the possibility of such diseases multiplying and taking many more lives have increased. Among the diseases which are water-related and are common in India, mention be made of diarrhea, dysentery, typhoid, jaundice and cholera.

Droughts and Floods

Natural calamities take a heavy toll of life and property in India. Among these, floods and droughts are rather quite common. With the ongoing deforestation in the Himalayas, the frequency and severity of floods have increased during the last few decades. Floods affect the health in a number of ways. Floods destroy crops and render people homeless. Apart from creating local and seasonal food shortage, they pollute the environment. Communicable diseases in particular follow the floods.

Droughts affect people in many ways. At times, they are long lasting and come in succession. Crops are destroyed; there is not enough to eat and under-and malnourishment a widespread phenomenon. Useful animals like bullock, cows, and buffaloes die because of shortage of fodder. People become easy victims of diseases. They may not die of starvation, but they do die of deficiency diseases and of diseases, which catch the under-and mal-nourished first. One-year drought is enough to push the rural economy back by three years.

Earthquakes, cyclones, hailstorms, lightening and cold waves are the other natural calamities. Earthquakes can take hundreds and thousands of lives and cause heavy damage to housing, roads, railways, etc. Cyclones can be equally destructive. They take a heavy toll of basic infrastructure like transport lines, electricity grids, drainage channels, etc, apart from housing, agriculture, industries, commerce and trade. Unfortunately, it is the poor who are affected most. With a low purchasing power, they are unable to make their two ends meet and succumb to many diseases. It may be mentioned here that each natural calamity is followed by the outbreak of a number of diseases (Fig. 6.3).

BIOLOGICAL ENVIRONMENT

Related to relief and climate is vegetation. More the rainfall greater the greenery, so goes the rule. India possesses one of the most diverse forest vegetation in the world ranging from the moist evergreen forests of the Northeast, along the West coast, Bengal Delta and the Andaman and Nicobar Islands to the temperate and alpine vegetation in the Himalayas. Indian culture has been closely linked to mountains and forests where the wise men had their Ashrams for contemplation and training of youth. As late as the eighteenth century, at least 40 per cent of land of India was under forests.

The forest wealth of India is dwindling fast because of wanton felling for commercial purposes, growing pressure of population on land, overgrazing, over-exploitation, encroachments, forest fires and indiscriminate location of development projects—dams, mines, roads, industries, etc. The current annual withdrawal of fuel-wood is estimated at 235 million cubic metres against a sustainable capacity of only 48 million cubic metres. The annual demand for industrial wood is about 28 million cubic metres against the production capacity of only 12 million cubic metres. The area affected by forest fires range from 33 per cent in West Bengal to 90 per cent in Manipur.

The forest resources of India declined fast during the twentieth century. As in 2000 AD only 23.3 per cent of the land area of the country i.e. 76.52 million hectares, is under forests. The actual forest cover is only 63.30 million hectares i.e. 19.30 per cent of the area. And if we consider only the dense forests with crown density of more than 40 per cent, the area covered is only 36.70 million hectares or just 11.20 per cent of the total area of the country. Fortunately, there has been no major negative change in the forest cover since 1981.

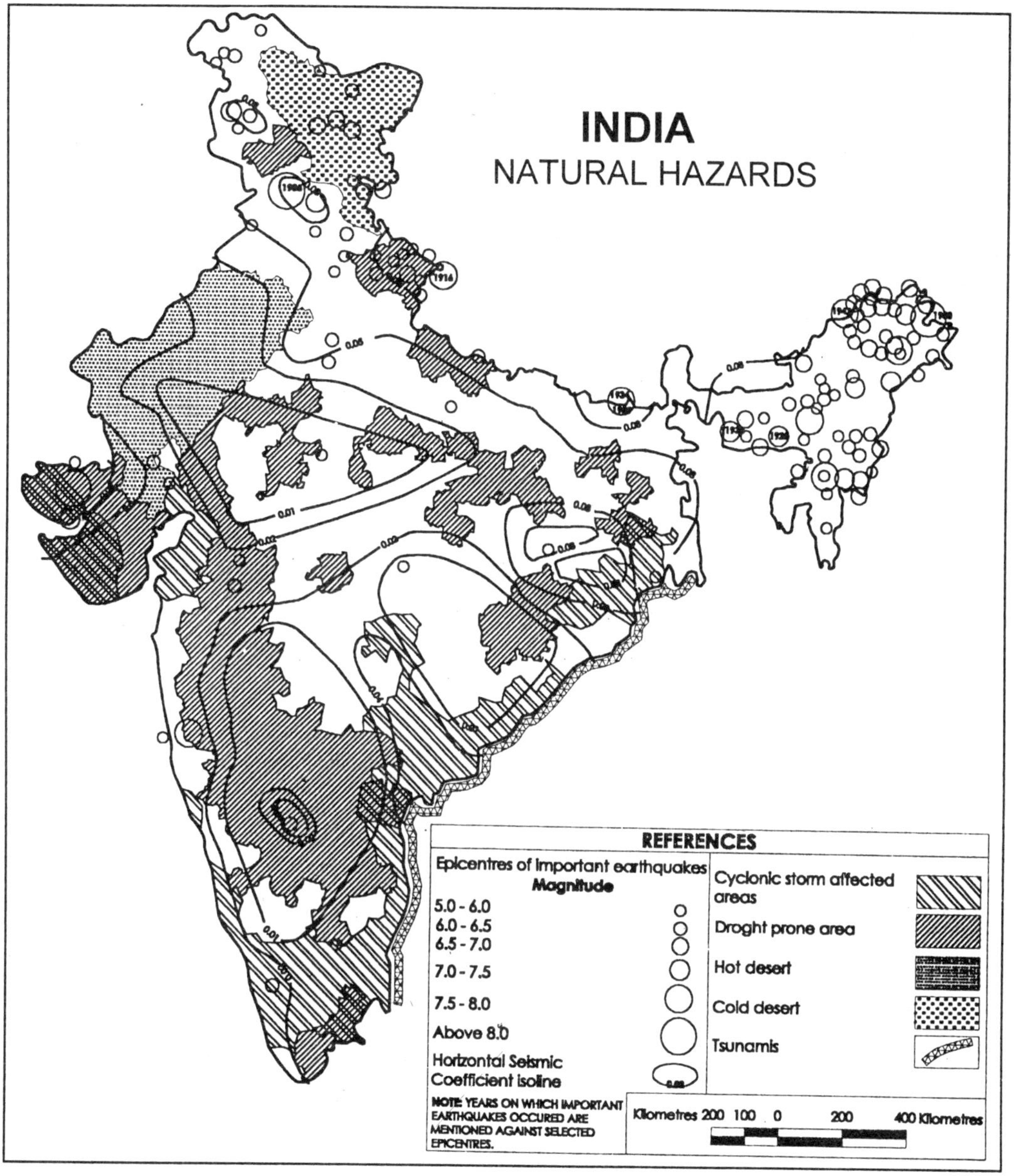

Fig. 6.3: India: Disaster Prone Regions

Source: National Atlas and Thematic Mapping Organisation, DST, Government of India 1991. Reproduced from Abdul Qaiyum, 'Planning for Disaster Mitigation: A basic Change in pproach is Needed', *Spatio-Economic Development Record*, Vol. 8, No. 1, Jan.-Feb, 2001, p. 5.

To maintain ecological balance, the National Forest Policy Resolution of 1952 and the National Forest Policy 1988 stipulated a target of 33 per cent of the land under forests. India has to make serious efforts to reach this target in the twenty first century. The problem becomes more complex when we consider the geographic distribution of forests. Much of the forests are concentrated in the Himalayas, Western Ghats, Sundarbans, the central Indian mountains and the sparsely populated islands. The states of Punjab, Haryana and Rajasthan have less than 10 per cent of land under forest. With the formation of the new states of Uttaranchal and Jharkhand, both UP and Bihar will be left with very little land under forests. The states with less land under forests are also the ones which are very densely populated or which are climatologically unsuitable for forestry (Fig. 6.4). As such the scope for increasing area under forests is limited. What however can be done is to encourage social forestry and tree cropping.

Most of the forests of India are broadleaved deciduous type. They can be broadly classified into five groups: tropical, subtropical, semi-desert, temperate, and alpine. Each of these can be divided into sub-types on the basis of thickness of cover, species of trees, etc. Certain human diseases are linked to the species of plants and trees as also to the nature of vegetation cover. Insufficient forest cover has its impact on temperature and rainfall apart from on soil fertility. Deforestation is an important contributory factor in soil erosion, and frequent occurrence of floods and droughts. Among the other natural calamities, which affect the life and property are earthquakes, cyclonic storms, hailstorms and cold waves.

ENVIRONMENTAL CONCERNS

Environmental degradation has turned out to be a major health hazard of modern civilization. It is far more lethal than the great wars for it does not discriminate; it affects all and often comes so slowly that the victims are totally unaware of the dangers they face.

Land Degradation

Land degradation has become a serious problem in India. Most of the land area of the country shows evidence of degradation, thus affecting the productive base of the economy. Out of the total geographical area of 329 million hectares, 175 million hectares are considered degraded.

Erosion by wind takes away the topsoil. This problem is quite acute in arid and semi-arid parts of the country. Desertification of land is a common feature in eastern Rajasthan. Water logging and resulting salinity is another way of land degradation. Over-irrigation in canal-irrigated areas is a major cause of salinity. It is said that more land is now lost per annum than gained by canal irrigation in India. Many developmental activities have opened even the densely forested areas to degradation. Table 6.2 gives the details of soil erosion and land degradation in India as in 1998.

Controlling the soil and land degradation is essential for food security and health of the people. Afforestation in catchment areas, watershed management, micro-planning, change in the land tenure system, direct involvement of the people in the land management, use of modern technology like remote sensing to identify the problem areas are urgently called for.

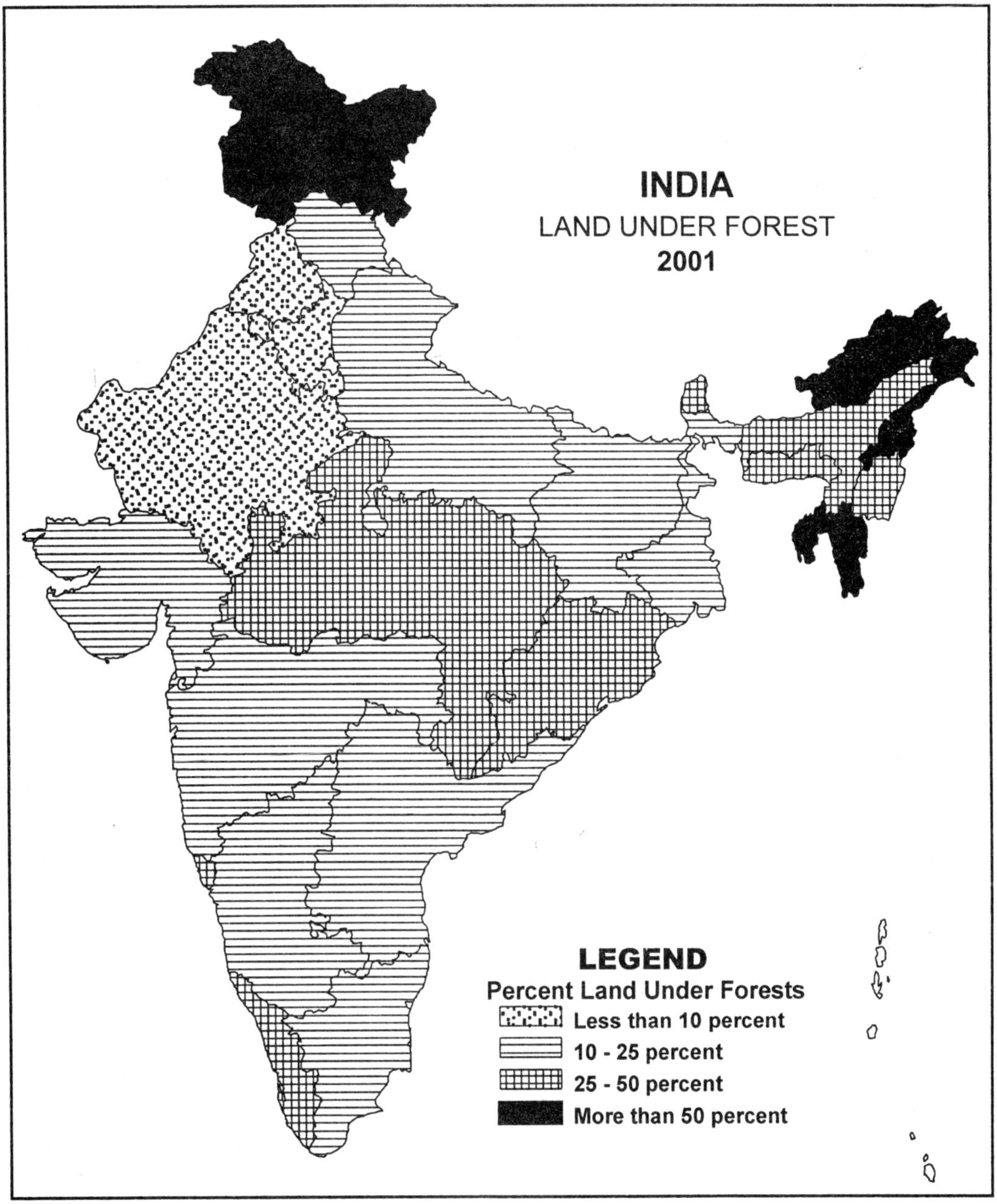

Fig: 6.4: India: Land Under Forest Cover

Table 6.2: Soil and Land Degradation in India

(*Figures in million hectares*)

1.	Total geographical area of the country	328.70
2.	Area subject to water and wind erosion	141.30
3.	Water logged area	8.50
4.	Alkali soil	3.60
5.	Acid soils	4.50
6.	Saline soil including coastal sandy areas	5.50
7.	Ravines and gullies	4.00
8.	Area under shifting cultivation	4.90
9.	Riverine and torrents	2.70
	Total 2 to 9	175.00

Loss of Biodiversity

India has a unique phytogeographical and agro-climatological diversity giving a wide variety of agro-climatic zones that harbour a rich repository of biological resources. With only 2.40 per cent of the total land area of the world, India contributes 8 per cent of the known global biological diversity. India is fourth among Asian countries and tenth in the world in plant diversity. It stands seventh in the world as regards the number of species contributed to agriculture and animal husbandry. It ranks tenth in terms of mammalian species and eleventh in endemic species of higher vertebrates. Forests produce many plants and herbs, which are used in manufacturing medicines. Depletion of the forest cover has, therefore, adverse implications for health. Forests influence climate, enrich soils, provide fodder for animals, and give shelter for wildlife. Since greater emphasis is now laid on herbal medicines, preservation of virgin forests must become a major component of environmental policy.

The Botanical Survey of India, after surveying 70 per cent of the country, has recorded 46,00 plant species; and the Zoological Survey of India has listed 81,000 animal species. They have current as well as potential importance for development in the field of food, medicine, textile, energy, recreation, eco-tourism, etc. The areas yet to be surveyed are the Himalayas, Andaman and Nicobar Islands and the Exclusive Economic Zone in the high seas.

This biodiversity is subjected to increasing pressure of population. Forests are cleared to give way to agriculture and variety of other activities. This has led to the extinction of many plant and animal species. According to some estimates, 1500 plant species, 79 mammals, 44 birds, 15 reptiles, 3 amphibians and several insects have now fallen in the category of endangered species. A network of 85 National Parks, 448 Wildlife Sanctuaries, and 10 Biosphere Reserves have been set up to protect these species. But this is not enough. There is a definite need for change in the attitude of the people towards nature. They must realize that nature is not only a resource but also a habitat for man. If it is used in a manner that destroys the habitat, then the resources will lose their meaning.

Atmospheric Pollution

Air pollution has become a major health hazard in the country. Until very recently, it was essentially an urban problem; it has now reached the rural areas also. The causes for the air pollution are well known; rapid industrialization, increase in the vehicular traffic and lack of hygieie life style.

Air quality is being monitored on a regular basis under the National Ambient Air Quality Monitoring system. The most prevalent form of pollution is suspended particulate matter (SPM). Sulphur dioxide (SO_2) and nitrogen dioxide (NO_2) are the other pollutants of importance. Table 6.3 gives average level of pollution in India's 19 metropolitan cities.

Table 6.3: Level of Air Pollution in Some Metropolitan Cities

(*micrograms/m3*)

City	SO_2	NO_2	*SPM*	*City*	SO_2	NO_2	*SPM*
Ahmedabad	5.4-110.9	3.6-70	72.4-575.4	Kochi	3.2-54.3	1.7-137	10.5-271.1
Bhopal	8.1-22	12.2-32.4	85-393.3	Lucknow	23.2-37.4	23-34.4	382.6-672.7
Kolkata	6-122	6-73.1	77.3-833.3	Mumbai	6.1-111.7	5.4-115.8	60.6-473.2
Chennai	2.4-161.6	1.8-55.5	26.6-351.4	Nagpur	4.3-18.8	3.2-43.2	38.2-403.2
Coimbatore	0-8.9	0.3-19.1	2.5-133	Patna	12.7-46.4	8.5-55.7	132-1307
Delhi	10.1-85.1	20.1-104.5	145.3-929.8	Pune	17.1-29	10.1-34	112-166.5
Hyderabad	5.1-70.7	7.5-124.13	59.3-458	Surat	22.4-304	10-135.7	81.7-1215.3
Indore	2.6-10.2	4.4-17.4	77-812	Varanasi	18.3-27.1	10.6-28.8	155-349
Jaipur	6.1-53.7	4-64.3	81.6-570.1	Vishakha-patnam	5.5-80	5.1-92	46.7-482.7
Kanpur	8.2-22.4	7.7-63	233.7-809.2	NAAQS	15-80	15-80	70-360

NAAQS = National Ambient Air Quality Standards.
Source: Central Pollution Control Board

Not very many people are aware of the health hazards associated with various kinds of pollutants. Lead affects circulatory, reproductive, nervous and renal system and is suspected of lowering learning abilities in children. Fine particulate matters may cause lung cancer. A strong correlation has been noted between SPM and infant mortality in urban areas. Carbon monoxide affects the fetal growth in women and tissue development of young children. It is known to impair perception and thinking in children, slows reflexes and causes drowsiness. In extreme cases, it can cause unconsciousness and even death. Sulphur dioxide exacerbates bronchitis, asthma and emphysema; it causes coughing and impairs lung function. The toxic substances are suspected to cause cancer, reproductive disorders and birth defects. Benzene is a known carcinogen. No wonder then that urban dwellers are prone to many diseases not so common in rural areas.

Noise pollution too is very high in the large cities of the country. It rarely conforms to prescribed standards. The chief sources of noise pollution are diesel generator sets, heavy vehicles, loud speakers, construction activities and crackers on festive occasions. No major city in the country has lower than the day time ambient noise standards prescribed by the Central Pollution Control Board for residential, commercial, sensitive and industrial parts of cities. In general, larger the city, more is the noise pollution.

Air-pollution has its implications for weather and climate too. Recent increase in air pollution has produced visible changes in the climates of the world and it is feared that if the trends do not change the world climates may become hotter as time passes. This may lead to the melting of the polar ice and consequent rise of level of the oceans and submergence of large tracts of low lying coastal tracts. Air pollution has also affected the Ozone layer, which reflects the ultraviolet rays back to the outer space. With the thinning of this layer, ultraviolet rays would reach the earth and produces skin diseases including skin cancer in animals as well as human beings.

The principal sources of air and noise pollution are classical industries using coal and oil and increasing number of transport vehicles. The clearing of forests on a large scale has also affected the air adversely. Trees are the only source of oxygen; they also absorb carbon dioxide. Thus they maintain balance among the gases that constitute the air we breathe. Air pollution has, therefore, serious consequences for the health of practically all life forms from plants to human beings. It affects the lungs and causes a number of lung diseases. Noise pollution adversely affects the eardrums.

Air pollution in India is the cause of many diseases. Given below are some of the pollutants and the diseases they produce.

Atmospheric Pollutants	*Associated Diseases*
Oxides of Nitrogen	respiratory tract infection, Bronchial hyperactivity, impaired lung defences, bronchitis obliterans
Hydrocarbons	Lung cancer
Ozone	Cough, substernal discomfort, Brancoconstriction, decreased exercise performance, respiratory tract irritation
Sulfur dioxide	Exarbation of asthma and COPD, respiratory tract irritation.
Lead	Impaired neuropsychological development in children

Water Pollution

Water pollution is a major health hazard in India. According to a 12 year study (1986-97) conducted by the Central Pollution Control Board, the biochemical oxygen demand (BOD) values in a sample of 4500 observations below 3mg/l were above 60 per cent during 1986-91 and below 54-58 per cent during 1991-97 showing some improvement in water quality. The number of observations having BOD more than 6mg/l, also increased from 7 per cent in 1889 to 16 per cent in 1997. The ranges of water quality parameters with respect to organic and bacterial pollution as observed in 1997 indicates that of the 4531 observations taken on the BOD, about 65 per cent had BOD less than 3mg/l; 21 per cent between 3 to 6 mg/l; and 14 per cent more than 6mg/l. State wise, most of the observations taken in Kerala were less than 3mg/l BOD, while in Maharashtra most of the observations recorded above 6mg/l BOD. UP had the maximum value of fecal coliform bacteria. Gujarat tops in chemical pollution followed by Maharashtra, Andhra Padesh, Tamil Nadu, Uttar Pradesh and Punjab.

The predominant sources of water pollution are domestic sewage and industrial effluents, which contain organic pollutants, chemicals and heavy metals, apart from run-off from the land based activities like agriculture and mining. The major water polluting industries are fertilizers, refineries, sugar, pulp and paper, leather, metal plating, paints and warnish and other chemical industries. Apart from point sources, the non-point sources such as fertilizer and pesticide run-off from agriculture has also now become a major source of pollution.

As the tempo of development speeds up, the industrial and domestic wastes increase polluting the water bodies such as rivers, lakes, ponds, reservoirs and even coastal stretches of seas. The groundwater sources are also polluted as untreated urban and industrial effluent is allowed to accumulate in low-lying areas. Water pollution is the main causative factor in the diseases of the digestive system such as dysentery, amibiosis, diarrhea, cholera, etc. About 21 per cent of all communicable diseases and 11.50 per cent of all diseases are water borne.

A survey of groundwater quality was carried out in 1994 at 138 sample locations in 22 industrialized zones of the country. The water was found to be unfit for drinking due to high bacteriological and heavy metal contamination. According to the Central Pollution Control Board, mean BOD values have shown a marginal increase in all the 28 major rivers between 1978-91. Minimum and maximum coliform values have increased manyfold over the same period indicating a very severe pollution load.

Urban Waste

Solid waste of cities is dumped in low-lying areas. As rainwater seeps through these deposits many chemicals injurious to health reach the groundwater and make it undrinkable. Further, the mining areas as also the brick kiln areas destroy fertile lands forever. This has its impact on food production and food security of the people living in these areas.

Municipal solid waste is a heterogeneous mixture of paper, plastic, cloth, metals and organic matter generated by households, public institutions like hospitals, commercial establishments and industrial enterprises. It amounts to about 50 million tonnes per annum. Our per capita waste generation is not very high. It is much lower than that of the developed countries. But it becomes enormous because we are more than a billion people and our capacity to clean it up is very low. Fly-ash, phosphor-gypsum, and iron and steel slag are the main industrial wastes in India.

Urban waste in sub-tropical climates like that of India becomes a major source of air and water pollution. On decomposition, it offers ideal conditions for flies to breed. It attracts rodents and vermin; the pathogens present therein have easy access to humans.

As noted earlier, nothing is waste in nature; nature recycles everything it produces. And hence there is no pollution in nature. It is only the human beings and their activities, which generate waste because our system of production and consumption does not follow the laws of nature. This waste leads to pollution of the soil, air, water and even human beings.

Coastal and Marine Pollution

India has a coastline of 7500 km. Depending on the climate and oceanic currents and waves, it harbours a great variety of marine and coastal eco-systems like mangroves, coral reefs, salt lakes and mud flats. These ecosystems constitute the habitat for many endangered marine species, and commercially important marine flora and fauna. These coastal areas are being increasingly polluted due to land-based pollutants being drained to the sea; fishing, esp^^ially the pran-culture; oil-sleek from tankers; improper development activities along the coast; shipping and sea-based activities and off-shore mining.

Heavy metals such as lead and cadmium have been found in the Thane Creek near Mumbai and Cochin coast has been polluted by petroleum hydrocarbons. Coral reefs, which are a very productive marine ecosystem, are being destroyed by indiscriminate exploitation for lime, recreational and ornamental trade. Mangroves cover over 6700 sq km. They are under constant biotic pressure due to land-based water pollution, change in land use, fishing and other related activities. Similarly, the wetlands, which cover an area of 1.45 million hectares, are being destroyed by weed infestation and encroachments by coastal farmers for agriculture. Various kinds of pollutants also are harmful to the wetlands. Of the 85 mangroves of international importance, 45 are under serious threat.

The short-term problems apart, in the long-run, much of the wetlands would be submerged under the sea and totally destroyed, if the looming threat of climatic change resulting from greenhouse-effect becomes a reality. Just one metre rise in the sea level will submerge 0.41 per cent of the land area; it would also render 1.68 per cent of the total population of India living in the coastal districts homeless.

Table 6.4: Area and Population Likely to Be Affected by Rise in Sea Level by One Metre

State	*% Area affected*	*% Population affected*
Goa	4.84	7.25
West Bengal	1.88	2.35
Gujarat	0.92	1.07
Orissa	0.81	1.75
A &N Islands	0.72	-
Tamil Nadu	0.52	2.91
Andhra Pradesh	0.19	0.93
Maharashtra	0.18	1.75
Karnataka	0.15	0.56
India	0.41	1.68

Source: Ministry of Environment and Forest: 1995

ENVIRONMENTAL POLICY

India does not have an all-embracing comprehensive environmental policy; but it does have sectoral policies, which impinge on environmental issues directly. The Ministry of Environment and Forests in the Central Government in collaboration with other sectoral ministries and institutions like state pollution control boards is responsible for the protection, conservation and development of environment. Environment (Protection) Act 1988 is the key legislation within the framework, which various programmes and projects are designed and implemented.

Efforts have been made in recent years to check environmental pollution through legislative means but the enforcement of laws so far enacted has been tardy. The judiciary however has been quite active in this area of public concern. It has made some impact on the deteriorating environmental scenario. What is needed is environmental education to make people aware of the dangers of pollution and the role they can play to stop it.

Among the various policy responses, the following deserve our attention.

1. Notification of pollution abatement, emission and effluent standards for air, water and noise for major polluting industries has been done and regular monitoring is carried out to identify the defaulters.
2. Apart from effluent and emission standards, national ambient air quality standards including ambient noise standards have also been notified.
3. In the field of forest management, participatory approach has been evolved with a view to enlist the support of the people living in and around forest areas for the protection and conservation of biodiversity.
4. Instead of end-of-the-pipe treatment, it has been decided to encourage the use of clean technologies.
5. All development projects have to be cleared on the basis of environmental impact assessment.
6. National River Conservation Plan, on the lines of Ganga Action Plan, covering 18 major rivers of the country, has been launched. Integrated development of all rivers of India has also been announced.
7. National Environment Tribunal Act providing relief, compensation and restitution to victims of accidents while handling hazardous substances and for environmental damages has come into force.
8. Efforts are afoot to estimate the money value of environmental damages. According to some estimates, the people of India have to suffer an annual loss of $10 to 13.8 billion, directly and indirectly, due to air-pollution, water-pollution, soil-erosion, land-degradation and deforestation.
9. System of Natural Resource Accounting, also known as Green Accounting, is also being tried with a view to give a balanced and realistic state of the economy.
10. Other steps include removing subsidies that encourage unsustainable use of natural resources, participation in global efforts at environmental protection and reconstruction, warding off climatic change, etc. and encouraging and financing sustainable development.

ENVIRONMENTAL LAW

One of the measures adopted all over the world to check environmental degradation is legislative. Laws are passed by national legislatures restraining people from polluting land, water and air; and from destroying vegetation. Laws are also passed to take certain positive steps to improve environmental quality. Then, there are International Conventions, which are binding on member states of the United Nations.

Indian culture has been very conscious of and sensitive to environmental quality but two developments of the last two centuries made this country a polluted and degraded land. British colonialism was the first major factor, which destroyed the natural ecology of India. Indiscriminate cutting of forest and diversion of river water for irrigation, have done incalculable harm to India. Much of the timber was exported out and the water withdrawn from rivers was meant to produce crops, at least partially, for export. Withdrawing water for irrigation or drinking purposes is necessary but its end use must not aim at export earning but food and fibre security. Moreover, it should not be used in a way that the land irrigated is destroyed forever.

The other factor for environmental destruction in India emerged more prominently after the Independence of the country. It was the mad rush for economic development. Instead of managing the available arable land better and distributing it more equitably, the country decided to bring under cultivation all the land under forests, grasses and trees obstructing the natural drainage, destroying the virgin forests and the animal life that lived there for millennia.

The culture of living with nature was gone and a new culture of living for material goods took its roots. In line with global thinking, a Ministry of Environment was established both at the Centre and the States and laws were passed to check environmental destruction. In fact, the need for such laws arose more acutely after the 1984 Bhopal Gas Tragedy, which took over 3000 lives and disabled many more. Given below is a list of important environmental laws, which are being amended from time to time to get over difficulties in coverage or implementation.

Environment in General

1. Environmental (Protection) Act, 1886,
2. Environment (Protection) Rules, 1986,
3. Hazardous Waste (Management and Handling) Rules, 1989,.
4. The Manufacture, Storage, and Import of Hazardous Chemical Rules, 1989,
5. The Manufacture, Use, Import, Export and Storage of Hazardous Micro-organisms/ Genetically Engineered Organisms or Cells Rules 1989,
6. The Public Liability Insurance Act and Rules, 1991,
7. National Environment Tribunal Act, 1995,
8. National Environment Appallate Authority Act, 1995,
9. Bio-medical Waste (Management and Handling) Rules, 1998.

Forest and Wildlife

1. Indian Forest Act, 1927 and Amendment, 1984
2. Wildlife Protection Act, Rules, 1973, and Amendment, 1991
3. Forest Conservation Act 1980 and Rules 1981

Water

1. The Easement Act, 1882,
2. Indian Fisheries Act, 1897,
3. The River Boards Act, 1956,
4. Merchant Shipping Act, 1970,
5. The Water (Prevention and Control of Pollution) Act, 1974,

6. The Water (Prevention and Control of Pollution) Cess Act, 1977,
7. The Water (Prevention and Control of Pollution) Rules, 1978
8. Coastal Regulation Zone Notification, 1991

Air

1. Factories Act, 1943 and Amendment 1987,
2. Air (Prevention and Control of Pollution) Act, 1981,
3. Air (Prevention and Control of Pollution) Rules, 1982,
4. Atomic Energy Act, 1982,
5. Air (Prevention and Control of Pollution) Amendment Act, 1987,
6. Motor Vehicle Act, 1988.

REFERENCES

1. Law, B.C. *Mountains and Rivers of India*, Calcutta: National Committee on Geography, International Geographical Union, India, 1968.
2. Pascoe, E.H. *A Manual of Geology of India*, Calcutta: Government of India Press, Volumes I-III, 1950-1964.
3. Singh, Gopal *Geography of India*, Delhi: Atma Ram & Sons, 1995
4. Wadia, D.N. *Geology of India,* London: McMillan, 1961.
5. Subramaniam, V.P., *General Climatology*, Vol. 3, Contributions to Indian Geography, New Delhi: Heritage, 1993.
6. ——, *Applied Climatorlogy*, Vol. 4, Contributions to Indian Geography, New Delhi: Heritage, 1993.
7. Suresh Misra and Rajvir Dhaka, *Environmental Law in India, New Delhi: Concept,* 1998.

7

Culture and Health

Socio-cultural factors play a very significant role in matters health. Culture includes worldview, values, beliefs, approach to life and living, code of conduct, behaviour patterns and social norms and practices. It also includes factors like population size, density, composition and economic factors like level of living, income, employment etc. This chapter is devoted to the health problems related to cultural patterns, social norms and economy. The demographic factors are discussed in the next chapter.

While discussing the issues of health and medicine, it is often said that the industrial societies are scientific while the developing societies are traditional in approach. This is, however, only partially true. Both societies suffer from misconceptions and irrationalities. The faith that the man in the developed world reposes in modern drugs, chemicals and doctors is as irrational as the faith the primitive man reposes in sorcerers and traditional healers. Both the societies are unhealthy, one because of over-nutrition and over-medication and the other because of under-nutrition and under-medication. What makes them stand on the common ground is the unhealthy style of life and equally unhealthy environment in which they live. Both have left their health to healers – modern or traditional.

We propose to discuss various dimensions of culture and their implications for health in the pages following.

FOOD INTAKE AND HEALTH

Food is the main source of nourishment for all life forms. It plays a critical role in survival, growth and development of human body and mind. There are two main reasons for the global spread of the Homo sapiens: search for food and curiosity to see new places and things. The type of food consumed, the way the food was gathered, assembled or produced; the way it was produced and shared among the fellow humans and the degree to which it was diversified and tuned to the needs of the human body, formed one of the key factors in the evolution of different cultures and civilizations in the world. The centricity of food in cultural configurations of various societies is no longer the same today. As man outgrew the hunting and gathering and subsistence agriculture stages and entered the modern post-industrial technological age, access to food is no longer the central concern but it continues to be important in maters health.

Food habits are closely linked to the natural environment in which people live. The staple food is usually the one that is produced locally or regionally but in societies where food has entered national and global markets it is universalized and homogenized. What the people eat depends on what is available in the market, rather than what is produced locally. And what they can get from the market and in what quantity depends on their purchasing power: their economic status. In the past one who produced food, was also its consumer. Today producer is not necessarily the consumer. What one choose to eat depends on a complex of factors such as attitude, the concept of good and bad, clean and unclean, religious prescriptions and prohibitions, past practices, and tastes as acquired from early childhood.

In India there are a number of problems relating to food and nutrition. The country produces over 210 million tonnes of foodgrains each year and the plan is afoot to double this quantity in the next 25 years or so. Apart from the food grains, India produces large quantity of milk and milk products, vegetables, edible oils, and fruits. But it does not mean that people have access to adequate quantity and quality of nutritious food. The purchasing power of at least one-third of the one billion people of India is so low that they cannot buy all the food they need to keep themselves healthy. Secondly, the food habits are such that even those who get enough to eat do not get all the nutrients they need. For example, the rice is polished in order that it looks better; wheat flour is sieved to remove the roughage; and vegetables are overcooked and fried to taste better. And thirdly, there is hardly a food item which is not treated with harmful chemicals. Added to all these are certain religious restrictions which debar people from eating some items of food. Vegetarians do not take any kind of meat; some non-vegetarians would not eat pork; others would avoid beef. The net result is that a number of people suffer from under-or malnutrition and deficiency diseases related thereto.

Food includes water. Man cannot survive even for a week without water. There are cases of people surviving without food for months. Sixty five per cent of human body and 85 per cent of the human brain consist of water. Any impurity or contamination in water has, therefore, an immediate impact on human health. Several diseases that afflict people in developing societies are water borne. Unfortunately, the quality of water people drink in India is not very good. This is particularly so in rural areas. The Environmental Hygiene Committee in 1949 reported that only 16 per cent of the urban population and six per cent of the rural population had access to potable water supply. Even in 2000 AD per cent of people who have access to potable water is less than 50.

Indian culture lays special emphasis on personal hygiene and cleanliness. Our forefathers were well aware of the adverse effects of impure water on health. That is why, they kept the drinking water in copper vessels, exposed it to the sunlight, and filtered through charcoal before drinking. Contaminated water was boiled, kept in the sunlight and further purified by dipping a hot piece of copper rod in it seven times. It was filtered and cooled before use. Even today large number of Hindu households have copper vessels for storing drinking water. But with the passage of time, these health-promoting practices were abandoned and unhealthy practices gripped practically the whole country.

Personal cleanliness is still a norm in Indian households, but the interest of the people in environmental cleanliness has considerably waned. They do not mind being surrounded by dirty and filthy environment. The general tendency is to clean up their own houses and throw the dirt on the street. The Environmental Hygiene Committee, 1949 said, "rivers, lakes and beaches have been revered and sanctified by religious traditions in India for centuries. However, as in other matters, practice is far removed from principle. These bodies of water are polluted by the discharge of wastes and excreta by individuals, municipalities and factories, without sufficient consideration for health of other users of the same water, or for the conservation of aquatic life or for beauty" (Kawata). The situation has not improved much in many parts of the country.

Diseases like cholera, hepatitis, gastroenteritis, guinea worm infection, fluorosis, goitre, diarrhoea, dysentery, fevers of various kinds including typhoid, paratyphoid, tuberculosis and several other diseases are caused by contaminated or mineral deficient water. Water pollution may also be responsible for transmission of leptospinosis and schistogomiasis in certain areas. Over six per cent of deaths in India are caused by the problems of the digestive system. Several animal diseases are also caused by contaminated water. Important among them are anthrax, hog cholera, bovine tuberculosis, and tape worms. Some of the agents are transmitted to man through the udders of buffaloes that cool themselves in dirty water during hot summers.

People have misconceptions about the purity of river waters. There is a feeling even in educated circles that running water has the capacity to clean itself and hence river water must be clean and potable. This misconception is based on the experiences of the past. When river ecology was not disturbed by man through massive withdrawal of water for irrigation and killing of fishes, crocodiles, tortoises and other aquatic lives, it was possible to maintain the purity of the running water. The discharge of liquid waste from urban factories and homes was also far less than what one notices today. Even rural areas become polluters. Part of thy chemical pesticides and fertilizers is carried to the rivers. Today the situation has undergone drastic change. Rivers are no longer their natural self: They have been over-exploited; and converted into natural drains to carry wastewater released by cities and factories to the sea. But the old notion that flowing water cleans itself remains fixed in the minds of the people. People throw their dead in the rivers and seas that are considered sacred, wash their clothes and allow wastewater to drain therein without any treatment. Even wells get polluted as they are rarely covered. Dust and other pollutants carried by gusty winds enter the wells without any hindrance and make the water unusable. People, however, use this water unmindful of the disease generating germs and other contaminants present there.

PERCEPTION OF DISEASES

Culture is the medium through which man looks at the world around him. What is a disease and how to get rid of it? These questions appear to be simple and innocent but they are not. Answers to these questions are not the same everywhere and all the times. They are also culture-specific to a great extent. The concept of disease has its implications for treatment. As stated earlier, modern approach to disease is centred on the germ theory. The traditional, but in no way less scientific, approach considers disease as a symptom of disharmony among certain forces that keep the body in healthy condition. The first approach looks for medicines that kill the germs either before they enter the body or after they got in. The second approach calls for the restoration of the lost balance in the system by change in the diet, style of life, use of biotic and mineral energizers and restorers. The medicines prescribed are in consonance with the climate, constitution of the body and the mental make up of the patient. In the first case, treatment is addressed to the disease; in the second case, it is addressed to the patient.

Many communities in India still believe that certain supernatural powers like ghosts, witches and planets are responsible for diseases. Some uncharitable gods and goddesses are also supposed to be in health business. In these communities, it is not uncommon to call witch doctors and sorcerers who are supposed to have direct communion with them. A trained and qualified physician is approached or the patient is taken to the hospital, only when the sorcerers fail and the patient's condition takes a turn for the worse. Then there are the quacks roaming around in rural and tribal areas who pose themselves as trained doctors. They are readily accessible to whosoever approaches them. They are aware of patented medicines for common diseases and know how to administer injections or glucose. Most of the people who fall sick get over the disease in the normal course; but the credit for cure goes to these quakes and thus their hold on the gullible people increases. Cases of people dying because of these messengers of death are not rare, but of those who have to get hospitalized because of wrong medication are numerous.

The traditional concept of health in India is holistic. Man must be in harmony with environment that includes supernatural powers, nature and society. Illness means some disturbance in the harmonious relationship. To restore the balance, people tend to use both modern and traditional methods. They go to the doctor to kill the germ, and to the sorcerer to propitiate the supernatural powers. Not infrequently, the latter is resorted to in order that the medicines work.

According to S.C. Dube, a well known social anthropologist of India, "most of the common diseases are interpreted as a 'fault in the physical system' and are treated with herbal medicines or modern drugs obtained from the dispensary. Common colds, headaches, stomachaches, scabies, gonorrhoea and syphilis are regarded as natural diseases, and an effort is made to cure them with medicine. But persistent headaches, intermittent fevers, continued stomach disorders, rickets and other wasting diseases among children, menstrual troubles, repeated abortions, barrenness, bearing of children, etc. are attributed to supernatural forces. In all such cases, medicinal cures as well as propitiation of the 'unseen powers' are attempted simultaneously. Similarly, such calamities as failure in undertakings, death of children in quick succession, and too many deaths in the family within a short time are taken to indicate misfortune and 'handiwork of supernatural forces.' Smallpox, cholera and the plague are always attributed to the wrath of various goddesses. For these diseases, worship is regarded as the only remedy; and no medicines are administered to the patient."

The situation is changing fast even in rural areas of the country. A reverse trend of over medication has started in a section of the Indian population. With diversification and commercialization of the rural economy, people have started spending more money on doctors and medicines. They take less care of their physique and equate health with absence of disease. They ask for strong medicines and injections. It is here that the quakes succeed. They administer multiple drugs of very high potency and thus pollute the body with toxins that produce new diseases. Over drugging has now become a major health hazard in the country. The worst part of the story is that people are becoming over dependent on doctors, medicines and hospitals. They are abdicating their own responsibilities towards their health.

TREATMENT OF DISEASES

Faith Healing

Throughout human history persons claiming powers to relieve pain and sufferings had an important place in society. These traditional healers command a respectable following even today. Even educated people with scientific background have some faith in the powers of these healers and not infrequently rely on them for relief. Healers who claim to have direct communion with supernatural powers abound in India. They perform certain rituals including walking on fire to cure the sick. They may chant some *mantras* given to them by some saint or *fakir* to ward of the evil. Some of them cure people by touching the affected parts of the body. The patients usually belong to traditional, illiterate and economically poor communities but those who are educated and know about modern science are not rare among the clients of these healers.

The number of people who visit temples, durgahs, churches and other religious places in the hope of getting rid of diseases they suffer from is surprisingly large. And it is there all over the world – developing or developed. The patients usually develop complete faith in the power of the deity and perhaps this faith, if not anything else, helps them recover from the ailments.

At some shrines the healers act as media between the supernatural power and the patient. The healer plays upon the psychology of the possessed and gives the impression of having succeeded in removing the evil spirit. At times, the faith that the patient reposes in the healer works; at another the shock treatments like walking on the fire, severe beatings, forcing the patient to inhale incensed smoke, etc. work. But in most cases nothing tangible results from these treatments. The patient ultimately goes to the hospital or dies. Such healers are still active in rural and tribal parts of India.

In the recent past, faith healing has emerged in a different and very sophisticated form attracting educated people. Those who suffer from systemic disorders and incurable diseases are attracted most. Among the various schools of faith healing is Rekki. There Are conflicting reports on the efficacy of theses practices. Some patients appear to have been cured, but many others have quite opposite experience. The fact, however, does remain that as the faith of the people in modern allopathic medicines declines, the popularity of faith healing increases.

Traditional Medicine

Practice of herbal medicine goes back to very ancient times. There are references to the curative properties of some herbs in the Rigveda, which was composed between 3500 and1500 B.C. A more detailed account is found in the Atharvaveda. Ayurveada, the Indian system of medicine, gives details of over 1500 herbs. The Chinese in Pen Ts'ao Ching, an ancient Chinese work dating back to 2800 BC describe 1000 plant medicaments and instructions on their use. Hippocrates (460 BC), the Greek physician and father of modern medicine, also listed several hundred of herbal remedies. The herbal medicine was based on scientific principles, but with the passage of time, its scientific base was lost.

Until very recently, herbal treatment was branded as traditional i.e. based on experiential rather than scientific knowledge. Medical scientists considered it as a relic of the distant past and branded it as quackery practised by old women in traditional families. It has proved to be a fallacious judgment on their part. Herbal treatment is scientific in approach and more in tune with the biology of the human body. Quite a large number of modern medicines are derived from herbs. As the damaging effects of unhealthy food habits and over-medication assume alarming proportions, inclination to go back to traditional cures based on various parts of medicinal plants and a more healthy style of life, has grown. The belief that more attention should be given to maintenance of good health from the day a child is born rather than to curing the diseases once they set in has grown in recent years. Further, people all over the world have come to realize that toxic chemical medicines while curing a disease give rise to new diseases. Herbs when used in right combination and doses and under the supervision of a trained physician can balance and strengthen the body's own healing mechanism, instead of suppressing or disturbing it as many modern medicines tend to do.

Modern Medicine

As stated earlier, the growing access to modern medical care has increased the use of chemical medicines. Improvement in medical facilities through primary health centres even in remote areas of the country has to be welcomed. But it has its negative implications too, particularly in a situation where economic conditions are changing for the better. People's belief in the efficacy of chemical medicines has increased. Maintenance of good health through nutritious food and healthy style of life has taken a back seat. People depend on medicines, which in most of the cases are toxic and give only temporary relief.

We have already noted the problem of over medication and under-medication. The former is responsible for weakening the whole immune system of the body, and the latter has made the germs more resistant to diseases. India, like the rest of the world, is steadily moving towards a health scenario wherein people would live longer, but with poor health. Modern medicine is becoming the cause of diseases.

SOCIO-ECONOMIC CONDITIONS AND HEALTH

The social and economic setting in which man lives has its own implications for health. Practically, all societies are organized hierarchically so that some people are better placed on the social ladder than the others. There is no hope of building a truly egalitarian society in the near future for that would require a fundamental change in the psyche and value system. Such changes take place slowly.

The basis on which social hierarchy is built and the number of tiers therein varies from country to country and place to place. It is difficult to pin point the factors that brought about these inequities. What is clear is that it is a historical legacy against which the marginalized have risen from time to time but without any lasting success. Marxism generated a new hope in the early part of the twentieth century. It produced Bolshevik Revolution in Russia in 1917, which threw away the Czar by violence. The Czar was killed brutally and a government led by toilers and workers vowed to spread the message of the Revolution the world over. The great socialist experiment known as the USSR miserably failed to eliminate social hierarchy. Gandhi in India used nonviolence to change the hearts of the people in favour of equality. After his death, his message was drowned in the mad rush for self-aggrandizement. This experiment also failed under the weight of the same forces, which introduced inequity in the society to begin with.

Our socio-economic system is iniquitous. There are dominant groups that hold power; and then there are groups deprived of these powers on one ground or the other. The form in which this iniquity shows up differs from society to society but it is there everywhere and all the time. Deprived of their legitimate opportunities, the deprived fail to take care of their health and hence they become victims of a variety of diseases. The rich, on the other hand, make wasteful uses of resources; clings to luxuries and comforts to deny their weaker brethren the basic needs; and lead an unhealthy style of life to invite systemic disorders and diseases. Both the groups are sick and unhealthy.

If people take care of their health from early childhood, they can avoid many of the diseases, which take a heavy toll of life. The first requirement for healthy life is balanced diet – a diet that gives all the energy and nutrients body needs to work at the optimum level of performance. The second important requirement is a healthy style of life. The nutrients one takes must be ingested; they must reach different parts of the body in the form and quantity body needs. For this, it is necessary that the body has enough exercise, mind is engaged in creative thinking and the environment in which one lives is healthy and peaceful. Most diseases come at the age of 35-45 because man is most callous about health during this period. The diseases show up only after the age of 45 or so when the resistance of the body is on the decline.

Health-Wealth Nexus

India is one of the low-income countries of the world. Its per capita income is US $340 per annum. Compared to Singapore ($26,730), or even Malaysia ($3,890), or Indonesia ($980), it is quite low. Only three countries in the Asia and Pacific region (Afghanistan, Bangladesh and Nepal) stand below India. China's per capita income is around $620 per annum. When we look at the per capita income of the USA ($27,980) or Japan ($39,650), we feel stunned at the abysmally low income of the average Indian. Even if we consider income in terms of purchasing power parity (PPP), the figure for India just touches US$ 1400. Probing deeper, we realize that per capita income hides more than it reveals for it is only an average. It does not mean that all individuals, households and areas get the same income all over the country. About half the people of India live on US$100 per annum. The lowest 20 per cent share only 8.5 per cent of the GDP, while the uppermost 20 per cent share 42.6 per cent (and the highest 10 per cent share 28.4 per cent). The gini index comes to 33.8 (where 100 = equal distribution, and 0 = everything concentrated in one person or group.

Poverty line is the simplest approach to find out the persons and families, which need support because they are too poor. In a sane society, there would be no poverty, no matter how we define it. Unfortunately, humanity has to go a long way before it becomes sane. It has just emerged from a feudal and imperial era; democratic vales are still only skin deep. It is passing through a series of crises. Democracy can succeed in a environment wherein each individual has almost equal opportunity for self-realisation. Inequitous distribution of means of production, wealth and opportunities for cultural and social development is injurious to democracy. Only in an environment of equality, at least with respect to basic needs – food, clothing, housing, education, health, security of life and property, and opportunity for self-realization—democratic values can grow. Equality does not mean uniformity. It recognizes that the potentials of each individual or group differ and when these potentials are realized, interpersonal, inter-group and inter-spatial differences would emerge and grow as well. So, in the present stage of our social development, the best that can be achieved is to ensure that everyone has access to the above seven basic needs equally. This would be the most practical way of defining the poor. Of course, one can sound very radical and call for full-fledged egalitarian social order, which the communists once vowed to achieve, but that would mean breaking one's head against a wall. Let us try to achieve the above goal in our time and leave further refinement of social order to future generations.

Of the seven basic needs, the first three (food, clothing and shelter) are the survival needs; the next two (education and health) are enabling needs; and last two (security and self-realization) are ennobling needs. Access to appropriate resources to meet all these needs is part and parcel of the needs. Which needs to be met first? This is a question that arises when the resources for development are limited and the number of poor is 'unlimited'. Apparently, the priority must go to the survival needs; next in order come the enabling and ennobling needs. But we must keep in mind that all the basic needs form a package; they cannot be separated from each other and hence except for emergencies, prioritization is not advisable.

India from the very start of the planned development process in 1950 put poverty eradication as one of its major programmes. Methods were, devised to measure poverty and identify the poor. The problem of poverty in India being so acute that millions of people did not have access to even two square meals a day. The line separating poor from the non-poor rests on survival needs particularly food and nutrition. The National Sample Survey Organization (NSSO) and the Central Statistical Organization (CSO) periodically collect data on private consumption expenditure in the country. The income required to meet the minimum of consumption needs is taken as the poverty line. People falling below this line are treated as poor and those above as non-poor (but not necessarily rich). According to the Economic Survey, 1998-99, the poverty ratio in 1973-74 was 54.90 i.e. more than half the people of India (321 million) were below the poverty line. It came down to 36.00 in 1993-94 but the number of people below the poverty line (320 million) remained almost unchanged. In this regard it would be pertinent to compare these figures with some of our neighbouring countries. The poverty ratio in 1975 and 1995 in China changed from 59.50 to 22.22, in Indonesia from 64.30 to 11.40, in Philippines from 35.70 to 25.50, in South Korea from 23.00 to 5.00, and in Malaysia from 17.40 to 4.30.

Figure 7.1 shows the per cent of people below the poverty line in different states of India. It is estimated that at least one third of the people of India live below the poverty line. That means that about 350 million people are undernourished and hence exposed to various kinds of diseases – deficiency as well as others. These are the people who cannot pay for medicines and healthcare. Even this generalized situation is not uniform all over the country. Some states have higher than average national per capita income, while others have much lower. And hence the per cent of people below the poverty line also varies from state to state.

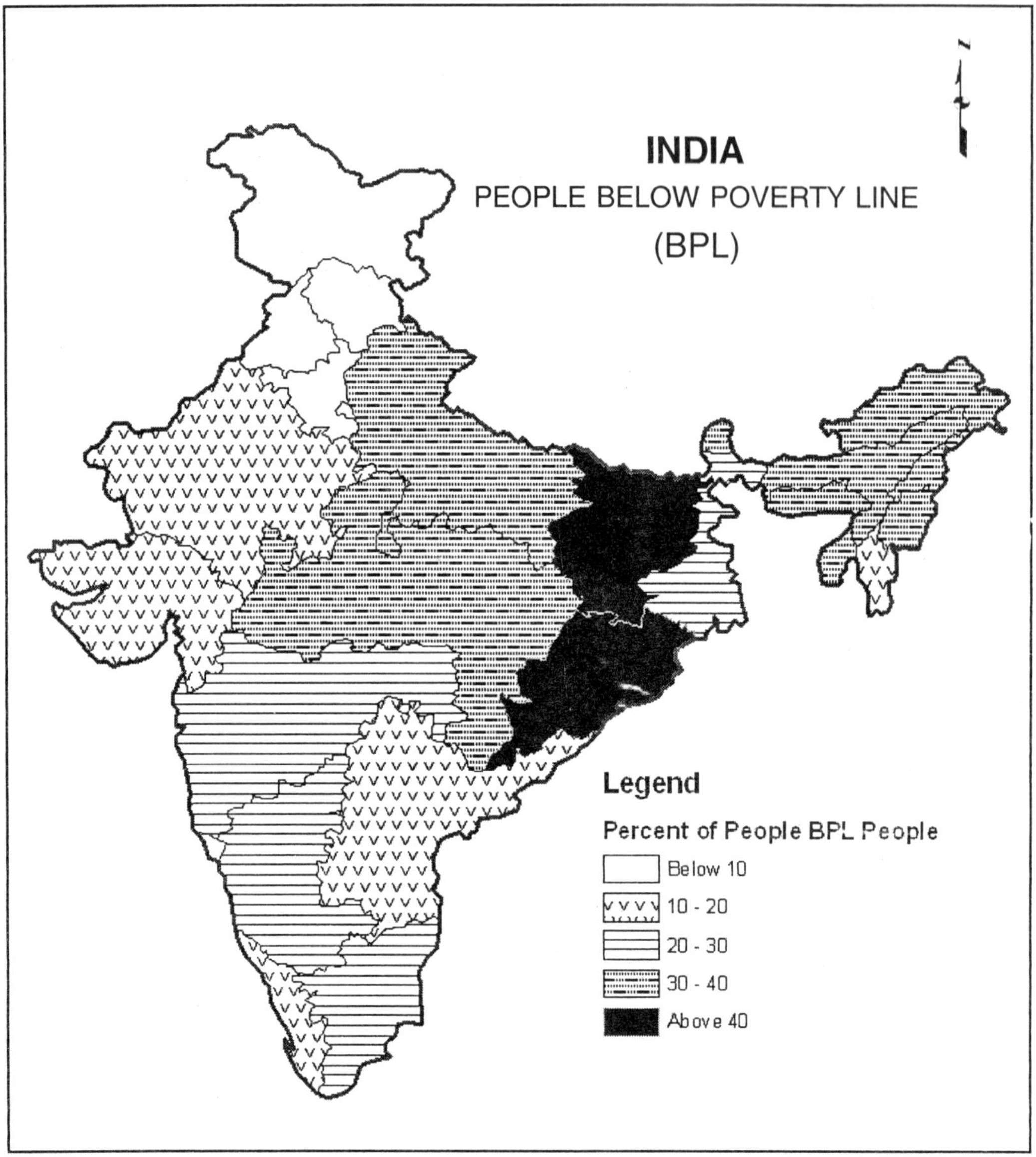

Fig. 7.1: India: People Below the Poverty Line

Then there are rural-urban differnces. (Fig. 7.2) The relationship between income and health becomes clear when we compare the per capita income with mortality or morbidity rates.

Per capita income is however not the only indicator of welfare of the people. The per capita income of Kerala (in 1996-97) was not very high (Rs. 9,066 as compared to Rs.18, 213 for Punjab and Rs. 17,295 for Maharashtra) but the life expectancy at birth in Kerala stood at 75 years and adult literacy at 92 per cent. So Kerala is far ahead of other states in human development index.

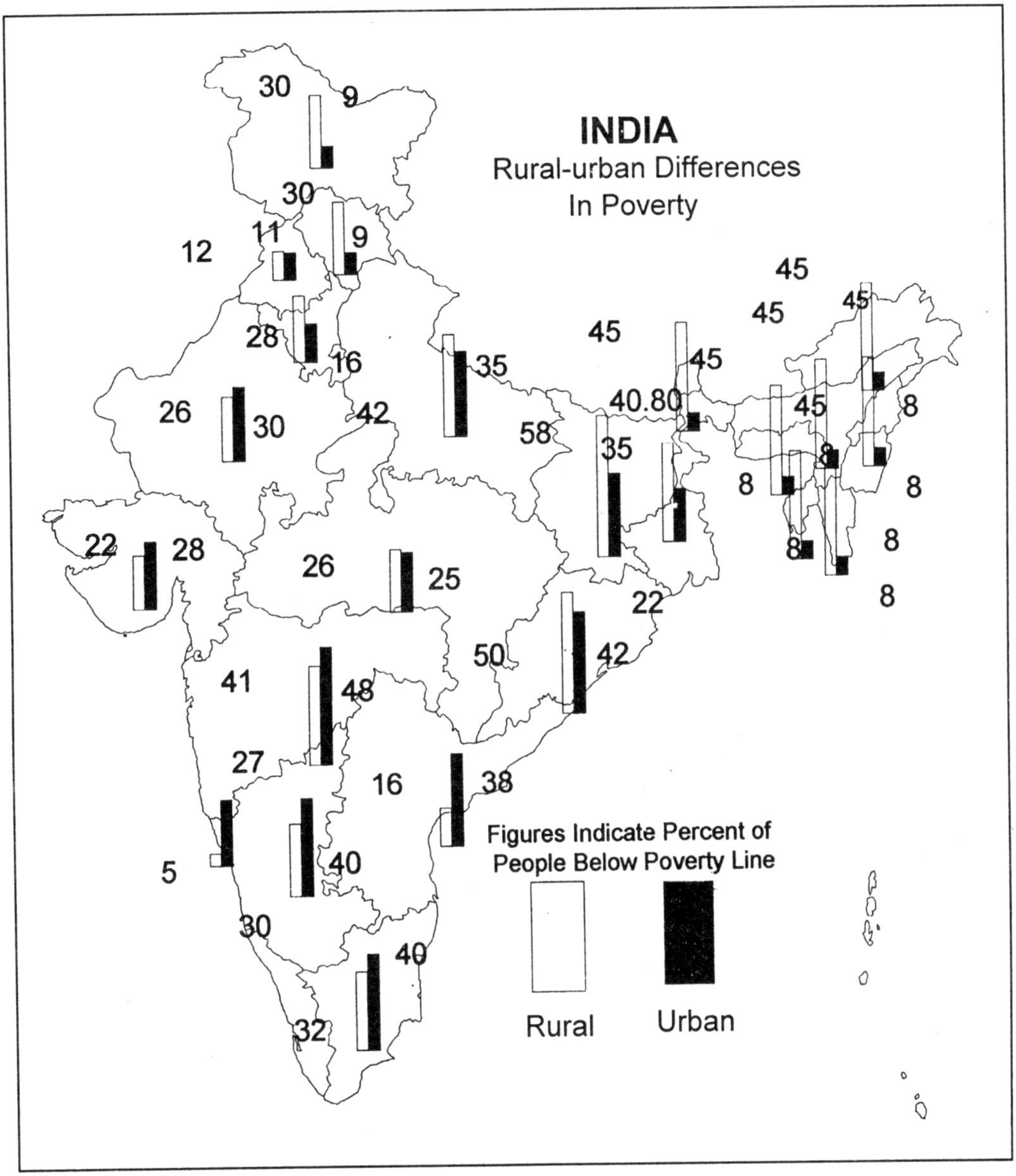

Fig. 7.2: India: Rural-urban Differences in Poverty

Source: NSS 50thRound (Jul 1993-June 1994)

If Kerala can do it, why not the other states. In Kerala, the government and the people have joined hands to promote human development. Whatever resources are available are effectively used. It is a model worth pursuing.

Development Style and Health

Process of development entails a series of positive as well negative changes that have direct impact on health. Among the positive changes include more and better education, more income, higher standard of living, increased willingness to spend money on health; it also means more hospitals, clinics, doctors, nurses, etc. Healthcare becomes an important activity of the civil society and more resources are diverted to this social sector. That is why, there is a positive correlation between development and health indicators. But it is not all that rosy. A number of byproducts of economic development have very adverse implications for the health.

Environmental pollution discussed in chapters 5 and 6 is one of the major byproducts of development. Development and environment need not contradict each other. In fact, they ought to support and strengthen each other. Unfortunately, it is not so. The reason lies in the style of development being pursued. Three factors constitute the foundation for economic development: natural resources, human beings and technology. For development to be sustainable all the three must work in concert to preserve and enhance each other. The current style of development considers natural environment to be just a factor of production. It is inert and hence should be exploited to achieve higher levels of material welfare.

Pollution of land, water, air and space is considered to be the price humanity must pay for development. It is yet to be realized that natural environment is not inert. It is live. Man is a part of it. He cannot live outside it. Development must, therefore, improve the quality of the environment; it must ensure that it is not polluted, destroyed or even misused. It is something that belongs to the whole humanity that includes not only those who are denizens of the earth today but also those who are yet to be born. The present generation is not its owner; it is its custodian.

Pollution of the environment adversely affects the health of the people, particularly in cities. Only 70 per cent of the people living in large cities get clean drinking water. The rest drink contaminated water. Air pollution caused by motorized vehicular traffic and urban factories has already overcrowded hospitals and dispensaries. No city in India is able to clear all the solid and liquid waste it generates. All this has made the urban environment unhealthy. If people still congregate there it is not because cities offer a better place to live, but because rural parts do not offer any scope for earning one's livelihood.

As the economy diversifies and shifts from primary to secondary and tertiary occupations, life becomes more sedentary. The manual labour, which agriculture requires gives place to mental work. Lack of adequate movement and exercise for the body and excess of fat and sugar coupled with physical and mental stresses have given rise to a number of systemic diseases like hypertension, obesity, diabetes, heart ailments, and diseases of the digestive system. As life becomes complicated and complex, joint families break and social system gets atomized. Many a people fail to cope with the speed and complexity of change. Psychosomatic cases are becoming too common to be ignored. According to some estimates, at least a quarter of the people of the world suffer from mental or emotional problems.

Development is also having its effect on priorities of the people. In times bygone, among the three desirable goals of life – wealth, health and character – the last one was accorded priority, followed by health and wealth. That is why the aphorism:

> If wealth is lost, nothing is lost.
> If health is lost, something is lost.
> If character is lost, everything is lost.

Development process has now reversed this order. Wealth now gets top priority; next in importance comes health, and character gets the last place. People are now prepared to use any means to earn wealth. Indian society has not remained untouched by this virus. It has become one of the most corrupt societies of the world. People do not mind even ruining their health, just to become wealthy. They treat human body like an engine to produce thrill and physical enjoyment. They are not at peace with themselves. They do violence to themselves as well to others at times in the name of God who, as a concept, is the embodiment of peace.

Development has brought people closer to each other. Newer and better means of transport and communication have enabled them to move fast and interact among themselves more frequently than ever before. The world is tending to become a global village, so they say. While this has brought people closer to each other and thus to benefit from each other's cooperation and experience, it has also enabled unhealthy traits of life including contagious diseases which travel fast and affect larger number of people. It so happens that bad things travel faster than good things. With greater mobility, the world is becoming homogenous in what is not good for health but highly fractured in what is good for health. AIDS, the most recent contagious disease, is no longer confined to few places and countries, it has become a global disease within a decade or so. Same is the case with systemic disorders like hypertension and diabetes which result from unhealthy styles of life. Terrorism, a social disease caused by warped minds, has now spread to the whole world. Even the mightiest country like the USA is a victim of it.

Social Structure and Health

All human societies are hierarchically organized. The gradations in the hierarchy differ from place to place and so also the principles of gradation. Not too far back in history, many western societies were divided on the basis of race, colour, language, occupation and so on. Slavery was abolished in America only in 1776. In ancient times, the Greeks had slaves and so did the Egyptians. Indian culture did not have slavery as a social practice. Instead it evolved a unique system of caste, which in the beginning must have been based on occupation.

It is plausible that the Aryans devised caste as a social means to bring in all peoples in their fold, irrespective of the level of cultural development. To begin with, the society was divided into four functional classes (*varnas)*: the intellectuals, the warriors, the producers of goods, and the producers of services. As time passed, these functional groups further divided and subdivided themselves to form hundreds of occupational groups or guilds called *jati* or castes. The Aryans wanted to assimilate all peoples irrespective of their cultural background into an overarching Indian culture still in making. They had three options. They could eliminate the less developed people as Europeans did with respect to the original inhabitants of Australia and Americas; they could make them slaves as the Greeks and Egyptians in ancient times and the Americans did in the eighteenth century with respect to the blacks. Or they could integrate them as partners, even if unequal, and allow them to carry on with their own life styles while accepting the broad parameters of the Aryan culture. The Aryans chose the last course. Each group thus carried on its functions as before and remained more or less endogamous but not insulated from the rest. In that non-literate and slow moving agricultural society, it must have worked to the advantage of the some but not necessarily to the disadvantage of others. The system got religious sanction so that even those who suffered had to accept it as their pre-ordained fate. In due course of time, each group started considering itself superior to some and inferior to others. And thus emerged the hierarchy of the so-called caste system of India.

The *varnashrama* system, to begin with, was based on the basic principles of division of labour and on the recognition that each individual or group had the right to live in a way it considered desirable. It had the option to move up the hierarchy, but those who acquired the social and economic power made it so rigid and unchanging that social mobility in the system stopped completely and one's position came to be determined by birth rather than merit. What we see in Indian society today is the continuation of this pernicious system under which a great majority of people is denied access to economic, social and political power. They are poor and hence cannot get enough to eat; they are under-or mal-nourished. When they get sick, they cannot afford to pay for medicines and doctors.

They are also illiterate and hence ignorant about modern developments in the field of medicine. It is these people who become victims of quacks, traditional healers and sorcerers. The so-called modernization, that is sweeping the rural parts of India, has not made the situation better. People do not give that importance to health and nutrition as they used to give a generation or two back. Now priority is given to non-food items of consumption; to things that add to the external look and bring prestige to the individual and his family. Poverty, ignorance and misallocation of whatever resources are available have led to a widespread nutritional deficiency syndrome particularly among the children and women in India.

During the last 50 years or so the discipline that could be imposed by the caste *panchayats* to maintain the status quo has very much loosened. With education and democracy, people have become aware of their rights. They do not accept caste as a binding force. They want to come out of it and desire to be treated as a human being without any label of caste.

With the installation of a democratic government in the country in the post-colonial era a lot of change occurred. Caste became a less binding force and new leadership cutting across caste and communal divides emerged. With the passage of time the pace of change, however, slowed down and the commitment of the Indian political leadership to bring about a social change and moral regeneration, which the Father of the Nation had laid stress on, took a back seat. A new tendency on the part of the people to identify themselves with caste as a pressure group to ensure appropriate share in economic development emerged and political parties on caste lines started taking roots in the 1970s. It was the time for the Indian leadership to rise equal to the occasion and to redirect the resentment of the neglected sections of the society to creative channels.

Rajiv Gandhi's short-lived administration did try to reverse the trends. His replacement by a revengeful politician suffering from megalomania put the clock back and fractured the country on caste lines almost completely. The ostensible purpose for which he did this was to ensure justice for those who were left behind, but the real purpose was different. He would have achieved the goals he wanted to achieve by heavily investing in education of the 'backwards' through special incentives and institutional arrangements. He could have put the poor in the forefront as Gandhi did and further weakened the caste system. In this endeavour, he would have got the support and backing of the whole country. But he chose a different path – a path that widened and cemented the age-old caste system. He did not last long as a 'hero' of the 'backwards' but he did add a new term to Indian sociology i.e. *Mandalization, to* express deliberate fracturing of society on caste lines.

Mandalization of Indian society in the 1990s was followed by its communal polarization dividing it on religious lines too. Both these undesirable developments ushered in a period of ill-governance in the country. Practically, all norms of good governance were given a good bye and in the confusion that reigned supreme the poor were the worst sufferers. Caste and religious animosities took violent turns in several states, particularly Bihar and Gujarat. People started resorting to extra-constitutional and extra-legal means to get even small and legitimate things done. The decade of 1990s was a socially unsettling decade in India. It fractured Indian society further.

Social Norms and Health

It would be pertinent to recall the definition of health we adopted in chapter one. Health is not just the absence of disease, nor it is confined to the state of the body. It has much to do with the behaviour of man in the society resulting from his worldview, his style of life, particularly with his approach to others. Human society constitutes a network of diverse peoples and equally diverse interests and concerns. It can function efficiently only if its individual members follow the rules of the social games.

Violence has become a major killer in India. The number of people being killed and maimed by other human beings at certain times and places exceeds those killed by diseases. Why do people kill other people? There may be several reasons, which can be bunched in two categories. Some individuals are mentally disturbed because of certain mental illnesses or their inability to adjust to the society at large. Alternatively, the social system is so oppressive that a good number of people cannot live honourably. In disgust, they resort to violent means and become highly destructive.

Those who are mentally sick can be treated in the mental hospitals. One should, however, keep in view that many of the mental patients get sick because of their inability to adjust to the prevailing social situation. But those who resort to unlawful activities knowingly and deliberately can be cured only if the factors, which promote such characters, are taken care of.

In India, as in other parts of the world, violence has become so common that unless a large number of people are killed, it does not become news. Killing is both individualized and organized. Then there are many other crimes such as inflicting injuries, looting, theft, etc. that are on the increase. Among the organized crimes, terrorism is the most serious ones. As our economy grows, the economic crimes involving highly respected and responsible people have come to the surface. High-level scandals to cheat the common men have now become too common to emphasize.

One can find many factors responsible for these tendencies. But the following factors appear to be the most pertinent. They are listed here not necessarily in order of their importance.

1. Religious intolerance,
2. Ethnic or caste animosities,
3. Discrimination against women,
4. General moral degradation, and
5. Economic poverty.

Religious extremism divided India in two in 1947; it has started raising its head again. Its tentacles have spread all over the world. The terrorist attacks in the name of Islam indicate how dangerous it can be for the humanity as a whole. Jehad has become a menace for the whole world. The destruction of the WTC in New York is not the last terrible thing done by man in the name of a religion. If the emerging scenario is any indicator, more such attacks are expected in future.

We have already discussed the *Mandalization* of Indian society and its social and political consequences. Atrocities against the weaker sections of the society have increased, particularly in the northern states. Violence against women has reached alarming proportions; bride burning and foetus killing has increased to an extent that the sex ratio in the country is seriously upset.

Let us hope that the surging tide of social destabilization would be checked and the inner strength of Indian polity would stem the rot we are in sooner than later.

Gender and Health

In most societies, women are not accorded status equal to that of men. Exceptions are few. It might have begun as a special treatment for women as they had to bear children and hence must be spared of arduous functions. In due course of time, they were confined to household activities and treated as inferior to men not only in physical terms but also intellectual. Interestingly, practically all religions gave legitimacy to this discriminatory practice. And some of them still prescribe veil for their women to ward off evil eyes of men. As late as mid-twentieth century, some of the European countries did not give their women the right to vote. The human society as it is constituted today is male dominated and women have yet to get their rightful place in it, recent struggles for gender equality notwithstanding.

Discrimination against women begins from early childhood; nay, from the mother's womb. Abortion of girl foetus is on the increase. Those who are born, do not get the attention they deserve. Boys get preferential treatment in all matters from food to health and education. Things have improved in the developed parts of the world in matters economic but progress in the social sector is still unsatisfactory.

As the economy of developed societies improved and income ceased to be a critical constraint on access to the basic needs, discrimination against girls in food, clothing, health, education and housing has considerably diminished. But the freedom with which boys develop their personality is yet to reach the girls in its all manifestations. Being a girl is disadvantageous in many ways even in developed countries.

The situation in the developing countries like India is quite alarming. Women are not only discriminated against but also exploited culturally, socially and economically. Boys get preference over girls in practically all respects including food, nutrition and health. In a situation where half of the population poor, shortage of food and health-care is not exceptional. The girls get access to these and other inputs only after the needs of the boys are adequately met. The reasons are many. Boys when they grow up are expected to support and take care of the old parents. It is the sons who inherit the parental properties as well as liabilities. The girls go away after they are married. Parents have to spend lot of money to get their daughters married. The last rites to lead the dead to the heaven can be performed by sons alone.

In a male dominated society, women's job is procreation to ensure the continuity of the family, and management of household affairs under the direction of the male members. She is not an earning member of the family even though she does tremendous amount of work and hence is dependent on the males for everything. She cannot determine the number of children she would bear. She is expected to give birth to male children and in the event of her failure to do so, she is looked down upon, ostracized and even divorced, although the reason for it may lie with the husband. The position of the bride in a joint family is not very envious. She does not get the same attention and treatment that she used to receive by her parents. Once her relations with the in-laws deteriorate, she becomes a victim of tortures, ranging from verbal abuses to beating and in extreme cases even bride burning. Premature termination of female foetus and strangulation to kill after the delivery, are no longer rare. Modern technology has given further fillip to these crimes. People can now know in advance the sex of the foetus.

In the rural parts of the country, early marriages lead to early pregnancies, that in turn lead to high rate of maternal deaths. Most women are malnourished, if not undernourished. They eat only after the men have eaten. They get only what is left after every one has finished eating. They do not get milk and milk products even if they are pregnant. They do not get adequate medical attention even when they are pregnant and most of the deliveries still take place at home without the aid of trained nurse or midwife (dai). Recent data indicate that women are victims of a number of gynaecological and deficiency diseases. No wonder, the sex ratio has been going against them.

Education and Health

Among the social factors that impact health, education is perhaps the most important. Education includes character building, literacy, knowledge of one's environment and the acquisition of the ability to earn one's livelihood. In 2001, 65.38 per cent of the people of India were literate. In 1951, the percentage stood at 18.33. Of this, only half of the people can be said to be educated. If we translate the percentages into absolute figures, we see that at least 296 million Indians were illiterate in 2001.

The literacy rate of 65.38 per cent is not uniform all over the country. States like Kerala are approaching the total literacy level (90.92 per cent) whereas the BIMARU states are still struggling hard to approach 55 per cent. Bihar registered only 47.53 per cent literacy in 2001 (Fig. 7.3). When we look at the literacy figures men and women separately, the situation gets highly distressing. Literacy among the males is invariably higher in the country. National literacy rate in 2001 was 76 per cent for males and only 54 per cent for females. It was only 35 per cent for women in Bihar as compared to 62 per cent for males. No wonder, Bihar has chosen an almost illiterate person to be its chief minister. And if we look at the data pertaining to rural-urban differences in literacy, we see that urban centers are far ahead of villages. Urban literacy in 2001 was 73.08 per cent as against 44.69 per cent for rural areas.

Knowing that education is essential for healthy life and living, the prevailing literacy scenario in India is really a matter of great concern. The whole of the Ganga basin states are in a mess, irrespective of the vantage point from which we look at them. Lots of resources have been and are being spent on adult literacy, but the situation has not changed much. What is needed is a single point agenda to invigourate, strengthen and restructure primary education. All the resources for education should be pooled to reach the target of 90 per cent literacy

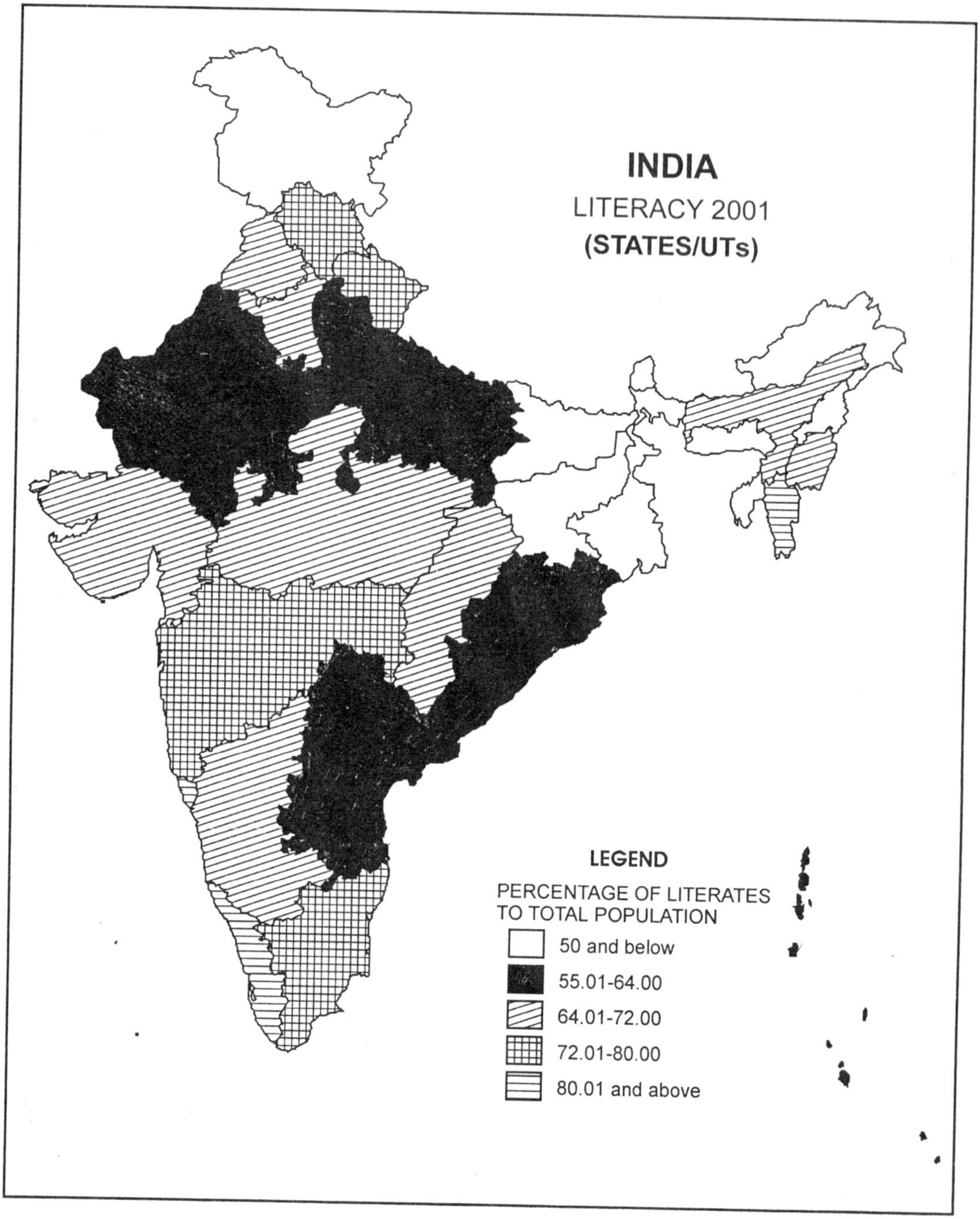

Fig. 7.3: India: Level of Literacy-2001

within two decades (let us say, 2000–2020 AD). The greatest hindrance in the way of complete literacy in the country is the lack of viable infrastructure and motivated teachers, particularly in rural areas. The official machinery is inert; it lacks missionary zeal.

It is not possible to make much headway in health unless the educational level of the people improves. Education of the girls is of prime importance; on it depends the health of future mothers and children.

Habitat and Health

Rural Habitat

Majority of people of India live in rural areas. In the past, simplicity was the hallmark of rural life. People were hard working; whatever they earned was spent on food, clothing and shelter in that order of priority. The priorities have now changed. Nutrition is less emphasized today than in the past. This naturally has its impact on the health of the people. The rural environment has also deteriorated. Haphazard developmental works have blocked the natural drainage pattern; natural plant cover has given way to agriculture; use of pesticides and chemical fertilizers has polluted the main sources of drinking water; density of houses even in small villages has increased and, therefore, the problems of sanitation have become acute.

Agriculture being the main occupation of people, maintenance of environmental cleanliness in rural areas is not easy. Everything including straw and cow dung has some value and hence is stored for future use very close to houses that are not very large. Humans and animals living side by side, sometimes in the same room or verandah, is still a common sight. Cooking is an arduous task in villages. Wood or cow dung cakes are the main fuels used for cooking. Practically, the whole household work is done by women and grown up girls. Until recently most houses were made of mud, otherwise called kutcha houses. (Fig. 7.4) Brick houses are becoming common but the basic layout has not changed much.

The physical layout of villages and village homes is also against the basic principles of hygiene and sanitation. The lanes are narrow, fortuitous and unpaved. Houses are usually above the level of the ground and hence household wastes, both solid and liquid, accumulate all around including the lanes. During the rains, the situation deteriorates further. Houses are built without any systematic planning. As family size increases, the parental house is divided, subdivided and expanded to accommodate new households. Due to shortage of space within the settlement, people encroach upon the village lanes till they become so narrow that they are unfit for any vehicular traffic.

Most rural houses do not have latrines (Fig. 7.5). People prefer to defecate in the open behind some bush or higher ground. Children ease themselves very close to the house along the street or in open ground. Women face the real difficulty. They have to get up very early in the morning and wait for the dark to set in the evening for nature's call. Pigs function as scavengers. In the absence of proper drainage, the waste, including human excreta, gets washed into the village tank that is used for bathing, washing clothes and cleaning kitchen.

In certain parts of the country, water tank is the only source of drinking water for humans as well as animals. The village wells are invariably polluted. With the introduction of hand pumps the situation with regard to drinking water has improved a bit, but frequent failure of the hand pumps and dilapidated condition of wells continue to pose serious problems (Fig. 7.6).

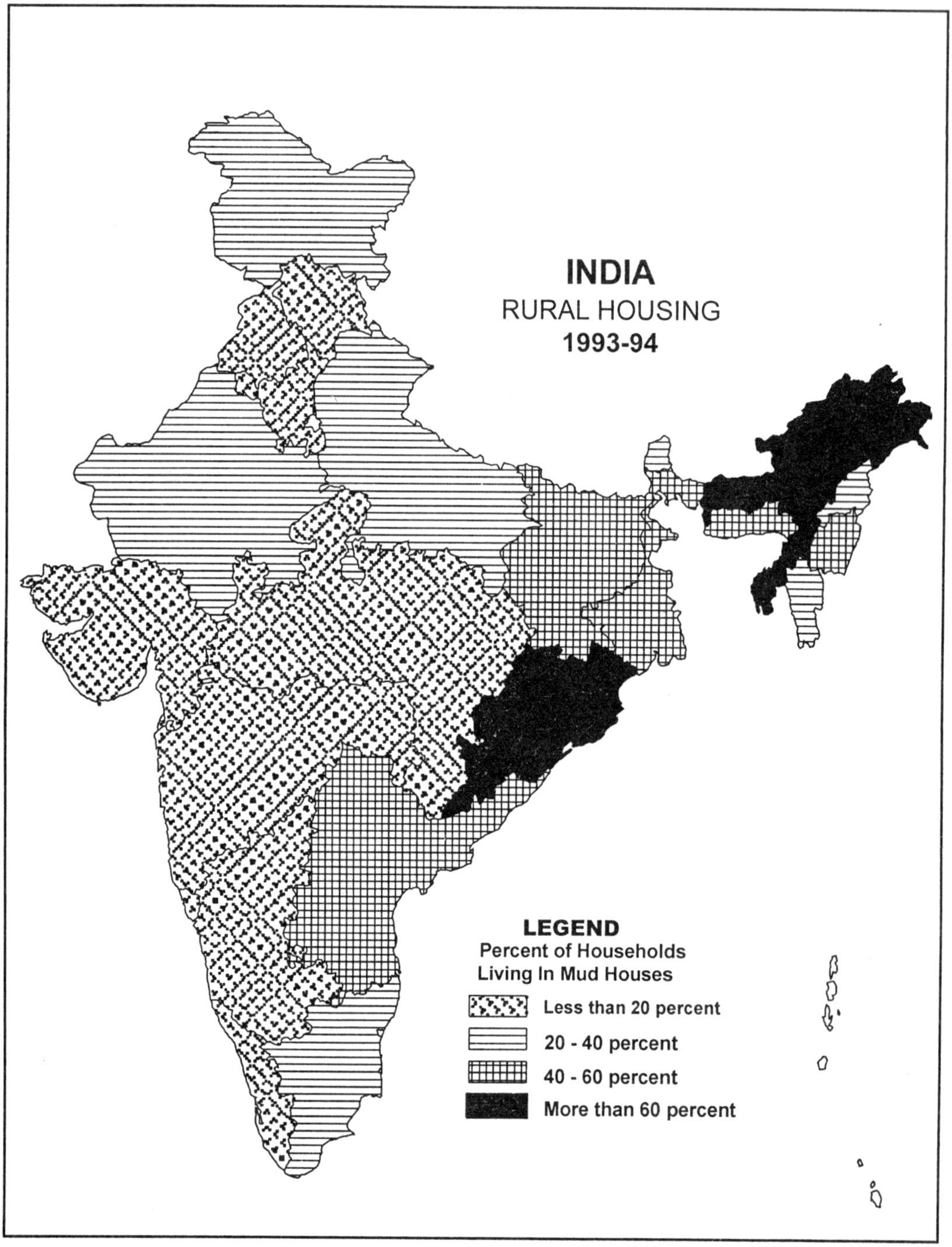

Fig. 7.4: India: Quality of Rural Housing

Source: NSS 50th Round (July 1993–June 1994).

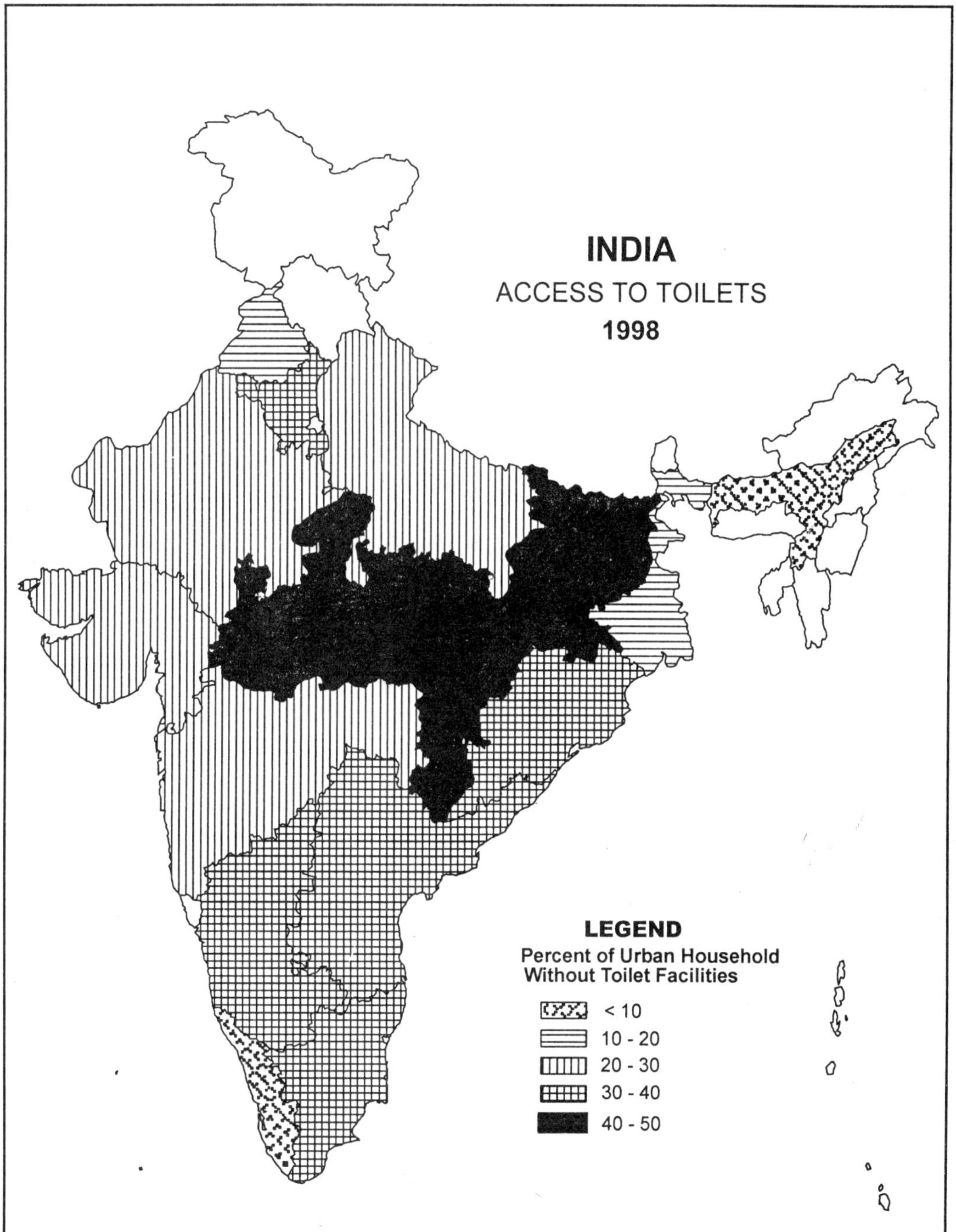

Fig. 7.5: India: Access to Toilet Facilities

Source: Statistical Abstract of India, 2001.

Village houses set an example in inner cleanliness. The kitchen is clean and so are the kitchen utensils. The first charge of the ladies of the household is to thoroughly clean the house early in the morning. Everyone takes bath daily and even children are not allowed to eat unless they have taken bath. The men folks clean the courtyard and cattle shed. Cow dung cakes are used as fuel for cooking. If the house is kutcha (made of mud) its floor is plastered with cow dung at least once a week. Cow dung has des-infective qualities.

The concept of cleanliness is, however, limited to personal hygiene and interior of the house. Beyond these limits, people behave differently. They spit wherever they feel like doing so; they urinate and defecate in open and thereby pollute the environment. After cleaning the house, they throw the garbage on the street or in front of neighbouring houses. These practices ultimately result in all houses surrounded by heaps of rubbish. During rains the solid and liquid wastes join together to create a real hell. Nothing could be more favourable to the spread of communicable diseases. As people switch over to brick houses, the sanitary conditions may improve in future but as long as this distorted concept of cleanliness remains unchanged, and local governments do not become functional, Indian villages will continue to have unhealthy environment and thus breeding grounds for diseases of various kinds.

Within the village, certain segments are better than others. The worst parts are those where the people of the so-called lower castes live. Indian village is still quite a cohesive community but behind the cohesiveness lies a great social chasm that has now started surfacing. The chasm is clear from the physical build of the village: its segmentation, house types, poverty and quality of life in general. The *dalit* houses are usually in one corner of the village, often a bit removed from it. It is not difficult to identify these areas as the layout of the streets, quality of the living quarters, sanitary conditions, and general look of the place are quite depressing. Changes have started creeping in, but they are slow and too disintegrated to make a major impact on the overall environmental situation.

Urban Habitat

The problems of living environment and health are not less acute in urban areas of the country; but they are different in nature and intensity. Cities, because of heavy concentration of population in a limited space, generate large amount of solid and liquid waste. Unless this waste is removed daily, it accumulates, spreads around, and gives foul odour. Disease causing agents – flies, flees, insects, bacteria and viruses – grow and multiply there. Rats, crows, vultures, dogs and pigs congregate there to excavate the rotten waste and to make their own contribution to the filth in the form of urine, excreta, flies, fleas and ticks. No wonder then, that the communicable diseases are so common in Indian cities. Cases of malaria, indigestion, dysentery, other intestinal diseases, hepatitis, typhoid, meningitis, etc. are common in cities. Not long ago, even a form of plague (or a disease resembling plague) struck the city of Surat in Gujarat; its source was the garbage that was allowed to accumulate for months.

As noted earlier, a huge chunk of urban population in India constitutes the recent migrants from villages. They live in slums of various kinds. Slums are much worse than villages in matters of hygiene, cleanliness, housing and living environment in general. They are the breeding grounds for the agents that cause diseases. Slum dwellers do not have access to clean water,

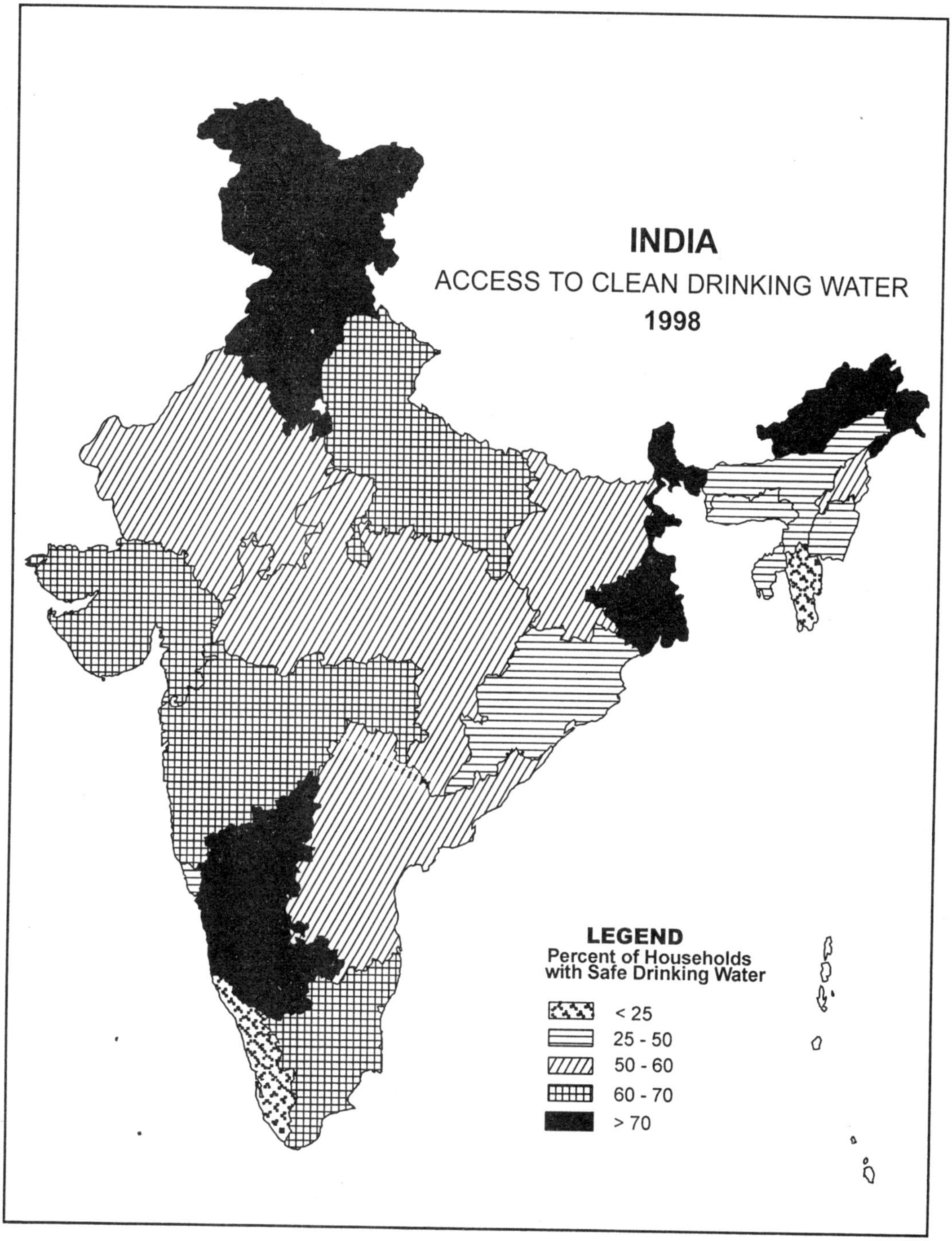

Fig. 7.6: India: Access to Safe Drinking Water

Source: Statistical Abstract of India, 2001.

proper housing, latrines, drainage, paved roads/lanes and hospitals. Most of them are engaged in non-formal activities and often live from hand to mouth. Health is not a priority concern for them, nor is cleanliness and sanitation. In fact, from psychological and sociological points of view, urban slums are not different from overgrown villages. They are the breeding grounds of diseases.

According to the WHO, a healthful housing both in urban and rural environments provides the following:

1. physical protection and shelter;
2. facilities for cooking, eating, washing and excretory functions;
3. mechanisms to prevent the spread of communicable diseases;
4. protection from noise and natural hazards;
5. safety within and outside the building; and
6. access to community and social institutions.

Poor housing is responsible for many ailments. Important among them are respiratory infections; skin infections; rat infection; diseases caused by arthropods like flies, mosquitoes, fleas, and bugs; accidents; and psychological stresses.

REFERENCES

1. Dube, S.C. India's Villages.
2. Kawata, K. *Report of Environmental Hygiene Committee,* 1949.
3. Registar General of India, Census of India, 2001, the data are published in various volumes.
4. World Bank. *World Development Report,* 1998.
5. Ministry of Home Affairs, National Crime Records Bureau, *Crime in India*, 1998.

8

Demographic Factors and Health

Various demographic parameters of population such as size, growth rate, density, age structure, sex ratio, occupational structure, urban-rural composition, ethnic and religious composition etc. have a great bearing on health and healthcare. Size, growth and density of population impact man-resource ratio, on the one hand, and access to health-care facilities on the other. Age structure determines the dependency ratio and need for age specific health services. For example, the growing child population demands more pediatric healthcare. A low and declining sex ratio calls for special attention to female children and women in general. Low literacy comes in the way of proper health and family welfare education. Lack of knowledge about nutritional needs, and about diseases and the available, healthcare facilities exposes people to various avoidable illnesses.

Unplanned urban growth is posing a serious threat to ecology and environment and over all quality of life in developing countries. Sedentary life style; pollution of land, air, water and social space; increasing psychosomatic stresses; unhealthy food habits; alcoholism and drug abuse; violence against nature, animals, children, women and other weaker sections of the society pose new challenges to human health in urban areas. Shift from primary to secondary and tertiary occupations has also its own impact on the health scenario. A brief outline of demographic profile of the country is, therefore, called for.

DEMOGRAPHIC CYCLE

History of world population since 1650 reveals that population changes take place in five identifiable stages. It is known as demographic cycle. All societies are expected to pass these stages. One must, however, be cautious in projecting the future on the basis of the past. Past need not repeat itself; often it does not. Yet, one can discern some future trends from a model like this. It is important that we should know at what stage in the cycle India stands today in order that we know the direction in which the country is likely to move in the future.

1. I stage: high stationary,
2. II stage: early expansion,
3. III stage: late expansion,
4. IV stage: low stationary, and
5. V stage: declining.

The first stage is marked with high birth rate and high death rate. Infant mortality is high yet, the dependency ratio is also very high. Of the many children born only some survive to their fifth birthday. High infant and child mortality prompts parents to have more children. The rate of growth of population is naturally low. India was in this stage until about 1920. The second stage sets in when death rates begin to decline, mainly because of control measures against epidemic diseases and general improvement in health facilities. Birth rates remain stationary at a high level; at times birth rates go up. In the third stage, the death rates decline further and birth rates also move down. India is in this stage since 1995.

The fourth stage is characterized by low birth and low death rate. The population does not grow; it remains stationary. Most of the developed countries are passing through this stage. In these countries growth rate varies from 0 to 0.5 per cent. The last stage is reached when population starts declining. It happens when desire for children lessens and many couples remain childless. Germany, France, and Scandinavian countries are passing through this stage (Fig. 8.1).

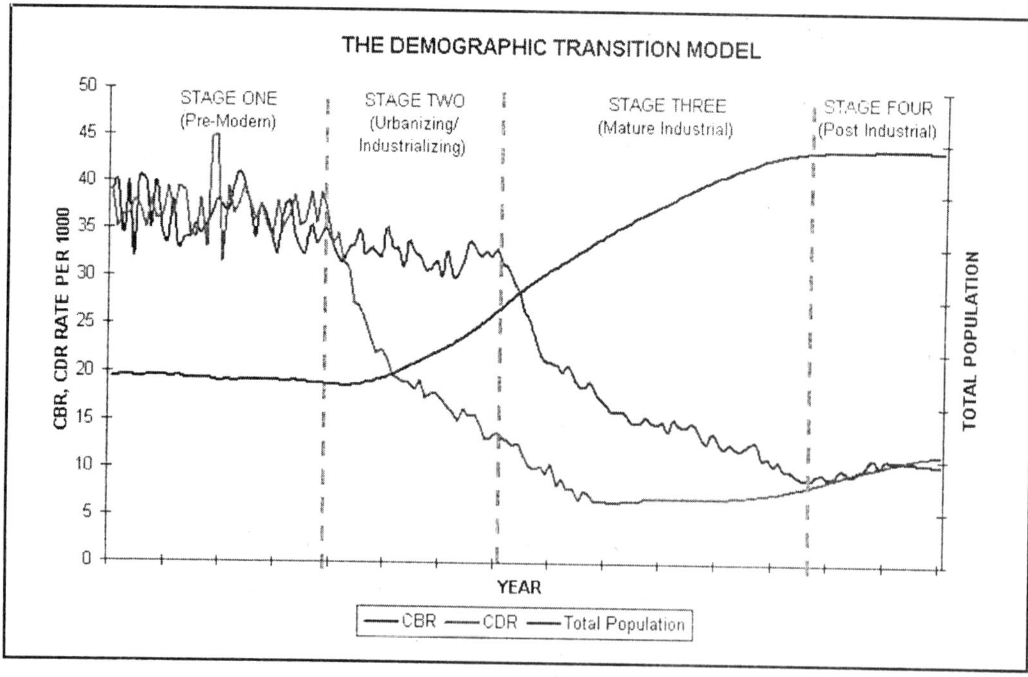

Fig. 8.1: Demographic Cycle

Different countries of the world are passing through different stages of demographic cycle. In general, most of the African, West Asian and Latin American countries are still in the first or second stage. Asian countries fall in the third stage, industrialized countries in the fourth stage; and a few countries of Europe in the fifth stage. Globally, the world is still at the junction of the second and third stages. Population is growing fast. India is passing through the third stage of demographic cycle. Growth rates are declining but absolute increase in population is still very high.

POPULATION EXPLOSION

The Number

With a total population of over 1027 million in 2001, India contains nearly 16.7 per cent of the world population in just 2.4 per cent of the land area of the world. It is the second most populated country, the first being China, which has about 1300 million people (Table 8.1). The annual net addition to the total population of India is approximately 18 million. The number of people added to the total population between 1991 and 2001 was 180 million. It was 160 million during 1981–1991. In other words, our population grows by about 45,000 persons each day i.e. 3 persons each minute or one person every twenty seconds. The annual addition of 18 millions exceeds the total population of Australia. Seventyfive countries of the world have less than 18 million persons each. According to some estimate India will overtake China by 2050 to become the most populous country on the earth.

Table 8.1: Population of Selected Countries

	Country	*Reference date*	*Population in millions*
1.	China	Feb. 1, 2000	1,277.6
2.	India	March 1, 2001	1027.0
3.	USA	April, 2000	281.4
4.	Indonesia	July 1, 2000	212.1
5.	Brazil	-do-	170.1
6.	Pakistan	-do-	156.5
7.	Russian Federation	-do-	146.9
8.	Bangladesh	-do-	129.2
9.	Japan	Oct. 1, 2000	126.9
10.	Nigeria	Feb. 1, 2000	11.5

Source: Reproduced from paper 1 of Census of India 2001.

This huge size of India's population is a big burden on its economy, ecology, polity and society; much of the economic growth has been gobbled up by population growth. Each baby born increases the demand for all that is necessary and desirable to lead a civilized life. The country has made impressive progress in practically all walks of life, but the net effect is minimized, if not neutralized by population growth. For example, India's food production went up from 50 million tonnes in 1950 to 210 million tons in 2001 (4 times) but the per capita availability of food grains increased by only 50 per cent because our population increased in the same period by three times.

It will be relevant to mention that India's population has not grown as fast as it is made out to be. The problem lies with its huge base. Even a moderate growth adds millions of people each year. Moreover, it is not unique to India. It has happened elsewhere in the world in similar circumstances. Population growth in Europe was far higher than that in India during the eighteenth and nineteenth centuries. But for the fact that they could export their growing numbers to the newly colonized lands of North and South America and Australia, Europe could not have avoided the Malthusian trap. To improve the quality of life of those who were left in Europe, the resources of the whole world were assembled at the cheapest possible rate. Had the present day developing countries like India got the opportunity to transfer their surplus population to other parts of the world, the crisis that they face today would have been considerably mellowed down. They would have got adequate time to change their fertility behaviour and stabilized the population much earlier. Unfortunately or fortunately, they did not get such escape routes.

Whenever man-resource ratio declines, human societies all over the world devise direct as well as indirect means to stop the Malthusian law from operation. In India, widow marriage was prohibited. People engaged in religious ceremonies including the last rites of their family members were prohibited from having sex for an extended period. Polygamy and extramarital relations were banned. Late marriages, rhythm system to avoid certain days for copulation when women were more likely to conceive were some of the traditional methods of avoiding pregnancy. In fact, as per the ancient religious rules, people should not indulge in sex unless they desired to have children. It was *brahmacharya* (abstinence from sex for pleasure) for the laity.

None of these norms of the bygone days are followed now. Modern thinking that sex is a natural urge that should not be suppressed has gained ground. There are a number of artificial ways to check conception: pills, condoms, visectomy, tubectomy, and if nothing works, termination of pregnancy through abortion. The old habits, however, do not change easily even when dangers ahead are in sight. Unfortunately, the dangers inherent in population growth appear to come slowly specially to those who are poor who have not much to lose whether the country is under-or over-populated. Population control for nation's sake is difficult to sell to the poor. Their energy is centred on earning wages to meet the basic needs. What would sell is the social and economic benefits the individuals and their families would reap from fewer rather than more children. It takes a generation or two to adopt fully to the new reproductive behaviour even if economic and social conditions improve appreciably.

There is a close relationship between birth and death rates. Unless small family norm becomes a conscious choice of people, high mortality rates are followed in quick succession by high birth rates. But when death rates decline, birth rates do not decline instantaneously: they are delayed by one to two generations. High birth rate is related to the survival rate of the newly born children also. If child mortality rate is high, more children must be produced to ensure the survival of the few. For the adoption of small family norm, people must be convinced that chances of survival of the children born are high. And this conviction must become part of the life.

Access to high quality health facilities, improvement in economic conditions resulting from higher rate of national economic growth, and social welfare measures make a big difference. All these, however, take time to have cumulative effect. One should, therefore, not be over sensitive to the current high rate of population growth and take imprudent decisions in panic. Investment in education and health, particularly in rural areas where majority of the people live, coupled with policies that reduce poverty and pestilence to a tolerable level are the only means to speed up change. Improvement in the law and order situation and effective mechanisms to protect the basic human rights of the common man also create favourable conditions for family planning.

Unfortunately, we have not done so well as our potentials empower us to do and have failed to integrate family welfare with social and economic welfare in a manner that can make people realize the advantages of small families. Keeping these points in perspectives, let us see how population has grown and what the implications of this growth are for the health of the people.

Growth Rate

India's population growth during the twentieth century can be broken down into four distinct phases:

1901-1921: Stagnant population,
1921-1951: Steady growth,
1951-1981: Rapid high growth, and
1981-2001: High growth with signs of decline,

One of the distinguishing features of India's population is its high rate of growth. It doubles almost every thirty years. But if we go into its demographic history, we find that its population growth has been fairly in tune with the classical theory of demographic transition. During much of the nineteenth century, India's population has been fluctuating: a decade or two of growth was followed by a decade or two of decline. It almost remained stationary. And this trend continued until 1921. Since then the country passed through all phases of demographic transition and has now entered the fifth phase of secular decline. How long it will take before its population stabilizes? Would the decline be fast enough to have its effect on the absolute population sooner than later?

When compared to the growth rate in many other developing countries, it does not seem to be unusually high. For example, it has hovered around three per cent per annum in Pakistan, Nigeria, Saudi Arabia, Israel and Kenya, a much higher percentage compared to India's 2.13 per cent. During 1941-1951, the exponential growth rate of population in India was 1.25 per annum; it increased to 1.96 per cent during 1951-61, 2.20 per cent during 1961-71 and 2.22 per cent during 1971-81. Between 1991-2001, the growth rate declined to 1.8 per cent.

The growth rate of India's population as noted above is not uniformly distributed all over the country. The states, which recorded higher growth than the national average were J&K, Haryana, Rajasthan, U.P., Bihar, Jharkhand, M.P., Maharashtra and all the mini states of the northeast. And those which recorded lower growth were H.P., Punjab, Uttaranchal, Assam, West Bengal, Orissa, Chhattisgarh, Andhra Pradesh, Karnataka, Kerala, Tamil Nadu and Goa. During the decade 1991-2001, it varied from 2.89 per cent J&K to just 1.4 per cent in Kerala. The states whose population grew faster than 2.5 per cent were Haryana, J&K, M.P., Maharashtra, Rajasthan and U.P., and those lower than 2.0 per cent were H.P., Kerala, Orissa and Tamil Nadu (Fig. 8.1).

The key determinant of population growth is the difference between birth and death rates. Both of these vary spatially as well as temporally in response to a number of social, economic, biological and environmental factors. As discussed earlier, birth rate is closely linked to the past experiences and practices, images of the future, present scenario with respect to social security, level of development, urbanization, age and sex composition of the population, importance attached to children and population policies pursued by governments. In general rural societies and poor household tend to have more children whereas the urban societies and higher income people prefer smaller families.

On the mortality front, the situation has been changing rather fast during the past few decades. The change started sometimes in the 1930s. The British government started investing more in healthcare; industrialization and urbanization diversified the agricultural economy to some extent making people shift from villages to towns. Scientific discoveries and inventions produced new medicines and methods of diagnosis and treatment. The mass killers like plague and small pox were won over. These developments upset the balance between high birth and high death rates. Earlier more children were born, very few survived; deficiency diseases, natural calamities and epidemics took a heavy toll of life. Average longevity of life was as low as 24 in 1901. With the birth rate remaining high and death rate going down steadily, the decadal growth blew up to reach the peak of 24.80 per cent in 1971. As birth rate too started sliding down, it came down to 23.85 per cent 1981-91 and declined further to 21.34 per cent during the decade 1991-2001. This is fairly good but when translated in absolute terms, it amounts to an increase of over 180 million people within a decade. Only a few countries of the world have more than 180 million people.

Table 8.2: India: Growth of Population, 1901-2001

Year	*Population (millions)*	*Rate of growth*	*Remarks*
		British India	
1600AD	100	–	Moreland's estimates
1750	130	–	Shirras' estimates
1850	150	–	Mukerjee's estimates
1872	206	–	First partial census
1881	254	1.50	Census of India
1891	287	9.60	-do-
1901	294	1.40	-do-
		Independent India	
1901	236	–0.2	Census of India
1911	252	5.76	-do-
1921	251	–0.31	-do-
1931	279	11.01	-do-
1941	219	14.22	-do
1951	361	13.31	-do
1961	439	21.50	-do-
1971	548	24.80	-do-
1981	683	24.66	-do-
1991	844	23.50	-do-
2001	1027	21.34	-do-

Source: Registrar General of India, Decadal Census Reports.

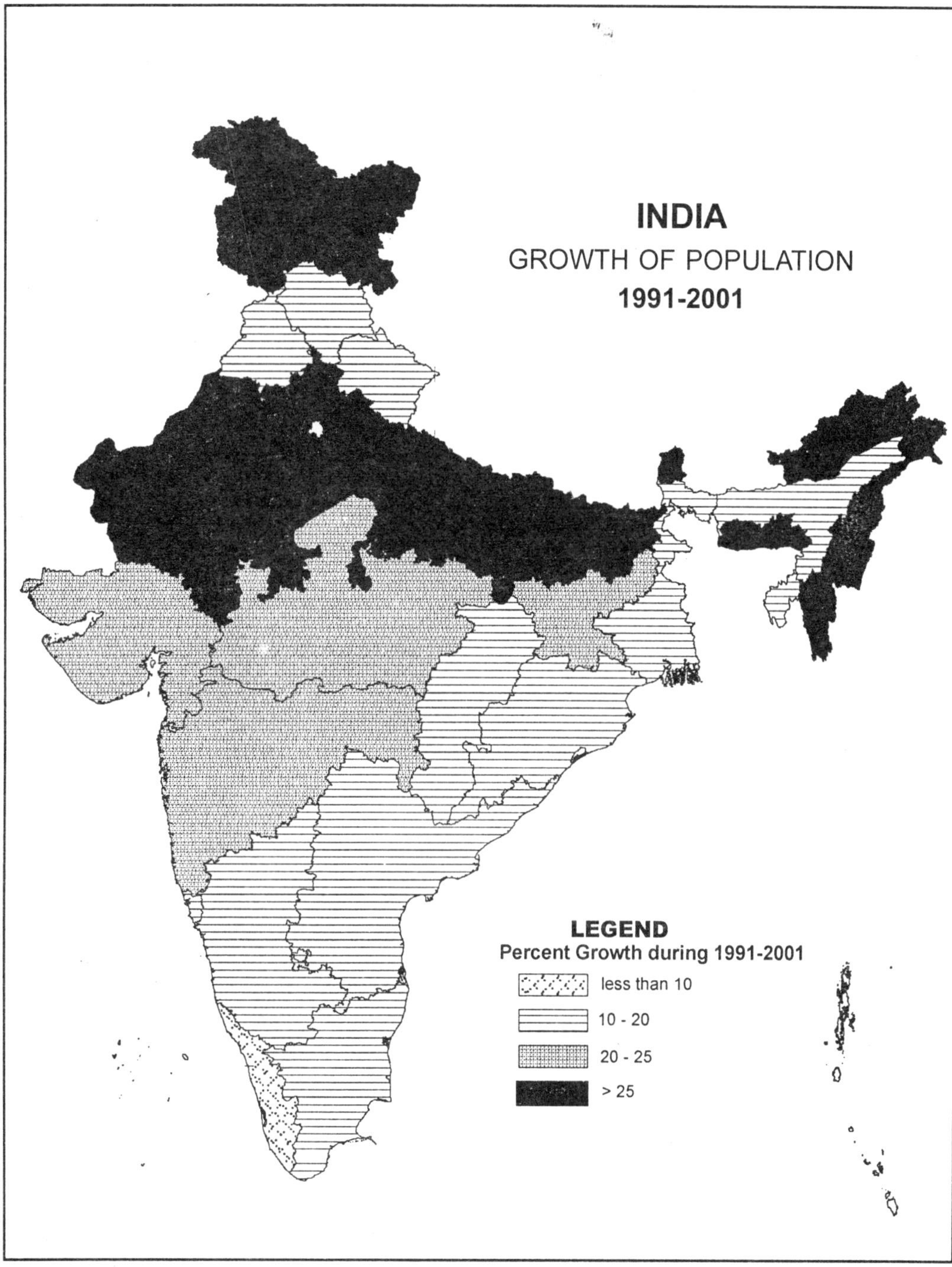

Fig. 8.2: India: Decadal Growth of Population: 1991-2001

Source: Census of India, Provisional Tables, 2001.

Density

As stated earlier, India contains 16.7 per cent of the world population but only 2.4 per cent of the land area. Its population is growing fast enough to add 18 million additional heads each year. Even though its population density is less than that of Netherlands, the man-land ratio is extremely adverse as a huge chunk of Indian population (about 70 per cent) depends on agriculture. The other sectors of the economy are still developing. Agriculture contributed 28 per cent of the GDP. High rate of growth of population and stationary land areas increases the density further. In 1961, density of population stood at 137 persons per sq. km; in 2001 it more than doubled to 324 persons. In 1901 it was 77 persons per sq. km. Table 8.3 and Figure 8.2).

The national level density figures are, however, too generalized to present a realistic picture. Density is not uniform spatially; it varies from state to state and within the state from district to district. Density is high in plains of Punjab and the Ganga valley. In the peninsular India, the coastal plains are thickly populated. Among the thinly populated areas are the arid lands of Rajasthan, and the mountainous areas of the northern states. Elsewhere the density is medium hovering around the national average. One-third of the people of India live in just one-tenth of the land area of the country.

Table 8.3: Density of Population: Major States in 1991 and 2001 (per sq. km)

State	*Density in 1991*	*Density in 2001*	*Per cent change*
West Bengal	767	904	17.86
Bihar	685	880	28.46
Kerala	749	819	9.34
UP	548	689	25.73
Punjab	403	482	19.60
Tamil Nadu	429	478	11.42
Haryana	372	477	28.23
Assam	286	340	18.88
Jharkhand	274	338	23.35
Maharashtra	257	314	22.18
A. Pradesh	242	275	13.64
Karnataka	235	275	17.02
Gujarat	211	258	22.27
Orissa	203	235	15.76
MP	158	196	24.05
Rajasthan	129	165	27.90
Uttaranchal	133	159	19.55
Chhattisgarh	130	154	18.46
HP	93	109	17.20
J&K	77	99	28.57
India	267	324	21.35

Source: Census of India: Provisional population Tables, 2001.

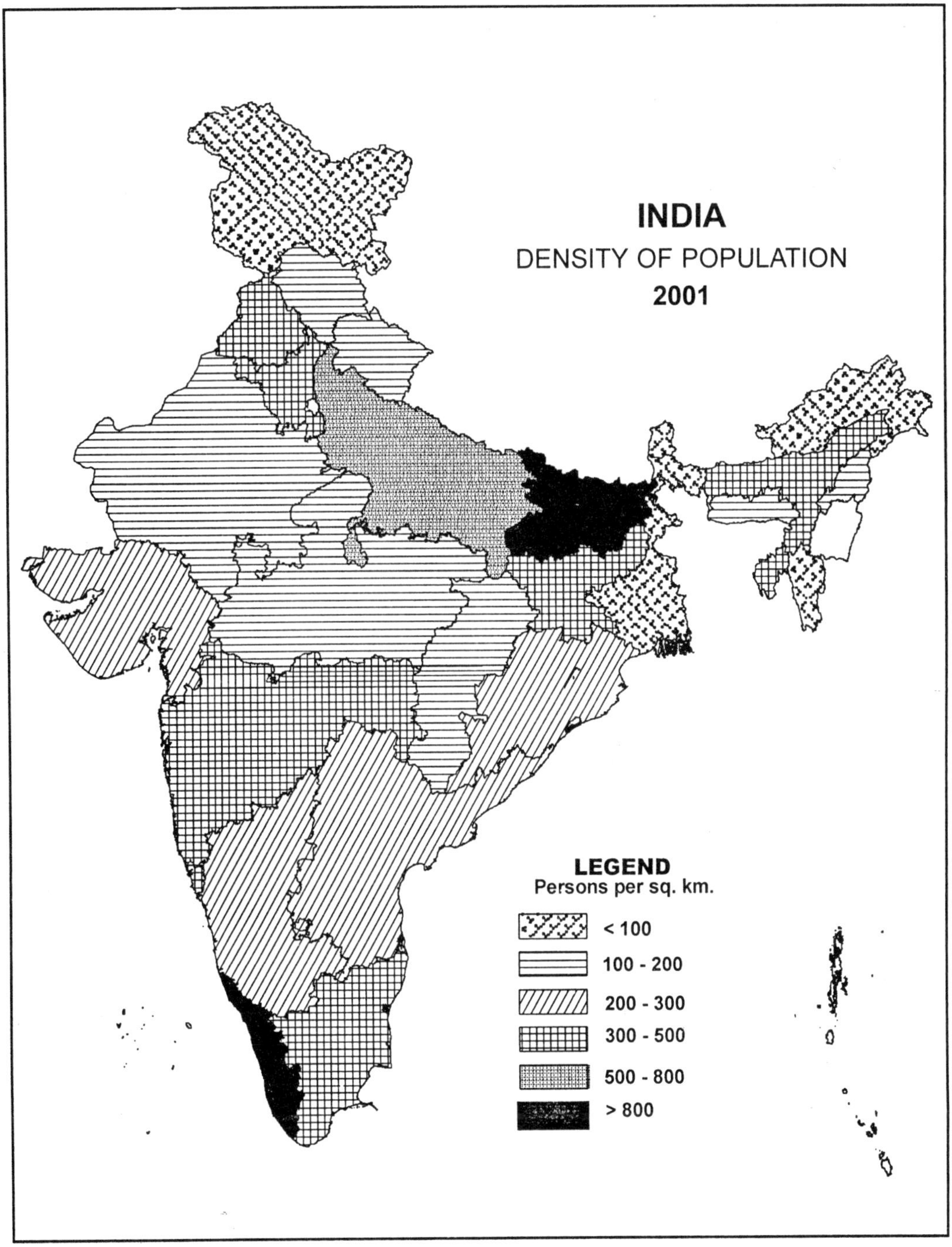

Fig. 8.3: India: Density of Population, 2001

Source: Census of India, Provisional Tables, 2001.

Density is a very crude indicator of pressure of population on land. To get a realistic picture we should qualify the quantity of people as well as land by quality. An area inhabited by healthy, educated and skillful people will definitely be far better than another inhabited by unhealthy, illiterate and unskilled people. Similarly, a good quality land can support far more people than a bad one. Parts of Rajasthan may have very low density but are over-populated. As such crude density figures should not be taken as indicators of over– or under-population of an area, region or country.

When we look at the density of population in relation to arable land, we get a more meaningful picture. Despite the fact than more than half (57%) of total area of India (3.29 m sq km) is under crops, the per capita availability of land is low and secularly declining. In 1981, the figure stood at 0.368 ha per head; it declined to 0.277 ha per head in 1991.

POPULATION COMPOSITION

Age Structure

Age group in which people fall has several socio-economic implications. Age determines the reproductive as well as working capabilities, apart from dependency ratio, family structure and objectives and contents of socio-economic development. It also has bearings on the health. The working force consists of people in the age group of 15-60 years. A high proportion of population in the age groups 0-14 and 60+ indicates high dependency and hence enhanced health needs. India has close to 40 per cent dependent population both males and females. It share in the total population is declining but not fast enough. The elderly population in the age group of 60+ years makes up about 7 per cent of the total population. The share is on the increase. In the developed countries the share of child and elderly population is 25 and 15 per cent respectively. In India the state of Kerala has almost attained this age structure.

In general, the age structure of Indian population has started moving away from the typical pyramid to a bulging pyramid reflecting a growing working and elderly population (Figure 8.2). More girls are entering the childbearing age group after surviving the vulnerable child age group. This would have impact on the fertility ratio in coming years.

Sex Ratio

Sex-ratio is a good indicator of changing health status of both males and females. A low sex ratio i.e. number of females for each 1000 males points to higher rate of mortality among the females of various age groups. It also points to lower social status of women and hence reduced accessibility to health facilities. Any improvement in the sex ratio indicates corresponding advance in the social or health status of women.

Sex ratio in India when compared to other countries of the world is really disturbing (Table 8.4). This indicates that women suffer from certain social and health infirmities which are peculiar to them. Since the women are biologically better equipped to cope with diseases, the situation should be just the reverse if both sexes are equally exposed to same kinds of hazards.

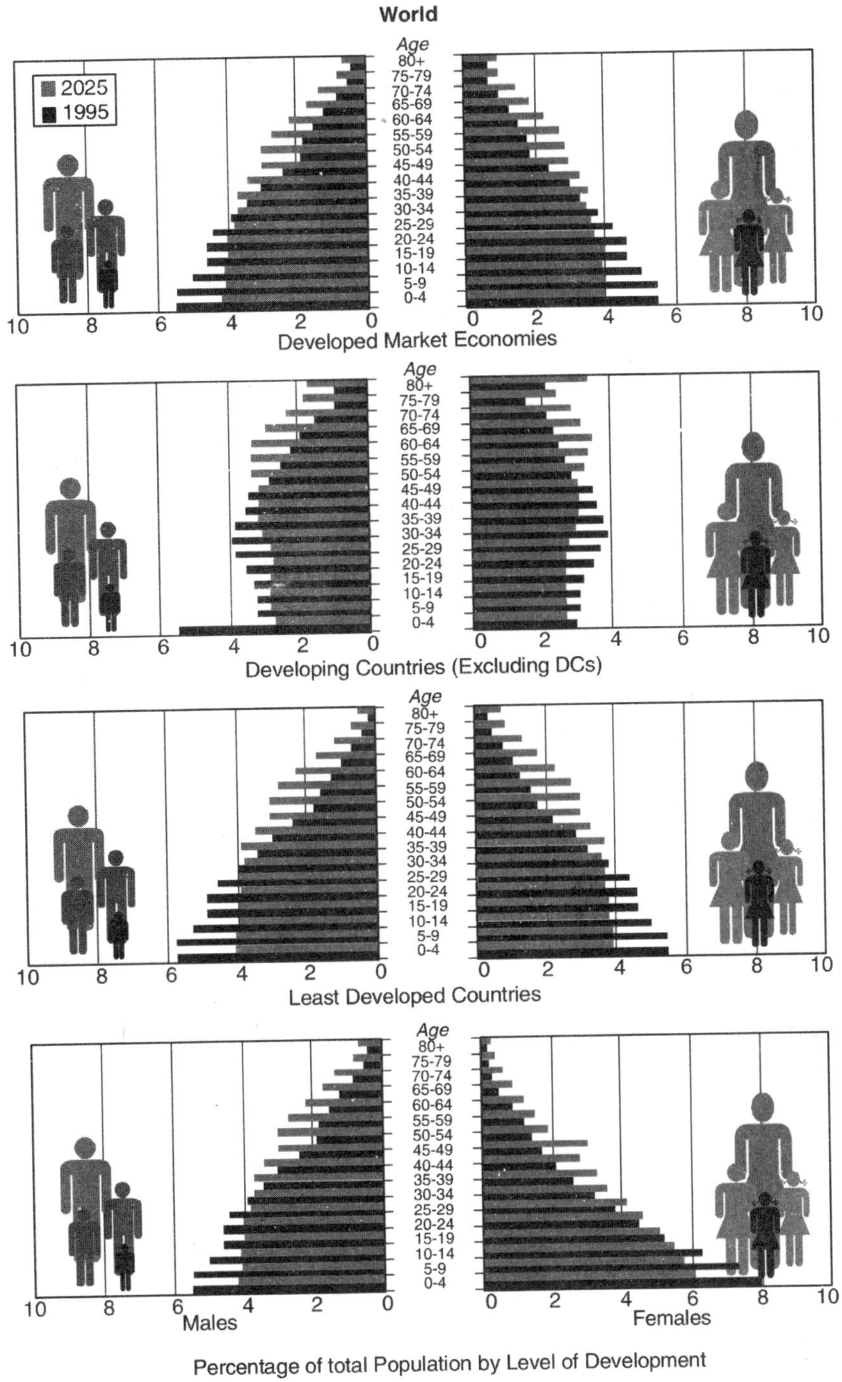

Fig. 8.4: World: Age and Sex Pyramid (1995-2025)

Source: World Health Report, 1998.

Available data indicate that the sex ratio in India is favourable to women up to the age of 12; thereafter it becomes favorable to males in the age group 12-45 and for the rest of the years it is again favourable to women. Apparently, the most crucial period for Indian females constitutes the childbearing age during which repeated pregnancies and abortions at short intervals and low nutritional status affect their health adversely. The risks involved in bearing and giving birth to children are further heightened when antenatal healthcare facilities are not within easy reach.

Table 8.4: Sex Ratio in Selected Countries

	Country	*Number of Women per 1000 men*
	World	986
1.	China	944
2.	India	933
3.	USA	1,029
4.	Indonesia	1,004
5.	Brazil	1,025
6.	Pakistan	938
7.	Russian Fed.	1.140
8.	Bangladesh	953
9.	Japan	1,041
10.	Nigeria	1,016

Source: WHO, World Health Report, 2002

The deteriorating sex ratio in India since 1901 is highly disturbing social phenomenon. It shows that our women live in worsening social and health conditions than their male counterparts. Sex ratio in India in 1901 was 972; it slid down to 930 in 1971. The following census returns showed an upward turn but in the decade succeeding, it came down from 934 (1981) to 927 (1991). The last census returns of 2001, once again pushed the ratio only slightly up to 933. Continuing low sex ratio clearly indicates that the programme launched by various agencies to improve child and mother care have had only a limited success.

Wide differences among the states and among the districts within the states in sex ratio indicate that the factors, which militate against the health of women are not the same all over the country. Kerala's sex ratio is 1071; most of the peninsular states are above the national average. Taking 950 as the standard sex ratio, we find the states of Himachal Pradesh, Uttaranchal, Manipur, Tripura, Meghalaya, Orissa, Chhattisgarh, Andhra Pradesh, Karnataka, Goa, Kerala, Tamil Nadu and Pondicherry above it. All other states are below it. And the states which are below the national average are: J&K, Punjab, Haryana, Chandigarh, Delhi, Rajasthan, U.P., Bihar, Sikkim, Arunachal Pradesh, Nagaland, Madhya Pradesh, Gujarat and Maharashtra (Fig. 8.3).

District level analysis, however, shows wide disparities within the states. Sex ratio is remarkably low in pockets of northwest India comprising parts of Haryana, Rajasthan,

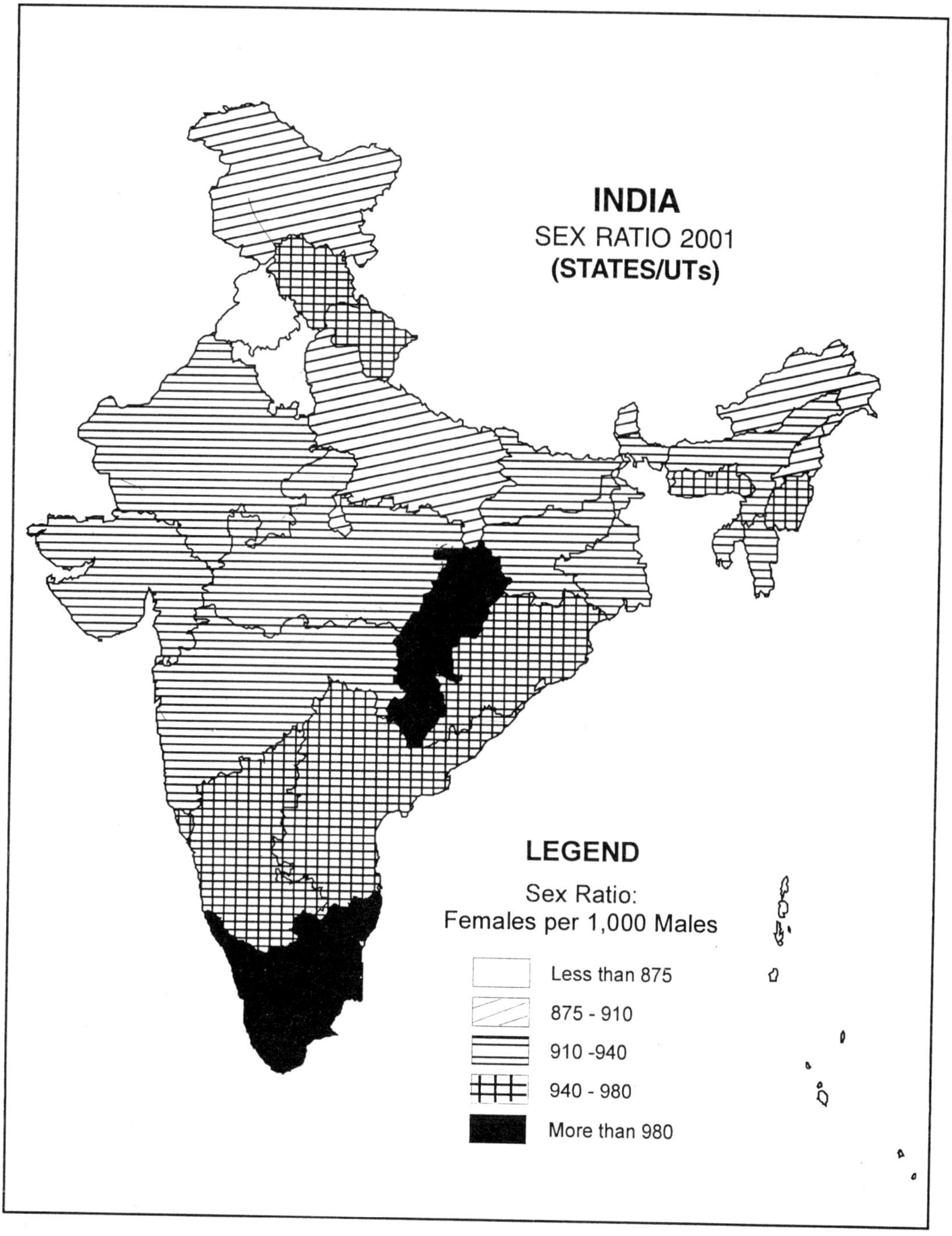

Fig. 8.5: India: Sex Ratio-2001

Madhya Pradesh and western Uttar Pradesh. Interestingly, it is the belt where agriculture is highly developed. The dominant farming communities favour sons who could work on their fields. This is also the belt that shows quite high differentials in male and female child mortality. If we exclude the culprit districts from the region, the sex ratios increase substantially. This means that low sex ratio in India and in many of the states of the country is, to a great extent, because of the abysmally low ratio in some districts. This situation calls for a selective spatial approach to this problem. There should be special child and reproductive care measures targeted to these districts to correct the situation.

The imbalance in the sex ratio poses a serious challenge to Indian society. Why is the sex ratio so low in certain pockets of the country? Is it only because of poor nutrition, health services, and maternal and childcare or there are other factors linked to social values, practices and preferences? A depth analysis of all these factors in cross-cultural situations may open up new opportunities for corrective action.

Religious Composition

Religion plays a very crucial role in the status of health. Food habits, the habitat and thinking of the people is highly influenced by religion. India has given rise to four main religions of the world: Hinduism, Jainism, Buddhism and Sikhism. It has substantial number of Muslims (12 per cent) and Christians (2.5 per cent). An overwhelming percentage (82 per cent) of Indians profess Hinduism, the oldest surviving religion of the world (For the latest available figures, see Table 8.5).

Table 8.5: Religious Composition of India's Population

	1961		*1991*	
	Number	*Per cent*	*Number*	*Per cent*
Hindus	366.50	83.50	687.60	82.00
Muslims	46.90	10.70	101.60	12.12
Christians	10.70	2.40	19.60	2.34
Sikhs	7.80	1.80	16.30	1.94
Buddhists	3.20	0.70	6.40	0.76
Jains	2.00	0.50	3.40	0.40
Others	1.60	0.40	3.30	0.39
Total	439.20	100.00	838.60	100.00

Source: Census of India, 1991. Figures for 2001 are not yet available.

Hindus constitute a majority in the country but there are states like Jammu & Kashmir where they are in minority. Islam predominates in Kashmir valley, Malappuram district of Kerala, Murshidabad distrct of West Bengal and the union territory of Lakshadweep. Christians form majority in Northeastern states of Meghalaya, Nagaland, Mizoram and several districts of Manipur. Sikhs form a majority in Punjab and Budhists in Ladakh region of Jammu and Kashmir.

Occupational Structure

Occupational pattern of a society has its own impact on the health scenario. People engaged in agriculture are more exposed to the vagaries of nature including natural calamities than those engaged in secondary and tertiary activities (Table 8.6). The income of the agriculturists is low as compared to the workers engaged in other sectors. This too has its influence on health through nutrition intake differentials and expenditure on health. Accessibility to health services in rural areas, where agriculturists live. is relatively poor. Floods and droughts affect the agriculturists more than any other occupational group. The natural calamities not only impact nutritional intake of the people, but also cause deaths and loss of property. There are occupation specific health hazards, particularly in the industrial sector. The Bhopal gas tragedy is still fresh in our minds. Workers engaged in mining develop diseases related to the respiratory system including lung TB. Mine blasts cause many injuries and deaths. Pollution of water and air caused by industries is also responsible for many diseases.

Table 8.6: Occupational Structure of India (Main Workers)

Activities/Sectors	*1991*			
	Number (millions)	*Per cent*	*Number (millions)*	
Primary Sector				
I. Cultivators	148.96	38.72	127.60	31.70
II. Agricultural laborers	99.72	26.09	107.50	26.70
III. Livestock, forestry, fishing, plantation and allied activities	7.30	1.90		
IV. Mining & quarrying	2.34	0.62		
Secondary Sector				
V. Manufacturing, (processing, Servicing), etc.	39.00	10.14		
VI. Construction	(9.16)	(2.38)		
	7.50	1.95		
Tertiary Sector				
VII. Trade & Commerce	28.70	7.46		
VIII. Transport, storage and Communication	10.81	2.81		
IX. Other services	39.70	10.32		
Total Main Workers	384.70	100.00	402.50	100.00

Source: Census of India, 1991 and 2001

According to the 1991 census, the working population of India was 316 million. Of these, 192 million (37.50 per cent) workers were engaged in agriculture and allied activities. The number of workers increased to 375 million by the year 2001. Two-third (62.50 per cent) of the people being non-workers, the dependency ratio is very high. Among the agricultural workers a great majority of them are marginal farmers or landless labourers. High dependency ratio and a large share of workers engaged in agricultural pursuits is indicative of underdevelopment and wide spread poverty in the country.

With rapid growth of population and the demise of the mass employing classical industries like textiles, sugar, steel, etc. the occupational structure of India has started changing. During the decade 1981-91, working population engaged in agriculture and allied activities increased by 40 per cent; that engaged in manufacturing by 67 per cent, and in construction, trade, commerce, transportation, communication and storage by 177 per cent. Agriculture continues to be the most important employer, its declining share in the GDP notwithstanding. These trends have by and large continued during the decade 1991-2001.

Rural-Urban Composition

Level of urbanisation is usually taken as an indicator of economic development. Health planners and social scientists interested in health issues relate cities with better and villages with poor health and health services. It happens because health facilities tend to get concentrated in urban places, particularly the large cities. Villages are spatially scattered and their income base is also low. With poor means of transportation and communication, the threshold population for healthcare facilities rarely reaches the optimum in rural areas. Investment in health services, therefore, goes to urban centres.

Within the urbanized areas, better health facilities exist at the district and state head quarters and metropolitan cities. Cities also offer better quality of water supply, sanitation and housing. Due to higher level of literacy, people have higher level of health awareness. In view of these factors, an urban resident is better equipped to face health hazards. The picture, however, is not that rosy. A large chunk of urban population in countries like India lives in much worse environmental conditions than rural population does. The outbreak of water borne diseases like cholera, hepatitis and gastroenteritis is, therefore, common in cities of many developing countries. Further, the urbanites live under more stressful and polluted environment than the rural inhabitants do. Sedentary lifestyle is another great drawback giving rise to a number of degenerative diseases.

Nearly one third of India's population lives in towns and cities, which number more than 5167. In 1991, the share of urban population in the total population of India (844 million) was 27 per cent. The 2001 census showed further increase in urban population. The share of urban population to the total (1027 million) was 27.80 per cent, which in absolute terms amounted to 285 million people, which is more than the total population of all other countries of the world except China and the USA.

The urban population of India is not uniformly distributed across states and size of cities. Leaving aside the city—states like Delhi and Chandigarh and various mini states like Mizoram and Goa, Tamil Nadu is the most urbanized and Bihar the least urbanized state of India. (Table 8.7). Practically, two thirds of urban population resides in Class I cites having 100,000 or more people. And almost half the population of these cities lives in 35 metropolitan cities with more than 1000,000 population each.

Table 8.7: State Wise Distribution of Urban Population in India (in per cent in 2001)

S.No.	*Major States*	*Per Cent*
1.	Tamil Nadu	43.86
2.	Maharashtra	42.40
3.	Gujarat	37.36
4.	Karnataka	33.98
5.	Punjab	33.95
6.	Haryana	29.00
7.	Andhra Pradesh	27.08
8.	Madhya Pradesh	26.67
9.	Kerala	25.97
10.	Uttaranchal	25.57
11.	Jammu & Kashmir	24.88
12.	Rajasthan	23.38
13.	Jharkhand	22.25
14.	Chhattisgarh	20.08
15.	Uttar Pradesh	20.78
16.	West Bengal	20.03
17.	Orissa	14.97
18.	Assam	12.72
19.	Bihar	10.47
20.	Himachal Pradesh	9.79
	India	27.78

Concentration of urban population in large cities is posing serious threat to urban environment. Growth of urban services and infrastructure is lagging behind the growth of population. Shortage of housing, drinking water, transportation, electricity, open space and what not, has made cities unlivable for at least half the urban population. Several attempts have been made to decongest large cities and to clear the urban slums, but nothing tangible has so far emerged. For rural migrants, city is the last refuge. Priority is not to live well but to somehow exist and use urban services as a means of survival in an otherwise very hostile environment. The solution lies in developing small towns and villages. Approaching the problem from the urban front would offer only palliatives. The problem has to be tackled at the source. And the source is rural underdevelopment.

The urban-rural composition of population is not uniform; level of urbanization in states like Punjab, Maharashtra, Gujarat, Tamil Nadu, and Karnataka is above the national average while states like Bihar, UP, MP and Orissa are far below the national average. In general, the states with higher level of urbanization are also high in health infrastructure and human development. The only exception to this rule is the state of Kerala that is not so highly urbanized but it stands very high in human development. It may be partly because of the fact that the density of population in this state is so high and availability of health and education services so ubiquitous that distinction between village and town has practically disappeared. It is not uncommon to find villages with over 20,000 population. The rural-urban divide that is so glaring in other states of India is practically absent in Kerala. It has thus become a rurbanized state. It is neither rural nor urban. It has a balanced settlement system (Figures 8.5 and 8.6).

LEVEL OF WELL-BEING

Well-being has two components: objective and subjective. Objective components are those, which can be standardized and measured. The valuation procedures are based on the criteria, which do not vary from person to person or group to group. Subjective components are those whose values vary from person to person or group to group, depending on the values of the individuals and groups. The first measurement gives indices like standard of living, while the second one gives measures like quality of life.

Standard of Living

In essence, it means the income we receive and the bundle of goods and services we consume. It includes level of education, employment status, food, clothing, housing, entertainment and other creature comforts. According to the WHO, "income and occupation, standards of housing, sanitation and nutrition, level of the provision of health, educational, recreational and other services may all be used individually as measures of socio-economic status, and collectively as an index of the standard of living."

Level of living is almost the same as standard of living except that it includes just nine items in its measurement. These are: health, food consumption, education, occupation and working conditions, housing, clothing, social security, recreation and leisure, and human rights. All the nine are objective criteria to be measured quantitatively. Both the concepts (standard of living and level of living) are, however, used loosely. Per capita income is often taken as proxy for standard of living.

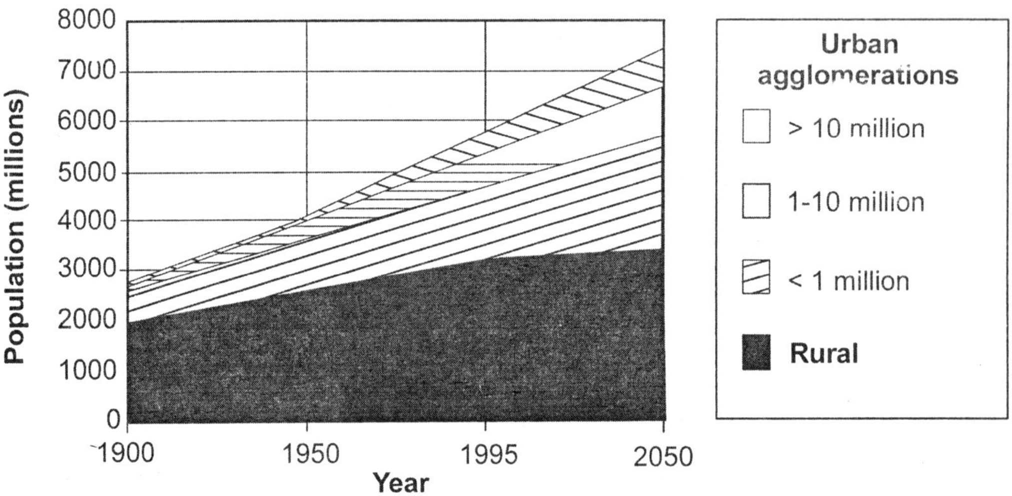

Fig. 8.6: World: Rural-Urban Composition of Populations
Source: Census of India, 2001.

Until very recently the only measure of well-being was standard of living, which in essence meant per capita income. There were several flaws in this approach. First, per capita income gives only an average that hides lot of realities with respect to the weaker sections of the society. Second, it does not reflect the purchasing power of the income holder, much depends on the ruling prices. Third, it does not take into account the services that are given at subsidized price or free as elementary education, primary health-care, etc. And fourth, it is an objective measure; it does not reflect the subjective value a person attaches to the goods and services he gets. Hence, social scientists have been in search of a better and more representative measure of human well-being. The concept of quality of life answers part, if not the whole, of the question.

Quality of Life

Quality of life signifies real level of living of people. According to the WHO, it means the "condition of life resulting from the combination of the effects of the complete range of factors such as those determining health, happiness (including those in the comfort in the physical environment and a satisfying occupation), education, social and intellectual attainments, freedom of action, justice and freedom of expression." According to Nagpal and Sell, it is a "composite measure of physical, mental and social well-being, as perceived by each individual, or by groups of individuals –that is to say, happiness, satisfaction and gratification, as it is experienced in such life concerns as health, marriage, family, work, financial situation, educational opportunities, self-esteem, creativity, belongingness and trust in others,"

In view of the fact that quality of life is difficult to measure, social scientists have scaled it down to measurable components and called it physical quality of life (PQL). It takes into account just three variables as surrogates of all other variables. These are:

1. infant mortality;
2. life expectancy at age one; and
3. literacy.

For each of the three components, the performance of the individual countries is graded on a scale of 0 (worst) to 100 (best). Averaging the three indices, gives a composite index. The resulting PQLI is also scaled from 0 to 100. It is clear that PQLI does not take into account per capita income.

Human Development Index

Unlike the quality of life index, the human development index is a mixed index of qualitative and quantitative aspects of life. Life expectancy at birth and knowledge level (as exhibited by adult literacy rate and mean years of schooling) cover the qualitative aspects, while income (real GDP per capita in purchasing power – PPP dollars) takes care of the quantitative aspects. Income can purchase a bundle of goods and services but it can not purchase life expectancy and knowledge except indirectly and in the long run.

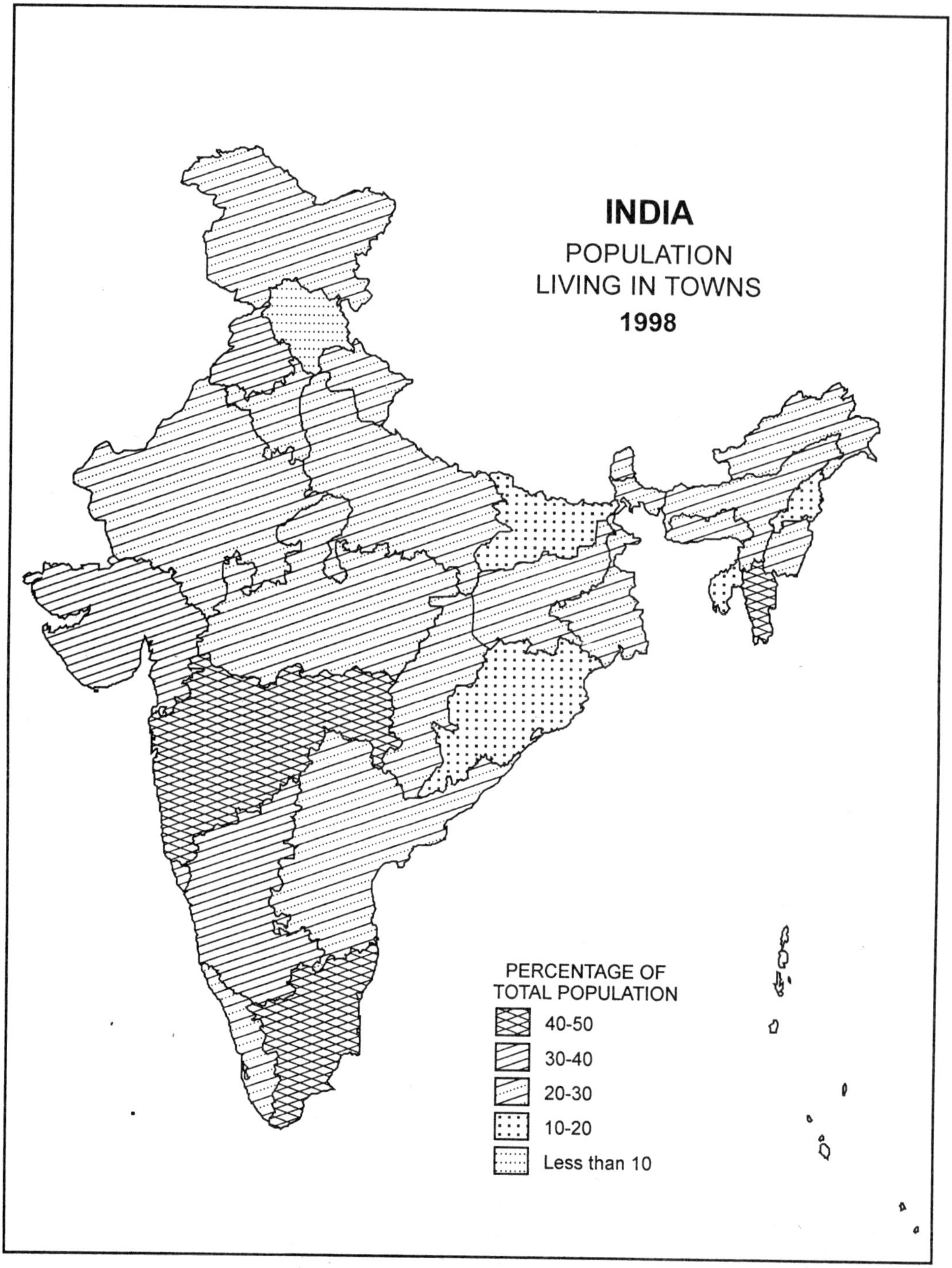

Fig. 8.7: India: Level of Urbanization (2001)

It would be useful at this stage to dwell on how the Human Development Index is worked out. Let us take any one of the three indices. We first find out, let us say, life expectancy at birth in India. It was 64 years in 2001. Deduct from it 25 which is the minimum prescribed for life expectancy. And then divide it by the maximum value prescribed for it, (in this case 85) minus the minimum value (in this case 25).

$$\frac{(\text{Actual Value}) - (\text{Minimum Value})}{(\text{Maximum Value}) - (\text{Minimum Value})} = \text{index}$$

For example:

$$\text{Life Expectancy Index} = \frac{(64-25)}{(85-25)} = \frac{39}{60} = 0.65$$

The same method is used to get literacy index also. It should be kept in view that knowledge component has two dimensions: literacy and combined gross enrolment. For both the components, the maximum and minimum prescribed are 100 and 0, while putting the two components together, the literacy component should be given a weight of 2, while the gross enrolment component a weight of 1 only.

Let us illustrate it:

India's literacy rate in 1999 was 55; so the literacy index would be

$$\frac{55-0}{100-0} = \frac{55}{100} = 5.55$$

For combined gross enrolment also we calculate the index the same way. In 1999 combined gross enrolment was also 55. So the index we arrive at would be:

$$\frac{55-0}{100-0} = \frac{55}{100} = 0.55$$

The two should be combined using the following formula:

$$\frac{[2\,(\text{literacy index}) + 1(\text{gross enrolment index})]}{3} = \frac{2(5.50)+1(0.55)}{3} = 0.54$$

For per capita income, the maximum is \$40,000 and the minimum is \$100. In 1999, India's per capita (PPP \$) income was \$1670. So the index for income will be:

$$\frac{\log(1670) - \log(100)}{\log(40{,}000) - \log(100)} = 0.47$$

$$\text{HDI} = 0.65 + 0.54 + 0.47 = 0.55$$

Note: Figures for the three indices should be for the same year.

In the year 2001, life expectancy at birth was 64 years; it was 32 years in 1951; literacy rate stood at 64, it was 18.30 in 1951; the per capita income increased from Rs. 1127 in 1950-51 to Rs. 11,014 in 2002-03 AD. The change is significant indeed but when we compare with that of the developed countries of the world, it was not so great. India is far behind even its Asian neighbours. For example, life expectancy at birth in China, Thailand, Malaysia and South Korea exceeds 70 years. And adult literacy rate is over 90 in Korea, Malaysia, Philippines and Thailand and between 80 and 90 in China, Indonesia and Philippines.

Education is the most important change agent. Let us, therefore, discuss literacy in India in some details. As stated earlier, about 65 per cent of the people of India are literate but there are vast differences among the states and sexes. Most of the densely populated states of the Ganga valley are pretty low in literacy both average and sex wise.

Even if literacy level of India goes up to 70 per cent by 2010, the problem of low percentage of female literacy will continue. This calls for a major effort to promote girl's education. Our past experience shows that adult literacy programmes do not produce expected results. Instead we should pool all our resources to expand and enrich elementary education. If all the children start going to school, illiteracy will disappear within the next two decades. This suggestion acquires greater meaning, if we look at the literacy figures from another perspective.

Education influences the health status of the people that in turn influences their earning capacities. An illiterate person neither understands the causes of diseases, nor he knows the nutritional requirements of the body. Knowledge of the health facilities is also poor. That is why, the countries, which are high on literacy, are also the countries that are high on longevity of life and low on child and maternal mortality. With so many illiterate mothers, it is not possible to bring up children well. No wonder then, child mortality in India is high and so is the expectancy of life.

According to the 2001 Human Development Report of the UNDP, India stood 127th among the nations of the world in HDI. This is not a very commendable status particularly in the context of improving economic potentials of India.

REFERENCES

1. Registrar General of India: Census of India, 1991 and 2001.
2. Nagpal, R. and H. Sell, *Subjective Well-being, Regional Health Papers*, No. 7, WHO, New Delhi, 1985.
3. WHO, *Promoting Health in the Human Environment*, Geneva, 1975.
4. Government of India, Economic Survey, 1998-99 and 2000-2001.

9

India: Selected Vital Facts

After examining the demographic structure of India, we now propose to discuss the fertility, birth and death rates, infant and child mortality, maternal mortality, expectancy of life at birth and sex ratios through time as well as space. Vital statistics denote the health status of people better than any other data. They constitute the most important bases on which health planning is done. The concept of human development is based on three indicators i.e. infant mortality rate, longevity of life at birth and literacy. Two of these pertain to vital facts. While discussing the vital data, special attention has been given to women and children because the health scenario of the future depends on their well-being.

A few demographic terms often used by us connote specific meanings. Let us understand them before we proceed further.

Crude Birth Rate $= \dfrac{\text{Number of live births during the year}}{\text{Estimated mid-year population}} \times 1000$

Crude Death Rate $= \dfrac{\text{Numbe of total deaths during the year}}{\text{Estimated mid-year population}} \times 1000$

General Fertility Rate $= \dfrac{\text{Numbe of live births in an area during the year}}{\text{Mid-year female population in the child bearing age-group in the same area and year}} \times 1000$

Age Specific Fertility Rate = Number of live births in a year to 1000 married women in any specified age-group

Pregnancy Rate = Number of pregnancies in a year to married women in the reproductive age-group

Abortion Rate = Number of abortions per 1000 women of child bearing Age

Crude Marriage Rate = $\frac{\text{Number of marriages within a year}}{\text{Mid-year population}} \times 1000$

Gross Reproduction Rate = Average number of girls that will be born to a woman through out the reproductive span, if she experiences current fertility pattern and there is no mortality

Net Reproduction Rate = Number of daughters a newborn girl will bear during her life time assuming fixed age-specific fertility and mortality rates.

BIRTH RATES

Leaving aside migration from outside, the growth of population is determined by the birth and death rates. India for over a thousand years or so witnessed a very high birth and death rates as a result of which the population of the country was stationary or grew very slowly depending upon the frequency and intensity of natural calamities and epidemic diseases. The years that were marked by negative growth of population were not rare. For example, the census of 1911 showed up a negative growth during the decade 1901-11. The plague epidemic and droughts appear to have taken a heavy toll of life. In fact, by the end of the nineteenth century the birth rate was very much stabilized at a very high level; it was the death rate, which fluctuated and thus determined the growth of population.

On becoming independent, the first task that the country took up was to stop people dying of preventable diseases and thus to reduce the death rate expeditiously. At the same time it launched the world's first official family planning programme to bring down the birth rate too to offset impacts of reduced death rates on the growth of population. The health services, that were earlier limited to urban areas, were extended to rural parts of the country. Technological advances in healthcare and increasing awareness of the people about these services brought the crude death rates (CDR) drastically down from 25.10 in 1951 to 8.90 in 1996. But the crude birth rate (CBR) did not follow the pattern set by CDR; it declined from 40.8 in 1951 to only 27.40 by 1996. As a result the annual exponential growth rate of population remained above 2 per cent during the last few decades. Some welcome signs on the birth front emerged during the 1990s so that the annual growth of population appears to have come down from 2.14 during 1981-91 to 1.90 per cent or less during 1991-96, but it was not substantial enough to give needed relief.

Our population problem emanates not only from a high growth rate but also and perhaps more importantly from a huge base so that even a modest growth adds more people per annum than the total population of a huge country like Australia. We cannot change the base, but we can certainly reduce its accelerated expansion by drastically cutting the CBR to the level of the CDR. Our crude death rate has practically reached the level of the developed parts of the world but we stand far behind in CBR. It has to be halved (about 15 per cent) to stabilize the population. While the death rates may further come down to 7-8 per cent by 2011, we do not see a fast track CBR reduction before that year. That should worry us because in the absence of population stabilization our investment in national development including that in health and education will stand neutralized. We may be better off on the mortality front, but that would not necessarily mean improvement in health: lower mortality does not ensure lower morbidity. The urgent need to bring down the high CBR, therefore, needs no further emphasis.

The national picture of the CDR (8.9 in 1996) more or less prevails all over the country. Only a few states cross the figure 10 per thousand (Bihar, 10.20; M.P. 11.10; Orissa, 10.70 and U.P. 10.20), and even this difference may disappear in the next one decade or so. With the virtual elimination of the classical epidemics and increasing tendency of the people to make use of modern health facilities, both public and private, death rates are sure to come down further all over the country, particularly because the infant mortality rate (IMR) which is still very high (72 per thousand) in India is declining fast. As the IMR declines, the CBR would also come down.

Interstate differences in the CBR are, however, still great. As against the national average of 27.40, three major states containing almost one third of the total population of the country cross 30 (Bihar 32.10, M.P., 32.40, U.P. 34.00). Even within the states, there are substantial differences among the districts. For example, Kerala, which had almost reached the standards of the developed countries in CBR, CDR and IMR, has higher than the national IMR in Idduki district and CBR in Mallapuram district. U.P. that is the worst state in birth and death rates has lower than national IMR in Almora district and lower than national CBR in Kanpur Dehat district. It means that the country has passed that stage when all states and districts were allocated proportional share of resources. There is need for spatial concentration in lagging states and districts (Fig. 9.1).

Causes of High Birth Rates

Social scientists attribute many interrelated causes for high crude birth rates in India. Important among these are:

1. high rates of fertility;
2. high rates of infant mortality;
3. low couple protection rate;
4. low literacy rate particularly among the females;
5. high percentage of people below the poverty line; and
6. low level of urbanization.

High Fertility Rate

The number of children a woman in the reproductive age group of 13-49 produces in her entire reproductive period at the current rate of fertility is called total fertility rate (TFR). The TFR of the world stood at 5 in 1970; 3.3 in 1991 and at 3 in 2001. The TFR of India was 5.8 in 1970; it came down to 3.9 in 1990, and was 3.3 by 2001. The TFR of the developed countries of the world is lower than 2. In general, the TFR and CBR go together.

The TFR in India is declining, but the trend is not uniform all over the country. Kerala with the TFR of 1.7 has already reached the levels of the developed countries, but Uttar Pradesh, the most populous state of the country, hovers around 5. Several other states are above the

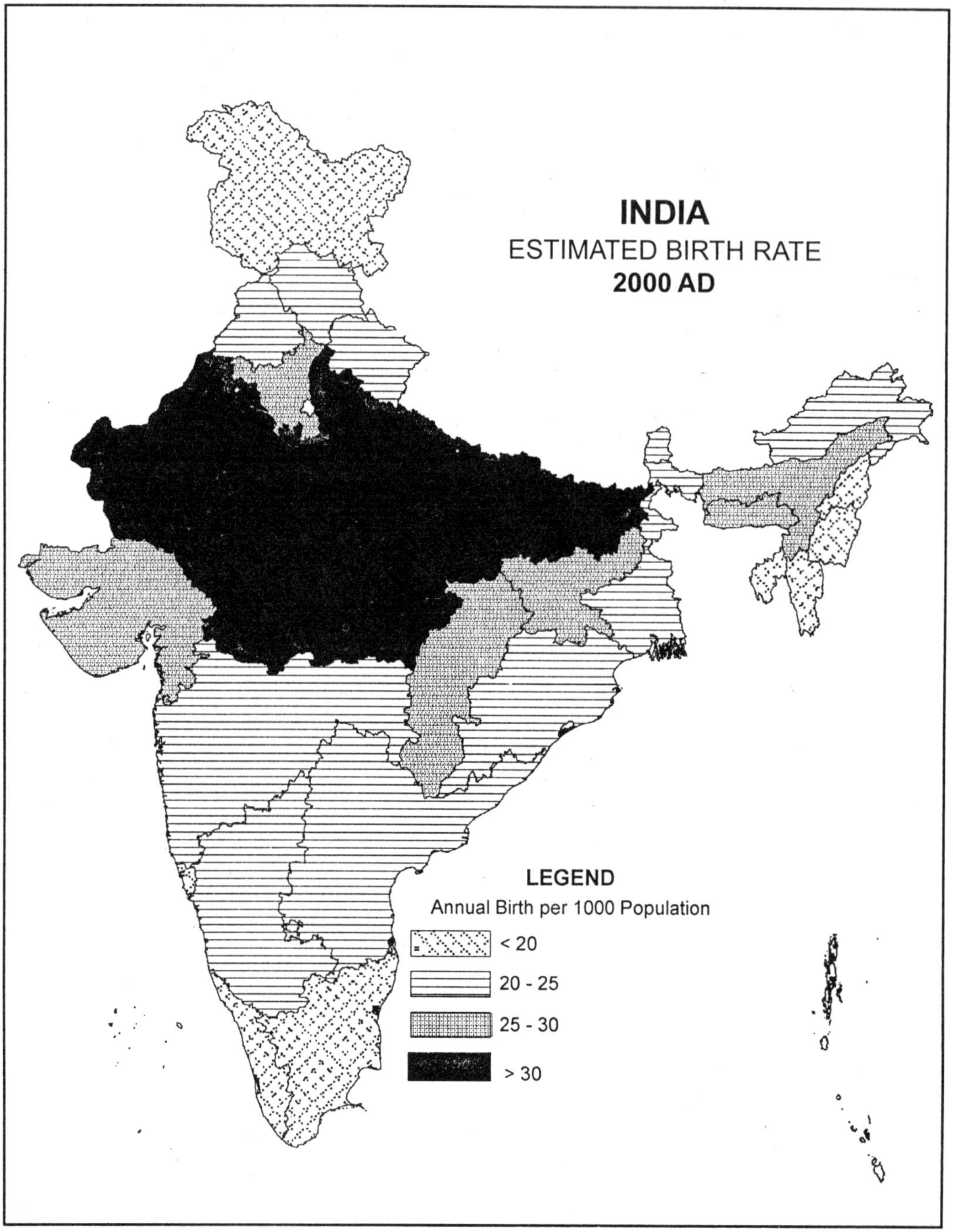

Fig. 9.1: India: Crude Birth Rate

national average. It is difficult to pin point the reasons for these variations. Perhaps, there is a very peculiar mix of reasons because the results differ even if the conditions remain the same. In general, early marriage is one of the important causes of high TFR in India. Most couples complete their family by the time they attain the age of 25. Unless family planning becomes a part and parcel of their life, there is no way of reducing the TFR.

High Infant Mortality Rate

Another reason behind high crude birth rate in India is the continuing high rate of mortality of children before they attain the age of one for the last several centuries. Infant Mortality Rate (IMR) means the number of infants dying within a year per 1000 babies born in that year. The IMR in India is still as high as 72. Although it is almost half of the one that prevailed in 1970 (137), it is too high as compared to the developed countries i.e. 8 per 1000 children born. If we add to it the death rate per 1000 children in the age group pf 1-4 years, the situation gets more alarming. Prevalence of high IMR in the country has given rise to a mindset that tends to offset high mortality by high fertility. With the introduction of a number of mother and child health programmes, the IMR has started sliding down but the mentality of a large section of Indian population has yet to undergo appreciable change in favour of small family. It is to be noted that more than one quarter of the infants have low birth weights.

One cannot get the real picture of infant mortality in India nor the potentials of its reduction in coming years unless the spatial differences in its rates are analyzed. The IMR is above 90 in the states of Orissa and Madhya Pradesh; between 80 and 90 in U.P. and Rajasthan; and between 72 and 80 in Assam and Bihar. Kerala has brought its IMR down to 13 indicating that given the right kind of policy, health infrastructure and popular participation, India can bring down its IMR rather fast in a decade or two.

Low Couple Protection Rate

High rate of fertility cannot be brought down without conscious attempt at family planning. IMR will go down further in the next decade or two to reach the level of the developed parts of the world. Early marriages are becoming less common. Other factors that promote high birth rate may also become less relevant as time passes. But unless family planning becomes a part of life of the people, birth rate cannot be brought down to a level that can stabilize the population. The percentage of couples fully covered by family planning is indicated by couple protection rate (CPR).

Between the two main methods of family planning, temporary contraception and sterilization, the former has not proved very effective in male dominated, only partially educated traditional societies. But it helps in spacing pregnancies and hence has its own importance. Sterilization is the real answer for quick results but here too there exists a growing imbalance between male and female sterilization. Females try to undergo sterilization through tubectomy only when more than two children are already born or when their health does not permit any further pregnancy. Men are reluctant to undergo sterilization through vasectomy because of a common belief that it leads to sexual impotency.

The CPR in India is improving but not at a desired pace. In 1951 it stood at 10.4; went up to 43.3 in 1994 of which only 30 constituted sterilization. In the next three years it inched up to 45.4 and stood at 50 in 2001. The birth rate declines fast once the CPR comes down to 60.

Low Literacy Rate

Literacy can be taken as a proxy for capacity to seek, know, comprehend and use information for one's own and society's benefit. It is true that given proper environment from early childhood, even an illiterate person can become cultured, knowledgeable and highly competent but in the world of modern science and technology such cases would be rare. Education is a must for all. Literacy is the cornerstone of educational structure including health education.

The 1991 census showed a very low literacy rate (39.3) in India. According to 2001 census, the percentage has gone up to 65.30. Even then when compared to the developed parts of the world, where literacy rate is invariably above 95, the country has to go a long way before it can take a relaxed view on this front. What is most disturbing, yet at the same time offering some hope, is the wide variation among the states of the Union in this regard. A state like Kerala with approximately 90 per cent literacy is not very far behind the developed parts of the world. On the other hand, the northern states like Bihar (47.53 per cent) fall behind even the underdeveloped countries of the world. The key to expansion of literacy in India, therefore, lies in the overpopulated states of the Ganga valley; it is here that our efforts and investments should be concentrated in years ahead. It is interesting to note that these are also the states that have registered highest growth of population in the country.

Poverty

Poverty is an important factor influencing birth rate. Children constitute an important resource of the poor. Moreover, the IMR being higher among the poor, the usual tendency to compensate higher mortality by still higher fertility comes into play. In India, at least one-third of the people are below the poverty line and two third of them live in conditions which are not very conducive to family planning. It is also clear from the fact that the states with very low per capita income are also the ones that are marked by high birth rate. Kerala appears to be the only exception but if we add to the per capita income the indirect contribution of almost free social services, and the influence of very high level of literacy, the exceptionality of the states gets very much tempered. Average Keralite may have low per capita income but his levels of life and living are high.

Low Level of Rural Development

Urban-rural differential in birth rate is a common demographic feature all over the world. The social and economic traits of urban societies are different from that of the rural societies. Rural is close to the nature; it is agriculture-based and informal; and is marked by close family and community ties; while urban is less natural; it is formal and non-agricultural; its family structure is unitary and living space limited. Urban sociology under certain conditions can penetrate rural areas too as is the case in Kerala which is far less urbanized. But the people of Kerala, even if living in rural settlements, possess many of those traits that the people living in cities possess. Hence, Kerala does not fall in the same category of least urbanized states of India in which Uttar Pradesh, Bihar, Rajashan, Orissa, etc. fall. The vice versa is also true. In states like Bihar even medium size cities still exhibit rural traits. Village life is transplanted in cities; a sizable number of people live in urban villages and slums; engaged in dairy farming, village crafts and manual labour, they belong to families which extend all the way to the villages they migrated from, may be a generation or two back. And they lead a semi-urban life: one-fourth urban and three-fourth rural combining the worst of both.

Pro-male Cultural Values

There is a general belief in India that sons alone can perform the last rites of the dead parents. This belief persists even today. As such many couples have multiple children in the hope of getting a son. It is quite common even among the highly educated persons to have 4 or 5 daughters waiting for the arrival of a son. Further, in a patriarchal society, only the male progenies inherit the parent's property. Naturally then, parents have preference for male children.

DEATH RATES

Mass scale deaths have been a common feature of Indian history. Epidemics, famines and wars have claims millions of life. Not much is known about the situation that prevailed in ancient times. The density of population being low and the resources plenty, scarcity of food must have been uncommon and the chances of communicable diseases spreading over large areas low. We do however get references of famines and epidemics even in ancient Sanskritic literature. The situation appears to have worsened during the last four centuries or so as population grew and density increased putting heavy pressure on the available resources. Disturbed civil life followed by the colonial rule damaged the basic foundations of Indian society and ruined the subsistence but sustainable economy of the people.

The British era was marked by several major disasters claiming millions of lives caused by famines and epidemic diseases. The 1918 influenza epidemic alone killed 12 million people. 1919 is often called the demographic divide in India. It is from that year onwards that the crude death rate (CDR), that was as high as 45, started declining. It was the first sign of India's entry in the first stage of demographic transition. By early 1930s, the death rate dropped to 35 or so. Thanks to the post-independence improvements in health services, the CDR continued to decline from 25.1 in 1951 to 9.8 in 1991and 8.9 in 1996 putting India in the last stage of demographic transition. The target is to reach the CDR of the developed countries or that of the state of Kerala i.e. 6 per thousand by 2010.

Mortality rates are not uniform all over India (Fig. 9.2). As given above, Kerala has already reached the level of the developed countries. But there are many states particularly those in the Ganga basin, which are way behind Kerala. The states of Orissa, Bihar, UP, Rajasthan and MP are at least two points above the national average. Kerala has the lowest mortality rate of 6.2, followed by Maharashtra (7.4), Punjab (7.5), Karnataka and Gujarat (7.6), West Bengal (7.8) and Tamil Nadu (7.9). Rural areas across the whole country showed higher (10.5) CDR than urban areas (6.8) in 1990. This applies to all age specific mortality rates. Mortality below the age of 35 is higher among the females than among the males. As the mortality of females in the reproductive age of 15-39 declines, the fertility rate would go up unless the CPR improves.

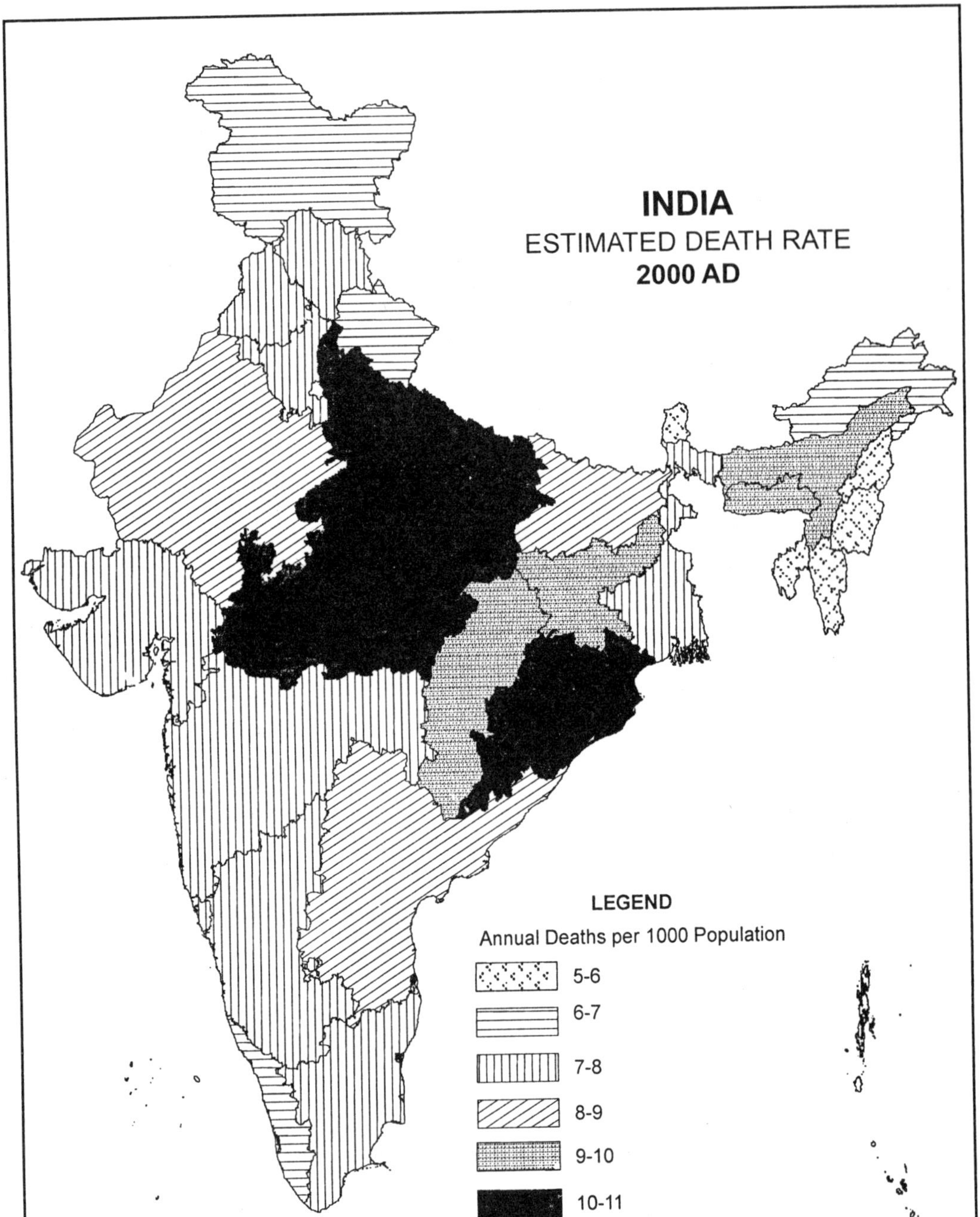

Fig. 9.2: India: Crude Death Rate

Age-specific Mortality

Children (less than 15 years of age) constitute 39 per cent of the total population but they account for two-third of total deaths in India. Half of the pediatric deaths accounting for one-third of the total mortality in the population occur during infancy (less than one year). Children in the age group 0-4 years form 13 per cent of the total population but they account for 50 per cent of all deaths in the country. This is the reason why the expectation of life at birth is so low in India. The mortality rate in this age group is 33. The death rates begin to rise again after the age of 55 and reach 94 per cent for the age group 70 and above. But there are rural-urban differences. Death rates are lower in urban areas as compared to rural areas in the age group of 55-70. Beyond the age of 70, the situation is just the other way round. The rural mortality rate in the age group 0-4 is double of the urban rate. Thereafter the differences tend to narrow down. The reasons for the above differences are essentially environmental and socio-economic. We will now examine the age-specific mortality in greater details.

Child Mortality

According to the WHO (1981), "more than the IMR, CMR reflects the main environmental factors affecting the health of a child such as nutrition, sanitation, the communicable diseases of the childhood and accidents occurring in and around home. It reflects even more than the IMR, the level of poverty and is consequently a sensitive indicator of socio-economic development in a community." The CMR in 1972 stood at 58; by 1982 it declined to 39; in 1993 it was 24. As in other cases, the rural areas show higher rates of CMR. In the mid-eighties, the rural and urban CMR were 41and 21.3 respectively. The sex-wise differences were also glaring. Female children invariably had higher mortality rate, often exceeding four per cent above the male children.

Inter-state differences in the CMR are quite significant. States like Bihar and UP are far above the southern states. CMR is higher where mothers are illiterate; child mortality declines as the level of education of mothers goes up.

Infant Mortality

Infant mortality rate (IMR) i.e. the number of infant deaths per thousand of births in a year is considered one of the most sensitive indicators not only of the health but also the socio-economic development of a society. In an uninformed traditional family with low or no formal education of mothers, tenuous sources of income and limited or no access to health services, the probability of giving safe birth and rearing the newly born in a manner that can ensure its survival is not high. The health of the child as well as of the mother is closely linked to the number of live births, stillbirths and abortions the mother undergoes during her fertility period.

IMR has been steadily declining in India for the last several decades. It was 204 in 1911; in 1996 it stood at 72. This should not however make us complacent. We are still worse than our neighbours like China and Sri Lanka. Until very recently investment in health was considered to be investment in consumption rather than production. The attitude has changed only recently and hence there exist several lacunae both in policy and management of health and family welfare services.

Infant deaths that take place before birth are called anti-natal; those taking place soon after birth are called perinatal; those within four weeks of the birth are called neo-natal, and those occurring between four weeks and 12 months of the birth are called post-natal. Based on the sample registration system, the Registrar General of India estimated the 1988 IMR to be 94 while the crude death rate was only 11. Of this, the peri-natal death rate was 49.6, neo-natal 56.8 and post-natal 37.7. If neo-natal death rates are reduced, the overall IMR will come down sharply. As the following rule of thumb expresses, the first few hours and days are most critical in the life of an Indian baby.

Half the deaths of the first day take place in the first hour;
Half the deaths of the first week take place on the first day;
Half the deaths of the first month take place in the first week; and
Half the deaths of the first year take place in the first month.

Seen regionally, the IMR is lower in southern states of Kerala, Tamil Nadu and Karnataka. Maharashtra in the west is also better off. Increase in female literacy, medical attendance at birth, and accessibility to primary healthcare and nutrition augmentation programmes for the mothers and children have helped in lowering the IMR. In this regard Kerala has reached the standards of the developed countries. The time-honoured tradition of personal hygiene and environmental sanitation in these states has also contributed to lowering of the IMR. Among the northwestern states, J&K, Punjab and Haryana also show low IMR. Rapid economic development appears to be the favorable factor. Neo-natal and post-natal mortality is highest in UP and lowest in Karnataka. In Himachal Pradesh and Tamil Nadu, post-natal death rates are higher than neo-natal death rates.

Rural areas in general record higher rates of IMR. But the poor in urban areas are not much better off. The urban IMR for the country as a whole is 61 but the city of Calcutta has 161, Delhi between 91 and 181, and Varanasi 127. These figures are higher than rural figures in many states. This shows that the rural-urban differences are not so relevant for the poor. No matter where they live, diarrhea, respiratory infections, pyrexia, asphyxia, pneumonia, septicemia, tetanus and anemia continue to take a heavy toll of their infants. In tribal zones some additional diseases inflict the babies. These are pherosis, sickling, red cell, bigot spots, bleeding and spongy gums.

No matter how good the medical and other facilities are, some of the babies born are sure to die in their infancy. The exact causes are not so clear. According to Chandrasekhar, "there are at least six biological factors connected with infant mortality. These are the general mortality and fertility rates, the mother's age, the birth order, spacing of births, lack of care of the mother during neo-natal and post-natal periods." Added to and in certain cases consequential upon the above, there are physiological complications arising from heredity and protein-energy malnutrition.

Maternal Mortality

Maternal mortality is also very high in India. The reasons are many. Important among them are:

1. pregnancy at a premature age,
2. poor health of the mother,
3. frequent pregnancies, and
4. home delivery unattended by trained dais or nurses.

The ratio of female/male mortality is still more than 1. In rural areas it is 1.02 and goes up to 1.45 in the reproductive age group of 15-29. Maternal mortality, according the WHO, has two aspects: one, direct obstetric deaths resulting from complications of the pregnant state-pregnancy, labour and puerperium and from interventions, omissions, incorrect treatment etc. and two, indirect obstetric deaths resulting from pre-existing or during pregnancy diseases aggravated by physiologic effects of pregnancy.

Almost two-third of the total deliveries in the country are still attended by only untrained *dais* who do not know even the basics of pregnancy or even hygiene; one-fifth of them are attended by trained dais; and the remaining one-fifth are institutional. Approximately 1.50 per cent of deliveries are complicated requiring the help of trained medical personnel. Among the major causes of maternal deaths in rural India as in 1989 are:

1. Bleeding during pregnancy including puerperal sepsis (23.8 per cent);
2. Anaemia (20.3 per cent);
3. Abortion (10.9 per cent);
4. Toxaemia (7.9 per cent);
5. Malposition of child (10.9 per cent); and
6. Not classifiable (20.3 per cent).

Shifts in Causes of Death

Typically, mortality patterns distinguish three major successive stages of epidemiological transition: one, age of pestilence and famine; two, age of epidemic diseases; and three, age of degenerative and culture-induced diseases. In the present context of very fast scientific and technological changes having bearings on health, the stages are not so sharply set aside from each other. India is passing through a very peculiar phase of epidemiological transition. While a sizable section of India's population is still in the grips of a variety of communicable and intestinal diseases, the number of those who are no longer afflicted by these diseases but are gripped by diseases attributed to senility and modernization syndrome is also fast increasing.

In 1979, the degenerative diseases such as the diseases of the circulatory system accounted for about 16 per cent of all deaths and were responsible for about one-third of total deaths in the age group of 45 and above. By 1997, the figure went up to 29 per cent. The developed and the developing countries are, however, still poles apart. Within the country, there exists vast difference among the states, between urban and rural areas and among the sexes. The changing pattern of mortality needs to be examined in different geographic situations and across various age, sex and socio-economic groups whereby pandemics of infections are gradually displaced by degenerative and man-made diseases.

During the epidemiological transition, the most profound change in health and disease pattern in the developing countries takes place among children and young women. Unlike the classical model, mortality decline has been substantially influenced by medical technology and organized maternal and child health drives. The transition is rapid in the urban sector of the population due to the clustering of medical and health facilities in cities, greater access to income and greater acceptance of small family norm.

Table 9.1: Main Causes of Death in Developed and Developing Countries

Diseases	*Developed Countries*		*Developing Countries*	
	1985	*1997*	*1985*	*1997*
Infectious and parasitic	5	1	45	43
Perinatal and maternal	21	21	10	9
Cancer	51	46	6	9
Circulatory system	4	8	16	24
Respiratory system	18	23	6	5
Others	5	1	17	9

Source: Survey of Causes of Death (Rural), 1997.

LIFE EXPECTANCY AT BIRTH

Life expectancy at birth is a good index and a comprehensive measure of the level of health of a population. It incorporates the mortality experience at all ages of life and estimates the probability of survivors. Life expectancy at birth in India is 60+ years. In 1901, it stood at 23.6 years; between 1911-20 period at 20 years and in 1951 at 36.7 years. We have definitely made a great progress but when compared to the developed countries of the world, we are far behind.

The increase in the expectation of life is not uniform all over the country. Again, the southern states of the country (Kerala, Tamil Nadu and Karnataka) together with Maharashtra and Punjab are far ahead of the northern states like Bihar, UP, MP and Assam. In this regard, the country can be divided into two macro regions. The western half has above the national average expectation of life while the eastern half has below average. A baby born in Kerala in 2000 AD is likely to live for 68 years but the one born in Assam may not live for more than 60 years (Fig. 9.3). Expectation of life of females is slightly higher than that of males all over the country, the unfavourable circumstances in which they are brought up and live notwithstanding. Apparently then, as the biases against them lessen, in years to come their life expectancy vis-a-vis their male counterparts will further improve.

Improvement in the longevity of life has significant implications for the society. In years to come the number of people above the age of 60 will increase. These people would be living on savings of their working life; they would require specialized hospitals, nursing homes and old age homes. With nuclear family becoming the norm, these people would be increasingly less dependent on their children for support and care in old age. As they advance in age, health will deteriorate and many of them may have to spend years in nursing homes and hospitals. Provisions will have to be made for them in any health plan of the future.

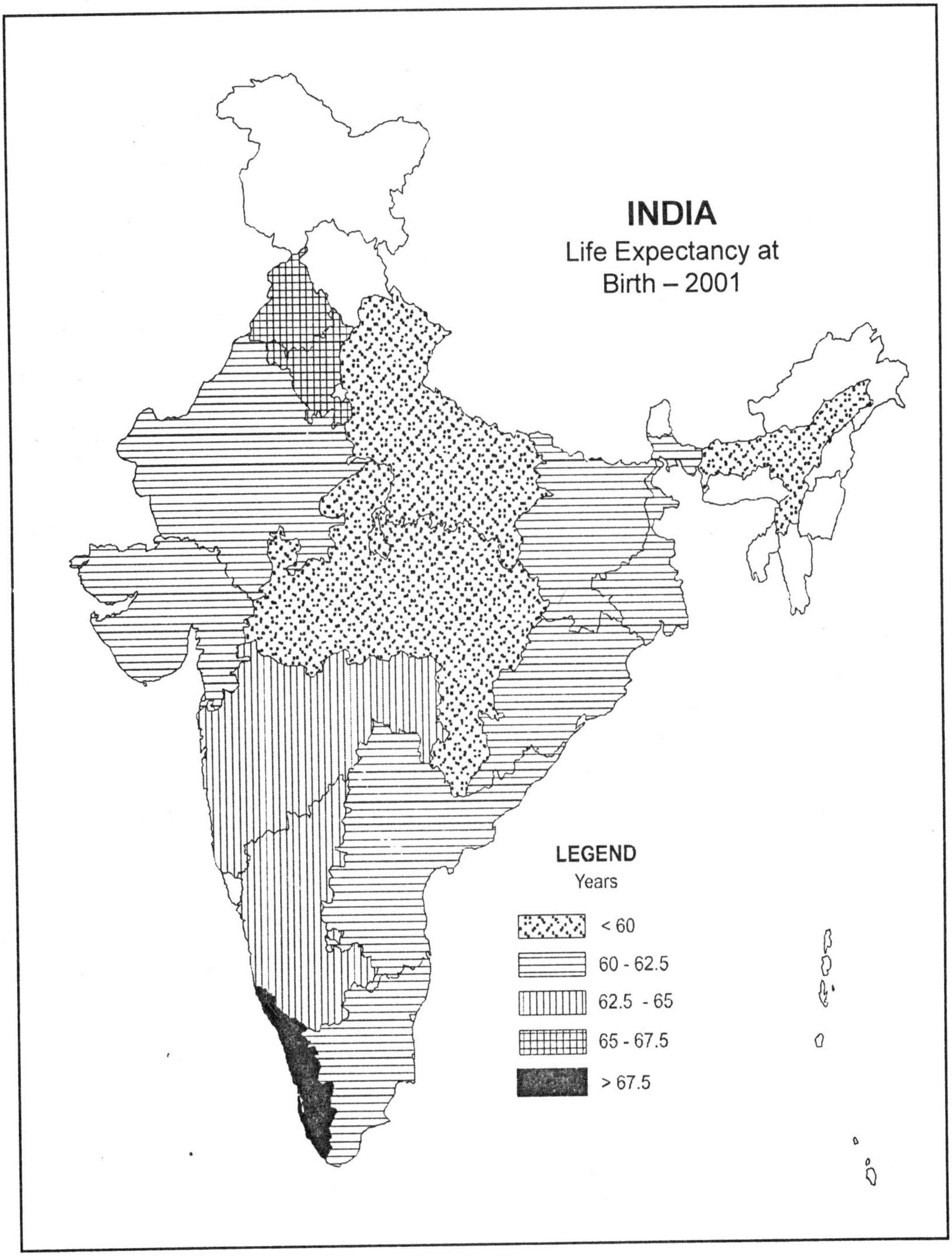

Fig 9.3: India: Life Expectancy at Birth – 2001.

In this connection the changing mood of the society with respect to the care of the aged has also its bearings on health planning for the senior citizens. So long as the joint family was a norm, age had its own advantages. The senior most member of the family was considered to be the head of the family even if he was crippled. With nucleation of the family, the aged do not have the position they occupied earlier. With increasing mobility of the youth, the aged cannot move with them for it involves cutting themselves off from their roots. They are often left uncared. The civil society has therefore to fill the gap and make institutional arrangements to take care of the aged.

SAMPLE SURVEY OF CAUSES OF DEATH (RURAL)

In order to get more reliable information about causes of death, the Registrar General of India has started an annual survey initially covering only rural areas. The survey results are published even after three years, they do provide good information on who dies, where and why?

The deaths caused by ten major killer diseases as revealed by the 1996 and 1997 surveys are given in Table 9.2. These are moving average figures for two years. The reader should take these figures with caution; they are good only in the sense that there is nothing better. They suffer from a number of limitations. They pertain to only rural areas; they are largely based on what people perceive as the cause of death; and the survey procedures are still being improved.

The idea of the annual survey of causes of deaths emerged from the recommendations of the Conference on Improvement of Vital Statistics held in 1961. It was called Model Registration Scheme (MRS). The third Conference of the Chief Registrars of Births and Deaths in the year 1980 suggested improvement in the scheme and recommended that the survey of causes of deaths (SCD) should cover two primary health centres per million rural population. The Technical Advisory Committee on Vital Statistics and Survey (1990-91) recommended that four PHCs per million rural population based on 1991 census be covered by the survey.

The procedure followed is something like this. A sub-centre of a PHC located at a distance of 3-6 km and having a population of about 5000 is selected. All the births and deaths related to the usual residents of the villages under the sub-centre, irrespective of the place of occurrence, are covered by the survey. Since 1994, the concept of population at risk was introduced to study the causes of death by age and sex also. "*The primary object of the survey is to build up statistics on 'Most Probable Causes of Death' for the rural India, states and union territories, using Lay Diagnostic Reporting (Post-death Verbal Autopsy) method through post-death enquiry based on symptoms, conditions, duration and anatomical site of the disease as reported by family members of the diseased" (HII, p. 2).*

The 1997 survey covered 2059 PHCs covering over 45 million people. Total number of deaths reported was 44,409; selected number of sample units was 1909 (it was 1305 in 1988. Number of deaths per PHC covered by the survey in 1997 was 23. The survey results are classified according to International Classification of Diseases (ICD).

The top ten killer diseases as revealed by the 1996 and 1997 survey are given in Table 9.2.

Table 9.2: Top Ten Killer Diseases: 1996-97

Rank	*ICD Code*	*Specific Causes of Death*	*Per cent*
1.	J 20 & 45	Bronchitis & Asthma	14.40
2.	I 21-25	Heart Attack	10.05
3.	A 15	TB of Lung	6.40
4.	G 80-83	Paralysis of Cerebral Apoplexy	5.25
5.	P 07	Prematurity	5.05
6.	C oo-97	Cancer	4.95
7.	J 18	Pneumonia	4.60
8.	D 50-64	Anaemia	4.00
9.	X 60-84	Intentional Self-harm (suicide)	2.95
10.	V 01-99	Vehicular Accidents	2.65

Source: Registrar General of India, Survey of Causes of Death (Rural), 1997

Age-specific Killers

Premature birth is naturally confined to infants and hence they claim all the deaths in this category. Pneumonia afflicts children most; more than 80 per cent of lives claimed by pneumonia pertain to children in the age group 0-4 years. Over 75 per cent of deaths due to bronchitis and asthma, and paralysis occur in the age group 60+ years. Other major killers of the aged are heart attack, cancer and anaemia. Suicide and accidents claim 40-50 per cent of deaths in the age group 15-44.

Infant mortality is an index of the quality of public health. It reflects the socio-economic and environmental conditions in which people live and the quality of health services they have access to. When the baby is born, it is no longer protected by the special environmental condition in which it had grown in mother's womb. If the difference between the environment of the womb and the new world it has entered is too contrasting, the baby's survival is jeopardized. That is the reason why infant mortality rates in the developing countries are so high.

Major causes of deaths vary according to sex too. Leaving aside the deaths caused due to contact with venomous animal contact (18 per cent of all deaths in the reproductive age group of women) the top ten killers of this group are:

- Suicide: 11.10 per cent,
- T.B. of Lung: 9.40 per cent,
- Cancer: 6.70 per cent,
- Heart Attack: 6.6 per cent,
- Burns: 6.50 per cent,
- Anaemia: 4.20 per cent,
- Vehicular Accidents: 3.30 per cent,
- Acute Abdomen: 3.10 per cent,
- Bronchitis and Asthma: 3.10 per cent, and
- Puerperium: 2.40 per cent.

The major killers of the reproductive age group are very unevenly distributed in India. The top ten killers of this age group claim 56.30 per cent of all deaths. The situation, however, varies from state to state. For example, in UP, these diseases claimed 70.60 per cent of all deaths in this age group in 1997. As against this, the percentage in Orissa was as low as 44. Bronchitis and asthma claimed 13.70 per cent of all deaths in the country in 1997. But in Maharashtra the percentage was as high as 24.50 and in Tamil Nadu as low as 7.00. Similarly, the second top killer (heart attack) accounted for 10.60 per cent of all deaths in the country. But in Punjab it was on the higher side (28.20 per cent), and in UP on the lower side (3.50 per cent). Similar was the case with T.B. of the lung. It claimed 6.20 per cent of all deaths in India but it was as high as 9.10 per cent in Gujarat and just 2.5 per cent in Kerala.

Paralysis was responsible for 5.40 per cent of al deaths in India; for Andhra Pradesh, the percentage was 9.60 and for UP, just 2.00. Cancer claimed 12.80 per cent of all deaths in Kerala; 2.70 per cent in Bihar and 5.20 per cent in India. Pneumonia claimed 11.10 per cent deaths in Bihar, just 0.50 per cent in Andhra Pradesh and 4.40 per cent in India as a whole. In case of anaemia, the percenage deviated from 8.60 for Bihar to 0.60 for Kerala; it was 3.80 for India.

REFERENCES

1. Registrar General of India, *Census of India, Provisional Tables*, 200.
2. ——, *Survey of Causes of Death*, 1997, 1998.
3. Government of India, Ministry of Health, *Health Information of India*, 1998 and 1999.
4. WHO, *World Health Report*, 1998 to 2002.
5. Statistical Abstracts of Various States of India, 2001.
6. World Bank, *World Deve' 'pment Report*, 1998 to 2002.

10

Major Diseases of the Past

The mankind has suffered from diseases since time immemorial. It is believed that the pathogens of most of the diseases have always been present in our environment. Their prevalence, ferocity and impact have, however, varied with the medical sciences, nutritional status of the people, public health delivery system and progress in attitude of the people towards health. Some diseases spread fast and take a heavy toll of life even today while others only weaken the body or mind of the afflicted making them unfit for normal routine of life, temporarily or forever. Diseases associated with high mortality attract greater attention of national governments as well as international agencies.

Diseases are classified in different ways. The ones that are transmitted through vectors like rodents, mosquitoes, water, air etc. are classified as communicable diseases. These diseases spread fast killing thousands of people. Fortunately, some of the major killers among them have disappeared; they have become the diseases of the past. The etiology and ecology of many of these diseases, although less known earlier, do, however, tell a great deal about their origin and the processes associated with their diffusion. Further, we must not forget that many of the diseases, which appeared to have been eradicated, are coming back. There is a real danger of the germs of some of them being used as biological weapon by misguided religious fundamentalists and criminals which are present in all societies.

The eradication of some of the major communicable diseases brought the death rates down rather significantly during the last few decades. But these rates are still very high in comparison to the developed parts of the world. It is partly because only some of the diseases have been eradicated and partly because new diseases earlier uncommon have now become common (Fig. 10.1 and 10.2).

India is in the midst of the epidemiological transition. It has eradicated many of the major killers but quite many of them still visit the people intermittently. The largest single cause of death until the 1920s was plague. One to two million people dying of plague in a single year was not rare. It was so wide spread that no part of the country remained untouched by it. Small

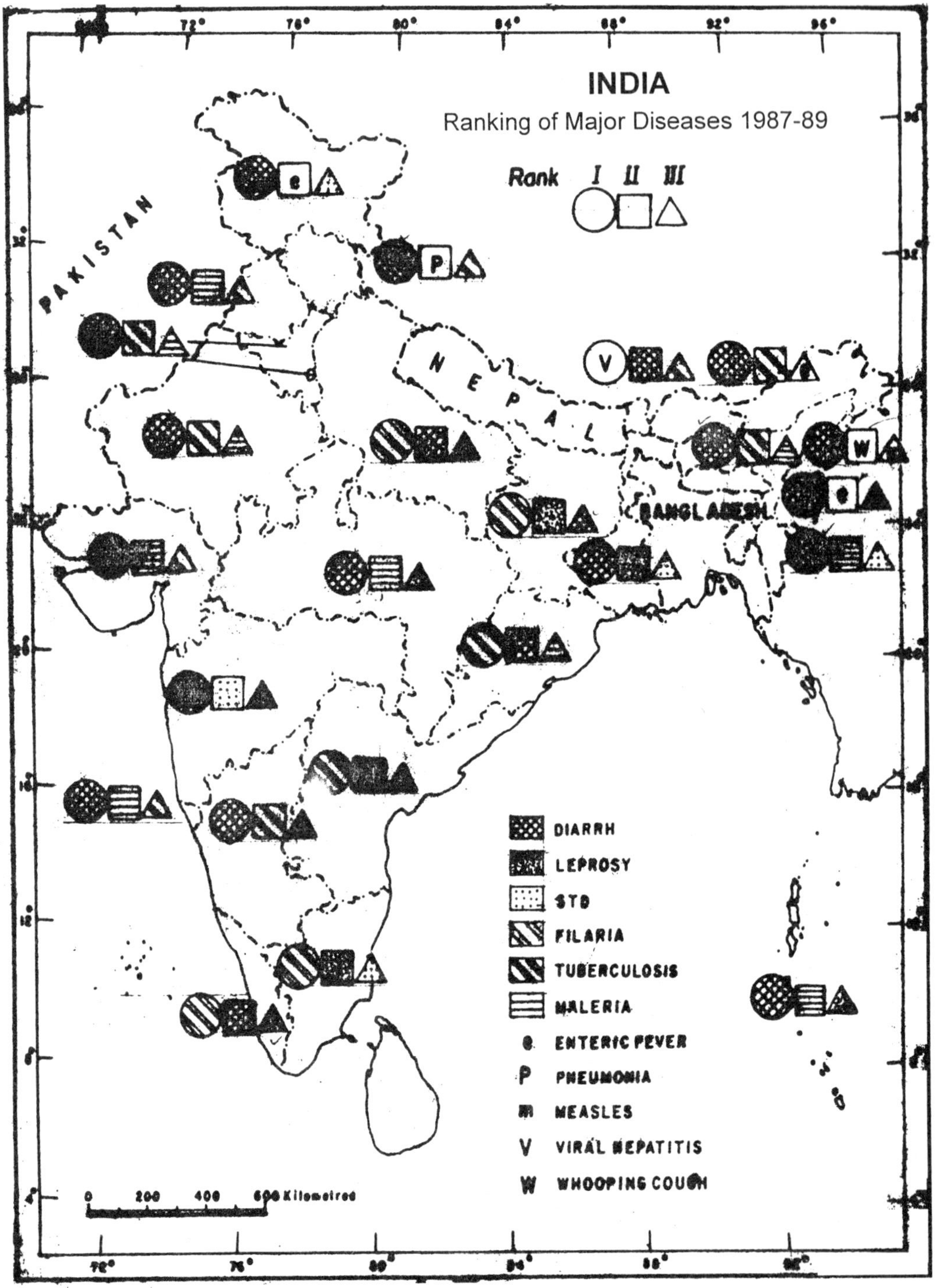

Fig.10.1: Ranking of Major Diseases in India

pox was another dreaded disease. It not only claimed thousands of lives but also debilitated thousands. It disfigured the face and blinded the victims. Cholera was also a great killer in the past. It persists even today in mild forms in small pockets here and there but has by and large remained controlled. Another major disease of the past is trachoma. It has been totally eradicated but needs constant vigilance lest it returns again. Guinea worm infection and anthrax are other diseases of the past discussed in this chapter.

BUBONIC PLAGUE

Epidemiology

Plague is a bacterial zoonoses; it has been a scourge of the ancient and medieval worlds, and is still a potential health menace for the whole humanity. Epidemics of plague are mentioned in Bhagwat Purana (800 BC); it instructs the people to abandon their habitats the moment they observe rats dying. It is also referred to in the Bible. It was known as 'Black Death' in Europe. It is also called Oriental plague, Pest, Pestilentia, Chuma (Russian), Yeki (Japanese), and Shu-Yi (Chinese). In India, plague was known as Mahamari (major killer disease) Death toll was so high and traumatic that plague became a generic term applied to all killer diseases and even those people who created social unrest. Medically, it refers to a specific infectious fever caused by *Pasteurella pestis,* also called *Bacillus pestis* and *Yercenia pestis.* The *pestis* was discovered by Alexander Yersin, a Swiss bacteriologist, and student of Louis Pasteure in 1894.

During the last 2000 years, three great pandemics have plagued the world. The first occurred in 542; it killed about 100 million people. The second began in 1346; it lasted for about three hundred years and claimed over 25 million lives. And the third began in 1894 and continued until 1930s. The natural foci of the disease has been located in Central Asia (Arabia and Iranian Khurdistan); Central and South Africa; South and Southeast Asia (Myanmar, Vietnam, Indonesia and India); South America; and Western United States of America. It declined considerably in the second half of the twentieth century: from over 40,000 cases in 1950 to 3000 in 1980-84. The fatality rates have consistently declined but they continue to be higher than five per cent in Africa and Latin America. The last case of plague in Asia was reported from Sri Lanka in 1938, Thailand in 1952, Nepal in 1968, and India and Myanmar in 1994. The danger of its attack still looms large. In India, It struck Surat in Gujarat in 1994, even if on a minor scale. News papers report cases of plague like diseases every year, but the proved cases are rare, if at all.

Plague is a disease that is transmitted by fleas, which attack the rodents first. From rodents the fleas then attack the human beings through physical contact. The disease in man comes in three forms. The most common is bubonic plague that is characterized by swelling of the lymph nodes (buboes). The next in importance is the pneumonic plague in which the lungs are severally infected by pestis. The last one is the septicemic plague in which the blood stream is so strongly invaded by the pestis that the patient dies.

The bubonic plague is a primarily bacterial zoonoses involving rodents and fleas. The Y. pestis exists in natural foci, and is transmitted by infected flea-bites to humans living in or visiting the environment. It is characterized by the development of buboes or swellings in the groin, armpits, or neck of the patient. It is relatively less severe and infectious than the other

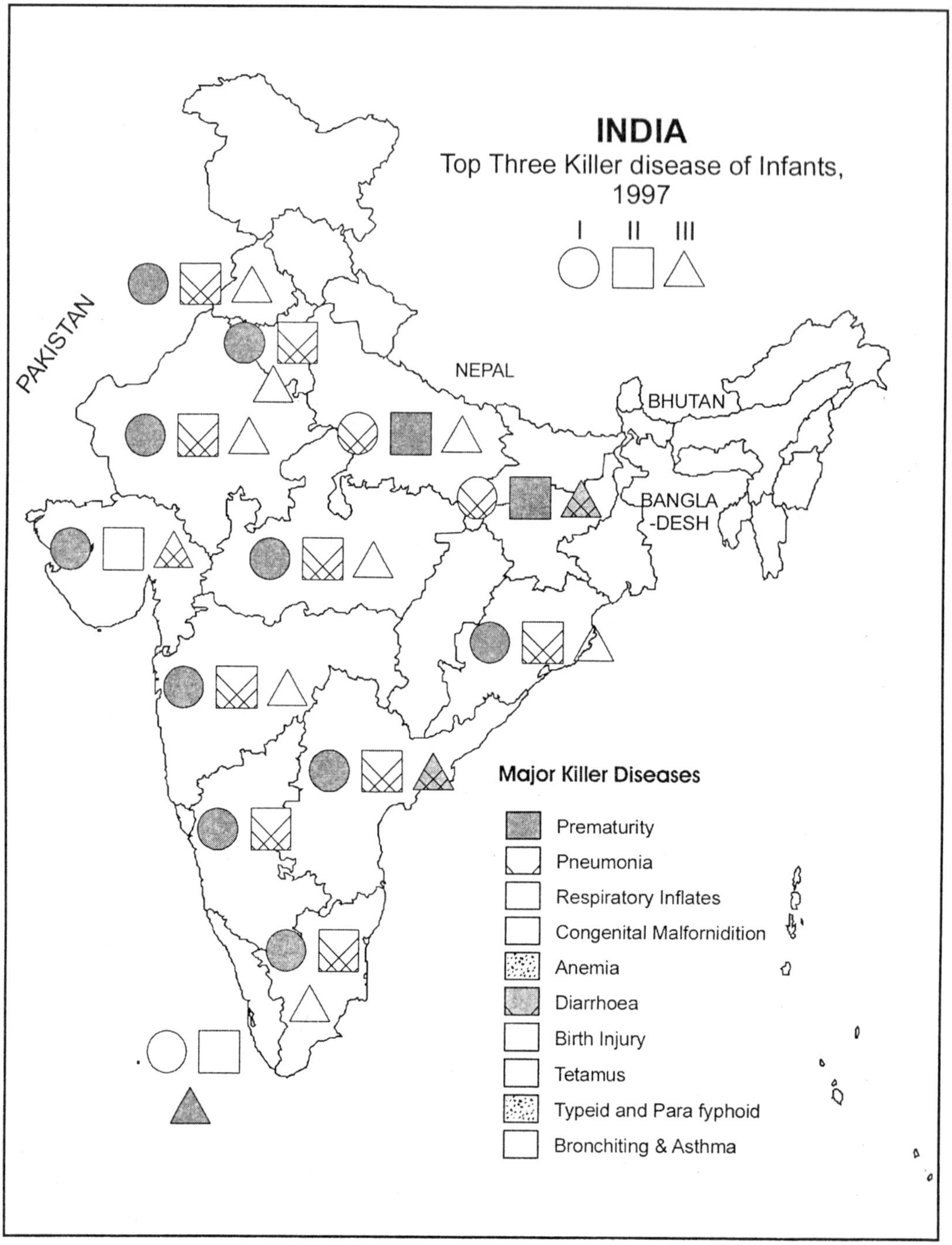

Fig.10.2: Major Killer Diseases of Infants

two varieties, yet the mortality may be as high as 60 to 70 per cent of those infected. The patient dies in a week or so. Domestic rats are responsible for spreading this type of plague.

Plague occurs in many forms: enzootically, epizootically, sporadically and in epidemics of various types including anthroponotic and pneumonic. Indian plague is mainly thc bubonic type but the pneumonic type is not uncommon. Bubonic plague attacks the human victims without serious warning. It starts with bodily pain, physical and mental depression, giddiness, feeling of coldness, palpitation of heart, low fever, headache, tiredness, and pain in the groin. Gradually, the patient staggers like a drunken person, drunkenness being accompanied by nausea and diarrhoea. After a incubation period of a week or so, the temperature of the body of the patient goes up reaching 40° to 42° C. His pulse and respiration rates go up and soon the face becomes swollen and the eyes sunken and fixed. His hearing is lost, the skin becomes dry and hot, the tongue gets coated with a creamy fur which later turns deep brown or black. He is unable to speak. Then come the bubos in the armpits and groin. Perspiration is often an indication of possible recovery. Death can come at any stage of the disease but usually it comes between the third and seventh day of the attack.

Pneumonic plague is more severe than bubonic plague. It is a respiratory track disease that appears as severe pneumonia set up by the plague germ. Because it attacks the lungs, plague bacilli are sprayed in the air each time the patient breathes out. Its infection is, therefore, transmitted from person to person through the air. The chances of contracting this type of plague are very high in cases of those who come in contact with a plague patient. Death occurs within four days of infection. The septicemic type is the most fatal of the three. It kills the patient within a few hours. It gives out no symptoms to warn the patient; bacilli enter the blood stream so fast that the patient dies before the appearance of external symptoms.

Plague is primarily a disease of the rodents. Wherever the infected rodents go, the chances of plague outbreak brighten. The primary cycle of the disease is: rodent (host)—flee (vector) – rodent (host). The bacilli multiply in the stomach of the flea. When the flea bites, it sucks the blood of the host and injects infected blood back in the host. When the mortality among the rats increases to a level that the fleas do not get enough blood, they infect the humans. Man thus enters the cycle only accidentally when he comes in contact with rodents. He does not get the disease from wild rodents.

Domestic rodent is the main carrier of plague. Among the domestic rodents, the rats are the most important as they are found everywhere. And among the rats, the Muridae variety is the one that retains endemicity and causes sudden and large outbreak of the disease. Among the other rodents that can cause plague are squirrels, rabbits, gerbils and hamsters. From the rodents, the infection can be passed on to pigs and cats too. The organism does not survive outside the human or rodent body. It is easily killed by heat. The rat furrows provide the ideal environment for multiplication and transmission.

Fleas prefer rats to humans as hosts and rarely attack human beings so long as there are enough rats to feed on. A rat flea dies within a week if it fails to get food. It sucks the blood of the host through a picker and passes it down its gullet by successive waves of muscle contractions. The pear shaped stomach of the flea can accommodate as much as 0.5 cc of blood at a time. A plague-infected rat carries about hundred million bacilli per cc of its blood. The flea can store about 5000 bacilli in its stomach at a time. The bacilli multiply in the stomach of the flea. Later they are passed out through the feces in order to relieve the choking overflow of the new generation of the bacilli. As it bites the new rodent, it sucks fresh blood and squirts old infected blood from its anus. The bacilli enter the victim through the wound.

As mentioned earlier, plague is a zoonotic acute infection affecting certain rodents. Human infection takes place on an appreciable scale only under certain favourable conditions that bring man and the rodent together. In India, the rodent in question is rat; in South Africa it is gerbil; in California, USA, it is ground squirrel and in South East Siberia and northern part of China it is tarbagan. "Man becomes infected from such animals through the bite of fleas, which live and feed on them. Opportunities for close association between the man and the special rodent responsible for keeping alive plague in the area concerned is a very important factor for the production of the disease in the human communities. Widespread outbreaks among such animals may lead to territorial extensions of the plague while the transportation of the infected rats or infected fleas through grain traffic or in other ways may result in the staring of the infection in areas far removed from the endemic foci of the disease" (Health Survey Report, 1946).

Rat fleas, also called *xenopsylla cheopis,* can travel from place to place in one of the three ways: on the natural host, the rat; hiding in merchandise like hay, cotton and grains; and on the human body. A temperature of 70° C is very favourable to the flea. 85° C or more kills the bacilli in the stomach of the flea and temperatures below 50° C kills the rat before the bacilli appear in its blood. High temperatures affect the breeding process in the flea; they are unable to lay eggs and eggs cannot become larvae.

As noted by Desai, "Breeding of the rats is vigorous during the off season which precedes the breeding of fleas. From this it is easy to see why plague is seasonal disease. First, a rat epizootic reduces the rat population considerably, leaving the immune rat proportion greater than the susceptible rats. The immune rats now begin to multiply and bring into existence a new race of susceptible rats. The fleas are breeding and as soon as a carrier rat has passed the path of the procreating flea, the epizootic begins. And after the epizootic, when the fleas have not enough rats to feed on, comes the turn of man and his epidemics. Plague comes and recedes automatically every year, unless we break the vicious circle of rats-flea-man-rat-flea and man again."

That the rodents !ike rats were responsible for the spread of plague became clear only in 1905-06 when the Plague Research Commission appointed by the then Government of India inquired into the causes of the outbreak of the disease in Bombay the same year. Earlier, people knew that rats died in large numbers before the spread of the disease but they could not find any logical relationship between the two. In India, the disease came to be known as Mahamari caused by goddesses and gods to punish the people for their ill-doings. In some European countries people believed that "God in this matter as in all others brought a marvelous remedy" to correct the women who attended tournaments dressed "in a variety of the most sumptuous male costumes, riding choice war-horses or other splendid steeds to the appointed place, and wearying their bodies with fooleries and wanton buffooneries." The general public believing in these and similar other superstitions sought scapegoats in men and women they did not like and indulged in brutal savagery against them. In Spain, it were the Moors, in France the English and almost everywhere the Jews. In Basle, all the Jews were penned up in wooden buildings and cremated alive. The citizens of Speyer murdered several thousands of them, and threw the bodies into the Rhine. Epileptics, village idiots, and old hags, all suspected of being in league with devils and spirits, were hunted down and put to death by vigilance squads.

The above narrative has been given here with some purpose in mind. Those who are engaged in human development activities in rural parts of India should understand that the superstition that prevails in rural society is not peculiar to India. It was present even in Europe just a hundred years ago.

Geographic Distribution

Global

When and where the plague originated is still a matter of conjecture. Archeological and historical records of the ancient times do not offer any definitive clue. On the basis of whatever information is available, indirect and fragmented as it may be, it is believed that origin of plague can be traced to North Africa in the first or second century BC. From this region it spread to the grasslands of Central Asia having abundant rodent population. It hit Constantinople in the second century AD and killed on an average 5 to 10 thousand persons per day. By the middle of the seventh century, it appeared in Europe in an epidemic form and killed over 100 million persons. England appears to have suffered three bouts of it within just 20 years (between 664 to 683 AD). The disease was nicknamed as Black Death. Thereafter it appears to have gone in hibernation once again to re-emerge in the fourteenth century. Striking at Constantinople first, it spread to neighbouring countries like Greece and Italy. It was the most important killer disease in Europe during fifteenth to seventeenth centuries taking as many as 25 million lives i.e. a quarter of the European population; and more than half of the population of Great Britain was wiped out by this scourge. The spread of the disease was facilitated by the migration of domestic rats from one part of the world to the other as trade through land and sea routes intensified. The infected rats moved from endemic areas to new areas as people and goods moved across countries and continents.

The plague of London killed almost one-sixth of the population of the city in 1664-65. From London it spread to other parts of England. In the late sixties of the seventeenth century, plague was quite widespread in much of Europe. It subsided on its own and by 1670 much of Europe was free from plague in epidemic form. But the disease spread to Central and East Europe, Turkey and North Africa. It continued to kill large number of people in Turkey, Greece, Syria, Egypt and other North African countries during the eighteenth and nineteenth centuries.

While practically the whole of Europe was in the grip of plague, it was absent from the Orient. It never crossed the Indus until the first decade of the nineteenth century when it attacked Kathiawar peninsula of the present state of Gujarat in 1815. It reached China in 1855; its southern ports became centres of plague distribution. By 1922, the disease spread throughout the world. Being a 'sea-faring' disease it struck the port towns first and then penetrated the interior. It reached Bombay in 1896; Calcutta in 1898; Japan and Philippines in 1897; Australia, Hawaii, Central and South America in1899; South Africa, and San Francisco, USA in 1900; Egypt and Singapore in 1901; Bangkok, Thailand in 1904; Java, Indonesia in 1910; New Orleans, USA and Colombo, Sri Lanka in 1914; Texas and Florida, USA in 1922; and almost all port towns of Europe and Asia during the first decade of the twentieth century. India suffered the most. Within a span of thirty years (1896-1917), practically the whole country was gripped by the disease; about ten million people died. Fortunately, the second quarter of the twentieth century saw the curve of mortality going down to reach just 162 in 1955. Other countries reporting plague deaths in that year were Kenya in East Africa, and Ecuador and Peru in South America. After 1937 no European country including the former USSR reported plague deaths.

India

Though plague is said to have entered India from Europe through trade routes in the nineteenth century, there are reasons to believe that it existed in the country from ancient times in endemic form. Bhagwat Purana composed sometimes before sixth century AD refers to a disease of human beings and rats. It recommends that human beings should desert the place when they see rats dying. There are also references to deaths by plague during the medieval times i.e. eleventh to seventeenth centuries. For some reasons it remained dormant for about one hundred years only to reappear in a virulent form in 1812 when the whole of the present day Gujarat was overrun. It struck Rajasthan in 1836. In both cases the disease appears to have come from Iran, which continues to be endemic even now.

Subsequent history of plague in India begins in 1896 when it was imported from China through the port of Bombay. It spread fast over a large part of the country. In 1904, more than a million (1,150,000) persons died of plague. The number of dead reached 1,315,892 in 1907 – a rate of 5.16 per thousand. It stayed put in the country taking a heavy toll of life practically each year until the mid-nineteen forties. In 1939-41, only 58,000 persons died of plague. During the next two decades, only four states of the country reported plague mortality; they were Andhra Pradesh 1, Bihar 90, Tamil Nadu 5, and Karnataka 35; in all 131 deaths. By 1979, the mortality figures came down to 12. And since early eighties, no one died of plague in India. In 1993, plague was reported to have struck the city of Surat in Gujarat. About 50 persons were reported to have died. The panic-stricken residents of Surat left the city by whatever means they could secure. According to some reports, at least 30 per cent of the citizens deserted the city within no time.

Table 10.1: India: Plague Mortality (1896-2002)

Period	*Total No. of Deaths*	*@ Annual Deaths*
1898-1908	6,032,693	548,427
1909-1918	4,221,528	422, 153
1919-1928	1,1702,718	170,272
1929-1938	422,880	42,288
1939-1941	58,041	19,347
1961-1962	331	166
19779-80	12	12
1993	25*	25*
2002	3	3

Note: Deaths not confirmed officially

There are conflicting reports about the nature of the disease that struck Surat and panicked the whole of India and even the world. The residents of Surat ran for their life but they did not realize that the disease was with them. It will strike no matter where they go. It will strike all those who tough and live with them. And thus there were plague cases in Delhi and other places too. Later, it was found that it was not a bubonic case that struck Surat. It was a post-flood communicable disease not dissimilar to plague. In March 2001, cases of pneumonic plague were reported from some villages near Shimla in Himachal Pradesh. The disease was controlled before it could spread to other places.

The plague mortality data indicate that the disease remained prevalent in large parts of both north and south India; it never reached the Northeastern states and Orissa though. Why the disease never entered the above two regions of different natural and socio-cultural backgrounds? It continues to be a medical geographic enigma.

Although the incidence of plague had practically disappeared in India, it exists in endemic forms in several parts of the country. As soon as conditions become favourable, the disease may reappear. We should, therefore, be alert and vigilant. The Surat experience of 1993 was caused by lack of vigilance. We had forgotten the plague. The moment someone floated a rumour, people were gripped by panic; they ran helter-skelter and tried to leave the city by whatever means of transport were available. The endemic areas are found in cool and moderately damp climates; the plague bacilli cannot stay alive in very high temperature regimes for more than a few hours. It extends from the foothills of the Himalayas to the southern districts of Karnataka and adjoining areas of Tamil Nadu through the central parts of the country. The endemic areas "are therefore fairly widely distributed and, in view of the past history of the plague, not merely in India but in other countries, which shows that during certain periods, the disease may spread widely and, at others, exhibit a contraction in the territory covered and a marked decrease in the number of cases occurring in the affected areas. These endemic centres may continue as potential sources of danger to the country as a whole unless they are effectively brought under control." (1946 Health Survey Report) The emergence of bubonic plague in Beed district of Maharashtra; and of pneumonic plague in Surat in Gujarat (and from Surat to Delhi, Kolkata and Mumbai) both in 1993-94 should be treated as reminders of the potential dangers ahead.

Environmental Factors

The outbreak of plague is seasonal: in North India it extends from September to May. It disappears in hot weather. Seasonality is related to the exposure of the human to the rats and of the rats to the fleas. During winter, the field rats, which are the main hosts of the pest remain inside the burrows and live on stored food. They do not infect the village rats nor do they infect human being directly. When the monsoon floods dry up by September end, the field rats come out of the burrows. The epizootic is revived in fields and then on to human beings. The disease in peninsular India was not marked by seasonality partly because of prolonged dry season and partly because of undulating topography, which did not allow the water to accumulate.

Temperature range of 20 to 25° C and mean humidity of 60 per cent appear to favour the spread of the disease. Flat topography and heavy rainfall are not favourable to the disease.

That may be the reason why Bengal never experienced major outbreaks of plague. Plague in India has essentially been a rural disease because field rats have safe habitats there. But once the disease spreads in urban areas, either because of the migration of people, or because of the introduction of infested rats through trade routes and vessels, it spreads fast.

Rodent plague is still firmly entrenched in its natural foci which is a "strictly delimited area where ecological conditions ensure the persistence of the etiological agents for considerable periods of time, and where epizootics and quiescence alternate, without introduction of infection from outside." The persistence of plague in some areas cannot be explained by a simple rat-flea-rat formula. A number of geographic factors still unknown may be involved. One has to look into the type of soil where burrows are made, microclimates with the burrows, nature of the stored food in the burrows and the process of movement of the field rats from burrow to burrow and burrow to human habitats.

Plague occurs in cycles of a decade or so. It may be because, once the disease is gone, it can come only by way of fresh infection, which naturally takes time. It may also be because the plague bacilli can survive in the burrows of rats for many years if micro-climatic conditions are favourable. They can slowly infect the healthy rats and cause the disease to re-emerge.

Prevention and Control

The prevention and control of plague requires three-pronged measures. First, appropriate sanitary measures against the host and the vector reservoirs are a must. Use of modern insecticides to kill the fleas should be taken up on a priority basis. And since the bubonic plague does not spread from patient to patient; it spreads from wild rat to house rats; and from house rats to human beings, the most effective step in its prevention is the elimination of the rodent, which functions as the primary reservoir of the bacilli. Keeping down the rat population, particularly in the endemic zones that are now well known, is, therefore, an extremely important preventive measure. Third, the immunity of the population in danger should be enhanced. Immunization with plague vaccine is an effective preventive measure. Vaccine to control plague was first developed in India in 1897 by Haffkine. The one used currently is an improved version of Haffkine vaccine. To be effective, it should be given at least two weeks before the outbreak of the disease. Immunity starts after 5-7 days of vaccination. Fourth, all infectious diseases have a tendency to select those as their fresh victims who are physically weak. Those suffering from under-or malnutrition become easy victims of this scourge. Improvement in the general health of the people will go a long way in immunizing the people against the disease. Inoculation plays a very critical role in the battle against plague. The vaccine, when injected, strengthens immunity and the person injected becomes less susceptible to the disease. And finally, the isolation of the sick is a must, particularly in pneumonic cases.

We should not lose sight of the fact that chemicals used as insecticides such as DDT are toxic and impact the environment very adversely. They kill not only the insects that are harmful to man, but also those that are helpful. What is needed is improved sanitation, clean environment, adequate intake of nutritious foods and timely medical attention in the case of suspected infection.

Plague is no longer a cause for concern. But it remains endemic in many parts of the world including India. It has the potentials to pose danger to human life in future. The danger gets enhanced as the fleas, due to frequent exposure to insecticides like DDT, may become resistant to these chemicals and re-emerge in new avatars. Yet another danger signal is related to the change in the rat population. In 1950s, it was reported that in Bombay *B. Bengalensis*, which is highly sensitive to plague infection, is gradually replacing *R. Norvegieus*, a more resistant species or rat. Such shifts in rat population can be expected to create favourable conditions for triggering of epidemics in the human beings. Plague is a dreaded disease. With the growing menace of terrorism, the possibility of terrorists using *bacillus pestis* to spread the disease is no longer a theoretical proposition. The world is, however, not prepared to face it if it comes as an epidemic. Here is a new problem in medical geography, which is the outcome of a peculiar mixture of health, bacteriology, sociology, politics and technology.

SMALLPOX

Smallpox is an acute respiratory infection caused by variola virus. Until very recently it was also a major killer of the world. Its onset is marked by very high fever followed by red rashes all over the body. The tongue of the patient becomes highly coated and he feels thirsty. He develops constipation and his skin remains red and dry. Within four days eruptions in the form of papules appear first on the face and then on the arms, and finally on the whole body. Gradually, the temperature of the patient's body falls. The papules, which pass through the stages of vesicle, pustule, and scab, leave more or less distinct scars. The vesicles are full of clear fluid first and later with pus. Body temperature goes up again; and eruptions become visibly swollen and hemispherical. Finally, the desication begins in which eruptions shrink and dry up. Dark brown crusts are formed on the eruptions that fall off gradually leaving behind deep-set pits. But not many who are attacked by smallpox live to shed the scabs off. Quite many of them die within a week of attack. Of those who survive, not all live a normal life. Some develop broncho-pneumonia, encephalitis, meningitis, melancholia with suicidal tendencies, and partial or complete blindness of one or both eyes. When in mild form, it resembles chicken pox (varicella) and leaving no visible scar on the body.

According the WHO, smallpox cases are classified into variola major and variola minor. The former is more acute and has fatality rate ranging from 20 to 50 per cent while the latter is benign and has a fatality rate of 1 per cent or less. The disease has been traced to a filterable orthopox virus, a genus that also includes cobra, monkey pox and vincina viruses. These are brick shaped viruses and cannot be destroyed easily. The smallpox virus enters the body via nisiss membrane of the upper respiratory tract and by direct face-to-face contact.

Smallpox can occur in all climates, tropical or temperate, dry or wet, but its attack is more severe in hot climates or summer seasons in cold climates. Its incidence increases with increase in humidity. The virus is highly contagious. It can be conveyed in secretions of the mouth and nose. It persists in the scabs that fall off from the drying eruptions. It can also be carried on the clothing or hair of the person coming from a small pox area or patient. Flies and domestic pets can also transmit it.

GEOGRAPHIC DISTRIBUTION

Global

Smallpox is one of the oldest diseases of the world. As late as 1967, smallpox was endemic in no less than 33 countries. The faces of some of the Egyptian mummies entombed over 3000 years ago show clear signs of the legacies this disease leaves behind with the person who becomes its victim. Persian physician Rhazes wrote an account of the disease in 900 AD. Several Europeans had mentioned about it much earlier such as Eusebius of the disease in Syria in 302 AD, Bishop Marius in France and Italy in 570 AD, and Gilbert in England in 1200 AD.

Smallpox was pandemic in Europe in 1614, epidemic in England during 1666-75, and there were scattered outbreaks in the New England states of the USA in the seventeenth century. On account of their habits of living together, the American Indians became easy victims of the disease. Some scholars ascribe smallpox as a very critical contributory factor in Englishman's success against them. The death toll from smallpox in England and other European countries was so terrific and suffering of the people so acute that Macauley considered it to be the "most terrible of the ministers of death. The havoc of the plague has been far more rapid; but the plague has visited our shores only once or twice within living memory; and small pox was always present filling the church yard with corpses, tormenting with constant fear all whom it had not yet stricken, leaving on those whose lives were spared the hideous traces of its power, turning the babe into a changeling at which the mother shuddered, making the eyes and cheeks of the betrothed maiden objects of horror to the lover" (Desai). It reached the Americas with Spaniards in sixteenth century. About three and a half million people became its victims. The American Indian population was reduced to half. Cities like Boston lost at least half of their population

India

Smallpox appears to have been present in India from times immemorial. The Ayurvedic physician Charak referred it in seventh century AD. Apparently, he wrote on the basis of medical knowledge handed down from the past. It was considered to be a *Mahamari* all over the country. It has been eradicated from the whole world including India. No one is reported to have died of smallpox in India since 1975.

The disease was prevalent all over the country but came in more virulent forms in the northwestern states like Rajasthan, Punjab, Haryana, Gujarat, UP and MP. Morbidity and mortality data for the year 1961 show that the above states followed by AP and Karnataka were the most severally affected parts of the country. In 1962, the spatial variation in the mortality from smallpox ranged from 0.01 per thousand of population in Assam to 0.3 per thousand in Punjab. The national average was 0.07 per thousand. The spatial variability of mortality was not the only characteristic of the disease; it was marked by temporal variability also. It ranged from 0.001 to 0.8 per thousand of population per annum.

The smallpox incidence in India was one of the highest in the world. It accounted for almost two-third of the total deaths of the world during the twentieth century. During 1932-41, the mortality was as high as 69,475 per annum. It was doubled in 1951, the year India launched its first five year plan. Thereafter, the number of deaths fell rather drastically to reach 10,931 in 1956. In subsequent years, it doubled and trebled only to come down to just 196 in 1975. Through a concerted effort, supported by the WHO, the complete eradication became possible in May 1975. Since then, there might have been some sporadic cases here and there in endemic areas, but nothing has been confirmed so far (Table 10.2).

Table 10.2: Smallpox Morbidity and Mortality 1932-2000 AD (in Numbers)

Year	*Incidence (World)*	*Incidence (India)*	*Deaths (India)*	*% of World Cases in India*
1932–41	–		69,475	–
1951	–	253,332	94,580	–
1952–53	–	60,883	–	–
1954–55	–	66,198	–	–
1956–57	–	123775	34081	–
1958–59		215909	68031	–
1960–61		76471	20393	–
1962–63		139018	41408	–
1964–65		70058	19099	–
1966–67	131,697*	116559	34707	64.40
1968–69		49434	10422	37.90
1970–71	33706#	28777	4946	64.90
1972–73	135859@	115516	20891	86.10
1974	218367	188003	31262	7.40
1975	19278	1436	196	–
1976	995	Nil	Nil	–
1977	3234	Nil	Nil	–
1978	2	Nil	Nil	–
1979	Nil	Nil	Nil	

Note: * for the year 1967; # for the year 1970; and @ for the year 1973
Source: Health Information of India and other relevant reports.

Environmental Factors

Smallpox had a definite seasonality; the incidence reaches epidemic proportions in spring months. The virus can survive for 12 to 18 months outside the human body in relatively low temperature and humidity. Sun light kills it quickly. Variable climates of India can keep it alive throughout the year. However, the ideal season is winter and spring. In the state of West Bengal, and in Bangladesh the impact of season is so strong that the disease is called Bashunto due to its occurrence during the spring. The disease also appears to come in cycles of five to six years perhaps because of the accumulation of susceptible cases. Laxity in vaccination or absence of a definite scheme of vaccination might have been the reason for it. Children are more susceptible to smallpox attack. However, by the time the disease disappeared from the Indian scene, its choice of victims had changed and even the adults were being caught in its net.

Although small pox is not as infectious as plague, its diffusion often reaches epidemic proportions in areas of crowded living conditions and frequent social contacts. Concentration of people at locations such as market places and festivals facilitated the spread across settlements and communities. The intensity of the disease, however, depends on previous exposure to smallpox, history of vaccination, standard of medical institutions, frequency of movement, and living conditions.

Prevention and Control

Public Health Measure

The best treatment of smallpox is care of the patient and cleanliness around him. He should be kept in a separate room, given only light and digestible foods, should be given complete rest in bed, and his body should not be exposed to sun or open air. He should be given as much liquid food as he desires. Vaccination, after eruptions, does not help and hence should not be resorted to. After the pox has been formed, a solution of potassium permanganate can be used to remove its bad odour. A doctor must be consulted if complications affecting lungs or heart are foreseen.

Vaccination

It is now well known that vaccination is the sure means of preventing smallpox. The story of the vaccination is a fascinating one. Introduction of the smallpox virus in the body of healthy persons by grafting was practised in Turkey and China in ancient times. Lady Montague, the wife of British ambassador to Turkey, introduced it in England in the hope that some lives will be saved by its use. During the first quarter of the eighteenth century, it was taken to the USA by Cotton Mather and Bolyston. People in England as well as the USA considered it something very outrageous. Lady Montague was ridiculed and ill-treated. Bolyston was mobbed and Mather had hand grenade thrown at his window. Yet this primitive method of inoculation became common in France by 1720, in Germany by 1725, and not many years later in other European countries. In Russia, it was used in the great epidemics of 1771 to prevent its spread.

The method at times proved fatal because it was not possible to determine the exact dose that ought to be introduced in the body. Knowing that the dairy maids, who milked cows suffering from cowpox did not get smallpox, Benjamin Jesty of Dorsetshire, an English farmer, vaccinated his wife and two sons using the pus from the pustules on the udders of the cows suffering from cowpox. The sons had a mild attack of smallpox but Mrs. Jesty hovered between life and death. Her condition alarmed the neighbours. They cursed Jesty for indulging in such mal-practices!

Twenty-two years after Jesty's experiments, Edward Jenner, a pupil of the famous physician John Hunter, but a complete failure as a medical practitioner, caught the idea of vaccination and experimented again by vaccinating James Phipps on May 14, 1796 with the pustules on the hands of a milkmaid named Sarah Nelmes. He developed a mild attack. Phipps was vaccinated again with the pus from a smallpox patient. This time he did not get any attack. Thus was proved the effectiveness of vaccination in the prevention of smallpox.

Eradication of Smallpox in India

In India smallpox was linked to Goddess Kali. Once the signs of smallpox became clear, the patient was kept in a very clean and cool place separate from the rest of the family members. Neem leaves were kept near the patient; they were also used as fan to cool the body. Neem is a known disinfective plant. Incense was burnt to keep the whole room disinfected. The visitors were not allowed to go near the smallpox patients and environment around him was kept clean and disinfected.

The European countries were able to control smallpox by mid-1950s. It took another 25 years for developing countries to eradicate the disease. India was the last stronghold of the disease even though vaccination was introduced first in India at Bombay in 1830. But until the vaccination process was improved to become less painful, it remained very unpopular among the people, especially in the rural parts of the country. A vaccinator was a real terror for children.

Systematic efforts to eliminate the disease began in 1962 when the National Smallpox Eradication Programme through mass vaccination was launched. Some 500 million people were vaccinated during 1962-66. The program was, however, only a partial success due to large population base, dense settlements, large number of foci, frequent movement of the people from place to place and leakage from the neighbouring countries like Bangladesh. School going children were the main target of the programme but they could not be covered fully in rural areas where many of children did not attend school. Efforts were further intensified in 1967 as a part of the WHO initiated Global Intensified Smallpox Eradication Programme GISEP). The programme started with universal mass vaccination all over the country. Later, it was modified to focus on certain target areas where identification and surveillance of the cases was considered easier and scientific.

The GISEP was carried out in four phases to arrest the disease: preparatory, attack, consolidation and maintenance. The preparatory phase included identifying the villages in an administrative zone with smallpox cases, training of the field personnel and mass education for acceptance of vaccination. Under the attack phase, mass vaccination, follow up and surveillance, were carried out to cover individuals and local areas. The consolidation phase covered the newly born, migrants and other suspected cases. By the end of this phase, about 80 per cent of the population was covered and the incidence rate declined to just 5 per 100,000 persons in a year. The maintenance phase was completed when there was no endemic smallpox in the selected target areas for more than two years. By 1973, the disease was eliminated from the world barring three countries of Africa and the Indian sub-continent. India began a third campaign called Intensified Smallpox Campaign in October, 1973 and succeeded in eradicating the disease within two years. During 1974, active searches were launched to track down unreported cases especially in the endemic areas of West Bengal, Bihar, UP and MP. Three such searches were conducted within a year. In December 1974, 'Operation Smallpox Zero' was launched and on May 24, 1975, India was declared free from smallpox. Six years later, on May 8, 1980, the WHO declared the whole world free from smallpox.

Future Prospects

Smallpox has been eradicated from the world but the final chapter of its history is yet to be written. The smallpox virus has not been completely eradicated. Stocks of the virus were held in 76 laboratories in the world in 1976. By 1983, only two of them – the US Laboratory, Atlanta and the Research Institute of Viral Preparation, Moscow, had the stocks of the virus under the supervision of WHO. The World Health Assembly in its 1999 meeting recommended the destruction of the stocks by 2002. But whether it is desirable to destroy the stock is still being debated. The stocks may be needed for future researches. The smallpox can come back in future through laboratory infection as it happened in Birmingham, UK in 1978. There are a number of other viruses, which are similar to smallpox virus (monkeypox, camelpox, cowpox, tanapox, tateropox, etc) but whose natural history and geography is yet to be understood. They can prove dangerous to man in future. Who knows, the answer to these poxes may lie in smallpox virus.

Human monkeypox is a disease, which was recognized only after the smallpox was eradicated. Monkeypox virus is different from variola virus. The number of persons suffering from monkeypox is increasing every year. And several countries have come under its attack all over the world. Smallpox vaccination is effective in the case of monkeypox also but with decreasing immunity against smallpox, the chances of the disease spreading fast are very much there.

Tanapox is another disease, which resembles smallpox but is quite different from it. The reservoir of the virus is unknown. It is also a zoonotic disease found in East and Central Africa. Smallpox vaccination does not protect people against tanapox.

TRACHOMA

Not long ago trachoma was one of the major surface infectious diseases of the eye the world over. In India, almost all had to undergo the agonies caused by this disease. It was not a killer disease but it used to disfigure and blind many. After smallpox, trachoma was the next most important cause of blindness in India. It was a disease of the summer months and was highly infectious. Children were the easiest victim of the disease for they, being highly mobile and carefree, contacted the disease from fellow children in school, during play, or just by using towels of the infected persons in the family.

According May, it "is a chronic disease of conjunctiva and cornea characterized by a sub-epithelial cellular infiltration with a follicular distribution, the natural resolution of which is by cicatrization involving potentially much visual disability and gross deformity. Its importance as a sources of human suffering, as a cause of blindness, and as a national economic loss over large tracts of the world surface is second to none among the diseases of the eye, or, indeed among diseases of all kinds." Trachoma attack is mild in the beginning but it becomes serious after bacillary infection. Repeated secondary infections complicate the disease to produce blindness of one or both the eyes.

The viruses responsible for trachoma are known as *chlamydozoa trachomatis* and *C. oculogenitale*. It is relatively easy to detect them through microscopic examination, both in the early and acute phase of the disease. In chronic and cicatricial cases, it is absent or rare and hence difficult to detect. These viruses die within 15 minutes if subjected to 45° C temperature but can resist cold or even prolonged freezing for weeks. They pass from man to man; there is no known intervening vector or reservoir in which they grow before infecting the human eye.

The viruses do not enter deep into the eye; they remain confined to the epithelium of the conjunctiva or cornea. It does not, therefore, confer much immunity after the first or subsequent infections. It is a disease of childhood and the infection is more common at a very early stage of life. When the virus attack takes place, the conjunctiva becomes thickened and roughened. Its extension to cornea may lead to opacity and blindness. Transmission occurs during the acute stage by infective ocular secretions being transferred from person to person through bodily contact or use of common handkerchief/towel/pillows or other clothes. It is a disease of poverty, poor environment and hygiene, unbalanced diet, lack of sanitation and healthcare.

Geographic Distribution

Global

Trachoma is a global disease; it is endemic all over the world. No race, region, country, climate or individual is immune to it. It is believed to have originated in Mongolia in prehistoric times. As the Mongoloid people moved to the present day west Asian region in the west and through the isthmus connecting Asian and American continents to the Americas in the east. Some contend that the disease originated in West Asia and from there it spread to the rest of the world following human migration and trade routes. Since the disease is endemic and present in mild form all over the world, it must have been there for quite a long time to acquire the current stage of maturity.

In North America, a mild form of the disease is prevalent among American Indians. As late as 1970, a quarter of the school-going children in Mexico were victims of trachoma. In South America, Chile was the most infected country. In Europe, the Mediterranean and East European countries have mild infection syndrome. The North African countries from Egypt to Morocco are still hyper-endemic. It is quite common in China, Mekong river basin countries, Indonesia, Malaysia, Myanmar and of course India and other South Asian countries.

According to recent estimates, about 540 million people are at risk of infection; 150 million suffer from the disease and need treatment; and about 6 million people suffer from reversible blindness because of trachoma. It has been eliminated from North America and Europe. In Southeast Asian region, the cases of trachoma are declining fast but in some parts of the region like Myanmar, Nepal and India, it is still an important factor contributing to total load of blindness.

India

According to the survey of trachoma conducted in 1956 under Trachoma Pilot Project at least half of the total population of India had experienced trachoma. The prevalence rate varied from region to region. It was much higher in the western and northern states than in the southern states. The rate varied from 38 to 70 per cent in Rajasthan, UP, MP, Bihar, Punjab and Gujarat. Elsewhere the prevalence rate was 25 per cent or so with pockets of high endemicity in J&K, Karnataka and Assam. The Pilot Project also studied the extent of visual impairment brought about by trachoma and associated bacterial infections. It was revealed that 12 to 42 per cent of the population examined was 'economically blind', that is, they could not count fingers at a distance of two meters with both eyes open. It was also revealed that five times the number of economically blind persons suffered from mild or moderate degree of visual impairment. The estimated number of economically blind persons due to trachoma and related infections was as high as 450, 000. And the number of those who had a mild degree of visual impairment touched 2.7 million.

Environmental Factors

In India, April-May and July-September are the months during which trachoma is most rampant. It is also the time when eye-seeking flies flourish. High temperature and rainfall favour the growth of flies. Apart from the weather conditions, trachoma is associated with solid waste and poor housing.

Studies in UP, one of the most severely affected states of the country, revealed that 85 per cent of the people examined had signs of active or healed trachoma. The age of onset was 1 to 3 years; the children under 10 years were the main victims. The incidence was higher in March-April and July-September indicating clearly the influence of natural environment on the disease. High temperature, humidity and rainfall give rise to flies that are excellent carriers of the virus from the eyes of the infected person to those of still safe. It is the poor people living in rural areas and in the slums of cities that suffer most.

Trachoma is not yet eradicated from India but its severity and spatial spread are very much reduced. There were many cases of trachoma in the country even in 2003. The source of infection is the ocular discharges of infected persons, usually children, but adults too. Poverty, ignorance, poor personal hygiene, squalor and illiteracy favour trachoma infection. The first priority in any measure to control the disease has to go to hygiene and public health. Creating conditions in which flies do not multiply fast is conducive to control of trachoma.

Prevention and Control

The World Health Organization has targeted trachoma for eradication by 2020 through long lasting antibiotics. About six million people living in Africa and Asia have been irreversibly blinded by it and another 150 million suffer from the disease and need treatment. During 1997, a WHO Alliance for the Global Elimination of Trachoma was established to intensify action against the disease together with interested non-governmental organizations and other partners (UNICEF, UNESCO, FAO, UNDP, Rotary International, and governments of a number of countries) making use of new methods for rapid assessment and more effective treatment of the disease.

India has done fairly well in the control of trachoma; it is no longer the most important cause of blindness. That is why the trachoma eradication programme in India is now merged with blindness control programme. A national survey conducted in 1986-87 showed that blindness in the country was 1.49 per cent. The National Programme for Control of Blindness aims at bringing this percentage down to 0.30 by 2000. To achieve this target a minimum of 21 million cataract operations had to be performed. The target has been achieved but new cases have also cropped up. So the Programme continues. (for greater details, see chapter 11).

GUINEA WORM DISEASE

Also known as dracontiasis, it is a vector borne parasitic disease on its last leg of journey. In 1989, the number of Guinea worm cases in the world amounted to 892,005; the figures came down to 96,293 in 1999 recording a drop of over 89 per cent. It has been practically eradicated from all over the world except 13 African countries. The main areas of the disease in Africa are Sudan, Ghana and Nigeria. There has been increase in cases in these countries. But the transmission has almost stopped in Kenya, Camaroon and Senegal. Asia is now free of the disease since February 2000. In India, the last reported case of guinea worm was in 1999.

The adult parasite involves the viscera to begin with, and then manifests in the subcutaneous tissues and the skin. The causative agent is dracunculus medinensis, a distant relative of filarial worm. The disease is endemic in India, West Asia and tropical Africa. The adult worms mature in the viscera and deeper tissues. The male worm is very minute (just 2 to 3 cm) but the female can attain a length of 55 to 120 cm. Once pregnant, the female worms migrate to the skin of the extremities of the human body and produce a blister. On contact with fresh water, the blister bursts and a swarm of larvae get into the water. The larvae can survive in water for 3 to 6 days. The water fleas (cyclops) swallow these larvae and enter the human body when flea-infected water is taken orally by human beings.

Digested by gastric juice, the released parasites; penetrate the duodenal wall and in due course migrate through the viscera to various parts of the body. It takes about 9-12 months before they become adult. The clinical manifestation of infection appears when the female migrates from deeper tissues to the skin. The long tunnel in which the female worm resides gets readily infected with bacteria. It is not easy to pull it out. The biological control of the disease is possible by stocking plankton-feeding fish in the infested water. The fish eat away the cyclops.

Guinea worm infection is no longer a health hazard in India. It has been controlled but not eradicated. At least six states of the country, namely, Andhra Pradesh, Gujarat, Karnataka, Madhya Pradesh, Maharashtra and Rajasthan reported guinea worm cases as late as 1991. These are also the states that have endemic areas requiring surveillance and periodic dis infection. As on January 1, 1990, 63 districts of the above states were considered endemic. After a three-year surveillance, 12 districts were deleted from the list and one new district (Buldana in Maharashtra) was added to bring the total down to 52. The state of Tamil Nadu became free from the disease in 1984-85.

As stated earlier, there has been no guinea worm case in India since 1996. But being an endemic area, India has to remain vigilant. The endemic areas are almost coterminous with the areas, which had guinea worm cases in 1990-1991. These areas along with the number of cases and villages affected are given in Table 10.3 and Fig.10.3.

The reservoir of infection is the human being. No animal has so far been found harbouring the guineaworm female. A person infected once can be infected several other times. The main link in the transmission of guineaworm disease is water infested with cyclops. The larvae of cyclops develop best in 25 to 30° C temperature; they cannot grow in temperatures below 19° C. In areas of step wells, the peak season of transmission is March to June. In areas where ponds are the main source of drinking water, the peak season of transmission is the rainy season (June to September) when ponds have enough water. Surveillance data show that children of both the sexes are equally susceptible to guineaworm disease but adult males are more susceptible than adult females. It may be because males are more likely to drink infected water while working in the fields especially in rainy season. Apparently, the main strategy for the eradication of the disease has to be based on adequate supply of clean drinking water. No drug is suitable for effective mass treatment.

Table 10.3: Distribution of Guinea Worm Disease in India: 1990-91

Endemic States	*Affected as on 1.1.1990*				*New/re-infected in 1990*				*Affected as on 1.1.1991*		
	Cases in 1989	*PHCs*	*Villages*	*Pop. in 000*	*PHCs*	*Villages*	*Pop. .in 000*	*Cases No 1990*	*PHCs*	*Villages*	*Pop. In 000*
Andhra Pradesh	224	26	150	348	3	15	50	18	22	88	266
Gujarat	6	30	52	319	3	6	8	14	11	15	41
Karnataka	896	34	313	627	-	17	17	31	32	249	505
MP	1408	61	825	921	-	13	23	-	51	485	659
Maharashtra	475	89	289	153	11	32	109	150	67	190	180
Rajasthan	4872	76	2009	164	3	135	104	471	70	1565	1213
Total	7881	316	3638	4005	20	218	310	684	253	2592	2864

Source: Reproduced from Ashok Kumar *et al*: *Current Guinea Worm Disease Situation in India*, National Institute of Communicable Diseases, New Delhi., 1991

India launched its National Guineaworm Eradication Programme in 1984 with technical assistance from the WHO. The strategy was to provide safe drinking water and to intensify surveillance through PHCs. All the endemic districts were asked to submit periodic reports even if no cases were noticed. The district administration was advised to treat the sources of unsafe water with temephos eight times a year. Fine nylon mesh and double cloth stainers were distributed to household in all guinea worm affected villages. Self-sticking wall posters and identity cards were issued to all the villages and individual. Students from colleges and schools were mobilized to impart health education to the people. Ten epidemiological teams were deployed during 1990 in the endemic states and districts to monitor GW situation and GWEP implementation. As in 1992, the number of cases of guinea worm had come down to 1081. In February 2000, the International Commission for Certification of Dracunculiasis Eradication recommended that India be certified free of the disease. The surveillance of the endemic districts, however, continues lest it returns under favourable conditions.

ANTHRAX

Anthrax is one of the oldest recorded diseases of animals. It has been eliminated from the world. But there is always a danger of its virus being used clandestinely to infect human beings, as has been the case recently in the USA and several other countries. Knowledge about the disease is given below.

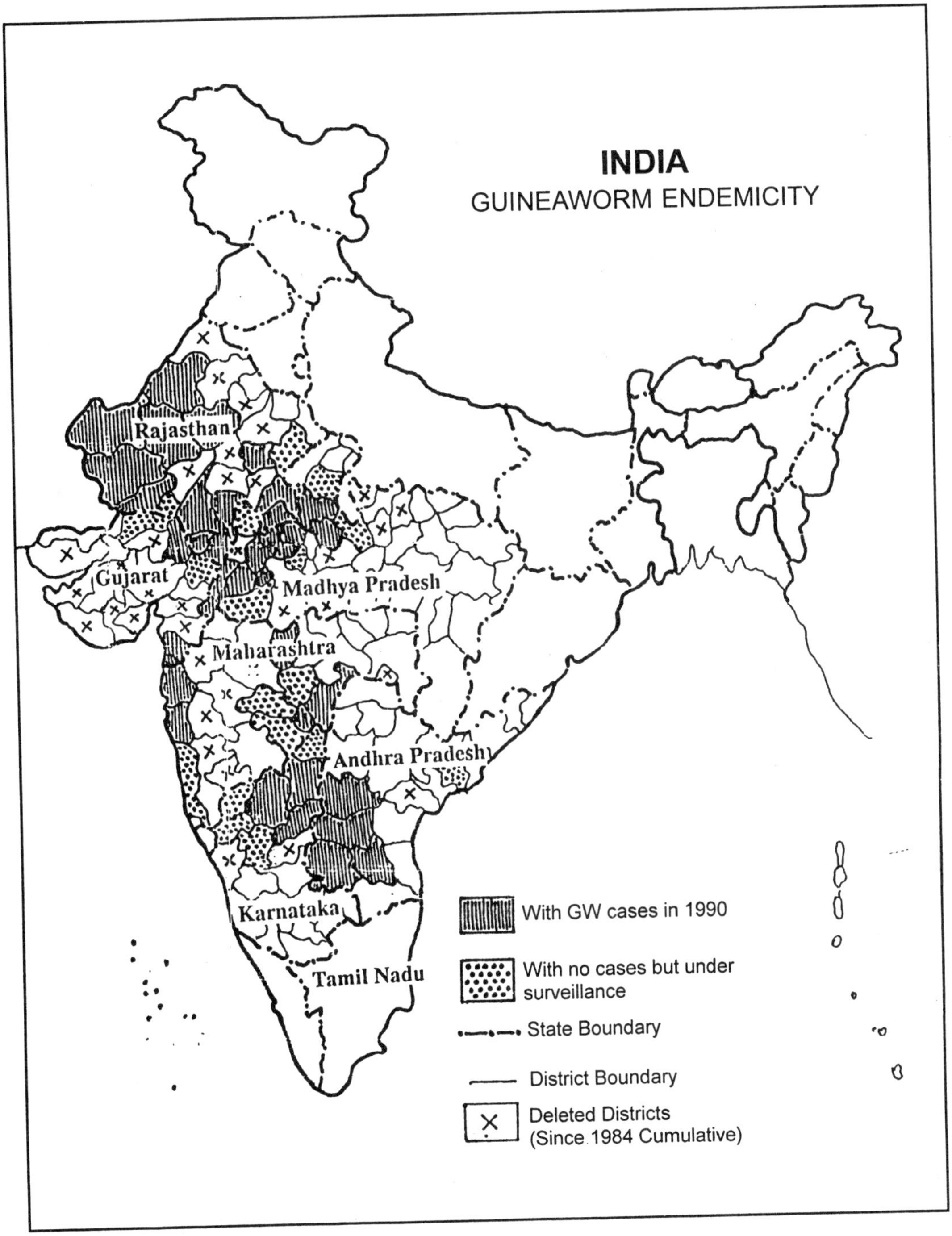

Fig. 10.3: India: Guinea Worm Affected Areas (1990-91)

During the eighteenth and nineteenth centuries it spread like plague over the southern part of Europe taking a heavy toll of human and animal life. It was the first disease whose causative agent was diagnosed to be a micro-organism by C.J. Davaine in 1863. Robert Kotch isolated the organism in pure culture in 1876. It was also the first bacterial disease against which a vaccine was found to be effective by Louis Pasteur in 1881. These discoveries led to the origin and development of modern science of bacteriology and immunology.

Anthrax is caused by spore-forming bacterium *Bacillus Anthracis*, an organism, which under certain conditions, forms highly resistant spores that may persist and retain their virulence in contaminated soil and other materials for many years. Anthrax spores can be produced in dry form and stored into particles. Eating under-cooked meat of animals infected with the bacilli is one of the important ways of getting anthrax. It is not communicable from human to human and as such the disease does not spread very fast. Recently, the disease has come to prominence because there are distinct possibilities of terrorists producing the spores and sprinkling them in populated cities. The incubation period of the infection is 2 to 6 days.

Anthrax attacks in three ways: skin infection, inhalation and intestinal. Most people suffering from the disease can recover. Deaths are few if treated in time and adequately. The skin infection begins with itchy bumps as it happens in the case of insect bites. Within a day or two it develops into vesicle and then painless ulcer one to three centimeter diameter with a black spot in the centre. Lymph glands in the adjoining areas also swell. One-fifths of the untreated cases of cutaneous anthrax end in death. If treated with antibiotic medicines in time, patients generally survive.

The initial cases of inhalation anthrax resemble common cold. Soon they become serious cases of respiratory obstruction. Usually, these cases result in death after 2-3 days of serious infection. The intestinal anthrax may result from consumption of half-cooked meat of infected animals. It is characterized by an acute inflammation of the intestinal tract. To begin with, the patient feels nausea, loss of appetite, vomiting and fever. These are followed by diarrhea, vomiting of blood, and severe abdominal pain. Quarter to two-third of patients infected by intestinal anthrax die.

Anthrax is a universal disease even if more concentrated in certain parts of the world. Repeated epizootics of the disease resulted in heavy contamination of the soil in southern Europe, and parts of Asia, Africa and Americas. A number of countries have regions of periodic contagion in Australia, Japan, China, Thailand, India, Iran, Saudi Arabia, Morocco, Egypt, Italy, Poland, Russia and its associated Republics of Central Asia, Mexico, Argentina, Brazil, Uruguay, USA and many other countries such as U.K. During the last ten years (1990 to Feb. 2000), India had 35 cases of anthrax in Pondicherry. It took an epidemic form in Orissa in 1997 when a cyclonic storm brought heavy rains. The disease is not uncommon in those parts of the country where people eat uncooked or semi-cooked or dry meat.

A sort of epidemics of human anthrax occurred during World War I when large number of British and US troops and many persons in the civil society of England and USA were infected by the use of shaving brushes imported from Japan. It can be transmitted through clothes, furs, woolens, etc. The hazards of the disease can be minimized or even eliminated by better hygiene and careful handling of the materials suspected to be contaminated. Once the symptoms of infection appear or there is danger of attack, surveillance of the disease and immediate treatment should be the first priority. Prompt diagnosis can avoid many a tragedy. Penicillin is the best medicine for it, particularly because it is available almost everywhere at a reasonably low price.

Practically all animals are susceptible to anthrax. They usually get the infection while grazing in contaminated soil. The pet animals get the disease through contaminated food. The disease may occur in peracute, acute, sub-acute form (internal anthrax) or chronic and localized form (external anthrax). The peracute form usually leads to instant death; the acute forms take two days before the animal dies. In sub-acute cases it takes three to four days before the animal dies.

Prophylactic vaccination is extensively used in preventing anthrax in animals. If treated early, most of the animals survive.

YAWS

Yaws is a chronic contagious non-venereal disease, which stands almost eliminated from India. Yaws is caused by *T. Pertenues,* an agent, which is too small to be distinguishable, even microscopically. The disease usually comes in childhood. It starts with a primary skin lesion, followed by several eruptions and destructive lesions of the skin and bones.

Yaws is a disease of the tropics: between Tropic of Cancer and Capricorn. It used to be a major public health problem in Central America, Southeast Asia and America. Much of Africa is free but the resurgence of the disease is very much visible in West African countries like Ghana. Small foci are found in Brazil, Colombia, Ecuador and Guyana in South America. In Asia, it occurs in Indonesia, Papua New Guinea and Pacific island countries like Fiji.

In 1950, about 400 million people lived in yaws affected zones and 50 to 100 million persons had active yaws. With intensive mass treatment supported by WHO and UNICEF, the prevalence rate has come down to less than 1 million. The disease, however, remains endemic; it is yet to be eradicated. In some countries, it is on its come back trail.

In India yaws was endemic in Andhra Pradesh, Madhya Pradesh, Maharashtra, Orissa and Tamil Nadu prior to mass campaign against it in 1950s. According to 1985 survey, it is still prevalent in Andhra Pradesh (districts of West Godavary, Khammam and Vijianagaram), Madhya Pradesh (Bastar district) and Orissa (districts of Keonjhar, Mayurbhanj, Dhenkanel, Phulbani, Balasore and Koraput) even if at a very low level. Only 1349 cases were detected in these districts of three states during 1983-85. As at present, yaws in India appears to be in its last stage of existence but this situation is not likely to change. Yaws, unlike smallpox, is not amenable to eradication because the cases of yaws are contagious for years after the onset of symptoms. The agent remains in the body even after cure. The disease is not fatal. And there is no vaccine against it.

The causal agent of Yaws (*T. Pertenue*) measures about 20m in length and is coiled in 8-12 rigid spirals. It dies outside human body. There is no reservoir where it grows before entering human body. Transmission takes place from one infected person to other. As moist lesions break out, transmission increases. Yaws is primarily a disease of childhood; most of the cases occur before the age of 15 years. It is more prevalent among the men than women. There is no natural immunity from the disease. It is, however, noted that the disease provides some immunity against syphilis.

Yaws is a disease of the humid and hot tropics. Average rainfall of 1000 cm and high humidity for half of the year produce favourable conditions for the growth of yaws. Yaws is endemic among the tribal people of India. Scanty clothing, poor hygiene, over-crowding, poverty and poor housing are important socio-economic conditions for the yaws. It is a crippling disease; lesions on the palms and soles can disable the patient.

Yaws is transmitted through direct contact and secretions from the lesions of affected persons. It may also get into the soil and infect people when they sit or walk on it. For the first five years, it does not take a very serious form. But thereafter, the lesions enlarge, expand and break to deform the affected parts of the body. Palms and soles are invariably affected. Face is distorted particularly near the nose. WHO recommends three types of treatments: mass treatment, juvenile treatment and selective mass treatment.

REFERENCES

1. WHO, *Technical Report Series,* No. 447.
2. Government of India, *Health Survey* 1959-60.
3. Ashok Kumar *et al*: *Current Guineaworm Disease Situation in India,* New Delhi: National Institute of Communicable Diseases, 1991.
4. Government of India, Health Survey Report, 1946.

11

Diseases on the Way Out

This chapter aims at discussing the geographic aspects of the diseases, which are on the way out. They are yet to be eradicated but if the trends of the last decade are indicatives, they should not last for more than a decade. Most of these diseases are infectious ones; they are amenable to modern antibiotic drugs and improvements in public health facilities.

POLIOMYELITIS

The causal agent of poliomyelitis is known as *poliovirus hominis*. It attacks animals too. The attack of the virus may take place in one of the following four ways:

1. the virus may be released through tonsils or feces producing just a light infection of intestinal tract;
2. it may get lodged in the intestines and produce sub-clinical levels of infections with such symptoms like soar throat, fever, headache, nausea and vomiting;
3. it may produce serious though non-paralytic infection involving the central nervous system; and
4. it may paralyze various groups of muscles, particularly the legs, feet, arms, hands, face, etc. The bulbur paralysis is the most deadly among them.

Poliovirus hominis is 25 to 30 mu in size; it is resistant to 20 per cent ethyl ether in the cold. It is stable in PH medium in the range of 4 to 10. It is inactivated by disinfectants like chlorine, potassium permanganate and formalin and highly sensitive to ultraviolet light and heat. When exposed to 50° C temperature, it dies within minutes but it can survive for many weeks at room temperature, for many months under refrigeration, and for many years in 50 per cent glycerine solution. It is indeed one of the most resistant viruses that attack human beings.

The virus enters the human body through nasal and pharyngeal portals or through digestive tracks and intestines. It attacks the unterior horn of the spinal cord and the motor and premotor areas of the cerebral cortex. It is not found in any other animal. Inoculation of the virus in monkeys does, however, produce a response.

People in all age groups are not equally susceptible to this disease but the age at which people get infected by the virus is not the same for all. Originally, it was the disease of infants. It is no longer so. It can attack the children of all age groups but rarely after the age of five. Although researches do point to some families and races being more susceptible to polis, it has not been proved that is an inherited disease, or it occurs more in certain families and races than in others. One of the most important factors determining the severity of the attack is the physical condition of the host. Too much stress or fatigue just prior to attack favours severe attack. Pregnancy and high fever may also create conditions for polio attack.

How is the virus transmitted from one person to another is not yet known. Most probably, it is through the oral route. In areas where children in early age are exposed to the virus, they acquire some immunity against severe attack as the virus creates sub-clinical disease in the host. If the cultural conditions postpone the encounter with the virus to later years of childhood, epidemics may occur. It has also been noted that eradication of infectious diseases like cholera, dysentery and typhoid had been followed by severe attacks of polio. J.R. Paul warned as early as 1955 that cultural developments were changing the ecological relations between poliomyelitis and man. A.M.M. Payne in 1955 said, "any large scale disturbance of the ecology of the natural processes may be followed by unexpected and often undesirable side effects."

Polio is found all over the world. But certain areas are endemic where more children below the age of 5 get this infection than elsewhere. There are several areas in industrialized as well as other countries where polio came in epidemic forms until 1950 crippling thousands of children every summer.

Man is the only reservoir of the virus. Its hosts are infants and children. Its life in sewage is just 48 hours. In cold water, it can survive for 4 months; and in faeces for six months.

The situation started improving with the development of anti-polio vaccine in 1954. The World Health Assembly in 1988 passed a resolution to eradicate the disease. It started losing its grips on the developed countries by 1980s. Polio was eradicated from Americas in 1994, and there have been no cases in Europe and Western Pacific since 1999. South-East Asian region is the greatest reservoir of polio. The polio eradication programme has been a great success in this region also and the number of polio cases is on the decline. Sub-Saharan Africa is another area of concern. As such even the polio free countries are always at risk of re-infection. Full benefit of global eradication programme will be realized only when polio has been eradicated from the remotest areas of all endemic countries (Table 11.1 and Fig 11.1).

In India, polio is on the way out. In 1988, India reported 25711 cases; in 1998 the number of cases came down to 1934; in 1999, to1126; and in 2000 to less than 300. India plans to eradicate polio by 2005. A few districts in the northern states especially in UP, however, pose some problems. Polio cases have increased in these districts during 2001. Intensive administration of polio drops has been launched in these areas. Even in 2002, there were over 500 reported cases of polio in the eastern and central districts of UP. A special programme to administer polio drops has been launched but not all the children are covered (Fig. 11.2).

Table 11.1: Number of Poliomyelitis and Acute Flaccid Paralysis Cases in 1996

WHO Regions	*Confirmed Cases*		*AFP Cases*
	1995	*1996*	*1996*
Africa	2192	455	142
Americas	0	0	1550
Eastern Mediterranean	789	182	1328
Europe	206	166	1133
South-East Asia	3359	933	1207
Western Pacific	492	203	4497
Global total	7038	1939	9857

Source: WHO, World Health Report, 1998

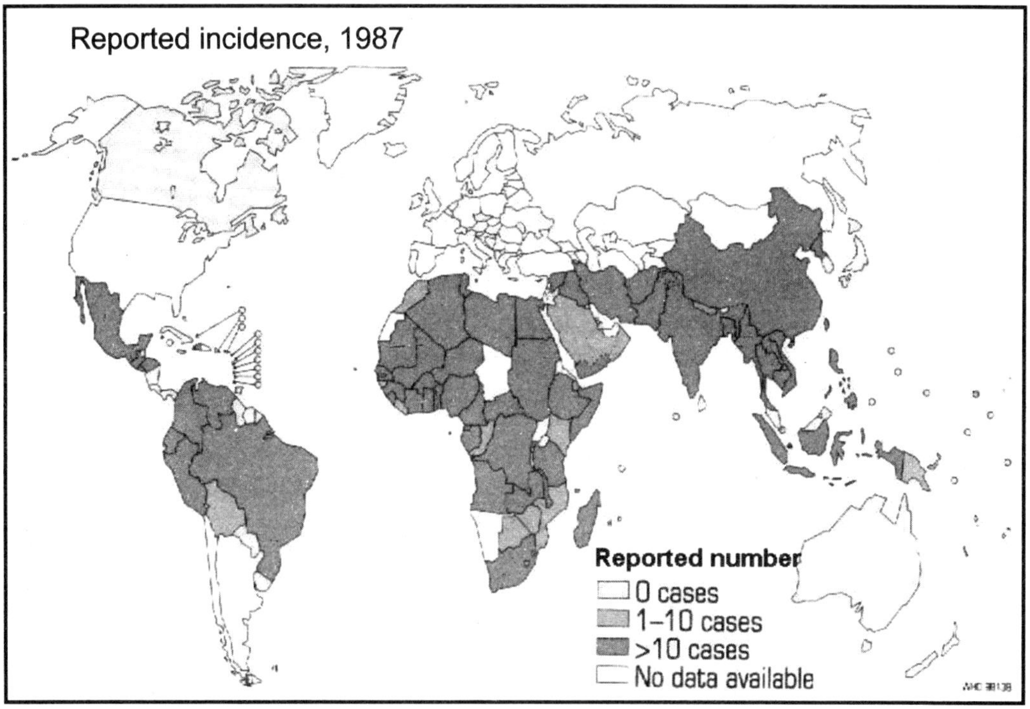

Fig. 11.1: Global Incidence of Polio:1987 and 1997

It is now possible to bring some paralytic polio cases to normalcy through surgery. Hospitals have been opened in India to reach out to the patients living in far-flung areas. The first such facility was at Waltair, Andhra Pradesh. Now there are several centres rein by religious and charitable organizations.

LEPROSY

Leprosy is probably the oldest and also one of the most baffling diseases of humankind. No one knows its place of origin. It affects the mucous membrane and peripheral nerves making the patient's face, hands and feet so deformed that he is not only crippled but also disabled physically, psychologically, socially and economically. In India, leprosy is traditionally considered to be a worst disease and incurable too. It is believed to attack only those who have committed heinous sins in this or previous life. The patients are expected to atone for their sins by suffering and begging. Even close family members shun and discard them.

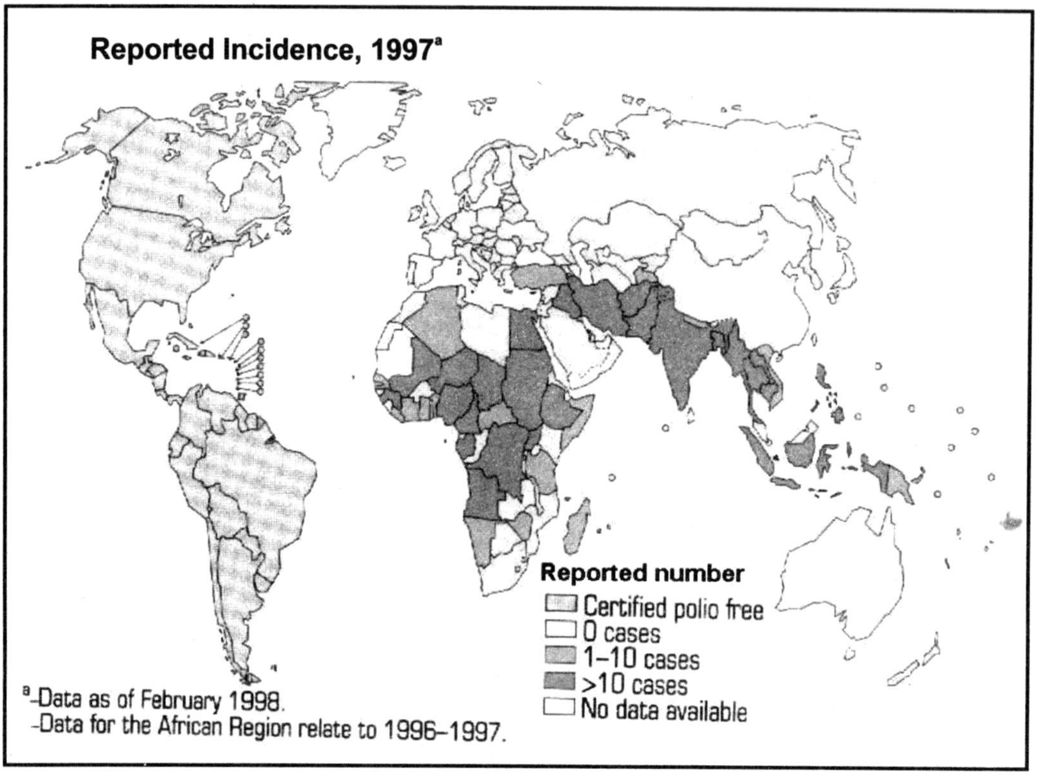

Source: World Health Reoprt, 1998

Fig. 11.2: India: Polio Cases (1997-2002)

Leprosy is caused by *Mycobacterium Leprae*, which morphologically resembles *Mycobacterium Tuberculosis*. Discovered by A. Hansen in 1875, the bacterium measures 1.5 to 5 microns in length and 0.2 to 0.5 microns in width.

The lepromatous variety is highly infectious. Its bacilli are lodged in the tissues of the body of the host and have a tendency to form globi. It affects the mucous membranes of the larynx, the eyes, the skin and also the peripheral nerves, and abdominal viscera. It spreads fast in the body. The second variety (tuberculoid) has a high degree of resistance to infection. The bacilli grow in the tissues. It is relatively less contagious. The last one (intermediate type) is marked by various degrees of resistance to infection. Only a few bacilli are present in the tissues and its symptoms are localized in skin and the nerves. In most cases, it is non-infectious.

Leprosy is a human disease; it is not found in animals. The bacilli have to penetrate the human tissues and only gradually they spread along the nerve fibers. Children are more susceptible to leprosy than adults because their developing body produces changes in the skin, and hence their cutaneous nerve plexuses are easily damaged. That is why, about 30 per cent of all leprosy attacks take place before the age of 15. Those who are exposed to infection before the age of five are most likely to contact the disease. It is, however, not a hereditary disease and the children of lepers do not get leprosy if they are separated from their parents in early childhood.

Studies show a close relationship between the incidences of leprosy and tuberculosis. Immunity from tuberculosis also makes a person immune from leprosy. That is perhaps the reason why multiple drug therapy (MDT) has gained importance in recent years. It is also observed that men are more susceptible to leprosy than women. The reasons may be physiological or environmental. It has also been suggested that dark skinned races are less susceptible to leprosy than white and yellow races. Whatever may be the case, leprosy has been eradicated from European, American and Australian continents. It has also been eradicated from other developed regions and countries like Japan. The only region where it still poses a health challenge is South and Southeast Asia.

Types of Leprosy

Leprosy is classified in different ways. The three most accepted and used classifications are: Madrid; Ridley-Japling; and Indian. Indian classification is a clinico-bacterial classicification evolved by the Hind Kushta Nivaran Sangh (Indian Leprosy Association). It recognizes five types: undeterminate type, tuberculoid type, borderline type, lepromatous type, and pure neuritic type. The Madrid system of classification recognizes only the first four types.

The indeterminate type covers cases with just one or two hypopigmented macules and definite sensory impairment. The tuberculoid type covers those cases, which have one or two well defined anaesthetic and bacteriologically negative lesions. Cases with four or more lesions with sensory loss are classified as borderline type. The lepromatous type are those which have several bacteriologically positive lesions. And the last category (pure neuritic) consists of the cases, which show nerve involvement but no lesions. They are bacteriologically negative.

Taking the use of the MDT as basis, WHO has divided leprosy cases into three types: paucibacillary single-lesion leprosy; paucibacillary leprosy (2-5 skin lesions); and multibacillary leprosy (more than five skin lesions). The first can be cured without MDT; the other two need MDT.

Environmental Factors

The risk of leprosy transmission is controlled by environmental factors. Humidity appears to favour the survival of laprae in the environment. The laprae can survive in moist soil for 46 days; and in the nasal secretions for 9 days. Moist climate is favourable. Over crowding is another favorable factor in the transmission of the disease.

Laprae enter the body only through cuts and injuries. The environment in which chances of injuries are higher is more favourable to the transmission of the disease. Laper mothers do not give birth to leper babies. Contact with the mother, however, makes the baby susceptible to infection. Children are known to get leprosy through their parents.

Geographic Distribution

Leprosy is a communicable disease but not common everywhere. Why does it occur in some places more than elsewhere, is yet to be fully understood. Climatic factors like temperature and humidity do appear to have some relevance because it is more common in hot and humid climatic zones. It has also been noticed that more patients come to clinics during March-September and inflammatory changes in neuromuscular lesions increase during March-May. This shows some co-relation between high temperature with high humidity and increased bacterial activity. It is, however, not clear as to whether the climatic factors work on the agent or the host or something else. It may be that the agent and the host come together more frequently during these seasons and hence the high rate of infection.

Since there is a close morphological affinity between mycobacterium leprae and the other mycobacteria such as mycobacterium tuberculosis. It is possible that the increase or decrease in one may have implications for others. In any case, environmental sanitation along with preventive measures do play a crucial role in controlling the disease. Segregation of the leprosy patient is often considered essential for stopping its spread, but it is not a very practical proposition. It promts the leprosy patients to hide themselves from detection. Solution lies in early detection, treatment and rehabilitation and of course intensive health education to make lepers acceptable in the society.

Global

For the first time since global statistics have been collected, the number of registered cases of leprosy has come down to less than 1 million. Further, all registered cases have access to MDT. Total number of cases on treatment in the world in 1999 was 753,263 i.e. 1.25 per 1000 population. Number of new cases reported was 738,284 (12.30 per 100,000 population). Thus there is a hope that leprosy will be eliminated sooner than later.

Table 11.2: Global Prevalence of Leprosy, 1999-2000

Region	*Total Cases on Treatment*	*Rate**	*Number of New Cases*	*Rate@*
Americas	90,447	1.10	45m599	5.70
Europe	846	(-)	172	(-)
E. Mediteranean	8,755	0.20	5,757	1.20
Africa	64,490	1.00	55,635	8.60
South-east Asia	574,924	3.80	621,620	41.30
Western Pacific	13,771	0.10	9.501	0.60
Total World	753,263	1.25	738,284	12.30

* Rate per 10,000 population; @ Rate per 100,000 population.

Source: WHO, World Health Report; Govt. of India, Health Information of India.

It is estimated that there are about 1.32 million leprosy patients in the world. The figures given in Table 11.2 refer to only those cases, which were registered. Thus about half a million cases are yet to be diagnosed. Most of them live in Asia and Africa. By January 2000, about 10.70 million cases were cured with MDT. About 2.30 million people in the world are disabled due to leprosy. They need rehabilitation.

The global trend of decline in leprosy is visible in Southeast Asian region too even if less spectacularly. In 1985, the number of registered cases amounted to 5.50 million; in 1999, the number came down to 0.50 million. About 10 million people have been cured since the introduction of MDT. The leprosy load in the Southeast Asian region is given in Table 11.3.

Table 11.3: Incidence of Leprosy in Southeast Asia (1999)

Country	*Registered Cases (Jan.1, 2000)*	*Rate per 10,000*	*Cases Detected (in 1999)*	*Rate per l lakh*
Bangladesh	11,092	0.90	14,336	11.40
India	495,073	5.00	537,956	54.30
Indonesia	23,156	1.10	17,477	8.30
Myanmar	28,404	5.90	30,479	62.90
Nepal	13,572	5.70	18,693	78.70
Sri Lanka	1,260	0.70	1,757	9.40
Thailand	2,291	0.40	864	1.40

Source: WHO, Regional Health Report (South and South-East Asia), 2001.

India

State of health in India at the time of Independence was grim. In 1950 there were 1.37 million leprosy patients in the country; the number went up to 4 million by 1981. Prevalence rate was 57 per 10,000 population. The number increased partly because of the increase in population; partly because of better reporting; partly because of the weak public health programme and partly because of increased mobility of lepers. With the introduction of the MDT since 1983, a large number of cases have been treated and discharged. In 1987, the number of cases cured exceeded the number of new cases. In 1998-99, the number of cases discharged was 0.78 million and number of new cases detected stood at 0.77 million.

So far, the leprosy eradication programme has been able to treat over 12.19 million cases out of which 8.33 million cases were treated with MDT. In March 1999, there were 0.509 million patients in the country giving a prevalence rate of 5.19 per 10,000. people. India today accounts for as much as 60.9 per cent of all recorded leprosy patients in the world. About 15 per cent of these patients are children. The proportion of multi-bacillary cases is 56 per cent; among the new cases, it is 32 per cent. The deformity among the newly discovered cases is 3 to 4 per cent.

At present only about one fifth of leprosy patients fall in infectious category. They are the ones who have not been given Multi Drug Therapy and are in prolonged contact with healthy persons. Only 5 per cent of the total population in a community is susceptible to the disease. Even a single dose of MDT kills 90.9 per cent of the bacilli in laboratory conditions. It takes anywhere between six months to one year to completely cure the patient. Unlike most other bacteria, the leprosy bacilli multiply very slowly, and hence have a very weak potential to cause the disease. A single dose of MDT can cure a patient with a single lesion. Deformity caused by the disease is not infectious. It is like post-scar on skin after the attack of smallpox.

As stated earlier, India accounts for over 60 per cent of global recorded cases of leprosy. The prevalence rate has, however, come down from 5.7 per 1000 population in 1981 to 0.50 per 1000 population in 2000 (Fig. 11.3). The total recorded cases have decreased to about 5 lakhs. And the cases cured are less than the new cases detected. About one fifth, of the patients are children below the age 15 years. The deformity rate is still high ranging from 6 to 8 per cent.

The prevalence rate of leprosy is secularly declining: it was 2916 per 1000 population in 1986. It came down to 770 in 1999. At the same time, the detection rate is improving each year. It was 528 in 1999 as against 477 in 1986 (Fig. 11.3)

Leprosy is an all-India disease; it is prevalent in every part of the country. The distribution is, however, uneven. Inter-state variations in the prevalence rate and the proportion of population at risk are quite substantial. (see Table 11.4 and Figures 11.3). Among the states, West Bengal, Bihar, Orissa, Uttar Pradesh and Madhya Pradesh are marked with greater prevalence of the disease. These five states contribute 71 per cent of the leprosy load of the country. Earlier, Tamil Nadu, Maharashtra, Andhra Pradesh and Pondicherry had high caseload but it is no longer so. If we look at the report of the Special Committee on 'Leprosy and Its Control in India', 1941, there used to be a very high incidence in the east coast and peninsular states like West Bengal, Jharkhand, Orissa, Andhra Pradesh, parts of Karnataka and Tamil Nadu and the whole of Kerala. A belt of moderate incidence ran through the Himalayan foothills. The incidence was lower in central part of India but there were several local foci that spread the disease far and wide. The situation has changed since then but all these areas continue to be endemic requiring regular surveillance.

In the highly endemic areas leprosy incidences may range from 2 to 5 per cent of total population. But incidence rate reaching 20 per cent in some areas is not rare. In non-endemic regions like Rajasthan, Punjab and Haryana, leprosy cases are rare; the incidence rate may not go beyond 0.01/1000. Only about one-fifth of the total cases in India are lepromatoes. It is unusual to find areas in India where leprosy is both common and severe. In Bengal, Bihar, Orissa and north-eastern parts of the country, it is common but mild. In the foot-hills of the Himalayas and in Rajasthan and Punjab, it is uncommon but severe. In the southern states of Tamil Nadu and Andhra Pradesh, it is very common but the severity is moderate. (Fig. 11.3)

Leprosy Control Programme

Government of India launched a National Leprosy Control Programmr as early as 1955. It targeted the rural areas of high and moderate endemicity. Centres for detection and treatment were started in areas where the incidence rate of the disease was 10/1000. Each centre served a population of 80,000 living within a compact area of 8 to 16 sq. km. By 1960, as many as 125 centres were established: four main treatment and study centres were located in Madhya Pradesh, Tamil Nadu, Uttar Pradesh and West Bengal, and 111 subsidiary centres in Maharashtra (22), Bihar (17), Andhra Pradesh (15), Tamil Nadu (14), Karnataka (8), Uttar Pradesh (8), West Bengal (7), and Madhya Pradesh. The programme was further strengthened in 1969; it

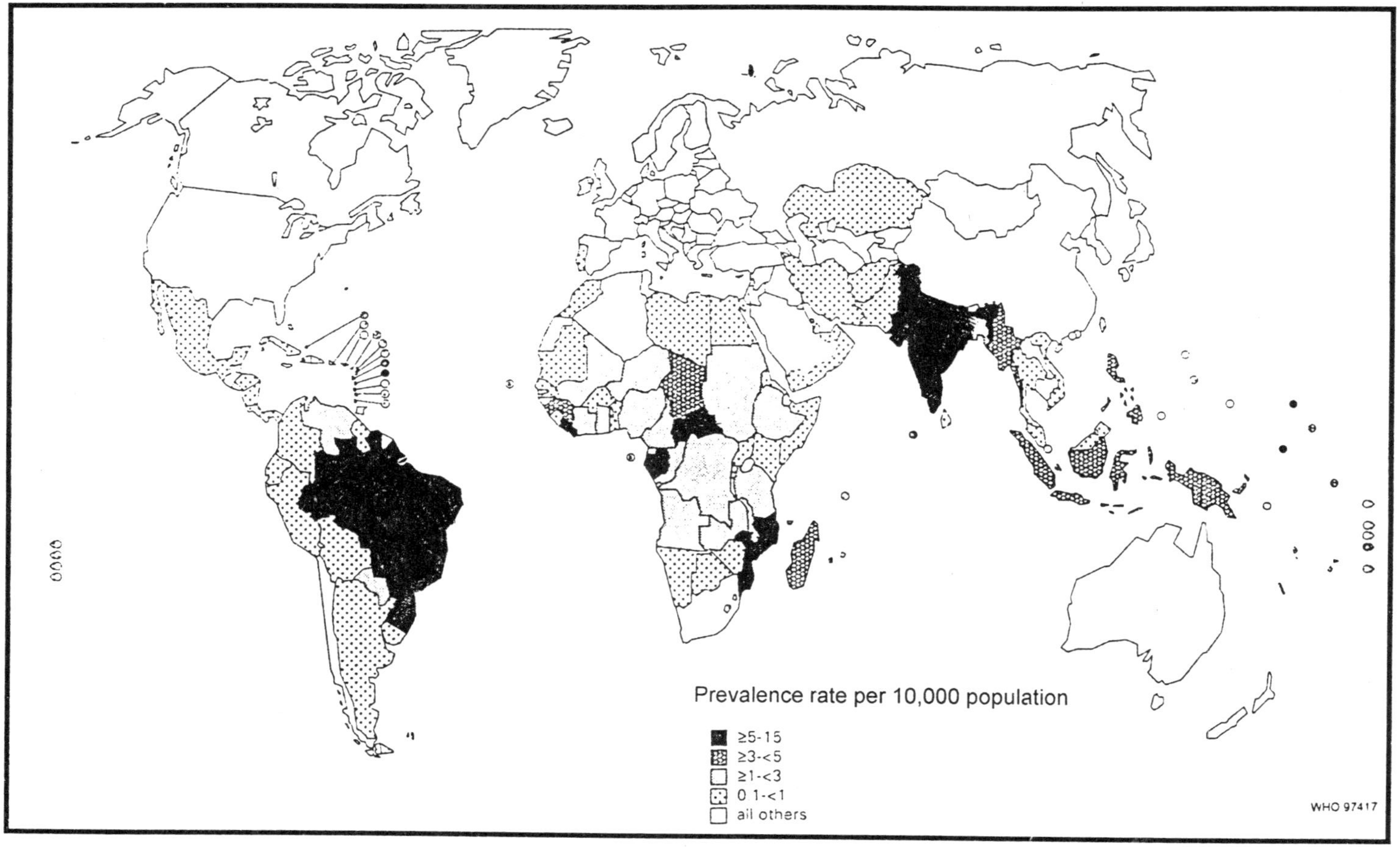

Fig. 11.3: Global Incidence of Leprosy (1997)

Source: WHO, Weekly Epidiological Report, 1997.

was converted into a central government activity but the focus continued to be Domiciliary Dapsone Monotherapy. With the availability of highly effective treatment of leprosy by MDT, the programme was redesigned as a National Leprosy Eradication Programme in 1983. After the World Health Assembly Resolution of 1991, it aimed at reducing the caseload to < 1/1000 population by 2000 AD. World Bank, in 1993-94, assisted India to the tune of Rs. 3020 million to meet the following objectives:

Table 11.4: Distribution of Leprosy in India in 1997-98

States	*Cases Detected (Number)*	*Cases Discharged (Number)*	*Cases Detected per 100,000 Population*
Andhra Pradesh	53,418	55410	74.20
Arunachal Prasesh	151	328	15.00
Assam	1765	4204	7.20
Bihar	104478	121688	100.00
Goa	436	380	36.30
Gujarat	15567	19436	32.00
Haryana	148	162	0.70
HP	258	1053	1.30
J & K	739	1447	0.12
Karnataka	17766	22997	35.50
Kerala	4699	6606	15.70
MP	31449	51444	40.32
Maharashtra	62473	51229	67.20
Orissa	99341	58722	296.00
Punjab	1198	1250	5.40
Rajasthan	3037	2748	5.73
Tamil Nadu	29649	26162	49.50
UP	55859	67157	35.00
West Bengal	38134	60440	50.00
Delhi	2170	6125	18.00
India	524504	572812	57.80

Source: Health Information of India, 1997-98

1. to cover the whole country by MDT and to create facilities for domiciliary treatment in endemic districts;
2. to extend the services to moderate and low endemic areas through mobile units;
3. to intensify health education to remove the stigma attached to leprosy; and
4. to create facilities for the treatment of deformity and rehabilitating of the needy.

In endemic rural areas, Leprosy Control Units (LCUs) have been set up at the rate of one unit for a population 0.45 million. A LCU has a complement of one medical officer and a supporting staff of 24. The survey, education and treatment (SET) units attached to Primary Health Centres (PHC) have one para-medical worker each. Each SET takes care of about 25,000 people. For urban areas, there are Urban Leprosy Centres (ULC), each covering 50,000 people. Each ULC

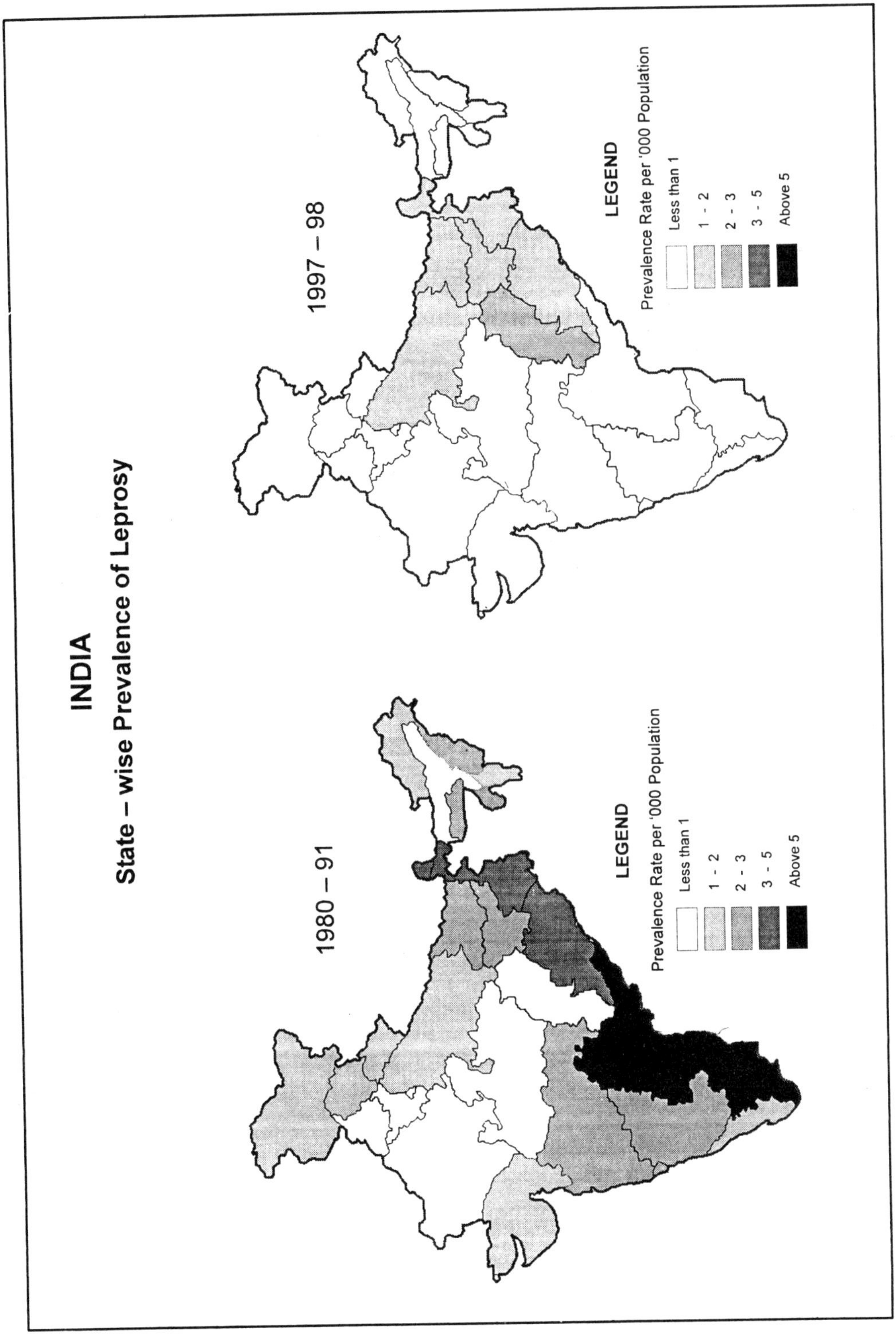

Fig. 11.4: India: Leprosy Cases per '000 Population

Source: Centre for Social Sciences Research in Leprosy (CCSRL), Wardha

has one para-medical worker. As in 1999, there were 778 LCUs, 907 ULCs, 5744 SETs, 290 Temporary Hospitalisation Wards, 75 Reconstruction Surgery Units, 40 Sample Survey-cum-Assessment Units, and 350 Mobile Treatment Units.

WHO has set the year 2005 as the target year for the eradication of leprosy in the world. It is providing support for supply of anti-leprosy drugs for meeting the entire need of the country. In addition to this, it is providing assistance to eradicate leprosy from all the five endemic states. The other international agencies helping India in this regard are DANIDA, German Leprosy Relief Association, Damien Foundation, Lepra India, Italian Leprosy Relief Association, and Swiss Emmaus.

CHOLERA

Cholera is a disease that manifests itself as acute diarrhoea with watery non-faecal stools causing loss of salt in the body. Death from dehydration is common. It is a communicable disease known in India from ancient times. During the nineteenth century, several pandemics of cholera originated from India and spread to Europe. The last pandemic started from Indonesia; it has yet to be overcome. It is endemic to India and hence we have to be vigilant lest it overruns the country again in a far more virulent form than before.

Cholera is not choosy among its potential victims: it attacks persons of all ages and sexes, both in rural and urban areas, and in western or eastern countries. It is, however, more prevalent in areas where hygienic and sanitary conditions are poor and diarrhoeal diseases common.

Etiology

The agent of cholera is vibrio discovered by Koch in 1883. Measuring 4 by 3 microns, it is mobile and possesses a complex chemical structure. These vibrios are of three types: A (inaba), B (Ogawa) AB (Hokojima), and El Tor. Most cholera vibrios can grow and develop in temperatures ranging from –55° C and 16° C in an alkaline medium (PH 7 to 8) containing oxygen. They can survive in both cold and dry climate. Acid medium destroys the vibrio. If a person having normal proportion of hydrochloric acid in the gastric juice swallows the vibrio, he will not get cholera, but if the proportion is low, the vibrios will pass down to the bowels and produce cholera.

An attack of cholera begins with discomfort, fatigue and diarrhea. The water of the stool becomes colourless like rice water. Soon a profuse vomiting of the water of the same colour appears along with excruciating cramps in the abdomen and the calf muscles of the leg. The victim collapses; his eyes sink in the sockets; his nose stands out thin and pinched above his sunken eyes and hollow cheeks. His looks become frightening; the skin of the fingers become loose; voice turns husky; body becomes cold; and pulse rate slows down and becomes erratic. The body temperature sinks below the normal, but when measured in rectum, it rises to 105 degree F. The victim is unable to pass urine and he is ever thirsty.

In August 1854, John Snow, while investigating the epidemic in Broad Street, London, found out how the disease spread from place to place. He traced the infection in the stools of a child patient washed off in a cesspool which discharged in a well just three feet away through a leakage. By the end of August, most of the people who drank water from that well were down with cholera. Two days later a woman died of this disease in Hampstead. She had taken water from the same well because she liked its taste. She gave the contaminated water to her niece; she also died. Dr. Snow concluded that the disease was water borne and the germ emanated from the linen or excreta of the patient (D. Stamp). Macnamara, a scientific observer, later confirmed that cholera germ multiplied inside the stomach of the patient and passed out with his or her stools. When water was contaminated with such stools, the germ entered other persons' bowels where they multiplied to start the vicious circle of death through the stomach of other victims.

The credit for tracing the germ goes to Dr. Koch, a German scientist. And the place where he traced it was none other than Calcutta, India. The germ was called comma bacillus. Dr. Koch concluded that, "cholera never rises spontaneously. No healthy man can ever be attacked by cholera unless he swallows the comma microbe, and this germ can only develop from its like, it cannot be produced from any other thing or out of nothing. It is only in the intestine of man, or in highly polluted waters, like those in India, that it can grow."

Human beings alone can be infected with vibrio cholera. Any person, on becoming a host of vibrio cholera, can develop the disease if he does not have natural immunity or is not temporarily protected by excess of hydrochloric acid in his stomach or has not been inoculated or did not have cholera earlier within a span of a year or so.

The complex mechanism governing the occurrence of endemic, epidemic and pandemic cholera is still obscure. The influence of factors like climate on the agent or the host and on the agent-host relationship is still to be fully understood. Nor is the role of genetics and ecology known. Available data and the experiences of the past do indicate a close relationship between environment and cholera incidence. The outbreaks of the disease take place during the same season of the year in any given place. The first major outbreak of cholera in India occurred in 1816. That was an exceptionally hot and dry year. The preceding and succeeding years were the years of heavy rain, floods and famines when a large section of the population was famished.

History and Geography

Reference to diarrhoeal diseases in historical literature is not infrequent. Susruta in the seventh century AD mentions of a diseases quite akin to cholera. There is mention of a similar disease in Greek literature of fifth century BC. All these references could, however, be for ordinary bacillary dysentery. It was only in the fifteenth century AD that we find mention of an acute diarrhoeal disease that might have been cholera. According to the Chinese literature of the early seventeenth century, cholera reached China from India.

Cholera is believed to be endemic from ancient times in the deltaic areas of Bengal in India. From India, it reached Russia through Persia by land route and to China by sea route. It reached Egypt and Turkey through Arabia and thence on to Europe. It appears there was a parallel endemic centre in the valley of Yuan, a tributary of Yangtze Kiang in China.

The first great cholera pandemic started in India in 1817 and spread by land to China in 1818, to Sri Lanka the following year and by sea to Mauritius and East Africa in 1820, to Philippines, China and Japan in 1822 and by land to Iran, Arabia and Russia in the next two years. It, however, did not reach Europe. Another pandemic began in India in 1826. It reached China the same year and then on to Manchuria, Mongolia and Russia by 1830. It was in

Edinburgh, UK by 1832 via Germany and then on to Canada the same year. By 1836, cholera was present in almost the whole of the United States and it remained there until 1838.

There were five more pandemics originating in India that reached practically the whole world. One of them started in 1840 and ended in 1849, the other started in 1863 and ended in 1866, the third started in 1879 and ended in 1883, the fourth stared in 1891 and ended 1886 and the fifth started in 1902 and ended in 1908. After 1910, no pandemics occurred but the epidemics spreading in different parts of India were many.

Global experience shows that cholera cannot be stopped from moving from place to place or country to country but it would not be a major health hazard unless public health situation favours. Cholera outbreak is generally abrupt. By the time measures are afoot to control it, its decline from the peak is already visible. The epidemic has its roots in water but mere improvement in water quality after the outbreak of the disease does not stop it. Transmission continues through contacts. The seasonality of the disease is not fixed; it differs from place to place and also from time to time in the same place. Cholera does, however, occur at intervals even in epidemic areas.

Number of cholera cases and deaths are given in Table 11.5.

Table 11.5: Cholera Cases and Deaths in the World: 1961-97

Year	*Cases*	*Deaths*	*Fatality Rate %*
1961	62,000	30,560	49.30
1971	176,000	26,048	14.80
1981	51,000	2,448	4.80
1991	595,000	19,040	3.20
1995	208,000	5,034	2.40
1996	143,000	6,689	4.67
1997	147,000	6274	4.26

Source: Health Information of India, 1998

The chances of controlling cholera, thanks to international cooperation under the leadership of WHO, have improved in recent years, but a new strain of the diseases code named O139 cropped up in 1992, making its eradication a long drawn process. It has spread to Pakistan in the west and Bangladesh in the east. It was responsible for 10,000 deaths in southern Bangladesh in 1993.

As already mentioned, cholera appears to have originated in India. It has been its home and it still persists in South Asian countries. It knocks at the door practically every year but fails to acquire epidemic or pandemic status because of the constant vigilance maintained in these countries to ward off its onset. It followed the trade routes to reach the South-east and East Asian countries like Myanmar, Thailand, Cambodia, Indonesia, and China. To the west, it reached Europe through Iran, Egypt, Turkey and Greece. The main foci of endemicity continue to be located in India and China even to day.

Cholera has been a major killer in India for about two centuries and until 1921the annual number of cholera cases used to hover around 4000,000 and the number of people who died was 250,000 to 300,000 per annum. In certain years, the mortality figures were really staggering.

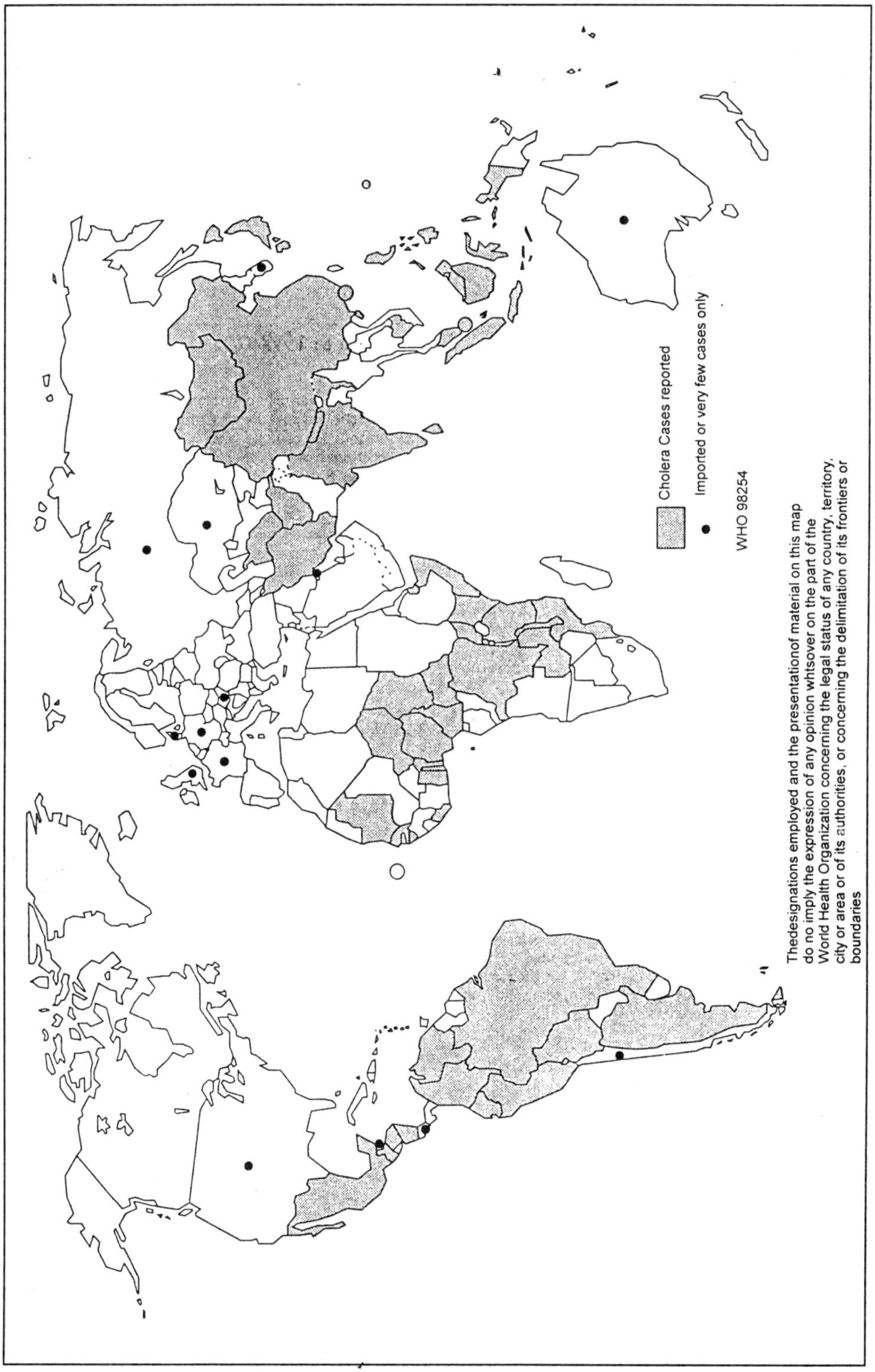

Fig. 11.5: Global Incidence of Cholera (1998)
Source: Countries of the World Reporting Cholera Cases, 1997.

In 1900 AD, it killed 805,698 persons; in 1906, 682,649 persons; and in 1919, 556,533 persons. Greater investment in public health after independence brought the incidence as well as deaths down. Recent figures of morbidity and mortality are given in Table 11.6.

Table 11.6: Cholera Morbidity and Mortality in India 1877 to 2000

Year	*Incidence (per year)*	*Deaths (per year)*	*Fatality Rate in per cent*
1877-81	288,950	–	
1887-91	400,934	–	
1907-11	397,127	–	
1917-21	392,070	–	
1927-31	297,756	–	
1937-41	147,423	–	
1950	176,307	86,997	49.34
1965	53,285	12,947	29.90
1975	21,955	2,320	10.50
1985	5,808	155	2.60
1994	4,973	32	0.64
1995	3,315	5	0.15
1996	4396	34	0.77
1997	2,768	16	0.58
1998			

Source: Health Information of India; R.P. Misra, *Medical Geography of India*, 1970.

When we look at the statewise data for the years 1994 to 1996, we find that the states that still have above 200 cases per annum are Gujarat, Karnataka, Maharashtra, Tamil Nadu, Uttar Pradesh, and Delhi. Incidentally, barring aside Uttar Pradesh, all these states have large metropolitan centres with ever expanding slums. Even a rural state like Uttar Pradesh has seven cities with a million or more population. Some four decades back in 1961-62, the mortality from cholera per 1000 population was highest in the states of West Bengal, Bihar, Orissa, Uttar Pradesh and Karnataka whereas the cholera cases per thousand population were highest in Bihar, followed by West Bengal, Maharashtra, Karnataka and Andhra Pradesh (Fig. 11.5).

According to the Expert Committee appointed by the Government of India in 1958 to review the question of cholera and to recommend ways and means to deal with it, the following were identified as highly endemic areas.

1. Lower reaches of the Ganga valley, particularly the deltaic districts of West Bengal;
2. Middle Ganga valley falling in the states of Bihar and Uttar Pradesh;
3. Coastal districts of Orissa; and
4. Deltaic districts of Godavary, Krishna and Kavery including the district of Tanjore, Tiruchirapalli, South Arcot, Krishna, West Godavary and Guntur.

Cholera is permanently present in these endemic areas. They, therefore, form a menace to the adjoining areas as they provide a permanent reservoir of infection.

The Committee, after studying the epidemics of 1957-59, concluded that the disease spread from one area to another in geographical contiguity, and that the appearance of cases in non-endemic areas depended entirely on the extent and intensity of infection in the neighbouring endemic zones, thereby indicating that the occurrence of cases in the former was triggered off by infection lurking in the endemic zones. The Committee also concluded that the disease appeared to spread from West Bengal to Bihar and Uttar Pradesh and thence to Orissa and from Orissa in two directions, towards the east and south. As it increased its coverage, subsidiary centres of infection were formed from which it moved radially to surrounding areas. These observations had practical as well as analytical value. Its practical value lay in the programme for control of the disease. From theoretical point of view it confirmed the conclusions reached by spatial diffusion theorists that the spread of communicable diseases could be predicted (T. Hagerstrand; R.P. Misra). During 1950s and 60s, a number of studies were conducted by geographers using Monto Carlo simulation model to predict the spread of a number of cultural, social, technological and other activities, events and innovations. They identified the city of Calcutta as the main focus of infection. A secondary focus was found in Puri-Balasore area.

A new biotype of cholera called Cholera El Tore entered India in 1964. It has considerably changed the geography of the disease in India. The old classical strain of cholera had its foci in West Bengal. The El Tor has spread in many states, which were earlier immune or had low intensity of the disease. It crossed the sea and invaded even Andaman & Nicobar Islands in 1966 and Rajasthan in 1969. Sudden outbreaks of the disease at the time of festivals and fairs, earlier a very common occurrence under the classical type regime, has now become rare. At present, Maharashtra, Tamil Nadu, Kerala, Gujarat and Delhi account for over 80 per cent of cholera incidence (Fig. 11.6).

Prevention and Control

'Prevention is better than cure' rule applies to cholera more than to any other disease. The dissemination of cholera is possible only if the infected faecal material reaches the mouth of the potential victim. The most common vehicle is water but raw or stale foods can also be responsible for it. The disease takes an epidemic form, if a large number of people simultaneously take contaminated water from a common source. If the epidemics occur in a non-endemic area the disease disappears after the last case. But in endemic areas, the infection persists even after the disease is gone and it returns even on a slight provocation.

Cholera in its initial stages of onset is often confused as acute bacillary dysentery. Only a clinical analysis can give a definite proof of the disease. Since it is not available everywhere and instantly, the best thing to do is to treat all such cases as cholera cases to begin with. Since the mortality from cholera results largely from dehydration, the replacement of fluid and maintenance of blood and tissue chloride are critical steps for survival of the patient. This could be done through intravenous administration of hypertonic alkaline salt solution.

In certain parts of the country, open tanks storing rainwater are the main sources of drinking water. Same tanks are used for bathing, washing of clothes and disposal of faecal material. The water of these tanks is not protected and hence carries bacteria and bacilli to the stomach of all

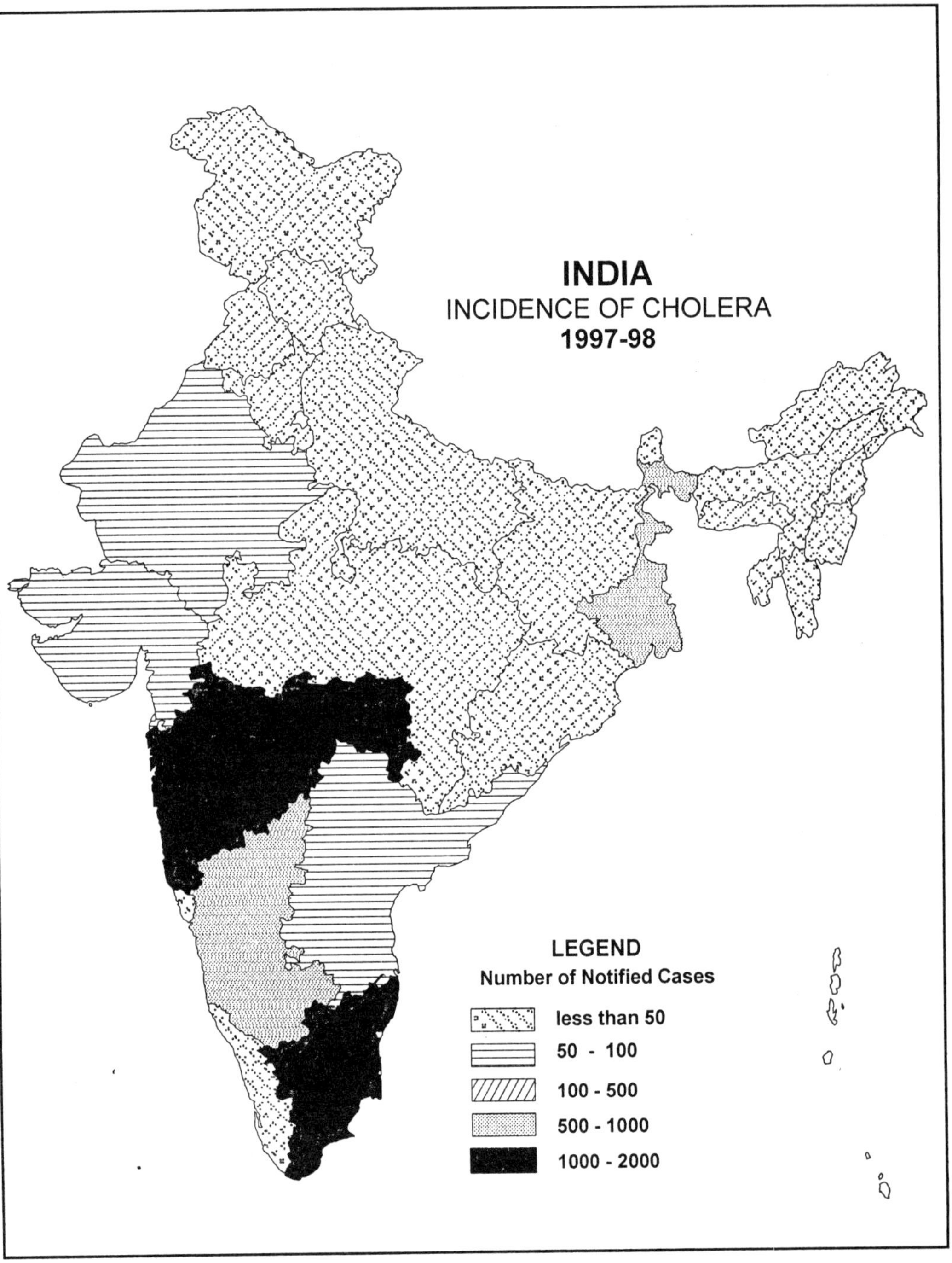

Fig. 11.6: India: Cholera Cases and Deaths (1998)

Source: Health Information of India, 1998.

those who use it. This is one of the major reasons why diarrhea and dysentery are so common in India. In endemic areas, it can produce cholera infection, which under favourable conditions takes the form of epidemics.

To conquer cholera forever, all that we need is effective measure of sanitation and hygiene backed by inoculation covering every potential victim especially in the endemic areas of the country. We have been able to inoculate almost everyone, but we have yet to win the battle on the hygiene front. We have yet to provide clean water to a large section of the population, particularly in rural areas. Required improvements in sanitary conditions are yet to take the form of national movement. The disease has been kept in check with the help of medicines. But we know that medicines are not the panacea for good health. They help us overcome the crisis but do not ensure its eradication. Healthy people are not likely to contract diseases and if they do, they can overcome them with a little aid from outside. So long as there is poverty in the country, so long as people fail to get nutritious food, so long as potable water is not available to each and every individual and so long as people remain unaware of the health hazards of their own behaviours and actions, the risks of contracting diseases like cholera remain. Cholera has been practically eradicated but the risk it poses for the future is yet to be eradicated.

MEASLES

Measles (morbilli rubeola) is an infectious disease of worldwide distribution. It breaks out at an interval of 2 to 4 years. It is a once in a lifetime disease; rarely does it attack the same person twice. If the mother had the disease, the infants up to the age of five months remain immune from it. It is seasonal, occurring in winter or spring, but can appear in any season. In each outbreak, almost all persons who did not have the disease earlier acquire it. It is disease of children, but adolescents and adults who did not have the disease in childhood are its potential victims. It is clinically characterized by fever and symptoms of catarrha in the upper respiratory tract. Soon, the rashes appear on the body.

The causative agent of the measles is a virus, which was isolated by Enders and his colleagues in the USA in 1954. Live measles vaccine was licensed in 1963. It is such a highly communicable disease that the slightest contact with an active case may infect susceptible persons. The disease spreads through the secretions of the eye and respiratory passages of patients. Infectivity is greatest just before the eruption appears and subsides with fading of the rash. Uncomplicated measles is seldom fatal. Deaths attributed to measles result from the secondary broncho-pneumonia caused by bacterial organisms entering the bronchial tree.

No signs of the disease appear for about ten days after infection. Before the end of the second week, the patient develops fever, redness and watering of the eye, lot of nasal discharge and congestion of the mucous membranes of the nose and throat. This state last for three to four days and then rashes appear as temperature of the body rises to 40 to 41° C. After a couple of days the rashes turn deep and red.

Measles lowers the immunity of the patient to secondary infections of bacterial origin. Bronchopneumonia is most common secondary infection. It develops as the rashs fade and the patient is relieved of the primary infection. Among the other complications is the flaring up of the pre-existing tuberculosis in the patient.

A mild form of measles called German measles (rubella) is still a health concern in Germany and neighbouring countries. It is also called a three-day measles. It has a longer incubation period and is not known for secondary complications. It is more common among the older children

Globally, about a million children die of measles. WHO has 'therefore' launched a special drive to eliminate the disease. The medical weapon being used is called MMR-an inoculation that fights measles, mums and rubella (German measles). It requires two injections, the first injection is given as soon as the child is one year old and the second one after the child starts going to school. The second inoculation is designed to close the so-called vaccination gaps. At least five per cent of the children even in the developed countries are left out of the first injection. In countries like India, it may be much higher. If the infection takes place in early or late adulthood, it is far more difficult to combat the disease. As such the inoculation target should be 95 per cent of the children.

According to WHO estimates the measles mortality and DALYs in various regions of the world totals 0.89 and 30.25 millions (Table 11.7 and Fig. 11.7).

Measles has been a wide spread disease in India. As late as 1995, there were as many as 43,373 reported cases and 239 deaths. The number of cases in 1996 was 85,914 and of deaths 298. In 1998, the figures went down to 47,522 cases and 147 deaths. The states having more than twenty deaths were Gujarat, Rajasthan, Uttar Pradesh, West Bengal and Delhi and those having more than 4000 cases were J&K, Kerala, Maharashtra and West Bengal. The reported cases, however, do not tell the whole truth, nor do the absolute number of cases and deaths. A large number of cases never reach the hospitals. Nor are they reported mainly because fatality rates are very low and most of those who get it, recover without medication. The disease spreads like an epidemic. It rarely kills but it does keep a huge chunk of manpower away from work.

Table 11.7: Measles Mortality and DALYs-1998

WHO Regions	*Mortality ('000)*	*DALYs ('000)*	*Rank in DALYs*
Americas	0	17	92
Africa	503	17132	6
Europe	7	234	67
Easern Mediterranean	96	3288	8
South-east Asia (-India)	256	8703	11
Western Pacific	26	882	48
India	190	6474	3
World	888	30255	10

Source: WHO, World Health Report, 2000

Measles is on decline in India and it may be eliminated by 2010. In 1987, there were 2.47 lakh cases; in 1999, only 39,000 cases.

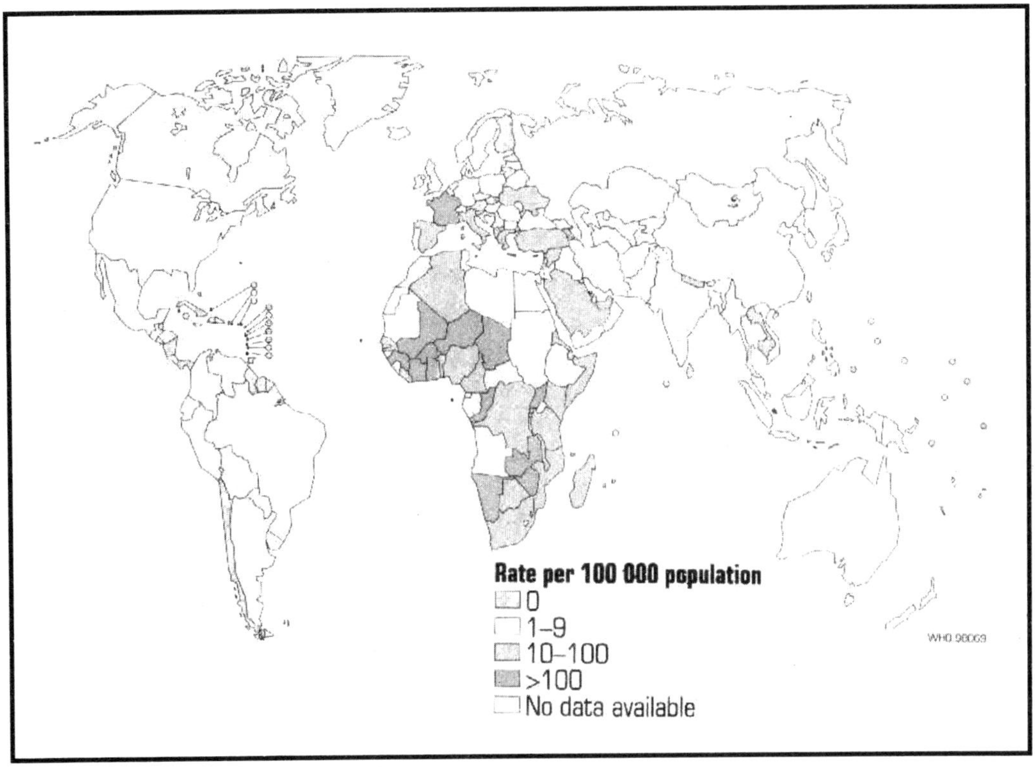

Fig. 11.7: Global Incidence of Measles (1996)

LYMPHATIC FILARIASIS

Filariasis is a major health hazard in many parts of India. Very few people die of filariasis but the ones who suffer from it have a miserable life; they cannot lead a normal life. It is a disease of the lymphs: it appears as swelling of the feet and legs (elephantisis) or testicles otherwise known as hydrocele.

Filaria is caused by the introduction of embryo of a small worm known as filariae that is conveyed to human beings by mosquitoes. The adult worms mature and live in the lymph nodes, subcutaneous tissue or cavities of the human body. The micro-filariae are produced by adult worms in these parts of the body and from there they get access to blood circulation and lymph. After entering the blood streams they exhibit three types of distribution: nocturnal, diurnal and continuous.

Filariasis is classified into several epidemiological types such as bancroftian filariasis, Malasian filariasis, loiasis, acanthocheilonemiasis, mansonelliasis, and dirofilariasis. Only the first two are prevalent in India. The bancroftian filariasis is caused by *W. bancroti,* which is of two types: nocturnal and continuous. The nocturnal type is transmitted by night biting mosquitoes of the genera *culex fatigans or anopheles.* In this type the microfilariae are present in a great number at night. The continuous type is transmitted by day biting *aedes.* In this type the mocrofilariae are present continuously in their peripheral blood but show an increase in the afternoons.

In contrast to malaria, also transmitted by mosquitoes, the filariasis parasite does not multiply extensively in the host. In this case, only one adult develops out of one infective stage larva that enters the host. At least one male and one female worm must join together in tissues for fertilization to take place. The worms become mature in 3 to 12 months – three months in case of the Malaysian type and 12 months in case of *W. bancrofti* – to complete the cycles. As such clinical infection can take place only after multiple mosquito bites.

The adult worms of both the types live in lymph nodes. They mature there and produce microfilariae which on entering the blood stream cause the disease. The primary symptoms of infection are usually lymphangitis and filarial fever. The most common of the secondary manifestations are elephantiasis of the limbs or genitalia, and hydrocele.

Filaria of one type or the other is prevalent in most of the tropical countries of the world. Its limits are set by 27° C isotherm and 60 per cent humidity. Both types (Malaysian and bancroftian) are found in East and South Asian countries such as Korea, Japan, China, Thailand, Malaysia, Indonesia, Sri Lanka and India. The bancroftian type is found in South America and Africa. The other types are typical to South America and Africa only.

Etiology

Several physical and cultural factors combine to create ideal conditions for the fileria infection. Among the inorganic factors, climate appears to play a significant role. A warm and humid climate, heavy rainfall, marshy landscape, poor drainage system making water stagnate, and high soil moisture constitute ideal conditions for mosquitoes to grow and lay eggs. The socio-cultural factors include propensity on the part of people already infested with filariasis to move and migrate, congested and poor living conditions, lack of clothing, and exposure to mosquitoes bite while sleeping, working, or at rest. Infected mosquitoes and potential victims must come together to facilitate infection. Those who sleep outside without mosquito nets or inside without wire mesh in doors and windows are very likely to get infested. Behaviour of the vectors also has its bearings on infection rate. Some of the vectors bite only at selected hours of the day and night. Male agriculturists working in the field often with minimum clothing are very likely to come in contact with filaria vectors. The female workers, on the other hand, are well covered with clothes and hence more protected. That is the reason why filariasis is more common among the males than females.

The infection of filariasis differs from that of malaria significantly although in both the cases mosquitoes are the vectors. And hence the strategies to fight this disease may have to be devised differently. In case of filariasis, there exists a long gestation period between infection and appearance of symptoms and hence the carriers of the disease move around in the community as normal human beings. This is not the case with malaria where symptoms develop fast and the patient is laid in bed. Filaria is, therefore, not amenable to any crash eradication programme. Control measures have to be long-drawn and sustained.

Filariasis is not a new disease. It was recorded by Sushruta, the father of surgery, over 2500 years ago. In 1707, Clerk nicknamed it as 'Malabar Legs' as the disease was quite common on the Malabar coast of Cochin. The disease, however, did not get the attention it deserved. People who contacted the disease just lived with it for the whole life. The mobility was restricted but rest of the daily routine was not much affected.

A questionnaire survey was conducted to determine the prevalence of filariasis in India in 1951. The survey revealed that apart from the Malabar coast, the other areas where the disease was prevalent were: Andhra Pradesh, Tamil Nadu, Orissa, West Bengal, Gujarat, UP, Bihar, A&N Isles, and Pondicherry. The spatial pattern of the disease. The survey, apart from giving useful data on the spread of the disease and its intensity, pointed out how it is spreading its tentacles beyond the known endemic areas. That the bancoftrian filariasis was spreading from urban to rural areas was a new revelation.

As a follow up of the survey, the ICMR initiated a research programme for the prevention and control of filaria. The prevention part was designed to kill mosquitoes through insecticidal chemical sprays while the control measures involved the intensive use of diethylcarbamazine as a medicine for filaria. The favourable results of these experimental researches produced a National Filaria Control Program (NFCP) in 1955. Under this programmr, survey and control units were established in each of the states where filaria cases were located in earlier surveys to carry out further research in the etiology and cure of the disease and to train professional as well as ancillary personnel. By 1961, there were 47 such units in the country.

The NFCP launched in 1955, continues to this day. But the achievements of the programme have been far below the expectations. Despite the fact that by 1996, there were 206 filaria control units, 27 survey units, and 199 clinics spread over 17 states, only 48 million people out of a total of about 428 million exposed to infection have been protected by the programme. Of the total population exposed, 315 million reside in rural and 113 million in urban areas. About 6 million persons suffer from acute lymphangitis due to filariasis. Chemotherapy and vector control measures have succeeded in reducing microfilaria rate and disease rate in most of the towns where the programmes have been in operation for 5 or more years. Nevertheless, the number of microfilariaisis carriers are as high as 28 million.

Currently, a four-pronged attack on filaria is on. It includes: single dose DEC mass therapy once a year in identified 13 districts and elective DEC treatment in filariasis endemic areas; continuation of DDT spraying; detection and treatment of microfilaria carriers; and intensification of health education. These steps include increase in the population protected, establishment of control and survey units, and filarial clinics. Approximately two-fifths of the population of India is at risk; the population protected is about 50 million. So, there is a lot of scope for further work and improvement. Table 11.8 gives details of population at risk, population protected, microfilaria carriers and diseases persons as on 31.12. 1997 and figure 11.8 gives the prevalence of the disease and its intensity in different parts of the country.

DENGUE FEVER

Also known as break bone fever and yellow fever, it is an acute infectious disease that is transmitted by mosquitoes. It incapacitates the patient temporarily though. Until very recently it was rarely fatal but now fatality rate has increased. Almost all the states of India report cases of dengue fever. The concentration was high in Uttar Pradesh and Bihar.

Dengue fever vector is mosquito of *Aedes aegypti* variety but there are other varieties, which are also responsible for it. A mosquito becomes infected only if it bites the patient during the first 3 days of illness. After biting, the mosquito incubates the virus for 8 to12 days before it becomes a carrier of the disease. Once infected, the mosquito remains infected for the whole of its life. To control the disease, the control of the mosquito is a must.

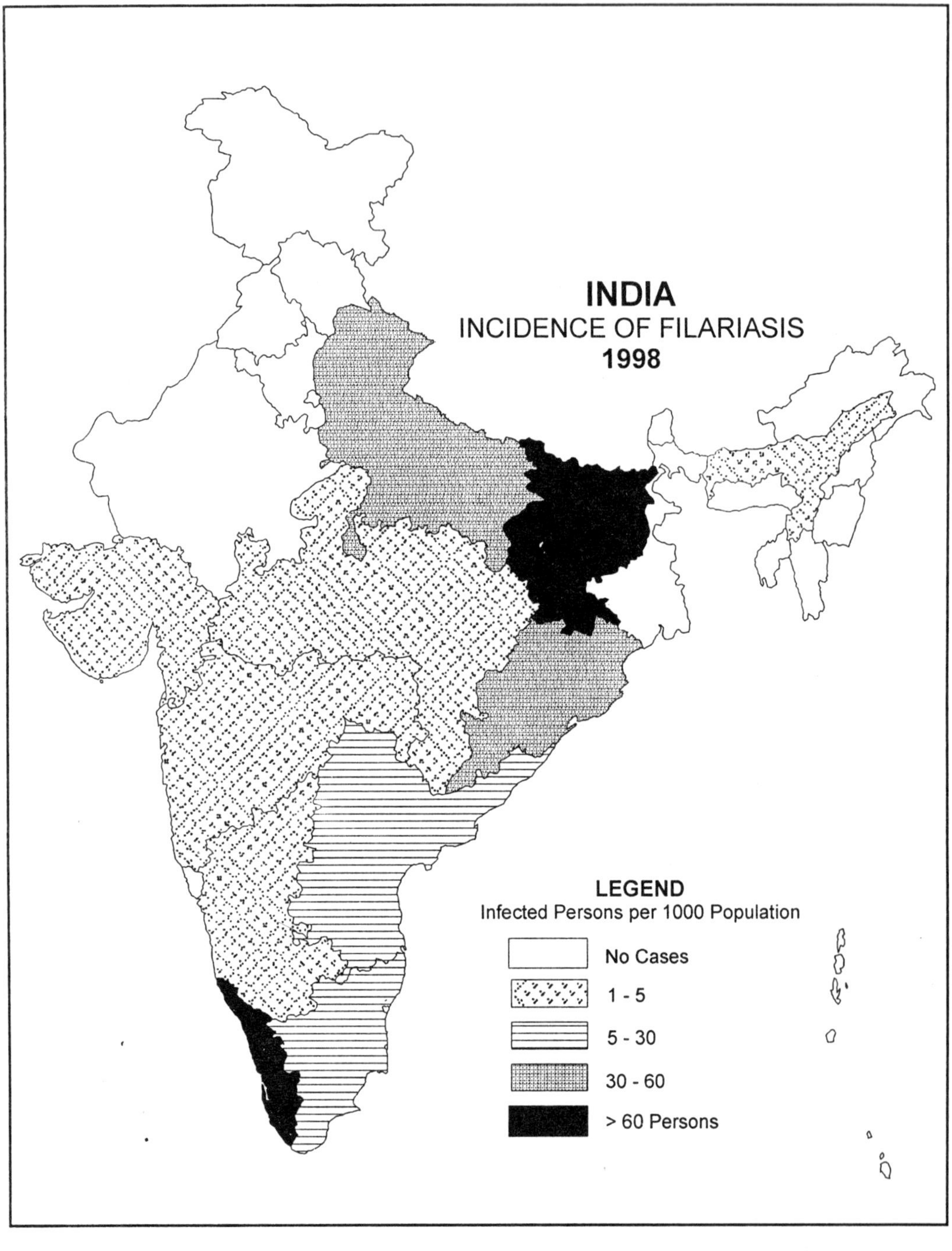

Fig. 11.8: India: Incidence of Filaria

Table 11.8: Incidence of Filariasis in India (1997)

(Figures in millions)

States	*Population protected*	*Population at risk*	*Microfilaria carriers*	*Diseased persons*
Andhra Pradesh	5.57	55.63	4.14	1.54
Assam	0.29	10.80	0.40	0.10
Bihar	7.76	66.54	4.51	6.19
Goa	0.35	1.28	0.01	0.00
Gujarat	3.61	19.03	1.15	0.15
Karnataka	0.66	12.27	0.79	0.08
Kerala	4.10	32.64	2.59	2.55
Mandhya Pradesh	0.67.	24.82	0.58	0.08
Maharashtra	6.03	19.30	0.99	0.18
Orissa	2.35	28.14	2.48	1.57
Tamil Nadu	8.72	40.46	2.55	1.35
Uttar Prasesh	6.77	103.74	7.30	7.82
West Benal	1.42	20.91	1.02	0.03
Pondicherry	0.50	0.79	0.03	0.01
A & N Isls	0.05	0.22	0.01	0.00
Dadra & N. Haveli		0.14	0.01	0.00
Daman & Diu	0.03	0.07	0.00	0.00
Lakshȧdweep	0.01	0.05	0.01	0.00
India	**48.89**	**436.85**	**28.57**	**21.65**

Source: Health Information of India, 1997 and 1998.

The virus is filterable; it prefers warm climates but can be found anywhere. The disease was first identified during an epidemic outbreak in Philadelphia, USA in1780 by Benjamin Rush. The causative organism was, however, identified only in 1907 by P.M. Ashburn and C.F. Craig in Philippines.

The virus is injected into the skin of the victim in minute droplets of saliva as the mosquito prepares to feed on his blood. As soon as the virus gets into the body of the victim, it starts multipling and during the incubation period of 4 to 10 days, penetrates all tissues particularly the linings of smallest blood vessels. The toxic by-products of the virus produce the symptoms of the disease. It starts with sudden onset of fever with acute chill, excruciating pain in the joints, loins, behind the eyes, and elsewhere in the body. The fever may rise even to 50° C and last for a week or so. Then the temperatures come down after profuse sweating, loose stools and at times bleeding from the lips and nose. The patient gets a feeling of relief but, in most cases, it is temporary. The fever returns and the patients get thoroughly exhausted. His white corpuscles in the blood decrease in numbers; in 3-4 days rashes appear in fingers and from there it spreads to other parts of the body. After a few days, the rashes disappear; and the patient slowly returns to normalcy in a few months.

Apparently, the best way to control the disease is to kill the mosquito before it bites or to cover oneself with proper clothing, to sleep with mosquito nets on, and fix wire or nylon mesh in windows and doors to ward this vector off human body. None of these is, however, a practical

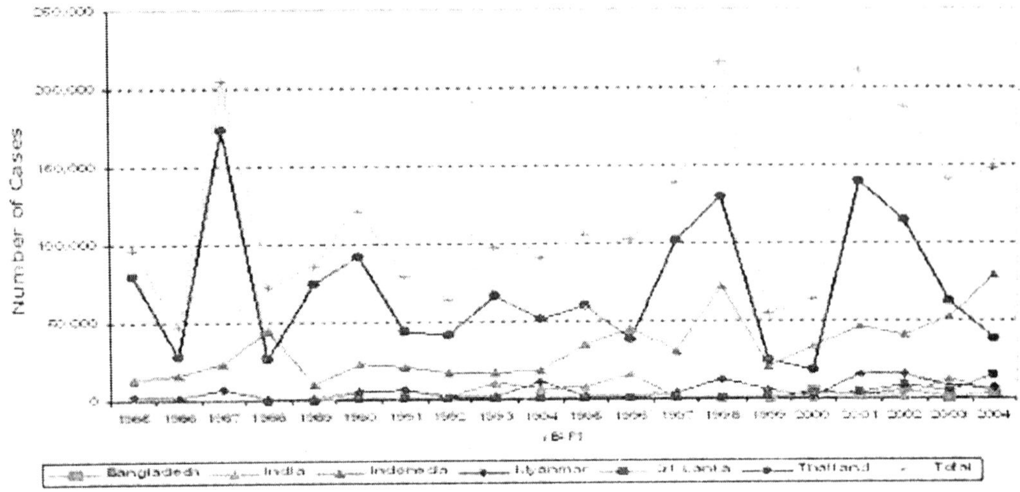

Data up to August 2004

Fig. 11.9: Dengue Fever in India

Source: WHO

proposition in countries like India where at least a quarter of the total population is malnourished. The other alternative is to eradicate the mosquito by spraying DDT (dichloro-dyphenyl-trichloroethane) or other insecticides around human habitations to destroy the breeding places of the vectors. The use of DDT is now banned, so other inexpensive and environmental friendly insecticides have to be developed. In temperate climates, the disease ends with the first snowfall and reappears in the spring. The tropics and semi-tropical areas, however, harbour it all through the year and hence the problem of control is far more difficult.

KYASANUR FOREST DISEASE (KFD)

Kyasanur Forest Disease (KFD) is associated with haemorrhages caused by an arbovirus flavivirus and transmitted to man by bite of infective ticks. The disease was first recognized in Shimoga district of Karnataka in 1957. Local inhabitants call it monkey disease. Later, it was named after the name of the locality: Kyasanur Forest.

Earlier restricted to Shimoga district, it is now diffused in the districts of North Kannada, South Kannada and Chikmaglur. Surveys reveal that a similar virus exists in Kutch and Saurashtra regions of Gujarat. Its outbreak in 1983-84 was so far the most severe one affecting 2167 people, 69 of them died. During 1991-97, 33 persons died of the disease. And number of those who contracted the diseases was 3309.

Small mammals specially the rats and the squirrels, are the main reservoirs of the virus. Monkeys too are hosts for the virus; but they die soon after contracting the disease and therefore are not very effective carriers. Cattle provide hymaphisalis ticks with required blood meals, which increases the population of the ticks. But cattle do not play any role as reservoir of the virus. Man is just and accidental host.

The hard ticks which function as reservoir for the virus of several varieties. The infection occurs mainly in the dry months. That is also the period when humans work in forests. Majority of the cases affected belong to the age group 20-40. Attack rate is higher among the men in comparison to the women. The transmission takes place by bite of the infected ticks. Control of the disease involves control of the ticks. Spray of insecticides and awareness among the people about the disease is the only solution.

TETANUS

Tetanus is an acute disease with very high mortality rate (40 to 80 per cent). It is induced by the exotoxin of *Clostridium tetani* and is clinically characterized by muscular rigidity with painful paroxysmal spasms of the muscles of the face, neck, back, and abdomen. It is of two types: neonatal and general. The neonatal type is a killer disease and is discussed in chapter XV: Health of the Children.

Occurrence of tetanus depends on the physical and ecological environment rather than on the presence or absence of infected persons. The agent Cl. Tetani is gram-positive, anaerobic, spore bearing organism resembling a drum-stick. The spores are resistant to heat (120° C for 15 minutes), phenol, cresol, and autoclaving. The spores can be destroyed at a temperature of 120° C for more than 20 minutes or by gamma radiation. The bacilli live in the soil and dust; it does not infect human through a vector. They are found in the intestines of many herbivorous animals. They come out with their faeces and remain in the soil for years. Wind often spread them around; even in operation theatres.

The bacilli produce a soluble exotoxin. It is very lethal. The lethal dose for a normal human being of 70 kg is just 0.1mg. The toxin acts simultaneously on four areas of the nervous system: spinal cord, motor and plates of the skeletal system, the brain, and the sympathetic system. It blocks the inhibition of the reflexes of the spinal cord.

Tetanus is a disease of the active age (5-40 years). It is the age when people are exposed to a variety of physical environmental hazards. Their activities and capabilities take them outdoor bringing them closer to the bacilli in the soil. Men are more prone to contract tetanus. Rural areas show more cases than urban areas. No age group is immune from the disease. The transmission process is simple. Any wound or injury including surgery exposed to dust or soil having tetanus spores will be a potential source of contamination. Once inside the wound, the spores germinate to produce exotoxin, which binds the receptor. The incubation period is 6 to 10 days; but it can be shorter or longer too.

The best and the only sure remedy of tetanus is active immunization with tetanus toxoid. It helps produce protective antitoxin. The best thing to do is to vaccinate the whole community and population. A combined vaccine, MPT is often used by public health agencies to immunize people. A monovalent vaccine is also available. Temporary or passive immunization can be provided by an injection of human tetanus hyperimmuneglobulin (ATS or TIG). It gives protection for about a month.

To prevent tetanus after injury, the wound or injury should be thoroughly cleaned with antiseptics; all foreign material should be removed; and it should be kept covered so that the chances of tetanus bacilli lodging in there are reduced, if not eliminated. ATS should be given; in case of reaction, adrenaline solution should be injected.

Note: Hepatitis B and Iodine Deficiency are also the diseases on the way out. Reader is referred to chapter XII for Hepatitis B, and chapter XV for iodine deficiency.

REFERENCES

1. Government of India, Ministry of Health, Health Information of India, 1993, 1998 and 1999.
2. ——, *Annual Health Report.*
3. Registrar General of India, *Survey of Causes of Death (Rural)*, 1998.

12

Persistent Diseases

In this chapter, we propose to deliberate on diseases, which, despite known cures, continue to persist. Some of them like malaria have developed new strains immune to antibiotic drugs efficacious earlier. With the introduction of antibiotic drugs, it appeared that tuberculosis would soon be listed as a disease of the past. It too has developed new strains, which get over even antibiotic medicines. Further, the disease has joined hands with other sever diseases including HIV to complicate the treatment further. Others like dengue fever come and go following a definite periodicity. In some cases like that of gastro-intestinal disorders, medicines are only a partial answer. They can be eradicated only if public health is improved and people exposed to them get better diet and environment; and are physically fit enough to counter the germs that cause the diseases. None of these improvements can be effected in the short run. And so the diseases persist, new medicines, better hospitals and more doctors notwithstanding.

The disease causing agents are becoming resistant to anti-microbial drugs earlier considered to be highly effective. No one now talks of penicillin as the panacea against all infectious diseases; nor the DDT as master killer of the viruses, insects and pests. The situation has really become alarming; it poses serious challenge to the already overburdened and malfunctioning healthcare system of the developing countries like India. Added to the woe is the ever-increasing population, not so much in terms of growth as in terms absolute number added each year, and resulting overcrowding and increasing burden on the natural as well cultural environment.

Most of the persistent diseases are the infectious once, otherwise known as communicable diseases. They claim 75 per cent of the morbidity and 50 per cent of the mortality in the country. Poor prescription practices and equally poor compliance coupled with poverty, lack of health education, low literacy, unsafe drinking water, unbalanced diet and unhygienic lifestyles are the main causes of the persistence and in some cases even resurgence of these diseases.

With advances in medical sciences and relative improvements in sanitation, the declining trends in the prevalence of communicable diseases should have been continued. However, irregular treatment or stopping the treatment before the agent of the disease has been completely eradicated from the body, immunizes the agent against the drug. These diseases spread fast if the mobility of the people increases. With accelerated industrialization and urbanization and consequent increase in rural to rural and rural to urban migration of the people, the chances of the diffusion of diseases from endemic to safer areas have increased.

Communicable diseases still claim a great number of incidences and deaths in most developing countries, India included. Data regarding reported number of cases and deaths attributable to some of the major communicable diseases in India as in 1997-98 are given in Table 12.1. Acute diarrhoeal and acute respiratory diseases alone claim over 22 million reported cases. The number of reported cases may not be more than 20 per cent of all cases.

Table 12.1: Major Communicable Diseases: Morbidity and Mortality (1997-98)

	Diseases	*Cases*	*Cases/lakh population*	*Total deaths*
1.	Acute diarrhoea	8,060,968	870.00	3,254
2.	Diphtheria	4,191	0.45	126
3.	Acute Poliomyelitis	2,295	0.25	60
4.	Tetanus-neonatal	4,487	0.46	485
5.	Tetanus-other	6,157	0.67	852
6.	Whooping Cough	33,860	3.68	94
7.	Measles	50,165	5.45	160
8.	Acute Respiratory Infection	14,060,859	1528.00	2,676
9.	Pneumonia	373,557	40.60	2,676
10.	Enteric Fever	266,383	29.00	260
11.	Viral Hepatitis	109,258	11.90	1,066
12.	Japanese Encephalitis	2,593	0.28	191
13.	Meningitis	5,745	0.62	632
14.	Rabies/dog bites	120,955	13.15	507
15.	Syphilis	28,540	3.10	10
16.	Gonorrhoea	80,650	8.75	29
17.	Tuberculosis	818,524	89.00	6,442
18.	Others including malaria	52,409,389	5696.00	87,317

Note: Figures Indicate Average of 1997-1998

Source: *Registrar General of India: Survey of Major Causes of Death (Rural) in India*, 1997-98.

MALARIA

The literal meaning of malaria is foul air. Malaria is a protozoal disease; it has a very long history because the female *Anopheline* mosquito that transmits the parasites of genus *Plasmodium* to humans also appears to have a long history. It is as old as 93,000,000 years and hence very adjusted to the environment in which it grows. The malarial parasite has four distinct species:

1. *P. vivax,*
2. *P. falciparum,*
3. *P. malariae*, and
4. *P. ovale.*

Plasmodium vivax is the most widespread malarial infection in the world. In India, about 60 per cent of the infections are due to *P. vivax.* It is a benign infection and rarely produces serious complications or death. Relapse of the infection due to persistence of inactive forms (hypnozoites) in liver tissues, which periodically invade blood stream producing clinical malaria, is, however, not uncommon. The gametocytes of this species mature in perpheral blood and are sucked by anopheles mosquito for completion of the cycle. *P falsiparum* is also widely distributed claiming about 40 per cent of the infections and nearly all the malaria related deaths. It produces serious complications such as cerebral malaria, jaundice, and renal failure. To become mature the gametocyte of *P. falciparum* invade deep circulation and clog the blood capillaries. *P. malariae* is restricted to only a few pockets. It is responsible for less than 1 per cent of the cases in India. *P. vovale* is a rare parasite as far as humans are concerned and is restricted to tropical Africa.

In highly endemic areas, two or more species of parasites may infect individuals at the same time giving rise to what is referred to as mixed infection. In India, 4-8 per cent of infections are of this category.

Depending on severity, malaria can be divided into two classes:

1. Benign: it is relatively mild, generally caused by P. vivax, is seldom fatal, and its chances of complications are few; and
2. Malignant: it is severe, is caused by P. falsiparum (rarely by P. vivax), has a rapid down hill course, and is marked by poor prognosis.

What is common among them is that they all are transmitted to humans by mosquitoes. *Plasmodium vivax* has the largest geographical distribution throughout the world. In India too, about 70 per cent of the infection belongs to this category. Next in importance is *P. falciparum,* which accounts for anything between 25 to 30 per cent of the infection. *P. malariae* is restricted to just 1 per cent of infection in India (mainly in Tumkur and Hassan districts of Karnataka). *P. ovale* is rare in India; it is confined to tropical Africa.

Mosquito is the first and the main host of the parasite (Fig. 12.1). Human beings are the intermediate host. When an infected mosquito bites human, the asexual cycle of the parasite begins. Each bite injects sporozoites, which produce thousands of merozoites in the human blood. Each sporozoite of P. falciparum produces 40,000 merozoites. Sporozoites from other species produce less than 15000 merozoites. Sexual cycle begins when the mosquito bites humans and sucks their blood containing gametocytes.

History

Hippocrates wrote about malaria in fourth century BC. It appears to have played significant role in some of the great events of the world such as the decline and fall of the Roman Empire and ancient civilizations of Egypt and Sri Lanka. Had Alexander not died of malaria, after his incursions in India, the world's history might have taken a different direction. Malaria must have been endemic in India, but very little is known about the medical history of the past.

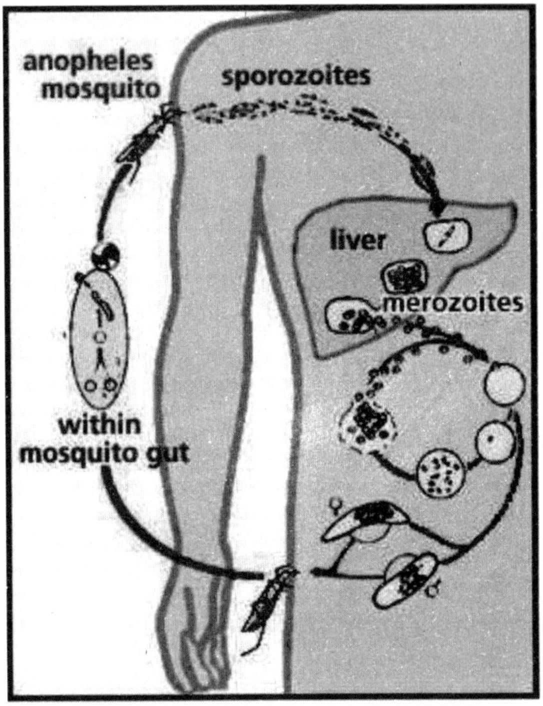

Fig. 12.1: Life Cycle of Malaria Virus

Malaria can be found in the Vedic writings of 1600 BC in India. Charak and Sushruta gave a vivid description of malaria and linked it with the bite of mosquitoes. In 1640, Huan del Vego first employed the tincture of the cinchona to treat malaria, although the aborigines of Peru and Ecuador had been using it even earlier. Morton (1696) presented the first detailed clinical picture of malaria treatment with cinchona and Laveran, a French physician identified the causative agent of malaria in 1880. Paul Muller discovered the properties of DDT in 1939.

Malaria is an anthropoid transmitted fever. Plasmodium, discovered by Ronald Ross, the son of a general in the Indian army, is its causative agent. Ross was born at Almora, in Uttaranchal. He started working on the theory propounded by Patrick Manson that malaria was caused by mosquitoes. While working at Secunderabad in Andhra Pradesh and later at Calcutta, he proved that the plasmodium was passed from one victim to another through the bite of mosquitoes and that it was a three factor disease – plasmodium as the causative agent, mosquito as the vector, and man as the host.

Until 1640, it was not possible to distinguish malaria from other fevers. The discovery of Ross linked it to mosquito bite, but what kind of mosquito bite produced malaria was not known. Ross experimented on birds in the final stages of his research but did not go far enough to understand that mosquitoes that caused malaria in the birds were not the ones that caused the disease in humans. It was Grassi, an Italian scientist, who obsessed as he was by the urge to eradicate malaria from Italy, proved that the disease was caused by the female Anopheles mosquito and not by the male of this species nor by any other type of mosquito.

As late as 1945, there were 80 million cases of malaria and 3 million deaths in South Asia alone. During the third decade of the twentieth century, 650 million people, one-third of the total population of the world, suffered from malaria each year. It is a major health hazard in many tropical countries of the world even today. Malaria took more lives (135,698 persons) in India than any other single disease in 1961. The number of malaria cases exceeded half a million. With the use of insecticides on a mass scale, incidence of malaria declined during 1960s and 1970s but now the disease has rolled back to become a serious public health problem. The antibiotic drugs and insecticides are no longer effective; the mosquitoes have adapted themselves to these drugs.

About 100 countries of the world are considered malaria infected and the number of people at risk exceeds 2.4 billion. It kills 1 to 3 million people per annum globally; a million of them are children under the age of 5 years who die of cerebral malaria and anaemia. Fatality rates exceed 30 per cent. Most affected region of the world is sub-Saharan Africa. Urban and peri-urban areas of South Asia, Latin America and Southeast Asia are still the home of malaria. Wherever there is war, internal disturbances, famines, floods and earthquakes, malaria along with intestinal diseases is the first to visit the sufferers.

In India, 2.2 million persons were infected by malaria in 1993; the number went up to 3 million in 1996; and declined to 2.2 in 1998. Number of deaths has, however, been just 354 in 1993, 1000 in 1996 and 660 in 1998. Malaria is no longer a major killer; but it is a major cause of debility and thus reduced immunity against many infectious diseases.

Geography

Lady Anopheles, though considered to be the cause of malaria, is only a vector or carrier of the germ. Mosquitoes need stagnant water to breed, human or animal blood to feed, and a moist and warm climate to live. Each of the various species of mosquitoes likes a different set of environmental conditions for all the three functions. If the conditions change, the mosquitoes related thereto would die unless the change is so slow that they are able to adapt themselves to the new conditions.

The moist climates create more breeding and living space for the vectors. Tropics are, therefore, notorious for malaria epidemics (Fig. 12.2). Optimum temperature for the sexual cycle of the parasite in the mosquito varies from 22° to 30° C. Malaria is not known to have occurred in epidemic form in regions falling beyond 16° C isotherm. Temperature also determines the time required by the mosquito to become infectious after absorbing the blood of the host. This is partly the reason why mountainous areas are free from malaria. The direction and speed of the wind influence the direction in which the mosquitoes fly to spread the disease. The relief of the land determines the amount of impounded water which mosquitoes must have to breed. The chemical content of the soil and the nature of vegetation impact the growth of vector population. For example, the breeding places of *A. gambiac* are confined to coastal swamps flooded by high spring tides and having arisennia mangroves and *paspalum vaginatum*, a coarse marsh grass. *A. funestus* enter houses only after midnight. Houses with curtains fitted in windows and doors are therefore better protected from them.

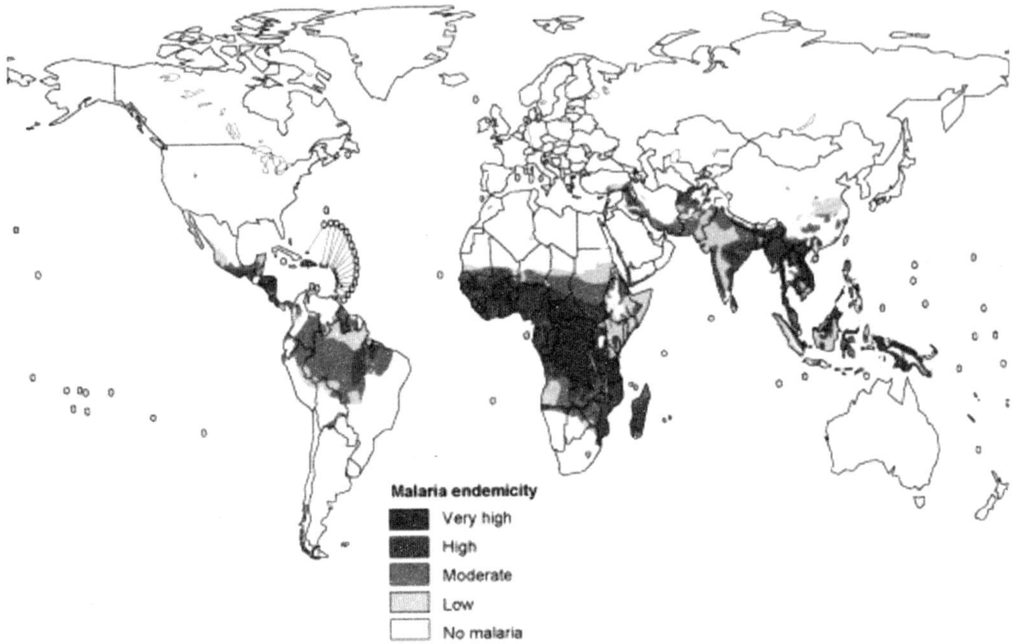

Fig. 12.2: Malarial Zones of the World

The world can be divided into seven zoo-geographic regions from the point of malaria:

1. Palaearctic Regions of Eurasia;
2. Neararctic Regions of North America;
3. Neotropical Regions of America;
4. Afrotropical Regions;
5. Oriental (Indian sub-continent and Mekong valley in Southeast Asia) Region;
6. Australasian Region; and
7. Antarctic Region.

Within each of these regions there is a remarkable similarity in the vector fauna, to which, the major palearctic malaria vectors belong. The *anopheles maculipenis* complex is found in a broad belt extending from Morocco to Easter Siberia but they are not present outside the Palaearctic region. Similarly *An. culicifacies*, an oriental vector, is present all along the Persian Gulf coast but malaria in the west of this region shows a greater affinity to malaria in other neighbouring Palaearctic areas compared to malaria in the main area of Indian subcontinent. Of course, the ecological determinants of malaria are in many ways associated with socio-economic environment. Ecology determines malaria; socio-economic conditions determine ecology.

As a rule, *Anophelines* are not found at altitudes above 2000 meters. The fact that malaria has disappeared from the developed parts of the world is indicative of the fact that the disease is closely related to the socio-economic conditions of the people and quantity and quality of public health facilities. The style of life of the people, the houses in which they live, the occupations they pursue, and the diet they take determine their susceptibility or otherwise to the disease. Those who sleep in the open in the night without mosquito nets are sure to be infected. It is particularly so if there are breeding place around. Farmers engaged in wet farming are far more exposed to mosquitoes than others.

Global Burden

As stated earlier, malaria kills about 2.5 million people in the world and infects 500 million people each year. It occurs in about 100 countries placing 40 per cent of the world population at risk. Ninety per cent of these countries are in tropical regions of Africa. Almost all South-East Asian countries are malarious. The *P. falsiparum* cases are on the increase but the number of deaths, thanks to the availability of modern drugs and medical facilities, have tended to decline.

The global burden of malaria, as that of other communicable diseases, is not equally distributed. The developing countries are worst affected. These are also the countries, which are poor and cannot afford to lose opportunity for work. The world estimates of the burden of malaria and the DALY lost due to malaria is given in Table 12.2. It is clear that 95 per cent of dead are Africans and that too under the age of 5 years.

Table 12.2: Malaria Mortality and DALY Lost

Region	*Mortality (000)*	*DALY Lost (000)*
Africa	961	35506
Americas	4	130
East Mediterranean	53	1854
Europe	0	0
South-East Asia	53	1608
India	20	577
Western Pacific	20	591
World	1110	39267

Source: World Health Report 2000.

The number of malaria cases and deaths in South-east Asian Countries is given in Table 12.3.

Malaria in India

India's climate is favourable to the transmission of malaria. It is a seasonal disease and most common in July-November. Atmospheric humidity has a direct effect on the longevity of the mosquito. Rainy season, when the relative humidity exceeds 60 per cent, is the most favourable period. Further, accumulated water in ponds and low-lying lands offer good conditions for breeding. It has been noticed that canal irrigation in Karnataka, Punjab, Haryana and UP has enhanced the chances of malarial infection. The urban slums that are so extensive in large cities are the breeding grounds for mosquitoes. It is particularly so if the slums are located in the low-lying areas, which they often are.

Table 12.3: Malaria in South-east Asian Countries: 1996

Country	*Estimated cases in '000*	*P.f. cases % of total*	*Estimated deaths*
India	15,000	39	19,500
Nepal	30	11	15
Bhutan	21	36	45
Maldives	0	0	0
Sri Lanka	190	24	50
Bangladesh	1,250	54	4,500
Myanmar	3,323	82	5,136
Thailand	100	53	870
Indonesia	6,010	47	700
Total	25,924	41	30,816

Note: Only reported cases and deaths. Actual cases may be ten times more and deaths four times more.
Source: WHO, Regional Health Report (South and South-East Asia) 1999.

Within India, the intensity of malaria is not uniform. Areas, which are forested, including the hills and foothills, and those harbouring developmental projects, are highly malarial. Newly cleared forest areas have high incidence of malaria because people with low level of immunity settle down there as part of the rehabilitation scheme. Some states have a heavy burden of the disease, while others are close to the national average. The states where malaria cases have increased in recent years are Goa, Madhya Pradesh, and Orissa. Elsewhere the number of cases is declining. Figure 12.3 and Table 12.6 give the incidence of malaria per 1000 population in 1998.

In India, one comes across several types of the disease. Forest malaria accounts for 30 per cent of the malaria cases. Tribal malaria is common in the tribal belts of Andhra Pradesh, Madhya Pradesh, Chattisgarh, Jharkhand, Maharashtra, Orissa, Northeastern states, Gujarat and Rajasthan. About half of all *P. falsiparum* cases occur in these areas. Infants, young children, pregnant mothers who move for fuel and other requirements in the forests are the frequent victims of the disease.

Rural malaria is predominant in those areas where irrigation facilities have been extended in recent years. These include the irrigated areas of arid, semi-arid and dry regions like Rajasthan, Punjab, Haryana, and west Uttar Pradesh, Madhya Pradesh and the coastal districts of Andhra Pradesh, Tamil Nadu and Orissa. Malaria in these regions is of mild variety produced by the vector *An. culicifacies.* The other active vectors are P. vivax and P. falciparum.

Urban malaria is found in million cities of the country, particularly in the slums of these cities where almost half of their population resides. The mild type of malaria that prevails here is of *P. vivax* and *P. falsiparum* variety and the vector prevalent is *An. Culicifaci.*

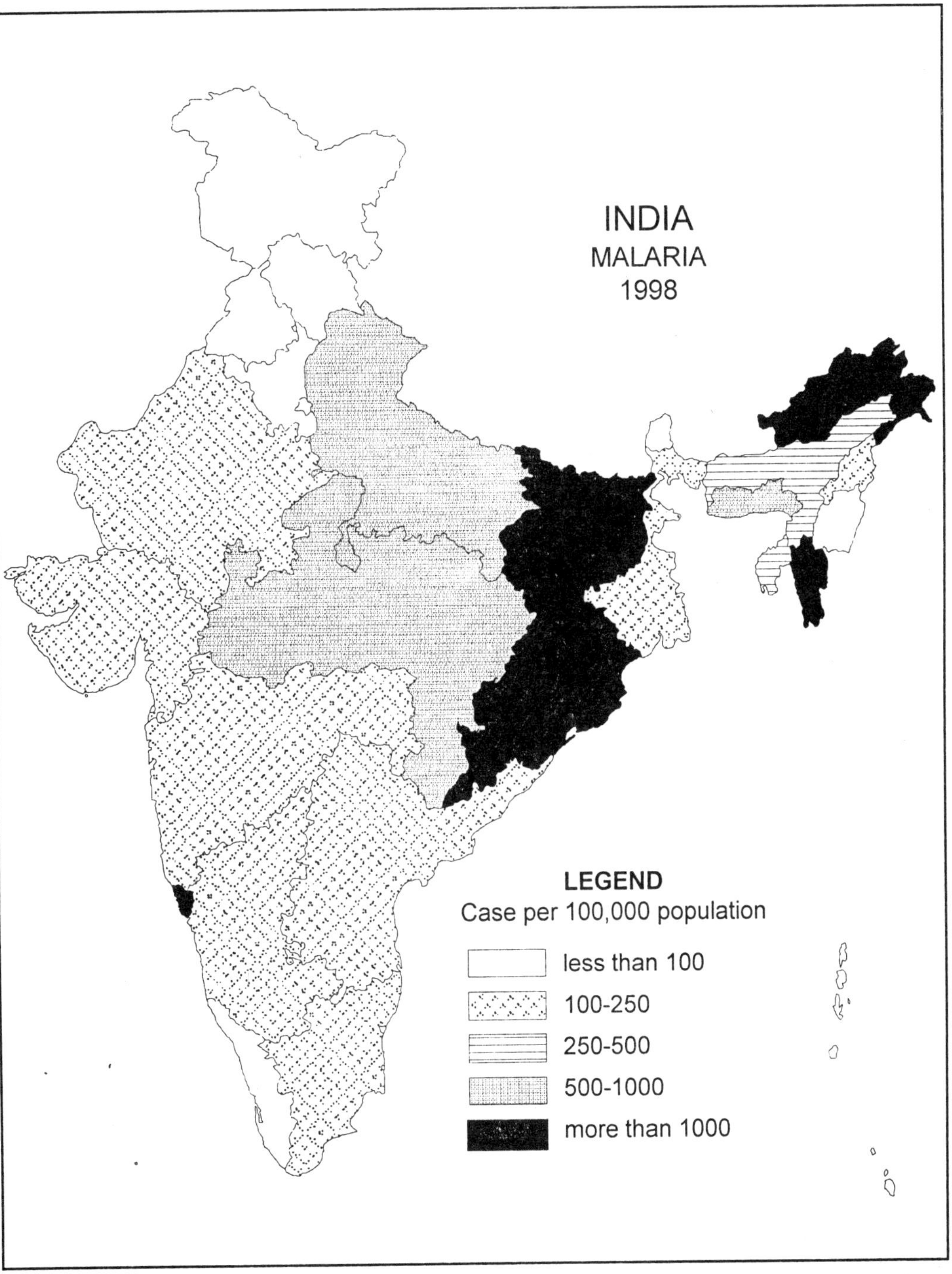

Fig. 12.3: India: Incidence if Malaria (2000)

Then there are other types: malaria in project areas and malaria in border areas. The latter areas are least served by public health facilities. The project areas have lot of in-and out-flow of population and accumulation of water in newly dug foundations, canals, ditches, etc.

Malaria Eradication Programme

The epidemic of malaria prior to the Second World War has been well documented by Lieutinent Colonel J.A. Suiton in the report of the Health Survey and Development Committee, 1946. According to his estimates, "at least hundred million individuals suffer from malaria every year in India." And that malaria was indirectly responsible for 25 to 65 million additional deaths. The mortality rate per 1000 population was not less than 8. This accounted for almost one-third of the total deaths from all causes. Since that time, the situation has materially changed. In 1963, there were only 67,707 reported deaths attributable to malaria out of which 61,786 pertained to the rural areas. In 1996, the number of cases went up to 2.87 million but reported deaths declined to just 2803. Malaria is on the come back trail.

To combat the menace of malaria, a nation-wide Malaria Control Programme was launched as early as 1953. As a result, both mortality and morbidity rates declined. To further intensify the fight, the government launched a National Malaria Eradication Programme in 1958. The success of this program can be gauged from the fact that the number of cases came down from 75 million in 1947 to 0.10 million in 1965. The programme, however, could not be continued with the same vigour and sincerity and hence the number of cases increased again in the nineteen seventies. Another programme called Modified Plan of Operation (MPO) was launched in 1977 with three fold objectives: first, to retain the achievements gained earlier; two, to bring down malaria morbidity; and three, to prevent death due to malaria.

The malaria eradication programme did improve the situation so that the number of malaria cases by 1989 had come down to a little over two millions, but thereafter it reached a plateau. From 1994, the situation worsened again. The number of both morbidity and mortality cases started going up again. The main reason for this situation is focal intensity and outbreak, despite declining trends in the rest of the country. Since 1997, the number of deaths has come down once again, but morbidity continues to be high (see Table 12.5).

During 1995, there were 2.93 million cases of malaria; 1.14 million of them being *P. falciparum (Pf)* as compared to 2.51 and 0.99 million cases respectively in 1994. *Pf.* cases are those, which are clinically confirmed drug resistant cases. The number of deaths in 1994 was 1122; in 1995, it increased to 116. However, in 1997 and 1998, there was a marked decline in total morbidity, *Pf.* and deaths.

Incidence of malaria in India is, however, not the same all over the country. Table 12.6 gives the total number of cases, cases per 100,000 population and total number of deaths in each state in 1998. Figure 12.3 gives the spatial pattern of malaria cases. Only reported cases have been taken into account. The number of cases, which go unreported, may be 4 to 5 times more. (Fig. 12.3)

Table 12.5: Malaria in India: Morbidity and Mortality (1961-1998)

Year	*Cases (number)*	*Deaths (number)*
1961	49,151	–
1965	99,667	–
1970	694,017	–
1975	5,166,142	99
1980	2,898,140	207
1985	1,864,380	213
1990	2,018,783	353
1992	2,125,826	422
1995	2,926,197	1151
1997	2,660,057	879
1998	2,222,789	666

Source: Health Information of India, 1998

Reasons Behind Malaria Roll Back

The main reason for the return of malaria is the immunity the mosquitoes have acquired against insecticides like DDT. This results largely from the tendency in government circles to spread disease eradication programmes mechanically all over the country ignoring geographical realities. It is presumed that a national programme must be truly national in coverage: every part of the country must participate in it, irrespective of the intensity of the disease. Medical geographers have been pointing out this lacuna in programme formulation and implementation for a long time. Thanks to the intervention of the WHO and the lessons learnt from the past mistakes, there is definite change in approach. Now the focal places, areas and regions are being identified and the intensity of the disease is being matched by the intensity of the programmes. It is called *Stratified Malaria Roll Back Programme.*

The World Bank has come forward to assist India in combating the menace of malaria. Apart from the rural focal areas, a large number of urban centres have also been included in the programme. All these measures can, however, succeed only if people cooperate and consider the programmes their own. Unless they take responsibility of their own health, governments can do precious little. Let us also keep in view that killing the mosquito is not the final answer to the problem. Disease vectors get used to many of the insecticides we use and they re-emerge in due course of time stronger and more resistant to the chemicals that could kill them earlier. If diseases like malaria have come back, it is because of this factor. The final answer to the problem lies in healthy body and mind, environmental cleanliness and alert and efficient health services. So long as these conditions are not satisfactorily met, the risk of contracting malaria will remain.

Bio-scientists are trying to evolve vaccine for malaria. It is expected to be in the market by 2005. The process involves spreading of a synthetic gene throughout the population of malaria carrying mosquitoes making it impossible for them to pass on the virus to the humans. Again, it is a process which nature takes millions of years to achieve. Hence, there are inherent dangers mainly because the process would be irreversible. It amounts to interfering with the nature without fully understanding the implications of the change.

Table 12.6: State-wise Incidence of Malaria in 1998

States	*Number of cases*	*Cases/1000 population*	*Total deaths*
Andhra Pradesh	118,800	1.60	12
Arunachal Pradesh	49,554	54.00	2
Assam	94645	3.60	34
Bihar	114958	10.50	34
Goa	25975	17.30	19
Gujarat	106825	2.10	3
Haryana	12115	0.60	0
Himachal Pradesh	1433	0.25	0
J & K	5451	0.55	0
Karnataka	118753	2.30	3
Kerala	7439	0.20	9
Madhya Pradesh	475098	5.90	26
Maharashtra	165985	1.75	32
Manipur	1306	0.55	1
Meghalaya	17618	7.70	2
Mizoram	10137	11.40	56
Nagaland	1989	1.00	0
Orissa	478056	13.30	349
Punjab	5316	0.20	0
Rajasthan	76438	1.40	0
Sikkim	15	0.05	0
Tamil Nadu	63915	1.05	2
Tripura	12595	3.95	5
Uttar Pradesh	112291	6.45	0
West Bengal	132088	1.65	77
A & N Isls	1247	3.55	0
Chandigarh	1675	0.10	0
D. & N. Haveli	6225	28.30	0
Daman and Diu	625	3.90	0
Delhi	4050	0.30	0
Lakshadweep	4	0.10	0
Pondicherry	168	0.20	0
India	2,222,789	2.65	666

Source: Health Information of India, 1997 & 1998.

The process being tried is bi-directional. In one case, the gene is attached to a bacterium called *wolbachia.* Once the mosquitoes is infected by the *wolbachia*, it becomes ineffective as a vector. When genetically modified (GM) females mate with males, they produce GM offspring. But the non-GM females cannot have offspring with GM males. Ultimately all mosquitoes will become harmless. The second process involves attachment of the gene to a freakish chunk of DNA called transposable element, which hops between chromosomes during reproduction. The GM mosquito will always pass on the added gene to more than 50 per cent of the offspring – eventually covering the entire population.

TUBERCULOSIS

Diseases of the chest take more lives annually than any other disease in India. What is worst is that they are on the increase and pose serious threat to our health in the 21st century. Yet comparatively less attention is paid to these diseases. Pneumonia has remained the main killer for children under-5 for decades even though it is completely curable. Asthma cases are growing rather fast; the cases of childhood asthma have alarmed the health authorities in India to join the International Study of Asthma and Allergies in Childhood (ISAAC). Cases of tuberculosis and cancer of the lung are going up. TB kills one person every minute in India; pneumonia claims life of a child every half a minute, one lakh new lung cancer cases are reported each year, and almost one per cent of the children fall prey to bronchial asthma every year.

Tuberculosis of the lung is perhaps the most serious and fast spreading disease of the chest in India. It is especially in large cities. Malnutrition, overcrowding and poverty (MOP) syndrome is the main cause of disease. Malnutrition makes body susceptible to infectious diseases, overcrowding makes air highly polluted, particularly in large cities where vehicular traffic releases so much of hydrocarbons in the air and poverty makes it difficult for the people to buy medicines and pay to the physician.

The 1999 WHO report gives a very grim picture of the prevailing situation. It warns that if TB patients are not treated promptly and effectively, they will infect the "succeeding generations and the cycle of infection, disease and death will continue." It is impossible to escape the disease carrying microbes that travel in the air that we inhale. They infect two million Indians each year, half of them having infectious and fatal TB. A person with TB infects 15 others every day. The burden of TB in India is 36 times higher than leprosy, 12 times more than malaria, and 35 per cent more than AIDS. It will go out of hand if the ambitious revised national tuberculosis control programme (RNTCP) is not made a success. Unfortunately, we will know the success or failure of the programme only after two decades. Cases of lung cancer are also increasing. Any one who gets the diseases is sure to die. Survival rate is close to zero.

Etiology

Tuberculosis is a symptom in human beings or animals whose tissues have been invaded by mycobacterium tuberculosis. It was discovered by Robert Koch in 1882, eight years after Hansen discovered mycobacterium leprae. The tubercle bacillus resembles a minute rod 1 to 4 microns in length and 0.3 to 0.6 microns in diameter. Tuberculosis is not an exclusively human disease. The agents that cause the disease are of three types: human, bovine and avian. The human and bovine types can infect human and animal hosts reciprocally. Avian infection in human beings is not very common. In areas where tuberculosis is common among the cattle, infection of human beings by the bovine type is not infrequent. The bovine type can be transferred to man through milk, meat or contact with infected animals. The bacteria are acid-fast; when subjected to strong acids or alcohol, they retain stains. Heat and ultraviolet rays however destroy them.

Morphologically, the three types are not very dissimilar from each other. The human type is generally found in lung tuberculosis, the bovine type in lymph nodes, bones and intestines. The human type enters the tissues through inhalation while the bovine type through the milk of cows or buffaloes. In countries where milk is taken only after pasteurization or boiling, the TB of the lungs, bones and lymph is rare. Possibility of a 'virgin' human host contacting the disease depends on the susceptibility of the body to succumb to the attack. The agent breaks through the tissues, but if the defence is strong it gets temporarily or permanently imprisoned in the scar created by it. As the number of bacilli increases, new foci are created eventually covering a major portion of the lung or intestines as the case may be, ultimately resulting in the death of the person. The degree of immunity or allergy resulting from it depends partly on the degree of virulence of the agent and partly upon the genetically determined resilience in the host.

Tuberculosis does not discriminate on grounds of age, sex, race, or region. The disease attacks with virulence if the person has never been exposed to it. That is the reason why tribal people coming into contact with persons from areas where tuberculosis has been rampant become easy prey of the disease. Amerindians who were not exposed to tuberculosis become easy victims of the disease. As against this, people living in areas having tuberculosis develop some immunity to the disease and unless the attack is really virulent, they do not contact it. This does not, however, apply to children below the age of five. Relatively speaking, men are more exposed to tuberculosis than women. Those who lack adequate amount of protein and vitamin D in the diet are also more likely to contact the disease. Those who live in small communities and get fresh air all the time are less likely to get the disease. Living with TB patients, particularly in houses that are not well ventilated, considerably increases the chances of infection. Children living with or close to the patients are the first victims if the sputum charged with tuberculosis bacilli is not disposed off properly. The chances that they would inhale the bacilli coming out of the air exhaled by the patient will also be high if they remain in close contact with him.

During mid-seventies, 7 to 8 million people were estimated to have contacted tuberculosis. Annual mortality exceeded half a million. Today, there are about 14 million cases of active tuberculosis in India, a quarter of them being highly infective. With HIV-TB co-infection, the incidence rate may increase much beyond the present rate of 1.8/1000.

What causes tuberculosis is not yet fully understood. There is combination of factors that appear to create conditions for its onset and spread. It may be that the tuberculosis in endemic form might have been there from ancient times. Its occurrence in epidemic form is however a relatively recent phenomenon. Before it became epidemic, it used to attack those who led a very luxurious and licentious life. Apparently some new situations developed that favoured it to become the disease of the common man. Two new developments point to these new conditions. First, the environmental setting has very much changed. To day people do not live in open dwellings and spaces as their forefathers used to do. Earlier the dwellings were perhaps poor but they were well ventilated and open. Now with rapid growth of population, settlements have become highly congested particularly in urban slums and small towns in rural areas. Second, the importance people used to give to health is no longer there. Food has become a second priority even in middle class families. Moreover, even the food that is eaten is not of good quality: it may even be adulterated and mixed with toxins that weaken and damage the body.

Among the contributory factors, we may list increased mobility of the people. A large number of persons went out to cities for work in classical factories producing cotton or woolen textiles, steel or mining iron ore, coal, bauxite, etc. The workplace as well as the living space of these workers was such that diseases like tuberculosis were but to come. They contacted the disease but did not know what they were suffering from. They perceived it as common cough and returned home to recover and recoup. They died prematurely leaving new patients in the family to meet the same fate. Look at what Arthur Lankester had to say in his report on the first survey of tuberculosis conducted in 1916.

"The impression left over the mind after careful inquiry with comparison of statistics as are available that many large areas in India, which 40 years ago were practically 'virgin soil' to tuberculosis, have now become to a considerable extent infected; that this has been for generations, probably centuries, a common disease of the larger cities, yet even in these there has been a considerable actual increase during the last 40 years; that while in smaller towns and village districts it was formerly comparatively rare or even absent, yet in these during a similar period the disease has made its appearance and spread widely. The increase has been most marked in connection with those centres which have shown greatest commercial and educational development, and in village districts which have been linked up with them by direct lines of communication."

The reservoir of infection and the size and density of population of hosts harbouring the agent are important factors in the diffusion of tuberculosis. Unfortunately, even today the detection of infected cases is not an easy job. The hosts harbouring the agent without any visible signs of the disease are not uncommon. The only indirect evidences such as hardened lymph nodes, dried sinuses, scarred tissues in the lungs, etc. offer some chances of detection.

Several studies indicate relationship between physical geographic factors like temperature, humidity, sunshine and altitude and tuberculosis but it should not be construed as causal relationship. Recovery of patients suffering from tuberculosis is faster in dry and sunny climates and higher altitudes. As stated earlier, poverty is the greatest promoter of tuberculosis. Repeated infective contact of people suffering from malnutrition is one of the most potent factors in the spread of the disease. Urban cores of the disease are the slums where the urban poor live.

Tuberculosis is not hereditary and hence its occurrence at birth is rare. The child of a tubercule mother should be free from the disease if it is segregated from her immediately after birth and is not nursed on her milk. It is an acquired disease. Most of its victims fall in the age group 18-45 often contacting the disease before 18. Tuberculosis is a disease of modern civilization; it was unknown in Americas before the arrival of Europeans there.

Global Incidence

Tuberculosis remains a global problem even though its causative agent and medicines, which can cure them, have been known for a long time. The estimated number of infectious tuberculosis cases in the world may touch even 20 millions. About 3 million tuberculosis patients die each year and about 7.5 million new cases are added; and about 5 million jump out of the pool after treatment. So the infective pool remains almost constant.

In the economically advanced countries, tuberculosis is declining at a rather fast pace. For example, tuberculosis death rate has declined to 0.5 per 100,000 in the USA; it used to be about 200 in 1900. The decline started before BCG was discovered. It means that good health attributable to nutritious food and better living environment is more important than medicines. This applied not only to tuberculosis but to almost all diseases. This also explains why 95 per cent of cases of tuberculosis occur in developing countries of Asia, Africa and Latin America.

The global magnitude of tuberculosis burden is given in Table 12.7. The disease killed about 1.49 million people in 1998, four-fifths of them being in the productive age group of 15-49. It kills more adults than any other infectious disease. Drug resistance has acquired serious proportions in these counties. Those who are treated do not go through the full course of the treatment. Increase in migration for work from rural to urban areas, as also from rural to rural areas has created conditions for infected persons to infect more people. The disease has also joined hand with HIV to make the situation still worse. Rarely can any one survive their joint attack.

Tuberculosis in India

Tuberculosis in endemic form might have been in India for quite a long time but it became a public health problem only in the early part of the twentieth century. Since then it has ranked very high as a public health problem in India. In olden days, it was a disease of affluence and was called *Raj Roga* (disease of the rich). It is no longer so. It has now become Rayyat Roga, disease of the poor. It is also called *Chhaya Roga* or a disease that

Table 12.7: Global Burden of Tuberculosis: 1998

WHO Regions	*Incidence in '000*	*Mortality in '000*	*DALY '000*	*TB cases with HIV in '000*
The Americas				
High income	17	1	8	4
Middle & low income	213	53	1,213	22
Europe				
High income	72	7	53	8
Low and middle income	357	53	853	2
Eastern Mediterranean	607	139	3,188	4
Africa	1,047	209	5,442	510
South-East Asia				
India	1,794	421	7,577	46
Other countries	1,146	261	4,438	16
Western Pacific				
High income	86	10	80	1
China	1,411	259	3,878	5
Other countries	478	86	1,459	3
World	7,393	1,498	28,189	619

Source: WHO, World Health Report, 1998.

Slowly and steadily consumes the body. The disease started shifting its focus from rich to the poor in the early part of the twentieth century. It was also the period when the people of India went through a number of famines and diseases like plague. Physiologically they were very much weakened and ready for the onslaught of contagious diseases like tuberculosis.

Reliable data on morbidity and mortality of that period are lacking, but the disease had caught the attention of the health specialists and workers as early as 1916. Disturbing information started coming after 1935. As in 1998, about 14 million people are afflicted by this disease, of whom 3 to 3.5 million are highly infectious. Each year more than 2 million new cases are added to the disease load. India accounts for nearly one third of the global TB burden. Of the 3 million people who die of TB each year, nearly one-fifth of them are Indians i.e. almost one person each minute. Figure 12.4 gives the state wise distribution of TB morbidity and mortality in India.

Incidence of TB in India is 187 per 100,000 population. The countries, which show higher rate than India are South Africa (392), Philippines (314), Indonesia (285), Ethiopia (260), Bangladesh (246), Nigeria (214). India has more TB patients than China even though latter has more population. India has the largest number of new cases of infection per annum i.e. 805,000; China has only 630,000 cases.

Soon after independence in 1947, more effective steps were taken by the government of India to control tuberculosis. Two of these activities deserve our attention. One was aimed at isolating the infected cases and treating them in hospitals and health centres; the other at covering as much population as possible under BCG (Basille Calmette Guerin) vaccination to minimize new infection.

A national sample survey was conducted during 1956-61 to assess the incidence of TB in the country. The method of the survey was miniature X-ray. The findings of the survey were as follows:

1. prevalence rate of active tuberculosis ranged between 13 to 25/1000 population;
2. rate of positive cases ranged between 2 to 8/1000 population;
3. the difference in the prevalence rate in cities and towns was negligible;
4. females were less susceptible to the disease;
5. older the people, more likely to have the disease;
5. in urban areas people living in mud houses were more exposed to the disease; and
6. most of the active cases had reached an advanced stage of the disease.

As in the case of other diseases, tuberculosis is unevenly distributed in India. Its intensity depends largely on the environmental conditions and availability of health facilities. The office of the Registrar General of India conducts a sample survey of causes of deaths each year. According to the report for the year 1997, this disease accounts for 6.2 per cent of all deaths in rural areas in India. Some states show higher while others show lower than national average. The states of Rajasthan, Gujarat and Madhya Pradesh are the worst off (above 8.6 per cent) while those of Kerala, Tamil Nadu, Maharashtra and Haryana are better placed (below 4.6 per cent) in this respect. The survey also reveals that as age advances, the chances of contracting tuberculosis are increased. Almost 60 per cent of deaths take place after 45 years of age. For more details see Table 12.6.

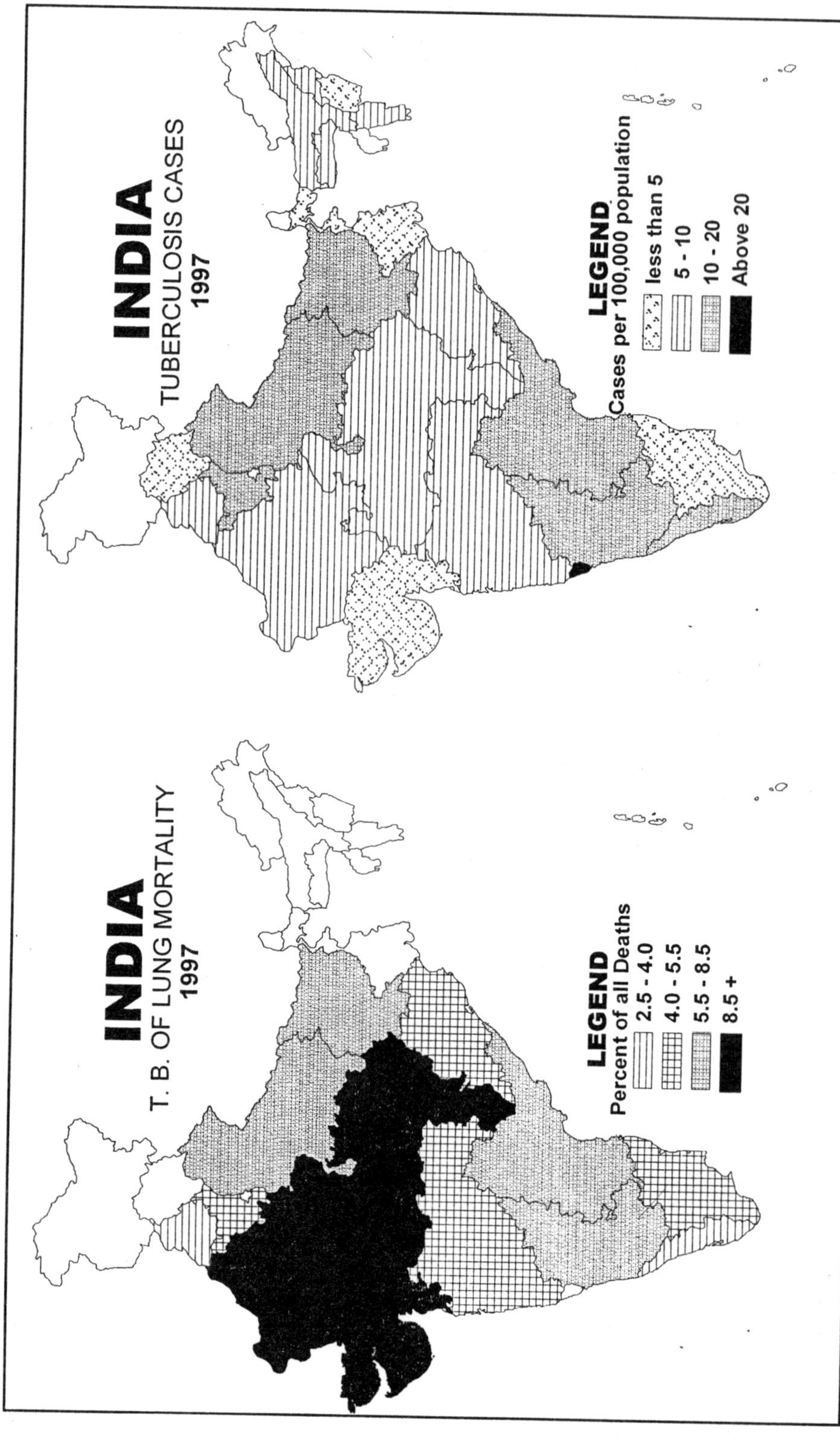

Fig. 12. 4: Tuberculosis in India-1998.
Source: Statistical Abstract of India, 2001.

Control of Tuberculosis

Studies conducted by Indian Council of Medical Research (ICMR) during 1950-65 concluded that BCG was not so effective in disinfecting adult patients, but if given soon after birth it did give some immunity against the disease in infancy and early childhood. It was also found that domiciliary treatment with anti-TB drugs was safe and effective. Armed with the feedbacks mentioned above, the Government of India launched the National Tuberculosis Control Programme (NTCP) in 1962 to detect early cases in symptomatic patients through sputum microscopy and X-ray and to initiate effective domiciliary treatment with standard chemotherapy. BCG vaccination at birth was part of the programme. The NTCP was implemented through 446 District Tuberculosis Centres.

To remove the shortcomings that hampered its success, the programme was modified in 1983 to introduce a short course of nine-months duration in chemotherapy. The new programme is in operation in 293 districts but the disease did not slow down.

Table 12.6: India: Age-wise Mortality Attributable to T.B. of Lung (1997)

States	*Per cent of total deaths*	*Age-group 0-14 yrs*	*Age-group 15-44 yrs*	*Age-group 45+ yrs*
India	**6.20**	**3.10**	**38.20**	**58.60**
Andhra Pradesh	5.80	1.80	30.50	67.70
Bihar	7.50	5.80	36.20	62.80
Gujarat	9.10	1.00	30.50	66.00
Haryana	4.60	4.80	35.70	59.50
Karnatak	5.50	5.10	40.50	54.40
Kerala	2.50	0.00	22.70	57.30
Madhya Pradesh	8.60	3.30	43.50	53.30
Maharashtra	4.40	2.10	47.30	50.60
Orissa	5.40	4.20	49.30	46.50
Punjab	3.50	0.00	43.20	56.70
Rajasthan	9.00	2.50	38.90	58.40
Tamil Nadu	4.60	4.00	30.80	65.40
Uttar Pradesh	7.20	6.40	35.00	58.60

Source: Survey of Causes of Death (Rural): 1997.

After a thorough review of the programme, a Revised National TB Eradication Programme (RNTCP), designed to improve the completion of the short course chemotherapy rates to 85 per cent and case detection to 75 per cent of potential cases, was launched in 1993. After pilot testing of the strategy, the new programme is being implemented in 102 districts spread over 15 states of the country and covering a population of 272 million. In addition to this, the old NTCP has been further strengthened in 203 districts with a population of 447 million.

In spite of all these efforts, only 2 per cent of the total population of the country was covered by the RNTCP by mid-1998. By the end of 2000, the coverage increased to 290 million living in 13 districts. About 15,000 patients are being placed under RNTCP treatment each month.

With a view to achieve the target of 1/1000 infection rate as early as possible, the current tuberculosis control programme is being revised again. The idea is to bring the patient to the clinic by personal contact. The patients should be registered by the PHC by personal visits to villages and they should be brought to the clinic and given medicine in the presence of the staff of the clinic. The present practice of giving medicines to the patients to be taken at home has not worked.

INFLUENZA

Influenza is perhaps the oldest and most persistent disease of human kind. It is an international disease in the sense that it is found all over the world. It is an acute respiratory tract infection caused by a virus of three types: A, B and C. A type ($H_1 N_1$) is, however, the most virulent one and almost all pandemics of the past have been of this type. Its symptoms are: chill, followed by malaise, slight fever, muscle pain and cough.

Influenza pandemics comes every 10-15 years; and epidemics every 2-3 years. The B variety comes every 4-5 years. But the periodicity is not as certain as that of measles or whooping cough. The pandemics of 1957 and 1968 were really serious. The disease starts with a few stray cases of children. It is then spreads fast to infect both children and adults and reaches its peak in 3-4 weeks. The rate of incidence varies from 10 to 50 per cent depending on the general health of the people, immunity, nutritional status, density of population, frequency of contacts, etc.

Its control is not easy because the antigens involved are of different varieties having no commonality in so far susceptibility to drugs is concerned. Immunity from one type of the antigen does not give immunity from other two types. It has been found that A type, discovered in 1933, is not stable; it changes. Since then it has emerged as $H_2 N_2$ in 1957 and H3 N_2 in 1968. Between 1946 and 1957, it transformed itself into $H_1 N_1$.

The reservoir of the antigen has been traced to animals and birds. It is nasopharynx one or two days before and after the onset of the infection. It attacks both sexes equally and attacks the adults less. The transmission chain runs from person to person, usually from children to elderly persons (65+ years old) and then on to others. The incubation period of the infection is 18-72 hours. Complications can lead to pneumonia.

The transmission, as stated earlier, is through the secretions of the respiratory tract and hence more crowded a place, and more mobile a person, greater the chances of getting the infection. It is more common in winter months in the northern hemisphere; and in winter and rainy months in the southern hemisphere. In India, it comes in summer months too.

India has the facilities for the isolation appears to be better than cure. Avoidance of crowded places, covering the mouth while sneezing or coughing, less exposure to sudden changes in temperature and eating easily digestible foods do reduce the chances of infection.

The disease is not confines to any area or climatic zone as such but it is more likely to strike in winters and rainy seasons. In India, the northern states, which experience severe to mild winter are more prone to influenza. It often attacks at the junction of winter and summer. Urban slums are the most severely affected areas.

ASTHMA

Asthma is a widely prevalent respiratory disease. Chronic obstructive pulmonary disease, a grouping of chronic bronchitis and emphysema, for which cigarette smoking is the most important risk factor, kills 2.9 million adults each year in the world. At least 15 per cent of the middle-aged smokers in the developed countries have abnormal lung function.

Asthma is a Greek word; it means breathing hard. It is a major chronic airway disorder affecting 155 million people of all ages worldwide. Very often it appears quite early in childhood and if it is inadequately treated, the life-long consequences can be substantial and disabling. The major burden of asthma, however, falls on the developing world.

The mechanics of the attack of asthma is something like this. A healthy respiratory system breathes air in and out of the lungs through an intricate web of air passages called the bronchiole network. Trouble starts when a minor allergen, also called trigger, sets off an immune system and releases antibodies which attach themselves to the cells in the air passage leading to the inflammation and mucus, the bronchiole becomes asthmatic. The attack of asthma begins when the body's immune system becomes so sensitised to an allergen, mainly through heavy exposure in childhood, that it starts treating it as a threat. Whenever this allergen enters the body, the renegade immune system triggers the release of a cascade of antibodies called IgE. These antibodies surge through the blood stream fastening themselves to cells that react by poring out inflammatory chemicals. Confined to the nose at first, this reaction only leads to a runny nose. But when it extends down to the lungs, the result becomes lethal. The bronchioles that are the small airways fill up with mucus leading to laboured breathing. As more airways get choked, the attack becomes severe.

A person can be predisposed to asthma, but unless the allergen triggers the attack nothing happens. A range of factors can act as allergens, the most important among them being air pollution. The rise in asthma is directly proportional to the number of automobiles, density of population and industrial growth. Ozone, diesel fumes and suspended particles all act as irritants to the air passages. Other important irritants are pet animals like cats and dogs, and some household items. The indiscriminate use of pain-killing drugs like aspirin and brufen can trigger off asthma. Preservatives, perfumes and mosquito repellents can also spur attack of asthma. Other factors that induce asthma attacks are viral and bacterial infections, weather changes, dust mites, insects like cockroaches, moulds, and pollens.

Children are also victims of asthma. Prevalence rates among children range from 1.5 to 12 per cent. The rates are relatively lower in the developing countries. Globally, both the prevalence and hospitalisation rates have increased by 40 per cent during the decade 1985-95. The long-term prognosis of asthma is now a major global health problem. It is believed that a majority of children who get asthma grow out of it in their teens. Recent epidemiological evidences are however less optimistic about it. Between 30 to 40 per cent of the asthma children, who get rid of the disease at puberty, get it back in adulthood. The remaining children continue to suffer throughout their life. Asthma in childhood is an example of a chronic disease, which can impair children's socialisation, school performance and later life. Self-management and care are essential if the asthmatic child is to lead a normal life. Such persons should therefore be doubly careful. They should not consider themselves as immune from the disease.

There is no medicine for asthma. A variety of inhalers have been developed which give instant relief. Tablets and injections are also available for serious cases. Steroid inhalers prevent the attack. Then there are the inhalers that dilate the bronchioles. There are breath-actuated inhalers also which release medicines the patient breathes in. To predict the onset of the attack, a peak flow meter is also available. Scientists have found a genetic master switch that they hope to use to ward off asthma attack. They have identified a group of genes that evolved to protect the children against intestinal parasites, but which in more sanitary, modern environment, cause a misguided attack on the respiratory airways.

More information on Asthma is given in chapter 30 dealing with the health problems of the aged.

INTESTINAL DISEASES

If the number of patients treated in hospitals and primary health centres is any guide, the group of contagious diseases clubbed together under the head dysentery and diarrhoea, is the third most important disease after fevers and respiratory diseases. It may not be a great killer, but it does weaken the immunity of a large number of people, specially the poor living in rural areas and urban slums, and thus exposing them to become victims of many other diseases. Five per cent of the total deaths in India are ascribed to these diseases. But the morbidity rate may be as high as 20 per cent.

Literally, dysentery means dysfunction or impairment of the functioning of the intestines. Medically speaking, it means the passing of blood or mucus in the motion. It may result from a variety of causes. When it results from organisms like S. Shiga, S. Flexture, etc., it is called bacillary dysentery. Endamoeba Histolytica can also cause dysentery.

Acute Diarrhoeal Diseases

Diarrhoea can be defined as the passage of loose and watery stool at an abnormal frequency (more than 3-4 times a day). Diarrhoeal diseases denote a number of diseases with same or similar symptoms. WHO defines acute diarrhoea as a sudden attack lasting for 3-14 days.

The process of development of diarrhoea and dysentery runs something like this. The food consumed first reaches the stomach where it is retained for a variable period of time depending on the nature of food. A rhythmic contraction and expansion of the stomach wall muscles move the food around and mix it with gastric digestive juices consisting of hydrochloric acid and pepsin. The former softens and dissolves the tough fibres while the later separates the proteins to form amino acids.

After the digestive process in the stomach is completed, the food passes into the first port of the small intestinal tack, the duodenum, through the pyloric sphincter. It is then mixed with enzymes (digestive juices) brought from the lever and the pancreas through tubes to the duodenum. The mixture become quite watery and easily passes along the track to the colon or large intestines. While moving through the small intestine, it is digested into its basic chemical parts and transferred through the intestinal walls into the blood vessels. Only the residue goes to the large intestine for final processing before its elimination. The main function of the colon is to absorb and return to the blood the water which is mixed with the food during the digestive process. If this water is passed off with the roughage through the colon, man would die of dehydration. As roughage passes through the colon, the cells in its walls transfer back water into blood vessels. The blood vessels then push it back into general circulation.

If something interferes with this process abnormalities in the form of dysentery, diarrhoea or even constipation may occur. Irritation in the walls of the colon resulting in a quick movement of the food material through the intestines is one of the causes of this disease. Irritation can be caused by chemical taken with food or by action of bacteria, which infect the digestive tract. It starts with cramping pain and frequent expulsion of watery motions. Majority of dysentery cases are bacterial.

Diarrhoea is one of the most important causes of morbidity in the developing countries, next only to respiratory diseases. It is estimated that about 3 million children die of diarrhoea, four-fifth of them under 2 years of age; and the total number of diarrhoea episodes run to over 1.8 billion.

In 1998, the estimated number of deaths due to diarrhoea was 22 lakhs. The developed countries of Europe and Americas accounted for less than 1.5 lakhs. India alone accounted for 7 lakh deaths. Within the country, the distribution of diarrhoeal cases is quite variable. For details, see Table 12.7 and Fig. 12.5.

Bacillary Dysentery

Bacillary dysentery is also a form of diarrhoea. Genus Shiglla is a group of bacteria, which can infect the colon to cause dysentery. They look like small rods, 1 x 0.50 microns; they do not move, and prefer to live in human intestines. The optimum temperature in which the bacteria thrive is 37° C, which is the normal temperature of the human body. Temperatures above 55° C are fatal for them. It must, however, be noted that the presence of shigellae is not the only necessary condition for dysentery to set in. A filterable organism called bacterophase, always present in the intestines, keeps the shigellae in check.

The agent shigellae are carried to man by flies. Thus, the conditions, which favour the growth of flies, also favour the onset of bacillary dysentery. "The breeding of the flies is closely related to the temperature. At 16 ° C temperature, the average time required for a housefly to develop from egg to adult stage is 44 days. The hatching times drops to 16 days at 25° C, and to10 days at 30° C. Although the exact nature of the chemicals needed for optimal development is not known, it is well established that flies multiply faster in decomposed organic material. Under optimal conditions of breeding and development a pair of flies beginning operations in April may be progenitors, if all were to live, of 191,010,000,000,000,000,000 flies by August. Allowing one-eighth of a cubic inch to a fly, this number would cover the earth 47 feet deep", says W.B. Herms. Fortunately, ideal conditions never exist for the flies to survive to swamp the earth.

The proboscis or the tiny trunk of a fly has fine hairs, which collect germs while picking up food from human excreta and other filthy materials. Its feet also have hairs, which secrete a glue to collect microscopic organisms. As it sits on food to be consumed by humans, it releases the microscopic organisms like shigellae collected earlier. Once in the stomach, they become the cause of bacillary dysentery. The infection rate is high if personal hygiene is neglected due to water shortage. It is thus a disease of unwashed hands and unclean environment.

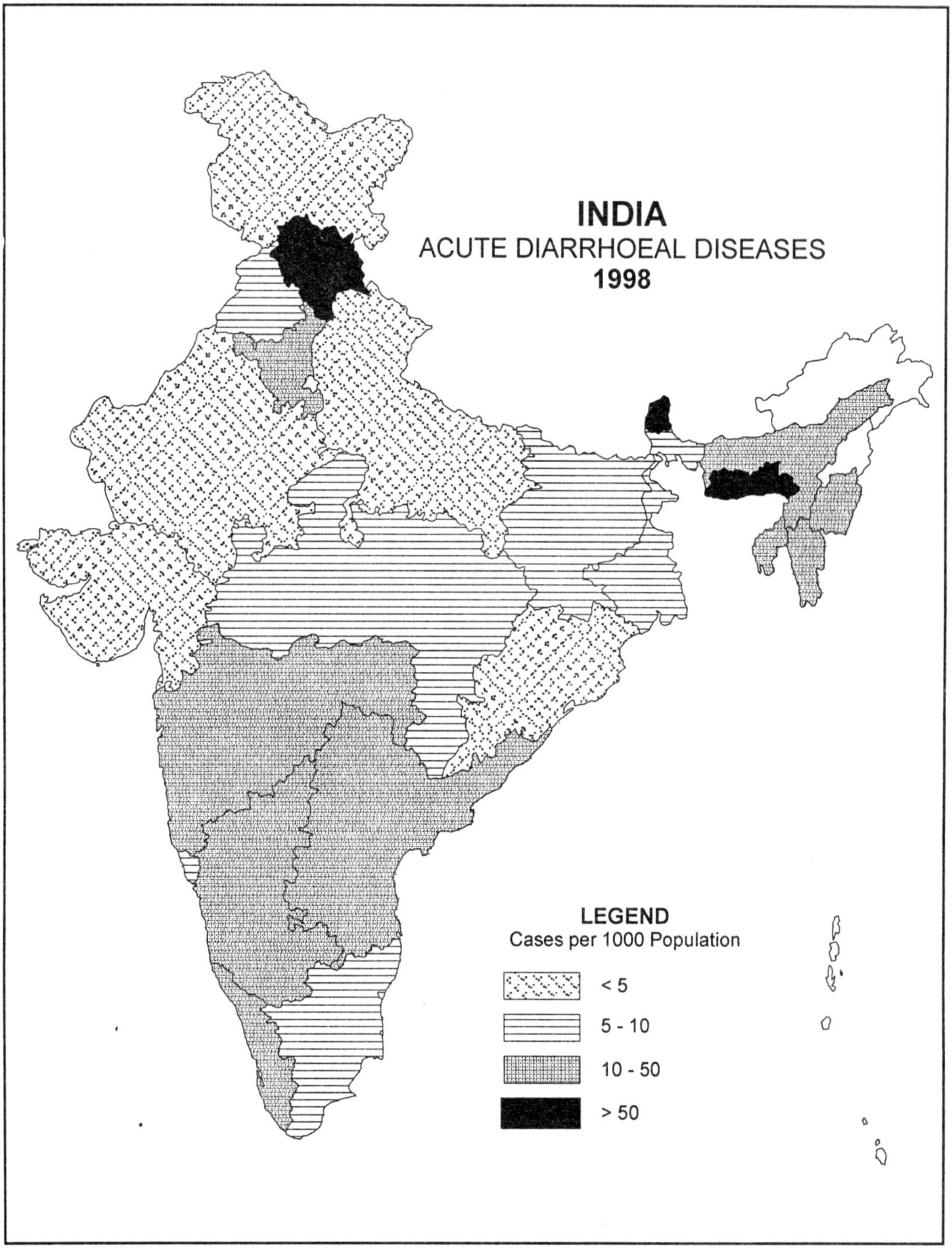

Fig. 12.5: India: Acute Diarrhoeal Diseases (1998)

Source: Statistical Abstract of India, 2001.

Table 12.7: Reported Cases and Deaths Due to Diarrhoeal Diseases: 1998 India: State-wise

	States	*Reported Cases in thousands*	*Cases/1000 population*	*Reported deaths*
1.	Andhra Pradesh	1853	25	674
2.	Arunachal Pradesh	–	–	–
3.	Assam	596	23	121
4.	Bihar	–	–	–
5.	Goa	11	8.6	3
6.	Gujarat	207	4.10	50
7.	Haryana	375	17.80	85
8.	Himachal Pradesh	433	72.0	58
9.	J & K	138	3.7	–
10.	Karnataka	675	13	366
11.	Kerala	351	17.4	49
12.	MP	479	6.25	260
13.	Maharashtra	1099	11.5	556
14.	Manipur	32	12.9	12
15.	Meghalaya	152	66	42
16.	Mizoram	9	10	12
17.	Nagaland	15	–	8
18.	Orissa	793	4.23	453
19.	Punjab	196	8.2	57
20.	Rajasthan	212	3.9	64
21.	Sikkim	41	75	9
22.	TN	57	9	112
23.	Tripura	108	34	74
24.	UP	565	3.25	405
25.	WB	720	9	3635
26.	A & N Isls	23	6	9
27.	Chandigarh	–	0.2	–
28.	D & N Haveli	51	198	7
29.	Daman & Diu	4	2	0
30.	Delhi	133	9.6	8
31.	Lakshadweep	5	85	2
32.	Pondicherry	120	120	21
	India	9635		7152

Source: Health Information of India: 1997-1998.

Amoebic Dysentery

Amoebic dysentery is caused by the invasion of human intestines by *Endamoeba Histolytica.* This organism is unicellular averaging 15-25 microns in diameter. It often contains red blood cells acquired from the host. It is a tissue parasite and multiplies by fission, one amoeba dividing into two. It enters the human intestines in the form of a cyst by ingestion. After reaching the intestines the cyst ruptures to release the young mobile trophozoites, which penetrate the walls of the intestines. When they reach the distal end of the large intestines, the process of encysting begins again. This is particularly so in the event of dehydration of the intestines.

They can be transmitted through sewage contaminated water or vegetables irrigated with sewage water or grown in land fertilized with night soil. They can also be passed on to the food by cyst bearing flies, cockroaches, soiled clothing and by careless food handlers.

Several factors including the general health of the host determine the susceptibility of a person to the disease. When the trophozoites enter a new host, they can infect it only if the stomach is devoid of gastric juices. In general, males are less resistant than females; and pre-school children show a lower infection rate than those in the older age group. The people in the age group of 25-30 years appear to be most vulnerable. But these differences may be more apparent than real. Much depends on the frequency of exposure people of difference age and sex groups are subjected to and overall health conditions.

Amoebiasis is quite wide spread in India but relevant data to map out its core areas just do not exist. Available data pertain to combined group of dysentery and diarrhoea. According to some estimates, at least half the cases of dysentery and diarrhoea are amoebiasis (Fig. 12.5)

For some pathogens that cause diarrhoea, man is the principal reservoir and thus most of the infections originate from human factors. There are some who originate in animals too. Usually, it is the faeces of humans or animals from where transmission starts. Faecal-oral transmission may be food borne, water borne or direct.

Oral rehydration therapy can take care of most of the diarrhoea cases. In complicated cases, chemotherapy is resorted to. Sanitation is the most important and effective preventive measure. But this is not easy to achieve in countries or regions, which are economically and socially poor and deprived.

SEXUALLY TRANSMITTED DISEASES (STD)

The most recent sexually transmitted disease is AIDS, which is discussed in the next (14) chapter. We propose to discuss in this section other venereal diseases common in India. Infection of these diseases results from sexual relations between man and woman or between man and man when one of the partners suffers from a venereal disease. Syphilis and gonorrhea are the two most common diseases of this group. Of minor importance are three other diseases: chancroid, lymphogranuloma venereum, and granuloma inguinale. The causative agents of these diseases are different but there are considered together because they are transmitted through sexual intercourse, specially of promiscuous nature. The organisms involved are: spirochetes for syphilis, cocci for gnorrhea, bacilli for chancroid, viruses for lymphogranuloma venereum, and bacterium for granuloma inguinale.

During the last few decades, considerable changes have taken place in the nature of transmission and number of pathogens responsible for these diseases. There were five classical pathogens, which were considered responsible for these diseases. Now their number has gone up to 20; and they are of different types ranging from bacterial to ectoparasites. In between are viral agents, protozoal agents and fungal agents. Many of the STD cases are outside the classical cases; they are the second generation cases requiring different approaches to treatment.

STD are global diseases found in both developed and developing countries. In India, they used to be more common in industrial cities where workers lived away from their families for extended periods. But with the breaking down of the social norms regarding sex, these diseases are not uncommon in other areas including rural areas. The problem with these diseases is that the infested persons tend to hide it and hence they are difficult to detect. Since promiscuous relations are the main sources of infection, each infested person infects many others before his case become serious enough to become clinical.

Like other infectious diseases the STD agents are also becoming resistant to antibiotics like penicillin giving new strains of the disease.

Syphilis

Syphilis is considered to be a destroyer of life. Its causative agent is an organism called *spirichaeta pallida* or *treponema pallidum.* It looks like a corkscrew varying in length from 5 to 25 microns and two to three times the diameter of a red blood cell. It dies easily when exposed to heat or chemicals like detergents in soap. It can, however, survive cold. The syphilis organism lives in the tissues of the infected person for his whole life.

Syphilis is of two types: venereal and endemic. The latter is found in certain climatic, social and economic conditions and shows up in the form of skin eruption without involving the nervous or cardiovascular systems. It is mild in effect and remains endemic. It erupts under favourable conditions and then subsides.

The causative agent of the venereal syphilis is spirochete, which enters the body through sex organs. Once inside, it reproduces itself at the entrance site and in no time begins to spread along the blood streams throughout the body. Its first symptom is a form of primary sore at the site of the entrance of the germ. As it multiplies and spreads to other parts of the body, it affects the mucous membranes of eye and the nervous system without any visible symptoms. After the wounds are healed, the disease becomes dormant and can be recognized only by routine blood test. About 25 per cent of the cases develop late manifestations, which may incapacitate or even kill the patient. These manifestations may appear as cardiovascular syphilis involving heart and blood vessels, neurosyphilis involving the brain and the spinal cord, the ocular syphilis involving the eyes, and gummatous syphilis involving the skin, mucous membranes and the bones.

It is not yet known as to where did syphilis originate? Some medical historians feel that its original home is Europe; but many others trace it to Americas. Whatever the case, the diseases came to India from Europe, probably through Portuguese. There were about 25 million cases of syphilis in the world in the 1970s; the current estimates put the figure at ...?...million. The disease is endemic in several parts of the world; its occurrence is however more in islands and coastal areas. Penicillin is the common drug for syphilis.

Gonorrhoea

Gonorrhoea is one of the oldest diseases of man. While syphilis is considered to be a destroyer of life; gonorrhoea is called the preventer of life. It was traced to sexual exposition only in 1790. Unlike syphilis, gonorrhoea is a common disease and is spreading fast. Mortality from the disease is rare, but its indirect effects including the sterilization of both the sexes are very common. Infection results from direct deposit of organism at or near the susceptible tissues of the genitalia, rectum, or the eyes. Eye infection takes place either at the time of birth or by hand.

The first symptom of the disease is the burning of the urination or slight vaginal discharge. If not treated in time, the infection involves the posterior part of the urethra or the fallopian tubes and ovaries. Arthritis is the most common extra-genital manifestation of the disease. Penicillin is the drug for this disease also.

Other Sexually Transmitted Diseases

Among the other sexually transmitted diseases are genital chlamydial infection, chancroid, genital hepes, genital human popilloma and trichomoniasis. HIV is also a partly sexually transmitted disease. It is however not discussed here (see chapter 14).

Global Incidence of STD

How many persons have STD will perhaps be never known. People maintain secrecy until the disease is so advanced that they cannot hide the reality. More often than not STD means extramarital sex. And this is something that the married persons try to hide. What is known is that these diseases are spreading fast and rate of incidence varies from 1 to 15 per cent depending on the vulnerability of the population.

According to the WHO about 333 million new cases of STD occurred in the world in 1997. These figures do not include HIV cases. They comprised of bacterial STD-165 million; viral STD-50 million; and trichomoniasis – 170 million.

STD in India

No accurate incidence of venereal diseases in India is available. It is, however, well known that these diseases constitute an important public health problem in the country. Many neonatal deaths, apart from cardiovascular and mental cases, are ascribed to these diseases. In 1933, Sir John Megaw, the then Director General of the India Medical Service, estimated that there were 5.5 million cases of syphilis and 7.6 million cases of gonorrhoea in the country. According to him, "syphilis and gonorrhea appear to be more common than has been usually believed; Bengal and Madras easily head the list. The data suggest that something like 5.5 million people in India actually show signs of syphilis so that if account be taken of those who have had the disease and have lost all obvious signs, it would probably be well within the mark to assume that 10 to 15 per cent of inhabitants suffer from syphilis at some time or the other during their lifetime. The striking low rates of venereal diseases in Punjab are entirely in keeping with impressions based on other sources of information" (Health Survey and Planning Committee).

As in 1970, the incidence of venereal diseases was very high in the states of H.P., present Uttaranchal, Orissa, Andhra Pradesh, Tamil Nadu, Gujarat and Kerala (see Fig. 12.4). The number of syphilis cases in India is declining because of the availability of antibody drugs, safer sex, and greater awareness among the people. It nevertheless continues to be a major health hazard in the country, particularly for the women, because sexually transmitted infections in the women appear with or without specific symptoms.

The STD cases seen and treated in specialized clinics give some indication of the problem. Each year about 1.3 million cases are registered in these clinics. The number of those who get treatment confidentially elsewhere would be six to seven times more and those who never get treatment or depend only on home medicines would be twice of those treated in clinics. Thus the STD load in India would be more than 15 million but the known cases are only 1.3 million as in 1989. The figures came down to 1.14 million in 1990. Stat-wise distribution of the cases is given in Table 12.8 and Figure 12.6.

Table 12.8: STD Cases Seen and Treated in STD Clinics: 1986-98

States	*1986*	*1990*	*1998*			
			Syphilis cases	*Gonococcal Cases*	*Total cases*	*Cases/lakh population*
Andhra Pradesh	75548	86316	18052	46731	64783	89
Arunachal Pradesh	–	–	–	–	–	–
Assam	1036	2812	44	268	312	1.25
Bihar	34587	18423	–	–	–	25 (1990)
Goa	1884	3014	1	1	2	
Gujarat	124813	98382	76	170	246	0.5
Haryana	807	5306	39	152	191	1.0
Himachal Pradesh	2530	3907	133	463	796	12.8
J & K	34854	16282	2724	319	3043	33.2
Karnataka	72285	87114	4012	6701	10713	21.40
Kerala	19483	28201	135	474	609	1.95
MP	18541	31479	1347	3284	5631	7.5
Maharashtra	423794	227822	1194	662	1856	2.10
Manipur	1181	3012	22	220	242	10.5
Meghalaya	3094	4518	1	17	18	0.8
Mizoram	3932	2532	7	34	41	4.8
Nagaland	506	1981	3	193	196	13.0
Orissa	94439	91643	681	1315	1996	5.75
Punjab	2743	2321	7	37	44	0.2
Rajasthan	14914	26508	98	1839	1937	3.80
Sikkim	0	0	0	14	14	2.80
Tamil Nadu	223746	243871	70	67	137	0.02
Tripura	3173	4012	61	46	107	3.14
Uttar Pradesh	26705	36037	724	3035	5379	3.36
West Bengal	26773	43491	–	–	–	–
A & N Islands	0	0	14	4	18	0
Chandigarh	246	231	–	–		
D & N Haveli	0	0	0	0	0	0
Daman & Diu	*		0	30	30	–
Delhi	31647	38315	93	85	178	1.45
Lakshadweep	0	0	0	0	0	0
Pondicherry	8780	9612	26	11	37	0.37
India	1,275,822	1141740	29,564	66,172	95,736	

Note: Rate is based on 1990 cases and 1991 population. * includes Daman & Diu.

Source: Health Information of India, 1998

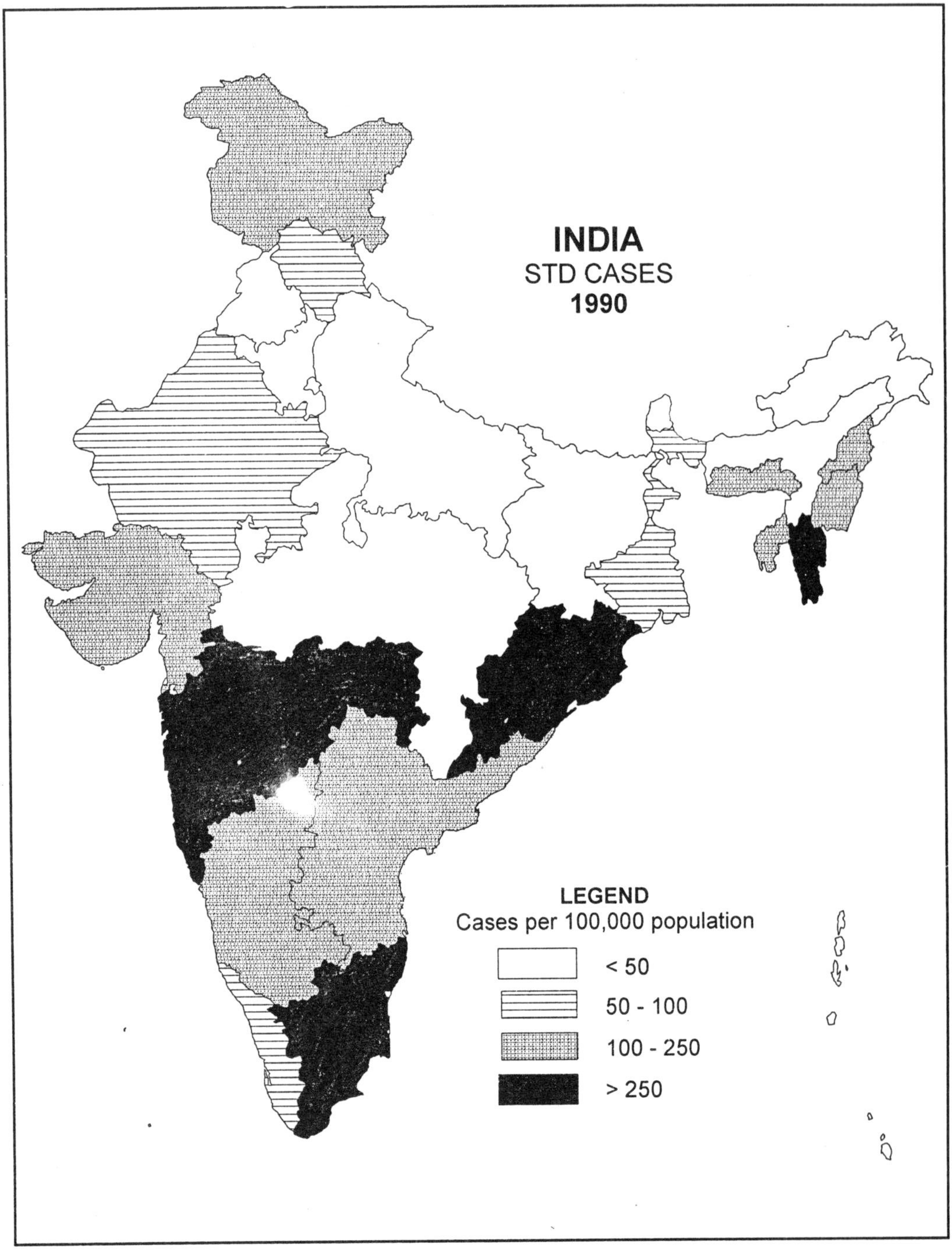

Fig. 12.6: India: Incidence of STD

MENINGOCOCAL MENINGITIS

Meningitis is an inflammation of the membranes covering the brain and spinal cord. It does not come under the category of communicable diseases. Nevertheless, it has been discussed in this chapter because some sort of infection is involved in it. Any micro-organism that reaches the membranes and causes inflammation produces meningitis. The term is, however, most commonly used for a specific disease caused by the meningococcus that is contagious and often comes as epidemics. It received medical attention when it appeared in epidemic forms during World War I. It is known to attack only human beings.

Meningococcus meningitis occurs all over the world. Barring a few cases, it now comes in the form of an epidemic recurring in a cycle of 8 to 12 years. It is not a seasonal disease but it appears to prefer late winter and early spring. It is primarily a disease of the early age, especially of children below the age of 5, but it does not discriminate on the basis of age or sex. Infants are its main victims. The disease is disseminated by carriers of meningococcus through nasopharynx droplets. Only those who have week immunity get the disease. It also depends on how often and in what dosage the infection has been transmitted.

The symptoms of meningococcus infection generally appear in three to five days depending upon the severity of the infection and the susceptibility of the victim. At first, the meningococcus enters the nasopharinx and multiplies there. In many cases, the infection does not proceed further and the patient get all right after a few days. If it does proceed further, it enters the blood and the patient develops the symptoms of toxaemia, irregular fever, and hyper-sensitivity to any external stimulus, he does not like to be disturbed, curls himself up, and becomes apathetic. Count of white cells in the blood increases to 15000. Rashes caused by haemorrhage appear all over the body. The blood culture at this stage can show the miningococcus.

If the infection does not stop, the patient dies within a few hours. In case the infection does not cause miningitis, it does not mean that causal factor of the disease is gone. Or even if the patient recovers from the disease, the danger of repeat infection remains if prescribed doses of medicine are not taken. The miningococcus should not only be removed from the blood but also from the meninges where it remains lodged waiting for the next epidemic to occur.

Meningitis usually begins with vomiting and severe headache, both caused by the inflammation of the meninges and increased pressure of the cerebrospinal fluid. Constipation and stoppage of urine may also take place in the early stages. The neck becomes stiff and in case of small children the spine together with the neck may bend backwards like a bow. Convulsions are common among the children. Both the pulse and the respiration are slow. If the purulent cerebrospinal fluid becomes too thick, it fails to reach the brain. This may swell the nerves arising from the brain causing temporary blindness in one eye and deafness. The brain itself is rarely damaged.

In the early stages, this disease may be easily confused with many other common diseases. It is therefore desirable to get blood examination done particularly by those who live in endemic areas. Early diagnosis is a must for cure. As soon as the symptoms of the disease appear, cerebrospinal fluid should be drawn without delay to identify the organism involved. Hospitalization and treatment by a qualified physician is a must. The patient should be given water to avoid dehydration; urine should be taken out regularly; the surroundings should be kept clean and the patient should not be disturbed or irritated.

Other bacteria can also cause meningitis if they reach the spine. Tuberculous meningitis and syphilitic meningitis fall in this category. Meningitis cases are on the decline all over the country.

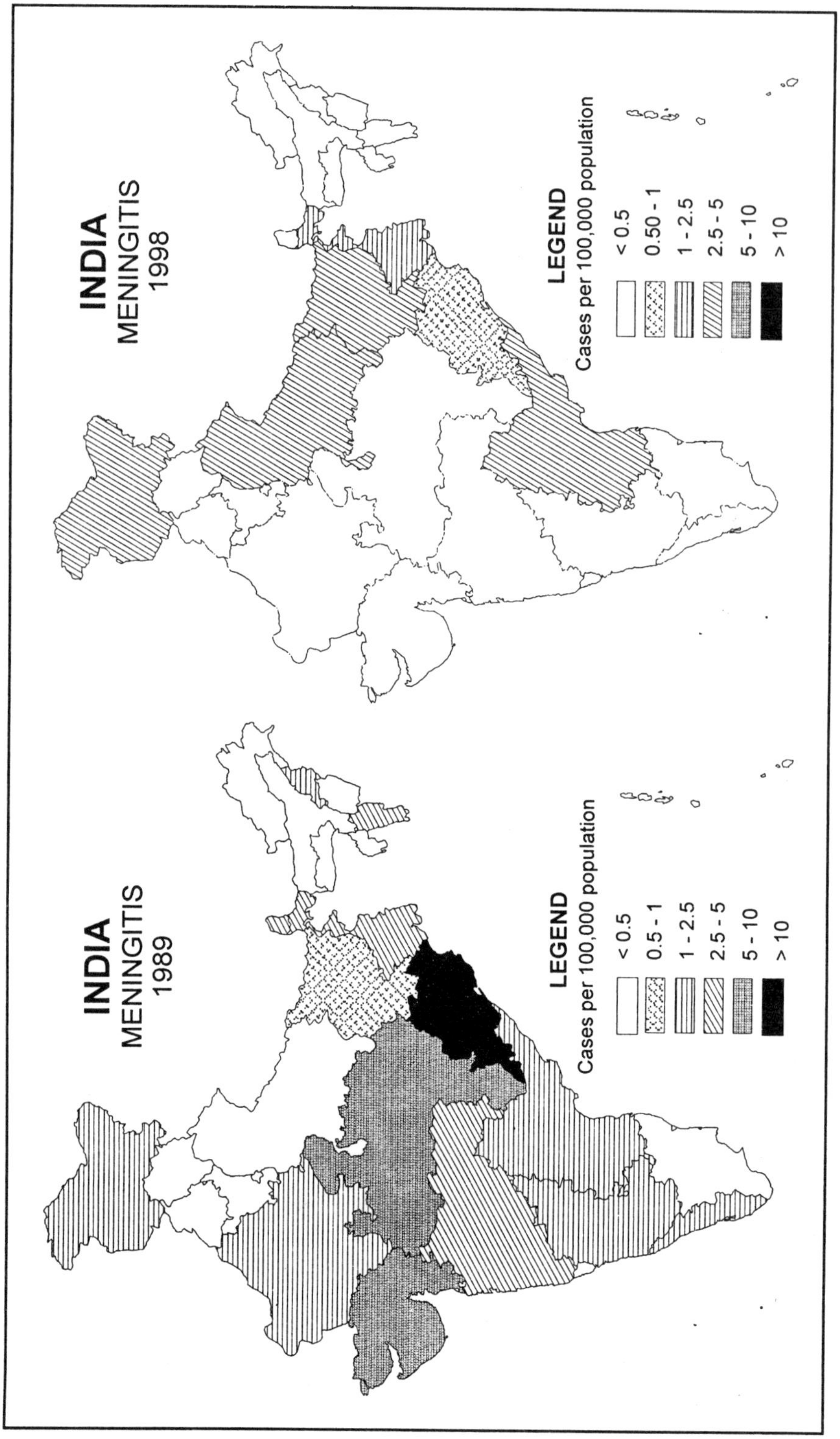

Fig. 12.7: India: Incidence of Meningococal Meningitis
Source: Health Information of India, 1998

JAPANESE ENCEPHALITIS (JE)

Japanese encephalitis has been reported in India since mid-nineteen fifties. With the expansion of irrigation facilities and flooding of low-lying areas, number of states reporting JE cases has steadily increased. During 1980s, 12 states and union territories covering 378 million people nad reported cases of JE. In 1992, there were 2432 cases of JE in the country and the number deaths attributed to the disease was 888. In 1996, the number of cases declined to 936 and deaths to 294. The states, which are totally or partially affected are Andhra Pradesh, Assam, Bihar, Haryana, Karnataka, Manipur, Tamil Nadu, Uttar Pradesh and West Bengal (Fig. 12.7).

Like malaria, JE is also on resurgence trail. In Uttar Pradesh, it has spread to 20 districts; a year back, it was confined to only 14 districts. It appeared in Gorakhpur first; from there it spread its tentacles to the Terai districts of the state. Over 600 cases of JE were reported from the state last year. 125 persons died of JE in eastern districts alone. In 1999-2000, three other districts namely Lakhimpur Kheri, Pilibhit and Bahraich came under its influence. Number of cases was 510; and number of deaths reached 116.

Efforts to control the disease have been hampered by non-availability of the vaccine. Gorakhpur has a branch of the National Institute of Virology since 1998 but it does not appear to have any impact on the diffusion and intensity of the disease.

KALA-AZAR

Kala-azar literally means black fever. Also known as visceral leishmaniasis, it is an infectious disease caused by a parasitic micro-organism of the genus *Lieishmania.* It is characterized by fever, reduction in white blood cell numbers, mild anaemia, wasting, gross enlargement of the lever, and especially of the spleen and derangement of amounts and kinds of serum proteins. Symptoms appear after two or more months of infection and gradually become more intense. In untreated cases death is almost sure within two years. The apparent cause of death may be pneumonia or any of the deficiency diseases.

Lieshmania discovered by William Leishman in 1900. It is an unusual parasite in the sense that it lives in the phagocytic cells of the lymphoid-macrophage system of the vertebrate host. Since these cells are part of the host's mechanism of defence against the invading organisms, it gets protection against them. Three species of the leishmania infect man: L. lonovani causing deep organ or vicsceral infection, L. tropica causing skin infection, and L. brazilienesis causing American cutaneous infection. Kala-azar is caused by the species L. lonovani only.

Kala-azar is one of the oldest diseases of man. It was quite prevalent in Europe in medieval times. In England alone lakhs of people died of this diseases in the fourteenth century. It has been wiped out from the developed parts of the world but continues to be present in India, Bangladesh, northern China, Kenya, Sudan, Brazil, Paraguay, Venezuela, Mediterranean coast and part of West Asia. All varieties of Leishmanial infections are transmitted by small blood sucking sand flies of the genus phlebotomus, but the species of flies involved differ from place to place. The host of the Indian Kala-azar leishmaniasis is man himself. Unlike the other varieties of the disease, the Indian Kala-azar takes epidemic proportions and becomes a serious public health hazard. In India, it is essentially a disease of the young adults; in the Mediterranean region it attacks children below the age of 5 years.

Two major states of India, Bihar and West Bengal, constitute the main endemic areas of the country. The disease might have been present in dormant form in these states for quite a long time. It emerged with a bang in the early seventies of the twentieth century in four Gangetic districts of Bihar. Currently, about 36 districts of Bihar, 10 districts of West Bengal and 2 districts of UP, and parts of the state of Sikkim are affected by this disease. Over 90 per cent of the reported cases and over 95 per cent of the reported deaths are, however, from Bihar alone. Kala Azar is more prevalent in districts adjoining River Ganga.

Table 12.9 gives the incidence of Kala-azar from 1994 to 2001. It shows that the incidence of the disease in general is declining but it is fluctuating. A Kala-azar control programme was launched in 1990. It was modified in 2001 under which the spray of DDT is being intensified in the endemic areas.

Table 12.9: Incidence of Kala-Azar in India 1994 to 2001

Year	*Cases*	*Deaths*
1994	24,391	377
1995	21.045	259
1996	25,056	874
1997	15,948	251
1998	12,411	215
1999	11,627	277
2000	12.909	130
2001	9,905	196

Source: Health Information of India (1998)

Kala-azar is spreading fast in India and deserves urgent attention. In 1986, total number of reported cases was 17,806 with only 72 deaths. By 1992, the number of cases went up to 77,102 and deaths to 1,419. During 1998 and 1999, the number of cases declined to 17,429 and 13,542 respectively, and the number of deaths to 255 and 221.

Government of India launched a programme to control Kala-Azar, in 1992. The strategy included: indoor residential spraying of insecticides like DDT to reduce vector population; early diagnosis and complete treatment; and health education for community awareness. The programme did have some effect and the number of deaths declined substantially. It has now been strengthened and DDT spraying has been intensified in the endemic areas. Fortunately the vector of Kala-azar is still sensitive to DDT.

Effective treatment of the visceral infections required intramuscular or intravenous injections of certain pentavalent organic antimonials such as sodium antimony gluconate or aromatic diamedines such as pentamidine or stilbamidene. Since the disease in India too is becoming resistant to the above medicines as also to DDT, it is likely to further spread unless prompt action is taken forthwith to prevent its occurrence. Prevention of access of flies to infected reservoir or of infested flies to the susceptible human beings leads to control. The spray of insecticides to habitations where transmission occurs indoors should be taken on top priority basis before it is too late. India has the means to control the disease.

HOOKWORM INFECTION

Hookworm constitutes a group of parasites that include *Ancylostoma duodenale, necator americanus, and Ancylostoma braziliense.* A closely related group of parasites of *stongyloidedae* family produces symptoms similar to those produced by *Ancylostomatidae* group except that the latter cause a very remarkable form of anaemia. The global prevalence of the disease in 1992 was 150 million; and 65000 persons died.

Ancilostoma duadenate was identified in 1843. It measures 8-10 mm in length and 0.40 to 0.50 mm in width. The female measures 10-13 x 0.6 mm. Its mouth has strong dental plates that enable it to penetrate of the walls of the intestine. It feeds on blood, mucous, membranes and serum. Each worm can suck 0.10 to 0.70 ml blood. Degree of anaemia a victim suffers from depends on the number of worms in the intestines. One female produces 30,000 eggs per day. N. Americanus produces 9000 eggs per day.

While in the intestine, *A. duadenate* lay and fertilize their eggs. The eggs are expelled through the faeces. "Once in the outside world, they hatch only under favourable conditions.The faeces need to be diluted with a moist earth of a sandy texture and at a temperature of about 25°C. Little happens if the faeces lie on dry or highly acid earth or in direct sunlight.

Under favourable conditions of moisture, oxygenation, temperature, shade and PH, a rhabditoid larva emerges which after a few days moults into a new form, slightly bigger. After another lapse of time (five to eight days) and under favourable circumstances, a second moulting takes place that results in filariform larvae that infect the human host.

After certain time, the larva is ready for skin penetration. If it encounters a human host, it will proceed through the skin and venous circulation to the heart and lungs, into the bronchi and trachea, on to the top of the hostesphagus and thence down through the pylorus to the worm's implantation area in the duodenum. There it grows into another adult." And thus the cycle continues. It takes five weeks until the newly entered larva is able to lay eggs. The larvae can develop on ground only if the faeces do not dry and are diluted by rain. Excessive rain is however not favourable because it can wash off the eggs. Stagnant water is also unfavourable because it gives rise to a variety of microorganisms, which eat away the eggs.

Average number of eggs per gram of stools gives the Endemic Index (EI).

Below	200 Not serious
200-250	Potential danger
250-300	Minor public health problem
Above 300	Serious public health problem

Chronic blood loss and depletion of iron leading to anaemia is the most important symptom of hookworm syndrome. It results from the loss of blood from the bite of the worms. This loss manifests itself through the loss of iron in the blood. If the body is healthy and the person affected takes nutritive food, anaemia may not occur. Hookworm anaemia is most prevalent among the poor who neither live in hygienic conditions nor eat iron rich food. Hookworm affects people of all ages and sexes. Those who are malnourished and weakened for some other reasons are its immediate victims.

Climate, hygiene and socio-economic conditions of the population are the main determinants of the occurrence and geographic distribution of the agents. Hot and humid climates are very favourable for it. In India and many other developing countries, cultural factors like defecating in the open play an important role in infective process. Coastal areas of the Indian peninsula offer favourable conditions for the spread of this disease.

Among the favourable environmental factors are:

1. moist and sandy soil,
2. temperature 24-32° C,
3. adequate amount of oxygen for the growth of the larvae,
4. adequate moisture: rainfall 100 cm,
5. adequate shade to avoid ultraviolet rays of the sun, and
6. poor hygiene and sanitation.

The disease is quite common in India. In the southern states nector americanus is the agent while in northern states it is the Ancylostomaduodenale. The Assam tea gardens, West Bengal, Bihar, Orissa, Andhra Pradesh, Tamil Nadu, Kerala and Maharashtra are the most severely affected states. According to some estimates, 60-80 per cent of the population of the coastal states (200 to 300 million persons) are under the risk of the disease.

TYPHOID FEVER

Prevalence of typhoid or entretic fever indicates substandard water supply and sanitation. As these factors change for the better, the cases of typhoid also decline. It is not longer prevalent in developed pars of the world. The only cases that occur are the imported ones. In UK, the prevalence rate is 1 per million of population. But in Asia, Africa and Latin America, it is a major health hazard. About 600,000 persons die of typhoid in the world each year; 80 per cent of them in Asia, 15 per cent in Africa; and 5 per cent in Latin America.

Typhoid is caused by systemic infection by *S. typhi.* It is found in man alone. Its symptoms are high fever for 3-4 weeks and brandicardi involving lymphoid tissues. The organism has a tendency to become resistant to antibiotics, so much so that half of the strains of the bacteria are now resistant to drugs. It is the resistant strains, which cause frequent outbreaks of the disease.

There are two other agents: *S. paro A* and *S paro B*. There is no commonality among the three. The *S. typhi*, the most common of the bacilli, survives intra-cellularly in the tissues of various organs of the body. It is readily killed by high temperature, freezing temperature and common disinfection. Man is the only known reservoir. He becomes infectious if the bacilli appear in stools and urine of the carrier. Those who excrete bacilli for more than a year after a clinical attack are called chronic carriers. The bacilli stay in the gal bladder and kidney tract. The primary source of infection is faeces and urine of the carrier. Among the secondary sources are water, food, fungus and flies. It attacks the males more than females (because males are more mobile) and has special preference for those in the age group of 5-19 years (Fig. 12.8).

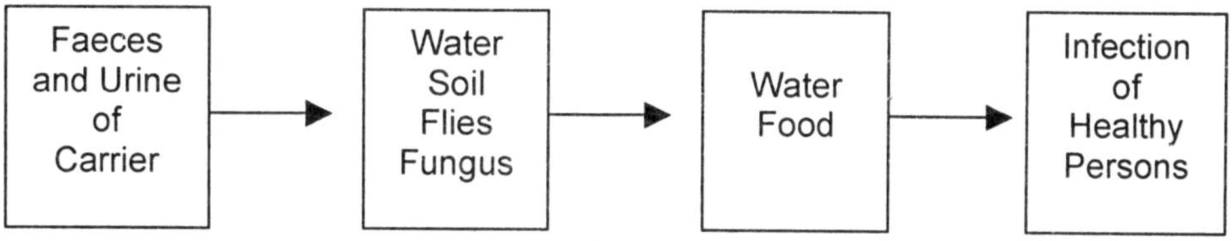

Fig. 12.8: Diffusion of Typhoid Fever

It should be noted that the bacilli are found outside the human body in water, food, milk and soil but they do not multiply in water. They do not live for more than 24 hours but may survive for 7 days in favourable conditions. In ice they can stay alive for over a month; in soils with sewage water for 70 days. They grow rapidly in milk.

Typhoid is endemic in India. One to three per cent of children are estimated to suffer from the disease at one time or the other. There are more than 300,000 reported cases each year; in 1998 the number of cases was 318510 and number of death, 328. The states with more than 25,000 cases were Andhra Pradesh, Karnataka, MP, Orissa and UP. For state wise prevalence of typhoid see Figure 12.9.

RABIES

Rabies or hydrophobia is an acute highly fatal zoonotic disease of the central nervous system. It is caused by Lyssavirus type 1. It is a disease of the warm-blooded animals specially the carnivorous ones such as dogs, jackals, wolves and cats. The virus is transmitted to man by bite or lick. Classical hydrophobia is characterized by long incubation period, followed by short period of illness and death.

Globally speaking, some countries do not have the disease; there are others which have controlled it or eradicated by mass immunization. Water is the most effective barrier for rabies. Almost all island countries are free from rabies. Even Portugal, Spain, Finland, Norway and Sweden are rabies free. In some of the western countries, rabies is spreading despite all precautions being taken in this regard.

Almost all (99 per cent) rabies infection to man is causes by domestic dogs and cats. But in most other developed countries, it has been eradicated long back. Of the ten million persons, who need post-exposure treatment, about 60,000 are reported to die of rabies the world over. In Southeast Asian countries 35,000 to 50,000 persons die of rabies each year. India and Bangladesh have high incidence of rabies; Maldives is free from it. Other countries of the region belong to intermediate or low intensity of rabies. The figures given above are, however, not to be relied upon, because most of the rabies patients in the developing countries do not die in the hospital. Such cases are never reported.

Within India, the island states of Andaman & Nicobar Islands and Lakshdweep Islands are rabies free. Data pertaining to the geographic spread of rabies are not available. But since the dogs, which are the main transmitters of the disease, are uniformly distributed in relation to the density of population all over the country, the cases of rabies should also be uniformly distributed in proportion to population. According to some estimates, over 100,000 persons die of rabies but the reported cases are less than 30,000. In 1998, reported cases were 12575 and deaths

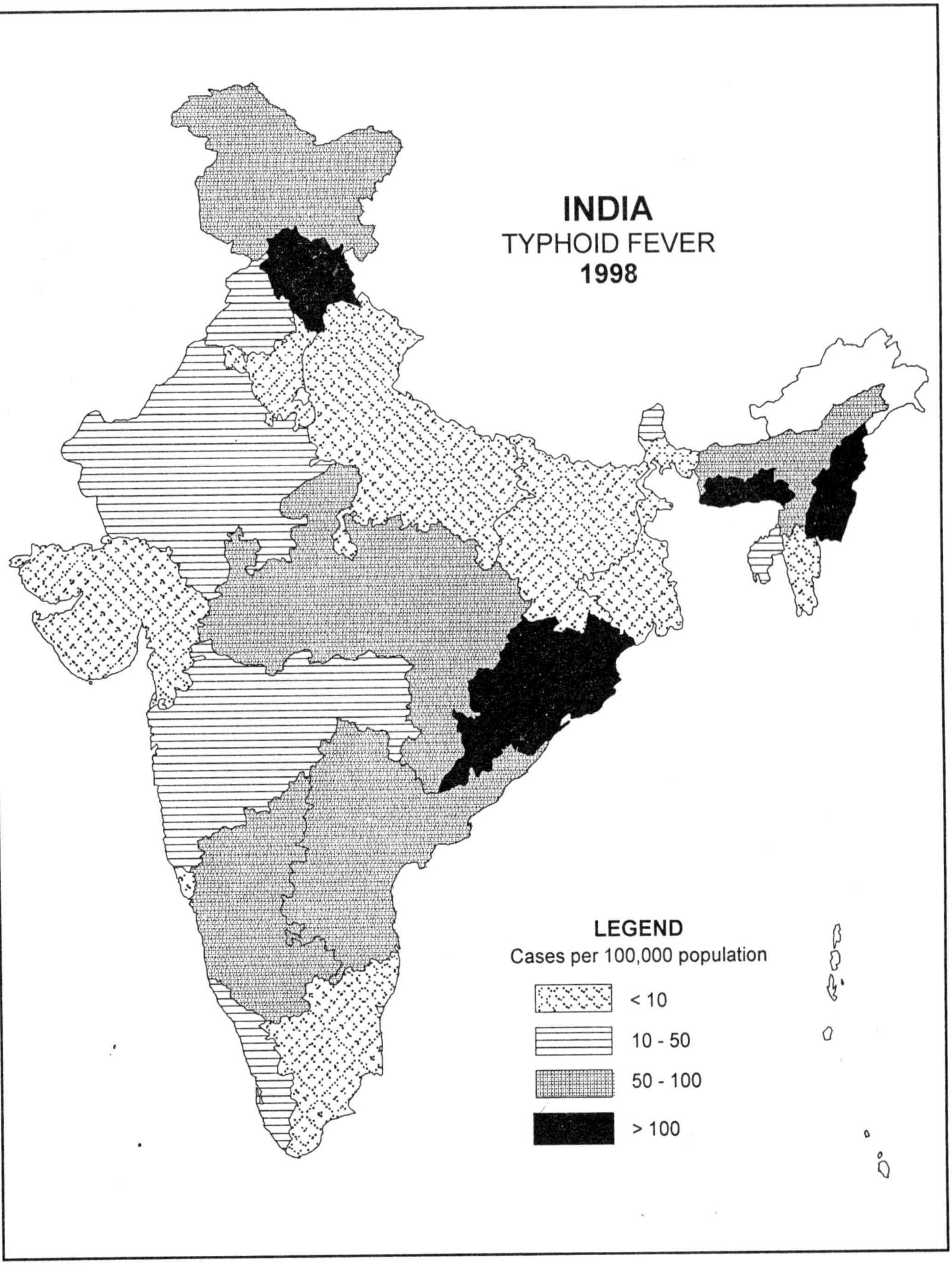

Fig. 12.9: India: Incidence of Typhoid Fever

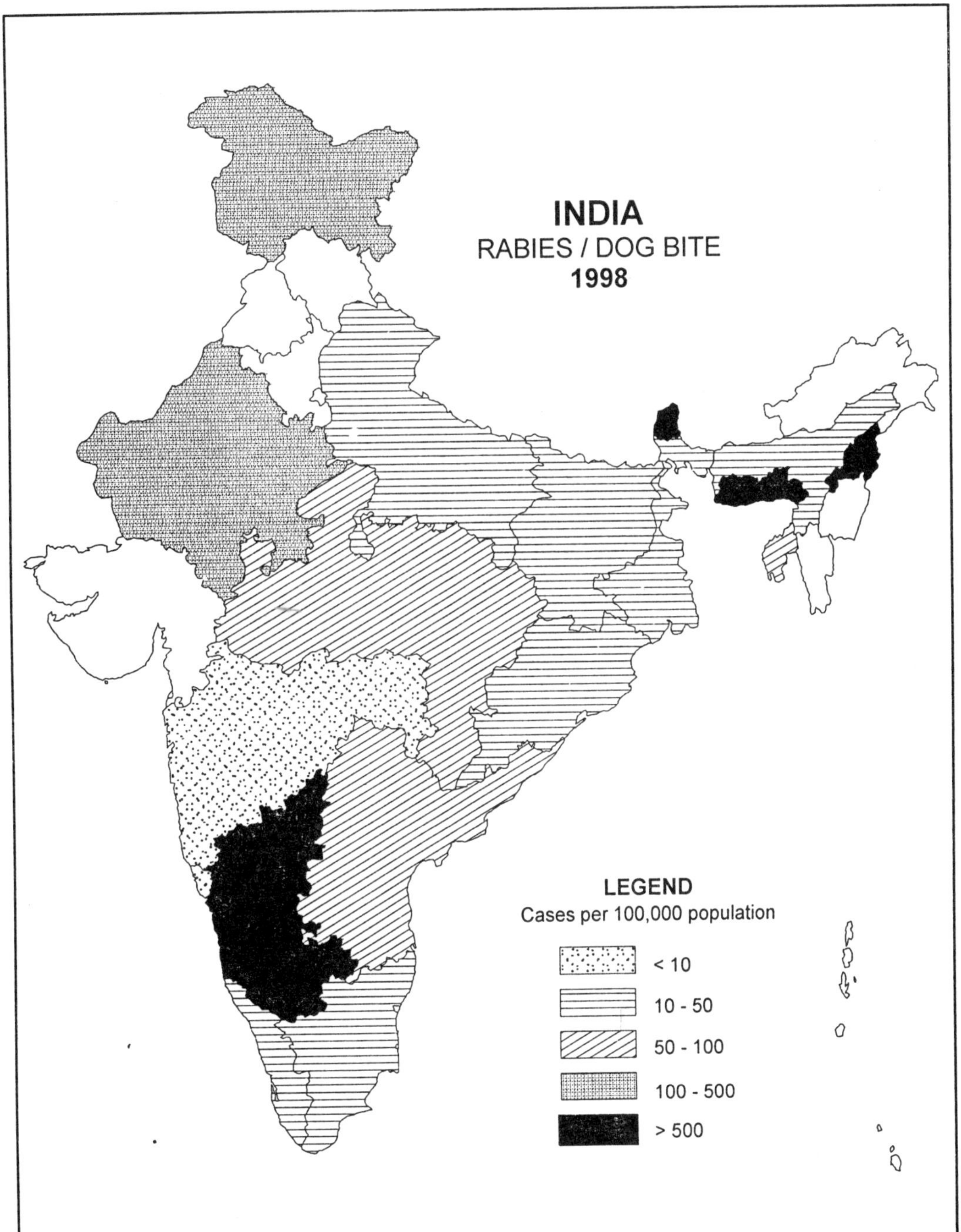

Fig. 12.10: India: Incidence of Rabies

566. About 1 to 1.5 million persons receive post-exposure treatment each year. Most of them (95 per cent) are dog bite cases (Fig. 12.10).

The causative agent (Lyssavirus type 1) is bullet shaped. Available vaccines are not always effective against the virus. The virus is excreted in the saliva of affected animals. Its incubation period in the body of the patient is 20-60 days. The disease has three strains: urban rabies, wild rabies and bat rabies. A single dog can infect a large number of people. The infected dogs runs helter and skelter in areas ranging from 2 to 25 km. It bites without notice. Rabies dogs have straight tails and usually look sickly. They may live for several years and continue to infect people.

Rabies survives in warm-blooded mammals including humans. It is a dead end infection and has no survival value for the virus. Most people infected in India fall in the age group 1-24 years. It can be transmitted by bite, by licks, by aerosols, and by person to person also, although the latter case is rare.

The disease begins with preliminary symptoms like headache, sore throat, pain at the site of the bite and fever for about 3 days. This stage is followed by stimulation of the nervous system, followed by the fear of the air and water. Fear of death, anger, irritability and depression are the other symptoms. Only 3 persons are recorded to have survived the rabies infection in India.

Various kinds of vaccines are now available which ensure survival after rabies infection, if treatment is given in time and the patient follows the instructions of the doctor. One of the problems in rabies is the estimation of the risk. Whether a dog is rabies or not, none knows. Many dogs appear sickly but are not rabies; many others appear healthy, but are rabies. One can be sure only after watching the dog for about 10 days, but by that time, it may be too late if it proves to be rabies.

REFERENCES

1. Government of India, Ministry of Health, Director General of Health Services, Health Information of India, 1998, 1999.
2. WHO, World Health Report, 1998 to 2002.
3. WHO, *Regional Health Report (South and South-East Asia),* 1997 to 2001.

13

Diseases of Modern Civilization-I

Modern civilization is a great leap forward in human progress in many ways. It has bestowed man with enough intellectual and technological powers to banish poverty and pestilence and to usher in an era of peace and prosperity. Would he use this power for the survival and further development of human race or he would continue to use his energy to pollute the earth, to promote social, economic and political strife, and to move from one crisis to the other? The record so far has not been very laudable. Materially, he is richer today than ever before, but he is not at peace with himself; he has created an iniquitous world – a world compartmentalized into classes, rich and poor, educated and illiterate, developed and undeveloped, and forward and backward. He has started exploring the outer space and has already set his foot on the moon and may soon land on the mars. But he has lost the capabilities he had inherited from his ancestors to explore his inner self to know what he is, what he stands for, and direction in which he must move to make this earth a better place to live.

Many of the great strides he has made are being questioned by perceptive thinkers the world over, not because the achievements are insignificant but because they are producing unintended direct and side-effects which have the potentials of destroying the very bases of life on planet earth. Development, progress, advancement, etc. carry no meaning in a world of the dead. The reality is that in the name of development we are making progress on the material front, but losing fast on the human front. In the long run, we may become so dehumanised that like mythological Bhasmasura we may become the cause of our own destruction.

Let us look at the health scenario. Man has been able to control many of the dreaded diseases. Death rates have come down drastically all over the world even in the developing countries. Food production has gone up and hence nutritional problems should not be the major concern of the humanity, at least in the short run. We have accumulated a vast amount of scientific knowledge to treat diseases. The number of medicines available in the market and the new ones coming up almost daily is mind-boggling. Our health infrastructure has penetrated even the remote areas of the world. But in the process of achieving all these and other good things, we have given rise to monsters that threaten our survival. One of these monsters is a group of diseases that do not appear to have conventional medicines. They are also called systemic disorders. Once we get them, we have to live with them and lest they immobilize us we take daily doses of chemical stabilizers, which produce unknown and unexpected side-effects. Can such disorders be prevented, controlled and cured by changes in lifestyles and by engendering harmony between body, mind, emotions and actions? Some say, yes. But how?

In ancient and medieval times, the diseases that afflicted people appear to be few. Many diseases were not known and even those, which were known, had no medicines as far as the common man was concerned. Sanitary conditions being better because of unpolluted natural environment and density of population and habitation being low, communicable diseases were few and their diffusion from place to place not fast enough to create conditions for diseases to acquire epidemic proportions. With increase in population density, distances were shortened and mobility of people increased. Diseases took the form of epidemics, and epidemics of pandemics killing millions of people. Nineteenth and twentieth centuries were the centuries of epidemic diseases. While the Third World countries are still in the grip of these diseases, systemic diseases like cancer, diabetes, heart failures, etc. have spread their tentacles all over the world. The last quarter of twentieth century witnessed the ascendancy of these diseases. The speed with which man is interfering with the natural environment, on the one hand, and his own body, on the other, is posing serious threat human health.

The systemic disorders are not diseases; they cannot be cured. They become part and parcel of our biology. We can only keep them in check by drugs, which take the place of natural processes in keeping the body system in order. The moment the drugs are stopped, body becomes dysfunctional. Unfortunately, people are not given true information about these disorders. They are made to consume tonnes of medicines although every one knows that are not effective. They can only give temporary relief and reduce feeling of pain.

The systemic disorders are the products of our socio-economic progress; the gifts of modern civilization. More we try to control them by medicines and surgery, less successful we appear to be in preventing them. With increasing longevity of life, these diseases are likely to pose new and more serious challenges than ever before. Very soon one-third of the human population will be above the age of 60. Body is most susceptible to diseases in this age group. But systemic disorders are most common in this age group. What is worst is the fact these disorders are genetically transferred to the children. As such some of diseases like diabetes, which were earlier confined to the aged, have become common among the children.

We propose to discuss the geography and related issues of these diseases in this chapter.

CANCER

Cancer is one of the most important causes of death in the world. Barring a few diseases like AIDS, most of the major killers of the world are on the decline. Cancer is, however, on the rise. In Japan it is the number one killer; it is going to be so all over the world if the present trends continue. What is interesting to know is that its causes are well known, yet not much is being done to prevent it. Attention is focused on cure rather than on prevention, as is the case with other diseases. The science of cancer is better known today but how to prevent the disease is only partly within the realm of science. It is in the realm of social sciences.

The term cancer is frequently used as a synonym for malignant tumour in contradiction to the benign tumours that are localized without tendencies to spread to other cells, tissues and organs. Further, they are not fatal unless they are located in or close to a vital organ. Cancer cells are endowed with tremendous growth energy; they lack growth restraint, which characterises normal cells. Faults in the controls of the cell division are what cause cancer. Instead of dying, the mutated cells keep on dividing and eventually forming a tumour. Cancer may invade normal and adjacent tissues by direct or contiguous growth or it may infiltrate within the blood or lymph vessels in which cells are broken off and carried to distant organs. There they lodge themselves through filtration, a process known as metastasis. Malignant tumours are the outcome of the ability of the cancer cells to grow when deposited elsewhere.

Cancer is not one but more than 200 different types of diseases and far too complex for any quick fix. There are as many cancers as the human organs and tissues within the body. Each type and subtype of cancer has a histological appearance peculiar to it and is identifiable on microscopic study. Its behaviour and natural history is now well known.

Cancer is not a new disease; it has a long history and finds mention in the ancient literatures of both west and the east. The causes of the disease, however, appear to have changed. In 1761, pipe smoking was recognized as the cause of lip cancer. Percival Port, a physician, pointed to the London's chimney sweeps suffering from scrotal cancer. Early in twentieth century, cancer was more common among the women; it is now more common among the men. Tobacco is said to be responsible for this change.

Causal factors for cancer are basically three: geographical, occupational and cultural (life style), which in real terms mean bad environment, bad habits, bad working conditions and in some cases bad luck (heredity). Some associative factors that may give clues to the causes of cancer are:

1. Chewing betel nut and tobacco causes cancer of the mouth and upper G.I. tract;
2. Sikhs who do not smoke rarely get lung cancer;
3. Cervical cancer is most common among the women, particularly among the sex workers, lower among the Muslims, and rare among the nuns;
4. Lung and gut cancer is common among asbestos workers;
5. Cancer of bladder and stomach is common among dye workers;
6. Many of the electrical and utility workers get brain cancer;
7. Lower G.I. tract cancer is higher among the meat eaters;
8. Stomach cancer is more prevalent in Japan where pickles, salt and soybeans constitute an important ingredient of daily food;
8. Liver cancer is common in Africa, particularly in Guam where food is often contaminated with aflatoxin;
9. G.I. tract cancer is common in Kashmir and places where people are habituated to green tea. Tea is anti-carcinogen but carcinogens of tea leaves are leached out in the process of boiling it in acidic water.
10. In the USA, cases of cancer among the Mormons who do not smoke or drink coffee is lower by 20 per cent;
11. Blacks in the USA have relatively higher incidence of cancer than whites (it may be because poverty among the Blacks is more rampant);

12. Again, in the USA, the Seventh Day Adventists have lower rates of breast, colon and rectum cancer;
13. In India, Parsees have 2.7 per cent more breast and spleen cancer and 1.5 times more skin cancer than persons of other communities.

According to available evidences, 30 per cent of all cancers are related to smoking. About 200 million people in the world get the disease because they do not get clean water. The high rate of cancer that one notices among the Africans and the Blacks of the USA is perhaps not because of race but because of high prevalence of poverty among them. Childhood cancers have increased by 10.5 per cent during the last two decades and the cancer of the nervous system has gone up by 35.1 per cent. During this very period, 35000 new chemicals have been introduced in the environment.

Some recent studies show that genetic factors are important only in a few types of cancers such as the cancer of the breast and prostate. All other cancers are linked to environmental factors such as chemical pollution of air, water, and food, diet, infection, smoking and chewing of tobacco, drinking of coffee, tea and alcohol.

Cancer is widespread throughout the vegetable and animal kingdom, but it is pre-eminently a human disease. It is a disease of the middle and old age but it can occur at any time in the life cycle. Certain varieties of cancers are more common among the children. Heredity factor cannot be ruled out: in certain families grandmother, mother and daughter are seen to have cancer of the breast. Cancer of the stomach also appears have hereditary links. Environmental factors appear to be most important causes of cancer but let us not count out the heredity. Mutation in TP53 gene is almost the defining feature of a lethal cancer. In over 90 per cent of lung cancer cases, TP53 gene was found broken. In 55 per cent of all other cancer cases, it was found broken. Like all other genes it was found inherited as a pair. Those born with the faulty versions of the two have a very high susceptibility to cancer at an early age. But this susceptibility can be very much lowered by removing environmental pollution and changing the style of life to conform to the laws that govern the biology of human body.

According to Nobel Laureate Sir Paul Nurse (Reuter, Feb. 25. 2002), some 6 million people each year die of cancer. Scientists are winning the fight against the disease, but it may never be eliminated. "It is an immensely complex disease. Much more complex than most other (diseases) we have to deal with. ... The single most major hit we can get for short-term cancer rates is to eliminate the use of tobacco. We have to try to do that." And "if you understand the genetic make up better, we will be able to sort out the environment more easily. That is a new type of approach that will be able to increasingly used over the next 10 or 20 years, and I think that could lead to significant improvement in prevention."

Cancer in India

India has one of the lowest cancer rates in the world. But the situation is changing fast. There are about two million cases of cancer at any given time and each year 0.75 million cases are added to the backlog. Tobacco related cancers, especially cancer of oral cavity, and of lung and cervix, form more than half of the cancer burden in India. Greater exposure to environmental carcinogens released by fossil fuels, increasing use of chemicals in industry and agriculture, continued use of tobacco in various forms, life styles unsuited to human biology, and increase in life expectancy are some of the important factors responsible for increase in cancer cases. A study by the National Academy of Sciences in the early 1980s found that 78 per cent of chemicals in highest commercial use are minimally tested for toxicity. There is every possibility of cancer cases going up in years ahead.

The chances of getting cancer in rural areas of India are fifty per cent less than those in urban areas. It is easier to prevent cancer than to cure it. In the USA, cases of lung cancer have declined because less people smoke cigarettes. But given the speed and scale of environmental pollution in the developing countries like India and given the highly toxic economic model adopted by these countries, cancer is going to be most important killer in not too distant a future. If gene is not the main cause of cancer, then the answer lies not in investing in hospitals to cure the disease but in health education and other preventive measures that nip the disease in the bud. Since cancer is in the environment, the civil society must force the politicians and medical profession to change the strategy of control. Though some cancers like leukaemia, Hodgkin's disease, the testicular cancer, malignant melanoma, and several other lymphomas can be cured if detected early, most others are incurable. There is no cure for advanced cases of any cancer. The existing therapies are not without risks; some of them increase chances of getting diseases such as leukaemia.

In 1996, the number of cancer cases reported by various specialised hospitals in the country was 60,518. Of these, 22.22 per cent pertained to genito-urinary organs; 15.60 per cent to liporal cavity pharynx; 13.65 per cent to bone connective tissues, skin and breast; 12.79 per cent to digestive organs and peritoneum; 9.25 per cent to lymphatic and haemopoietic tissues and 7.70 per cent to respiratory and thoracic organs. The rest i.e.19.2 per cent pertained to cancers of other organs of the body. There are wide differences among the states with respect to the prevalence of various kinds of cancers. Hospital figures do not give a true picture of the spatial incidence of the disease; it does however give some idea of possible distribution (Fig. 13.1 and Table 13.1).

Table 13.1: Per cent of All Deaths Attributed to Cancer

S.No.	*States*	*% of Deaths*
1.	Andhra Pradesh	6.4
2.	Bihar	2.7
3.	Gujarat	6.5
4.	Haryana	8.8
5.	Karnataka	7.7
6.	Kerala	12.8
7.	Madhya Pradesh	3.4
8.	Maharashtra	4.9
9.	Orissa	3.3
10.	Punjab	6.4
11.	Rajasthan	3.9
12.	Uttar Pradesh	5.4
13.	West Bengal	2.9
14.	India	5.2

Source: Survey of Major Causes of Death, 1997-98.

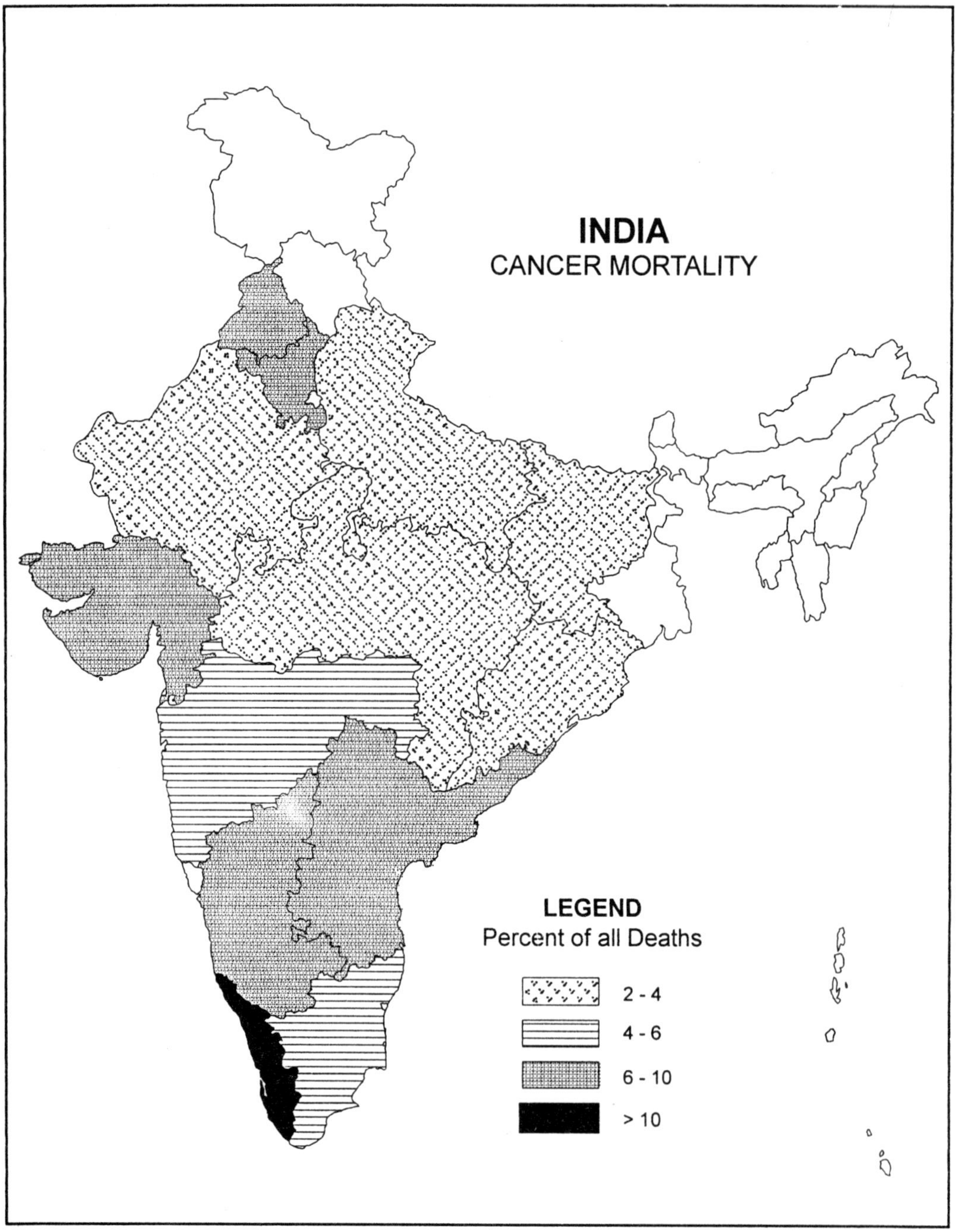

Fig. 13.1: India: Deaths Attributed to Cancer

Source: Annual Survey of Casuses of Deaths inRural Areas, 1998.

Growth in the number of cancer patients in India as depressing as it is alarming. The annual increase in the number of patients who come to Lok Naik Jai Prakash Narayan Hospital, New Delhi (which gets cancer patients from all over northern states of the country), for radiotherapy is around 500. Increase in the number of such patients between 1999-2003 was almost 100 per cent. This is a highly disturbing situation particularly because it is possible for man to control the spread of this disease by changing his life style. The common cancers and their causes mostly related to tobacco and food intake and both can be avoided, if not totally eliminated.

Common Cancers	*Causes*
1. Eye	Air pollution, eye infections
2. Nose	Frequent infection in nostrils, sinus
3. **Inner cheek**	**Chewing tobacco.**
4. Gum and palate	Smoking; chewing tobacco.
5. Tonsils	Chewing tobacco.
6. Lower lip	Smoking; chewing tobacco.
7. Throat	Smoking; chewing tobacco.
8. Breast	Rich food, first pregnancy after the age of 30; inadequate breast feeding.
9. Lung	Smoking and air pollution.
10. Liver	Insecticides.
11. Oesophagus	Smoking and chewing tobacco.
12. Stomach	Excessive consumption of alcohol and spicy foods.
13. Gall Bladder	Excessive fat in food.
14. Large intestine	Excessive consumption of red meat, family history of ulcerative colitis, and constipation.
15. Urater	Smoking, adulterated food and chemical pollution.
16. Genitals	Unhygienic conditions, STD
17. Cervix	Early marriage, frequent Pregnancy, STD, unhygienic. Conditions of genitalia, smoking and Malnutrition.
Prostrate Skin	Excessive consumption of fat.

National Cancer Control Programme

The National Cancer Control Programme was started in 1975. Under this programme, cancer hospitals and wards were started in the metropolitan cities of the country. Tobacco being one of the main causative factors of lung cancer, concerted campaign was launched to educate people about its harmful effects. The programme was revised in 1984 to meet the following three objectives.

1. Primary prevention: health education and prevention of intake of tobacco.
2. Secondary prevention: early detection of common cancers such as the cancer of the cervix, mouth and breast and other tobacco related cancers. And
3. Tertiary prevention: strengthening of existing institutions for comprehensive therapy including palliative care.

As a part of this programme all the twelve regional centres were strengthened and oncology wings were started in several medical college to improve infrastructure for early detection of the disease. Each district of the country has been assisted to intensify health education and to give advice and relief to those suffering from the disease. With the assistance of WHO, cobalt therapy units were located in major hospitals of the country.

Nature's Way to Meet the Challenge

According to Nobel laureate Nurse, we will always have cancer with us because of natural mistakes in the natural body; so it will never be eliminated." But we can reduce to the natural level by adhering to the biological laws of nature. We must treat human body as a biological phenomenon and stop over stressing it or stuffing it with poisonous things like tobacco and toxins of various kinds. Cancer cases will come down drastically if the internal and external environments in which we live is allowed to remain suited to biology of human body.

Tobacco smoking and chewing is the major cause of lung cancer. About 1.10 billion people in the world smoke tobacco. A good number of them will die of cancer if they fail to quit its use. Each year tobacco accounts for some 4 million deaths in the world: half of them in the developing countries. China with 20 per cent of world population consumes 30 per cent of cigarettes of the world. Sixty per cent of adult Chinese smoke and there is every chance of at least one-third of them dying of cancer and related diseases. Over a million people die in China from tobacco related diseases. In India, some 40 per cent of adults smoke beedis or cigarettes. Half of them may die of tobacco related diseases, if they do not stop smoking. If the situation does not change, the death toll from smoking may touch 1 billion by the turn of the century.

Among the developing countries, Thailand has proved to be a leader in curbing smoking. It has reduced the number of smokers by 25 per cent within a few years primarily through the efforts of high-ranking politicians, ban on tobacco advertising, and anti-smoking media campaign. India has had little success in this regard. In fact, the number of smokers is on the increase.

Let it be clear that cancer is the disease of modern civilisation. It is caused by the internal as well as external pollution. The external pollution has been discussed earlier. It includes the pollution of the environment in which we live. The internal pollution results from the intake of foods both solid and liquid, human metabolism is not able to digest to keep the body in normal state of functioning. It also results from the pollution of mind by anger, hatred, greed and so on.

The amount of money spent in treating cancer is indeed enormous. But not even a small fraction of it is spent on prevention; and the one spent on its cure through alternative medicines is negligible. Persons having family history of cancer should be doubly careful. They should have a style of life, which promotes health and should consume copious amount of fresh fruits, vegetables, preferably raw or boiled, and whole grains particularly in sprouted form, nuts and seeds. To restore the immune system, one should use highly alkaline foods. Wheat grass juice, tulsi, neem, lime, pudina, ginger and some other herbs retard the growth of cancer. Dark reddish violet grapes, raw onions, green tea (lemon grass) are anti-carcinogen and a powerful anti-oxidant against lung cancer. Soya beans, in whatever form one likes to consume, can block the cancer causing genes and cabbage and cauliflower help in overcoming breast and colon cancers. Cancer patients turning to grapefruit diet and beetroot juice can get back to health. Liberal use of garlic destroys malignant cells. Spinach, tomatoes, beet root, apples, sweet potatoes and carrots contain beta-carotene that is anti-oxidant. Among the fruits, beta-carotene is found in plenty in melons, plums, peaches, cherries, papayas, mangoes, and apricots. The red pigment 'licopene' helps destroy cancer precipitating free radicals.

DISEASES OF THE CIRCULATORY SYSTEM

Diseases of the circulatory system, specially the heart attack, pose the biggest risk for life of adults. These diseases account for at least 15 million deaths or around 30 per cent of the annual total each year. Five out of 12 deaths in the developed countries of the world are accounted by them and are emerging as major killers in the developing countries too. Already, they account for one-fourth of the deaths in developing countries (10 million out of 40 million deaths).

A large number of those who die of these diseases are under the age of 65. Millions of people are disabled. The important circulatory diseases are high blood pressure, coronary heart disease, and cerebrovascular diseases. High blood pressure or hypertension is not a killer disease as such. It is symptomatic of heart ailments. The other two are the real diseases that take millions of life.

High Blood Pressure

One of the major causative factors of heart diseases is high blood pressure that results from the hardening of the arteries. The hardening takes place because of unhealthy food habits, lack of exercise, obesity, mental tension and a variety of other related factors. There are two approaches to the cure of this disease: change in the lifestyle to soften the arteries or thinning of the blood through diet and medication. Which approach should be adopted depends on the severity of the problem and the risk factors involved.

Obesity is a major cause of heart problems. Earlier, this problem was limited to adults and elderly persons. Now it has brought even children in its grips. Overweight and obesity are not the same but they are not dissimilar. Most persons who are obese are also overweight but one can be overweight without being obese.

Obese are those who weigh 20 per cent more than what they should normally. They become susceptible to diabetes, heart diseases, high blood pressure and stroke. Obesity has become an epidemic in the developed parts of the world. Over 200 million people in the world fall in the category of overweight. It includes 22 million children under-5 years of age. Obesity affects about 10 per cent of the school going children in the West and one third of them grow into obese adults. The number of obese children in countries like the Netherlands had doubled between 1965 and 1980. The rate has not come down despite increasing awareness of the dangers inherent to obesity. More than one-third of the adults or about 50 million people in USA, are obese. By 2025, the number is likely to go up to 300 million. Obesity is however not confined to developed countries alone. With increasing sedentarization of life, people in developing countries too have come under its sweep.

Coronary Heart Ailments

Over 7.5 million people die of coronary heart diseases each year in the world. In the developed parts of the world, the coronary heart disease has started ebbing; its peak reached sometimes in 1970. The main risk factors are smoking, high blood pressure, unhealthy diet, diabetes and lack of physical exercise.

Cerebrovascular Diseases

Stroke and other cerebrovascular diseases are the second most common cause of death among the persons aged 65 and above. These diseases account for over 4.5 million deaths per annum in the world. High blood pressure is the most important risk factor for these diseases.

Over the past 40 years or so, stroke mortality has declined in many developed countries of the world. The possible reasons may be better management of high blood pressure, change in the diet, decreased severity of the disease and lower rate of obesity in the population. In contrast, stroke mortality has increased in the developing countries and Eastern Europe for the converse reasons. Lowering of stroke mortality may, however, be more apparent than real. As the longevity of life increases, the proportion of population in the age group 65+ is increasing and the proportion of persons surviving the stroke is also increasing. Thus, the morbidity rate may not be declining. The chances of more persons not leading a normal life after the stroke are going up. This situation would increase the morbidity burden on the society.

Heart Diseases in India

According to a recent report of the Registrar General of India (Vital Statistics Division), 21.4 per cent of deaths in India are caused by the diseases of the circulatory system, that is 6.2 per cent higher than the deaths caused by the infectious and parasitic diseases. India is thus caught in the double burden of diseases. While the infectious diseases continue to be major killers, the incidence of the diseases of the developed world like heart ailments and AIDS are surging ahead. Indians are 4 per cent more prone to heart diseases than Americans and 20 per cent more prone than Japanese. Indian culture has always laid emphasis on balance, avoiding extremes in all walks of life. The fast foods and fast styles of life are telling on the heart more than on any other organ of the body.

The diseases of the circulatory system rank third among the major causes of death in rural India during the period 1993-1997. The first and second ranks are the non-specific causes, and the diseases of the respiratory system. If we exclude the first, the diseases of the circulatory system stand second. In 1993, only 7.60 per cent of all deaths in the country were due to this group of diseases; in 1997, the per centage went up to 12.10. What is worrisome is the fact that the increase is secular and consistent.

According to 1997 survey of causes of death in rural India, heart diseases stand second claiming 9.50 per cent of all deaths. Bronchitis and asthma stand first (15.10 per cent). A quarter (25.60 per cent) of all deaths due to heart related diseases occurred in the age group of 45-59; and 58 per cent in 60+ age group.

Per cent of deaths claimed by heart diseases is however not equally distributed in the country. Whereas in India as a whole, it is 10.60 per cent, in Punjab it is 28.20 per cent and in UP only 3.50 per cent. These figures pertain to rural areas only, but they indicate the variations that must be in a vast country like India. The state-wise per centages of total deaths due to heart diseases is given in Table 13.2 and Figure 13.2.

Table 13.2: Per cent of Deaths Claimed by Heart Diseases (State Wise)

	States	*Per cent deaths*
1.	Andhra Pradesh	14.8
2.	Bihar	7.2
3.	Gujarat	11.3
4.	Haryana	8.7
5.	Karnataka	10.2
6.	Kerala	22.5
7.	Mandhya Pradesh	5.7
8.	Maharashtra	10.8
9.	Orissa Punjab	7.8
10.	Punjab	28.2
11.	Rajasthan	6.3
12.	Tamil Nadu	15.8
13.	Uttar Pradesh	3.5
	India	10.6

Source: Health Information of India, 1998

Age-wise, 15.8 per cent of all deaths in 1997 in the age group 60+ were due to heart attack; the first being bronchitis and asthma, and second being paralysis of cerebral apoplexy.

Prevention and Cure

Treatment of heart diseases is a costly affair. As far as modern medicine is concerned, open-heart surgery or angioplasty is the only option. Of the 30 million Indians who suffer from heart ailments; only 1 per cent can afford these expensive treatments. In India, it costs around Rs. 2.5 lakhs to undergo open-heart surgery and Rs. 1.5 lakhs to undergo angioplasty. From American and European standards, they are very inexpensive but from Indian standards, they are beyond the reach of a great majority of people.

The solution lies in lifestyles most conducive to good health. Human body is biological phenomenon; it is run by biological rules. There is threshold beyond which it cannot take interference with its biology. We have to rediscover that life style. Why is it that our forefathers, who survived the communicable diseases, lived more healthily and happily than we do? Apparently, they evolved a system of living, which gave enough exercise to the body and mind to remain healthy and alert. Everything they did was conducive to health: walking long distances, eating self-produced foods, living in open or well ventilated houses, and having less mental tension because of a feeling of contentment. Our life is just the other way round. The

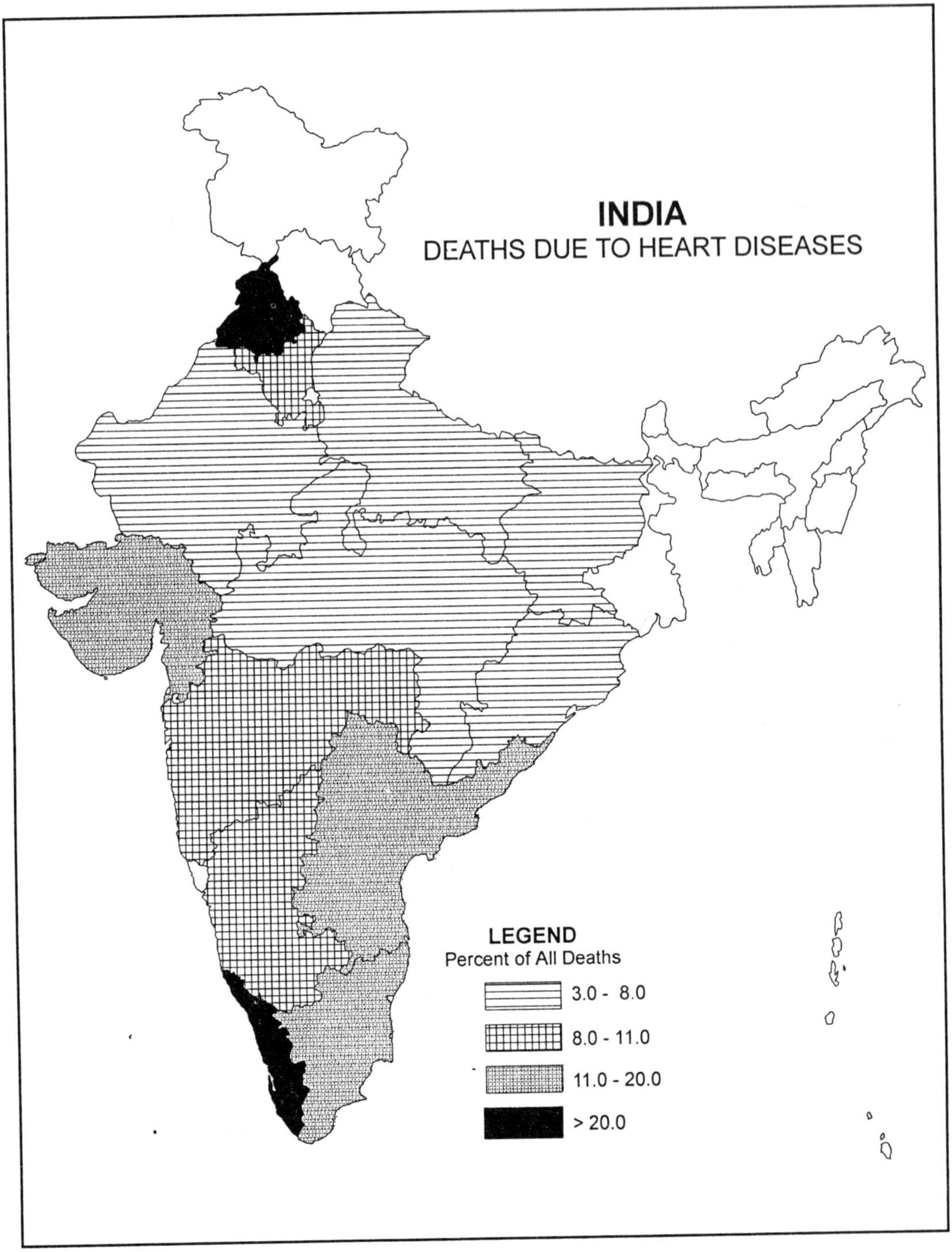

Fig. 13.2: India: Deaths Due to Heart Diseases

time has come to realize that medical cure is not a substitute for good health. We should depend less on curative medicine and more on preventive medicine, but not the preventive medicine of modern days. In the vocabulary of modern medicine, immunization is preventive. But in reality, it is not. It prevents the onset of disease, but the viruses, which cause diseases, develop immunity from the drugs and make them ineffective. So we resort to more powerful drugs. Each time we orally take or inject drugs in our body, we weaken its natural capacity to ward against diseases. Real immunity occurs only when we move from culture of medicine to the culture of natural life and living. Lest natural life and living are interpreted as primitive ways, let me emphasize that it means leading a life in consonance with the biological requirements of human body and mind.

This new culture is being promoted by many western physicians and surgeons, important among them being Dr. Dean Ornish of California. According to him, polluted environment, unhealthy style of life, unsystematic breathing habits and toxic medicines are the root causes of heart disease. He has pioneered a new approach to treating heart disease: reversal of the disease by changing the style of life and living more healthily. His method has now become a mainstream medicine. According to him, blocked arteries of the heart can be opened by yoga, meditation, group support, low fat vegetarian diet, and selected ayurvedic medicines. Yoga-*asanas* and *pranayam* increase blood supply to the heart and thus opening up the blocked arteries.

The patients treated under his system are not haunted by the fear of future the operated patients have. They can lead an active and long life, for the disease is taken off from its root.

DIABETES MELLITUS

Diabetes is not a disease; it is only a manifestation of a systemic disorder. It can also be said to be a heterogeneous group of diseases characterized by a state of chronic hyperglycemia resulting from different aetiologies, environmental factors and genetics working together. There is no cure for it but it can be prevented and also controlled if a person suffering from it is willing to follow a given regime of diet, exercise and medication. It results from the inability of the blood to properly absorb food containing glucose, a common form of sugar, fully and continuously because the pancreas stop producing insulin, a hormone that controls the sugar in the blood. Absorption of the glucose in the blood is a vital process in the creation of energy for the cells of the body. Glucose is a chemical derivative of the carbohydrates in food after they have been ingested. Carbohydrates are of plant origin and may be called starch saccharine, sucrose or simply sugar. Under the normal circumstances glucose is stored in the form of glycogen or animal starch in the lever and muscles for later use at which time it is reconverted to glucose. Insulin is necessary for both storage and reconversion of glucose.

The metabolic failure may result from one or both of the following reasons: insufficiency of insulin or the inability of the body to respond normally to insulin. In either case, the blood accumulates excess glucose. As the glucose accumulates above the normal levels in the blood stream, kidneys filter it and pass it on to the urine. Additional urine is produced to contain the excess glucose. That is why, diabetics pass copious and frequent urine and feel dehydration and insatiable thirst.

Just twenty-five years ago, diabetes mellitus was considered to be an uncommon disease with a prevalence of no more than 1-3 per cent even in the industrialised countries of Europe and North America. In the developing countries like India it was never a health concern of the common man. But the situation has now changed drastically. According to the WHO, about 145 million persons are already in the grip of this disease. By 2025 AD, the number of persons suffering from the disease will go up to 300 million. This increase will be accounted by population growth, urbanisation and higher longevity of life. In 1997, 63 per cent of the diabetics were in the developing countries. By 2025, the proportion will rise to 76 per cent. In 1997, the top country with diabetes was India, followed by China and the USA. The situation will remain the same in 2025.

No one knows why diabetes occurs. Researches are still on to find its real cause or causes. But everyone knows that it is a disease of modern civilisation as it is closely associated with urbanisation, industrialisation and lifestyle. In the past, diabetes was a disease of developed countries. It is, however, no longer so. In 1997, only 37 per cent of diabetics were resident in the developed countries. This proportion will further decline to 24 per cent by 2025. This means that by 2025, more than three quarters of the people suffering from diabetes will be in the developing countries. By 2025, the number of diabetics in the world will be 300 million, 228 millions of them in the developing countries. India will account of for a quarter of the diabetes patients in the developing countries (57 million). With just 19 million diabetics in 1997, the disease is expected to grow by 195 per cent in just 20 to 25 years.

Apart from the fact that the disease is shifting from developed to developing countries, its age preference is also changing fast. In developed countries, it has a preference for people in the age group of 65 and above, in the developing countries, it attacks those in the age group of 45-64 years. This tendency is likely to grow further so that increasing number of persons in the developing countries will be affected by diabetes in their prime productive period of life and would have a long gestation period during which to develop further complications leading to blindness, kidney failure and heart diseases.

Types of Diabetes

There are several types of diabetes and causes of each type may be different. Here we propose to discuss only two main types. Type I (insulin-dependent) diabetes primarily due to autoimmune-mediated destruction of pancreatic beta cells, resulting in absolute insulin deficiency. The total number of type I diabetes is on the increase, doubling every decade. It is commonest among Europeans is rare among Asians. Native Americans, Pacificislanders and Blacks. It can occur at any age but is most common in youth. It used to be called juvenile-onset diabetes. One in every 2500 children suffers from this disease. As the pancreas produce very little or no insulin, such patients have to depend on outside sources of insulin.

Type II is characterized by insulin resistance and or abnormal insulin secretion, either of which may predominate accounts for over 90 per cent of cases of diabetes globally. It is also called non-insulin-dependent diabetes. According to American Medical Association, somewhere between 60 to 90 per cent of the American diabetes patients falling in this category are obese. Patients with Type II diabetes produce some or at times even excessive insulin in their pancreas, but it is either not enough for proper functioning or is not being produced quickly enough to influence glucose levels in the blood effectively. This type of diabetes can be controlled by proper diet, coupled with exercise and oral medication. More details of the two types are given in Table 13.3.

Table 13.3: Characteristics of Type I and Type II Diabetes

	Type I	*Type II*
Age of onset	Usually during youth	Usually during adulthood and old age
How noticed	Generally appears abruptly and progresses rapidly	Gradual in onset; it may go unnoticed for years
Family background	Usually not present in other family members	Often present in other family members
Treatment	Insulin injection; diet, exercise and emotional control	Diet, exercise, and emotional control. Insulin injection may be required in some cases
Complications	Problems affecting blood vessels, eyes, kidneys and nerves may occur at any age	Problems affecting blood vessels, eyes, kidneys and nerves may occur at any age
Related to obesity	Not necessarily	80 per cent of patients are overweight at the time of diagnosis

Causes of Diabetes

As mentioned earlier, the causes of diabetes are still unknown but heredity is known to be an important factor. Heredity makes a person prone to the disease; he need not necessarily get the disease. Genetic coding prevents a disease from appearing in every generation and hence a child of non-diabetics can become a diabetic because one of his grand parents might have been a diabetic. The vice versa may also be true. What really set the stage for the onset of the disease is the stresses that affect the nerves. Important among these is overweight. Obesity affects the utilisation of insulin. That is the reason why 80 per cent of diabetics are also overweight. Among the other stresses are surgery, accident, serious infection, pregnancy and emotional shock.

Type II diabetics are seen to suffer from high blood pressure too. Older persons are more likely to get the disease than the younger ones, as are the women as compared to men. Nearly 2 per cent of all deaths in the age-group 60+ years are due to diabetes. This is a disease, which does not come singly; it is accompanied by many other diseases and systemic disorders. As such many people die of heat attack but the basic cause, to begin with, may be diabetes.

Geographic Distribution

Diabetes, as mentioned earlier, is a disease that is perhaps as old as humankind, but its spread on a mass scale is a recent phenomenon. That is why, it is classified as a disease of modern civilisation. It is also apparent from the fact that more developed a country is greater are the chances of it having more diabetic patients. As economic development spreads to the present day developing countries, this disease is likely to engulf even those areas that are still untouched by it. For example, Mongolia and a number of countries of West Africa and Southwest Africa have a very low incidence of diabetes. According to WHO estimates, many of these countries also will have very high rates of prevalence in decades ahead. The two world maps given here tell the prevalence rates of diabetes in different countries of the world in 1997 and the estimated prevalence rate in 2025 AD (Fig. 13.3).

The prevalence rate in different WHO regions in 1995, 2000 and 2025 is given in Table 13.4

The South-East Region is likely to be most seriously affected by diabetes. By 2025, about 80 million people are likely to have diabetes if the current trends continue. In this region males are more prone to diabetes, and urban dwellers are less likely to get diabetes than their rural counterparts. India with 19 million cases in 1998 tops the list. China had 38 million cases. The US with 14 million cases stands third in the world.

According tp the WHO some 228 million adults will suffer from diabetes in developing countries by 2025, a 170 per cent increase over the 84 million registered in 1995. The top ten countries with high diabetes cases in 2025 will be:

1. India 57 million
2. China 38 million
3. USA 22 million
4. Pakistan 15 million
5. Indonesia 12 million
6. Russia 12 million
7. Mexico 12 million
8. Brazil 11 million
9. Egypt 9 million
10. Japan 9 million

Region Wise prevalence of diabetes in 1995 and 2025 is given in Table 13.4.

Table 13.4: Prevalence of Diabetes in WHO Regions: 1995-2025

(*in millions*)

WHO Regions	*1995*	*2000*	*2025*
Africa	3.40	4.00	9.80
Eastern Mediterranean	13.80	16.70	42.80
Western Pacific	26.40	30.40	56.00
South-East Asia	27.60	32.70	79.50
Americas	30.70	34.80	63.50
Europe	32.60	35.30	47.50

Source: WHO, World Health Report, 2000

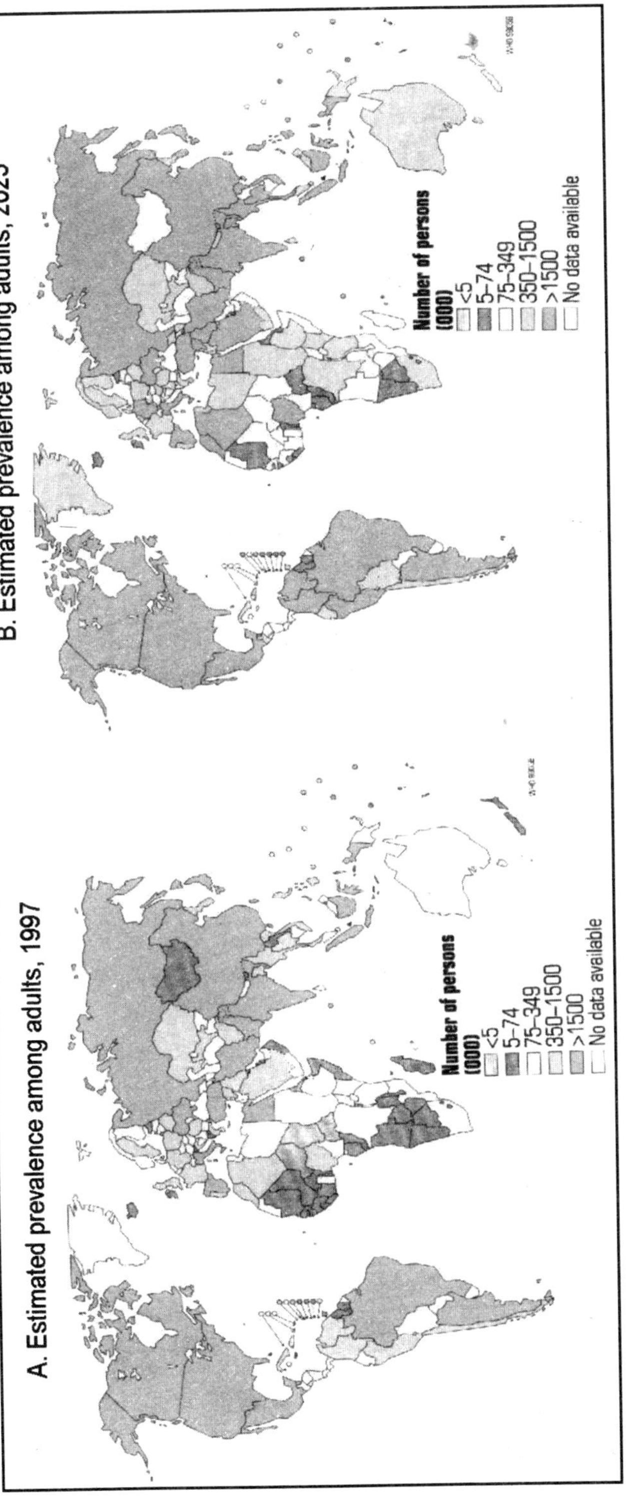

Fig: 13.3: Global Prevalence of Diabetes (1998).

As mentioned earlier, the Asians are likely to share far higher burden of diabetes than other racial groups in years to come. Table 13.5 gives data for the East and South Asian countries.

Table 13.5: Prevalence of Diabetes in Southeast Asia: 1995

Countries	*Per cent*	*No. (000)*	*Ratio U/R*	*Ratio M/F*
Bangladesh	2.20	1,285	0.80	1.42
Bhutan	2.10	17	0.11	1.21
DPR Korea	2.90	443	3.30	1.19
India	3.80	19,397	1.38	1.35
Indonesia	4.10	4,546	0.84	1.05
Malaysia	2.50	2,70	0.93	1.45
Myanmar	2.20	588	0.72	1.17
Nepal	2.20	225	0.31	1.25
Sri Lanka	2.50	225	0.61	1.15
Thailand	2.40	863	0.68	1.19

Note: U = urban; R = rural; M = male; F = female
Source: WHO, Regional Health Report (South and South-East Asia), 1999

Diabetes in India

India is already marked as a country with a very high prevalence of diabetes. The disease is spreading very fast not only in India but the whole sub-continent. India today leads the world with its largest number of diabetic subjects in any given country. According the WHO there were 19.4 million diabetics in India in 1995 and these figutrd are likely go up to 57.2 million by 2025 – one sixth of the world total. And by 2030 the diabetic population of India is likely to shoot up to 80.90 million i.e. about one fifth of all diabetics of the world. Within a period of just 5 years (from 1993-1997), the mortality attributable to metabolic diseases increased from 0.60 per cent to 1.10 per cent.

In urban India the situation is alarming. It (type II) is reaching epidemic proportions. In rural areas the prevalence is 4-5 times lower than in urban areas. In 1970s the prevalence of diabetes among urban Indians was reported to be 2.1 per cent. A ecent study of 26001 samples in Chennai district reveals that the prevalence rate is as high as 16 per cent. The National Urban Diabetic Survey (NUDS) reveals that the diabetic prevalence rates are 13.5 per cent in Chennai, 12.4 per cent in Bangalore, 16.6 per cent in Hyderabad, 11.7 per cent in Kolkata, 11.6 per cent in Delhi and 9,3 per cent in Mumbai. The prevalence rate is higher in southern cities, relatively lower in eastern and northern cities and lowest in western cities.

The main reasons for increase in diabetes in India are increasing incidence of obesity. Further, the Asians specially the South Asians are metabolically more prone to get this disease. In the past, Type II diabetes was considered to the disease of the adults specially the elderly. But it has the tendency to catch the young and children too overtaking the Type I variety. It is now considered as significant and emerging public health problem not only in India but also the world over.

Diabetes develops at a younger age in Indians – at least a decade or two earlier than in the Western population. Maturity Onset Diabetes of the Young (MODY) is a monogenic variety of Type II diabetes. It is characterized by an autosomal dominant inheritance and an age of onset at 25 years or younger. It is estimated that at least 2.5 per cent of Type II patients have MODY variety in India.

The above estimates are based on partial information. Once more detailed and reliable data become available, India would have problem very hard to grapple.

Figure 13.4 gives the chart showing increase in estimated cases diabetics in India.

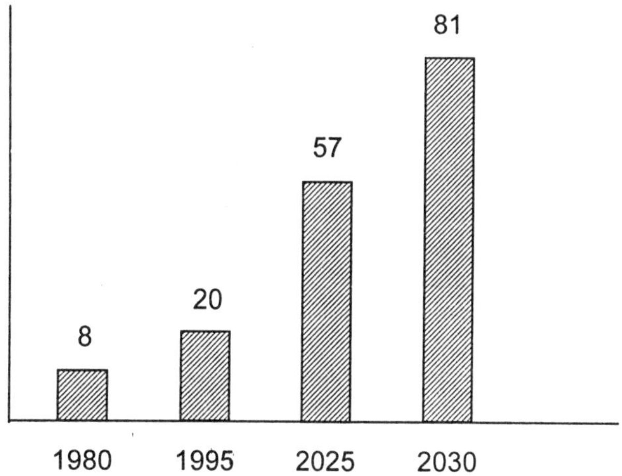

Fig. 13.4: Estimated Cases of Diabetes in India
Note: Figures above the columns show cases in millions.

The increase in the diabetes cases cannot be attributed to genetic factors alone. India is going through what is known as epidemiological transition with more urbanization and a rapid shift in the economy and employment. Dietary habits are changing fast and manual labour which was part of life of the people in the past is becoming scarce activity among those who are economically better off. Obesity and excessive consumption fats are also contributory factors. The close relationship between obesity and diabetics has given rise to a new term 'diabesity'. The health burden is shifting from communicable diseases to non-communicable diseases, particularly diabetes.

Despite the alarming rise in diabetes in India, the level of awareness about it and its consequences remain abysmally low. To many it is just an increase in blood sugar which has to be controlled by sugar free diet and some medication. Not many are aware of the more serious implications of the disease. If not treated properly and at the right stage, diabetes can affect eyesight and lead to renal failure, heart attack and amputations.

The cure of the disease is often attempted within the modern medical paradigm of thinking. This is not a correct approach. It is not the vaccines which would solve the problem; nor would be genetic manipulation. The secret lies in a more healthful style of life and living in an environment that is tension free and conducive to peace and tranquillity.

True, we should have more vaccines and medicines for those who are already sick need support. But all this should be done with a clear understanding that drugs would not solve the problem. People must change their life style: eat less fatty foods, return Indian vegetarian dishes without fats, exercise, reduce tensions, and follow Gandhi and engage in manual labour as a matter of principle.

Fortunately, type II diabetes is life style related and hence easy to control. Simple living and high thinking should not treated as an empty slogan. It has now to become part of our life. Indigestible fatty nutrition and lack of exercise are the primary causes; non-fatty nutrition and regular exercise are therefore the primary methods for recovery from the disease.

CHRONIC RHEUMATIC DISORDERS

Chronic rheumatic disorders include a group of about 100 diseases that involve the inflammation of joints and discomfort in connective tissues throughout the body. Important among them are osteoarthritis, rheumatoid arthritis, low back pain, gout, osteoporosis, and several other diseases of the joints and soft tissues. The term arthritis is derived from two Greek words arth = joint, and tis = inflammation or infection. Thus the arthritis means inflammation of joints.

Rheumatic diseases are on the increase in India. According to some estimates, half of the senior citizens of the country suffer from a variant of these diseases. Since there is no cure for these ailments, people suffering from these diseases are condemned for life long incapacity and pain. In the United States about 40 million people that is about 15 per cent of the total population had some form of arthritis in 1995 and the number is likely to go up to 60 million by 2020. Earlier, it was a disease of the senior citizens. While this old pattern continues, it has started afflicting even the children.

Rheumatic diseases are very personal diseases. In most cases they do not show up visible symptoms at least in the early stages; only the person who gets it can feel agonies associated with them. As opposed to an acute disease, which is serious for a while, is treatable, and goes away after proper medication, the rheumatic disorders do not go away. Treatment can help alleviate pain to some extent. Arthritic patients in India resort to Ayurvedic treatment, which does give some relief. There are no modern medicines except pain relievers.

Osteoarthritis

Osteoarthritis is a wear and tear disease. It affects more people than any other type. It is also called degenerative joint disease. Patients know it as old age arthritis. In a normal joint a smooth elastic material called cartilage covers the ends of the bones where they meet to help the bones glide smoothly across each other. As the cartilage wears away, the bones rub each other when in motion give pain that is often unbearable. In reaction to the pain the muscles near the joint may become tense and contract. In due course the shape and structure of the joint may change making the movement difficult or even impossible. While the disease can affect any joint, the ones most commonly affected are those bearing the load such as knees, hips and lumber spine. The joints of the fingers, toes and the base of the thumb are also affected.

Women are more prone to this disease. It has also been seen that in some families it is more common and acute than in others. Heredity may have something to do with this. It is a disease of the old age but it can occur at an early age of, let us say, 30 years. Reduction of weight, removal of obesity, physical exercises as recommended by experts, and changes in the lifestyle do help. Since the disease is very closely related to the life-style one leads, a change in it has a beneficial effect.

Rheumatoid Arthritis

It is an inflammatory disease. It begins slowly but sometimes sets in suddenly. Symptoms may appear, go away and return again. Even though it is systemic disease, the most noticeable symptoms are the sore joints of the hands and feet. It begins with the inflammation in the synovial membrane, a thin tissue that lines the capsule surrounding the joints. The inflammation may spread to other parts of the joints and ultimately spread to cartilage surrounding bone ends. As the cartilage disintegrates, scar tissues take its place. The joints are finally fused and the patient cannot move the joints.

The person suffering from rheumatoid arthritis feels lot of pain and stiffness in the morning. Usually more than one joint is affected by it. As joints stiffen full motion becomes painful and difficult. The fingers affected by the disease may get deformed. Since it affects all joints and connective tissues all over the body, it may produce fever, loss of appetite, anaemia and weight loss.

The disease can occur in any age-group but it is most common in age group 20-40 years. Apart from heredity, infection is also considered to be a possible causative factor for rheumatoid arthritis. The treatment for this disease is also similar to oesteoarthritis. The purpose of the therapy is to reduce inflammation and pain, to preserve the function of the affected parts and to prevent deformity. Life style changes, mix of exercises and rest, use of hot and cold water, ultraviolet heating, and use of anti-inflammatory drugs do help. In some cases even surgery is helpful.

Other forms of Arthritis

The other forms of arthritis discussed in this chapter are spondylitis, gout and rheumatic fever. In the case of ankylosing spondylitis, the small joints of the spine and the sacroiliac joints are affected first. Pain in the lower back and legs is often the first symptom. The spine may become progressively stiffer and develop curvature forcing the patient to stand in a stooped position. It can really cripple the person if the treatment is delayed or is inappropriate. It is different from osteoarthritis of the spine. It attacks younger people in the age group of 20-30 years. Men are more susceptible to the disease than women. Further, unlike the osteoarthritis, it is an inflammatory disease. It affects the eyes and heart also. Heredity appears to be the major cause of this disease.

Gout develops only when serum uric acid remains elevated for a number of years. It can happen due to heredity or use of certain medicines for a prolonged period. Around 10 per cent of the people, who have this elevated serum acid, develop needle like crystals in their joints producing severe inflammation, swelling and tenderness. Often it starts with the large joint of the big toe first. Gout can be controlled if the level of the uric acid in the system is reduced. There are medicines to do that. It can also be controlled by appropriate diet.

Rheumatic fever is also considered to be a form of arthritis because it inflames the joints and damages the heart. Antibiotics and aspirin do help. The disease is painful but it does not cripple. Rheumatic fever is associated with urban crowding. In 1-3 per cent of the cases it is followed by common streptococcal group A sore throat resulting in life long crippling rheumatic heart disease. It is a disease of the children and can be prevented and treated. Its prevalence rate is 2-11 per 1000 population in the age group of 5-16 years. Penicillin is quite efficacious in this disease.

Geographic Distribution

Rheumatic disorders are almost uniformly distributed the world over. With increasing longevity of life, the prevalence rate is also increasing. There is a close relationship between climate and incidence of these diseases. Humid climates have relatively more cases. In India, the coastal states have relatively more cases of arthritis. But of more significance is the style of life. The foods people consume, the nature of the work they do, and psychological pressure they undergo have much to do with arthritis. Sedentary lifestyle, junk food, and mental tension are important causes for the spread of arthritis in the world.

Data on the incidence of arthritis and related diseases are scanty as the mortality rates are very low. Since it is not a killer disease, public health institutions pay less or even least attention to it. This is a debilitating disease; it restricts the patient's mobility and affects his psychology too. He feels diffident and becomes an easy victim of other diseases both infectious and systemic. Estimates of those suffering from the disease are

Vary widely but if we take into account only the senior citizens, the prevalence rate is at least 30 per cent.

Prevention and Cure

Rheumatic disorders have become very common all over the world but the mortality rates attributable to these diseases is very low. That might be the reason why not much attention has been paid to them in developing countries like India. In the West, apart from various therapies that do relieve the pain, surgical methods have also been developed to cope with this growing menace for the health. The situation has become so serious that the WHO has dedicated 2000-2010 AD as the bone and Joint Disorder (B&JD) decade.

The WHO, in collaboration with the International League against Rheumatism (ILAR), has launched a project called Community Oriented Programme for Control of Rheumatic Disorder (COPCORD). The purpose of the programme is to study the causes, control and remedies of rheumatic problems and of creating awareness among the masses about the serious consequences of the disease. The Project came into existence in July 1999 and more than 60 seed centres have been created in the world. Most of the centres are in the developing countries. India has two such centres, one at Pune and the other at Lucknow.

According to benchmark survey of four villages selected by the Lucknow Centre, the most common ailment was cold and cough and next in order was rheumatic disorder due to which most of the patients were not able to earn their livelihood. About 8 per cent of the villagers were suffering from bone and joint disorders and none of them have visited any orthopaedic specialist. Out of these patients, 30 per cent suffered from back pain, 27 per cent had body ache, 27 per cent had ostrocerosis and 9 per cent had post injury pains.

HEPATITIS

Hepatitis is one of older diseases but its current severity, spread and universality are recent phenomena. It is an infectious disease of the liver. More than 40 million people are infected and over 200,000 lives are lost each year. Contaminated water and blood products are the two root causes. It is caused by viruses, which can thrive only in human lever. It renders the vital organs vulnerable to chronic diseases as it destroys the immune mechanism of the body.

Hepatitis is not one disease; it has 7 types: A to G. Type A and E are milder; they are water borne and are not fatal, if the patient gets appropriate treatment.

Hepatitis A

HAV is a benign virus. It belongs to the picornaviridae family of viruses. It is quite resistant to heat and other climatic elements. It can survive in well water for more than 10 weeks and can withstand 60 degree C heat. It is inactivated by 5 minutes of boiling and ultraviolet rays of the sun. Case fatality is low (0.10 per cent). The patient recovers a few weeks. The incidence rate is 10-50 per 100,000 people. Popularly known as jaundice, the disease wanes with time if proper medication is available (Fig. 13.4).

HAV is excreta borne. It attacks children more than adults. A person, infected by HAV once, never gets the disease again in his lifetime. It thrives in heavy rainfall and poor sanitary conditions. It is thus a disease of poverty and poor living conditions. Its route of transmission is faeces-water-stomach-intestines. It is not a blood borne disease; the virus is homosexual; and its incubation period ranges from 15-45 days.

Hepatitis B

HBV is water or blood borne virus. It is the most common among the seven sub-types of hepatitis viruses mentioned above. More than 20 million carriers of the disease living in areas inhabited by two-third of the world population keep the infection level high. Over 2 billion people the world over have evidence of past or current HBV infection and 350 million people are chronic carriers of the virus, harboured in the lever. The virus is responsible for 60-80 per cent of all primary liver cancer, which is one of the three main causes of cancer death in East and South-east Asia, the Pacific basin, and Sub-Saharan Africa. Vaccine is the only means to prevent it. It is, however, not accessible to all. Ninety most seriously affected countries have now integrated it into national immunization programme.

Many countries have not yet started the immunization programme because of the high cost of the vaccine of HBV ($0.50 per dose). A minimum three doses are needed for complete immunity. Once a person is infected, he becomes a potential carrier even if he is treated and apparently cured. He can transmit it to others through food, water, body fluids and also sexual contact. It is

200 times more infectious than HIV and is more common, but not much has been done to create awareness against it. Ninety per cent of the babies infected remain carriers all through their life. Only recently it has been included as a part of the universal immunization programme.

According the WHO, all those countries, which have carrier frequency higher than two per cent should include Hepatitis B in their immunization programme. India has over four per cent carrier frequency rate; 2 to 5 lakh infants are infected each year. According to Children's Lever disease Awareness and Support Programme (CLASP), 4 lakh children suffer from serious lever ailments in India.

Taiwan has reduced its infection rate from 14 per cent to 1 per cent within a decade. China, Singapore, Italy and Zambia too have reduced their rates substantially but India still has to go a long way before it can make a dent in the increasing cases of Hepatitis B (Fig. 13.5).

Hepatitis C

HCV is the most fatal type. It is transmitted by blood transfusion or drug injection and has no cure so far. Hepatitis C (HCV) virus has therefore become a major public health problem. According to the estimates of the WHO, 3 per cent of the world population is infected with HCV and about 170 million individuals are chronic carriers at the risk of developing liver cirrhosis and lever cancer (Fig. 13.7). The professional blood donors have a very high prevalence of HCV infection, especially in the developing world. Although this virus does not infect people as easily as HIV or HBV, it has a peculiar tendency to induce chronic liver disease in three-fourths of the cases. It also has the characteristics of genetic diversity enabling it to escape the host's immune system.

The HCV was identified in 1989. It is a single strand RNA virus with properties similar to those of flavivirus. Inferon is the only drug, which can be depended upon to some extent.

Hepatitis E

HEV was discovered in 1990. It appears to have originated from blood donors in Saudi Arabia and Egypt. The virus causes a mild disease with mortality rate of less than 4 per cent. It was responsible for the 1955-56 epidemic in Delhi due to flooding of Jamuna. China reported 100,000 cases in 1986 and 1998. Since then, the disease has been noted in India, Indonesia, Borneo, Mexico and Nepal.

HEV is faecus borne and reaches human body through food and water. The virus is self-limiting and hence does not have chronic carriers. Its incubation period lasts for 2 to 9 weeks. It infects pregnant women more probably because they are weakened by the burden of pregnancy.

Hepatitis G

The clinical significance of HGV has so far remained uncertain. It is usually mild with only modest or no rise in transaminasis. However, HGV has been associated with fulminate hepatitis of unknown aetiology in Japan.

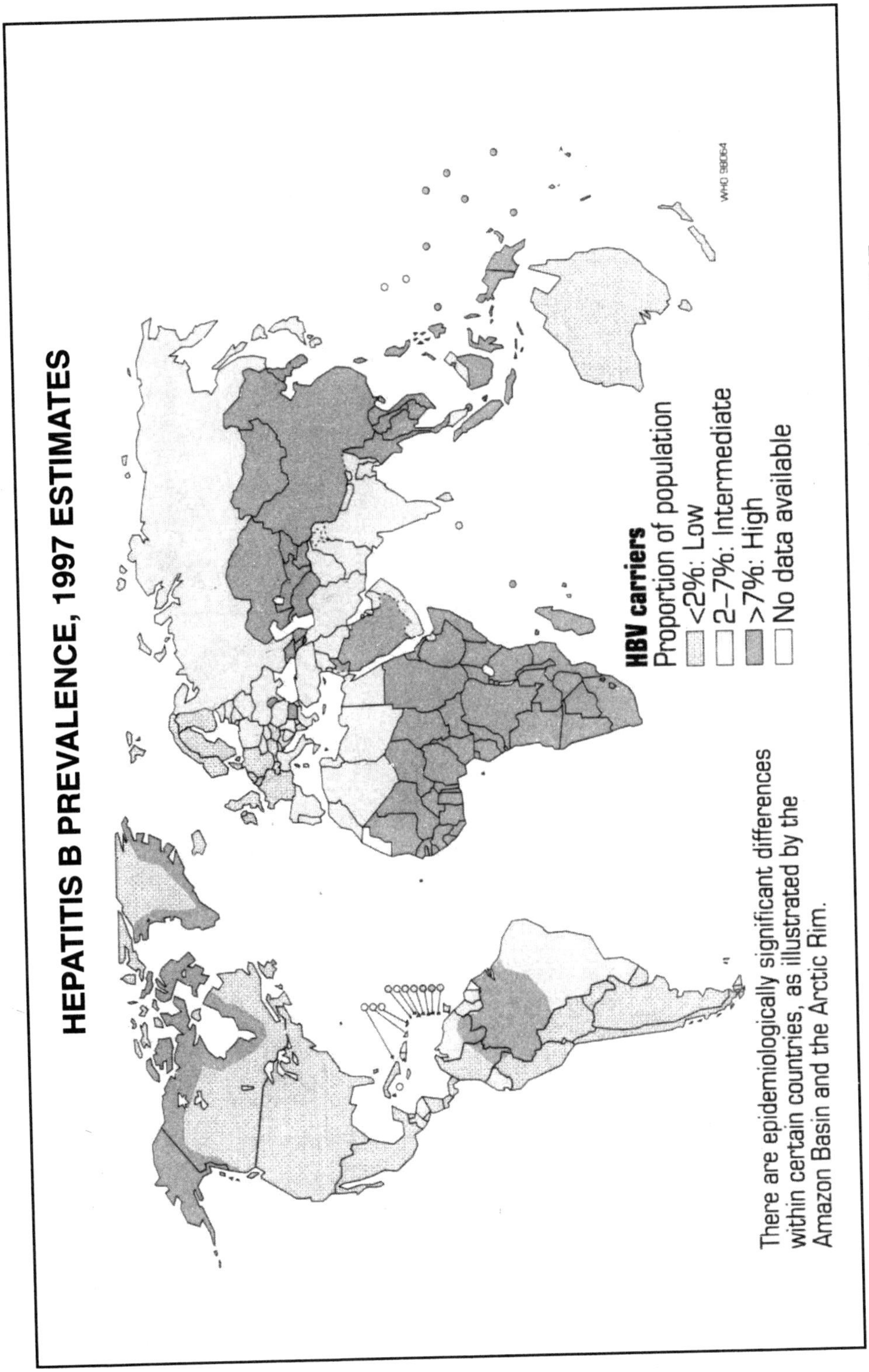

Fig. 13.5: World map showing the estimated of Hepatitis B virus carriers as per cent of total population in 1997

Source: World Health Report 1998.

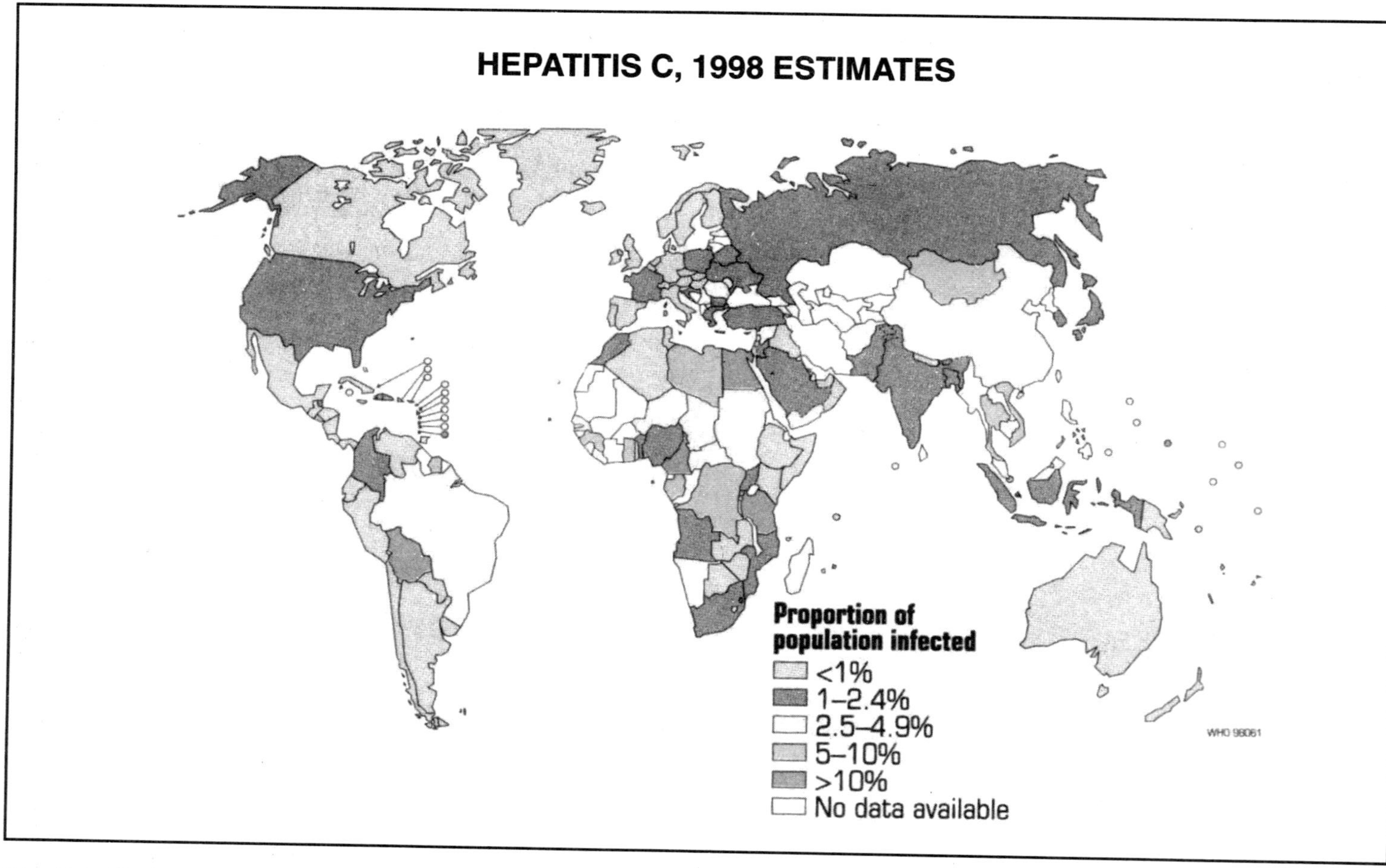

Fig. 13.6: World map showing estimated proportion of population infected with hepatitis c virus (HCV), 1998.

Source: World Health Report 1998

Geographic Prevalence in India

As in 1997, there were 1,33,594 reported cases and 1218 deaths of viral hepatitis in India. The actual cases were definitely several times more. Presuming that underreporting is uniformly distributed across the states, we take cognizance of these figures as useful indicators of te prevalence of the disease. The states with more than 20,000 cases were Andhra Pradesh, Maharashtra and Orissa. Kerala had 19000 cases. The states with more than 90 reported deaths were Andhra Pradsh, Madhya Pradesh. Maharashtra, Orissa and West Bengal. Maharashtra was the most seriously affected state with 515 lives (42 per cent of all deaths in the country). More details about each of the states can be found from Table 13.6 and Figure 13.7.

The states with moist climates have relatively higher rates of incidence hepatitis per 100,000 population. Moist climate means lower level of sanitation, which in turn means greater chances of infection. Blood transfusion or reuse of syringes is not really the ultimate cause of infection. The virus first has to enter the liver of the host and then only the host becomes the source of infection. The natural conditions in which the virus survives and then enters the water stream or foods are the most crucial factors.

Unfortunately, the environmental conditions in rural areas and urban slums in India are far below the standards required for a healthy life. This is the main reason for increase in the incidence of HAV and HBV cases in India.

Hepatitis C is not so common in India. According to World Health Report, 1998, the regions most affected by HCV are East Asia, Central and North Africa and North Eastern South America (Fig. 13.6).

Table 13.6: Incidence of Viral Hepatitis in India: 1998

Viral Hepatitis in India	*States*	*Number of Cases*	*Cases/100,000 Population*	*Number of Deaths*
1.	Andhra Pradesh	25514	35	93
2.	Arunachal Pradesh	13	1.30	0
3.	Assam	10038	29.36	7
4.	Bihar	–	–	–
5.	Goa	144	9.60	0
6.	Gujarat	3552	7.70	44
7.	Haryana	1632	8.50	17
8.	Himachal Pradesh	1946	30.00	9
9.	J&K	1479	15.73	3
10.	Karnataka	4452	8.80	61
11.	Kerala	19013	60.20	7
12.	Madhya Pradesh	11836	15.70	135
13.	Mahrashtra	20531	23.40	515
14.	Manipur	1492	66.00	0
15.	Meghalaya	1271	60.50	0

(Contd.)

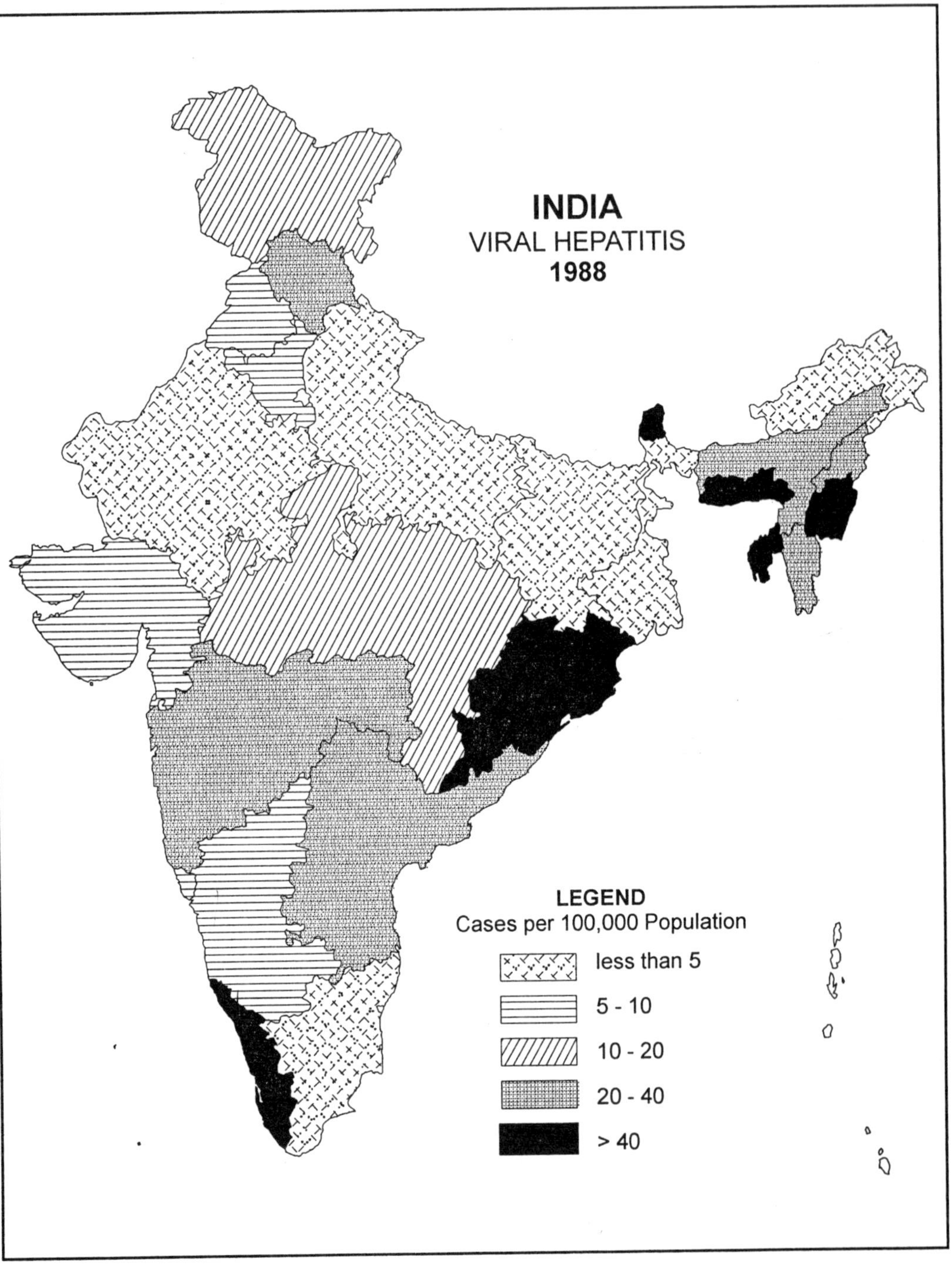

Fig. 13.7: Prevalence of Viral Hepatitis in India

(*Contd.*)

Viral Hepatitis in India	*States*	*Number of Cases*	*Cases/100,000 Population*	*Number of Deaths*
16.	Mizoram	320	40.00	1
17.	Nagaland	466	31.00	0
18.	Orissa	22459	64.00	125
19.	Punjab	–	–	–
20.	Rajasthan	1774	3.50	19
21.	Sikkim	449	90.00	2
22.	Tamil Nadu	1679	2.80	6
23.	Tripura	400	118.00	3
24.	Uttar Pradesh	355	0.20	10
25.	West Bengal	1727	2.30	93
26.	A & N Isls	382	109.00	7
27.	Chandigarh	215	27.00	1
28.	D & N H.	153	90.00	6
29.	D & D	346	266.00	0
30.	Delhi	1799	14.62	2
31.	Lakshadweep	15	2.50	0
32.	Pondicherry	132	13.20	2
	India	133,594	14.00	1,218

Source: Health Information of India, 1998.

REFERENCES

1. Government of India, Director General of Health Services, *Health Information of India,* 1998 and 1999.
2. Registrar General of India, *Survey of Causes of Death*, Rural, 1998.
3. WHO, *Regional Health Report*, 1998 (South and South-East Asia).
4. ——, *World Health Report*, 1998 to 2002.

14

Diseases of Modern Civilization-II AIDS

AIDS is the latest and most dreaded disease afflicting humankind. Recognised only in 1980s, it has established itself throughout the world and is likely to endure and persist well into the twenty-first century and may be even beyond. Evolving from a mysterious illness having no known cure, it has now acquired the form of global pandemic infecting tens of millions in less than twenty years. It is now prevalent in virtually all parts of the world.

AIDS, an acronym for Acquired Immune Deficiency Syndrome, is a disease that is caused by a virus known as HIV (Human Immunodeficiency Virus). According to the findings of Bette Korber and colleagues at the Los Alamos National Laboratory, University of California, San Diego, USA the epidemic appears to have started sometimes around 1930. She arrived at this date after analysing the rate of the mutation in the genes of the virus. Genes in any organism mutate and evolve at a constant rate. This gives the age of the disease to no more than 70 years as in 2000 AD. Korber arrived at the same conclusion when the mutation rate was taken as varying. James Moore, an anthropologist at the same university and a specialist in the study of genetics of humans and chimpanzees, agreed with Korber and asserted that the HIV was first transmitted to man through chimpanzee bite; and it was some time around 1930 in Africa. The chimpanzee blood contains SIV (Simian Immunodeficiency Virus). The oldest case of HIV was found in blood taken in 1959 from a man who died the same year in what is now known as Democratic Republic of Congo. Most recently in January 2000 AD, Sylvie Corbet of the Institute of Pasteur in Paris found HIV in several chimps from Cameroon that was very similar genetically to the HIV strain that infects people in that country. In early twentieth century, Africa was the host to many destructive activities like deforestation, new plantations, forced dislocation of people, and changes in hunting practices, which might have facilitated the spread of the HIV.

HIV thrives mainly in blood, seminal and vaginal fluids and the infection takes place most easily when the virus has easy access to the blood stream of an individual. This can happen when infected blood is transfused to a patient in the hospital or when needles used by HIV positive persons to inject medicines or drugs, are reused by a healthy person. It is also transmitted through sexual intercourse specially when there are untreated reproductive tract infections (RTIs) and sexually transmitted infections (STIs). Such infections are open invitation to HIV. Empirical evidence from all over the world suggests that reproductive health care leading to reduction in RTIs and STIs has proved to be first line of defence against HIV.

Sex is a means to procreate necessary for continuation of the species. Nature has added an element of pleasure in the process to ensure that no one fails in this essential duty. Man in his wisdom created a series of rules and laws to regulate sex relations and to give rise to family as the basic unit of social formation. Institution of marriage was created for this very purpose. There were exceptions to the rule and the men and women who violated rules were not rare. In order to save the society from the scourge of such deviations, the violators were given a separate identity. These days they are called sex workers. Of late, the tendency among the people to violate the rules of the game and to opt for extra-marital sex relations for enjoyment and pleasure has increased; procreation has become incidental. Here lies the fundamental problem of HIV infection.

So long as sex is confined to married couples, chance of contacting HIV through the sexual channel is remote. The other ways of infection include transfusion of HIV infected blood to patients and reuse of syringes used by HIV infected persons by others. Compulsory and statutory testing of the blood before transfusion and banning the reuse of syringes has made some difference. Unfortunately, it is on the sex front that the control is difficult. With increasing mobility of people for work and pleasure and growing tendency to have extramarital sex, the HIV infection is spreading rather fast all over the world. With no drug or vaccine in sight in the foreseeable future, AIDS acquiring epidemic proportions in the world. The rate of the new HIV infection is increasing rapidly even among those sections of the society that were hitherto supposed to be outside danger. Our focus should no longer therefore be confined to the prostitutes, truck drivers, migrant labourer, and other vulnerable sections of the society. Even commoners and innocent children and adolescents have to be protected. Active social and policy interventions will now have to include the bulk of sexually active population–old, young, married, unmarried, single, gay, men, women, perhaps even children.

Symptoms and Diffusion Process

The HIV virus is a virtually invisible passenger that uses the human body as a vehicle throughout its long incubation period before causing illness more than ten years later, in many cases. During this time, the virus can be transmitted by an infected person without any symptoms of infection to other persons who likewise become its unwitting vehicle to ensure its wider diffusion. An infected person becomes a potential transmitter as soon as he is infected without himself knowing that he has HIV infection. This is unlike other sexually transmitted diseases like syphilis or gonorrhoea where the symptoms appear in the first few weeks or months of infection.

The HIV is not resistant to heat. At 56° C, it dies within five minutes if left outside the living system. But its longevity increases as temperatures decrease. It can mutate within an individual's body, so that by the time it is transmitted to someone else, it has changed some of its characteristics. This lack of stability is part of the complex constitution of HIV, which in turn makes the development of effective drugs, and possibly vaccines, very difficult. It cripples the immune system of the individual infected by it. Even a minor case of influenza may get complicated and may take the life of the infected person. It certainly exposes the infected persons to life threatening ailments like T.B. and cancer that can never be cured once associated with it. It takes three to ten years before HIV infection turns into AIDS.

The process of transmission takes one of the following forms. When people engage in sexual intercourse, there is an exchange of genital fluids. With one of the partners being infected, the transmission rate may be as low as 1 out of 100 episodes of intercourse. Higher the promiscuity greater are the chances of transmission. Elisa test and Western Block technology for testing HIV can detect infection in the blood between 6 weeks to 3 months after infection with the margin of error ranging from 1 to 20 per cent. The tests have to be repeated. Sex, particularly the promiscuous one, is considered to be too private an affair to be disclosed even to a doctor. This false sense of privacy in a situation where the social norm of limiting sex relations to married couples alone is being increasingly broken, is an important reason for the rapid spread of the AIDS.

Global Prevalence

There are ten types of genetically known HIV. They are numbered from A to J. There are outliers, O-type, which are very heterogeneous. Type C is the cause of over 80 per cent of infections in India. Along with type E, it is associated with heterogeneous sex. Type B associated with homosexuals and intravenous drug use.

The disease that struck the world just two decades back has already claimed over 10 million lives. There are 42 million HIV infected persons in the world. And over 6 million new infections occurred in 2000 AD alone. Since the beginning of the epidemic, there have been an estimated 20 million deaths from AIDS. Women with HIV transmit the virus to the newly born children too. Adolescents and young adults who are becoming sexually active for the first time are particularly exposed. AIDS patient is destined to die sooner than later. All that modern science can do is to make the process of dying less painful and more humane. Efforts are on to find a vaccine that can combat the virus, but nothing hopeful appears to be in sight.

According to WHO estimates, the twenty-first century has begun with a load of 30-40 million HIV infections out of which approximately 3 million will die each year. And this load will grow at the rate of 15 per cent per annum. In 1994, the number of HIV cases in the world was approximately 14 million. In 2000 AD, it went up to 30 million. Global distribution of these cases is given in the Table 14.1. The annual update of the United Nations Programme for AIDS 2000 shows that the global epidemic continues unabated. As many as 5.3 million people contacted the virus and another 3 million people died from the disease during 2000 AD (Fig. 14.1). In 1997, the WHO estimated 2.3 million AIDS related deaths and 30-60 million HIV/AIDS infection in the world (Fig. 14.2).

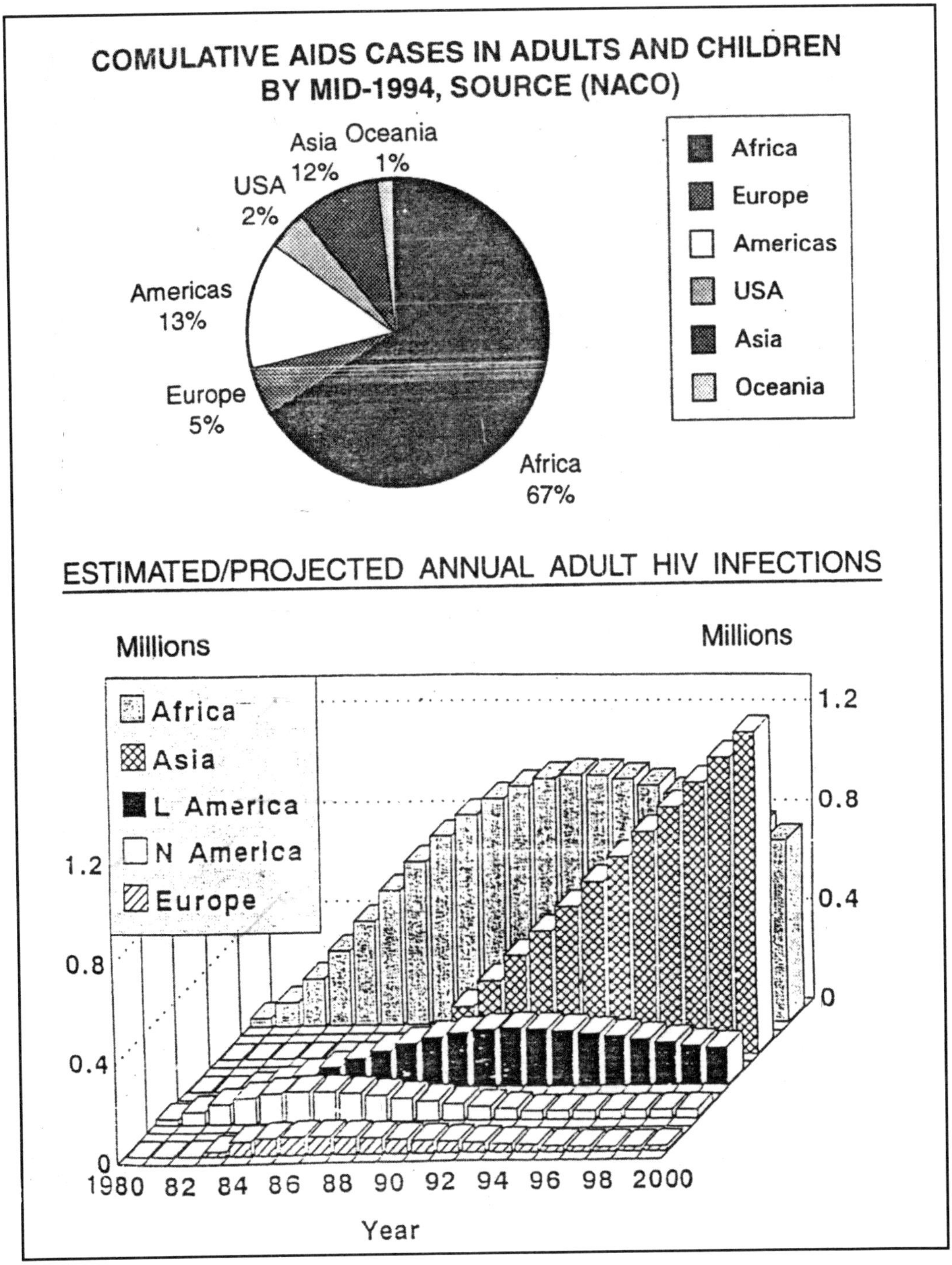

Fig. 14.1: HIV Infections and AIDS cases.

Source: World Health Organization.

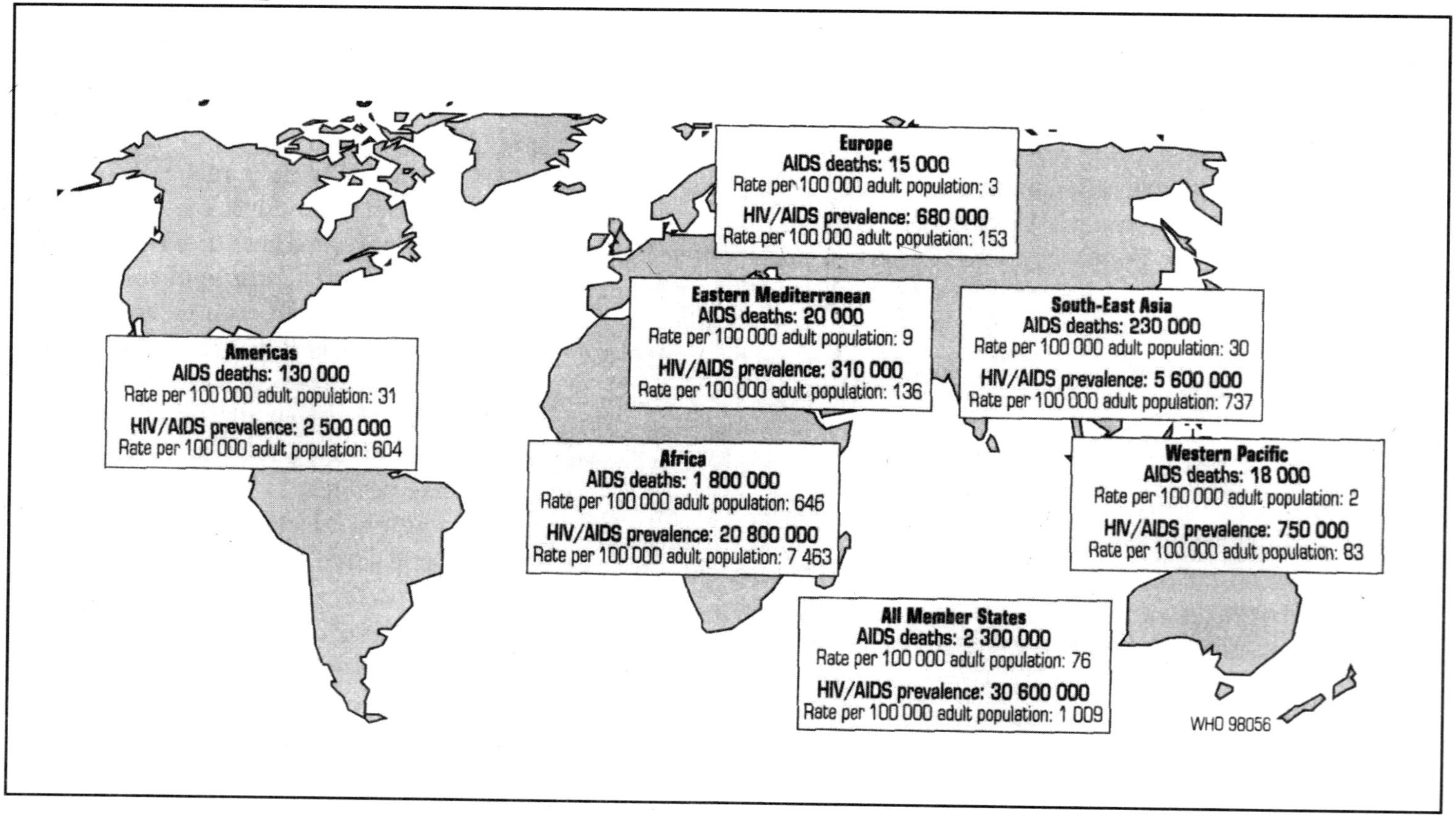

Fig. 14.2: World map showing AIDS death and HIV/AIDS prevalence among adults aged 15-48 by WHO regions.

Source: World Health Report, 1997

Table 14.1: Estimated Cases of HIV Infections By Macro-regions: Mid-1994

Macro-regions	*Total Cases*	*Cases Alive*
North America	> I million	800,000
West Europe	>0.50 million	>400,000
Latin America and Caribbean	>5 million	1.5 million
North African and West Asia	>75,000	>75000
Sub-Saharan Africa	> 7 m	7 million
South and South-east Asia	> 2 m	> 2 million
Eastern Europe and Central Asia	>50,000	>50,000
Australia	>25,000	>20,000
East Asia and the Pacific	> 25,000	>25,000
World	>14 million	>11-12 million

Source: WHO, World Health Report, 1996

According to the estimates of the WHO, the number of adult HIV infections and AIDS deaths per annum in 1997 was 2.3 million and number of HIV infected persons was 30.60 million. Macro-regional deaths as well as prevalence of adult HIV as in 1997 are given in Table 14.2 and Fig. 14.2. And the number of annual infections in the world by the turn of the century was expected to be 1.97 million: Asia 1.1 million, Africa 0.70 million, Latin America 0.1 million, North America 0.05 million, and Europe 0.02 million. It is only Asia where the number of infections would continue to grow so that the number of infected persons in the world was expected to be around 40 million by the year 2000 AD.

Table 14.2: AIDS: Global Prevalence and Mortality 1997.

WHO Regions	*AIDS Deaths*	*HIV/AIDS Prevalence*
Americas	130,000	2,500,000
Europe	15,000	680,000
Eastern Mediterranean	20,000	310,000
Africa	1,800,000	20,800,000
South-East Asia	230,000	5,600,000
Western Pacific	18,000	750,000
All Member states	2,300,000	36,000,000

Source: WHO, World Health Report, 1997

AIDS has serious implications for economic development. The countries afflicted by it have a very bleak future if they fail to control it. It wipes out the economically most active segment of the population. In Africa, the disease has left wide swathes of area where much of the active population is gone leaving behind children and aged. According to some estimates, 0.3 to 0.5 per cent of the GDP of South Africa is lowered because of this disease. Botswana, another hot spot in Africa, will have 30 per cent lower GDP by 2010 because of AIDS. India already has a surfeit of poverty and sufferings. It should avoid having more of both because of AIDS.

An important effect of AIDS is deterioration in the quality of life. For example, in Botswana, the life expectancy rose from 44 years in 1955 to 58 years in 1990. Now with 25-30 per cent of the adult population infected with HIV, life expectancy is expected to drop back to the level of 1960s. Zimbabwe has already brought its life expectancy of a child born in 1990 down by 10 years. Several sub-Saharan African countries show similar trends.

The other potentially explosive countries are in Southeast Asia and the Pacific. Cambodia, Thailand, Myanmar, Bangladesh, India and several other countries of the region may go the African way if corrective measures are not adopted forthwith. In Easter Europe, drug injection is behind the dramatic surge in HIV infection. In Ukraine, 70 per cent of the new cases pertain to drug addicts. In Latin America and the Caribbean, AIDS has already overtaken traffic injuries as a cause of death. In North America, AIDS dropped to second place as the leading cause of death in people aged 25-44 years in 1996. Similar trends are visible in Western Europe and some of the Latin American cities like Sao Paulo. Thailand has successfully reduced infection rate because of increasing use of condoms. This reversal has resulted mainly from anti-retroviral therapy that is yet to become easily available to the people in most of the developing parts of the world. The ideal situation will be one in which extra-marital sex relations are minimal. It is good for human society not only from the point of view of infection but also from family and social stability. But if it is not possible to achieve, mechanical devices like condoms must be popularised to minimise, if not totally stop, HIV infection.

AIDS in India

Once confined to red light areas and roadside dhabas (folk restaurants), it has now entered even the remote rural areas and even the most conservative households. Of the 2.90 million people tested by the National AIDS Control Organisation (NACO), about 50,000 were found HIV positive. And 3161 of these cases had progressed to AIDS. The NACO figures are limited to only high-risk groups – prostitutes, homosexuals, drug addicts, truck drivers and migrant labourers. But based on prevalence rates and sample surveys, the Joint United Nations Programme on HIV/AIDS estimates point to HIV positive persons in India being between 3.5 to 4.0 million, perhaps the largest in any country in the world. Other countries in order are Uganda (1.5 million cases), South Africa and Nigeria (1.2 million cases each).

What is worrisome in India is the transmission chain by which the virus quietly percolates through social substrata and affects low risk individuals like housewives and children. Unprotected sex with the so-called high-class call girls by the rich has led to many positive cases and deaths in recent years. One out of ten positive cases in India is now a housewife. Promiscuity may be a taboo in India, yet two-thirds of the HIV positive cases are accounted for by heterosexual transmission. In the Western world, the situation is just the reverse; 70 per cent of the cases result from homosexual transmission.

While in the West, having multiple sexual partners is now considered a high-risk behaviour, in India it is becoming fashionable. Every young man desires to be a James Bond. Sexual promiscuity is considered to be a sign of liberation and upward mobility. Teenagers and those in the early twenties constitute one-third of the HIV positive cases in the country. Peer pressure makes young Indians desperate for sex. While sex is increasingly available in the campuses of the colleges and universities, it is not so free; so they go to the brothels.

Mumbai is considered to be India's AIDS capital. In 1992, 0.7 per cent of the samples of the pregnant women were found to be HIV positive. In 1996, the per centage went up to 2.7 per cent. In Chennai, the disease is quite common among the educated persons. Of the 79 infected cases the Asia-Pacific Network of Peoples with HIV removed 79 infected men and 46 infected women from private HIV clinics across the city of Chennai and found 65 per cent of them graduates, 25 per cent post-graduates, and 7 per cent Ph. Ds. In Bangalore, 58 per cent of the 420 cases the Samaraksha is looking after come from the middle class families. In Pune, the National AIDS Research Institute (NARI) reports that 14 per cent of the women who come to its clinic are housewives. In Ahmedabad, the number of middle class women coming to the clinics of Gujarat AIDs Awareness and Prevention Unit has increased by 30 per cent. In Maharashtra, the HIV prevalence rate among pregnant women under 20 years of age has gone up from 2.5 per cent to 3.5 per cent between 1994-96.

According to Monitoring the AIDS Pandemic (MAP), India has over 2.5 million HIV positive cases (in 1996), which is more than that of any other country in the world. By 2000 AD the number increased to 3.8 million. The rate at which AIDS is spreading in India is, however, alarming and, according to some estimates, by 2010, India may have as many as 25 million HIV/AIDS cases. Delhi alone had 2200 HIV positive cases in 2002. But in the context of its huge absolute population of 1.10 billion, it cannot be said to have acquired epidemic proportions. That works out to only 0.32 per cent prevalence rate. But when seen in absolute terms, it is half of the infections in the whole of Asia. Some social scientists question the figures given out by international agencies and feel that the situation is not as alarming as it is claimed to be. But, estimates apart, one cannot but be disturbed that the HIV infections are on the increase in India.

The distribution of HIV infection and AIDS cases is not uniform all over India. The very adversely affected states are Maharashtra, Tamil Nadu, Andhra Pradesh, Gujarat, Karnataka and Manipur. It does not however mean that other states are immune from it. In fact, the virus is spreading fast in all parts of the country. For example, the rate of seropositivity in UP has gone up from 1.7 to 2.46 between 1992 and 2000. The first case of AIDS in UP was detected in 1987 and AIDS control programme was launched in 1992. Unfortunately, the disease has been found more prevalent in the 21-30 age-group. The second largest number of the seropositive cases belongs to 30-40 age-group. The disease is more common among the males. Of the 238 AIDS cases detected, 196 were males and 42 were females. The largest number of cases is reported from Allahabad and Varanasi. This is because of the transmission through truckers and commercial sex workers. The NACO has now put Uttar Pradesh in the high prevalence category.

Madhya Pradesh is a low prevalence state as far as HIV/AIDS is concerned; it is fast entering the moderate category. The state has only one per cent of its people infected with HIV; its western districts have much higher infection rate. 180 AIDS cases have been reported from Indore city alone. There were 89 such cases in Ujjain. In fact, all the districts of the state adjoining moderate (2-3 per cent) to high (4-5 per cent) HIV prevalence states of Maharashtra and Gujarat, are marked with high to moderate HIV prevalence rate (Fig. 14.3).

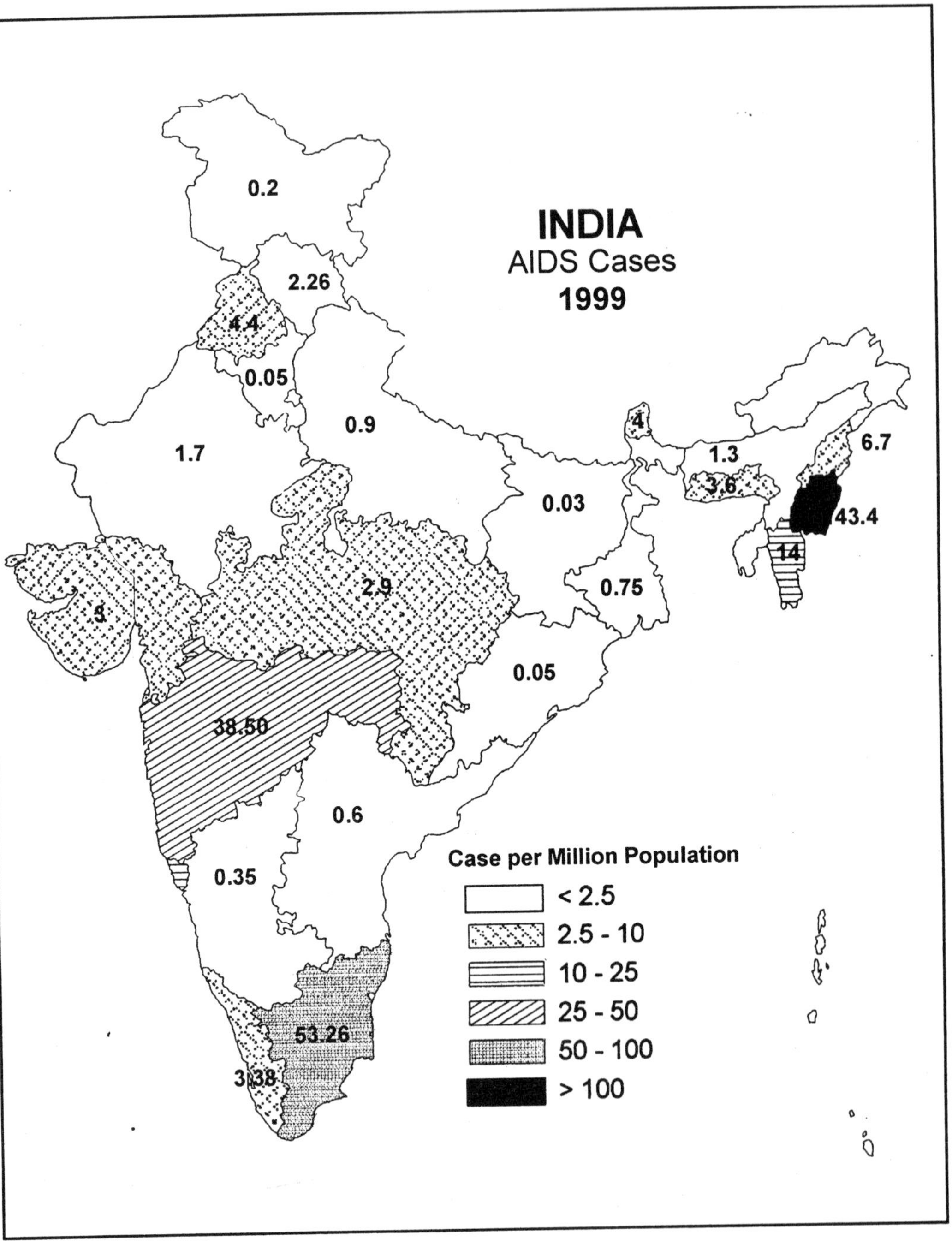

Fig: 14.3: Map of India showing state-wise incidence of AIDS per 1000,000 population in 1999.

Source: Health Statistics of India, 1998.

Table 14.3: Per cent of Screened and Found HIV Positive Cases-1994 and 1996

States	1994		1996	
	AIDS cases (Number)	*Per cent found HIV positive*	*No. of persons screened*	*Per cent found HIV Positive*
Andhra Pradesh	1	5.50	4173	5.15
Asam	1	1.30	10288	1.30
A & N Isls	–	0.94	8960	0.94
Bihar	–	0.04	8401	0.04
Delhi	54	0.32	309506	3.2
Daman &Diu		3.20	250	3.20
Goa	12	1.29	58203	1.29
Gujarat	18	0.14	369960	0.14
Haryana	1	0.14	122537	0.14
Himachal Pradesh	9	0.51	13767	0.51
J & K	2	0.28	7009	0.28
Kerala	76	0.43	41334	0.43
Madhya Pradesh	21	0.37	71552	0.34
Maharashtra	246	2.17	298547	2.17
Manipur	54	9.98	39957	9.98
Pondicherry	6	2.74	64166	2.74
Punjab	47	7.14	56	7.14
Chandigarh		0.34	54578	0.34
Rajasthan	1	0.19	33685	0.19
Tamil Nadu	194	0.49	575172	0.49
Uttar Pradesh	8	0.70	94856	0.70
West Bengal	25	0.25	102505	0.35
Sikkim	–	43.54	147	43.54
Karnataka	12	0.62	355736	0.62
Lakshadeep		0.88	566	0.88
D&N. Haveli	1	–	–	
Orissa	1	0.28	62780	0.28
Mizoram	–	0.38	14013	0.38
Meghalaya	–	0.38	14013	0.38
Nagaland	–	7.80	3344	7.8
Tripura	–	0.77	16889	0.77
India	803		2798521	

Source: Health Information of India, 1998

In mid-1994, the number of AIDS cases and the HIV infections amounted to 803 and 22,389 respectively. The figures for the HIV infection were based on just 2.8 million screenings. The AIDS figures were also partial in the sense that the chances of many of the patients hiding themselves were not remote. The state-wise distribution of these cases is given in Table 14.3 and Figure 14.3.

Six years later, in 2000 AD, there were as many as 3.86 million people in India living with HIV. Only one per cent of them use anti-retroviral drugs because they are too costly for them.

Minimum cost is approximately Rs. 2000 per month (in 2000 AD). With antiretrovirals improving the quality of life of HIV-infected people by bringing down opportunistic infection, making drugs available cheaper has become the overriding concern. The enforcement of the Intellectual Property Rights by 2005 will make HIV drugs more inaccessible for the poor.

Though rights of countries to circumvent patent rules in case of health emergencies such as AIDS is recognized, unless they become applicable for all situations, developing countries will remain at disadvantage. The cost of the triple-dose antiretroviral therapy came down drastically from $1400 to $350 per month when the Indian generic drug manufacturer Cipla offered its generic version to some African countries in 2000 AD. But even this is too high a price for the poor or for free distribution by any agency. The National AIDS Control Organisation (NACO) has decided to give one dose of Nevirapine free to both mother and child in 2001. This may help in controlling transmission of HIV from mother to child but unless at least three doses are taken, the drug is not very effective.

A major fraction of the HIV/AIDS aid has gone to Africa. South-east Asia has an adult prevalent rate of 0.56 per cent with 5.8 million infections and 470,000 deaths in 2000 AD. India accounts for 11 per cent of HIV infected persons, it gets only one per cent of the global resources. The UN set aside $1.5 billion to fight the disease globally; it is only a fraction of the $7.10 billion required annually to eradicate the disease. There is a lurking fear that much of this fund may never reach the poor.

National AIDS Control Programme

Sexually transmitted diseases have been a global problem from time immemorial. May be the humans invented the institution of marriage only to ward off diseases like AIDS. Endogamous sex relations were perhaps given up in all cultures when transfer of certain diseases from one generation to the other became too common. This also may be reason for the reluctance of the society to accept children born of illegitimate relationships. Whatever the other reasons, the fear of contracting STDs and may be even HIV has been the major deterrents against promiscuous multi-partner sex relations in the past. However, the old social controls weakened as geographic mobility of people consequent upon urbanisation, industrialisation, and improvements in the means of transport and communication increased. Sexual mores in most of the countries of the world have undergone a major change during the last five decades. The ready availability of antibiotic to cure STD and the contraceptives to prevent pregnancies on the one hand encouraged the youth in particular to indulge in promiscuity and on the other kept STD cases down. AIDS has however changed the situation rather drastically because there is no cure for it and the old sexual behaviours because of inertia do not change fast enough to cope up with the new situation.

In India, the National STD Control Programme has been in operation since 1967 but its outreach and coverage have been sub-optimal. In the absence of any nation-wide surveillance system until 1986, the estimates of 40 million new cases per annum could not be treated as reliable. With the emergence of AIDS as a major threat, the Indian Council of Medical Research initiated a national sero-surveillance programme in 1986. It was the first nation-wide survey in the silent phase of the HIV infection in the world. The results of the survey indicated the existence of all three modes of transmission of HIV in India: heterosexual transmission; reuse of syringes by drug addicts; and contaminated blood or blood products and vertical transmission from infected mothers to their off-springs.

Realising the gravity of the situation, the Central Government of India initiated a National AIDS Control Programme in 1992 to combat and minimise the magnitude of HIV epidemic. The major components of the programme include sentinel sero-surveillance and AIDS surveillance, strengthening HIV/AIDS control, improving clinical facilities for AIDS cases, ensuring safety of blood and blood products, and improving awareness through health education. This programme has been carried out more seriously during the ninth five year plan ending in 2000-01 AD. The surveys conducted under the programme revealed that HIV infection existed in all the states of India both in urban and rural areas. The difference among the states in this regard might be attributed to the level of exposure or to the varying number of sero-surveillance cases. According to the ICMR estimates for 1997, the number of HIV infected persons were 3 million, half of them being women and children. About 30,000 deliveries took place among sero-positive women and 6000 to 8000 infants had peri-natal HIV infection. The sources of HIV infection in India as in 1997 were as follows:

Heterosexual 73.1 per cent,
IV Drug users 8.2 per cent,
Blood transfusion 6.9 per cent,
Spouse infection 1.3 per cent.
Blood products 0.8 per cent,
Homosexual 0.7 per cent,
Others 9.0 per cent.

The cumulative HIV sero-positive rate per thousand has gone up from 10.2 in 1986-92 to 16.8 in 1996. It is estimated to be 20+ in 2001.

What Next?

Control of HIV/AIDS is possible only if human beings adhere to the norms of sexual behaviour as prevalent in different societies of the world. No culture permits promiscuity but no culture is bereft of it. The need for promoting a more healthy social life, therefore, cannot be over emphasized. The other but less preferred way to develop a vaccine which can be mass injected to check infection from person to person. Efforts are on to develop vaccines and it appears that the microbiology department of the All India Institute of Medical Sciences, New Delhi is in an advanced stage of developing a vaccine for C-type HIV. It has already been successfully tested on mice. After its test on monkeys, it can be tested on human beings.

MENTAL DISORDERS

Mental disorders are not the major killers but they are a major source of global burden of diseases. Mental disorders are attributable to a variety of factors ranging from malnutrition of pregnant mothers to heredity. With improvements in antenatal and postnatal care of mothers and children and better availability of nutritious foods, the cases of mental retardation among children are declining fast in the developed parts of the world but improvements in the situation, if at all, in the developing countries is slow and tardy.

"Mental health is influenced by both biological and social factors. It is not a static condition but subject to variations and fluctuations." says the WHO. A mentally healthy person is able to form harmonious relations with others. He participates and constructively contributes to the living environment around him; he is able to harmonise his own conflicting needs, aspirations and drives and to adjust them with that of others so as to maintain peace and harmony.

Mentally sick were considered to be the people possessed by devils or some angry little gods. Patients were locked and confined so that they do not harm others or run away. This situation has not changed even at present in many developing societies like India. Developments in the field of psychology and psychoanalysis have revealed that mental disorder is a disease and it is curable like any other disease. '

Among the mental diseases are included mental retardation, depressive disorders, mental dementia, schizophrenia, post-traumatic stress, epilepsy, and alcohol and drug abuse. Mental disorder in the newly born is either hereditary or because of malnutrition of the mother or the child in the early age. Depressive disorders are more common among the younger persons. It happens because of their inability to cope with the fast changing social and economic situations. These cases are likely to increase in number in transitional societies like that of India.

William C. Manninger, president of Menninger Foundation, Kansas, USA, has given a set of question for screening the mental cases. If the response to any of the questions is 'yes', the person is a potential mental case.

1. Are you always worried?
2. Are you unable to concentrate without any known reason?
3. Are you continually happy without any justifiable cause?
4. Do you loose you temper easily and often?
5. Are you troubled by regular insomnia?
6. Does your mood fluctuate widely between depression and elation?
7. Do you continually dislike to live with people?
8. Are you upset if the routine of your life is disturbed?
9. Do your children consistently get on your nerves?
10. Are you constantly bitter?
11. Are you afraid without cause?
12. Are you always right and other persons wrong?
13. Do you have numerous aches and pains for which doctors fail to find a cause?

If we use the standards set by Dr. Menninger, the per cent of people who can be categorized as mentally sick would go up to anywhere between 10 to 20 per cent in the world.

Number of Mental Cases

According to a worldwide survey carried out by the WHO, mental disorders are likely to become major health problem of the twenty first century. According to the World Health Report 1995, about 500 million people in the world suffer from neurosis, stress related, and somatoform;

another 200 million people suffer from mood disorders like chronic and maniac depression. Mental retardation affects about 83 million; epilepsy 30 million; dementia 22 million, and schizophrenia 16 million. In India morbidity related to mental diseases stands between 1.5 to 2.0 per cent. That means that there are at least 15 million mentally sick in the country. Three fourths of these patients need psychiatric treatment but the number of hospital beds in the country, as in 1991, was only 21147.

In view of growing cases of mental diseases, the WHO declared 2001 as the Year of Mental Health. Five out of ten leading causes of disability include mental health problems such as depression (36.5 per cent) and alcoholism (11.3 per cent). By 2020, depression is likely to emerge as the second most important factor contributing to the increase in the number of unproductive years in an individual's life.

The rapid economic, social and technological changes going on in the world, the number of young people not able to adjust to the changes is likely to increase further. WHO has identified children and adolescents, abused women, abandoned elderly and poverty-stricken people in the high-risk category. Since most of the mental problems start in the teenage, the affected persons suffer for the whole of their life.

One of the outcomes of mental disorder is increasing suicide rate. It has increased by 60 per cent during the last 45 years. Attempted suicide cases are 20 times higher. According to a report, the cases of suicide in the most highly and thickly populated state of UP in India has doubled during the last four years and there is an increasing number of teenagers taking their own lives. In 1995, the number of suicide cases was 108; it jumped to 207 in 1999. What is most disturbing is the fact that children in the age group of 9-10 are also taking this extreme step to get rid of their assumed or real problems. Many of them belong to far-flung rural areas, which, in days bygone, rarely heard of suicide. While earlier the main causes of suicide were psychological, presently they are factors like sheer anger, immediate provocation, inferiority complex, failure in examination, and general feeling of an insecure future.

The stresses and strains on average man in India have increased so much that at least a quarter of the people need psychiatric counselling. Disturbingly, many of these people do not know that they needed counselling. About 10 million persons in India suffer from schizophrenia. And the number is likely to increase further as the pace of mobility, urbanisation, industrialisation and unemployment accelerates. Unfortunately, because of the stigma attached to mental disorders, most of the patients hide their disease until it become incurable.

Facilities for Treatment

In spite of the fact that anywhere between 1.5 to 2.0 per cent of the population of India suffering from mental problems, qualified professionals providing mental health care are few and the outreach of the services in rural areas is very low. The National Mental Health Programme was started in 1982 with a view to improve the mental health services at primary, secondary and tertiary levels for early diagnosis, treatment and rehabilitation of patients with mental health problems within the community or in the hospitals. Not much progress could, however, be made until 1995. The Mental Health Act, 1987 was notified only in 1993. The Act enjoins on all states of the Union to set up its own Mental Health Authority. Most of the states have now set up the Authority and state level mental health institutions have been created to take care of the patients with mental health problems. During the last five years (1995-2000) District level counselling, treatment and referral facilities have also been created in most of the states.

Statistics on the number of mentally sick persons in the country are scarce. According to some estimates, one out of every five persons in India needs psychological counselling or disorder treatment. Each year only about 30,000 patients are treated in specialised hospitals and the number of those who go to private doctors and those who never visit any doctor or hospital and spend their life on the streets begging for food are certainly far more than this. Of the patients who get treatment, those suffering from psychoses constitute over 86 per cent, from neurosis about 12 per cent and those from mental disorder only about 1.2 per cent. Among the patients treated the proportion of men to women was 2:1, showing that even in this matter women are discriminated.

The lot of the mental patients in India is really miserable. There is common belief all over the country and cutting across all communities and castes that mental diseases are caused by certain supernatural powers. The moment a person gets mentally sick, he is taken to the sorcerer, temple, *dargah*, or church to invoke supernatural powers for recovery. Recent (2001) burning of scores of chained mental patients in a dargah at Erwadi in Tamil Nadu points to only the tip of the iceberg. It came to light because the death toll was high and it was caused by accidental fire.

Three main reasons appear to be responsible for this state of affairs.

1. Belief that the mentally sick are "possessed" by some supernatural power. More mentally ill are taken to faquirs, peers, sadhus, sorcerers etc. than other patients. Among the magico-religious treatment are: chaining, beating, flogging, fire-walking, drinking ones urine, etc. It is done with the belief that it does not hurt the patient; it hurts the ghost.
2. Lack of trained professionals who can treat the mentally sick.
3. Tendency to hide even such diseases as schizophrenia either because of ignorance or because of stigma attached to the disease.

In the pre-independence era, mental asylums were either jails or torture centres supervised by police officers. Until 1980s, the inmates were invariably chained so that they did not go out of control. India has only 37 institutions where mentally sick are housed and treated. Families approach these institutions only as a last resort. First they approach the men and women who are believed to have supernatural powers, or the dargahs and other shrines which have cured some patients earlier. It has been found that most of the patients who are cured in these institutions continue to reside there because their family members do not want to take them back. There are no rehabilitation centres where they can be shifted.

To take care of 15 to 20 million patients, India needs about 40,000 trained personnel, 20,000 day-care centres, and 10,000 half-way-homes or rehabilitation centres. As in 1995, it had only 3,500 trained professionals, 37 day-care centres, and no rehabilitation centres. How bad the situation is can be gauged from the fact that the Ranchi Institute of Neuro-psychiatry and Allied Sciences (RINPAS) caters to the patients originating in Bihar, West Bengal, Orissa, Manipur, Tripura and Mizoram. In 1997, just 1210 patients were admitted; in 2000-01, the number of new admissions was 3116. The general conditions prevailing in the RINPAS can be gauged from the fact that in May 2001 one of its employees is alleged to have raped a female patient from Manipur; a patient tied to a cot was bludgeoned to death; one patient lost her cheeks to dog in 1981; some patients were caned and driven out by hospital employees in 1984; 134 patients escaped the centre in 1992; and each year about 20 patients escape it. The conditions prevailing in mental hospitals elsewhere are none better.

ALCOHOLISM AND DRUG ADDICTION

Alcoholism and drug addiction is also a sort of diseases. According to the WHO, drug means 'any substance that, when taken into the living organism, may modify one or more of its functions'. 'Drug abuse' means self-administration of a drug for non-medical reasons, in quantities and frequencies that may impair an individual's ability to function normally, and that may result in social, physical or emotional harm. 'Drug dependence' means a psychic or physical state "resulting from interaction between a living organism and a drug, characterized by behavioural and other responses that always include a compulsion to take the drug on a continuous or periodic basis in order to experience its psychic effect, and sometimes to avoid the discomfort of its absence."

Non-medical use of alcohol and drugs has become a major problem all over the world. It is spreading like an epidemic. While alcohol has now become a social necessity, the number of drug addicts is on the rise. In the USA alone, about 20 million people are addicted to marijuana. Drug smuggling is the major source of income of the underworld.

Apart from alcohol, the drugs which surreptitiously find their way in the market, include:

1. Opioids,
2. Cannabinnoids,
3. Cocain,
4. Sedatives or hypnotics,
5. Hallucinogens,
6. Tobacco,
7. Volatile solvents, and
8. Pan Masala in India

The most commonly used drugs are:

1. Amphetamines (Benzedrine, Dexedrine, Methedrine, etc,): These are synthetic drugs; they act on the central nervous system. They boost self-confidence.
2. Cocaine: It is derived from leaves of coca plant. It produces a sense of excitement.
3. Barbiturates: These are sedative drugs.
4. Cannabis: This is the most widely used drug. It is derived from hemp plant. Almost every part of the plant is used for preparing drugs. Hashish or charas is derived from flowering female plants; bhang is derived from dried leaves; ganja and marijuana is also derived from leaves and other tender parts. It produces a dreamy state of mind with tendency to laugh, greater awareness of colours, and disproportionate perception of time and space.

5. Heroin: It is a narcotic analgesic. It produces cravings, and unless taken in higher doses, its effects decrease with time. It is therefore the most harmful drug.
6. LSD: Lysergic acid ediethylamide was synthesized by Hoffman in 1938; its psychic properties were however known only in 1943. It alters the normal structuring of perception so that the individual sees the world differently. Seconds become minutes and minutes become hours. Sounds become louder, body size bigger, fantasies and visual illusions become common.
7. Alcohol: It has marked effect on the central nervous system. Alcoholics develop psychic and physical dependence.
8. Tobacco: It is the most commonly used intoxicant. It is responsible for 3 per cent of all deaths in the world and 30 per cent of cancer deaths. It is the only drug that is chewed smoked, and sniffed, and is prevalent all over the world. It creates withdrawal symptoms.
9. Volatile Solvents: They include glue, petrol, diethyl ether, chloroform, nitrous oxides, etc.

ACCIDENTS AND INJURIES

Sufferings and deaths caused by external causes such as accidents, injuries and venomous contact with animals account for about 8 per cent of all deaths: 7.90 per cent in developing countries and 7.5 per cent in developed countries. Approximately, 8,85,000 lives are lost each year in transport-related accidents, domestic injuries, occupational injuries, burns, etc. And most of them fall in the age group 10-24 years. Children in the age group 5-14 years being highly mobile and risk taking are the ones who are the common victims. Sex-wise, males account for 57 per cent of deaths on this category in the age group 5-14 and 43 per cent, female. More details of the sex-wise deaths are given in Table 14.4.

In India, natural hazards like floods, earthquakes, cyclones claimed about 20,000 lives in 1996. Unnatural causes like air crashes, house collapse, drowning, electrocution, explosions, falls, fires, injuries caused by animals, poisoning, traffic accidents, etc. claimed about 200,000 lives. 80,000 people, accounting for about 2.70 per cent of all deaths, died in road accidents alone. As mobility of the people increases, both morbidity and mortality related to injuries etc. tend to increase further. According to the survey of causes of deaths (rural) in 1997, these causes were responsible for about 10 per cent of all deaths in the country.

Table 14.4: Sex-wise Per cent of Accidental Deaths (Global)

Causes of Death	*Males (Per cent)*	*Females (Per cent)*
1. Motor Vehicles	23.80	23.20
2. Poisoning	7.80	6.40
3. Falls	6.50	16.60
4. Burns	2.10	3.40
5. Suicide	22.20	20.20
6. Homicide	8.40	7.10
7. Other violence	5.70	4.90
8. Other accidents	22.50	19.40

Source: WHO, World Health Report, 1999

Some states of India appear to be highly accident-prone. For example, mortality due to vehicular traffic in the western states of Punjab, Haryana, Rajasthan and Maharashtra is above the national average. The southern states and the states of the Ganga valley are low intensity accident rate, not because people are drive better or the roads are better but because the vehicle/ population ratio in these states is lower.

The cases of suicide are, however, higher in the peninsular states. 3.1 per cent of all deaths in India in 1997 were ascribed to suicide. Percentage in Tamil Nadu. was 7.50; Kerala 5.9; Andhra Pradesh 4.70; and Karnataka 4.30. The only other state above the national average was Haryana (4.40 per cent). The combined percentage of suicides and vehicular vehicles is again high in the southern states. Punjab and Rajasthan in the north-west are also above the national average (Table 14.5).

Table 14.5: Per cent of Deaths to Total Deaths Caused by Accidents and Injuries

States	*Per cent deaths due to vehicular accidents*	*Per cent deaths due to suicide*	*Combined % of suicides and vehicular accidents*
India	2.70	3.10	5.80
AP	2.10	4.70	6.80
Bihar	1.20	0.80	2.00
Gujarat	1.90	2.60	4.50
Haryana	5.60	4.40	10.00
Karnataka	2.10	4.30	6.40
Kerala	3.20	5.90	9.10
Madhya Pradesh	1.70	2.10	3.80
Maharashtra	3.00	1.60	4.60
Orissa	1.10	1.90	3.00
Punjab	6.70	1.70	8.40
Rajasthan	5.20	1.40	6.60
Tamil Nadu	2.60	7.50	10.10
Uttar Pradesh	3.20	1.70	4.90

Source: Annual Survey of Causes of Death-1997.

Emerging Problems

As we develop new weapons to combat epidemic and infectious diseases, new dangers to health appearing almost daily. Many new bacteria and viruses have emerged and many of the old ones have developed new strains, immune from the antibiotics, which save millions of people today. It is not inconceivable that we may face a pandemic of a communicable disease for which we have no cure.

The hospitals, which are centres where the sick are treated, have become sources of infection. The medicines, which cured us earlier, have become sources from where new diseases emerge. We are very close to a global crisis in infection. Development activities, which are supposed to improve the quality of life of the people, have been instrumental in fouling our natural and social environment to an extent that it is almost impossible to lead a healthy life. Unplanned urbanization and resulting overcrowding and mobility of people have further increased the chances of infection and rapid diffusion of diseases. Poor sanitation, despite trillions of rupees spent on developmental activities, is claiming more lives than ever before.

Man appears to be so gripped by death wish that all that he does to promote his welfare does just the opposite, irrespective of the scientific knowhow he uses and the technology he applies. The basic premises and paradigm of his thinking appear to have gone haywire. While the economy grows, the man decays; knowledge expands but the man shrinks; world is integrated but the man is broken into pieces; longevity of life has gone up but health has deteriorated; the dilemma of human survival and development is more confounded than ever before.

In matters health, classical diseases are on the way out but new strains of the same and newer diseases now afflict humanity. Man has entered a new transition that is taking him from diseases to disorders and physiological to physio-psychological ailments, which are systemic and for which there is no cure as such. Cancer, diabetes, hypertension, mental disorders, etc. are not diseases. These are biological disorders. The only way to ward them off is to lead a more natural lifestyle; a lifestyle that is more in conformity with the laws of nature than with the laws of economics and politics.

Man, it appears, has reached a turning point in matters of health, as matters economics, technology and sociology. He has to realize that the development model pursued so far by him has failed and more he pursues it, greater the danger to his survival and future development. He has to go back to the laws and principles of biology, which govern human body and life more than the laws of physics and economics and thereby save himself from his impending annihilation and extinction. Would he do that before it is too late, is still a moot question.

REFERENCES

1. Government of India, Ministry of Health, *Annual Report*, 1998 to 2002.
2. Government of India, Ministry of Health, *Health Information of India,* 1998 and 1999.
3. WHO, *World Health Report*, 1998 to 2002.
4. ——, *Regional Health Report (South and South-East Asia)*, 1997 to 2002.

15

Food Security and Health

All forms of life, from single-cell organisms to complex mammals, require food to sustain themselves and to lead an active life and successful reproduction. Nutrition is concerned with what these foods are; what they contain; how they impact human body on ingestion in amounts less or more than needed; and what happens to them after ingestion. The study of foods, nutrients in foods, and their relation to health is called the science of nutrition.

Food is a fundamental physiological human need. It is enjoined on all societies, peoples and nations to ensure food for all. Hunger and malnutrition still stare over 1000 million people in the world. Perhaps the most outstanding achievement of India ever since it became independent is the great strides it made on the food front. At the time of independence, it was a ship to mouth case. But for the timely assistance by the United States of America under its PL 480 programme, millions of people would have died of hunger. Within five decades, the country has become surplus in foodgrains. Its population has grown by three times while the food production has gone up by four times.

By increasing food output, India has won a major battle on the food front but it is yet to win the war. Increased food production does not necessarily ensure its availability to each and every person. Food is a survival need. Everyone needs food but everyone cannot produce it. Those who do not produce must have enough money to buy it from the market. Unfortunately, in countries like India, a sizable number of people are poor; they do not have enough income to buy adequate quantity and quality of food to lead a healthy life. Food may be there in the storage bins; it may even be exported; people may still go hungry. It can happen in abnormal times of calamities – natural or man-made when production is precipitously low and/or the distribution system is disrupted. It can also happen and does happen in normal times when people do not have enough resources to purchase food.

Hunger caused by poverty and famine has been a major killers in the past. It still persists in many developing countries. In India, it is no longer a major cause of mortality but it continues to be a major cause of morbidity, which is another name for slow but sure death. Poverty, under-nutrition, malnutrition, diseases and poor health go together. So long as the people are poor, self-reliance in food at the national level is not a sufficient guarantee against hunger and malnutrition.

Food security has to be looked at not only in terms of self-sufficiency at the macro scale – global or national – but also at micro scale of communities, families and individuals. Man must get enough quantity of food to quench his hunger but that alone would not ensure good health. Human body needs a large number of micronutrients to remain healthy. It is the quality of food that ensures adequate supply of the nutrients. If the body is deprived of adequate quantity and quality of food, it becomes an easy prey of a number of diseases.

This chapter examines the energy and nutritional requirements of human body. It also discusses the geography of the deficiency diseases, which follow the non-fulfillment of energy and nutritional needs of the body.

FOOD INTAKE AND HEALTH

"The soldier at the front never fights a lone battle. Behind him stands the might and will of the entire nation. Behind him stands the spirit of resistance. Just as this resistance behind the lines has to be carefully built up in a total war, resistance has also to be built up against the enemy attack in a total war against disease.

"If any one factor has to be singled out as basic for building this resistance, one would unhesitatingly place one's finger on nutrition. What is this nutrition and how does it help build up resistance against disease in human body? The human body is a complex machine. Just as a modern machinery requires fuel, lubricants and so on, the human system requires nutritive elements for the building up and proper maintenance of bones and muscles, arteries and nerves and all the other constituents of the human body. It also requires aids like enzymes and hormones for adapting the nutritional elements to the body's needs.

According to Borker, "Nutrition and diet are not synonymous though they are popularly used in that fashion. Diet consists of various articles of food, which are ingested and converted for use in the body for building up and maintaining it in a vital condition. Nutrition is the end of the process by which these are assimilated and produce the desired result." Man's physical and mental development and growth and his capacity and fitness for work depend on the quantity and quality of the food he takes. Nutritional deficiency if not recouped in time appears in the form of a number of diseases called deficiency diseases. We will discuss these in a separate chapter. But even before it shows up as a disease, it makes man dull; he loses interest in the world around him; he does not want to exert; he becomes short tempered; and acts without thinking of the consequences of his action. He loses the balance of the body and mind.

Nutritional deficiency can be caused by two factors singly or jointly: inadequate quantity of food, and poor quality of food. Man must eat enough to satisfy his hunger. Failure to do this for an extended duration of time can lead to under-nutrition. And a person who is undernourished must necessarily be malnourished also. Malnourishment can of, course, be caused by under-nutrition but it can also result from insufficiency in the diet of all those micronutrients which human body needs. It can also be produced by over-nutrition. If the overweight is caused by the accumulation of fat in the body, the man is called obese. Obesity is a systemic disease of modern urban dwellers consuming more food than the body needs and leading a sedentary life style – no physical exertion. It is caused by over-nutrition or lack of exercise.

We can, therefore, know the nutritional status of a man by finding out how much and what kind of food he eats. The quantity of food indicates the caloric value of his diet. And the quality of food he takes indicates the amount of various nutrients he gets from it. Calorie is a measure of energy supplied by the food articles we consume. Caloric requirements vary from person to person in accordance with age, sex, weight environmental setting, style of life, occupation, nature and amount of physical activity etc. Inadequacy of caloric intake leads to a state of under-nutrition. Malnutrition is not the consequence of low caloric intake alone. Apart from energy, our body needs fats, proteins, salts, calcium, vitamins, phosphorus and some other nutrients. The absence or insufficiency of any of these nutrients can cause malnutrition, even if all other nutrients are over supplied. Some of these nutrients like fats, when consumed in quantities higher than what a particular person needs, can cause over-nutrition. As stated earlier, over-nutrition is also a kind of malnutrition.

CONSTITUENTS OF NUTRITION

All living organisms have two basic nutritional requirements: compounds that give energy, and substances that fill the structural and functional needs. Some of them fulfill both the needs. But the sources from which they are derived differ from one form of life to another. Further, all the species do not need the same nutrients in same quantity and quality. For example, the plants do not need proteins and vitamins. They convert the simple compound of elements such as carbon dioxide, nitrogen and water into complex molecules that are used by higher forms of life, to once again break them down into simpler compounds to be consumed by still higher form of life (the human beings). In this process, only energy is expended. This is called food chain. If this chain is broken for an extended period of time, there will be no life on planet earth. This is one of the important reasons why we are concerned about the anthropogenic changes in ecology and environment taking away increasingly larger number of life forms from the earth's gene pool.

The nutritional requirements of higher animals and human beings are different from those of plants and microorganisms. First, they require a number of preformed complex organic compounds in their diet for their survival. Second, each cell and tissue needs different set of nutrients. Third, the nutrients they consume are derived from plants or animals. Four, the caloric requirements are higher due to greater muscular movements. And last, unlike plants and microorganisms, the food requirements of the humans is greatly influenced by appetite, habits, or idiosyncrasies that make their nutritional requirements variable and complex.

Energy (Calories)

The fundamental requirement of the cell and therefore of the whole body is energy measured in terms of calories. Without calories the functioning of the cells as well as the body as a whole would stop. In the event of starvation, the body would, for some time, depend on the reserves of the fats, carbohydrates and proteins. Once these reserves are exhausted, it would be dead. Calories are needed to keep the body active. Additional calories are needed, if the body undergoes additional stresses such as hard work, pregnancy and lactation or is in the process of growth as in the case of children.

As stated earlier, the main sources of calories are fats, carbohydrates and proteins. Each gram of these yields nine, four and four calories respectively. To find out the caloric value of any food, we have first to find out the amount of fat, carbohydrate and protein in that food and then translate those amounts into calories. How many calories a person needs depends on his age, height and weight. But this is a very rough way of finding caloric needs. To be more specific, the unit used to calculate is the surface area of the body, which can be found out by the formula:

$$HWa$$

Where H = height
W = weight
a = constant to be derived from empirical findings

Enzymes (The Catalysts)

Enzymes are substances that cause and direct the chemical reactions that occur in living cells or organisms. They are the catalysts of the living cells. Practically, all reactions in human metabolism are mediated through enzymes, but their role is most crucial in the digestion of food. Some enzymes are secreted by cells: for example, enzyme ptyalin, secreted by the cells of salivary glands, is discharged into the mouth to break complex starch molecules down into simple molecules of sugar maltose. The cells of the stomach secret enzyme pepsin that helps degrade proteins into amino acids and polypeptides. Trypsin, secreted by pancreas glands, also degrades proteins. The process of degradation is called hydrolysis since water is used to break down the bonds of atoms of complex molecules to form simple molecules.

They also help join together the atoms of simple molecules to create complex molecules. Glands do not secrete all enzymes; some of them are present in the cells. They direct the process of cellular metabolism. Enzymes are very sensitive to heat. They are inactivated when exposed to a temperature of 120 degree F for a few minutes. They are also very sensitive to acidity and alkalinity. Many toxic materials inactivate the enzymes; these materials cannot be ingested and therefore cause toxicity in the body. Many modern drugs prove harmful in the long run because they contain toxins, which inactivate the enzymes.

Carbohydrates (The Sugars)

Present in most foods, these compounds constitute sugars of two kinds: disaccharides such as cane sugar, and polysaccharides such as starch. When ingested they must be converted into simple monosaccharides i.e. simple sugars – fructose, glucose and galactose – before they are absorbed in the body through the blood stream. A proper utilization of sugar is essential for health. The first step in their absorption involves enzymatic reactions that results in the formation of sugar phosphates, which in turn are converted into carbon dioxide and water. Insulin is essential for the phosphorylation of the glucose. If not available in sufficient quantity, as it happens in the case of diabetes mellitus, the glucose concentration in the blood increases.

Some of the sugar is passed off through the urine. Another hormone called adrenaline causes the breakdown of the carbohydrates in the lever and muscles as glycogen. Shortage of glycogen can cause ketosis in human adults.

Fats

Fats are derived from edible oils, milk and milk products, meat, chicken, fish and eggs. Nothing happens to fats until they reach the intestines. There, they are emulsified and go through enzymatic hydrolysis by an enzyme called lipoprotein lipase to form mono-or diglycerides and fatty acids. Apart from being the source of energy, fats act as insulating material against cold and mechanical shocks. They also function as carriers of fat-soluble vitamins. It is very rich in calories. A normal adult human male engaged in manual work can take about 100 grams of fat per day in Indian setting.

Proteins

Proteins also provide calories to the body. But their main function is to yield amino acids for the maintenance and synthesis of the body protein. When ingested, protein is converted into peptides and peptides into amino acids. This conversion takes place in the stomach through the action of the enzyme pepsin. The rest of the degradation takes place in the intestines through the action of the enzyme trypsin. The amino acids so formed are carried to the tissues through the blood streams. Here they are incorporated in the tissues or undergo further degradations to end up as water, carbon dioxide, ammonia, urea, uric acid and related compounds. The species having ample water supply, excrete urea through the urine; but those, which get less water, excrete uric acid. The person is said to be in nitrogenous equilibrium if the intake and secretion of urea in all possible forms is equal. The amount of protein ingested has important bearings on the nitrogen balance.

Salts

Constant replenishing of the minerals and the electrolytes, excreted by the body in various forms, is essential for health. Among these are calcium, magnesium, iron, iodine, potassium, sodium, phosphorus and chlorine. The quantity required varies from species to species. For adult human beings 1 gram of calcium and 15 mg of iron is sufficient. The trace elements like zinc, copper, cobalt and the manganese are also needed in very minute quantities. For example, a patient suffering from pernicious anemia needs as little as < 0.0001 mg of cobalt in the form of vitamin B_{12} to keep normal. To oxidize copper, ascorbic acid i.e. vitamin C is needed; while magnesium is needed in the metabolism of carbohydrates. Phosphorus is a major constituent of bones and teeth.

The metabolic processes, which go on in our tissues, produce sulfur and phosphorus. Sodium, potassium, calcium and magnesium neutralize these acids and enable the kidneys to maintain a balance. Excessive loss of sodium chloride can prove dangerous as it happens in the state of abnormal discharge through sweating.

Approximately 85 per cent of the mineral matter in the body is concentrated in the bones. Other parts of the body draw on this reservoir as and when needed. Excessive drawl may, however, weaken and soften the bones. The remaining mineral matter is found in the blood plasma. The ratio of potassium and calcium to sodium in the blood plasma is identical to that in the primeval ocean water of pre-Cambrian formations. That is the period when life appears to have originated on planet earth some 600 million years ago.

Vitamins

Vitamins are specific organic compounds that are required in diet in very minute quantities ranging from 0.005 to 0.00002 per cent. That is how they are differentiated from other organic substances such as amino acids required by human body. Shortage of these compounds can retard growth and lead to deficiency diseases. Beriberi, scurvy, rickets, pelagra, pernicious anemia and xerophthalmia are some of these diseases. We propose to discuss them in some detail in latter sections of this chapter. Recent researches have discovered a number of new vitamins so that their total number has enormously gone up. We propose to discuss here only a few of the most common ones.

Vitamin A

It is a fat-soluble vitamin. It is readily destroyed by exposure to light and air. It is found in butter, fish, and liver fats of various animals. It does not occur in plants, but many of the vegetables and fruits containing carotenoid pigments (yellow and red colour) can provide all the vitamin A man needs. The yellow colour of carrots is caused by presence of beta-carotene in it.

Lack of vitamin A can lead to night blindness, then on to xerophthalmia and finally to complete blindness. It is required in very small quantity – just 4000 IU of vitamin or 2.4 mg of beta-carotene per day can meet the requirements of an average man.

Thiamine or Vitamin B

It is a nitrogenous alcohol of great variety. Like other vitamins, it has several variants. Thiamine, also called Vitamin B_1, is a water-soluble alcohol. It is the substance that was first called vitamin. It occurs most abundantly in most of the cereal grains. It helps convert carbohydrates into energy. About 1 mg per day meets the vitamin B_1 requirements of an average adult. It prevents beriberi. Severe deficiency may also lead to loss of appetite and certain types of neuritis.

Vitamin B_2

Also known as riboflavin, Vitamin B_2.is a yellow nitrogenous alcohol abundantly found in whey egg white and a variety of plants. A normal human being needs about 2 mg per day to lead a healthy life. Deficiency of this vitamin retards growth and produces changes in the skin and tongue. It is a part of enzyme systems that oxidize carbohydrates.

Niacin is nicotinic acid. It is pellagra preventive vitamin. Pellagra is a disease that is common among the people whose staple food is corn. It is a vitamin that is very stable even under very high and low temperatures. It is widely distributed among plants and animals. A person requires 5 to 15 mg niacin each day to remain healthy and to be free from pellagra.

In addition to the above acids classified as vitamins, there are several others which have some role to play in keeping human body healthy. Among them are: vitamin B_6, pantothenic acid, biotin, folacin, cobalamine and several others.

Vitamin C

It is a water soluble and easily oxidizable carbohydrate like lactose that prevents scurvy. Only a few species like humans, monkeys and guinea pigs need to supplement this vitamin: animals can synthesize it themselves. Fresh fruits, particularly of citrus variety, vegetables, and other plant materials are the main sources of this vitamin

Vitamin D

This is also a fat-soluble alcohol derived mainly from sunlight, which is a free gift of nature. It is produced by the irradiation of various sterols with ultraviolet light. It is therefore not necessary to take this vitamin in the food. But those who are not exposed to sun light must supplement it orally. About 400 international units (400 IU or 10 ug) are needed for a growing child. Cod liver oil and sun light are the main sources of this vitamin.

Tocopherols or Vitamin E

It is a fat-soluble phenol found in certain vegetable oils. It improves sexual potency in men and childbearing capacity in women.

Vitamin K

Present in green leaves, this vitamin reduces prothrombin in the blood and thereby reduces clotting time of blood. It increases naphthoquinone and thus acts as an anti-hemorrhage substance.

Water

We have discussed the importance of water in chapter on natural environment. As a reminder, let it be restated that water constitutes 60 per cent of our body weight. Apparently, it must play an important role in the metabolic processes. Although some forms of life require little water, none can exist without it. Practically, all chemical reactions related to the life of living organisms take place in solution. Quality of water is therefore an important determinant of health of the people. Water contamination due to industrialization, urbanization and increasing use of chemicals and other toxins has now become a major health hazard in the world.

BALANCED DIET

Foods and nutrients almost go together but they are not the same. Bread, rice, pulses, vegetables, milk, butter/ghee and fruits are examples of foods. Nutrients are chemical substances or compounds, usually derived from foods. They enter our body in the form of carbohydrates, fats, vitamins, minerals and proteins. A wholesome food is capable of providing all nutritional requirements of human body. If we consume adequate quantity of foods of different varieties, we will get all the nutrients our body needs. All the foods give more than one nutrient but the granulated sugar, being an isolated carbohydrate, gives only calories. The whole wheat bread is a multi-nutrient food. It gives protein, iron and vitamin B. Milk gives almost all basic nutrients – calcium, proteins, carbohydrate, fats, minerals and vitamins. Milk is said to be man's most nearly perfect food because it supplies a great variety of nutrients-fats, carbohydrates, iron, calcium, proteins, minerals, etc.

Foods are divided in five basic generic groups in accordance with the nutrients they supply: 1. cereals and cereal products, 2. meat, eggs, poultry and fish, 3. milk and milk products, 4. vegetables, and 5. fruits. If the food that we consume is drawn from each of these groups, then it would roughly be balanced i.e. all the needed nutrients i.e. carbohydrates, proteins, fats, minerals and vitamins will be present in it in required quantities. A balanced diet is the one that provides adequate quantity of calories and nutrients to the human body.

Human beings, however, differ widely according to age, sex, occupation, physical environment, cultural setting, etc. The food requirements of children are different from that of adults; of pregnant and lactating women are different from that of other women. A sedentary man needs less food than a manual worker. The same man in different stages and styles of life needs different quantity and quality of food. So what is balanced diet for one person may be unbalanced for another. This calls for scientific study of diet. The discipline that pursues this study is called dietetics. Dietetics involves a knowledge of foods, their composition and preparation, and nutrients they contribute for tissue repair and growth, for heat and energy, and for normal functioning of the body.

Even if the food we consume contains all the nutrients our body needs, it may not be a wholesome food. Food to be wholesome must meet three other requirements. First, it must be free from harmful bacteria. Milk in particular is a carrier of a number of harmful organisms. We are aware of the fact that many diseases spread through water. Secondly, food should be clean. It should be free from insect parts, hairs and excreta. All raw foods must be cleaned or even rinsed in clean water before they are used. And finally, foods should BE free from harmful chemicals like DDT and other insecticides and pesticides.

The method of preparing foods has its own implications for its wholesomeness. Cooking makes foods more palatable, easy to eat and also easy to digest. Cooking kills unwelcome micro-organisms and eggs of parasites. It, however, reduces or destroys some of the vitamins sensitive to heat such vitamin C (ascorbic acid). That is why, salad of fresh fruits and garden vegetables is recommended as essential ingredient of balanced diet. Cooking time for vegetables should be as short as possible and a minimum of cooking water should be used to obtain desired results. Throwing away of the cooking water amounts to oozing out of the vegetables much of the nutrients they contain. The same applies to cooking of rice.

Constituents of Balanced Diet

A stated earlier, there is nothing like a balanced diet for all. Age, sex, occupational and cultural as well as geographic differences do not permit meaningful averaging. And hence the prescriptions that one often finds in health guides should be taken as indicative rather than prescriptive. Each individual has to have his own chart of balanced diet. But the matter is not as complicated as it may appear to be. If a person takes adequate quantity of all the five groups of foods, he is sure to get all the energy and nutrients he needs.

An average man's balanced diet (see Table 15.1) prescribes at least 2400 to 2600 calories in addition to various other nutrients. But as stated earlier, the amount of energy needed depends on the age, sex, nature of work, and several other factors. As such an average female needs only 2100 calories, but if she is pregnant, the requirement may go up to 2500 calories, and if she is nursing, it may touch as high as 3000 calories. For infants, we can calculate the energy requirements by multiplying weight in kg by a factor of 100 for 0-3 month olds; a factor of 90 for 3-6 month olds; and a factor of 80 for 6-12 month olds. To determine the calorie requirements of children, some standard coefficients have been worked out (Table 15.2).

Table 15.1: Balanced Diet Chart for an Average Male

	Items of food	*Amount per day in grams*
1.	Cereals	400
2.	Pulses	85
3.	Green vegetables	85
4.	Root vegetables	85
5.	Other vegetables	85
6.	Fruits	85
7.	Milk	300
8.	Sugar/gur	60
9.	Veg. Oil/ghee/butter	60
10.	Fish/meat	60
11.	Eggs	One piece

Source: National Institute of Nutrition and other sources.

Similarly, the protein requirements have also been standardized for general guidance of the people. In this regard, age and weight of the body are the main determinants. For a child of 1-3 years, the protein requirement per kg of the body weight is 3.5 grams. It is 3 grams for 3-5 year olds, 2.5 grams for 5-15 years olds, 2.0 grams for 15-17 year olds, 1.5 grams for 17-21 year olds, and only 1,0 grams for 21+ year olds. For pregnant and nursing women it is 2.0 grams.

Table 15.2: Calorie Requirements of Children

Age group (in yrs.)	*Co-efficient*	*Number of Calories/day*
1-2	0.3	720
2-3	0.4	960
3-5	0.5	1200
5-7	0.6	1440
7-9	0.7	1680
9-11	0.8	1920
11-12	0.9	2160
12+	1.0	2400

Source: National Institute of Nutrition

It is important to know that balanced diet need not be a costly proposition. Even a poor man can eat balanced diet if he is conscious about what he eats and when. Human metabolic system requires 14 hours to digest food. Most of us eat three meals a day. This means that we keep our body engaged in digestion without rest, repair and recharging the vital batteries. We should take only two meals a day. The breakfast should be light and so also the lunch. Raw foods are most nutritious. We should try to eat as many raw foods as we can. Even cereals in sprouted forms become highly nutritious. The whole wheat contains 14.5 per cent water, 11 per cent nitrogenous mater, 1.2 per cent fat, 60 per cent starch and sugar, 2.6 per cent cellulose and 1.7 per cent minerals. Just imagine that 100 grams of sprouted wheat, 50 grams of pounded almond, 10 grams of whole almond, 200 grams of green vegetables, 250 grams of seasonal fruits, 25 grams of lemon, and 50 grams of honey will constitute a wonderful balanced diet. It is better to avoid refined sugar. Instead, Jagary or gur should be preferred if honey is not available. Jagary ccntains 47 per cent cane sugar, 20 fruit sugar, 2.7 per cent coloring and other matters, 2.6 per cent salts and 27.3 per cent water. Potato is a highly nutritious root vegetable. It gives more vitamin C, calcium, phosphorus, iron and vitamin B than most of the cereals. Milk is a very wholesome food item very rich in calcium, salts and phosphates apart from vitamins B1, B2, and A.

In view of the increasing popularity of junk or instant foods, it would be desirable to say few words about them. Junk food includes burgers, pizzas, hot dogs, aerated drinks, potato chips, french fries, chats, golgappas, samosas, chhole bhature, etc. Junk foods are very rich in fats and calories but very poor in vital nutrients like proteins, calcium, iron, minerals and vitamins. Children are easily attracted to these foods. In the USA, obesity among the children and youth has become a major disease. In India too this disease is spreading fast among the children as well as adults of well off families and the whose style of life is sedentary. The synthetic food dyes, artificial flavourings, and preservatives used in most junk foods can play havoc with the body causing a host of physical, emotional and mental problems. If the physical growth is not normal, the mental growth also suffers.

How Balanced Is Indian Diet?

It is difficult to talk of Indian diet without taking into account the great variations in the food eaten in different parts of the country. Apart from regional differences, there exist social differences. A quarter of Indian population is well fed and in some cases over fed too. Another quarter of the population is ill fed; half of it does not get enough calories and practically the whole of it is short of micro-nutrients. And the remaining half stands in between. It manages to get adequate amount of calories but the cases of nutritional deficiency are quite common. When we talk of the diet of the average India, we keep in view this 50 per cent of the population that falls in the middle-income group.

Average Indian diet consists primarily of cereals and pulses which together account for nearly 75 per cent of calories, 85 per cent of proteins, 75 per cent of iron, 30 per cent of fats, 40 per cent of calcium, 15 per cent of vitamin A, 50 per cent of riboflavin, most of thiamine and niacene and some negligible per cent of vitamins C and D. Due to the absence or shortage of other sources of nutrients like milk, fruits, green vegetables, fish, eggs and meat, it is not a balanced food.

What constitutes a balanced diet for average Indian is still a debatable question. "Nutritional experts have collected basic data on ethnic, climatic, socio-economic and other considerations and have fixed norms for each type of person and for each type of activity. A sedentary worker requires less calories than a hard working woodcutter. A man living in colder regions naturally requires more calories than his brother in the tropics. Though the requirements may vary from individual to individual, they can certainly be fitted into a pattern of requirements for different regions and people and many variations warranted on individual considerations can be allowed according to circumstances" (see G. Borker).

The food items produced locally or regionally still have their influence on diet. This applies to both rural and urban areas. Some changes have however started taking place that may alter the food habits of the people. With the extension of irrigation facilities and universal availability of fertilizers, etc. wheat is being produced in rice growing areas like West Bengal and rice is produced in wheat dominant areas like Punjab. Moreover, with increasing urbanization people are getting exposed to a much greater variety of foods than they were earlier. The supply of subsidized food-grains through public distribution system is also changing food habit of the people. Nevertheless, the general pattern of diet continues to be geography specific.

Rice is the staple food in Kashmir valley (in the Himalaya), East UP, Bihar and West Bengal (in the lower reaches of the Ganga valley), Assam (in Brahmaputra valley), Orissa in (Mahanadi delta), coastal districts of Andhra Pradesh, Tamil Nadu, Kerala, Karnataka and Maharashtra, and the canal irrigated areas of Punjab and Central UP; wheat dominates in Punjab, Haryana, Delhi and West UP; and Jowar and Bajra in interior Maharashtra, Gujarat and Rajasthan. The pulses, supplemented by fish in the coastal areas and meat in the urban areas, are the main source of protein throughout the country. Egg, another source of protein, is now included as an essential item in the diet of at least 20-25 per cent of the people of India. Milk has always been a part of Indian dietary but the quantity of intake came down rather drastically during the twentieth century. Milk production in the country increased at an accelerated rate during the last three decades. After meeting its domestic requirements, India has started exporting milk products. This does not however mean that every Indian gets enough milk and milk products to meet his nutritional requirements. A large number of people do not have the income to buy milk and hence they remain deprived of it. That might be the reason why the country is able to export milk products.

Vegetables have always been important ingredients of Indian diet. There are over 100 varieties of vegetables in India – 40 varieties of leafy vegetables and 20 varieties of root vegetables and over 40 varieties of other vegetables. Green vegetables are a great source of carotene, vitamin C, calcium and phosphorus. Unfortunately, they are not very popular among the people. They are considered to be poor man's vegetables. Even the other vegetables do not get the importance they deserve partly because of poverty and partly because of the ignorance about their nutritional value. In this regard, the people living in rural areas and having cultivable lands are better off.

Which of various food items one should include in his diet? It is a question that cannot be answered definitively. But if natural principles and the biology of human body are any guide, one should prefer locally produced foods. This does not mean that one should be religious about it. Since humans and plants have always gone together, the biology of man must be tuned to the biology of plants. Man is after all 'son of the soil.' The second principle to be followed is that we must eat a balanced diet. Thirdly, we should eat only those foods, which can be easily digested. Fourthly, we should consume as much of raw foods as possible. And finally, we should not consume things that disturb the normal functioning of the digestive system such as liquors, intoxicant drugs, etc.

ACCESS TO FOOD IN INDIA

India is one of the major producers of food-grains, vegetables, fruits, milk and other animal products. It is also almost self-sufficient in most of these products if we look at self-sufficiency from actual demand and supply point of view. The county produces 210 million tonnes of food grains, 150 million tonnes of fruits, 85 million tonnes of vegetables, 70 million tonnes of milk, 28 billion eggs, and 5 million tonnes of fish. It ranks first in fruit production in the world accounting for 10 per cent of the world output and, second in vegetable production accounting for about 15 per cent of the world output. The above figures, however, become less impressive when seen against the total requirements of the country. India has 1.10 billion people and at least a quarter of this population is either poor or too ignorant of nutritional value of various foods to consume all the food items it needs. The country is nevertheless far better in food security today than it ever was during the last 200 years.

India's global position in regard to various food items gives a better idea of the needs and potentials of the country. Figures relate to the year 1997-98.

Global Food Production: 5000 m tonnes

98 per cent on land
  cereals 52 per cent
  animal products 20 per cent
  fruits, vegetables, fish 28 per cent
2 per cent from inland waters and oceans

Wheat: 550 m tones (world total):

52 per cent developed countries,
48 per cent developing countries
  China 96 m tones,
  USA 80 m tonnes,
  India 76 m tonnnes

Rice: 565 m tones (world total):

95 per cent developing countries
4 per cent developed countries
  China 180 m tonnes
  India 83 m tonnes
  Indonesia 50 m tonnes

Milk: 575 m. tones (world total)

India 74,5 m tonnes
USA 71 m tonnes
Russia 33 m tonnes

Fruits: 350 m tones (world total)

India 46 m tonnes
Brazil 36 m tonnes

Beef and Veal:

USA 11 million tonnes
Russia 5 m tonnes
Argentina 3 m tonnes

Vegetables: 400 m tones (world total)

China 97 m tonnes
India 71 m tonnes

Fish: 100 m tons (world total)

Japan 11 m tonnes
China 10 m tonnes
Russia 7 m tonnes
India 5 m tonnes (7th in the world)

Per capita availability of food-grains in India has consistently improved during the last 50 years. In 1951, the availability of cereals was 395 grams per head daily; now it stands at 450 grams per head daily. But the position with regard to the pulses, the main sources of protein in Indian diet, has deteriorated. Per capita daily availability stood at 60 grams in 1951; it came down to 33 grams in 1998. This is quite a disturbing trend. Unless the intake of other sources of nutrients such as milk and milk products, other animal products, fruits, vegetables, etc. increases correspondingly, the problem of mal-nourishment plaguing India for generations would remain unresolved. India is on the verge of attaining food security; but not nutritional security. To ensure that not a single individual goes without food and dies of hunger and malnourishment, India has a long way to go. So long there is poverty in the country, starvation deaths would be a common phenomenon, particularly in times of droughts, floods, earthquakes and other calamities, natural or manmade.

India's population has grown from 361 million in 1951 to 1100 million in 2001 i.e. three times. The food production in the same period has increased from 50.82 million tons to 210 million tonnes (in 2001) i.e. four times. It, however, appears to have reached a plateau unless scientists are able to usher in another green revolution by producing hybrid seed of rice. Another possibility to be explored is the genetically engineered quick maturing high yielding crops otherwise known as GM crops. So far, the food production in India increased because of four contributory factors: increase in area cultivated, increase in irrigated areas, introduction of high-yielding varieties of seeds, especially wheat and corn and increasing use of chemical fertilizers. The area under food-grains increased from 97.32 million hectares in 1951 to 125 million hectares in 1998. Production of food-grains increased by 4.8 per cent during 1951-61; 2.8 per cent during 1961-71; 1.8 per cent during 1971-81; 3.5 per cent during 1981-91; and 1.7 per cent during 1991-98. The 1981-91 period was the period of Green Revolution.

The decade of 1990s witnessed a downward or oscillating trend in food-grains production. This is a disturbing development as there is still a huge chunk of Indian population that is poorly fed. Moreover, our population is growing at the rate of about 1.8 per cent. It is likely to be 1.5 billion by 2040 or so. Even to maintain the present level of food consumption, India should produce at least 300 million tonnes of food gains to meet the growing needs. In fact, it should have a target of 400 million tonnes. In this connection, it should be noted that of the total production of food-grains, 12.5 per cent is deducted for reinvestment, wastage etc. Similarly, in case of fruits, vegetables, animal products, and other perishable food items, 37 per cent is deducted for wastage, etc. And then there are exports too. So all that is produced does not enter the consumer's basket.

While our agricultural production has gone up, the increase is not consistent. It is rather erratic. There are years of low production leading to shortage of some commodities and bringing the growth rate of Indian economy down. Indian agriculture is still very much dependent on the monsoon. Irrigation facilities have improved but a huge quantity of water is wasted. Water logging is leading to soil destruction, which ultimately tell on the overall production.

In the mad rush for industrialization on Soviet Union model, India neglected agriculture on which over 70 per cent of the people depended at the time of Independence in 1947. This neglect continued until about mid-1970 when Green Revolution was belatedly introduced in the country. India should have another look at it policy of agricultural and rural development to make frontal attack on poverty and malnutrition. Rural planning should become a necessary component of Indian planning system with great emphasis on agricultural resource development and introduction of both agribusiness and non-farm activities in rural areas. India may face a great challenge on the food front if it fails to stop the migration of youth from rural areas.

Let it be understood that India is not a land of rich resources inhabited by poor people. It is a land of poor resources inhabited by poor people. India must double its food production within the next decade or so. This is however possible only if its resources are conserved and further developed by necessary scientific and technological inputs. China with lesser land under cultivation produces nearly 400 million tonnes of cereals. Crop yields in India are really low. In 1995-96, per ha yield of rice was 1910 kg in India; it was 4178 kg. in China. Yield of maize was 1459 kg per ha in India; it is 4520 kg per ha in China. Per ha yield of wheat was 3734 kg in China as against 2553 kg in India. So the scope and potential to produce additional food-grains without bringing new land under cultivation does exist in India. This applies not only to food-grains but also to other items of food such as fruits, vegetables, animal products, etc. India produces 50 million tonnes of fruits. That gives only 80 grams per head per day. Total output of vegetables of various kinds amounts to 81 million tonnes i.e. only 125 gm per head per day (Table 15.3).

India's output of mills per annum is heighth in the world (Fig. 15.1).

Table 15.3: Availability and Requirements of Major Food Items

(per head per day)

Food Items	*Availability in 1951*	*Availability in 1998*	*Required (Vegetarian)*	*Required (Non–vegetarian)*
Cereals	395 gm	450 gm	450 gm	450 gm
Pulses	60 gm	33 gm	150 gm	100 gm
Edible oils*	3.2 kg	9 kg	12kg	10 kg
Sugar*	5 kg	15 kg	20 kg	20 kg
Fruits	–	80 gm	200 gm	150 gm
Vegetables	–	127 gm	200 gm	150 gm
Milk	124 gm	205 gm	250 gm	200 gm
Eggs*	–	26 per head	–	200 per head
Fish/meat		20 gm	–	100 gm

**Per head per annum availability/requirement.*
Source: Nutrition Foundation of India

Per capita energy requirement of an average Indian is 2400 calories. The WHO has recommended only 2110 calories but in view of the fact that two-thirds of Indian labourforce is still engaged in agriculture, a higher allowance to compensate for the strenuous work has been suggested. Even if the present rate of food-grains production continues in years ahead, India would be able to meet its food-grain requirements from within. There is however no reason why the country cannot increase its food production at the rate of 4 per cent per annum to produce enough surplus for export. While planning food production, India has to go for fruit, vegetable and milk production in a big way to meet its nutritional requirements adequately in years to come. With the declining production of pulses, country should plan for securing at least 30 per cent of the caloric requirements from proteins and fats. India already has a rich experience of organizing small and marginal farmers to put the country on the dairy map of the world. Anand cooperative venture is being followed elsewhere in the world. What is needed is the extension of this experiment to every village of the country.

Malnourishment in India

India is self-sufficient in food-grains but one-fifth of its population remains malnourished. Several intervening factors stand between availability in the market and availability in the households of consumers. Very poor people do not have the means to buy food. Even those who can meet their both ends meet, have social pressures to spend less on food and more on other real or perceived needs. Even poor people now tend to spend more on clothing, housing, entertainment, utensils, bicycles etc. to enhance their social status than on food.

During the early seventies, about 276 million people (47 per cent of the total population) consumed less than 2110 calories per day, which was the basic minimum recommended by the WHO. In the eighties, this percentage declined to about 25 per cent. Even now at the turn of

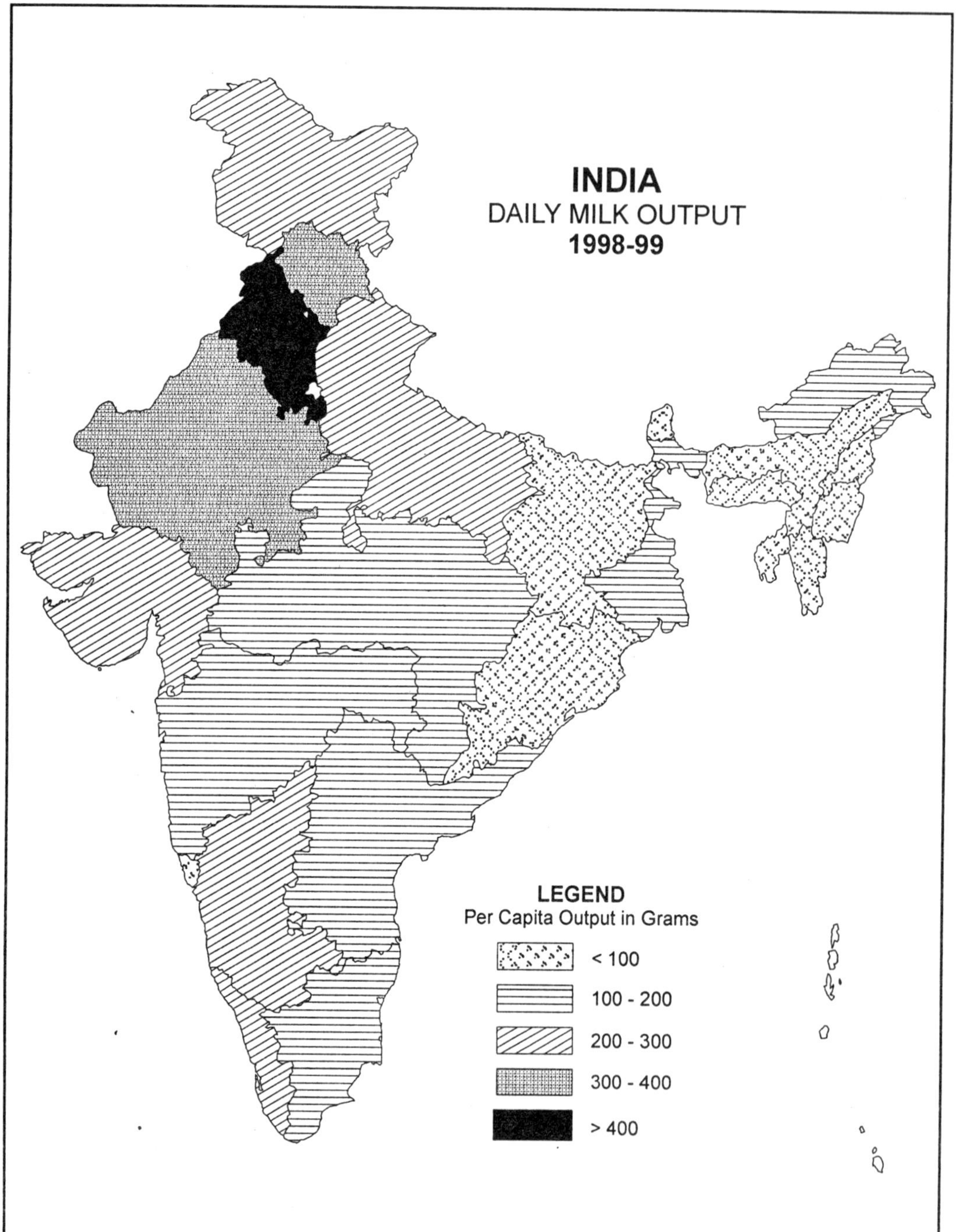

Fig. 15.1: Daily Milk Output in India

the twentieth century, the number of undernourished population has not declined even though the percentage has come down marginally. According to the surveys conducted by the National Institute of Nutrition, Hyderabad, about 40 per cent of the rural households in rural India does not meet their caloric requirements. The Thirty-eighth Round Survey conducted by the National Sample Survey (NSS) also gives the same results. (Vishwakarma) In states like Bihar and Orissa the situation is much worse.

Malnutrition among children and pregnant women is quite common in India. As given in Table 15.4, children in two-third of the households in the country suffer from calorie-protein malnutrition. If we take into account the other nutrients too, the percentage will increase further.

Table 15.4: Children with Calorie-Protein Deficiency in Selected States

(per cent households)

S. No.	*States*	*1975*	*1989*
1.	Kerala	65.50	62.80
2.	TN	37.60	65.30
3.	Karnataka	19.60	26.10
4.	Andhra Pradesh	38.60	36.70
5.	Maharashtra	45.30	48.50
6.	Gujarat	45.90	30.90
7.	Madhya Pradesh	26.40	19.20
8.	Orissa	36.00	27.50
	Average	38.50	40.40

Source: UNICEF, Children and Women in India, 1990.

Recent data show that almost 50 million children in the age group of 1-5 years get inadequate calories in their diet, the average deficit being as high as 350 calories. The main reason for it is the inability of mothers to breastfeed the babies and inadequate supplementary baby food after nine months of birth. In this connection, it has to be noted that there has been no appreciable improvement in the situation for the last 50 years. The same applies to maternal health. The body weight of a quarter of the women in the reproductive age group, places them in high-risk category. Remarkable improvement is possible in the nutritional status of mothers, foetus, and infants if the actual age of marriage of girls is raised to 18 years. Pregnant and nursing women need at least 300 additional calories per day, as their basal metabolic rate is higher by 10-20 per cent. Some surveys indicate three quarters of expectant mothers suffering from nutritional deficiencies and over 90 per cent were anemic requiring supplementary doses of minerals and vitamins.

NUTRITIONAL CONTENTS OF MAJOR FOODS

It would be useful to learn something about the nutritional contents of major foods commonly consumed in India. This would also help us identify the regions and people who might be exposed to deficiency diseases for most of the people eat what is locally produced. It would also help in planning diet reform.

Cereals constitute the bulk of the daily diet. Cereals contribute 70 to 80 per cent of the total energy and half of the protein intake. Since cereals are poor in proteins, pulses are traditionally used to make diet balanced in matter of proteins. Cereals provide about 350 kcal per 100 grams consumed.

Table 15.5 gives the energy and nutritive value of each of the cereals and pulses consumed in India.

Table 15.5: Nutritive Value of Cereals and Pulses (per 100 grams)

Food Items	*Energykcal*	*Protein (g)*	*Fats (g)*	*Carbo-hydrates (g)*	*Calcium (mg)*	*Iron (mg)*	*Thiamine (mg)*	*Ribofin (mg)*	*Niacin (mg)*
Cereals									
Rice	345	6.8	0.5	78.2	0.12	2.0	0.06	0.06	1.9
(milled)	346	11.81	1.5	71.2	25.0	4.1	0.45	0.17	5.0
Wheat	342	11.1	3.6	66.2	42.0	8.0	0.42	0.10	1.8
(whole)	349	10.4	1.9	72.6	344.0	3.9	0.3	1.3	3.5
Maize	361	11.6	5.0	67.5			0.3	0.25	2.3
Jowar	328	7.3	1.3	72.0			0.2	0.18	2.3
Bajra									
Ragi	360	17.1	5.3		202		0.3	0.15	2.9
Pulses	347	24.0	1.4		154		0.42	0.20	2.0
Bengal	335	22.3	1.7		73		0.45	0.19	2.9
gram	432	43.2	19.5		240		0.73	0.39	3.2
Black gram									
Red gram									
Soyabean									

Source: Gopalan, C. et. al. (1989). *Nutritive Value of Indian Foods*, Hyderabad: National Institute of Nutrition.

DEFICIENCY DISEASES IN INDIA

Diet of low caloric and nutritional value causes a number of diseases, especially among the children and expectant mothers. Apart from diseases, these deficiencies have serious implications for mental make up, thinking and attitude towards life and the world beyond. Malnourished people are dull, unwilling to exert, negative, short tempered, fearful and easy prey of various diseases. Nutritional surveys indicate that half of the children in India are malnourished. Retardation of growth – a direct result of protein deficiency – is quite a common symptom in Indian children. Anemia is the next most important deficiency disease that afflicts Indian children. It is caused by iron deficiency. Anemia of pregnancy is responsible for many maternal deaths. It is also responsible for many abnormal, premature and stillbirths.

Goitre is quite a common disease in the lower Himalaya and Terai districts of UP. It is caused by iodine deficiency. Night blindness, bitot spots, xerosis and keratomalacia caused by the deficiency of vitamin A are quite diseases in rural parts of the country, particularly among the pregnant women and old persons. Lack of thiamine (vitamin B1) causes cardiac and neuritic diseases; and that of B2 complex causes angular stomatitis, cheilosis, glossitin, nasolabial seborrhoea, anogenital syndrome and pellagra. Beriberi is common in areas where rice is the staple food and people prefer polished rice. Rickets caused by the lack of vitamin D is common all over the country. Iron deficiency is the main cause of anaemia. Deformed and softened bones are the indicators of the onset of this disease.

According to the WHO, 834 million people suffered from goiter in the world in 1995; and 3580 million suffered from iron deficiency. If the current programmes are continued, it is hoped that food security in the world would improve and by 2025, the number of persons suffering from goiter would decline to 350 million, and from iron deficiency to 2750 million.

Distribution of various deficiency diseases in India as in 1970 and 1998 is given in figure 15.2. The pattern has not changed since then, although intensity and morbidity has changed, hopefully for the better.

Vitamin A Deficiency (VAD)

Vitamin A deficiency produces ocular problems such as night-blindness, Bitot's spots, conjunctival and corneal xeroses, and keratomalacia. It is caused by unbalanced diet, frequent diarrhoea and dysentery leading to weakness, and general lack of health education. It can be controlled and treated by balanced diet rich in vitamin A and oral intake of vitamin A concentrates available in the market. The world over, 2.85 million people suffered from vitamin A deficiency in 1995.

The National Institute of Nutrition, Hyderabad has played a pioneering role in developing a community-based intervention against night-blindness which was so common in India until very recently. This method has now been adopted by many other developing countries of the world. The strategy is to administer a heavy dose of 100,000 IU vitamin A in edible oil orally every six months to children in the age group of 6 months to 1 year, and of 200,000 IU to children in the age-group of 1-6 years. It is highly effective in controlling even keratonalacia.

Night-blindness

The first and immediate effect of vitamin A deficiency is night-blindness i.e. inability to see in darkness. Children, pregnant and lactating mothers, and elderly are the common victims of this disease

Bitot's Spots

Bitot's spots are white or yellow spots on the sides of the cornea. When found in the eyes of the children, it should be taken as a sign of vitamin A deficiency.

Conjectival and Corneal Xerosis

In the case of conjunctival xerosis, the conjunctiva becomes dry, muddy and wrinkled. The corneal xerosis is far more serious a disease; it may end up in corneal ulceration

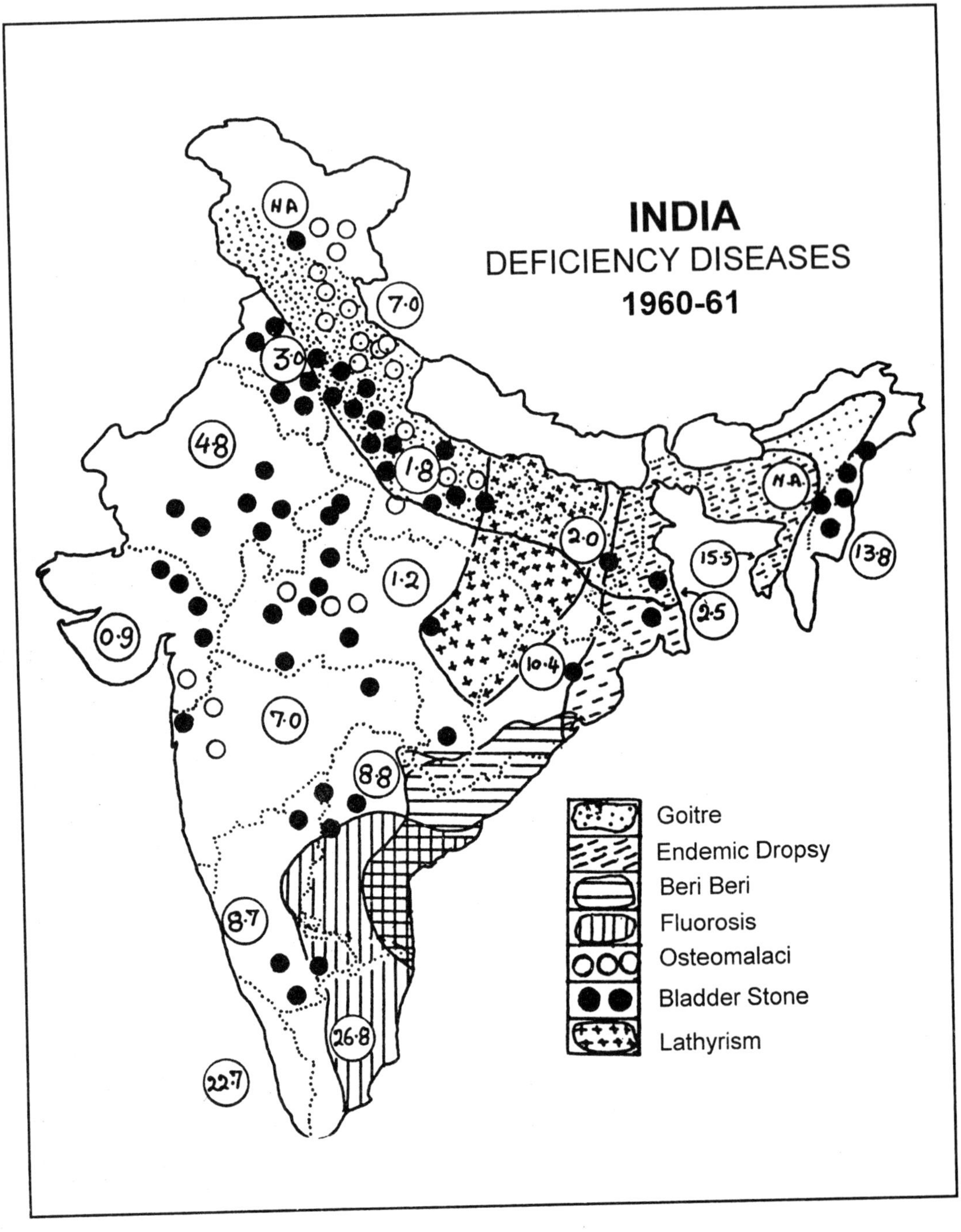

Fig. 15.2: India: Prevalence of Deficiency Diseases (1960-61)

Notes: Figures in circles show cases treated per 1000 population

Source: Reproduced from R.P. Misra, (1970) *Medical Geography of India*, National Book Trust of India, New Delhi.

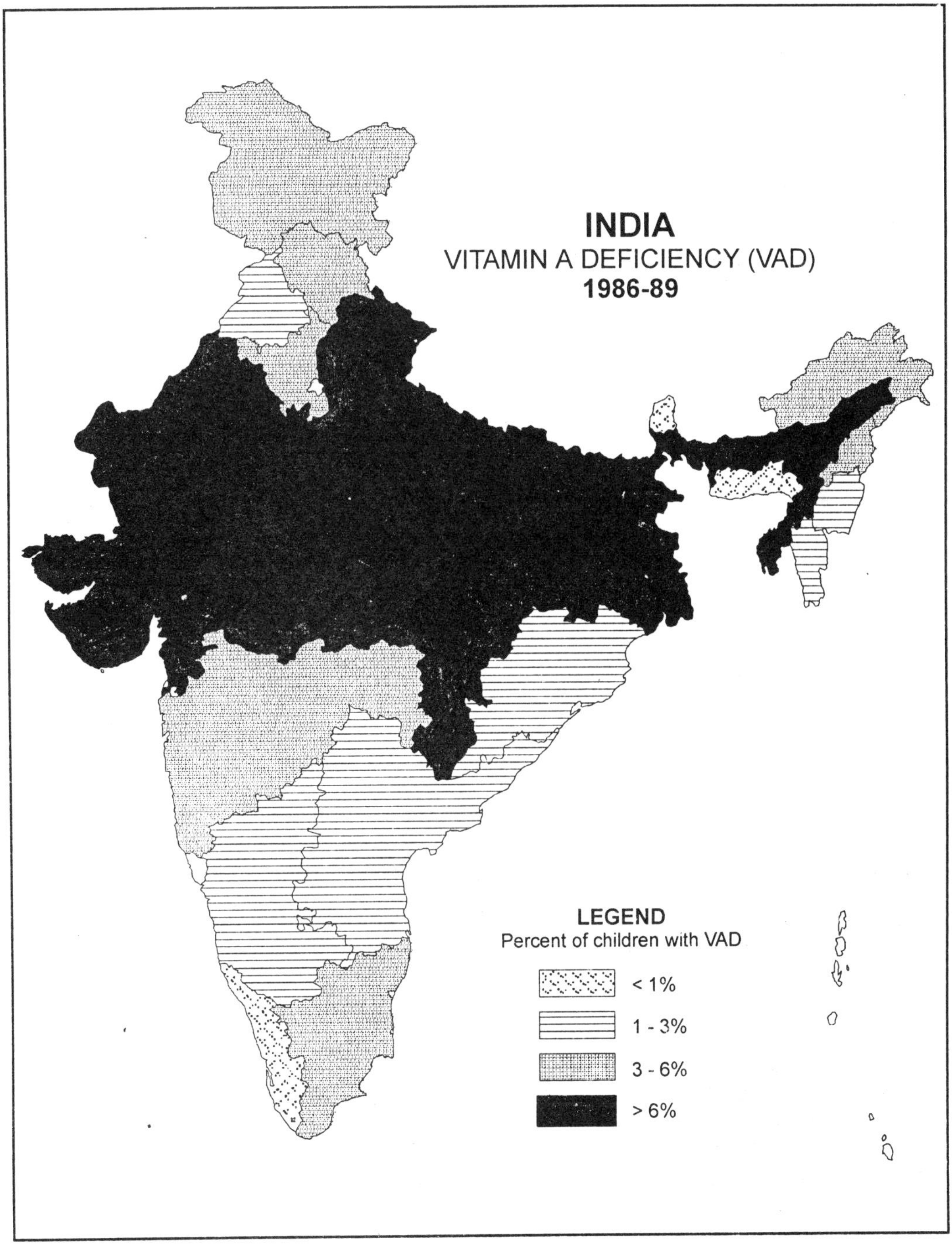

Fig. 15.3: India: Prevalence of Vitamin A Deficiency

Keratonalacia

It is a very serious disease. The cornea becomes soft; it may even burst open; the eye collapses and the vision is lost forever. Its causes are more complex. It occurs when vitamin A deficiency is combined with protein energy malnutrition.

Other Manifestations

Vitamin A deficiency retards growth. It also causes diseases like anorexia and follicular hyperkeratosis. It is linked to high child mortality and susceptibility to infectious diseases.

Geographic Prevalence

VAD is more common among the children and aged. According to the WHO, it is prevalent among the school going children all over the developing countries. In India, it is considered to be a public health problem. A nation-wide survey conducted in 1986-89 revealed that about 6 per cent of the children under six years of age were affected by VAD. State-wise prevalence rate is given in Table 15-6 and Figure 15.3.

A 1971-74 survey of blindness in India showed that VAD accounted for 0.30 per cent of all blindness. According to a similar survey in 1986-89, the percentage had declined to 0.04.

Table 15.6: Prevalence of Vitamin A Deficiency in India

	Group of States	*Per cent of blind*
Group I	Kerala, Meghalaya, Sikkim	Less than 1 per cent
Group II	Andhra Pradesh, Karnataka, Manipur, Orissa, Punjab, Chandigarh, Lakshadeep, Mizoram	1-3 per cent
Group III	Haryana, Himachal Pradesh, J & K, Maharashtra, Nagaland, Tamil Nadu, Arunachal Pradesh, Delhi, Goa, Pondicherry	3-6 per cent
Group IV	Assam, Bihar, Gujarat, MP, Rajasthan, Tripura, UP, West Bengal, Andaman & Nicobar Isls	More than 6 per cent

Thiamine (Vitamin B_1) Deficiency

It is water-soluble vitamin occurring in all natural foods. It helps in the utilization of carbohydrates. Thiamine deficiency leads to over occumulation of pyruvic and lactic in the tissues and blood.

Important sources of thiamine are cereals, whole grain cereals, pulses and nuts. Small quantity of thiamine can be derived from meat, eggs, vegetables and fruits also. In India, the main sources of thiamine are cereals (wheat and rice). They account for 60-70 per cent of thiamine intake.

The thiamine content of various foods are given in Table 15.7

Table 15.7: Thiamine Content of Various Foods

Foods	*Mg/100g*	*Foods*	*Mg/100g*
Gingelly seeds	1.01	Almonds	0.24
Ground nut	0.90	Unpolished rice	0.21
Bengal gram dal	0.48	Mutton	0.18
Whole wheat	0.45	Hen's egg	0.10
Liver of sheep	0.36	Polished rice/Cow milk	0.06/0.05

Thiamine, being water soluble, is easily lost in washing and cooking. This is specially the case with rice. Prolonged storage of fruits and vegetables destroys thiamine. Anything cooked with baking soda loses thiamine.

Beriberi is the main thiamine deficiency disease. Wernick's encephalopathy is also associated with thiamine deficiency. Beriberi is of three types. Type one, alled dry beriberi affects the nerves. The second, called wet beriberi affects the heart. And the last type called infantile affects babies of 2-4 month. Infantile variety is caused by milk of thiamine deficient mother. Wernick's encephaopathy is often found in alcoholics.

Beriberi was not uncommon in the coastal districts of Andhra Pradesh where people used to eat polished rice. It is now rare even there. The problem of thiamine deficiency has not however disappeared from the country. It is endemic and found to exist in milder forms in many parts of the country, especially among the poorer sections of the population.

Daily requirement of thiamine for an average person is 0.50 mg per 1000 kcals of energy intake.

Niacin Deficiency

Niacin, also known as nicotinic acid, is required in the metabolism of carbohydrates, protein and fat. It is also needed for normal functioning of skin, nerves and intestines. It differs from other vitamins of B complex group in two ways: an amino acid, tryptophan, acts as its precursor, and it is not excreted in urine. About 60 mg of tryptophan is required to produce one mg of niacin. It is an anti-Pellagra Vitamin B Complex.

The sources of niacin/tryptophan are groundnut, legumes, fish, poultry and meat. Milk is rich in tryptophan but relatively poor in niacin.

Niacin deficiency results in pellagra, a disease characterized by the Ds: diarrhoea, dermatitis, and dementia. Glossitis and stomatis are the other diseases associated with niacin deficiency.

Pellagra was once a very wide spread disease in areas where staple food was maize. It has practically disappeared from the world except some parts of Africa and West Asia. In India, it has been reported in Telangana region of Andhra Pradesh where Jowar is the staple food.

Pellagra is a disease related to poverty. It is a preventable disease. A mixed diet containing milk and/or meat cures the disease. A daily allowance of 6.60 mg/1000 kcal ensures immunity from pellagra.

Vitamin B_{12} Deficiency

It is a complex organic-cum-metallic compound having cobalt atom. It helps in the synthesis of DNA and fatty acids. It is not found in foods of vegetable origin. Its main sources are milk and milk products, fish, eggs, poultry and meats. Lever is the main storage site for this vitamin. It is heat stable and its deficiency is not common.

Pernicious anaemia (megaloblastic anaemia) is the most important B12 deficiency disease. Vegetarians should be careful about their diet; they should supplement their diet with animal products.

ICMR recommends a daily intake of 1 to 1.5 mcg for adults and 0.20 mcg for infants and children.

Vitamin B_2 Deficiency

Also known as Riboflavin, vitamin B_2 is a co-factor in several enzymes involved in energy metabolism. It is found in milk and milk products, leafy vegetables, eggs and meats. In India, the main source of riboflavin is cereals. Although cereals contain very little of this vitamin, when consumed in bulk, they provide enough to meet body's requirements. Sprouted cereals and pulses contain good quantity of riboflavin.

Riboflavin deficiency or ariboflavinosis is quite common in those parts of India where rice is the staple food. Angular stomatitis, which is so common in malnourished children, is associated with riboflavin deficiency. According to the estimates of the National Institute of Nutrition in India, about 80 per cent of children coming from poorer sections of the society suffer from riboflavin deficiency. It invariably occurs with deficiency of other B-complex vitamins. An average person needs about 0.60 mg per 1000 kcal energy consumed.

Vitamin B_6 Deficiency

This vitamin exists in three forms: pyridoxine, pyridoxal and pyridoxamine. It is important for the metabolism of carbohydrates, fats and amino acids. Present in practically every food we eat. Adults need about 2-2.50 mg/day.

Vitamin C Deficiency

Vitamin C facilitates the absorption of iron from vegetables by converting ferric iron into ferrous iron. It needed in the formation of collagen, which accounts for 25 per cent of total body protein. Collagen supports blood vessels, bones and connective tissues. In case of shortage of this vitamin, bone fractures and local haemorrhages are common occurrences.

The main sources of vitamin C are fruits and green vegetables. Sprouted pulses are also good source. One gets very little of this vitamin from cereals and only a bit more from meats of various kinds. Amla and guavas are excellent sources of vitamin C; they are found in plenty and are inexpensive. Mango carnel and Jamun are good sources of vitamin C.

The dietary sources of vitamin C are given in Table 15.8.

Table 15.8: Dietary Sources of Vitamin C (mg per 100 g)

Fruits	*mg*	*Vegetables*	*mg*
Amla	600	Cabbage	124
Guava	212	Amaranth	99
Lime	63	Cauliflower	56
Orange	30	Spinach	28
Tomato	27	Potatoes	17
Germinated pulses	16	Raddish/Brinjal	15/12

Deficiency of vitamin C leads to scurvy with symptoms of swollen and bleeding gums, delayed healing of wounds, subcutaneous bleeding or bruising anaemia and general weakness. It is no longer a major health hazard anywhere in the world. Normal human body contains about 5 g of vitamin C.

Vitamin D Deficiency

Vitamin D comes to human body in two forms: vitamin D_2 (calciferol) and vitamin D_3 (cholecalciferol. The former is derived from irradiation of plant sterol, ergosterol, while the latter can be derived from ultraviolet rays of the sun, which converts the cholesterol in the skin into vitamin D. Animal fats and fish oils are other sources. Vitamin D is largely stored in the fat deposits.

In tropical countries like India, vitamin D need not be a dietary requirement. Body can get all the requirements of vitamin D if exposed to sunlight even for 5 minutes daily. In the recent past questions have been raised on vitamin D being a vitamin at all because it cannot be obtained from dietary means. It is now treated as a hormone of the kidney.

Vitamin D is stored in the fatty tissues and in the lever. An excessive intake can prove harmful and produce vomiting, thirst, drowsiness, and nausea. Administration of D vitamin in excess of requirement is therefore counterproductive. Daily requirement for adults is 100 IU, for infants and children about 200 IU and for pregnant and lactating mothers about 400 IU (1 IU = 0.025 micrograms).

Ricket

Ricket is the most important vitamin D deficiency disease. It attacks children in the age group of 6 months to 2 years. Reduced calcification of the bones is the most important sign of it. It is characterized by growth failure, bone deformity, muscular hypotonia, tetany and convulsions due to hypocalcemia. Increase in the concentration of alkaline phosphate in the serum is also common.

Ricket is on the decline all over the world, particularly because of the expansion of child and mother health services and also because of improvements in living conditions of the women.

Osteomalacia

It is disease of vitamin D deficiency that affects adults, particularly the pregnant and lactating mothers. Osteomalacia is not uncommon in India but not to the extent that it poses a public health problem.

Vitamin E Deficiency

Vitamin E is represents a group of closely related fat-soluble compounds called tocopherols. It occurs naturally and is distributed widely in foods. Edible oils, butter, egg yolk and meat are the important sources. It is one of the least understood vitamins in so far as its role in human metabolism and health is concerned. Its shortage leads to peripheral neuritis. Tuberculosis patients receiving INH are also given vitamin E injection because INH is antagonist of the vitamin.

Vitamin K Deficiency

Vitamin K stimulates the production and release of certain coagulation factors in the blood. In the or shortage of this vitamin, prothrombin in the blood is reduced and the blood clotting time is prolonged. This leads to excessive and prolonged bleeding in the event of injuries.

Vitamin K is stored in the lever. It is of two types: K_1 and K_2. K_1 is derived from fresh green vegetables, some fruits, and cow milk. K_2 is synthesized in the intestine by bacteria. Over use of antibiotics can stop the intestinal production of vitamin K_2. This may lead to vitamin K_2 deficiency.

Newly born infants are deficient in vitamin K because prothrombin at birth is stored in minimal quantity. Soon after birth infants should be administered a single intramuscular dose of a vitamin K preparation.

Iron Deficiency

An adult human body contains only 3-4 g of iron. Since iron circulates and recycles in the body only a small amount is needed. Iron requirement is more in childhood, adolescence and

Table 15.9: Haemoglobin Levels Prescribed by WHO

Individuals	*g/dl*	*Requirement per day in mg*
Adult male	13	0.9
Adult female	11	
Menstruation		2.80
Pregnancy		0.80
First half		3.50
Second half		2.40
Lactation		0.70
Post-menopause		
Infants (5-12 months)		0.70
Children (6month-6yrs)	11	
(1-12 years)		1.00
Children 6-14 years	12	
Adolescents (13-16 years)		
Males		1.80
Females		2.40

Source: WHO (1968) Technical Report Series, No. 405 SK Sood and U. Rusia. (1986). *Annals National Acad. of Med. Sciences, India.* 22 (4), p. 235.

pregnancy. WHO has prescribed certain amount of haemoglobin in the blood to remain healthy (Table 15.9). It could be a case of anaemia, it falls below the prescribed level.

Iron is lost through excretion etc and haemorrhage. It varies from 1mg to 2mg per day. Iron deficiency leads to anaemia, which in essence is not a disease. Anaemic persons feels week and withdrawn; his immunity against infection is impaired.

Iodine Deficiency

Iodine is essential for normal growth and development of human body. It synthesizes triodothyrine (T_3) and thyroxine (T_4), the two thyroid harmones. They respectively contain 3 and 4 atoms of iodine. An adult body contains about 50 mg of iodine. Iodine deficiency occurs because of the presence of substances in foods, which interfere with the utilization of iodine. They are called goitrogens because they produce goiter. Some of the vegetables like cauliflower and cabbage also contain goitrogens. Recent studies indicate that iodine deficiency can result in a number of other disabilities including physical and mental retardation. That is why the term 'endemic goitre' has been replaced by 'iodine deficiency disorder' (IDD).

In view of the wider ramifications of IDD, a national programme for its control is already on in India. Figure 15.4 gives the endemic areas of IDD in India.

Fluorine Deficiency

Fluorine is the most abundant substance in nature. About 96 per cent of fluoride is concentrated in bones and teeth. It mineralizes the bones and gives enamels to the teeth. The source of fluorine drinking water but it occurs in traces in some foods, particularly the sea foods, also. Normal water contains about 0.50 mg/L of fluorine. If the level of fluorine is high in the water, it gives rise to skeletal and dental fluorosis. Some of fluorosis endemic areas in India contain 3 to 12 mg of fluorine per liter of drinking water. Goitre is the most obvious symptom as well as result of fluorine deficiency or should we say excess.

Other Mineral Deficiencies

Most human diets provide enough of other minerals but due to special circumstances shortages of minerals like calcium, zinc, copper, cobalt, chromium and molybendinum, even if needed in very minute quantities, do have effects on the growth, functioning and development of the body.

WOULD GM FOODS HELP?

To improve access to food, Green Revolution was ushered in the 1950s and 60s. It involved a combination of food production practices specially improved variety of (hybrid) seeds of wheat and maize, chemical fertilizers and irrigation. It was possible to tide over food deficiency in newly independent countries like India. As population grew, the demand for food increased. Many countries in Africa and elsewhere could not cope with the problems. Moreover, the

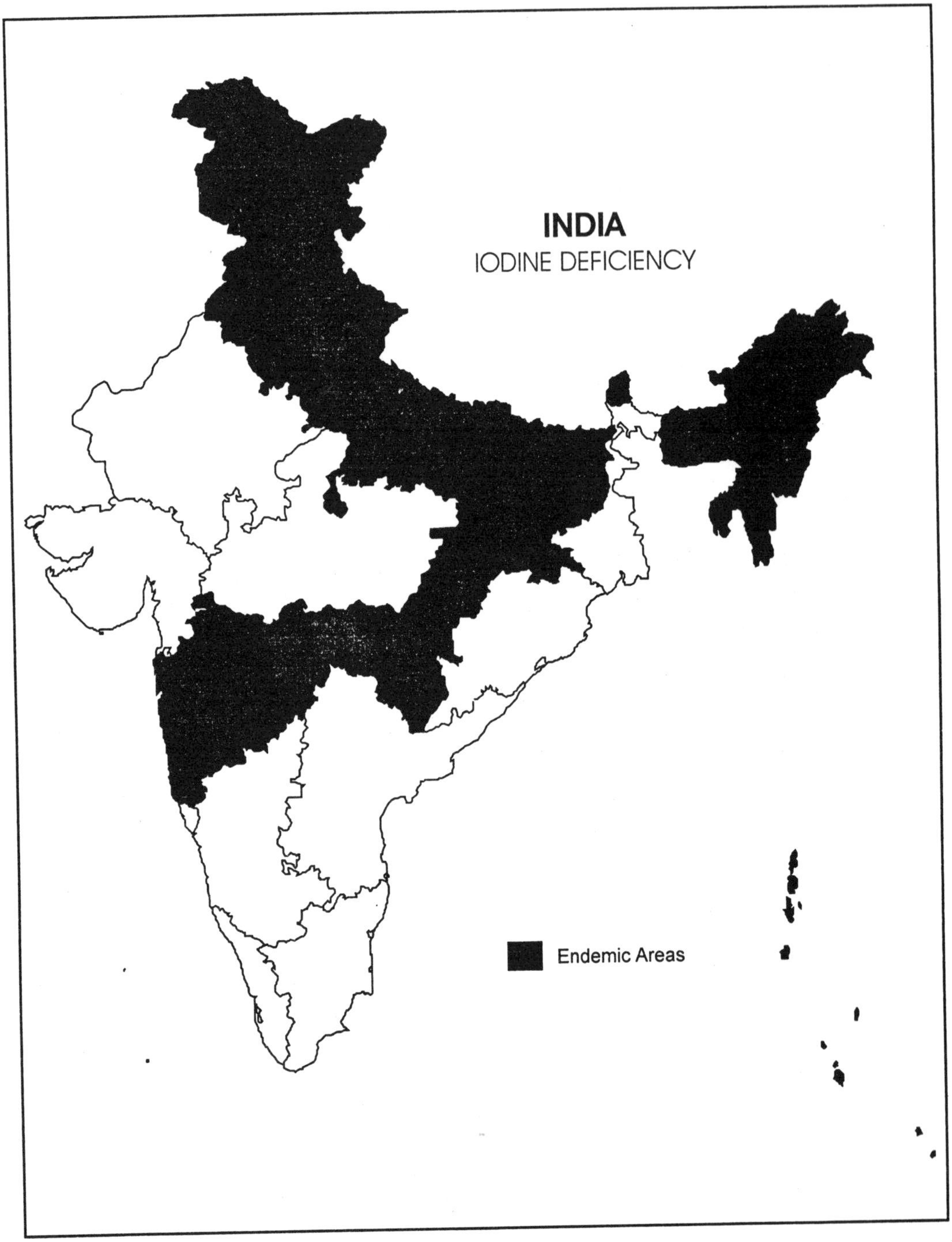

Fig. 15.4: India: Endemic Iodine Deficiency Areas

increase in food production could resolve only one problem i.e. to reduce or eliminate the under-nutrition (quantitative shortage of food). It could not eliminate malnutrition in densely populated countries of Asia and thinky populated by agriculturally backward countries of Africa.

In the 1990s, the scientific advances in the field of biotechnology opened up new opportunities to produce foods and other products having required nutritional and other contents. Commonly known as genetically modified food (GM) foods. They are produced by recombinant DNA (rDNA) techniques and are also known as transgenic or biotech foods. The traits of the plants The plant traits which are modified are: increase in yield, herbicide and insect tolerance; viral fungal and bacterial resistance, time of ripening, change in oil and fat contents and improvement in nutritive values.

The production of GM plants is growing fast. During the last four years, the world production has gone up by twenty times. USA, Canada and Argentina are the leading countries. Maize, Soybean, cotton and rapeseed are the major crops, which have been genetically modified. The technique would cover the other crops too if it is assured that it would have no adverse effect on health. There is significant public opinion against the adoption of GM plants. It is perceived, not unreasonably, that risks involved in the insertion of genes and their expression products could be serious for human health. The effects of the inserted genes and the proteins they produce is unknown. The promoter and terminator elements required in the genetic modification process are derived from various viral and bacterial genes whose effects are still unknown. The possibility of various antibiotic resistance genes used as markers in the production of GM plants entering the human gut microflora cannot be ruled out. Allergenic potentials of the transgenic proteins have yet to be determined.

GM foods are considered to be suitable for human use if they prove to be equivalent to the conventional foods in three respects, they are considered safe for use.

1. chemical content,
2. allergenity, and
3. nutritive composition

This is, however, not considered as sufficient ground for accepting GM foods as safe by many countries and, therefore, no international consensus has been arrived at and the doubts about the efficacy of these foods for human health continue unabated all over the world.

Given the doubts about GM foods, the question of regulating their use and sale has been debated at many a forums. In the USA, Japan and Europe GM foods are sold in both whole and processed forms. Polymerase Chain Reaction (PCR) techniques is used to detects the inserted alien DNA sequences and immunoassay methods is used to detect the proteins. The Food and Drug Administration (FDA) in the US regulated only the GM plants using the above three criteria. The products derived from these plants are not regulated. The EU, on the other hand, regulation of GM foods is process based.

In India, the department of Biotechnology has issued Guidelines for Research in Transgenic plants. Under these guidelines, appropriate rules and procedures are adopted to handle Genetically Modified Organisms (GMO). The Institutional Biosafety Committee (ISBC) and the Review Committee on Genetic Manipulation (RCGM) look into any proposal of the governmental or private institution to develop rDNA products. GM foods are not yet approved for sale in India.

There is growing resistance to the introduction of GM plants from environmentalists, ecologists and health specialists. While it is true that increase in food production would reduce malnutrition in developing countries and thus improve welfare and reduce expenditure on health, the genetic modification process involves gene transplantation, which may prove dangerous for health in the long run. The process takes the following form. First the gene coding for specific characteristics is identified where it occurs naturally and then transferred to another species where the desired characteristic is required. The selected gene is spliced from one organism and introduced into another by means of carrier that is frequently a viral vector. The vector having the selected gene is then multiplied in bacterial cells to obtain many copies of the transformed gene. This vector DNA is then introduced into the cell of the host plant with the help of agrobacterium tumefaciens as the carrier.

It is obvious that that the gene is introduced into the plant cell in a transformed state which contains the various genetic elements as promoters and terminators necessary for the expression and function of the inserted gene. Most of these elements are derived from viral sources. It is possible that these elements may promote over-expression of genes and induce cancer. Another matter of major concern is the effect of GM plants on the immune system of the people consuming it. Insertion genes that code for novel proteins, not found in traditional foods, may result in increased allergic reactions.

What is needed is rigorous testing of GM plants and foods derived there from before they are introduced in the market. There is, however, no doubt that the GM foods have the potentials to eradicate hunger and malnutrition from the world. The 'golden rice' being developed can revolutionize the whole nutritional situation for the better especially in Asia. It will wipe oit vitamin A deficiency within no time. Similarly rapeseed with b-carotene gene can replace vitamin A even if used in small quantity. Because of its potentials to remove under and malnutrition countries like India and China are taking keen interest in GM foods. But there are lingering doubts about their long-term implications for health of the people.

CONCLUDING REMARKS

It is quite clear that healthy life without healthy food is just not possible. And healthy food is one that gives all the calories and nutrients human body needs, apart from being clean and easily digestible. India is almost self-sufficient in cereals but is short of pulses, fruits, vegetables, milk and other animal products. This does not, however, mean that all the people get enough energy to lead a healthy life. There are several constraints that keep at least one fifth of the total population of India under-nourished. First, income level of the people is so low that they cannot afford to purchase enough cereals to meet their caloric requirements. Second, the cooking of food in India involves frying; it destroys many of the nutrients raw foods have. Third, people do not give importance to timely and regular food intake. And last, because of ignorance a good number of people prefer to spend money on medicines that cure diseases than on foods that prevent diseases.

The number of people who suffer from malnutrition is far more than that in the grips of under-nutrition. Here again, it is not so much the lack of nutritive food but the ignorance about the diet that is the main cause of this problem. Fruits, vegetables, milk and other nutritive foods are not taken as necessary ingredients of balanced diet, but as luxuries. They are not taken occasionally and in variable quantities. If people are alive of the need to supplement their caloric intake by proteins, fats, calcium, minerals, iron and vitamins, the demand for fruits, vegetables and dairy products will go up. The farmers will respond positively as they have done near the urban centres and there will be enough supply of these supplementary food items. Poor health education, apart from poverty and unhealthy practices, are the major causes of mal-nourishment in India.

Increasing Food Demand

India has enough land and water resources to produce twice the food it produces at present with just a slight improvement in the agricultural technology, resource management and education. It is tragic that in a rural country like India, there is no trace of rural planning. The village setting is anti-developmental and the rural development administration is so corrupt and ineffective that it cannot usher in any new improvements in rural life including agricultural development. The time has come for a freh thinking on rural development. Some fifty years back, Community Development and Extension Service was introduced in the country. It has now degenerated into a self-serving revenue service. India should now launch a new programme of rural reconstruction drawing from Gandhian praxis on the one hand, and the emerging nuances of physical planning, resource management and technological developments, on the other hand.

Change in Food Habits

Some recent developments in the field of health and medicine call for a change in our food habits. There is a growing belief that vegetarian food is better for health. Should people be vegetarians? Without entering into the ethical issue surrounding vegetarianism; we must stress here that human physiology is not designed for meat eating. Man has started eating meat in the primitive stages of his evolution. Then he was to a great extend only an improved animal. Researchers have linked non-vegetarian foods to many diseases. The evidence, even though inconclusive, is strong and recurring. Fats derived from edible oils and animal products like milk, eggs, fish and red meat, in the absence of adequate exercise of the body, have become major killers. Problems of overweight, coronary diseases leading to heart failure, cerebral hamoerrahge and a number of other diseases are traced to fatty foods. Sugar is another bad element in our food. Over consumption of it leads to diabetes, a disease that is incurable. In reality the problem does not lie in the fats or sugars; it lies in the absence of corresponding amount of manual work or exercise to digest them. Since in this era of instant foods and medicines, it is not possible to convince people to do hard work or to exercise, doctors suggest reduction in the intake of foods containing fats and sugars.

In spite of the great advances in the field of biological sciences, particularly the medical sciences the number and severity of diseases are on the increase. It is being realized that the root cause of these diseases is the environment, both external and internal, in which human body functions. The pollution of air, water, sound and foods eaten is taking a heavy toll of life. The internal metabolism of the body is also disturbed. The food taken by the people is not balanced. Many nutrients are absent or over eaten. The style of life people lead has its own implications for health. Hard manual work requires foods rich in fats and proteins apart from calories. A sedentary worker has to have a balanced light food.

While discussing nutrients, we tend to ignore the role that the enzymes play in human health. We cannot live without enzymes; they are the body's labour force. Metabolic enzymes keep our body system in order. They break down everything we eat to make the nutrition present in the food available to the body. If they are not functioning, we will not get nutrients from the food we eat. The basic sources of enzymes are the foods that are not cooked. Cooking in any form destroys the enzymes. Diet that is short of enzymes can produce such symptoms as gas, bloating, irritable bowel syndrome, tiredness, diverticulitis, allergies, headaches, and even fertility problems. Eating more fruits and green vegetables do help but they must be supplemented by 'living foods' like millet, alfalfa, green barley grass, parsley, flax seeds, sea weeds like dulse and nori, stevia or honey leaf, sunflower oil, and wild blue green algae. They are unknown and unpopular but their presence in the food is enough to digest anything one eats. The sprouted seeds of alfalfa, moong, gram, wheat, groundnut etc. offer good amount of enzymes.

Adverse Effects of Factory Farming

Factory farming, especially in the field of animal husbandry has appreciably increased productivity, but there are apparent signs of dangers emanating from it. Poultry and cows kept in stressful conditions and slaughtered in a manner that is neither nor human, have given rise to diseases like meningitis, dysentery and wasting syndrome in many European counties. The animals are dozed with powerful antibiotic drugs which can create super bugs with potentialities to wipe out the whole humanity in a bid to keep themselves alive. The horrendous conditions in which the animals are kept before they are slaughtered is indeed appalling. If the psychological and environmental conditions have effect on the body, then the meat that comes out of such animals cannot be suited to humans.

The Effects of GM Food

GM foods hold out a great future in so far as food security is concerned but as noted in this chapter one has to move cautiously lest the very existence of man on planet earth is endangered. While being cautious, India should not lag behind in further research in biotechnology involving genetic engineering.

REFERENCES

1. Planning Commission, Government of India, *Ninth and Tenth Five Year Plans.*
2. Government of India, *Health Statistics of India*, 1998.

3. Anon, 'Scientists Back GM for Third World', *Nature,* 406, 2000, pp. 115.
4. Conner, A.J. and Jacobs, M.E., 'Food Risks from Transgenic Crops in Perspectives', *Nutrition,* 16 2000, pp. 709-711.
5. Government of India, Ministry of Agriculture, *Annual Reports.*
6. Indian Council for Agricultural Research, *Annual Reports.*
7. Misra, R.P. (ed) *Contributions to Indian Geography, Vol. Agricultural Geography of India by (V.P. Subramaniam),* New Delhi: Heritage, 1994.
8. *Ibid, Vols. 3: General Climatology by* V.P. Subramaniam, New Delhi: Heritage, 1993. See also his Vol 4: *Applied Climatology.*
9. Brahmananda, P.R., *Fifty Years of Free India's Economy,* New Delhi: Indian Economic Association Trust for Research and Development, Habitat Centre, 1997.
10. ——, *Planning for a Wage-Goods Economy,* New Delhi: Indian Economic Association Trust for Research and Development, Habitat Centre, 1995.

16

Maternal Health

Three sections of the society, women, children and aged, need specialized health care facilities. Women suffer from reproductive health problems; men do not. The children are tender and innocent; they cannot cope with their health problems without outside support. And the elderly suffer from a weakened physiological system; they too need support and understanding. All the three need specialists who can understand their problems and treat them appropriately. They also need special facilities for treatment. In this and the following two chapters, we would discuss the health problems of these sections of the society.

Maternal health can be taken as a proxy for the health of a people in general. To a great extent, children's health depends on mother's health. A sick and famished mother can rarely, if ever, raise healthy children. A society that has unhealthy children must be a sick society. It's future cannot be a rosy one. Hinduism, the dominant religion of India, lays great stress on the well being of women. "God resides where women are worshipped.' But in actual practice, the situation is other way round. Women suffer from many disabilities. Physiologically, they are less prone to diseases but social and environmental conditions in which they grow from early childhood make them easy prey of many a disease. The diseases that afflict human beings in general afflict women too. Pregnancy and maternity related diseases are, however, peculiar to them.

FEMALE MORTALITY

High rate of female mortality is a matter of great concern all over the world. High rates of female deaths in the reproductive age group are largely accounted by high rates of maternal mortality. A single pregnancy consumes about 60,000 kcal of energy over and above the normal metabolic requirements. Lactation demands about 550 kcal a day. If the mother fails to get additional nutrition to meet the above demands, she becomes malnourished and vulnerable all kinds of diseases.

Maternal mortality rate in India is 408 per 100,000 live births. This amounts to more than 4 million female deaths due to pregnancy related causes each year. Two factors account for most of these deaths: malnutrition among the pregnant women and large number of deliveries unattended by trained personnel. Lack of adequate referral facilities to provide emergency obstetric care for complicated cases is also an important contributory factor.

According to the annual survey of causes of death conducted by the Registrar General of India in rural areas, the most important cause of female mortality in the reproductive age group is venomous animal contact (Table 16.1). This problem is more serious in rural than urban areas. Eighteen per cent of all female deaths, in 1997, were accounted by this group of causes. Next in importance were: infectious and parasitic diseases (15.1 per cent), diseases of circulatory system (11 per cent), and pregnancy, childbirth, and peurperium (9.3 per cent). Among the other important causes were neoplasm, injuries, and poisoning.

Table 16.1: Female (15-44 years) Mortality: by Major Cause-groups, 1997

ICDCodes	*Major Causes of Death*	*Percentage*	
		1996	*1997*
X	With venomous animal contact	17.3	18.0
A	Infectious and parasitic diseases	16.9	15.1
I	Diseases of circulatory system	10.2	11.0
O	Pregnancy, childbirth and peurperium	9.2	9.3
T	Injuries, poisoning & external causes	7.0	7.4
C	Neoplasm	5.7	6.8
R	Symptoms, signs and abnormal clinical causes not elsewhere mentioned	7.1	6.7
J	Diseases of the respiratory system	6.2	5.0
D	Diseases of the blood and blood forming organs	4.6	4.3
G	Inflamatory diseases of the central nervous system	4.4	3.7
B	Viral infection	5.0	3.6
V	External causes of mortality	1.8	3.3
K	Diseases of the digestive system	1.8	2.3
F	Mental and behavioral disorders	0.9	1.3
N	Diseases of the genitourinary system	0.7	0.8
W	Other external causes of accidental injuries	0.7	0.8
E	Metabolic diseases	0.5	0.6
	Total Deaths	100	100

Source: Registrar General of India, *Survey of Causes of Death (Rural)*, 1997.

Female mortality attributed to top ten causes in the reproductive age group, as given in Table 16.2, adds to 56.3 per cent of all female deaths. Suicide is the top killer in AP, Gujarat, Kerala, Orissa and TN, while TB of the lung is the predominant killer in Bihar, MP and Rajasthan. In Haryana and Karnataka, cancer is the top killer accounting for 20.5 and 13.2 per cent of all deaths in this category. Heart attack in UP and Punjab and burns in Maharashtra are the top killers.

T.B. of lung is the second major killer disease at the national level, followed by cancer, heart attack, burns, anaemia, vehicular accidents, acute abdomen, bronchitis and Asthma and puerperium. The percentage given for each disease is not the same for all age groups. For example, suicide is most common in the age group 15-34 (82 per cent); while TB of lung in the age group 25-44 (85 per cent). All other diseases follow the same pattern. A medical geographer should examine these data in details with respect to region and age group to arrive at any conclusion on why the intensity of the diseases vary from region to region.

Female morality is very high in the states of Bihar, MP, Rajasthan and UP, relatively low in Gujarat and fairly low in the states of Haryana, Andhra Pradesh, Karnataka, Kerala, Maharashtra, Punjab and Tamil Nadu. Surprisingly, it is moderately low in the states of Assam, Orissa and West Bengal (see Tables 16.2 and 16.3 and Figure 16.1). It will be useful to correlate mortality data with the access to health facilities. The states, where mortality is high, are also known for poor accessibility to the health facilities.

Table 16.2: Top Ten Killers of Females in Reproductive Age-group: Major States, 1997

States	*Suicide*	*TB of Lung*	*Cancer*	*Heart Attack*	*Burns*	*Ana-emia*	*Veh. Acciden ts*	*Acu. Abdo.*	*Bron.& Asthma*	*Pauperi sm*	*Total*
ICD	X 60-84	A-15	C 00-97	I 21-25	T 20-32	D 50-64	V 1-90	R 10	J 20-45	O 10	
INDIA	111	94	67	66	65	42	33	31	31	24	563
Andhra Pradesh	148	71	79	93	79	08	29	37	29	03	577
Bihar	16	114	16	65	33	89	00	89	65	73	561
Gujarat	146	104	63	73	83	10	42	21	10	00	552
Haryana	115	64	205	128	77	00	64	13	26	00	692
Karnataka	186	23	140	140	23	23	47	00	00	00	581
Kerala	124	124	132	74	41	25	33	08	25	25	612
Maharashtra	38	14	38	44	31	74	13	32	42	38	490
Madhya Pradesh	57	90	70	20	152	35	27	25	45	20	541
Orissa	84	76	34	17	34	50	00	50	50	45	440
Punjab	56	11	44	267	44	22	00	22	33	14	513
Rajasthan	14	128	64	00	99	35	72	14	28	36	490
Tamil Nadu	371	38	45	22	24	48	17	19	19	12	615
Uttar Pradesh	230	165	34	50	55	52	18	45	31	26	706

Source: Registrar General of India, Survey of Causes of Death, 1997

CAUSES OF HIGH RATE OF MATERNAL DEATH

While discussing the causes of maternal deaths in India, it would be useful to take a global look first. According to data given by the WHO, 25 per cent of maternal deaths the world over were caused by severe bleeding. Toxaemia accounted for 15 per cent. The figures for India were 29 and 18 per cent respectively in 1995. Figure 16.1 gives the comparative picture of global and Indian situation in regard to maternal health.

Causes of Material Deaths: World

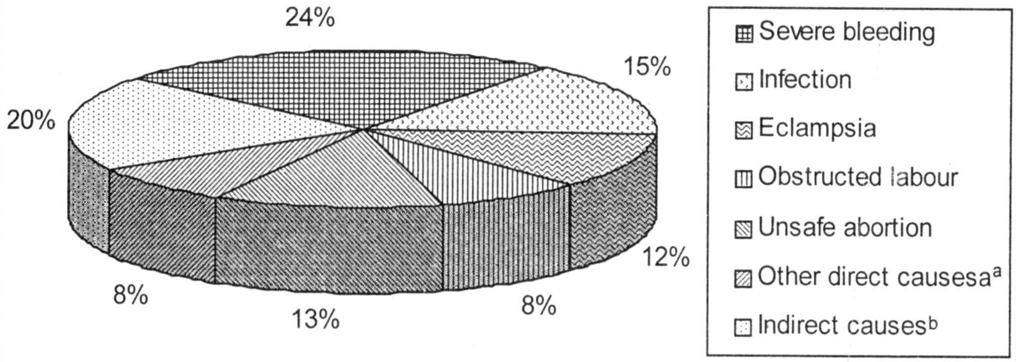

[a] Other direct caused including, for example: ecotopic pregnancy, embolism, anaesthesia-related.

[b] Indirect causes including. For example: Anamia, malaria, heart diseases.

Source: World Health Report, 1998.

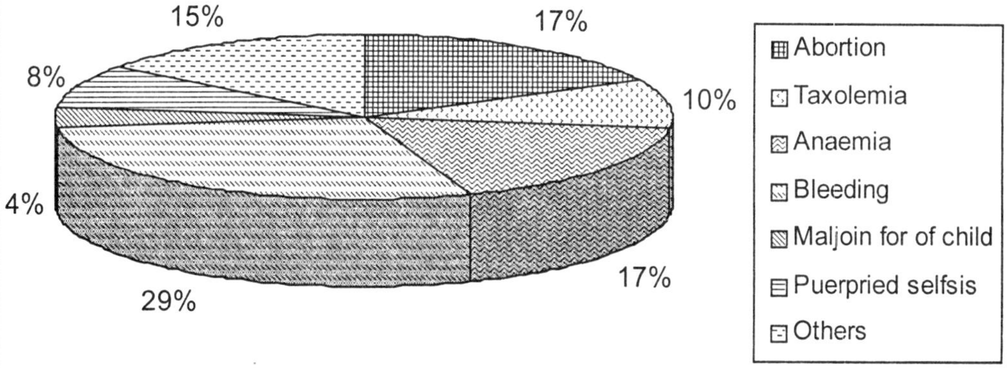

Fig. 16.1: India: Causes of Maternal Deaths.

Source: Health Infulormation of India, 1998.

PREGNANCY AND CHILD BIRTH

Pregnancy related causes of deaths cover a fairly large number of disorders such as abortion, toxaemia, anaemia, bleeding during pregnancy and puerperium, malposition of child leading to death of mother, puerperial sepsis, and several other less known and unclassified afflictions. They together account for 15 per cent of all deaths of women in the reproductive age group of 15-44 years and about 3 per cent of all female deaths in the country. Where women have many pregnancies, the risk of related deaths over the course of a lifetime is compounded. Pregnancy in early age is an important contributory factor.

Over half a million women die of pregnancy related causes in the world, 99 per cent of them in the developing countries. Risk is higher in regions where childbirth takes place at home and is not attended by trained medical and paramedical personnel. In Africa, the risk is 1 in 16, in Asia 1 in 64, in Europe and 1 in 1400. About 80 per cent of maternal deaths are due to direct causes such as obstetric complications of pregnancy, labour and peurperium, or due to interventions, omissions, incorrect treatment or a combination of several of them. While the maternal mortality rate in Gujarat in 1998 was 29, it was as high as 707 in Uttar Pradesh.

Table 16.3: India: State-wise Maternal Mortality Rates-1998

States	*MMR*	*% India*
Andhra Pradesh	154	37.75
Assam	401	98.30
Bihar	451	110.55
Gujarat	29	07.00
Haryana	105	25.75
Karnataka	195	47.80
Kerala	195	47.80
Madhya Pradesh	498	122.00
Maharashtra	135	33.10
Orissa	361	88.50
Punjab	196	48.00
Rajasthan	677	166.00
Tamil Nadu	76	18.60
Uttar Pradesh	707	173.30
West Bengal	264	64.70
India	**408**	**100**

Source: Health Information of India, 1998

Maternal mortality rates in India are still very high (Table 16.3 Fig. 16.2). Inter-state disparities are wide and some of the states with large population size are far below the national average. Maternal cycle begins even before a child is conceived. Cases of mothers' health not being good enough to bear children are not rare. It is specially so in the case of child marriage. Premature conception can lead to many complications. Miscarriage is only one of them. Maternal cycle consists of five periods; fertilization period, antinatal period, intranatal period, postnatal period, and inter-conception period. Problems can emerge in any of these periods.

Some of the main causes of maternal deaths are discussed below:

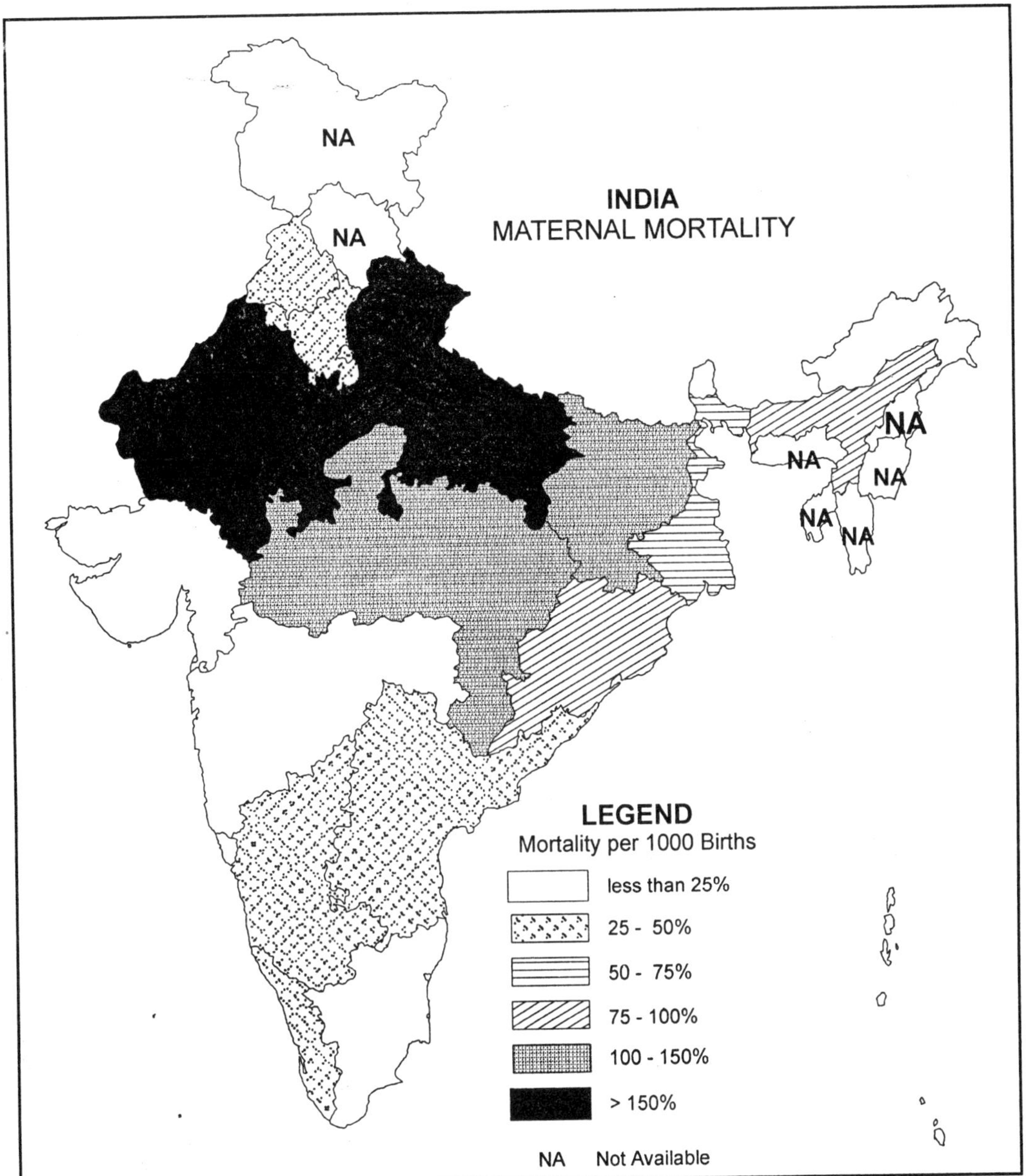

Fig. 16.2: India: Maternal Mortality Rates 1997.

Obstetric Haemorrhage

It is a common disease in most developing countries of the world. In India, it accounts for 25 per cent of all maternal deaths. It is a generally occurring postpartum; the patient dies rather soon unless prompt life saving care including treatment to control bleeding, and blood transfusion is available. Since these facilities are rare in rural areas, maternal mortality is very high there.

Unsafe Abortion

Unsafe abortion accounts for at least 13 per cent of maternal deaths in India. Abortions are resorted to in cases of pregnancies before marriage. Out of wedlock pregnancies are not accepted in most societies. It is particularly so in India. To avoid social stigma, parents of such pregnant girls take the help of quakes to abort the foetus. Traditional preference for boys over girls constitutes yet another reason. Modern technology enables parents to know in advance the sex of the foetus. Cases of abortion of female foetus are now becoming too common. This is also done surreptitiously and hence the chances of complications are high.

Puerperal Infection

Puerperal infection is caused by poor hygienic conditions during delivery. Untreated reproductive tract infections including the sexually transmitted ones account for nearly 15 per cent of maternal deaths in India. Such infections can be easily prevented but in a social context where child delivery is considered to be an unclean process, it is just not possible.

Mal-position of the Baby

Fairly good number of child deliveries end up in the death of mothers because of mal-position of the baby in the womb. Unless the patient is taken to hospital without delay, the chances of survival of the mother are bleak. At present, it is responsible for about 6 per cent of maternal deaths in India. Prolonged or obstructed labour accounts for 7 per cent of all maternal deaths.

Toxemia

Approximately 13 per cent of all maternal deaths are caused by hypertensive disorders of pregnancy particularly enclampsia (convulsions). They can be easily controlled if medical services are available at the time of pregnancy and delivery.

Anaemia

Among the indirect causes of death associated with pregnancy, anaemia is a major one in countries like India because the nutritional status of women is far worse than that of the men. This situation develops from the early childhood when the girl child is discriminated against in matters of health, education and many other aspects of general up-bringing. Approximately 20 per cent of all childbirth and pregnancy related deaths in the country are caused by anemia. Deficiency of iron is common among Indian women. During pregnancy and lactation the situation worsens and they fall prey of many common diseases such as malaria, typhoid, common cold, etc. Figure 16.2 gives the per cent of all deaths claimed by anaemia among all age groups and sexes; a good number of deaths, however, pertain to women in the reproductive age group.

Other Causes

Apart from the pregnancy and childbirth related deaths, women are prone to many other diseases common to their male counterparts. They are, more susceptible to coronary heart diseases and stroke, breast cancer, cervical cancer and violence. About 60 per cent of women in the developed parts of the world die of coronary heart problems. This disease has started taking heavy toll of life of senior female citizens in all developing countries, India included.

Breast cancer is another major disease of the women in developed countries. About 700,000 lives are claimed by breast cancer each year, 57 per cent of which occur in developed countries. It is now curable, if detected in time. The disease is coming to the developing countries alsò with a bang.

Cervical cancer takes away about 400,000 lives, largely in developing countries of the world. It afflicts the aged women more and is curable if detected in time through screening. And finally, a fairly good number of women die because of violence against them. Unfortunately, only a few cases of this category get reported and hence reliable data in this regard are scanty or even absent.

According to a survey conducted in 1999 in 252 districts of India, just 50 per cent of the women had safe deliveries and only 35 per cent had institutional deliveries. Only 67 per cent of women had had at least one antenatal check up (ANC) and only 15 per cent of them had full ANC. The survey also revealed that about 29 per cent of married women and 13 per cent of males had symptoms of reproductive tract infection or sexually transmitted diseases. State-wise information gathered from the above survey shows that some states are far better than others in matters of reproductive health. For example, 66 per cent of women (15-44 age group) in Kerala had full ANC; 97 per cent had institutional delivery; and more than 90 per cent of both men and women were aware of reproductive track infection and sexually transmitted diseases. As against this, in UP only 3 per cent of women had full ANC, only 17 per cent had institutional delivery and only 32 per cent of men and 21 per cent of women were aware of reproductive tract infection and sexually transmitted diseases.

PREVENTION AND CONTROL OF MATERNAL DISEASES

Many WHO activities now focus on women's health. It is realized that safety, protection and care of women are key to human development. Since they are socially disadvantage, improvement in their social status vis-à-vis the males is the first prerequisite. It has also been realized that low social status of women is not necessarily limited to the developing countries countries; it is not uncommon even in developed parts of the world. And hence a global movement to empower the women and to make health facilities accessible to them was the need of the hour.

In pursuance of the above realization, the WHO has appointed a Global Commission on Women's Health. The Commission focuses on three key issues: health education of girls and women; violence against women; and reduction of maternal morbidity and mortality. Programmes of reproductive and child health (RCH) have been launched in most developing countries of the world including India. Health facilities are being extended in rural areas to make maternal care accessible to mothers living in remote areas. The progress on these fronts is, however, slow. While it is easy to make physical infrastructure available even in remote areas, it is difficult to offer quality service due to reluctance of medical personnal to serve there.

Women constitute a majority of older population in virtually all countries. Their number is likely to grow by 150 per cent in the next 25 years or so. Women have different circumstances, challenges, and health concerns from men as they age. Older women are more likely to be

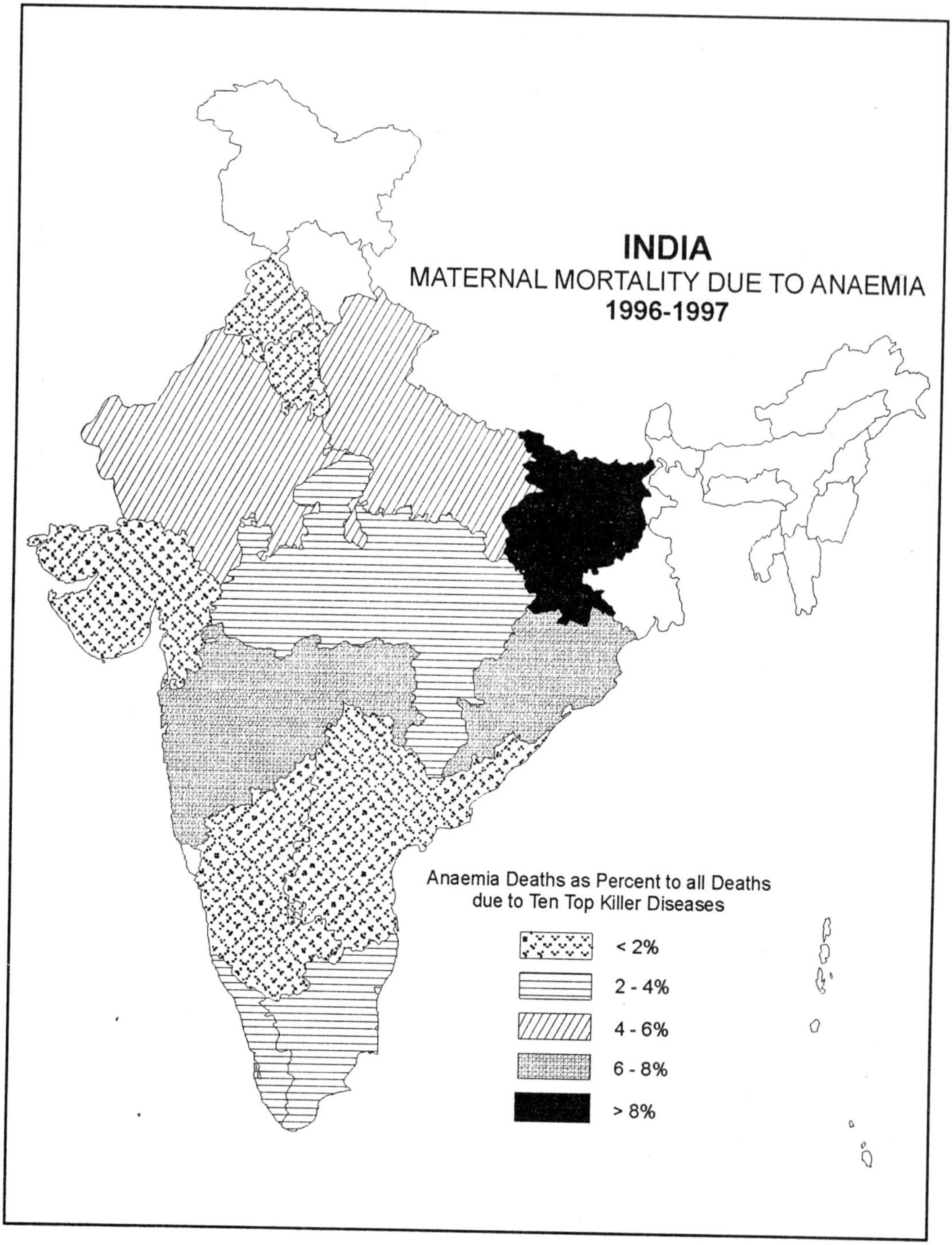

Fig. 16.3: India: Female Deaths Caused by Anaemia

widowed, to live alone and to live in poverty. It is partly because women live longer than men and partly because the siblings can no longer be depended upon for help and support. Although hereditary factors play an important role in determining life expectancy and health, the style of life one leads and the environment in which one lives do have catalytic effects. Habits and lifestyles conducive to a healthier old age are within the reach of every individual. This can produce what the WHO says 'Healthy Aging'.

Maternal health care was part of the family welfare programme in India from its very inception. Vertical schemes like National Anaemia Control; TT Immunization of Pregnant Mothers and Training of Dais (grassroots level female workers to assist in the delivery of babies) were introduced from time to time. In 1992 all these programmes were integrated into CSSM programme, which among others included:

1. early registration of pregnancy;
2. minimum three ante-natal care;
3. universal coverage of all pregnant women with TT immunization;
4. advice on food, nutrition and rest;
5. detection of high risk pregnancies and referral;
6. clean deliveries by clean personnel;
7. birth spacing; and
8. promotion of institutional deliveries.

These programmes were reorganized under the rubric RCH (Reproductive and Child Health Programme). The main elements of the RCH are:

1. essential obstetric care to all pregnant women through early registration of pregnancy, provision of minimum three antinatal check to detect any risk or complications, provision of safe delivery at home or at an institution, and provision of three postnatal cares to monitor the recovery. The states of Assam, Bihar, Madhya Pradesh, Orissa and Uttar Pradesh that lag behind in maternal care, have been identified for major attention;
2. arrangements to provide delivery services at the PHCs/CHCs all through the day and night; and
3. strengthening the referral units for emergency obstetric care.

The RCH programme did make an impact on health delivery for mothers and children but the results were not commensurate to the money spent. In fact, it has not risen done an one-shot project; efforts have been discrete and hence less effective. Unless there is continuity in the programme, peoples participation cannot bee ensured and unless people participation such programmes cannot succeed.

SPATIAL DIFFERENCES IN MATERNAL HEALTH CARE

There are wide differences in maternal health status and maternal healthcare facilities in India. A study of these differences is essential to get optimum results from the available human, technological and financial resources and also to fill the spatial gaps wherever they are. Unfortunately, literacy among the women in India is still very low. This negates many of the efforts being made by the government to reach out to the women with a view to help them improve their health situation. Yet, we cannot deny the fact that there is clear inadequacy of the physical facilities in much of the rural parts of the country. Even if physical infrastructure is readied, the people to man them are not in position or if they are, they are attending to their duties. It is clear from the fact that a large number of deliveries still take place at home often unattended by even trained dais.

India has just 55 medical practitioners and 65 nursing personnel per 100,000 population. The required number of obstreticians and gynaecologists in rural areas was about 3,000 in 1998; but only 780 of them were in position. Of the 23,000 positions of health assistants in PHCs, only 19,500 were in position. The shortfall in the case of female health workers amounted to 28,000; and in case of nurse midwives to 20,500. So the country has yet to go a long way in meeting the physical infrastructure and man-power needs of the women. True, this applies to a large extent to men too but in case of the women, lack of access to quality health facilities is more telling.

Generation Hexed

As if the glaring numbers of female foeticide weren't depressing enough, findings of a report come as a shock. The State of India's Newborns Report underlines the urgent need for drastic measures to reverse the persisting negative trend in neo-natal (within four weeks of delivery) mortality. The report states that of the 26 million die before completing the first four weeks of life. Over one-third of the deaths occur on the first day, and almost half within three days. Conducted by the Indian government (with the Unicef, WHO, the World Bank and the national Neonatology Forum), the study paints a dismal picture of the State of India's children, over half of whom are born without assistance at home where the mothers are young, poor and under-nourished. The staggering figure of 1.2 million accounts for 30 per cent of all neo-natal deaths in the world. For India, this is shameful and poses a big challenge.

Uttar Pradeh, Bihar and Madhya Pradesh account for over half the deaths and form 15 per cent of the global burden. In Orissa and Madhya Pradesh, 61 and 59 infants of every 1,000 live births die respectively. While the neo-natal mortality rate (NMR) had declined in the Eighties; it has inexplicably remained static since. In MP, the government has expressed concern at the state's maternal mortality rate being substantially higher than the national average. But clearly, it will take more than ministerial concern to change ground realities. For one, good intentions must be backed with concrete time-framed initiatives whose impact on mother and child health is measurable. Two, with health inexorably linked to poverty levels, the declining state expenditure on public health is having a direct negative effect on young mothers and their children. With limited or no access to family planning practices leading to frequent pregnancies, coupled with malnourished mothers, it's a marvel that children manage to escape death in their first five years of life in pockets of India.

What stops state governments from kick starting an integrated primary healthcare system to promote mother and child health? Governments—state and central—must create accountable administrative systems to ensure that we can, at least, keep our children alive in the 21st century.

Editorial of Hindustan Times, March 7, 2006
tells so vividly the problem of neo-natal and child mortality in India

REFERENCES

1. Government of India, Ministry of Health and Family Welfare, *Annual Reports,* 1998-2002.
2. WHO, *World Health Report*, 1998 to 2002.
3. National of Institute of Nutrition, Hyderabad, *Annual Reports.*
4. Government of India, Ministry of Health, *Health Information of India*, 1998 and 1999.

17

Children's Health

'Child is the father of man', said Wordsworth. A sick child cannot grow into a healthy man or woman to produce healthy children. Health of the child should, therefore, be the first social responsibility of any forward-looking society. The child mortality and morbidity rates have been discussed earlier. Infant and over-5 years old mortality rates are going down all over the world. The regions lagging behind now need special attention. The risk, of dying is influenced biologically by its gender, natural defenses and nutritional inputs; and by its physical, microbial, social and cultural environment. In this chapter we propose to take a look at the diseases our children suffer from and die of.

According to WHO, in 1995, as many as 10.4 million children in developing countries died before they could celebrate their fifth birth day. Just 40 years back in 1955, as many as 21 million children under-5 years of age had diet. We have made progress but let us not forget that child mortality rates are still as high as 200 per 1000 live birth. The causes of death as diagnosed by physicians are known but behind the apparent causes there is a hidden hand of malnutrition (Table 17.1). If children are given all the nutrients and energy they need to grow into full adults, the impact of these diseases will be negligible and at least 60 per cent of the 10 million deaths would be avoided.

"Depending on the highly variable conditions of living in India, the very first year of life, and the next two, could be an exiting phase of rapid growth and development of the budding brain and the body; or contrarily, a prolonged and unequal struggle for survival with an uncertain outcome. Maternal factors...are a determinant of which way the balance tilts. The factors related to an environment of poverty in its many forms are another, ...What is clear, on both these counts, is that a majority of the survivors are left to build their lives on less than firm foundations. "...Survival from severe mal-nutrition may constitute the event that starts a developmental path characterized by psychologically defective functioning, school failure and subsequent adaptive functioning. At the familial and societal levels, the ultimate result of this chain of events is what in an ecological sense could be called 'a spiral effect."[1] A low level of adaptive functioning, lack of modern knowledge, unhealthy social customs, widespread infections due to environmental pollution, insufficient or low quality of food intake lead to malnutrition results in a huge pool of survivors who function at sub-optimal levels. These survivors are not only themselves at risk, they also enlarge the pool by choosing mates of similar characteristics and rearing children under conditions and in a fashion totally programmed to produce a new generation of malnourished individuals.

We have already seen in chapter 9 that the infant and child mortality rates in India are declining, even if they are still high from international standards; and how they vary from region to region. In this chapter we propose to examine the nature of children's diseases and the deaths claimed by each of the major diseases. "The everyday nature of these deaths distinguishes the complex sequence of events leading to the remorseless process of repeated episodes of infections, often sequential, and not infrequently concurrent. Each episode is accompanied by loss of appetite and decrease in food intake, and each time the illness itself makes increased demands on the child's energy. Local health care facilities, if they exist, may be ill equipped and poorly supplied, and inadequately staffed, with patterns of care that are rarely optimal and may even be harmful. Often, the child struggles for life in a highly crowded, unhygienic and poorly ventilated environment that facilitates the transmission of respiratory infections and malaria."[2] The causes of death are, therefore, complex and the survey of hospital data need be taken with caution.

Table 17.1: Global Causes of Death of Children Under-5

Cause of death	*Number of deaths (millions)*	*Malnutrition associated deaths (%)*
Lower respiratory infection	2.1	44
Diarrhoea	2.0	70
Measles	1.1	65
Prematurity	1.0	40
Birth asphyxia	0.9	35
Malaria	0.7	40
Congenital anomalies	0.5	30
Pertussis	0.4	50
Meningitis + neonatal sepsis	0.4	30
Neonatal tetanus	0.4	20
Birth trauma	0.4	30
Malnutrition	0.3	100
Prematurity	0.1	40
Tuberculosis	0.1	60
All other causes	0.2	40

Source: The World Health Report, 1998.

In this connection, it is worth pointing out that the single-disease approach has so far not paid dividends. Children's diseases are multi-factorial and hence need a more holistic multi-pronged approach. A child does not come to the clinic as a case of something, but arrives sick and may have several conditions as such. Researches show that most childhood deaths are caused by five conditions: diarrhoea, pneumonia, measles, malaria and malnutrition. That is why, the WHO and UNICEF prepared a joint strategy called integrated management of childhood illness, which also includes environmental improvements, domestic hygiene, breast feeding, use of mosquito nets etc.

Five of the child diseases are vaccine preventable. These are polio, diphtheria, pertussis, NNT and measles. Because of strict surveillance, the cases of these diseases have gone down rather drastically during 1990-2000 and most of them are on the verge of extinction.

INFANT MORTALITY IN INDIA

Infant is a child below the age of one year. Infant mortality is often considered as an index of the state of public health and hygiene, environmental sanitation, and cultural and socioeconomic development. In the recent past, notable gains have been achieved in bringing down infant mortality but even in the most advanced countries, the risk of death immediately after birth remains high in comparison to that in later years. Infections and respiratory diseases are the major causes of infant mortality. Fig. 17.1 gives the state wise infant mortality rates in India.

The most important infant killer is a group of diseases called conditions originating in the perinatal period (claiming 62 per cent of infant deaths), followed by the diseases of the respiratory system (16 per cent). Next in order are infectious and parasitic diseases (5.5 per cent); congenital malformations, deformations, and abnormalities (3.1 per cent); diseases of the blood and blood forming organs (2.9 per cent); viral infections (2.6 per cent); inflammatory diseases of the central nervous system (1.7 per cent); symptoms, signs and abnormal clinical findings not elsewhere mentioned (1.4 per cent); diseases of the circulatory system (1.4 per cent) and others whose percentages are less than one.[3]

The top ten killer diseases of infants are prematurity, pneumonia, respiratory infection, congenital malformation, anaemia, diarrhoea, birth injury, tetanus neonatoram, typhoid and paratyphoid, and bronchitis and asthma. State-wise occurrence of each as recorded in the Survey of Causes of Death (1996 and 1997) is given in Table 17.2.

Prematurity

Almost a third of children are born premature or they are born dead. It happens largely because of the poor health of mothers caused either by neglect during pregnancy or malnutrition, frequent pregnancies, or teenage pregnancy. Many of these children die within a few days of birth. Some of them survive with stunted growth, mental retardation or several other abnormal formations. Such children become burden on the parents, family and society in general. Birth Asphyxia/trauma is caused by the lack of oxygen or over inhalation of carbon dioxide by the newly born child. Mortality from this cause can be curtailed if childbirth is attended by trained dais or it takes place in the hospital. Most of the premature births can be stopped if the pregnant mothers are given necessary nutrition, medical attention and family care.

Table 17.2: Causes of Infant Mortality in Rural India: 1996-97 (per 1000 deaths)

	Prema turity	*Pneu monia*	*Resp. Infec.*	*Cong Malf*	*Anae mia*	*Diarr hoea*	*Birth Inj.*	*Tetanus*	*Typhoid*	*Bronchitis Asth*	*Total*
Rank	I	II	III	IV	V	VI	VII	VIII	IX	X	
ICD Code	P 07	J 18	P 22	Q 00-99	D 50-64	P 75-78	P 10-15	A 33	A 01	J 20 &45	
India	305	155	109	3.2	30	33	17	16	8	10.5	716
Andhra Pradesh	266.5	28.5	190	33	0.6	31	24.5	8	1	26.5	614.5
Bihar	170	329	14	24	63	76	13.5	16	17	00	734
Gujarat	348.5	57	68	65.5	11.5	22.5	14.5	00	3	11.5	601.5
Haryana	197.5	234	52.5	43.5	58.5	10.5	3	12.5	11	0.3	626.5
Karnataka	441	22	175	44.5	0.5	35	29.5	15	00	0.3	770
Kerala	153.5	144	194	152	00	00	00	00	00	00	654.5
Maharashtara	554.5	,138	60.5	34	0.7	7,5	6	0.5	00	7.5	815.5
Madhya Pradesh	316	219.5	95.5	27	50	27	11.5	13.5	6	2	768.5
Orissa	371	123.5	67	0.5	81	2.5	5	25.5	4.5	50	734
Punjab	95	129.5	65,5	1.7	16	121.5	00	24	00	20	487.5
Rajasthan	221	248	69.5	2.9	67	45.5	13.5	6	19	.57	727
Tamil Nadi	216.5	98	249.5	49.5	5.5	39	29.5	4	01	12.5	700
Uttar Pradesh	186	228	89.5	19	34.5	52	21.5	49	24.5	-0.5	704.5

Source: Survey of Causes of Death (Rural), 1997.

Note: Figure show moving average for 1996 and 1997.

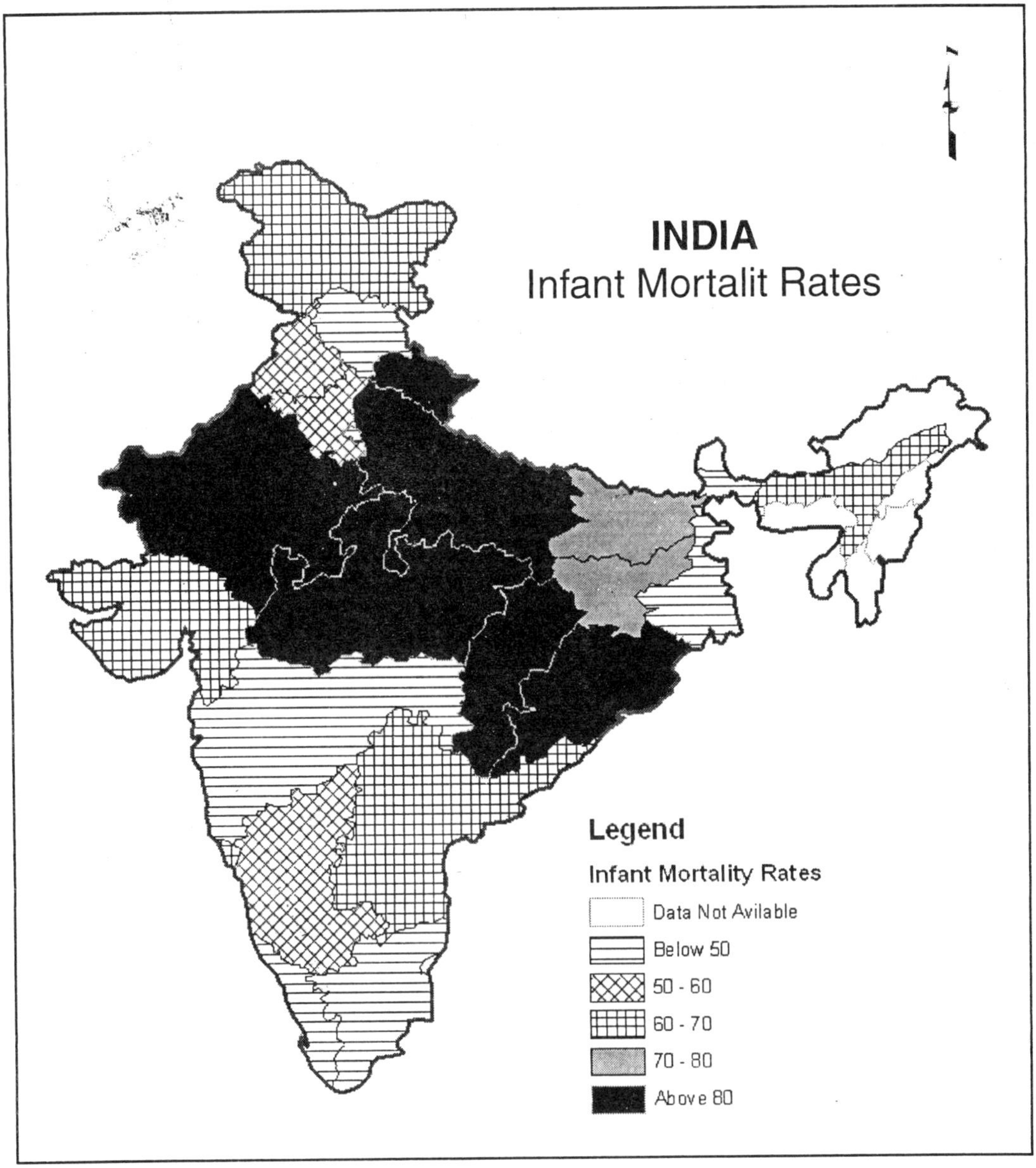

Fig. 17.1: India: Infant Mortality Rates (1998)

Pneumonia

Pneumonia is the second major killer of infants in rural areas. Pneumonia accounts for about 15 per cent of infant deaths; 10 per cent of those admitted in hospitals die. Morbidity on this account is extensive. Some children are known to have suffered 3 to 5 attakcs in a year each of 10 to 15 days duration. The Indian brand of pneumonia is not viral as in the West; it is caused by a bacterium. Microbial drugs are available in India in plenty; they are not expensive either. If given in time and in proper doses, the mortality can be reduced substantially. Per cent of deaths claimed by pneumonia in 1998 was 4.4. It stood eighth among the ten major killers of people in all age-groups; second most important cause of death of infants and top most killer of children in the age group 1-5 (Figure 17.1).

Congenital Malformations

Congenital malformation shows up as abnormal head, too big or too small; sometimes the urinary system is defective. In some cases, the stool cannot pass through the anus. In case of major abnormalities, the child does not survive beyond a couple of days.

Anaemia

Anaemia is caused by inadequate supply of mother's milk or some deficiencies in mother's milk due to poor diet. Many children are born under-weight i.e. weight at birth is less than 2500 grams irrespective of gestational age. It has an adverse effect on child survival and development, and may even be important risk factor for a number of adult diseases including diabetes and heart diseases. Even though the etiology of low birth weight is multi-factorial, poor maternal nutrition, certain infections, pre-eclampsia, arduous work after mid-pregnancy, short birth intervals, and teenage pregnancy are crucial factors. The preterm infant whose gestation period is less than 37 weeks is physiologically immature and at a higher risk of dying during the neonatal period. Low weight infants have poor sucking and swallowing reflexes; the retina of the eye is easily damaged by excess of oxygen and there is risk of intracranial bleeding as a result of birth trauma.

Diarrhoea

Diarrhoea of the newly born is responsible for around three per cent of all infant deaths. It may be of three varieties: acute, chronic and dysentery with some 20 etiologies. The anti-diarrhoeal drugs are not helpful; they produce several side effects. Many children die because of these drugs. To control this disease, Oral Rehydration Therapy (ORT) Programme was launched in 1986-87. It is a major cause of malnutrition among children.

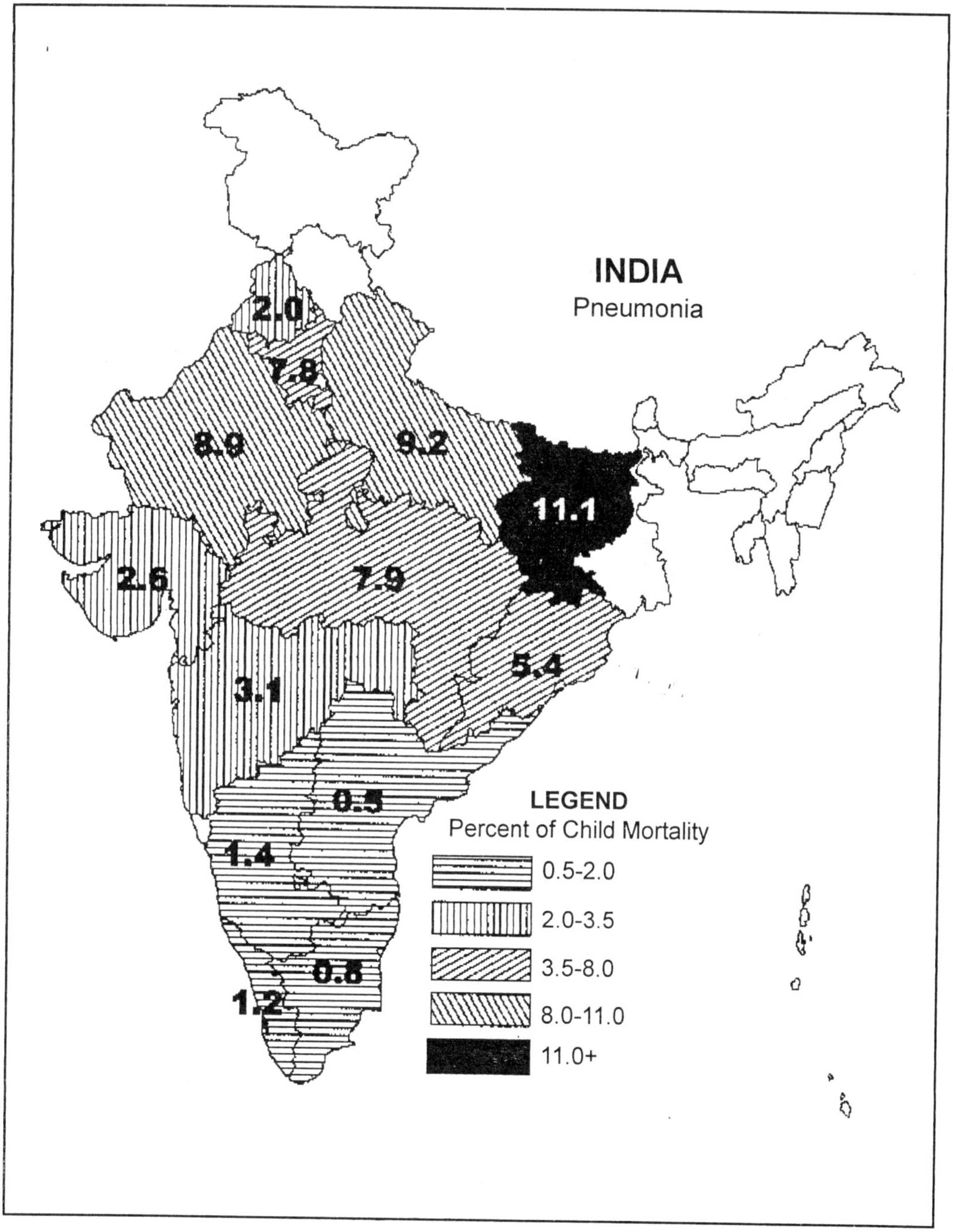

Fig. 17.2: India: Pneumonia Related Deaths Among Children (1998)

Birth Injury

Most children are born without any assistance from trained paramedical personnel, particularly in rural areas. There are chances of many of them being injured in the face, upper extremities, color bone, etc. Prolonged labour can be injurious to the child. Children with birth injuries are blue in colour and cry in a low voice. Frequent convulsions or facial paralysis are not uncommon.

Neonatal Tetanus

Tetanus of the newly born is called neonatal tetanus. Among the six EPI vaccine preventable diseases of children, it is the third major killer, first and second being measles and pertussis. Even if medical aid becomes available, the case-fatality rate is as high as 80-90 per cent. It is more common in socially backward areas and therefore it is one of the most underreported diseases in India. The WHO therefore estimates the number of cases and deaths using certain indirect socio-economic parameters.

Global Prevalence

In the 1980s, about one million children died of this disease each year. As a result of the efforts of the WHO, the global mortality figures came down from 408,000 in 1990 to 2,8,000 in 1997. Most of the deaths occurred in the developing parts of the world. Simultaneously, the number of cases of NT also declined from about 510,000 in 1990 to 355,000 in 1997. Table 17.3 gives more details of NT morbidity and mortality in India and its neighbouring countries. D.P.R. Korea, Maldives, Sri Lanka, Bhutan and Thailand are now NT free. The decline in NT cases and deaths in recent years is attributed to increase in the immunization coverage of pregnant women with tetanus toxoid. The World Health Assembly had resolved in 1989 to eliminate NT from the world by 1995 i.e. to reduce the incidence to less than 1 per 1000. The new target for the elimination of NT by the year 2000 was set in 1996.[4]

Table 17.3: NT Cases and Deaths in South Asia, 1990-97 (WHO Estimates)

Country	*1990*		*1997*		*Change in Mortality Rate %*
	No. of deaths	*Morality rate*	*No. of deaths*	*Mortality rate/1000*	
India	77,700	3.0	55,200	2.3	–23
China	75,700	3.2	12,800	0.6	–81
Bangladesh	38,600	9.9	16,300	5.0	–49
Pakistan	36,300	7.0	26,400	5.0	–29
Indonesia	22,800	4.7	6,400	1.4	–70
Nepal	6,700	8.8	5,800	7.0	–20
Myanmar	4,400	3.2	1,500	1.1	–65

Source: WHO (1999), Weekly Epidemiological Record No. 10.

NT in India

In India, as many as 3.5 lakh children died of NT before the national immunization programme was launched in the country. About 70,000 cases still occur in the states of UP, MP, Rajasthan, Bihar, Orissa and Assam. All of these are relatively backward states with low per capita income, poor public health facilities, low level of literacy and lower immunization coverage.

A new spatial strategy has been adopted to control this disease. The districts with high morbidity and mortality rates have been identified and classified on the basis of NT immunization coverage. NT high risk districts are those districts where NT rate is more than one per 1000 live births, or where TT_2 coverage is less than 70 per cent, or where attended deliveries are less than 50 per cent. NT control districts are those districts where NT rate is less than 1/1000 live-births or where TT coverage is more than 70 per cent, or attended deliveries are more 50 per cent. NT Elimination Districts are those which are marked with NT rate of less than 0.10 per 1000 live births, or where TT coverage is more than 90 per cent or where attended deliveries are more than 75 per cent.

NT in India is marked by seasonality. More than half of the total cases occur in the three rainy months: July-September. Tetanus is a positive environmental hazard. Adverse physical, social and ecological conditions are the main causative factors. Agricultural population is more prone to NT infection. Infection is acquired by contamination of wounds with tetanus spores. Unhygienic conditions at the time of delivery are responsible for high rate of NT cases in India.

Typhoid and Paratyphoid

These ailments are marked by long duration fever increasing during the day, severe headache, highly coated tongue, abdominal pain and constipation. Death occurs during the second or third week due to delirium, abdominal pain, or passing of blood in stools.

DISEASES OF CHILDREN (AGE GROUP 1-4)

According to the rural health survey 1997, child deaths in the age group 1-4 years can be ascribed to following groups of diseases: diseases of the respiratory system (29 per cent), infectious and parasitic diseases (22.3per cent), Viral Infections (11.5 per cent), diseases of the blood and blood forming organs (9.3 per cent), inflammatory diseases of the central nervous system (6.6 per cent), and other diseases or causes (14.7 per cent). More specifically, the top ten killers of children under-5 years are: pneumonia, anaemia, typhoid and paratyphoid, diarrhoea and gastroenteritis, dysentery, malaria, acute abdomen, drowning, jaundice, and meningitis.

One can get a comparative picture of the causes of deaths ascribable to each of the top ten killers of the children in the age group 1-4 years from Table 17.4, which gives the main causes of death of children under 5-years of age in the developing parts of the world.

Several other diseases that do not kill but maim children also deserve our attention: most important among them being poliomyelitis. Poliomyelitis, popularly known as polio, is a crippling disease of children. For quite a long time, it has been maiming and robbing the jest of life from millions of children all over the world; in developing countries in particular. It is of two varieties: paralytic and non-paralytic. The paralytic type is less common but highly debilitating. Children getting this disease have to lead a very miserable life. Very few among them get modern treatment and facilities for rehabilitation.

Table 17.4: Ten Major Killers of Rural Children in Age-group 1-4 Years, 1997 (per 1000 deaths)

States	*Pneumonia*	*Anaemia*	*Typhoid*	*Diarrhoea*	*Dysentery*	*Malaria*	*Acu. Abd.*	*Drowning*	*Jaundice*	*Meningitis*	*Total*
ICD code	J18	D 50-64	A 01	A 09	A 06	B 50-54	R 10	X 71	R 17	G-00 02	
AP	49	00	00	98	98	16	33	82	82	16	475
Bihar	393	121	37	47	19	47	28	09	19	09	729
Gujarat.	20	200	00	20	00	40	40	40	00	20	380
Haryana.	270	41	68	41	00	41	00	14	27	14	514
Karnataka.	155	127	42	42	28	00	14	28	127	28	592
Kerala	625	00	00	00	00	00	00	00	00	00	625
Madhya Pradesh	239	152	104	90	27	72	27	20	15	22	769
Mahaeash-tra	195	42	09	05	05	00	33	70	14	37	409
Orissa	225	113	14	70	00	14	28	28	70	14	577
Punjab	115	77	00	38	77	38	00	00	00	00	346
Rajasthan	254	136	77	30	18	24	12	18	24	06	598
Tamil Nadu	63	21	11	21	95	00	00	95	42	21	368
Uttar Pradesh	272	57	105	80	73	07	34	07	07	43	686
India	227	90	63	58	40	28	28	27	27	24	610

Source: Survey of Causes of Death (Rural), 1997

There were approximately 500 cases of polio in India, mainly in Uttar Pradesh during the first ten months of 2002. Figure 17.3 gives the distribution of polio cases in India during 1998-2002. Acute Respiratory Infection (ARI) is the most serious one that afflicts children in the age group 1-4 also. Most important among them is pneumonia. According to the WHO, 4.10 million children in the world died of ARI in 1998: 40 per cent of them being in India, Bangladesh, Nepal and Indonesia. It also includes Bronchitis and Asthma. ARI is caused by genetic factors or environmental factors. Difficulty in breathing, coughing of long duration, shortness of breath and breathlessness are the common symptoms.

Table 17.5: Global ARI Mortality and DALYs in 1998

WHO Regions	*Mortality in '000*	*DALYS in '000*
Africa	806	23369
Americas	139	3965
Eastern Mediterranean	348	10251
Europe	349	3810
South-East Asia	292	7176
Western Pacific	496	10976
India	987	25556
World	3507	85085

Source: WHO, Regional Health Report (South and Souh-East Asia), 1999

ARI is of two types: upper respiratory tract infection (AURI) and lower respiratory tract infection (ALRI). The former includes common cold, pharyngitis and otitis media, while the latter includes epiglottitis, laryngitis, laryngotracheitis, bronchitis, bronchiolitis and pneumonia. In both the cases, the usual symptoms are running nose, cough, sore throat, difficult breathing, ear problem, fever, etc.

ARI is global disease found in both developed and developing countries. Table 17.5 gives global figures of mortality and DALYs accounted by ARI. In India, 13 per cent of deaths in hospitals are ascribed to ARI. According to WHO estimates, about 987,000 deaths are caused by ARI. Of these, 10,000 deaths are ascribed to AURI and the rest to ALRI.

DIPTHERIA

Diptheria is another major disease that afflicts the children. It no longer a major health hazard though. It is an acute infectious disease caused by toxigenic strains of corynebacterium. The bacilli multiply locally, usually in the throat, and release powerful exotoxin, which form grayish or yellowish membrane over the tonsils, pharynx or larynx. Its fatality rate is medium not exceeding 10 per cent. It causes local congestion and tissue destruction, enlargement of lymph nodes and taxaemia.

Diptheria has been eradicated from developed parts of the world due to routine and regular immunization and improved living conditions. There was an outbreak of diptheria in Ukraine in 1990, and Thailand and Laos in 1996. About 5000 children died of diptheria in 1998.

Diptheria is endemic in India but it is weakening fast and may be said to be on the way out. In 1987, India recorded 12,952 cases; in 1999 only 2725 cases.

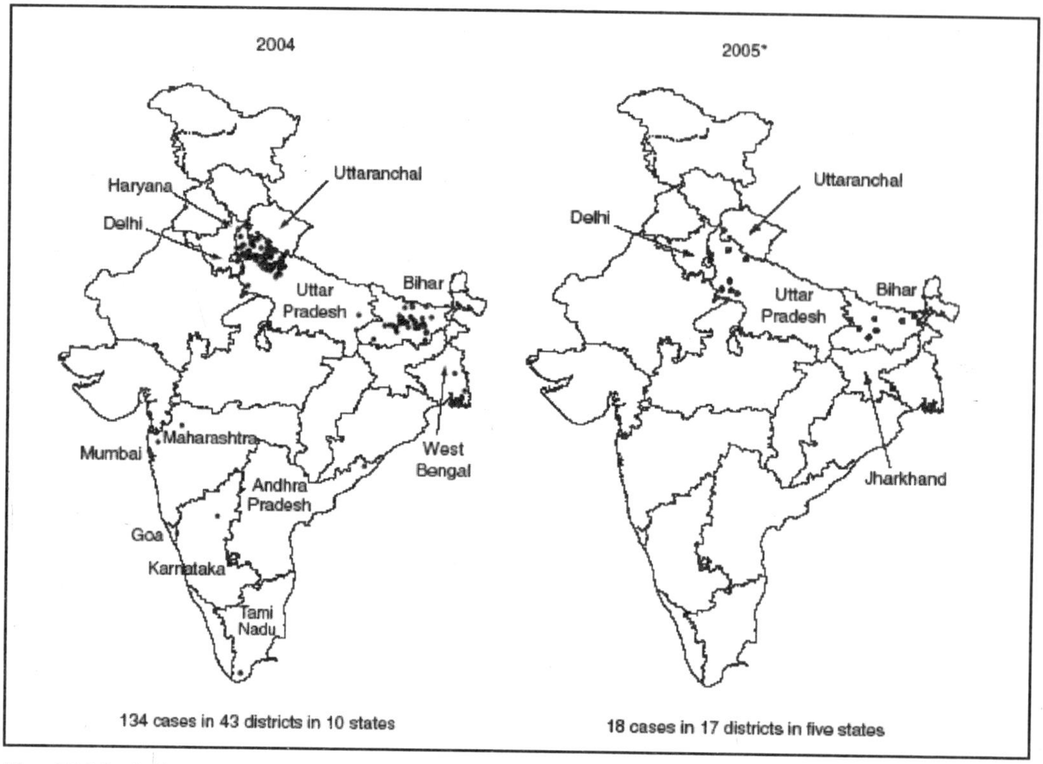

Fig. 17.3A: Laboratory-confirmed wild polio viurs cases — India, 2004 and 2005*
As on June 18, 2005

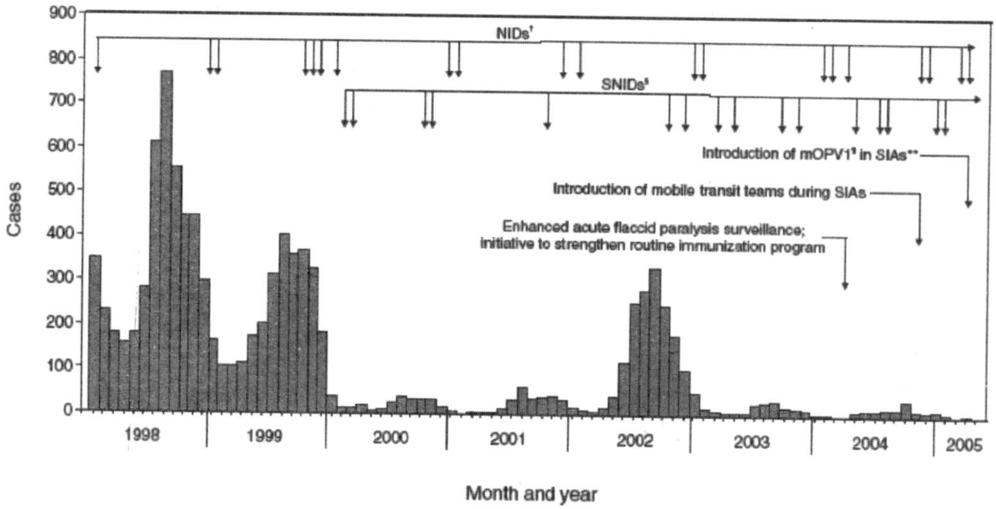

Fig. 17.3B: Number of Poliomyelitis cases, by month and year — Year, January 1998—May 2005*
As on June 18, 2005

The agents that cause diptheria are C. diptheriae. They are nonmobile and produce powerful exotoxin. It is very sensitive to penicillin, heat and chemical agents. It can survive in dust for a short period only.

The host of the bacilli are children of 1-5 years age. The babies of two weeks are however immune from the disease. It enters the body through the respiratory route, skin (if there are cuts) and wounds.

The attack of diptheria comes in winter months. But that is not a rule. In Kolkata it comes in August; in Mumbai in December-January; and in Delhi in August-October. The period of infectivity ranges from 14 to 28 days.

WHOOPING COUGH

This is a disease of the infants and young children. It is caused by B. pertusis. Its symptoms are mild fever, irritating cough with whoop (loud crowing inspiration). In China, it is called hundred days cough. It has been prevalent in practically all countries, but since the development of vaccine (DPT_4) in 1960, has been practically eradicated from developed countries. In developing countries of Africa, Latin America and Asia, it is still a disease to reckon with. In Eastern European countries also there is increase in the number of cases.

Whooping cough is one of the most lethal diseases of non-immunized infants particularly those suffering from malnutrition. Case fatality rate ranges between 4 and 10 but in case of infants it can touch 50 per cent. Immunity from whooping cough wanes with time and therefore booster doses are needed. In 1998, 346000 children died of the disease and DALYs lost amounted to 13.20 million. In India alone, there were 36700 cases and the DALYs lost was 2,69 million in 1999. Compared to the situation in 1987, there is definite improvement and the diseases may be on the way out. There were 163,000 cases and 71000 deaths in 1987.

The bacterium B. pertusis (in 5 per cent cases it is B. parapertusis) is a antigenically highly complex; it can survive for very short period in the human body. It is released through bronchical and nasopharyngeal secretions and becomes infectious after 3-7 days when catarrhal starts. The disease is more among the female children. It is more common in winter months. Poverty and overcrowding favour the onset as well as the spread of the disease. The transmission of the bacilli takes place through patients' coughs, sneezes or even talk.

As mentioned above, the disease is almost on the way out in India. The only states, which still have (1998) more than 1000 cases per annum, are AP, Assam, J&K, Karnataka, Kerala, Madhya Pradesh, Meghalaya, and Orissa. Of the 50,621 cases in 1995, 11,269 were recorded in Madhya Pradesh alone. The other states with more than 5,000 cases were Andhra Pradesh, Assam and Uttar Pradesh.

PAEDIATRIC AIDS

AIDS in children is substantially unrecognised and underreported because of the difficulty in diagnosing it in infancy. Moreover, the clinical features of AIDS overlap with a number of other diseases peculiar to children. In 1995 almost 95 per cent of AIDS deaths among children below the age of 15 years occurred in the under-5 age group. According to the WHO estimates,

30 to 35 per cent of children of HIV positive mothers contact the disease peri-natally. As half of the infected persons in 1995 were women, by 2000 AD about 13 million women had become HIV positive and 4 million of them died of AIDS. Their uninfected children would be potential orphans, as practically all their mothers would die within 5 to 10 years of their birth. So that there will be around 10 million children under 10 may be orphaned in sub-Saharan Africa alone and child mortality rates may go up by 50 per cent. The situation in Southeast Asia is also alarming as many women belonging to poorer families are at particularly high risk of infection. Paediatric AIDS will increase accordingly.

Women, who are HIV positive and are not under medication and breast-feed their babies, have a 15 per cent chance of transmitting HIV infection to their offsprings through breast milk. During the last two decades 1 to 1.7 million children are estimated to have contracted HIV this way. And almost all these cases were in the developing countries, especially sub-Saharan Africa. Such cases are rare in developed countries as all pregnant mothers are HIV tested and those found HIV positive are advised to desist from breast feeding. Moreover, they get quality medical care that includes the use of anti-retro-viral drugs. This strategy does work well in the developed countries where potable water is universally available. In the developing parts of the world, the situation is far more complex. First, most of HIV positive mothers are not aware of the infection, as they have not been sero-tested. *Second*, even those who are aware of the problems, try to keep it a secret. Third, the status of health services in many of the developing countries is too elementary to cope with HIV problems. Fourth, commercial infant formula as substitutes for breast-feeding is not accessible to the poorer sections of the population. And finally, even if such formula foods are available, the uncontaminated water in which they are prepared is not available. That is why, the formula-fed infants have 4 to 6 times greater chances of dying in developing countries. According to WHO estimates, about 1.5 million children die in the developing countries because of the lack of breast-feeding. In the interest of their babies, mothers infected with HIV or not sure of their HIV status, should opt for formula foods making it sure that only boiled water is used in its preparation. But all others should breast feed, and not opt for formula foods.

CHILD CARE IN INDIA

Children's health depends to a great extent on mothers' health. The present strategy is, therefore, to provide an integrated health service to both mother and child. The main focus of the services is reduction of mortality, spacing of pregnancies, limitation of family size, prevention of communicable diseases, improvement of nutrition and promoting acceptance of the services. It is known as Mother and Child Health Services (MCH). It has six components

1. maternal health,
2. family planning,
3. child health,
4. school health,
5. handicapped children, and
6. day care children.

Primary Health Care (PHC) units have been established all over the country to make health services accessible to the people. In these units the obstetric and pediatric units have been linked so that there are regular contacts between obstetricians, pediatricians, community physicians and health and social workers. Early detection of mothers and children with high risk for additional and more skilled care has been introduced. This approach enables the determination of priority activities within the MCH programme. Manpower has been augmented to include medical specialists, field workers such as multipurpose workers, health guides, dais, *anganwadi* workers and voluntary workers belonging to women's organizations.

Each PHC in rural areas covers a population of 30,000. There are 10 sub-centers each catering to 3000-5000 people. Each sub-centre has two health workers: one male and one female. They provide preventive and promotive healthcare in addition to MCH and family planning services.

The National Health Policy 1983 had set the followin; MCH goals for the year 2000:

1. Reduction in mortality rates	
(a) Infant mortality rate	60
(b) Perinatal mortality rate	35
(c) Child mortality rate	10
(d) Maternal mortality rate	2
2. Babies with birth weight below 2500 grams	10
3. Services	
(a) Immunization	
Infants	95 per cent
Pregnant	100 per cent
(b) Delivery by trained personnel	100 per cent
(c) Antinatal care	100 per cent
4. Incidence of blindness due to VAD	0.3 per cent

The immunization programme covers the following diseases.

Disease (vaccine)	*Recommended Age*
1. Tetanus (T.T.)	2 doses for expectant mothers
2. Tetanus (T.T./T.D.)	10 years, 16 years; 2 doses of TT to pregnant women
3. Diptheria Pertusis (whooping cough) Tetanus (D.P.T.)	Triple doses to cover sixth week, Tenth and fourteenth week, 16-18 months and 5 years.
4. Tuberculosis (B.C.G).	0-3 months;
5. Polio (O.P.V.)	Birth, sixth week, tenth week, 16-18 months, and 5 years
6. Hepatitis B:	Chosen date, one month after the first dose, 6 months after the first dose;

7. Measles	9 months (during epidemics, it can be given after 6 months);
6. Typhoid	2 years (should be repeated every three years thereafter;
7. M.M.R.	15 months (for better protection, it can be repeated after 5 years;
9. Hepatitis A:	Above one year (two doses are needed with a gap of 6 months;
10. HiB conjugate:	sixth week, tenth week, fourteenth week, 16-18 months;
11. Varicella, etc.	Above 1 year (only one dose needed;
12. Influenza Every year.	

In addition to the immunization programme, there are two other programmes to improve the health of mothers and children. These are:

1. prophylaxis (preventive treatment) against nutritional anaemia among women; and
2. prophylaxis against blindness due to vitamin A deficiency (five doses) starting from 1st year of birth.

INTEGRATED CHILD DEVELOPMENT PROGRAM (ICDP)

This programme was launched in 1975. It now covers almost all community development blocks. It aims at improving the nutritional and health status of children in the age group of 0-6 years; laying sound foundation of psychological, physical and social development of children; reducing morbidity, mortality, malnutrition, and school drop outs; imparting nutrition and health education to mothers for making them more competent in looking after nutrition and health needs of children. The beneficiaries of the programme are pre-school children and pregnant and lactating mothers.

This programme is carried out through anganwadis set up all over the country. Each Anganwadi serves a population of 1000 in rural areas and 700 in tribal areas. There are approximately 100 Anganwadis in each community development block. In some states like UP, the anganwadi workers are attached to primary schools.

Child Survival and Safe Motherhood Programme

This programme was started in 1992. It is designed to provide appropriate advice on infant feeding, control of vitamin A deficiency, control of acute respiratory infections, management of diarrhea in children, care of new born infants, antenatal care to pregnant mothers, safe delivery services, basic care to neonates, advice on nutrition and prevention of anaemia, tetanus immunization, antenatal care, delivery by trained persons, facilities for obstetric emergencies and birth spacing.

Reproductive and Child Health (RCH) Programme

The National Family Welfare Programme has been renamed as RCH. Among the services it provides are prevention and management of unwanted pregnancies; promotion of safe motherhood and child survival; nutritional supplements for the poor; treatment of reproductive tract infections and sexually transmitted diseases, reproductive health survey for adolescents, sex education, contraceptives, safe delivery, reduction of morbidity and mortality due to reproductive tract infection and prophylaxis against gonoccocal ophthalmia and maternal syphilis.

The department of Family Welfare has identified 80 poorly performing districts marked with high rates of birth and mortality. These districts are in the states of Bihar, M.P., Rajasthan, and U.P. Funds are being provided to construct well-equipped labour rooms, O.T., Observation Ward, electricity generator and ambulance in all the health centers.

CONCLUDING REMARKS

Considerable efforts have been made to reduce maternal and child morbidity as well as mortality in India during the last three decades. Support from UNICEF and WHO has been timely and substantial. If we look at the number of schemes and programmes, the scenario is very encouraging. But the ground realities are not commensurate with the efforts made and money spent. India is still far behind the developed countries in matters of maternal and child health.

From management point of view, there are two aspect of maternal and child health: self-management and professional management. Areas of self-management are: environmental cleanliness, personal hygiene, and nutrition. To make any progress, health education is a must and it must become a part of the primary and secondary school curricula. Self-management cannot take place in an economic vacuum. Only those who are above the poverty line can really take care of their health. Unfortunately, a large section of the Indian population is poor and even that which is not poor is poorly educated. As such many of the problems related to the health of mothers and children are rooted in ignorance and can be eased and removed only by proper health education.

Professional management is needed at the time of pregnancy, childbirth, sickness, and emergencies. A working network of primary health centres vertically linked with regional and specialized hospitals alone can meet this need. Unfortunately, the PHCs in rural areas rarely work efficiently either because the infrastructure is poor or because the needed personnel are not in position. Added to this drawback is the tendency among the people especially in rural areas to go to doctor or hospital only after the condition of the patient has become serious. Many of the mission-oriented health programmes like polio eradication drive make only a partial success because the parents do not take children to the polio-drop centres. The latest approach is to go to each of the communities to administer polio-drops. But there are problems here too. A rumour has been floated that the polio-drops were mixed with drugs that sterilize the children receiving it. As such many parents hide their children and refuse to get them immunized.

To remove these obstacles, a joint effort involving the government, local communities and NGO is urgently called for. Each village in the country must be linked to a competent NGO, which could work with government agencies and the local government to promote all development activities, health included. It is particularly important in a situation where the government machinery is slow and less responsive.

Many diseases are caused due to poor diet either because of poverty or ignorance. Nutrition has to be seen in two perspectives particularly for mothers and children. First, it has to be used as a means to maintain health at the optimum level. And second, it should be used as therapy to cure diseases. Diet therapy has certain very special advantages. First, the patient does not feel that he is sick; second, he does not have to take medicines, which generally are toxic; third, the patient gets personalized attention, and fourth, it is relatively inexpensive.

Diet therapy is most suited for children. In fact, if correct diet and clean environment are insured, children would grow healthy in India.

REFERENCES

1. UNICEF: *Children and Women*, p. 21.
2. WHO, *World Health Report*, 1998 to 2002.
3. Registrar General of India, *Survey of Causes of Main Death,* 1998.
4. WHO, *Weakly Epidemiological Report,* 1999.
5. Government of India, Ministry of Health and Family Welfare, *Annual Reports*.
6. C. Gopalan, 'Early Childhood Malnutrition in India-Interstate Differences', *Events Nutrition Foundation of India.* 2003.
7. Ministry of Health and Family Welfare, The Second National Family Health Survey (NFHS-2).

18

Health Care of the Aged

Not long ago most people died before they attained the age of 60. It is not so today. People now live longer than before although the prospects of aging with health do not appear to have become brighter. With improvement in health services, availability of new and more effective medicines, progress in surgery, more nutritive foods, and better care of the children and mothers, the age structure of populations is changing fast. The age and sex pyramid is widening in the middle as the bottom is narrowing. Earlier, very few children lived to celebrate their first birthday; now the situation is not so bad; very few of them are denied this privilege. Earlier, people who lived up to sixty years celebrated the occasion with festivities. Today, it is no longer a privilege; almost everyone expects to live up to sixty and beyond. People do live longer today than before; and the longevity of their life is increasing year after year.

Aging indicates wear and tear in the body and mind. Old age in itself is a disease, which has no cure. Man has always tried to find an elixir, which can stop aging, but he has not succeeded so far, nor is he likely to be in the future. Aging is a biological process; all that is born must age. Man cannot escape this law. Old age cannot therefore be healed; it can be protected, promoted and extended and made least painful. It should be accepted as a normal biological phenomenon. It has its own beauty and charm; age generally means wisdom. To enjoy it, one must accept aging as normal, not a curse. One of the preconditions for joyful aging is good health.

The study of the physical and psychological changes, which take place with aging is called gerontology. It covers a very wide field and is divided into many branches: social gerontology to experimental gerontology.

GLOBAL CHANGE IN AGE STRUCTURE

With increasing longevity of life, 60 years is no longer a cut off point to be called aged. Aged is one who is 65+ years old. The global population aged 65 and above is growing at the rate of

750, 000 per month. By 2025 there will be as many as 800 million persons in the age group of 65+ years, two-thirds of them in the developing countries and a majority of them will be women. There will be 274 million people over 60 years in China alone by the 2030. India will have almost the same number of senior citizens by that time. Thirteen per cent of US population is above 65 years; it was only 4 per cent at the beginning of the twentieth century. By 2030, the percentage will go up to 20. In 1950, France had only 200 persons above the age of 100 years; today there are 8500 such persons and the number is likely to go up to 150,000 by 2050. In India, about 6.67 per cent of population was above 60 years of age in 1991; in absolute terms it amounted to 56.50 millions. In another two decades this percentage is likely to go up to 15 which, when translated in absolute terms, will amount to 225 million people, that is almost the same as the total population of the USA in 1995.

By 2050 the world may have more elderly persons than children. It will have a profound effect on the society. With age, the ability of the people to take care of themselves declines. Parents can be relied upon to take care of the children but who should be relied upon to take care of the elderly? This question needs urgent attention. The elderly had a respectable place in a joint family system; the siblings were duty bound to take care of them. With the breaking of joint families, the elderly are no longer part of the family. Their position is becoming precarious even in countries like India where joint family culture is so deep rooted. Some parents have no sons and daughters to depend upon; some others have offspring but they do not live with them. In agricultural societies everyone was expected to live in the same place and residence generation after generation. It is no longer so. The number of sons and daughters who take care of the elderly parents is declining rather fast even in developing countries. Cases of old parents being left to die uncared are no longer rare.

Moreover, there will be less children to take care of and more elderly persons needing support from the civil society. The growth rate of the ageing population will be 88 per cent during the next two or three decades, but that of the working population only 45 per cent. This means that declining number of workers will have to support the increasing number of ageing dependents. Even in developing countries like India and China, the changing age structure of population is going to make a major difference in how we organize our medical and health services and allocate funds for various social welfare measures. In view of the many other current pressing problems, the global challenge of ageing has not yet been fully appreciated.

HEALTH PROBLEMS OF THE AGED

Health Requirements

With increasing cost of medical care, the problems of the elderly are multiplying fast. Most of the old and frail people even in rich countries like the USA cannot meet the healthcare expenses. With governments becoming more stringent about social security, problems of the elderly are sure to multiply. The civil society has come up with programmes and schemes for institutionalized care. Health insurance offers at least partial relief but it is still to reach the lower middle class and the poor. Homes for the aged are a must and special wards, doctors, nurses and other paramedical personnel have to be posted in hospitals to cater to the needs of elderly. Ageing people need long term, continuous, respectful and loving care and support.

Advanced age in itself is debilitating; disease stricken elderly face insurmountable problems. It is one thing to treat a disease which is a temporary setback in health, but quite another to deal with a long lasting problem and problem that escalates as time passes. It is beyond cure but not beyond care.

The WHO has launched a global initiative for the study of functioning and disablement called International Classification of Impairment, Disabilities and Handicaps (ICIDH) with emphasis on medical diagnosis and treatment of people suffering from disabilities of various kinds. It was however, realized that practically everyone becomes a victim of impairment and disabilities sooner or later, and hence the approach had to be universal. The ICIDH was therefore renamed as International Classification of Impairments, Activities and Participation (ICIDH-2) to cover all human beings. Further, because the environmental as well as personal situations in which the elderly people find themselves differ widely, ICIDH-2 takes into account the contextual factors too in the classification.

It is obvious that with the breaking down of joint family system, civil society has to come forward to take care of the elderly, particularly those who are disabled. This task, earlier came in the purview of individual families. It is no longer so. With the number of the aged people on the increase, it may not be possible for the governmental agencies under the present budgetary provisions to foot the bill. The global challenge of ageing has not yet been fully appreciated. It is going to change the whole gamut of our health scenario. The pertinent questions being asked are: Who should take care of the aged: governments, or private sector or both singly or jointly? Should the elderly be put in old age homes or they should be a part of the family structure? Should part of the wages people earn during their working life be paid as old age pension? Should there be a special tax to mop resources for this purpose? There are no clear-cut answers to these questions. Much depends on cultural contexts and traditions of social welfare. It is, however, clear that people must plan for a longer life span extending much beyond their working life. They must save far more than their parents did to meet their old age requirements. The civil society would have to find new ways and means to pay for the healthcare of the non-earning elderly needing frequent hospitalization and general healthcare at short notice.

Even if the problems related to the cost of meeting the health needs of the aged are satisfactorily resolved, there is no guarantee that they would get all the attention they deserve. No society will ever be able to take care of the ever-growing number of terminally sick, paralyzed, disabled and bed-ridden people. What is needed is a long life with good health. Doctors and hospitals cannot give good health; they can only cure diseases, if at all. If health is for more than absence of disease then medical care can be only a complimentary measure. Solution lies in:

1. Health promoting lifestyles.
2. Environmental cleanliness and serenity.
3. More active and less stressful living.
4. Reinventing joint family in which aged have a place. And
5. creating old age friendly living and medical facilities.

Healthy ageing is the new slogan coined by the WHO. It appears that the Rishis of ancient India had found a right way of healthy ageing. They prescribed four Ashramas (stages) of life:

the youth, the working age, the mature stage, and the old age. Youth ought to be spent in learning, the working age in raising family and earning money, the mature life in serving the family and the community at large, and the old age in teaching and meditation for peace and harmony. In those days, the number of people was limited, the natural resources were plenty, and the reverence for life was abundant. Society through the family took care of the aged who were considered to be assets rather than liabilities for they were supposed to possess wisdom.

Now things are different. Our style of life has changed enormously and many of the things we do are not good for our health. We smoke, chew and sniff tobacco knowing fully well that tobacco is injurious for health. We consume intoxicating drugs just to get a thrill, knowing full well that they weaken our nervous, mental and metabolic systems. It is rightly said that in youth man invites diseases; in old age diseases invite man.

Among the elderly, women have special problems. Women live longer than men and hence quite many of them are widows, poor and lonely. With reduced maternal mortality, longevity of life of women in developing counties like India is going up. The share of women among the oldest old of the (85+ year) is steadily increasing. Apart from the problems of impairment and disabilities, there are a number of diseases peculiar to elderly women. Important among them are diseases of the circulatory system, cancer, chronic obstructive pulmonary disease, musculoskeletal conditions, dementia, and visual impairment.

Let us look at these problems in some details.

Common Health Problems

Musculoskeletal Conditions

These conditions reduce mobility and, therefore, have a major adverse impact on self-care. For ageing men and women, exercise is an important preventive activity against all musculoskeletal conditions. In developed parts of the world, lack of exercise and improper nutrition leads to obesity; which in turn gives rise to musculoskeletal problems. In poorer countries too, causes are not very different. Malnutrition and sedentary life are contributory factors.

Osteoporosis

Bone fractures are major causes of disabilities among the elderly. As age advances, bones become porous and week and, therefore, fracture-prone. Women are more prone to bone fractures because after the menopause the rate of their bone loss is fairly high. Fracture of the hipbone is the most common disabling problem among the elderly. In 1990, about 1.7 million elderly men and women suffered hip fracture in the world; the cases are likely to go up to 6.3 million by 2050. Women represent 80 per cent of the cases. The only remedy is to decelerate bone loss by greater intake of calcium, adequate physical activity and bone strengthening diet.

Dementia

Dementia is a group of diseases that generate loss of memory; the most common among them being the incurable Alzheimer disease. Risk of the disease increases with age in people over

60 years. Its course runs from 5 to 20 years from the time of its onset to death. As the disease advances, the loss of memory and related behavioural changes follow.

So far there is no remedy for dementia. The disease being related to age, genes and family history, the possibility of a common medicine applicable to all cases is not in sight. In case of Alzheimer, certain portions of the brain start drying up and the process continues until the brain becomes practically inactive as far as cognition is concerned.

Blindness and Visual Impairment

Visual impairment is common among the elderly people. Apart from cataract, there are many other eye problems that are closely related to old age. Short sightedness and long sightedness are too common to be mentioned here. The very fact that a large number of aged people wear eye-glasses, is indicative of the universality of the problem. People who become totally blind are not few. There are about 20 million blind persons in the world and the number is likely double in a couple of decades.

HEALTH STATUS OF THE AGED IN INDIA

Information on the health status of the aged in India is hard to come by. The main causes of illness of the aged are: arthritis, cataract, bronchitis, hypertension, ear diseases, diabetes, rheumatism, psychiatric problems, bone fractures and dislocations, etc. A survey conducted by the ICMR in 1984-85 of people above the age of 60 years revealed that 88 per cent of them suffered from visual impairment, 40 per cent from locomotive disorders, 19 per cent from neurological and 17 per cent from cardiovascular diseases (Table 18.1)

Table 18.1: India: Aged Persons Reporting Specific Health Problems-1984-85

Ailments	*Reported Percentage*
Visual impairment/complaints	88.00
Locomotive disorders	40.00
Neurological complaints	18.70
Cardiovascular diseases	17.40
Respiratory diseases	16.10
Skin problems	13.30
Gastrointestinal/abdominal problems	9.00
Psychiatric problems	8.50
Hearing problems	8.20
Genitourinary problems	3.50

Source: ICMR

As apparent from Table 18.1, blindness and visual impairment is the most important health problem of the aged. Eighty eight per cent of the people surveyed complained about this disability. Notwithstanding the eradication of smallpox that used to be the major cause of blindness, there are 18 million blind persons in India. Out of these 15 million can be cured if they get right treatment. About 12 million of them are cataract patients who can be totally cured through an affordable and simple surgery. Cataract usually goes unattended because it is a disease of the old age and many of the senior citizens of the country remain neglected either because they are illiterate and poor or because their children do not care for them. About 3.5 million cataract surgeries are annually performed in India. As new cases add to the backlog of 12 million patients, the task of removing the problem is stupendous and requires special programmes carried out on war footings.

According to some estimates, there are 12.50 million economically blind persons in India, 80 per cent of them being cataract patients. At least 2 million cases of blindness are added each year. Most of the cataract patients are above the age of 60 years. Quite many of them are too poor to afford cataract operation. Those who cannot go out of their own locale for operation, even if they have resources, are not few. National Blind Control programme was launched in 1976 with the objective of providing comprehensive eye-care services at primary, secondary, and tertiary levels of health services and achieving substantial reduction in the prevalence of eye diseases in general and blindness in particular.

The programme was slated to bring down the rate of blindness from 1.4 per cent to 0.3 per cent by 2000 AD. During the 1970s its major thrust was ready access to cataract surgery free of charge. The number of operations increased from 0.55 million in 1981 to 1.14 million in 1984-85. Surveys carried out in 1986-89 showed that blindness caused by cataract was still rampant in A.P., J&K, M.P., Maharashtra, Orissa, Rajasthan, Karnataka, Tamil Nadu and U.P. A special drive was initiated for cataract surgery of 11 million persons within a period of 7 years (1989-90 to 1996-97). More than 10 million cataract operations were done during the eighth five-year plan period (1992-93 to 1996-87). A number of NGO's are actively induced in cataract operation.

The target of reducing blindness to 0.3 per cent of the total population could not, however, be achieved during the eighth plan period. The target for the ninth five-year plan period (1997-98 to 2001-02) has been set at 17.5 million cataract operations and 100,000 corneal transplants. These vigorous efforts should go a long way in reducing the burden of cataract blindness, but the speed at which the disease is spreading requires other supplementary and complementary measures along with surgery to handle the problem. At least half of the cataract cases have resulted from malnutrition, lack of health education and proper eye care. Cataract starts at the age of 55 or so. If the inadequacy of vitamin A in diet is eliminated, cataract cases would come down drastically. This vitamin is available from some of the very inexpensive food items readily available in the market but due to ignorance and prejudices, they rarely form an important item in Indian diet.

Given the situation as it is, the attack on blindness has to be double-edged. While the diet improvement is urgent necessity, there is also a need to make eye treatment available within a range of 5 km even in rural parts of India. Early detection and treatment can delay the onset of the disease and spare many an aged people from undergoing the trauma of impaired vision.

MAJOR KILLERS OF THE AGED

According to the annual survey of causes of death (rural) conducted by the Vital Statics Division of the office of the Registrar General of India, the top ten killers of the age (60+ years) in India

(1997) in order of importance are bronchitis and asthma, paralysis of cerebral apoplexy, heart attack, paralysis, cancer, lung TB, anaemia, diabetes, acuteabdomen, uraemia and peptic and gastric ulcers. The per cent of total deaths claimed by each is given in Table 18.2.

Table 18.2: India: Per cent of Deaths by Each of the Top Ten Killers of the Aged 1996-1997

	ICC Codes	*Causes*	*1996*	*1997*
1.	J 20 &45	Bronchitis & asthma	31.0	28.0
2.	I 21-25	Heart attack	14.4	15.8
3.	G 41	Paralysis	10.0	10.7
4.	C 00-97	Cancer	5.9	6.1
5.	A 15	TB of lungs	5.2	5.2
6.	D 50-64	Anaemia	4.9	4.3
7.	E 10-14	Diabetes	1.9	2.1
8.	R 10	Acute abdomen	1.4	1.5
9.	N-17-19	Uraemia	1.1	1.4
10.	K 27-28	Peptic or gastric ulcer	1.1	1.2

Note: 1. For International Code of Diseases (ICD) see Appendix A

2. The total percentage is less than hundred because cause like senility are not included in the causes of death.

Source: Survey of Causes of Death (Rural), 1997.

Bronchitis and Asthma

Bronchitis and asthma belong to the respiratory group of diseases. They together are responsible for almost a third (30 per cent) of all deaths in the age-group 60+. In fact, 92 per cent of total bronchitis and asthma deaths occur after 45 years of age. Heart attack claims 15 per cent of deaths. Among the other major killers of the aged persons are paralysis of cerebral apoplexy (10 per cent), cancer (6.0 per cent), TB of lung (5.2 per cent), anaemia (4.5 per cent), diabetes (2 per cent), acute abdomen (1.5 per cent), Uraemia (1.5 per cent) and peptic or gastric ulcer (1.2 per cent), Unknown causes claim the rest.

If we consider the deaths attributable to various diseases of all age-groups in rural India, we find a slight difference in the ordering of the major killers (Fig. 18.1). Bronchitis and asthma, however, continue to be top killers. 79.2 per cent of all deaths in the 60+ age-group, are caused by this disease. It is, however, not so all over the country. There are differences among the states ranging from 59 to 88 per cent. The states, which recorded higher than the national average, were Gujarat, Kerala, Madhya Pradesh and Maharashtra and the states, which have recorded below 70 per cent were Bihar, Orissa, Rajasthan and Tamil Nadu. States with wet climatic regimes appear to have higher mortality rates (Fig. 18.1).

Heart Attack

Heart attack is a cardiovascular disease, which afflicts the elderly group more than any other age group. It is also known as stroke because they both come under the same category of

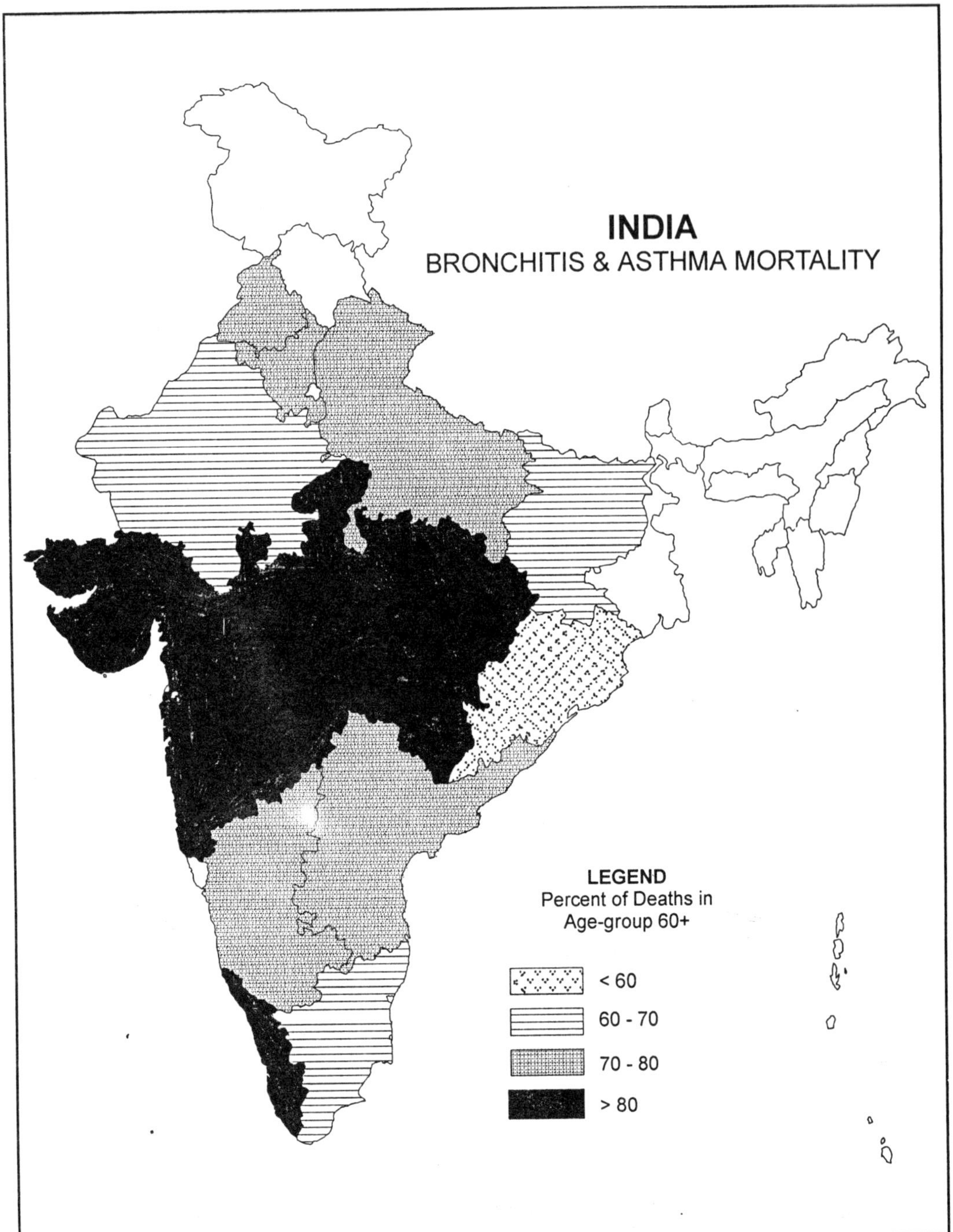

Fig.18.1: India: Old Age Deaths Due to Bronchitis and Asthma

diseases. But there is a difference in so far as the symptoms are concerned. Heart attack is caused by the clot in the arteries carrying blood to or from the heart; the stroke is caused when brain's blood supply is interrupted and lack of oxygen begins to damage the brain cells. A severe stroke can be fatal. Further. Heart attack is often accompanied by pain in the chest; stroke is sudden, without any warning. Before a person realizes that he had a stroke, the damage is already done. Fifty eight per cent of all deaths in India in the age-group 60+ is attributed to heart attack. Percentage is as high as 73.4 in Maharashtra and as low as 3.5 in Rajasthan.

Among the risk factors that increase the chances of heart attack are;

1. Diabetes;
2. Obesity.
3. Family History;
4. High Colestral;
5. Hypertension;
6. Deart Diseases;
7. Atrial Fibrillation;
8. Carotid Artery disease;
9. Smoking; and
10. Drinking (alcohol).

A very high burden of cardiovascular diseases (CVD) in older people is a cause for concern. World wide, it is the leading cause of death of people above the age of 65. Raised blood pressure and serum cholesterol leading to coronary heart diseases is quite common among them. Experiments show that 6 mm Hg reduction in blood pressure reduces the risk of stroke by 40 per cent and of heart attack by 15 per cent and that a 10 per cent reduction in blood cholesterol concentration will reduce the risk of coronary heart diseases by 30 per cent. Low salt and low fat diet will go a long way in keeping the heart of the elderly healthy. Mental peace, meditation and regular walking for 30 to 60 minutes, depending on age and ability, are a must for the elderly. Men appear to be at greater risk than women in matters of heart diseases but, as longevity increases, the difference, if any, tends to narrow down. These measures are helpful if the disease has already set in the person.

Paralysis of Cerebral Apoplexy

Paralysis accounts for over 75 per cent of all old age deaths in India. The states of Andhra Pradesh, Karnataka, Kerala, Orissa and Tamil Nadu have recorded higher than national average of 5.4 per cent of all deaths. As apparent from Table 18.2, the aged are the main victims of this disease. 76.8 per cent of deaths, due to paralysis, occur in the age-group 60+ years. It, however, varies from 53.9 per cent for Uttar Pradesh to 84.1 per cent for Andhra Pradesh. Coastal states show higher percentages (Fig.18.3).

Paralysis is caused by the damage to the portion of the brain, which controls particular parts of the body movement. Different regions of the brain handle different functions. The left sphere (half) control's body's right side: right hand, speech, written language, number skill and reasoning. The right hemisphere controls the left side of the body: left hand, special sense,

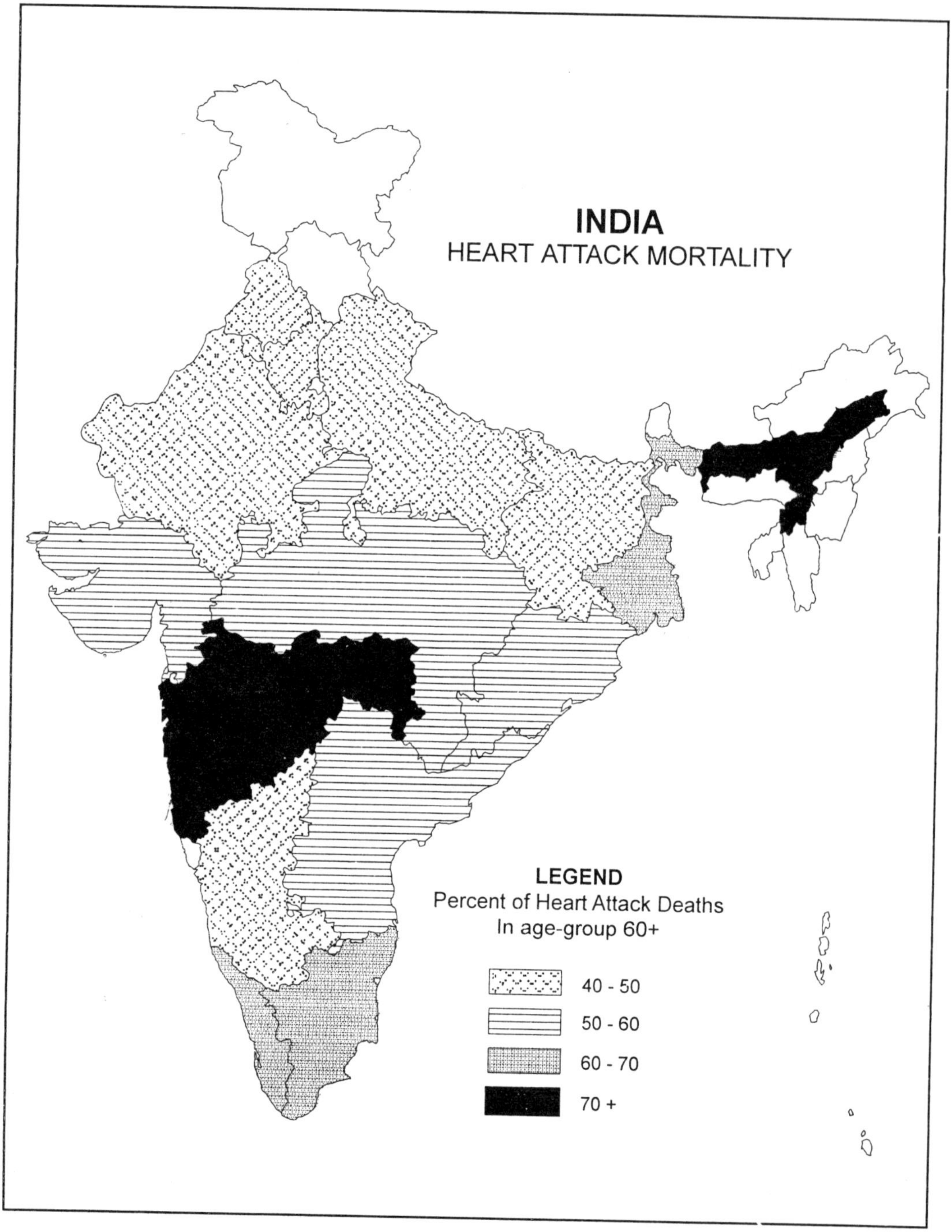

Fig. 18.2: India: Old Age Deaths Due to Heart Attack, 1998.

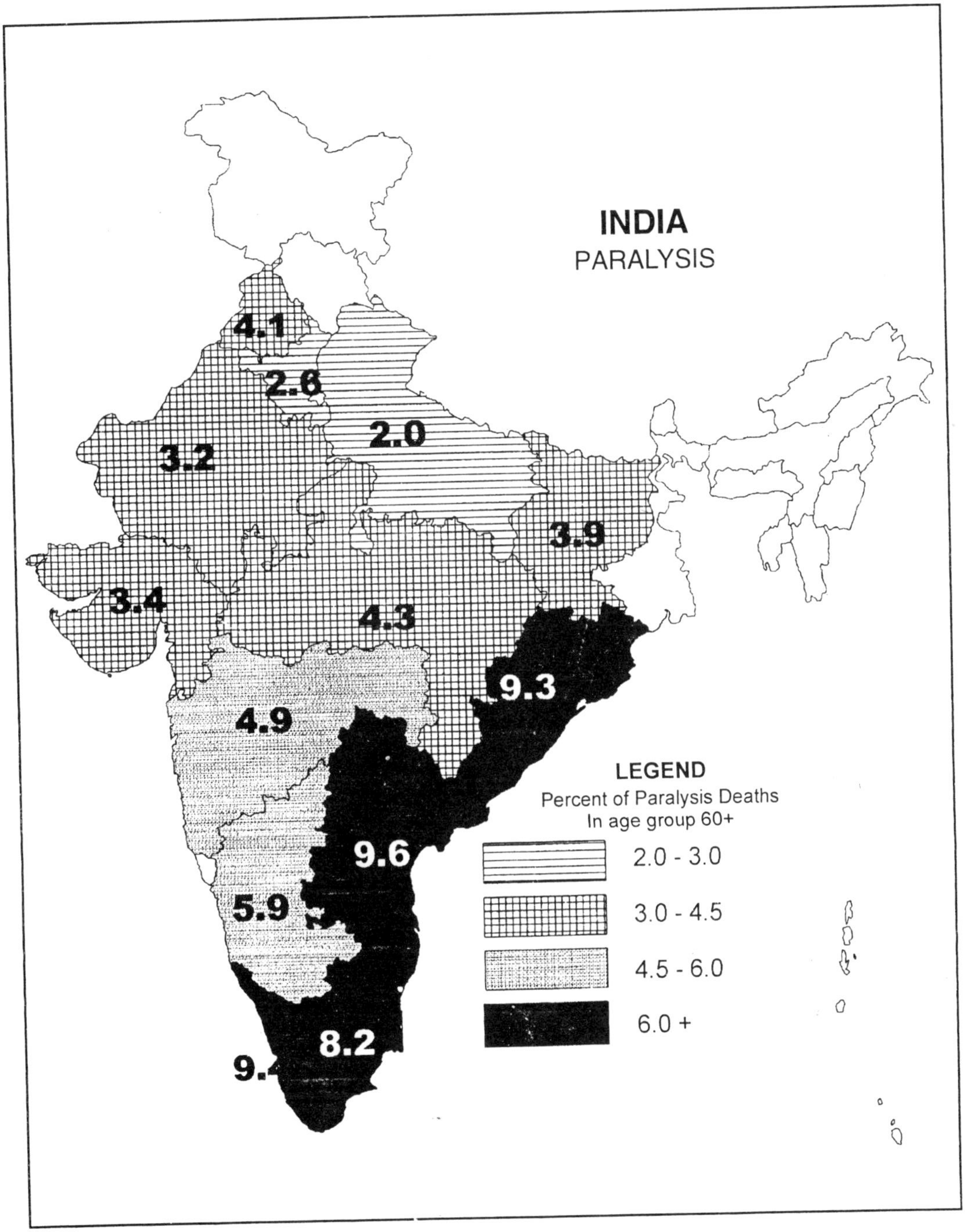

Fig. 18.3: India: Old Age Deaths Due to Paralysis

musical artistic ability, awareness, and creativity. Figure 18.4 gives a generalized map of the brain, which gives a picture of the structure of the brain, the muscles it controls and the sensation it generates in the body.

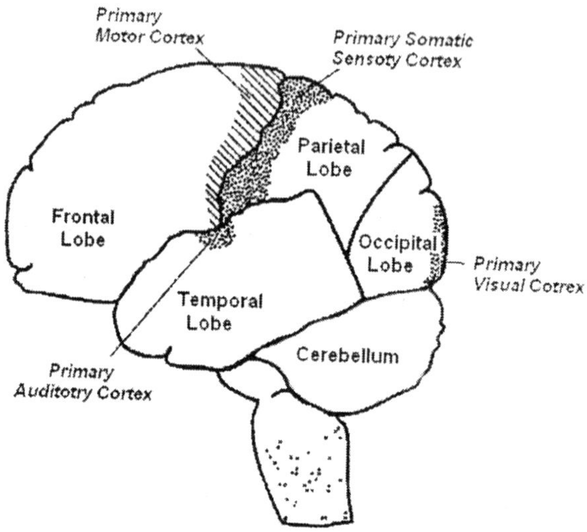

Fig. 18.4: Map of the Human Brain and Its Relation to Body Organs

Cancer

With increasing expectation of life, the risk of individuals developing cancer during their lifetime tends to increase. Most cancers arise at an advanced age and the risk increases steadily with age. Ground for the disease is generally prepared at the age of 35-45 years. Women have an additional burden of breast cancer. It reduces their age by about ten years. For men the eight most killer sites for cancer are lung, stomach, lever, colon-rectum, oesophragus, mouth-pharinx, prostate and lymphoma. For women they are cancers of breast, stomach, colon-rectum, cervix, lung ovary oesophagus and lever. In developing countries cancers of breast, stomach and ovary are the major killers. Lung cancer is related to tobacco consumption.

TB of the Lung

Use of tobacco and polluted environment are the chief causative factors for lung TB. It ranks third among the major killers of the aged in rural India. Aged account for 32-35 per cent of all deaths caused by it. States of Gujarat, Rajasthan, MP, Bihar and UP show higher prevalence than the national average. These data apply to much of the urban population too.

Other Diseases

Then there are other diseases, which are not age specific, but are quite common among the aged. Important among them are anaemia, diabetes, acute abdomen, uraemia, peptic and gastric ulcers

INSTITUTIONAL CARE OF THE AGED

There is no doubt that the elderly need special attention from the medical profession in the same way as children and mothers need. It is particularly so because their number is growing rather rapidly.

Old Age Hospitals

As stated earlier, the number of the aged persons is on the increase. By 2050 AD there will be over 300 million people in the 60+ age-group. To cater to the health needs of such a huge population having special health problems, the establishment of special hospitals for the aged needs no emphasis. There are two main grounds on which special hospitals are created: the peculiarity of the diseases people suffer from and the peculiarity of the group that suffers from the disease or diseases. There are military hospitals because the armed forces need very special type of attention: it must be prompt and often in very adverse circumstances. We have children's hospitals because the children constitute a sizable percentage of our population and they are unable to express their problems to the physician. Then we have specialized hospitals for women who suffer from reproductive problems. Such cases are also very large and they all need very specialized attention by gynaecologist.

With huge increase in the population of the aged and complicated health problems they suffer from, the re is a growing need for special hospitals for them. In fact, old age itself is a major 'disease' requiring constant and day-to-day attention. With increasing age, health problems multiply. Cases of people living in coma for years are not rare and those suffering from terminal diseases are on the increase. For the aged, it is not only the medical attention but also the way this attention is given is important. This is another reason why special hospitals for the aged should be planned.

Apart from the old-age hospitals, there should be special wards for the aged in all general hospitals. Geriatrics, a branch of medicine, which deals with diseases and physiological changes associated with aging and old people, should get greater attention. Every hospital should have increasing number of specialists in this field.

Old Age Homes

Elderly people suffer from a variety of disabilities. Apart from health problems, they have psychological problems too. Often they suffer from the feeling of neglect and helplessness. They want to be part of the social process; they don't want to be onlookers from a distance. While hospitals can take care of their health problems, their social and psychological problems can be taken care of by the family and community alone.

With the disintegration of the joint family system, particularly in the urban setting, the elderly people are left uncared. Even if they have enough resources to stand on their own feet, they are not secure. Cases of murder of the aged living alone in multi-storey flats of large cities are on the increase. Old age homes can meet to a great extent their social and psychological needs apart from taking due care of their health. These homes provide decent lodging, boarding, recreation, healthcare and other associated facilities.

India should plan a series of old age homes in all cities, district head quarters and community centres for the aged even in rural areas. Where the threshold of population is inadequate, there could be centres at the district level to begin with.

Health Insurance

Health insurance is a must for the aged. Healthcare is becoming a costly proposition. It will not be within the reach of common people. Governments too are short of resources. They cannot foot the bill in full. Health insurance alone can mitigate the problem. This should be so organized that everyone is made to contribute to health insurance policy. The governments, instead of giving variety of subsidies that never reach the poor, should contribute towards health insurance of the poor.

In a country like India where a great majority of people are engaged in unorganized sectors of the economy, where people care for today more than for tomorrow, and where a large number of people are un-or under-employed, participation in health insurance schemes is not easy. But a beginning has to be made. Life Insurance Corporation is already in the field but it covers only a fringe of the population.

INTERNATIONAL COOPERATION

Having realized the seriousness of the problems of the aged, the United Nations convened a World Assembly on Ageing in 1982. This initiative produced what is now known as Vienna International Plan of Action on Aging which the WHO implemented during1982-87 through its member states. After a series of meetings and consultations, the WHO published *The Uses of Epidemiology in the Study of the Elderly* in 1984. Since 1994, the programme has been oriented towards ageing and health. The new programme sees the aged as part of the life cycle and hence instead of treating them as a special category, it considers ageing as a tail end of the continuum of life. For smooth ageing and healthy old age, nothing will work unless a life-long endeavour is made. To lower the burden of ill-health and diseases in the later part of the life cycles, man would have to adopt a lifestyle that keeps the body system in tune with the laws of nature. True, there is a need to develop institutions that cater to health and other needs of the aged as also the need to promote cohesion between the aged and others to narrow the generation gap, the fact that the problem of the ageing is not just the problem of the aged, must be appreciated.

TOWARDS A NEW CULTURE OF CARE AND SHARE

The problems of the aged constitute only one spectrum of the overall societal problems humanity faces today. Our economic thinking during the last two hundred years or so has led us to a social mess wherein human values have taken a back seat. Humanity stands highly fractured – geographically, socially, economically and technologically. Violence against life in general is the rule rather than exception. The community solidarity that kept people united is loosened and the joint family, that was once a dependable source of strength and security against unexpected happenings, is no longer so. In this changed situation the children, the aged, and economically and socially weak become easy victims.

Only a new culture of care and share can fill the gap. Progress and development cannot be confined to economics for the end product is not money or more consumer goods but more happiness, satisfaction and self-realization. Money alone cannot raise the standard of life; it can only raise the standard of living when measured in terms of creature comforts. To raise the standard of life, economic growth must be accompanied by moral development. Then and then alone economic development will be able to create a happy and peaceful society.

Rapid economic growth in Europe, Japan and North America has not made these regions more happy, peaceful and fearless than before. Recent terrorist attack on the USA has proved the utter hollowness of the progress we have made so far. There are people who are prepared to commit suicide if only the people they consider to be villains can be killed. Here is a society wherein killing, death and destruction are normal features of life and living. Hundreds and thousands of innocent people are being killed only because a few others want to tell the world that what they say is the only thing that is right. All others are wrong and hence they deserve death and destruction.

This indeed cannot be the hallmark of development in any civilized society and hence the need for a new civilization, a new culture and a new meaning of development wherein the *the* right to life and living of each human being, may, each life is fully protected. It is then and then alone that the rights of the will be are protected and they would get due compensation for the contributions they have already made to the society.

REFERENCES

1. Government of India, Ministry of Social Welfare, *Annual Reports.*
2. Help-Age India, *Periodic Reports.*
3. Government of India, Ministry of Health, *Health Information of India, 1999-2000.*
4. WHO, *World Health Reports* (annual).
5. WHO, *Regional Health Report (South and South-East Asia),* annual.

19

Medical Education

India has been a forerunner country in matters of medical education. Soon after independence it started a number of institutions to train medical personnel, and to promote medical education and research. Among these were medical colleges, dental colleges, nursing colleges, colleges of pharmacy, research institutions and paramedical training institutions. India is one of the advanced countries of the world in terms of medical education. Indian doctors are spread over the whole world, both developed and developing.

As in 1998, India had 167 medical colleges admitting over 0.12 million students. 110 of these colleges were government run. In addition to these, there were 77 dental colleges, 290 institutions offering diploma courses in pharmacy, and over 1500 institutions for training of nurses and paramedical personnel. A number of regulatory bodies have been set up to maintain appropriate standards of medical education. Among these bodies, Medical Council of India, Dental Council of India, Indian Nursing Council, Pharmacy Council of India, National Academy of Medical Sciences, and Indian Council of Medical Research are the most prominent ones.

India had its own system of medicine from very ancient times. Ayurveda, the science of longevity, after 800 years of neglect, has once again emerged as a system of medicine most suited to human biology. There were other systems too: Siddha system, Unani system, Naturopathy, Yoga, and Folk medicine. Ayurveda, in olden days, received state patronage and spread all over the country through well-trained vaidyas who not only diagnosed the diseases but also prepared the medicines suited to each patient's temperament, body structure, state of health, etc.; Siddha system has been popular in South India. It is based on Yogic exercises coupled with some medications; Unani system is based on Greek medicine. It was transformed and further developed by the Arabs and the Persians. It had royal patronage in India during the periods of Sultanate and the Moghuls but received setback after the British introduced modern medicine during the nineteenth century. Nature cure continues to be popular in India because its mode of treatment has become a part and parcel of day-to-day life in India. In fact, folk medicine in many respects is naturopathy. Mahatma Gandhi was a votary of naturopathy. Now it is being treated as an important alternative medical science deserving promotion and encouragement. Yoga is a science and art of living that has become a household word all over the world. It helps in developing an integrated personality by establishing a balanced relationship between body, mind and heart (feelings). It has become so popular and its merits have been so widely recognized that attempts are being made to evolve a symbiotic relationship between Yoga naturopathy and modern medicine.

The British introduced allopathic system of medicine in India in eighteenth century. Physicians and surgeons were brought from England to treat British officers and servicemen and to man newly started hospitals. As the number of Englishmen increased, the communicable diseases also increased. Some were indigenous to which the British were not immunized; many others were brought by foreigners – the English, Portugese, French, Dutch, etc. Ayurveda, the indigenous systems of medicine, was not geared to cope with the new challenges. Diseases like plague, cholera and smallpox took a heavy toll of life. The British tried to send Indians to get medical education in England; but the task of maintaining public health system was so huge that they ultimately decided to open institutions within the country to train English educated Indians in allopathic system of medicine, nursing and pharmacy.

After Independence, the system introduced by the British has not only continued but also expanded. There were three important reasons for the policy of consolidation and continuation:

1. Indian systems of medicine have been rather stagnant for the last few centuries and hence they could not cope with the new health problems faced by the country;
2. health infrastructure, that the British developed during the last two centuries, could not be dismantled even if Indian systems of medicine were capable of dealing with the problems at hand; and
3. it was found out that no system of medicine could tackle all emergent and emerging health problems singly; all had their own strengths and weaknesses; and hence all systems needed encouragement.

As such it was decided to maintain the allopathic system and to simultaneously develop other systems also. Thus, India has five main systems of medicine and healthcare and for each there are institutions to train medical personnel.

1. Allopathic or Modern,
2. Ayurveda and Siddha,
3. Unani,
4. Homeopathy,
5. Naturopathy and Yoga, and

MODERN (ALLOPATHIC) SYSTEM

Education

Allopathic system, otherwise known as western system of medicine, was introduced in India in the mid-nineteenth century. To meet the growing demand of medical personnel, the British decided to establish medical training centres in India. The Medical Council of India was established as a statutory body under the provisions of the Indian Medical Council Act of 1933, later replaced by IMC Act of 1956, which was amended in 1993, to regulate medical education. The main functions of the Council include: maintenance of uniform standards of medical education, maintenance of Indian Medical Register, recognition of foreign medical degrees, and registration of medical practitioners. No medical college can offer medical education unless the Council is satisfied that it can meet all the requirements fixed by it. The Council has notified guidelines for the establishment of new medical colleges in the country.

There were 167 medical colleges in 1996, 163 of them were recognized by the Council. The annual intake of students in these colleges stood at 17,000. Until 1980s the policy of the government was to discourage opening of new medical colleges as the existing medical colleges were considered sufficient to meet the manpower needs of the country. With the extension of medical services to the rural areas and opening of primary health centres all over the country, shortage of medical personnel became visible. To fill this gap between supply and demand, the Medical Council Act 1956 was amended in 1993. It was decided to permit opening of new medical colleges. It was also decided to encourage private sector to enter medical education field. Between 1993 and 2000, 18 new medical colleges were started, 13 of them in the private sector. And many more are being planned.

About 12,000 students are admitted to various medical colleges in the country for bachelor degree (MBBS) course each year. It is interesting to note that the number of admissions has almost remained constant while that of the colleges offering the courses has gone up from 98 in 1971-72 to 165 in 1995-96. The distribution of medical colleges is very uneven no matter what the basis of assessment. Some states like Karnataka have too many of them and some states like Uttar Pradesh have very few of them.

In 19771-72, there were 98 medical colleges admitting 12,048 students; in 1995, the number of medical colleges increased to 165 and the students admitted to 122,500 almost a tenfold increase. Had this growth been distributed more evenly, the health service scenario in the country would have been a little better than what it is today flee speed with which new medical colleges are being set up in India, the regional disparities in the medical education facilities may not last for too long..

State-wise distribution of medical colleges is given in Figure 19.1.

Medical Research

Indian Council of Medical Research has a network of 21 permanent research institutes and six Regional Research Centres distributed throughout the country to conduct and promote research in communicable as well non-communicable diseases, nutrition and basic medical sciences like pathology, tumor biology, male fertility, haematology and several other fields.

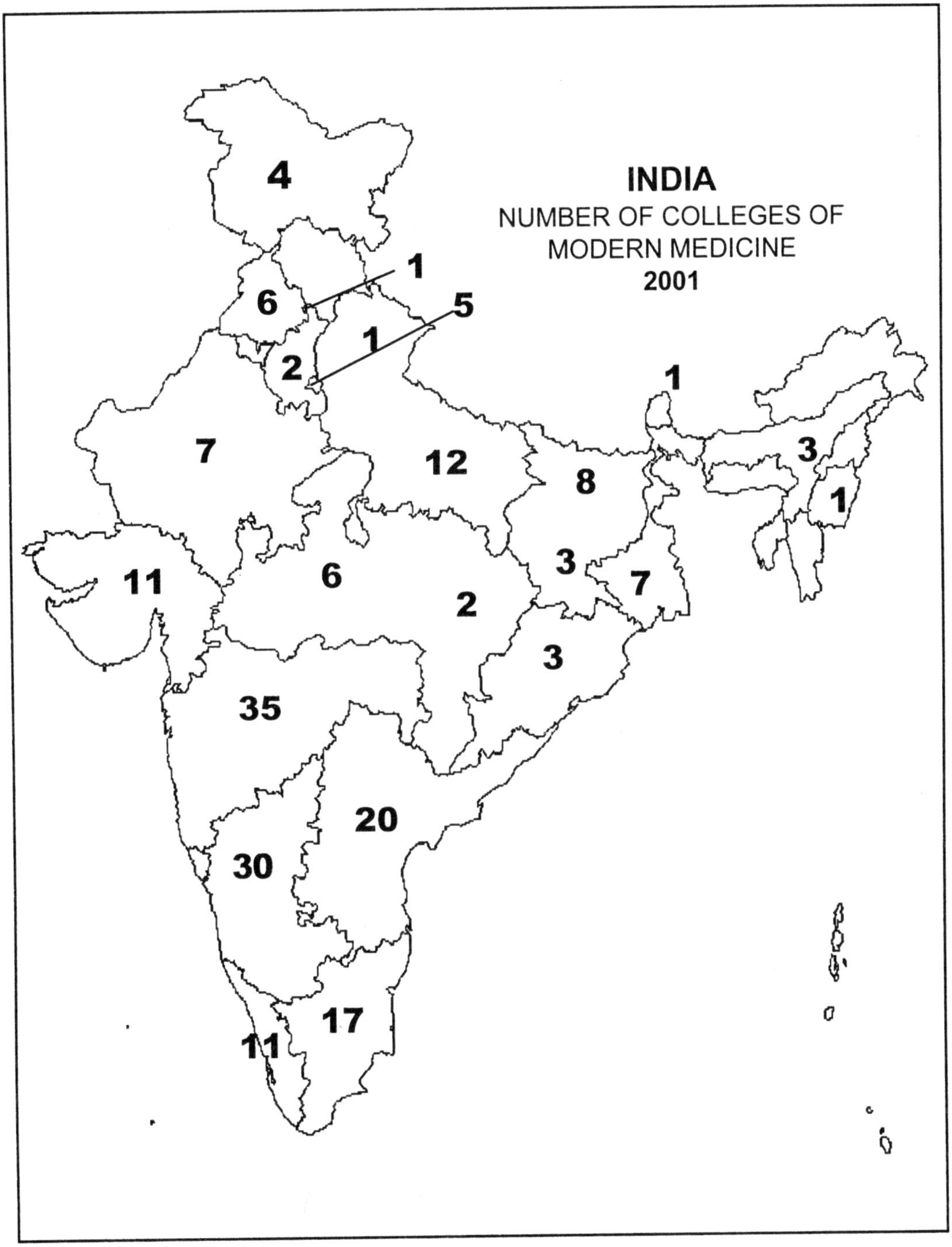

Fig. 19.1: India: Distribution of Colleges of Modern Medicine

A number of institutes have been set up in different parts of the country to conduct research in medical fields and on problems assigned to them. Important among them are Vallabhbhai Patel Chest Institute, Delhi; National Institute of Health & Neuro Sciences, Biological, New Delhi (to ensure availability of good quality of biological products like vaccine etc.); All-India Institute of Hygiene and Public Health, Kolkata; Central Leprosy Training and Research Institute, Chengalpattu; L.R.S. Institute of Tuberculosis and Allied Diseases, New Delhi; National Tuberculosis Research Institute, Bangalore; National Institute of Mental Health, Bangalore, Rural Health Training Centre, Najafgarh, Institute of Communicable Diseases, New Delhi; Pasteur Institute of India, Coonoor; All-India Institute of Physical Medicine and Rehabilitation; All-India Institute of Speech and Hearing; Central Institute of Psychiatry and Neurosciences, Ranchi; Central Research Institute, Kasauli (for production of bacterial, viral vaccines and sera); Central Bureau of Health Intellegence, New Delhi; and National Medical Library, New Delhi.

INDIAN SYSTEM OF MEDICINE AND HOMEOPATHY

The Indian system of medicine includes all those systems, which originated in India, as also those, which came to India from outside but were adopted and adapted to suit Indian conditions. These systems are Ayurveda, Siddha, Unani, Naturopathy and Yoga. All these systems are very closely related to each other and even go together. These systems are largely based on natural biological products and meditation and hence their medical formulations, prescriptions and practices do not produce side effects. This is the reason why these systems have become very popular and except in serious and emergency cases, people prefer to use these systems. There is another advantage that these systems possess. They lay emphasis on keeping good health through a good style of life, rather than getting good treatment once a disease attacks the body.

The Central Council of Indian Medicine is a legally constituted autonomous body under the Indian Medicine Central Council Act 1970. It was reconstituted in 1984 and 1995. The main functions of the Council are: to prescribe minimum standards of education in Indian system of medicine; to advise the government of India on the recognition of medical qualifications; to maintain a Central Register of Indian Medicine; to regulate practice in Indian medicine and prescribe professional conduct, etiquette and code of ethics.

Ayurveda

National Institute of Ayurveda was established in 1976 at Jaipur by the government of India as an apex institute charged with the responsibility of developing high standards of teaching, training and research in all branches of Ayurveda. The Institute has bachelor, master and Ph.D. level programmes. The post-graduate courses (Ayurveda Vachaspati) include Sharir Rachna, Sharir Kriya, Maulik Siddhanta, Rasa Shasta, Dravya Guna Vikriti Vigyan, Kaumarya Bhritya, Shalya Tantra, and Kaya Chikitsa. It is affiliated to the Rajasthan University, Jaipur.

Gujarat University of Ayurveda, Jamnagar is an Institute of Post-graduate Training and Research. It imparts higher education in all branches of Ayurveda and carries out advanced research leading to the perfection of Ayurvedic treatment. It has a well equipped hospital to treat patients and conduct Panchakarma etc. The Rashtriya Ayurveda Vidyapeeth, New Delhi was established in 1988. It is an institute that promotes Guru-shishya tradition of Ayurveda training. At present, it conducts two innovative courses. A 2-year post-MD acharya Guru-shishya training programme leading to membership of the Vidyapeethdiploma; and a one year Chikitsak-Guru training programme leading to the award of Cetificate of the Rashtriya Ayurveda Vidyapeeth.

There are 154 medical colleges of Ayurvedawith admission capacity of 6,300, one-fourth of them being in Karnataka alone. They offer BAMS degree, which is equivalent to MBBS degree of allopathic colleges. The states with more than one medical colleges are Karnataka (40), Maharashtra (37), Uttar Pradesh (12), Bihar and Gujarat (9 each), Madhya Pradesh and Punjab (8 each), Kerala and Rajasthan (5 each), Andhra Pradesh, Haryana and Orissa (4 each), and Tamil Nadu (3). States having one medical college are: Assam, Delhi, Goa, Himachal Pradesh, West Bengal., and Chandigarh. Figure 19.2 gives the location each of these colleges with their admission capacities. Thirty four Ayurvedic Colleges offer post-graduate degrees and admit 464 students each year. Half of them are located in Maharashtra.

Siddha System

Siddha System of Medicine is also one of the oldest in India. Siddha means a person who is selfrealized; a person who is saintly and who can restore health and vitality through Yoga. It is largely therapeutic in nature. It is based on18 siddhantas or principles. It originated in South India and much of its literature is in Tamil language.

Diagnosis of the problem involves the examination of the pulse, urine, eyes, tongue, voice, colour of the body and status of the digestive system. The system has worked out its colour, smell, density, quantity and oil drop spreading pattern. It involves the study of the disease together with the personality of the patient. Thus, the treatment is not general; it is individualized and differs from person to person, even if the ailment is the same.

The Siddha medicines contain silver, gold, arsenic, lead and sulfur. The system is quite effective in treating chronic cases of fever, skin diseases, rheumatic problems, anemia, prostrate enlargement, bleeding piles and peptic ulcer. It is efficacious in communicable diseases including HIV/AIDS.

A National Institute of Siddha was established at Chennai in 1999. It produces best quality physicians, teachers and researchers. It also ensures good standards of education and professional conduct and research in this branch of medicine. The Institute is located near Tambaram. There are two colleges with admission capacity of 150 students in Siddha imparting undergraduate courses; one of them offers post-graduate courses. Both are located in Tamil Nadu.

Naturopathy and Yoga

Naturopathy is not only a system of treatment but also a way of life. It is often referred to as drugless medical system. It is closely allied to Ayurveda and is an integral part of it. All ancient systems of medicine were naturopathic, to begin with. As diseases increased in number as well intensity, and people became more unnatural in their behaviour, therapeutic elements involving

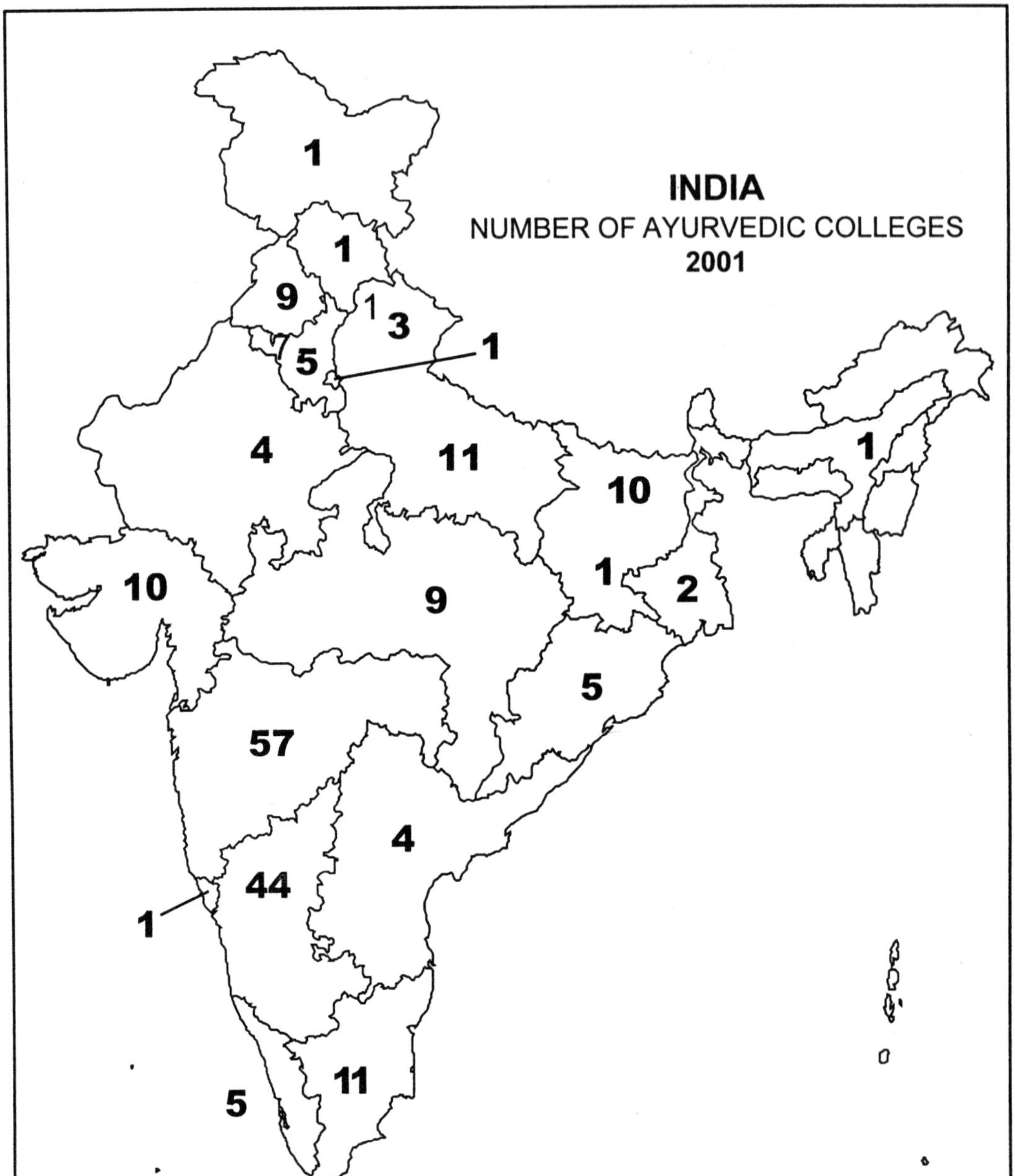

Fig. 19.2: India: Distribution of Ayurvedic Colleges

various types of drugs took deeper roots and nature cure became secondary. With the advent of modern industrial civilization, diseases multiplied further and the era of epidemics set in. Now a new situation has emerged wherein diseases are giving place to systemic disorders for which there are no cures. Change in the style of life to conform to the laws of nature is the only hope for humanity. Naturopathy has thus acquired a new and added importance for it promotes a healthy style of life and treats diseases with the help of exercises, yoga, physiotherapy, direct use of the Panchbhoota of Ayurveda and other non-toxic natural products. According to this system, a properly organized and conducted life gives rise to hountiful of energy, health and happiness.

Naturopathy and Yoga go together. Yoga is again a way of life propounded by Rishi Patanjali. It consists of eightfold rules of conduct: restraint, austerity, physical postures, breathing exercises, training of sense organs, contemplation, meditation and samadhi. These steps in the practice of Yoga improve the social and personal behaviour, enhance physical health by better circulation of oxygenated blood in the body, restrain the sense organs including the mind and induce tranquility and serenity of mind. Yoga prevents psychosomatic disorders and relieves stresses.

Yogic Asanas, if done regularly, improve physical health and prevent as well as cure diseases. Studies have revealed that Yogic practices improve memory power and intelligence and help accumulate energy to endure strains and stresses and develop an integrated psychosomatic personality.

Apart from the Central Council for Research in Yoga and Naturopahy, there is a National Institute of Naturopathy, Pune, which was established in 1984 at Bapu Bhawan with the objective of promoting naturopathy and to encourage research in chronic diseases; prevention of diseases; and development of human personality.

Morarji National Institute of Yoga has been set up at Ghaziabad, near Delhi to act a centre of excellence in Yoga, to develop, promote and propagate the science of Yoga, and to provide and promote facilities for training, teaching and research in Yoga. Vishwayatan Yogashram, New Delhi is also a national level institute to impart education and training in Yogic sciences.

Unani System

This system is quite akin to Ayurveda. Although it originated in Greece in the fifth to fourth centuries BC, it passed through many countries and civilizations before it reached India in medieval times. Arabs, Egyptians, Chinese and Syrians and Persians made significant contributions to its enrichment and growth. When it reached India in medieval times, it received official patronage and encouragement. Now it has become a indeginous medical system of India.

Unani system uses the naturally occurring, mostly herbal, medicines. It was documented by Sheik Bu-Ali Sina in short Avicina (980-1037 AD) in A.I. Qanoon, (medical bible) and in Al-Havi by Razi (850-923 AD). H.K. Azmal Khan, the illustrious Hakim of India, discovered (Asrol) Rawolfia serpentine for the treatment of blood pressure. It is based on humoural theory i.e. presence of blood, phlegam, yellow bile, and black bile determine the temperament of a person expressed as sanguine, phlegmatic, choleric, and malencolic. The medicinal plants too are assigned temperament. Any change in the humours affects the health. Medicines are meant to restore the humouric balance.

Treatment of diseases is carried out in four forms: pharmacotherapy, dietotherapy, regimental therapy, and surgery. For promotion of health and prevention and treatment of diseases, the Unani system lays emphasis on six essentials – exercise and rest, psychic movement and rest, sleep, wakefulness, evacuation and retention.

The National Institute of Unani Medicine, started by the Government of India at Bangalore in 1984, is charged with the responsibility of promoting the growth and development of Unani medicine in the country. The Institute runs post-graduate courses leading to M.S. and Ph.D.

There are 31 medical colleges imparting education in Unani System of Medicine, 3 of them offering post-graduate courses. They are located in the states of Maharashtra (6), Bihar (4), AP, Delhi, Karnataka, Rajasthan, J & K (2 each), Gujarat, MP, Tamil Nadu and W.B. (one each). Together, they admit 1252 students (see Fig. 19.3).

Homeopathy

Homeopathy is a specialized science of curing diseases by administration of drugs, which have been experimentally proved to possess the power of producing similar artificial symptoms on healthy human beings. Homeopathy is based on four fundamental principles: the law of similars, the law of direction of cure, the principle of single remedy and the theory of chronic diseases. These laws and principles were laid down by a German physician Dr. Christian Frederic Sammuel Hahnemann around 1700 AD.

The 'law of similars' states that a medicine, which can produce symptoms of a disease can also cure the disease. The 'law of direction of cure' states that in the process of treatment, the symptoms disappear in the reverse order of their appearance – from above downwards, from more important organs to less important organs. In Homeopathy, a single drug can cure the disease. Remedy is chosen for specific individuals. The 'theory of chronic diseases' states that most of the diseases are caused by three chronic latent affinities in human beings, which normally remain dormant but express their presence when the environment, caused by irregular lifestyle, exposure to unhealthy situation, emotional stress, climatic changes, etc. becomes conducive. These are called Psora, Syphilis and Sycosis.

Homeopathy does not attach importance to the nomenclature of diseases because it treats the physical, mental and spiritual expressions (symptoms) of the patient, not the diseases. The germ theory of diseases, which is the basic foundation of Allopathy, has no relevance in Homeopathy. It is very effective in the treatment of systemic disorders like diabetes, hypertension, arthritis, bronchial asthma, skin, allergic and immunological disorders, behavioural disorders, mental diseases and several other diseases for which there is no treatment in other systems.

Homeopathy was introduced in India by Dr. J.M. Honigberger. He visited India in 1839 and successfully treated Ranjit Singh, the Maharaja of Punjab. Later, Dr. Muller, another homeopath from Germany came to India; his work was reported in *Calcutta Review* of January 1852. Dr. Mahendra Lal Sarkar, a prominent Indian homeopath successfully treated among others Raja Radhakant Dev Bahadur and Ishwar Chandra Vidyasagar. He also started *Indian Medical Review*, the first homeopathic journal in India.

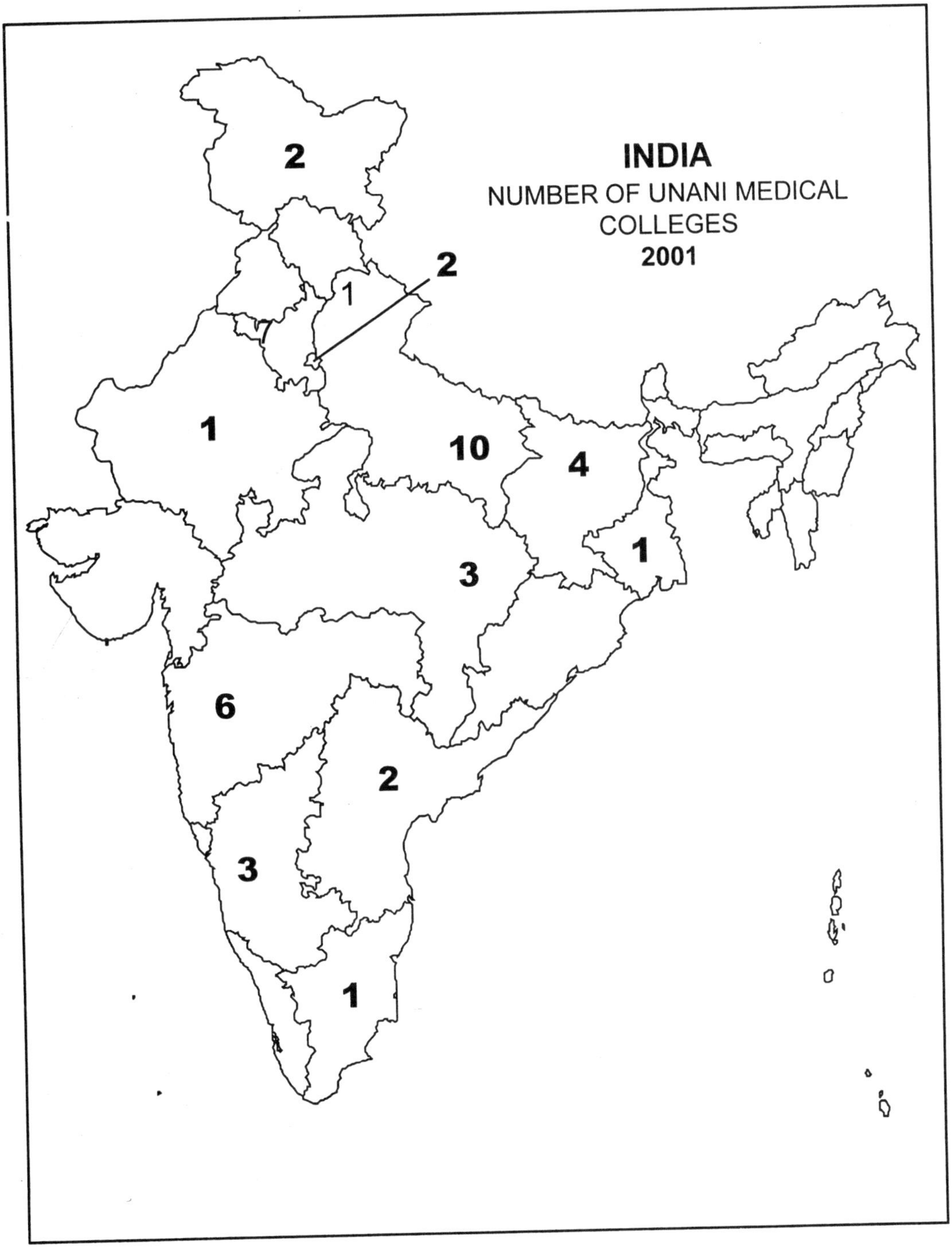

Fig. 19.3: India: Distribtion of Colleges of Unani Medicine

Dr. Salazar was the founder of Homeopathic Education in India. He, along with a few other prominent doctors, established the first homeopathic college in India in 1878. Dr. N.M. Chowdhery was its first principal. Dr. Chowdhery wrote the first book of the Homeopathic Materia Medica in India. Father Muller did pioneering work and treated people suffering from diseases like pneumonia, leprosy, etc. but the British government did not give recognition to Homeopathy. In 1937, it pushed a resolution in the Central Legislative Assembly to set up a Council for the promotion of Homeopathy. It was passed but was implemented only in Bengal.

After Independence, the government became more sympathetic and a resolution was passed by the Constituent Assembly of India in 1948 to set up a Central Council of Homeopathy to give recognition to this system. As a follow up of this resolution, a Homeopathic Pharmacopoeia Committee was constituted in 1962 to maintain uniformity in the preparation of drugs. After a decade or so, the Central Council of Homeopathy was established in 1974 and Central Council for Research in Homeopathy in 1975. The National Institute of Homeopathy affiliated to the University of Calcutta. was also established in Calcutta in 1975. The Institute conducts courses leading to bachelor and doctoral degrees. Kalyani Herb Garden situated 60 km from Kolkata city was set up to acclimatize exotic species of plants of homeopathic importance.

There are 118 colleges and institutions imparting training in homeopathy, ten of them offering post-graduate degrees. The state-wise distribution of these colleges is: Maharashtra (37), West Bengal (13), Gujarat and Uttar Pradesh (10 each), Karnataka (9), Madhya Pradesh (8), Orissa and Punjab (5 each), Andhra Pradesh and Kerala (4 each), Assam, Rajasthan and TN (3 each), Delhi (2), and Bihar and Chandigarh (one each) (Fig. 19.4).

Research in ISM&H

The Central Council for Research in Ayurveda and Siddha (CCRAS), an apex body constituted by the central government to promote research on scientific lines in Ayurveda and Siddha systems of medicine, has been set up. Among the major activities of the Council are: research in medicinal value of various plants, oral contraceptives for birth control and Yoga for treatment of various diseases. It has initiated projects to develop *vanaspati vans* (forests of medicinal plants) in different parts of the country.

STATE WISE DISTRIBUTION OF MEDICAL COLLEGES

Medical education in India as indicated by the location of medical institutions, is not uniformly distributed either in terms of area or population. States like UP, which have one-sixth of the total population of the country have very few colleges offering medical and allied educational facilities. Five peninsular states, Andhra Pradesh, Tamil Nadu, Kerala, Karnataka and Maharashtra together account for 31 per cent of the population of the country but between 55 to 80 per cent of medical education institutions: 60 per cent of allopathic colleges, 62 per cent of Ayurvedic Colleges, 35 per cent of Homeopathic Colleges, 58 per cent of Dental Colleges and 79 per cent of Nursing Colleges (Table 19.1).

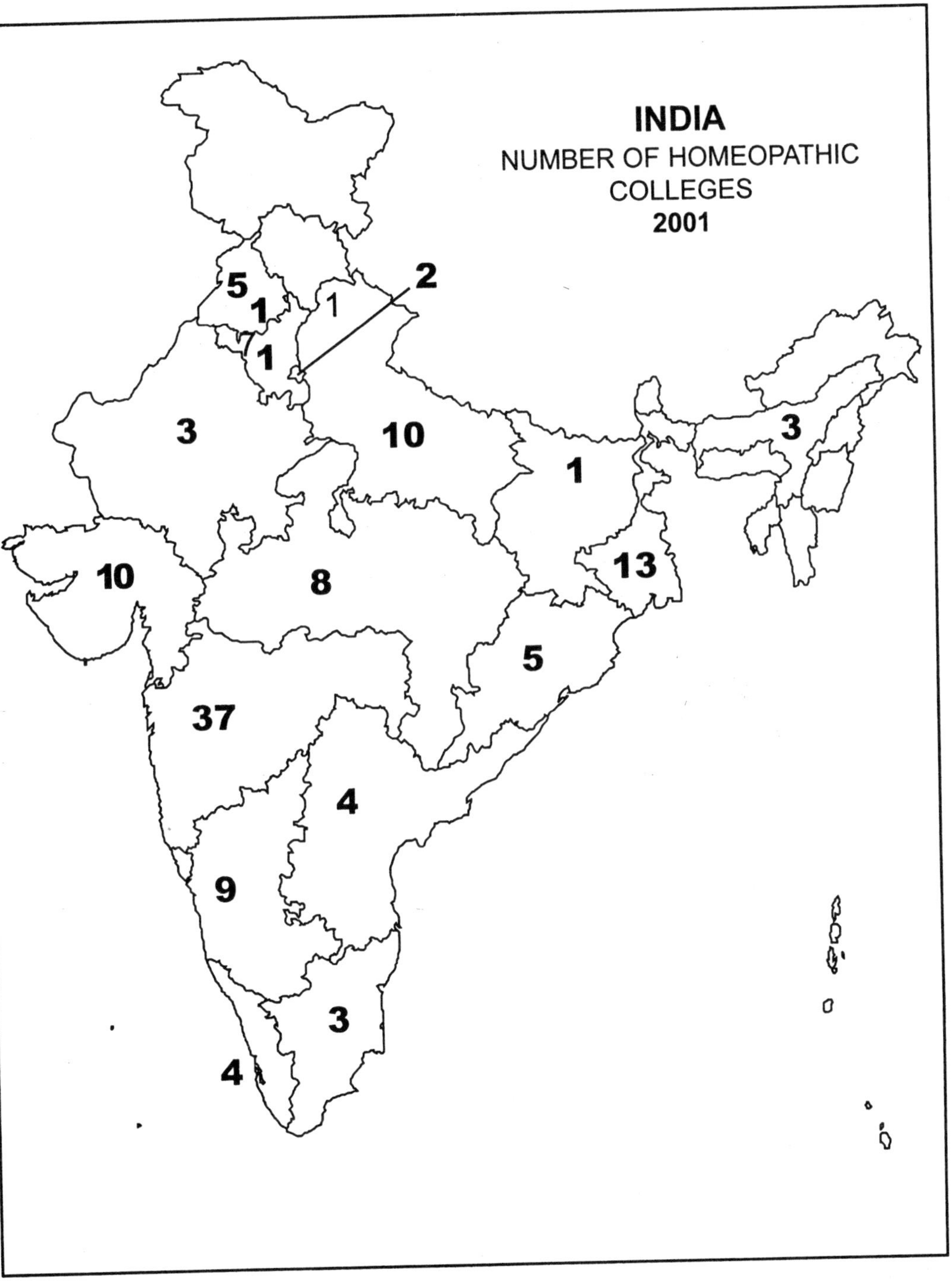

Fig. 19.4: India: Distribution of Homeopathic Colleges

Table 19.1: State-wise Concentration of Medical Colleges (2001) (per cent of national total)

States	*Total Population*	*Allopathic Colleges*	*Ayurvedic Colleges**	*Homeopathic Colleges*	*Dental Colleges*	*Nursing Colleges*
A. Pradesh	7.37	14.90	2.04	3.14	7.95	7.50
Tamil Nadu	6.04	8.18	5.60	2.36	8.55	41.50
Kerala	3.10	5.30	2.55	3.14	3.05	1.90
Karnataka	5.13	14.42	22.45	7.10	25.00	20.75
Maharashtra	9.43	16.83	29.10	29.10	13.40	7.50
Total	**31.07**	**59.63**	**61.75**	**34.84**	**57.92**	**79.15**

• Include 5 Siddha Colleges in T N

Source: Calculated from data given in Health Information of India and Other Relevant Sources.

Table 19.2 gives state-wise distribution of medical education facilities. A number of states are missing from the table because they do not have even a single institution. In an ideal situation, the number of colleges should conform to the size of population. But it is not so in India. The lopsided development matters little, if socio-economic level of population is egalitarian and all those who want to pursue medical education can afford to go anywhere in the country to avail of the opportunities. The situation in India is, however, not so. At least half of the people cannot afford to get professional and higher education because they do not have enough financial resources. And if the educational institutions are located far away from where they live, it becomes far more prohibitive to them. It is apparent from the fact that those communities with money have taken away the lion's share in medical services. Many talented boys and girls belonging to poorer sections of the society have been denied the opportunity to pursue medical education. Recent moves to reserve some seats for the certain communities has not helped much because only the well off candidates from these communities have benefited from reservation, not the poorer ones. There is clear need to develop a new criterion for affirmative action in favour of the poor.

Then there is the problem related to the sex composition of population. Girls in countries like India are less mobile than boys. If the institutions are located far away from the place of resident, girls have lesser access to education. This is the reason why boys outnumber girls in medical colleges. While the number of people belonging to the two sexes is almost equal, the number of medical graduates and medical personnel is highly favourable to the males. The solution lies not in reserving seats for the girls but in opening more institutions in states, which are left behind. The girls would always find their place; they do not need reservation. They are more hard working and sincere in studies than the boys.

It would be pertinent to mention that the above situation pertains not only to degree courses but also to research and post-graduate courses. Nor it is much better in respect of institutions engaged in training paramedical and related personnel like health visitors, radiologists, X'ray technicians etc. The mal-distribution of medical educational facilities has its implications for medical services too. Non-availability of medical personnel in primary health centres (PHCs) is far more acute in the northern than in the southern states of the country.

There is a clear need for a new spatial policy on medical education. The states, which are lagging behind, should start new medical pra-medical educational and training institutions of various types so that their citizens have better acces to quality health services

DENTAL EDUCATION

The Dental Council of India was established under the Dentists Act of 1948 with the purpose of regulating dental education, dental profession, and dental ethics in the country. New dental colleges can be started only after the recommendation of the Council to this effect to the Government of India. State-wise list of dental colleges is given in Table 19.2. Location of dental colleges is given in Figure 19.5.

Table 19.2: Number of Degree Level Medical Colleges in India (2001)

States	*Allopathic Colleges*	*Ayurvedic Colleges*	*Unani Colleges*	*Homeo. Colleges*	*Dental Colleges*	*Nursing Colleges*	*Pharmacy College*
Andhra Pradesh	20	4	2	4	13	4	2
Assam	3	1	0	3	1	1	1
Bihar	8	10	4	1	7	1	5
Chandigarh	1	1	0	0	0	0	0
Chhattisgarh	2	0	0	0	1	0	1
Delhi	5	1	2	2	1	2	2
Goa	1	1	0	0	1	0	1
Gujarat	11	10	0	10	4	3	4
Haryana	2	5	0	0	6	0	4
Himachal Pradesh.	2	1	0	0	4	0	0
J & K	4	1	2	0	1	0	1
Jharkhand	3	1	0	0	0	0	0
Karnataka	30	44	3	9	41	11	42
Kerala	11	5	0	4	5	1	1
Madhya Pradesh	6	9	3	8	4	1	3
Maharashtra	35	57	6	37	22	4	17
Manipur	1	0	0	0	0	0	0
Orissa	3	5	0	5	2	1	6
Pondicherry	5	0	0	0	1	0	0
Punjab	6	9	0	5	11	0	2
Rajasthan	7	4	1	3	4	1	3
Sikkim	1	0	0	0	0	0	0
Tamil Nadu	17	11*	1	3	14	22	25
Uttar Pradesh	12	11	10	10	19	0	4
Uttaranchal	1	3	0	0	0	0	0
West Bengal	7	2	1	13	2	1	1
India	**204**	**196**	**35**	**117**	**164**	**53**	**125**

• Including 5 Colleges of Siddha System.
Source: Health Information of India

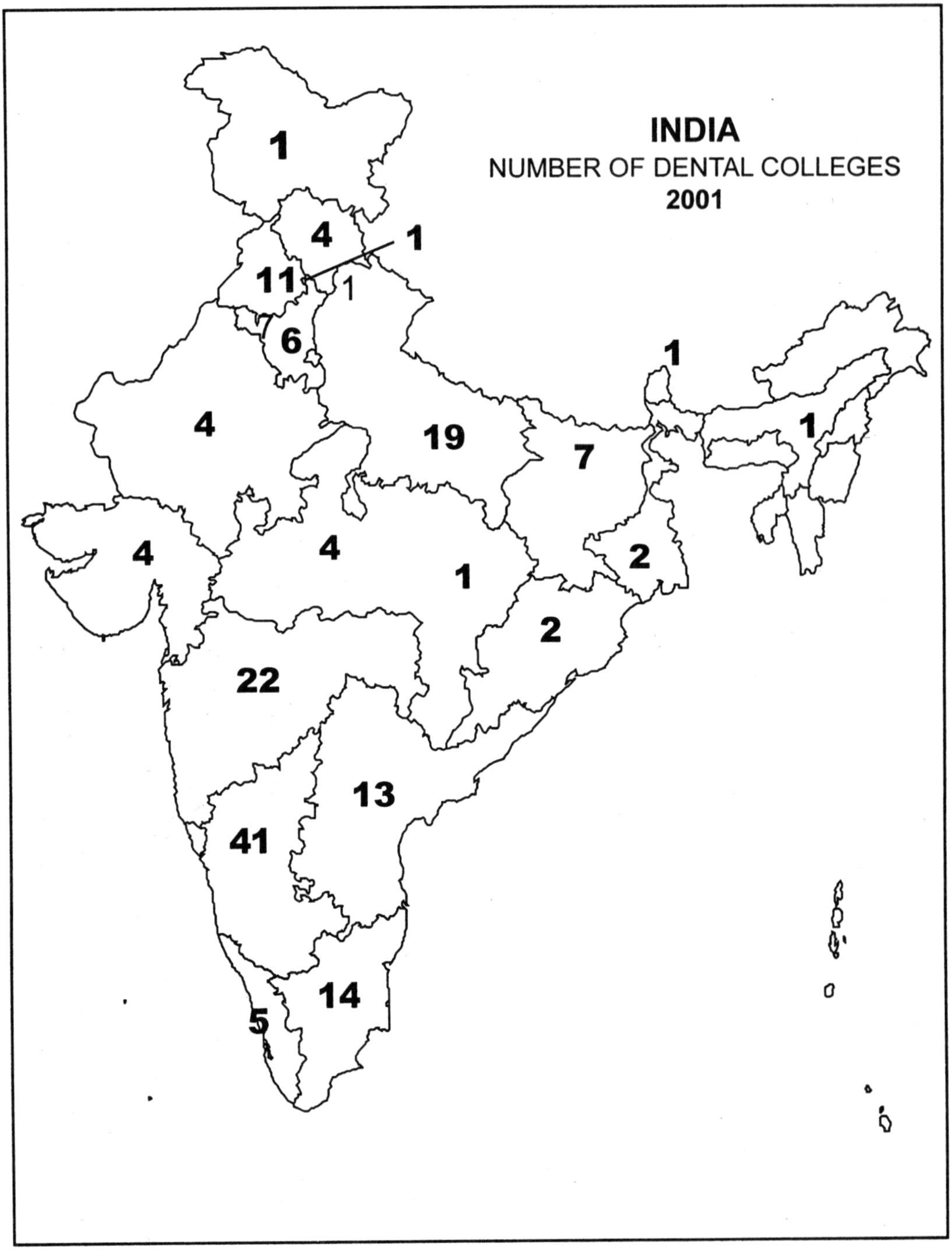

Fig. 19.5: India: Distribution of Dental Colleges

PARAMEDICAL EDUCATION

Nursing Education

The Indian Nursing Council is charged with the responsibility of regulating and maintaining uniformly high standard of nursing education and training. It is a statutory body constituted under the provisions of the Indian Nursing Council Act of 1947. Nursing includes nurses, midwives, auxiliary nurse-midwives and health visitors. We have already discussed the situation with regard to nursing.

In 1997, there were over one million nursing personnel in the country: 6,07,376 nurses, 3,01,691 nurses and midwives, and 24,824 health visitors. As in 1990, there were 2150 institutions admitting 6200 trainees each year. Among them were general nurses, midwives, auxiliary nurses, health and health supervisors, dental hygienist, dental mechanists, laboratory technicians, sanitary and health inspectors, radiographers, pharmacists, X-Ray technicians, operational therapists assistants, physiotherapists, occupational therapists, speech therapists, anthologists, opticians, refractionists, health workers, paramedical workers (leprosy), non-medical supervisors (leprosy), laboratory technicians (leprosy), physiotherapist technicians (leprosy) and others.

Each state has its own Nursing Council and Board of Examination. In all there were 603 general nursing training centres, 112 midwife training centres, 473 auxiliary nursing/midwife training centres, and 21 health visitor/supervisor training centres in various states in 1996. During 1998-99, 10 new nursing schools were recognized by the Council in the states of Tamil Nadu and J & K (3 each), and in A & N Islands, West Bengal, Madhya Pradesh and Himachal Pradesh (1 each). Figure 19.6 shows the relative position of each state of India in nurisng education and training. The figure gives the number of missing colleges in each state in 2001.

Diploma in Pharmacy

Constituted under section 3 of the Pharmacy Act 1948, it is meant to regulate the profession and practice of pharmacy. The Council prescribes minimum standard of education required for pharmacists; maintains uniformity in educational standards; approves courses of study and examination for pharmacists; gives recognition to foreign degrees; and maintains a central register of pharmacists.

There were 327 institutions admitting 19,016 students for diploma courses in pharmacy in the year 1996. Of these, just five states had 224 institutions: Karnataka 87; Maharashtra 56; Tamil Nadu 40; Punjab 21 and Orissa 20. In all, about 20,000 students were admitted. Three states (Karnataka, Maharashtra and Tamil Nadu) claim more than half the admissions. The state-wise distribution of the institutions and the number of students admitted is given in Figs. 19.7(a) and 19.7(b).

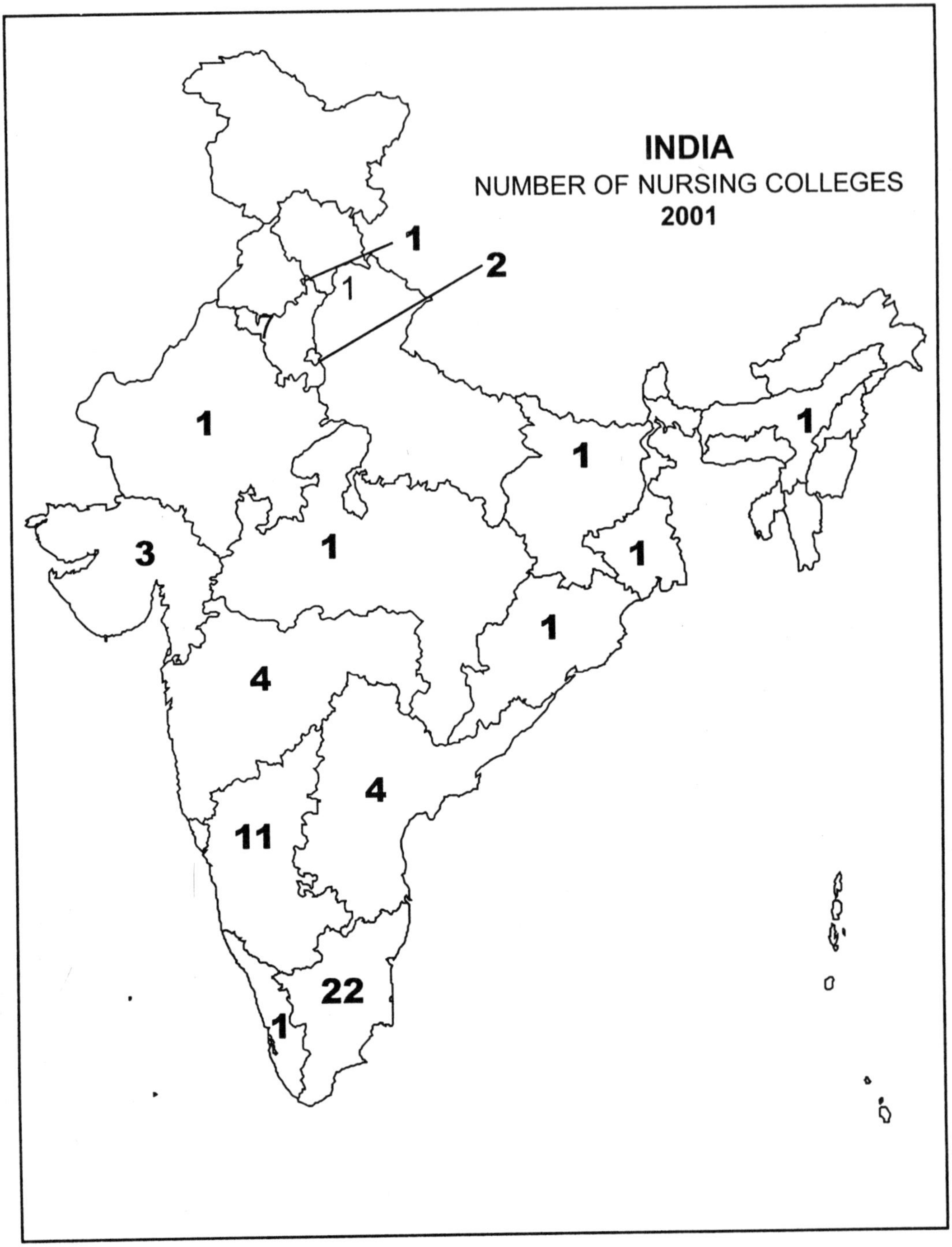

Fig. 19.6: India: Distribution of Nursing Colleges

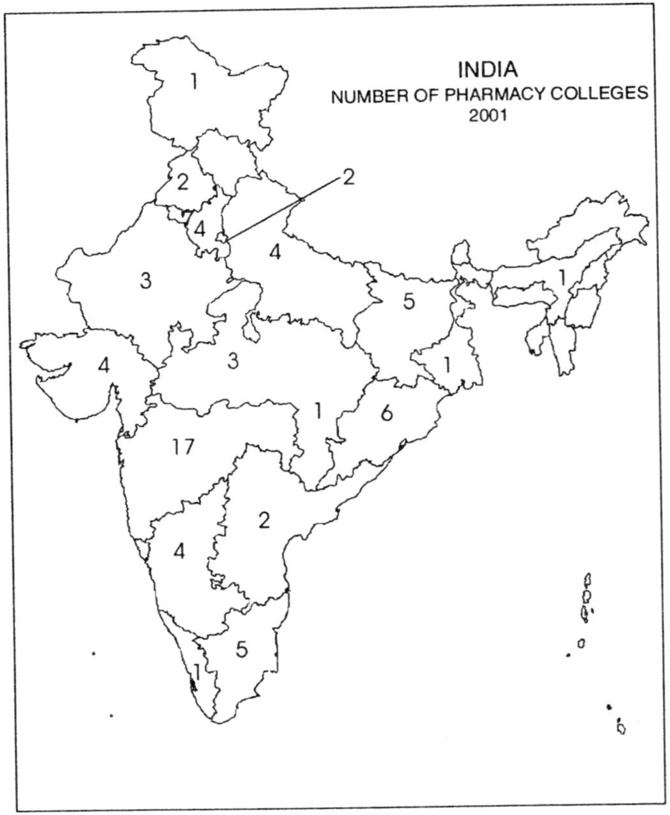

Fig. 19.7(a): India: Number of Pharmacy Colleges

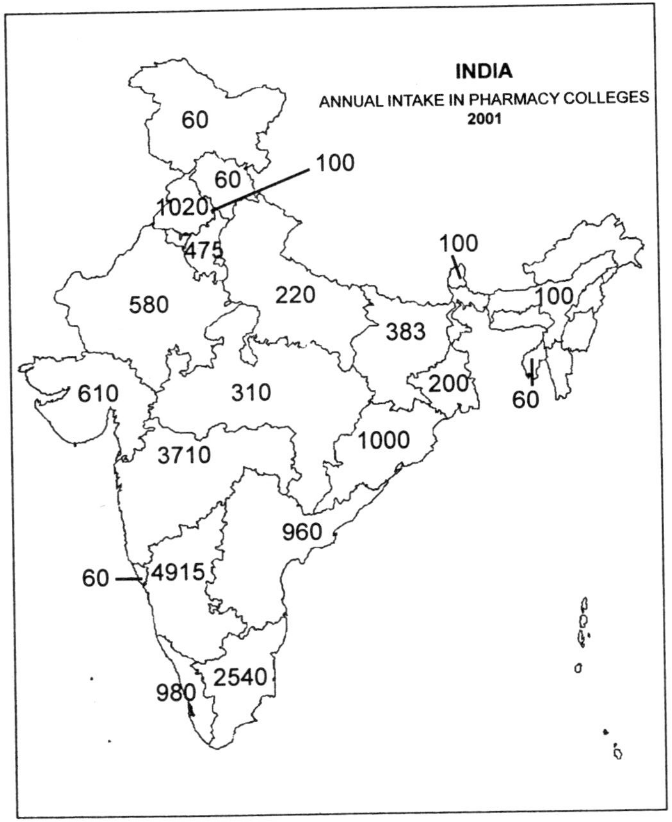

Fig. 19.7(b): India: Annual Intake in Pharmacy Colleges

Table 19.3: Number of Institutions offering Diploma Course in Pharmacy in 1996.

	States	*Institutions*	*Admissions*
1.	Andhra Pradesh	14	650
2.	Assam	2	160
3.	Bihar	9	563
4.	Goa	1	60
5.	Gujarat	9	610
6.	Haryana	10	710
7.	HP	2	45
8.	Karnataka	87	5208
9.	Kerala	13	780
10.	Maharashtra	56	3140
11.	Madhya Pradesh	2	120
12.	Orissa	20	1070
13.	Punjab	21	1100
14.	Rajasthan	9	540
15.	Sikkim	1	60
16.	Tamil Nadu	40	2690
17.	Tripura	1	60
18.	Uttar Pradesh	16	650
19.	West Bengal	3	180
20.	Chandigarh	2	100
21.	Delhi	8	460
22.	Pondicherry	1	66
	India	327	19016

Source: Ministry of Health, Health Information of India.

REFERENCES

1. Ministry of Health, Government of India, *Health Information of India.*
2. ——————, *Annual Reports.*
3. Indian Council of Medical Research (ICMR), Annual Reports.
4. Medical Council of India (MCI), Annual Reports.
5. National Institute of Nutrition, Annual Reports.
6. Annual Reports of Medical Councils of various states.

APPENDIX A

LIST OF COLLEGES OF MODERN MEDICINE (2000 AD)

Andhra Pradesh (20)

1. Andhra Medical College, Vishakhapatnam
2. Deccan College of Medical Sciences, Hyderabad
3. Gandhi Medical College, Hyderabad
4. Osmania Medical College, Hyderabad
5. Guntur Medical College, Guntur
6. Kakatiya Medical Collge, Warangal
7. Kurnool Medical College, Kurnool
8. Rangaraya Medical College, Kakinada
9. S.V. Medical College, Tirupati
10. Siddhartha Medical College, Gundala, Vijaiwada
11. Mamta Medical College, Khammam
12. Kamineni Medical College, Narketpalli, Nalgonda
13. SVS Medical College, Mahboobnagar
14. Narayan Medical College, Nellor
15. Government Medical College, Anantpur
16. ASRAM Medical College, Elluru
17. MNR Medical College, Sangareddy, Medak
18. Pratima Institute of Medical Sciences, Naganaur
19. PES Institute of Medical Sciences and Research, Kuppam
20. Ka'turi Medical College, Guntur

Assam (3)

21. Assam Medical College, Dibrugarh
22. Gauhati Medical College, Gauhati
23. Silcher Medical College, Silcher.

Bihar (8)

24. Patna Medical College, Patna
25. Nalanda Medical College, Patna
26. Katihar Medical College, Katihar

27. AN Magadh Medical College, Sherghati Road, Gaya
28. Darbhanga Medical College, Laheriasarae
29. Jawaharlal Medical College, Bhagalpur
30. Mata Gujri Medical College, Kishanganj
31. Sri Krishna Medical College, Muzaffarpur

Chandigarh (1)

32. Government Medical College, Chandigarh

Chhattisgarh (2)

33. Pt. J.N.M. Medical College, Raipur
34. Chattisgarh Institute of Medical Sciences, Bilaspur

Delhi (5)

35. Lady Harding Medical College (Delhi University), New Delhi
36. Maulana Azad Medical College (D. U), New Delhi
37. University College of Medical Sciences (DU), Shahadra, Delhi
38. All India Institute of Medical Sciences, New Delhi
39. Vardhman Mahavir Medical College, Safdarjang Hospital, New Delhi

Goa (1)

40. Goa Medical College, Panji

Gujarat (11)

41. Smt. NHL Municipal Medical College, Ahmedabad
42. BJ Medical College, Ahmedabad
43. Government Medical College, Bhvnagar
44. Medical College, Vadodara
45. Government Medical College, Surat
46. Pramukh Swami Medical College, Kaira
47. Sri MP Shah Medical College, Jamnagar
48. Government Medical College, Rajkot
49. C.U. Shah Medical College, Surendranagar
50. Municipal Corporation Medical College, Surat
51. Swami Vivekananda Institute of Medical Sciences and Research, Valia, Bharuch

Haryana (2)

52. B.D. Sharma Post-graduate Medical College, Rohtak
53. Maharaja Agrasen Institute of Medical Research and Education, Agroha

Himachal Pradesh (2)

54. Indra Gandhi Medical College, Shimla
55. Dr. Rajinder Prasad Government Medical College, Kangra

Jammu & Kashmir (4)

56. Government Medical College, Jammu
57. Acharya Shrichander College of Medical Sciences, Jammu
57. Government Medical College, Srinagar
58. Sher-I-Kashmir Institute of Medical Sciences, Srinagar

Jharkhand (3)

59. Rajendra Medical College, Ranchi
60. MGM Medical College, Jamshedpur
61. Patliputra Medical College, Dhanbad

Karnataka (30)

62. Adichunchangiri Institute of Medical Sciences, Bellur
63. Al Ameen Medical College, Bijapur
64. AJ Institute of Medical Sciences, Mangalore
65. Bangalore Medical College, Bangalore
66. Basaveswara Medical College and Hospital, Chitradurga
67. Dr. BR Ambedkar Medical College, Bangalore
68. Father Muller's Medical College, Mangalore
69. Government Medical College, Mysore
70. Jayajagatguru Murugharajendra Medical College, Davangiri
71. Jagatguru Sri Shivarateshwara Medical College, Mysore
72. Jawaharlal Medical College, Belgaum
73. Karnataka Institute of Medical Sciences, Hubli
74. Kasturba Medical College, Manipal
75. Kasturba Medical College, Mangalore
76. Kempegowda Institute of Medical Sciences, Bangalore
77. Khaja Banda Nawas Institute of Medical Hospital, Bangalore
78. KS Hegde Medical College, Mangalore
79. KVJ Medical College and Research Hospital, Bangalore
80. KVJ Medical College, Sullia
81. Mahadevappa Rampure Medical College, Gulbarga
82. MS Ramaiah Medical College, Bangalore
83. Navodaya Medical College, Raichur
84. S. Nijlingappa Medical College, Bangalore
85. Sri B.M Patil Medical College Hospital Research Centre, Bijapur

86. Sri Devaraj Urs Medical College, Kolar
87. Sri Siddhartha Medical College, Tumkur
88. St. John's Academy of Health Sciences, Bangalore
89. Vijaynagar Institute of Medical Sciences, Bellary
90. Vydehi Institute of Medical Sciences, Managalore
91. Yenepoya Medical College and Hospital, Chitradurga

Kerala (11)

92. Academy of Medical Sciences, Kannur
93. Amrita Institute of Medical Sciences, Kochi
94. Cooperative Medical Collge, Kodhi
95. Dr. Sumervel Memorial CSI Hospital & Medical College, Karkonam, Thiruvananthapuram
96. Malankara Orthodox Syrian Church Medical Mission, Kolencherry
97. Medical College, Kottayam
98. Medical College, Khozikote
99. Medical College, Trissur
100. Medical College, Thiruvananthapuram
101. Pushpagiri Institute of Medical Sciences and Reseach Centre, Tiruvalla

Madhya Pradesh (6)

102. Gujra Raja Medical College, Gwalior
103. Gandhi Medical College, Bhopal
104. Netaji Subhash Chandra Bose Medical College, Jabalpur
105. MGM Medical College, Indore
106. R.D. Gardi Medical College, Ujjain
107. Shyam Shah Medical College, Rewa

Maharashtra (35)

108. Annasaheb Churaman Patil Memorial Medical College, Dhule
109. Armed Forces Medcal College, Pune
110. B.J. Medical College, Pune
111. Bharati Vidyapeeth's Medical College, Pune
112. Dr. V.M. Medical College, Sholapur
113. Dr. Panjabrao Deshmukh Memorial Medical College, Amravati
114. Government Medical College, Aurangabad
115. Government Medical College, Kolhapur
116. Government Medical College, Nagpur
117. Government Medical College, Nanded
118. Grant Medical College, Mumbai
119. Indira Gandhi Medical College, Nagpur
120. Jawaharlal Nehru Medical College, Swangi, Wardha.
121. KJ Somaiah Medical College, Sion, Mumbai

122. Krishna Institute of Medical Sciences, Karad, Satara
123. Lokmanya Tilak Medical College, Mumbai
124. Mahatma Gandhi Mission's Medical College, Navi Mumbai
125. Mahatma Gandhi Mission's Medical College, Aurangabad
126. Maharashtra Institute of Medical Education and Research, Pune
127. Maharashtra Institute of Medical Sciences and Research, Lathur
128. Mahatma Gandhi Institute of Medical Sciences, Wardha
129. Meeraj Medical College, Meeraj
130. NKP Salve Institute of Medical Science and Research Centre, Nagpur
131. Nasik District's Maratha Vidyaprasarak Samaj Medical College, Adgaon
132. Padmashree Dr. DY Patil Medical College for Women, Pimpri, Pune
133. Padamshree Dr. DY Patil Medical College, New Mumbai.
134. Padmashree Dr. DY Patil Medical College, Kolhapur
135. Rural Medical College, Loni, Ahmednagar
136. Rajiv Gandhi Medical College, Thane
137. SRTR Medical College, Ambajogai
138. Seth GS Medical College, Mumbai
139. Sri Bhausaheb Hire Government Medical College, Dhule
140. Sri Vasanta Rao Naik Government Medical College, Yavatmal
141. Topiwala National Medical College, Mumbai
142. Tarna Medical College, Navi Mumbai

Manipur (1)

143. Regional Institute of Medical Sciences, Imphal

Orissa (3)

144. MKC Medical College, Ganjam
145. SCB Medical College, Cuttack
146. VSS Medical College, Burla, Sambalpur

Pondicherry (5)

147. Aarupadai Veedu Medical College, Pondicherry
148. Jawaharlal Institute of Medical Education and Research, Pondicherry
149. Mahatma Gandhi Medical College, Pondicherry
150. Pondicherry Institute of Medical Sciences, Pondicherry
151. Vinayaka Mission's Medical College, Pondicherry

Punjab (6)

152. Christian Medical College, Ludhiana
153. Dayanand Medical College, Ludhiana

154. Government Medical College, Amritsar
155. Government Medical College, Patiala
156. Guru Govind Singh Medical College, Faridkot
157. Sree Guru Ram Das Institute of Medical Scineces and Research, Sri Amritsar

Rajasthan (7)

158. Dr. SN Medical College, Jodhpur
159. Jawaharlal Medical College, Ajmer
160. Government Medical College, Kota
161. Mahatma Gandhi Medical College, Jaipur
162. RNT Medical College, Udaipur
163. SMS Medical College, Jaipur
164. Sardar Patel Medical College, Bikaner

Sikkim (1)

165. New Medical College (Sikkim-Manipal University) at Gangtok

Tamil Nadu (17)

166. Chennai Medical College, Chennai
167. Chengalpattu Medical College, Chengalpattu
168. Christian Medical College, Vellore
169. Coimbatore Medical College, Coimbatore
170. Government Kilpauk Medical College, Chennai
171. KAP Vishwanathan Government Medical College, Trichy
172. Mohankumarmangalam Medical College, Salem
173. Madurai Medical College, Madurai
174. New Medical College, Toothukudi
175. PSG Institute of Medical Sciences and Research, Coimbatore
176. Perindurai Medical College and Research, Perindurai
177. Raja Muthiah Medical College, Annamalai Nagar
178. Sriramchandra Medical College and Research Institute, Chennai
179. Stanley Medical College, Chennai
180. Thanjavur Medical College, Thanjasvur
181. Tirunelveli Medical College, Tirunelveli
182. Vinayak Mission's Kirupananda Variyar Medical College, Salem

Uttar Pradesh (12)

183. BRD Medical College, Gorakhpur.
184. GAVM Medical College, Lucknow
185. GSVM Medical College, Kanpur

186. Institute of Medical Sciences, BHU, Varanasi.
187. Jawaharlal Medical College, Aligarh.
188. King George Medical College, Lucknow
189. LLRM Medical College, Meerut
190. Maharani Lakshmibai Medical College, Jhansi
191. Motilal Nehru Medical College, Allahabad
192. PV Narasimharao Medical College, Dehradun
193. SN Medical College, Agra
194. Santoshi Medical College, Ghaziabad

Uttaranchal (1)

195. Himalaya Institute of Medical Sciences, Dehradun

West Bengal (7)

196. Burdwan Medical College, Burdwan
197. Bankura Sammilani Medical College, Bankura
198. Calcutta National Medical College, Kolikata
199. Medical College, Calcutta
200. Nilratan Sirkar Medical College, Kolikata
201. North Bengal Medical College, Darjeeling
202. RG Kar Medical College, Kolkata

APPENDIX B

LIST OF AYURVEDIC COLLEGES

Andhra Pradesh

1. Dr. BRKR Government Ayurvedic College, Hyderabad
2. Dr. NR Shastri Government Ayurvedic College, Vijaiwada
3. SV Ayurvedic College, TT Devasthanam, Tirupati
4. Government Ayurvedic College, Warangal

Assam

5. Government Ayurvedic College, Guahati

Bihar

6. Government Ayurvedic College, Patna
7. Government Ayurvedic College, Bhagalpur
8. Dri Ravindranath Mukherjee Ayurvedic College, Champaran
9. Sri Dhanvantri Ayurvedic Mahavidyalaya, Ahirauli, Buxur
10. Rajkiya Ayodhya Shiv Kumari Ayurvedic Mahavidyalaya, Begusarai
11. Swami R.T. Ayurved Mahavidyalaya, Manjhol, Gaya
12. Motisingh Jogeswari Ayurvedic College, Chhapra
13. Nitishwar Institute of Medical Science, Kanholi, Muzaffarpur
14. Rajkiya Maharani Rameshwari Bharatiya Chikitsa Vigyan Sansthan, Mohanpur
15. Ayurved Medical College, Gaya
16. Dayanand Ayurved College & Hospital, Siwan

Chandigarh

17. Sri Dhanvantari Ayurvedic College & Hospital, Chandigarh

Chhattisgarh

18. Government Ayurvedic College, Raipur

Jharkhand

19. Suryamukhi Dinesh Ayurved Medical College & Hospital, Ranchi

Delhi

20. Ayurved & Unani Tibbiya College, Karol Bagh, New Delhi

Goa

21. Bharatiya Sanskrit Prabodhini Gomantak Ayurvedic Mahavidhyalaya & Research Centre, Vaje

Gujarat

22. Government Akhandananda Ayurvedic Mahavidyalaya, Bhadra, Ahmedabad
23. JS Ayurvedic Mahavidyalaya Nadiad
24. Government Ayurvedic Mahavidyalaya, Baroda
25. Aryakanya Suddh Ayurved Mahavidyalaya, Baroda
26. Seth JP Government Ayurvedic Mahavidyalay, Bhavnagar
27. Government Ayurved College, Junagarh
28. Sri Balhanuman Ayurved Mahavidyalaya, Lodhra
29. Sri OH Nazar Ayurvedic Mahavidyalaya, Surat
30. Sri Gulabkunverba Ayurvedic College, Jamnagar
31. Gujarat Ayurved University, Jamnagar

Haryana

32. Sri Mastanath Ayurved College, Rohtak
33. Sri Manusingh Memorial Ayurved Degree College, Sonepat
34. Gaur Brahmin Ayurvedic College & Hospital, Rohtak
35. DET Murarilal Rasiwaria Ayurved College, Charkhi Dadri
36. Sri Krishna Government Ayurvedic College, Kurukshetra

Himachal Pradesh

37. HP Govt. Institute of Post-graduate Education and Research in Ayurveda, Paprola

Jammu & Kashmir

38. Jammu Institute of Ayurved and Research, Jammu Tawi

Karnataka

39. Govt. Ayurved Medical College, Mysore
40. ALN Rao Memorial Ayurved Mahavidyalaya, Koppa, Chikamagalore
41. Government Ayurvedic College, Bangalore
42. Govt. Taranath Ayurvedic College, Bellary
43. AV Samiti Ayurvedic Mahavidyalaya, Mrankeri, Bijapur
44. Ayurvedic Mahavidyalaya, Old Hubli
45. Sri BM Kanakradi Ayurvedic Mahavidyalaya, Shahpur, Belgaum

46. AEA's Ayurvedic College, Davangere
47. NKJ Ayurvedic College, Bidar
48. Dr. BNM Ayurved Medical College & Hospital, Bijapur
49. USS Ayurvedic Medical College, Mysore
50. SS Ayurvedic Medical College, Isarilakmapur, Haveri District
51. Sri Vijai Mahantesh Ayurvedic Medical College, Ilkal, Bagalkot district
52. Bapuji Ayurvedic College, Shimoga
53. TAME Society's Ayurvedic College, Hospet
54. TAME Society's Ayurvedic College, Bhadrawati
55. Amruta Ayurvedic College, Chitradurga
56. Bapuji Ayurvedic Medical College, Chitradurga
57. SDM College of Aurveda, Hassan
58. KVJ Ayurvedic Medical College, & Hospital, Sulliya, Dakshin Karnaaka
59. Sri JG Cooperative Hospital Ayurvedic Medical College, Ghataprabha, Belgaum
60. Sri Kalabhairaveshwara Swami Ayurved Medical College, Bangalore
61. Institute of Ayurvedic Medicine and Research, Bangalore Palace, Bangalore
62. Sri Guru Balmiki Maharshi Ayurvedic Medical College, Jaglur, Chitradurga
63. Alva's Ayurvedic Medical College, Moodbidri, Dakshin Kannada
64. SGV Ayurvedic Medical College, Bailhongal, Belgaum
65. Mahaganapati Ayurvedic Medical College, Hoysalnagar, Dharwad
66. Shivayogeswar Ayurvedic Medical College, Inchal, Belgaum
67. TSPS Mandal Ayurvedic College, Sindhagi, Bijapur
68. RET Ayurvedic Medical College, Raichur
69. Sri HES's Ayurvedic College, Bhawaninagar, Gulbarga
70. KPSVS Ayurvedic Medical College, Manvi, Raichur
71. SBVVS Ayurvedic College, Bagalkot
72. SBVMG Ayurvedic College, Jamkhandi, Bagalkot
73. Sri SBS Ayurvedic Medical College, Mundargi, Gadag
74. DGM Ayurvedic Medical College, Gadag
75. VVS Rura! Ayurvedic Medical College & Research Centre, Badami, Bagalkot
76. KBS's Rural Ayurvedic Medical College, Ramnagar, Belgaum
77. BM Jain Ayurvedic Medical College & Research Centre, Badami, Bagalkot
78. Kalidas Ayurvedic Medical College, Badami, Bagalkot
79. RGES's Ayurvedic Medical College, Ron
80. Muniyal Institute of Ayurvedic Medical Sciences, Manipal
81. Dhanvatari Ayurvedic College & Hospital, Siddhpur, Uttar Kannada
82. Ramakrishna Ayurvedic Medical College, Bangalore
83. Sri DM College of Ayurved, Udupi

Kerala

84. Govt. Ayurvedic College, Dhanvatrinagar, Ernakulam
85. VPS Variar Ayurvedic College, Kottakkal, Malappuram

86. Vaidyaratnam Ayurvedic College, Ollur, Trichur
87. Govt. Ayurvedic College, Kannur
88. Govt. Ayurvedic College, Thiruvanathapura

Madhya Pradesh

89. Government Ayurvedic College & Hospital, Gwalior
90. Government Ayurvedic College, Jabalpur
91. Government Dhanvantari Ayurvedic College, Ujjain
92. Pt. Shivashakti Lal Sharma Ayurved Mahavidyalaya, Ratlam
93. Government Ayurvedic College & Hospital, Burhanpur
94. Government Ashtang Ayurvedic College & Hospital, Indore
95. Government Ayurvedic College & Hospital, Rewa
96. Pt. Khushilal Sharma Ayurvedic Mahavidyalaya, Bhopal
97. Rajiv Gandhi Ayurved Mahavidyalaya, Shahpur, Bhopal

Maharashtra

98. Tilak Ayurved Mahavidyalaya, Pune
99. Ashtnag Mahavidyalaya, Pune
100. Sri Gangadhar Shastri Gune Ayurvedic

Mahavidyalaya, Ahmednagar

101. KVTR Ayurvedic College, Dhule
102. Vasant Dada Patil Ayurvedic College, Sangli
103. Ayurved Mahavidyalaya, Ahmednagar
104. MAMSBS Ayurvedic College, Pune
105. College of Ayurveda & Research Centre, Akurdi, Pune
106. SST Ayurveda Mahavidyalaya, Sangamner, Ahmednagar
107. VKRYoga & AS Siddhakala Ayurved Mahavidyalaya, Sangamner,

Ahmednagar

108. BSDT Ayurved Vishwashanti Dham, Wagholi, Pune
109. CSMSS Ayurved Mahavidhyalaya, Aurangabad
110. MSPM Ayurvedic College, Aurangabad
111. Govt. Ayurvdic College, Osmanabad
112. SCM Ayurvedic Vaidak Mahavidyalaya
113. SGR Ayurvedic Mahavidyalaya, Solapur
114. Yashvant Ayurved Mahavidyalaya, Kodoli, Kolhapur
115. Ayurved Mahavidyalaya, Peth, Basegaon, Kolhapur-
116. GES Ayurvedic Medical College, Ranklaves, Kolhapur

117. DCS Ayurvedic Mahavidyalaya, Deopur, Dhule
118. Dada SSN Ayurvedic Mahavidyalaya, Nandgaon, Dhule
119. Ayurved Medical College, Chalisgaon, Jalgaon
120. Chaitanya Ayurved Mahavidyalaya, Saketgaon, Bhusawal
121. RA Poddar Ayurvedic College, Worli, Mumbai
122. SKG Mittal Punarvasu Ayurvedic Mahavidyalaya, Mumbai
123. Ayurved Mahavidyalaya, Sion, Mumbai
124. YMT Ayurvedic Medical College, Navi Mumbai, Mumbai
125. RJVSBS Ayurved Mahavidyalaya Savanwadi, Sindhudurg
126. Nalsopara Ayurvedic Medical College, Nalsopara, Tahne
127. BSM Ayurvedic Mahavidyalaya, Nagpur
128. Government Ayurvedic Mahavidyalaya, Nagpur
129. Shri Ayurved Mahavidyalaya, Nagpur
130. Sri RK Tosniwal Qyurved Mahavidyalaya, Akola
131. Vidarbha Ayurved Mahavidyalaya, Amravati
132. Sri Gurudev Ayurved Mahavidyalaya, Amravati
133. DMM Ayurved Mahavidyalaya, Yeotmal
134. Sri GMS Ayurved Mahavidyalaya, Pushad, Yotmal
135. Gramin Ayurved Mahavidyalaya, Patur, Akola
136. Lt. SRC Ayurved College, Chikhili, Bildana
137. APESMS Ayurved Medical College, Kudwa, Gondia
138. SSSS Medical College, Yashwant Mandal, Nashik
139. LKR Ayurved Medical College, Khede, Kolhapur
140. VVPF Ayurvedic Medical College, Sevagaon, Ahmednagar
141. DY Patil College of Ayurved & Research Centre, Pimpri, Pune
142. Govt. Ayurved College, Wazirabad, Nanded
143. AD Ayurvedic Medical College, Islampur, Sangali
144. Manjara Ayurvedic College & Hospital, Latur
145. Dhanvantari Ayurved Medical College, Latur
146. EAR Ayurvedic Medical College, Manchi Hill, Ahmednagar
147. National Medical College of Ayurvedic Sciences, Sangamner
148. Chhatrapati Shivaji Ayurvedic Medical College & Hospital, Ashti, Beed
149. Sumananjali Pratisthan Ayurved Medical College, Aurangabad
150. NP Ayurved Medical College, Aurangabad
151. RP Ayurved mahavidyalaya & Rugnalaya, Puma, Prabhani
152. JJM Women's Ayurved Medical College, Jeysinghpur, Kolhapur
153. Jupiter Ayurved Medical College, Nagpur
154. BV College of Ayurveda, Shankarpur, Pune

Orissa

155. Gopalbandhu Ayurved Mahavidyalaya, Puri-
156. IGM Ayurvedic Medical College & Hospital, Jagamara,

Bhubaneswar

157. Mayurbhanj Ayurved Mahavidyalaya, Takhtapur, Mayurbhanj
158. KATS Ayurved Mahavidyalaya, Ankushpur, Ganjam
159. Govt. Ayurvedic College, Bolangir
160. Sri N. Ayurved College & Research Institute, Bargarh

Punjab

161. Government Ayurvedic Mahavidyalaya, Patiala
162. Desh Bhagat Ayurvedic College & Hospital, Amloh, Fatehgarh

Saheb

163. Sri SSMD Ayurvedic College & Hospital, Moga, Faridkot
164. Mai Bhago Ayurvedic College for Women, Muktasar
165. SKSES Ayurvedic Medical College & Hospital, Sarabha,

Ludhiana

166. Guru Nanak Ayurvedic Medical College& Hospital, Muktasar
167. Guru Nanak Ayurvedic College & Research Institute, Gopalpur,

Ludhiana

168. LN Ayurvedic College, Amritsar
169. Dayananda Ayurvedic College, Jullundhar City

Rajasthan

170. Parashrampuria Rajasthan Ayurvedic Mahavidyalaya, Sikar
171. National Institute of Ayurveda, Jaipur
172. MMMM Government Ayurvedic college, Udaipur
173. Sri Bhanwarlal Dugar Ayurvedic Vishwabharati, Sardarshahr,

Churu

Tamil Nadu

174. Sri Venkataramana Ayurvedic College, Chennai

Ayurved College, Coimbatore

175. Dharma Ayurved College, Sriperumbudur, Kanchipuram

176. Sri Sankara College of Ayurveda, Tiruchrirapalli
177. Sri Sairam Ayurvedic Medical College & Research Centre,

Poonthamdalam, Kanchpuram-

178. Sri Jayendra Saraswati Ayurvedic College, Thiruvallur,

Nazarathpet

Uttaranchal

179. Uttaranchal Ayurvedic College, Dehradun
180. Government Gurukur Kangri Ayurvedic College & Hospital,

Hardwar

181. Government Rishikul Ayurvedic College, Hardwar

Uttar Pradesh

182. Government Ayurvedic College & Hospital, Lucknow
183. Rajkiya Lalit Hari Ayurved College & Hospital, Pilibhit
184. Bundelkhand Government Ayurved College & Hospiotal, Jhansi
185. Government Ayurvedic College and Hospital. Atarra, Banda
186. SRM Government Ayurvedic College & Hospital, Bareilly
187. Swami Kalyandeo Government Ayurvedic College, Rampur,

Muzaffarnagar

188. Sri L B Shastri Memorial Government Ayurvedic College & Hospital, Handia, Allahabad
189. Sham-e-Ghausia Minority Ayurvedic Medical College & Hospital, Saheri, Ghazipur
190. Aligarh Ayurved and Unani Medical College & Hospital, Aligarh
191. Institute of Medical Sciences, Faculty of Ayurveda, BHU, Varanasi
192. Government Ayurvedic College & Hospital, Jagatganj, Varanasi

West Bengal

193. JB Roy Government Ayurvedic Medical College & Hospital, Kolkata
194. Institute of Post-graduate Ayurvedic Education & Research, Kolkata

APPENDIX C

LIST OF DENTAL COLLEGES

Andhra Pradesh (13)

1. Army College of Dental Sciences, Secunderabad
2. CVS Krishnamurthy Teja Institute of Dental Sciences & Research, Tirupathi
3. Government Dental College and Hospital, Hyderabad
4. Geetam Dental College, Vishakhapatnam
5. Kamiyeni Institute of Dental Sciences, Narketpally, Nalgonda
6. Leonara Institute of Dental Sciences, Rajamundry
7. Mamata Dental College, Khammam
8. NTR UHS Dental College, Vijaiwada
9. Narayana Dental College, Nellore
10. Sibar Institute of Dental Sciences, Takelpaddu, Guntur
11. Sri Sai College of Dental Surgery, Vikarabad, Rangareddy
12. St. Joseph Dental College, Dugirala, Elluru
13. Vishnu Dental College, Kovvadu, Bhimavaram

Assam (1)

14. Regional Dental College, Gauhati

Bihar (7)

15. Dr. B.R. Ambedkar Institute of Dental Sciences and Hospital, Patna
16. Mithila Minority Dental College and Hospital, Loheriasarai, Darbhanga
17. Patna Dental college and Hospital, Patna
18. Buddha Institute of Dental Sciences, Patna
19. Sarjang Dental College, Darbhanga
20. Dr. SM Naqvi Imam Dental College, Behera
21. Darbhanga Dental College, Darbhanga

Chandigarh (1)

22. Oral Health Science Centre, Chandigarh

Delhi (2)

23. Maulana Azad Medical College (Dental Wing), New Delhi
24. AIMS Dental Surgery, New Delhi

Goa (1)

25. Government Dental College and Hospital, Goa

Gujarat (4)

26. Government Dental College and Hospital, Ahmedabad
27. Government Dental College and Hospital, Jamnagar
28. KM Shal Dental College, Baroda
29. Manubhai Patel Dental College, Baroda

Haryana (6)

30. BRS Institute of Medical Sciences, Panchkula
31. DAV Centenary Dental College, Yamuna Nagar
32. Dental College (Medical Campus), Rohtak
33. Maharshi Markandeshwar College of Dental Sciences & Research, Mulana, Ambala
34. Sri Baba Mastanath Dental College and Hospital, Rohtak
35. Sri Govind Tricentenary Dental College, Hospital and Research Centre, Budhera, Gurgaon

Himachal Pradesh (4)

36. Bhojia Dental College & Hospital, Budh
37. H.P. Government Dental College and Hospital, Shimla
38. Himachal Dental College, Sundar Nagar, Mandi
39. MNDAV Dental College & Hospital, Solan

Jammu and Kashmir (1)

40. Government Dental College, Srinagar

Karnataka (41)

41. AJ Institute of Dental Sciences, Mangalore
42. AME's Dental College, Raichur
43. Coorg Institute of Dental Sciences, Coorg
44. Government Dental College, Bangalore
45. RV Dental College, Bangalore

46. Dr. Shyamla Reddy Dental College, Bangalore
47. Dayanand Sagar College of Dental Sciences, Bangalore
48. HKDET's Dental College & Hospital, Humnabad
49. VS Dental college, Bangalore
50. KGF College of Dental Sciences, Bangalore
51. Bangalore institute of Dental Sciences and Hospital, Bangalore
52. MS Ramaiah Dental College, Bangalore
53. Maratha Mandal's Dental College and Research Centre, Belgaum
54. Raja Rajeshwari Dental College, Bangalore
55. KLE Society's Dental College, Bangalore
56. Maruti Dental College, Bangalore
57. Oxford Dental College, Bangalore
58. Rajiv Gandhi College of Dental Sciences, Bangalore
59. Babu jagjivan Ram Dental College, Bangalore
60. NSVK Dental College and Hospital, Bangalore
61. Krishnadevraya College of Dental Sciences, Bangalore
62. Sri Sevalal College, Bangalore
63. PMN Memorial Dental College and Hospital, Bagalkot
64. SB Patil Institute for Dental Sciences, Bidar
65. SJM Dental College, Chitradurga
66. Bapuji Dental College, Davangiri
67. College of Dental Sciences, Davangiri
68. SDM College of Dental Sciences, Dharwad
69. HKE Society's Dental College, Gulbarga
70. A.L. Badar Dental College, Gulbarga
71. Sri SN Institute of Dental Sciences, Hassan
72. Shravathi Dental College, Shimoga
73. Farookquia Dental College, Mysore
74. ABSM Institute of Dental Sciences, Mangalore
75. College of Dental Surgery, Mangalore
76. Venepoya Dental College, Mangalore
77. College of Dental Surgery, Manipal
78. JSS Dental College, Mysore
79. Sri Siddhartha Dental College, Tumkur
80. AL Ameem Dental College, Bijapur
81. KVG Dental College, Sulia

Kerala (5)

82. Dental College, Medical Campus, Trivandrum
83. Dental College, Medical College Campus, Calicut
84. Government Dental College, Kottayam
85. PMS College of Dental Sciences & Research, Vittapara, Thiruvananthapuram
86. Mar Baselios Dental College, Thankalam, Ernakulam

Madhya Pradesh (4)

87. College of Dentistry, Indore
88. School of Dental Sciences & Hospital, Indore
89. Modern Dental College and Research Centre, Nainod, Indore
90. People's College of Dental Sciences & Research Centre, Bhopal

Maharashtra (23)

91. Armed Forces Dental College, Pune
92. Government Dental College and Hospital, Aurangabad
93. Government Dental College, Mumbai
94. Nair Hospital Dental College, Mumbai
95. Government Dental College, Nagpur
96. D.Y. Patil Dental College, Navi Mumbai
97. Bhartiya Vidyapeeth Dental College and Hospital, Pune
98. Pravara Rural Dental College, Loni, Ahmednagar
99. Jamnalal Goenka Dental college, Akola
100. V.P. Dental College and Hospital, Sangli
101. C.S.M.S.S, Dental College, Aurangabad
102. VYW Society's Dental College, Amravati
103. Mahatma Gandhi Vidyama NDIR'S Dental College & Hospital, Navi Mumbai
104. Sharad Pawar Dental College & Hospital, Wardha
105. Vidya Shikshan Prasarak Mandal's Dental College & Research Centre, Nagpur
106. Yerela Medical Dental College, Navi Mumbai
107. DY Patil Dental College & Hospital, Pimpri
108. MA Rangoonwala College of Dental Sciences& Research Centre, Pune
109. Tatya Saheb Kore Dental College & Research Centre, New Paragaon
110. Taena Dental College, Navi Mumbai
111. Anna SahebChudaman Patil Memorial Dental College, Dhule
112. Pandit Deen Dayal Upadhyay Dental College, Solapur
113. SMBT Dental College, Amrutanagar

Orissa (2)

114. SCB Medical College (Dental Wing), Cuttack
115. VM Lord Jagannath Institute of Dental Sciences & Research, Bhubaneswar

Pondicherry (1)

116. Mahatma Gandhi Dental College, Pondicherry

Punjab (11)

117. Punjab Government Dental College and Hospital, Amritsar
118. Government Dental College and Hospital, Patiala

119. Christian Dental College, Ludhiana
120. SGRD Institute of Dental Sciences and Research, Amritsar
121. Dashnesh Institute of Reseach and Dental Sciences, Faridkot
122. Guru Nanakdeo Dental College & Research Institute, Sunam
123. Baba Jaswant Singh Dental College, Hospital and Research Institute, Ludhiana
124. Khalsa Dental College & Hospital, Nangal Kalan, Mansa
125. Desh Bhagat Dental College, Muktsar
126. National Dental College & Hospital, Gulabgarh, Derabasi
127. Laxmibai Institute of Dental Sciences & Hospital, Patiala

Rajasthan (4)

128. SMS Medical College (Dental Wing), Jaipur
129. Darshan Dental College, Udaipur
130. Pacific Dental College, Udaipur
131. Jaipur Dental College, Jaipur

Tamil Nadu (14)

132. JKK Nataraja Dental Hospital, Komarpalayam
133. Tamil Nadu Dental College, Chennai
134. Savita Dental College and Hospital, Chennai
135. Rajas Dental College, Chennai
136. Sri Balaji Dental College, Chennai
137. Meenakshi Ammal Dental College, Chennai
138. Sri Ramchandra Dental College, Chennai
139. SRM Dental College, Chennai
140. Thai Moogambigai Dental College & Hospital, Chennai
141. Rajah Muthiah Dental College and Hospital, Annamalainagar
142. VMS Dental College, Salem
143. Rajas Dental College, Vadakankulam
144. Shri Mookambika Institute of Dental Sciences, Nagarcoil
145. Shri Ramkrishnan Dental College & Hospital, Coimbatore

Uttar Pradesh (19)

146. Awadh Institute of Dental Sciences, Lucknow
147. KGMC Faculty of Dental Sciences, Lucknow
148. Sardar Patel Institute of Dental Sciences, Lucknow
149. BHU Institute of Medical Sciences (Dental Wing), Varanasi)
150. Rama Dental College and Hospital, Kanpur
151. Subharati Dental College, Meerut
152. Santosh Dental College, Ghaziabad
153. VMS Internationasl Dental College, Mau, Sitapur

154. Saraswati Dental College, Lucknow
155. Kothiwal Dental College & Research Centre, Moradabad
156. DJ College of Dental Science & Research, Modinagar
157. Dental College, AMU, Aligarh
158. UP College of Dental Sciences & Research, Lucknow
159. ITS Centre for Dental Studies & Research, Muradnagar, Ghaziabad
160. Harsharan Das Dental College, Ghaziabad
161. Career Institute of Dental Sciences & Hospital, Lucknow
162. Kantidevi Dental College, Mathura
163. Institute of Dental Studies and Technologies, Modinagar
164. Institute of Dental Sciences, Bareilly

West Bengal (2)

165. Dr. R. Ahmed Dental College, Kolkata
166. North Bengal Dental College, Darjeeling

20

Health Policy and Planning

HEALTH POLICY

Policy is a well-conceived framework for administrative action to achieve a set of goals and objectives within a given timeframe. It is something like an image of a house, which satisfies the requirements of the person who would live in it. Health policy means a broad picture of the health system, which would satisfy the needs of the people. This picture is created by the parliament. The government uses its health infrastructure to prepare a design that would meet the requirements set in the policy and executes the same to give shape to a new health structure or system of health.

Need for Health Policy

In a democratic country like India, policy formulation is the responsibility of the elected representatives of the people. But behind the decisions of the people's representatives is the will and desire of the masses, on the one hand, and expert advice of the institutions created for policy research and strategic planning, on the other. This applies to the health sector also. Health of the people is one of the primary responsibilities of all constitutional authorities. Without clear-cut policies and associated strategies and tactics, the governments can do precious little. Government bureaucracy tends to get involved in its own survival and promotion; it loses sight of the purposes for which it was created. It needs direction, objectives and targets to be achieved from time to time. Policies are meant to give this direction.

India has done fairly well in the health sector during the last few years. But for clear-cut policies, this could not be achieved. If the attention of the government has shifted from curative to preventive measures, it is again because of the policy shifts during the last 25 years. And if the goals of HFA are to be achieved in shortest possible time, further changes in the current health policies would have to be carried out.

Health Policy in Colonial Era

Health policy in India during the British era was a subdued and a belated extension of the health policy adopted in England. Their first and immediate concern was the health of the British soldiers posted in India. A Royal Commission was appointed in 1859 to investigate the causes of extremely unsatisfactory condition of health in the British army stationed in India. As a follow up of the report of the commission, Sanitary Commissioners were appointed in the three provinces of Bengal, Madras and Bombay.

Soon, the British realized that the health of the army and general public could not be separated. Vaccination Act was passed in 1880; and in 1888, the local bodies were directed to look after sanitation also. The 1896 plague epidemics forced the government to give more attention to public health. Central Malaria Bureau was set up in Kasauli, and Indian Research Fund was established in 1911 at New Delhi. Later, the Fund was converted into AIIMS.

In 1919, following the Montague-Chemsford Constitutional Reforms, the subjects of health and sanitation were transferred to the provinces. All India Institute of Public Health and Hygiene was set up in Calcutta in 1930. Health Survey and Development Committee (Bhore Committee) was set up in 1943. Its recommendations came very handy for the new government to initiate action after independence in 1947.

The British government did not have a clear-cut policy on health but it did know what it had to do. Its involvement in matters of health increased with time, particularly in the area of prevention of epidemic diseases. It also paid some attention to health services in general. The idea behind the delegation of authority to provinces and local governments was to enable each region and locality to evolve its own system.

Health Policy: 1947-1983

After the independence of the country, ministries of health were established at the centre and the states. The Planning Commission of India allocated funds for health also and a number of innovative measures were taken to improve health infrastructure, education, and research, and services especially in rural areas.

It would not be out of place to give a gist of the activities undertaken in this period as a part of a policy to reach out to remotest corners of the country and to eradicate epidemic diseases which took a heavy toll of life. The first five-year plan (1951-56) allocated 5.9 per cent of planned expenditure for health. It was a very progressive step indeed. Community Development Programme was launched in 1952; each block of about 100 villages was given a health educator and steps were taken to start primary health centres at each block headquarter. National Malaria and Filaria Control Programmes were launched in 1953 and 1955 respectively.

During the second five-year plan period (1956-61), health received 5 per cent of the total plan fund. Family planning and demographic research received greater attention during this period. The Malaria Control Programme was converted into National Malaria Eradication Programme in 1958. A pilot project for the eradication of smallpox was launched in 1960.

During the third five-year plan (1961-66 plus 2 non-plan years), School Health Programme, Smallpox Eradication Programme and National Goiter-Control Programme, were launched. It was also the period when Applied Nutrition Programme, National Institute of Communicable

Diseases, and National Trachoma Control Programme were started. Family planning and population control received added attention during the period.

The fourth five-year plan (1969-74) was again marked by a number of initiatives on health and family planning front. Allocation for health and family planning was Rs. 840 crores (5 per cent of the total). Legislation to check water pollution was enforced and registration of births and deaths was made mandatory. Medical Termination of Pregnancy Act was passed in 1969. And soon the minimum needs programmr with several health related components was launched. The idea of multipurpose health worker was given a practical shape.

Launching of the fifth five-year plan in 1974 proved quite auspices. India was declared free from smallpox in July 1975. Integrated Child Development Scheme was set in motion on October 2, 1975. The sixth five-year plan started in 1980. The WHO launched the Health-For-All (HFA). Air (Pollution and Control) Act was passed in 1981 and India joined the global effort to provide sanitation and adequate drinking water for all. And in 1983, the country launched a new health policy.

The description given above proved beyond doubt that India tried to reach out to all aspects of health: preventive, curative, rural, urban, etc. and all dimensions of it: education, infrastructure, manpower, administration and management, and international relations. The country had reached a stage where a more integrated and coherent policy on health was felt necessary.

Health Policy – 1983

Being a welfare state, India has been deeply concerned about the health of the people. Concerted efforts had been made to make health services available to all, irrespective of where they lived: rural or urban settlement. Shortage of funds, manpower, equipment and medical infrastructure in general had, however, come in the way of achieving this goal. In order to reorient health delivery system to meet the emerging needs of the country and also to strengthen both preventive and curative health, the government of India formulated a Health Policy in 1983.

Major steps envisaged in the policy were:

1. Establishment of well-dispersed network of primary healthcare services;
2. Induction of health volunteers having appropriate knowledge, simple skills, and related technical backup;
3. Establishment of a well organized multi-tier referral system to keep the patient-burden on higher level hospitals light; and
4. Setting up of evenly spread speciality and super-speciality services with the participation of the private sector.

The above initiatives led to the establishment of a network of primary health centres. But for these centres it would have not been possible to launch campaigns against malaria, trachoma, smallpox, guineaworm disease, polio, etc. Steps taken to control leprosy, kala azar and filariasis were also facilitated by these policy initiatives. Substantial improvements have been recorded in life expectancy; birth rates have declined and so have the death rates; epidemiological situation has changed for the better.

These success stories were accompanied by some disturbing developments too. Of the communicable diseases, malaria staged a comeback in 1980s due to increasing level of insecticide resistance of the malarial vectors. Its incidence was stabilized in 1990s at a rather higher level. Another disturbing development is the increase in the incidence of P-falsiparum malaria, which is 50 per cent more deadly. With regard to T.B., the pool of infection has remained almost stagnant and drug resistance has increased rather significantly. HIV/AIDS has emerged as a new and fast spreading infectious disease. The old water-borne infections – gastroenteritis, cholera and hepatitis continue to add to the pool of morbidity.

The period between 1983 and 2001 saw increase in the mortality caused by life-style diseases like diabetes, cancer and cardiovascular diseases. The trauma cases also increased significantly. The number of people who died in accidents also increased secularly. As such, the health scenario in the country changed considerably (Table 20.1). This called for a new policy initiative on the part of the government.

Table 20.1: Demographic Changes in India: 1951-2001

Indicators	*1951*	*1981*	*2001*
Life expectancy	37.7	54	64.6
Crude birth rate	40.8	33.9	26.1
Crude death rate	25	12.5	8.7
Infant mortality rate	146	110	70
Leprosy cases per 1000 population	38.10	57.30	3.74
Smallpox (no. of cases)	>44887	nil	nil
Guineaworm (no. of cases)	–	>39,792	nil
Polio (no. of cases)	–	29709	265
No. of SC/PHC/CHC (1999)	725	57,363	1,63,181
No. of dispensaries & hospitals (1995-96)	9209	23,555	43,322
No. of beds (both private and public)	117,198	569,495	8,70,161
No. of allopathic doctors (1998-99)	61,800	2,68,700	5,03,900
No. of nursing personnel (1999)	18,054	1,43,887	7,37,000

Source: National Health Policy-2001

Health Policy – 2002

In order to face the new challenges, a new health policy was formulated in 2002. The main objective of the policy was to achieve an acceptable standard of good health amongst the general population of the country by augmenting existing health infrastructure so that access to health services across the social and geographical expanse of the country becomes more equitable. The private sector has been given greater role in the provision of health education and research, health infrastructure and health delivery system. The idea appears to be to involve the private sector in the provision of services to those who can afford to pay. This would allow the government to pay greater attention to those who are poor and more needy.

The policy accords primacy to preventive and first-line curative initiatives at the primary health level. Eradication of communicable diseases like T.B., increased attention to the health of women and children, and treatment of diseases like cancer, heart ailments, asthma, AIDS, etc. will receive priority attention.

The policy goals to be achieved during the first 15 years are given in Table 20.2.

Table 20.2: Policy Goals to be Achieved by 2015 AD

Goals	*Year*
Eradicate polio and yaws	2005
Eliminate leprosy	2005
Eliminate kala zar	2010
Eliminate lymphatic filariasis	2015
Achieve zero level of growth of HIV/AIDS	2007
Reduce mortality on account of various vector and water borne diseases by 50 per cent	2010
Bring blindness down to 0.5% of population	2010
Reduce IMR to 30/1000 and MMR to 100/lakh	2010
Reduce LBW babies from 30 to 10 per cent	2010
Increase use of health services from less than 20 to more than 75 per cent	2010
Establish an integrated system of surveillance, national health accounts, and health statistics	2005
Increase health expenditure by government from 0.9 to 2.0 per cent of the GDP	2010
Enhance central government grant to 25 per cent of health expenditure	2010
Increase the share of health sector in state budgets from 5.5 to 8 per cent	2010

Source: National Health Policy, 2001

Access to Health Services

Access Across Social Grqups: Access to, and benefits from, public health system in India continues to be uneven socially as well as geographically. This is particularly true with respect to women, children and socially disadvantaged sections of the society (Table 20.3).

Table 20.3: Health Status of Under-privileged Groups

Indicator	*Infant mortality/1000*	*Under-5 mortality/1000*	*Under-weight children %*
India	70	94.9	47
Scheduled Castes	83	119.3	53.5
Scheduled Tribes	84.2	126.6	55.9
Other Disadvantaged	76	103.1	47.3
Others	61.8	82.6	41.1

Source: National Health Policy, 2001

Physical Access: Despite notable achievements in the provision of health services during the last fifty years, some areas remained poorly served and differences among the states and urban and rural areas continue to be wide (Table 20.3). These differences acquire significance when we see them against the already low level of health services in the country. Health Policy 2001 tries to bridge these gaps. One of the ways of bridging this gap is higher investment in primary health sector. The new policy aims at increasing investment in the primary sector to 55 per cent of the total investment in health. The secondary and tertiary sectors will get 35 and 10 per cent respectively.

Table 20.4: Differences in Health Status among the States

Sector	*%Pop BPL*	*IMR**	*< 5 yr MR**	*Weight@ <–2SD*	*MMR #*	*Leprosy cases $*	*Malaria cases&*
India	25.1	70	94.9	47	408	3.7	2200
Rural	27.09	75	103.7	49.6	–	–	–
Urban	23.62	44	63.1	38.4	–	–	–
Kerala	12.72	14	18.8	27	87	0.9	5.1
Maharashtra	25.02	48	58.1	50	135	3.1	138
Tamil Nadu	21.12	52	63.3	37	79	4.1	56
Orissa	47.15	97	104.4	54	498	7.05	483
Bihar	42.60	63	105.1	54	707	11.83	132
Rajasthan	15.28	81	114.9	51	607	0.8	53
Uttar Pradesh	31.15	84	122.5	52	707	4.3	99
Madhya Pradesh	37.43	90	137.6	55	498	3.83	528

* Infant mortality rate per 1000 population and below 5-year mortality rate per 1000 population; @ Weight of children under 3 years; # Maternal mortality rate per 1 lakh population; $ Leprosy cases per 10000 population; & Malaria Cases in 2000 AD in thousands.

Global experience shows that the quality of health services depends among others on the quantum of investment through public spending in primary health sector (Table 20.5). The Health Policy 2001 envisages increased central government health sector expenditure to 6 per cent of the GDP with 2 per cent of the GDP being contributed as public health investment by the year 2010. The state governments would increase their budgetary allocation for health to 7 per cent by 2005 and to 8 per cent by 2010.

Table 20.5: Public Health Spending in Select Countries

Indicator	*Per cent population with daily income <1 $*	*Infant mortality rate/1000*	*Per cent of health expenditure to GDP*	*Per cent of public exp. on health to total Health expenditure*
India	44.20	70	5.20	17.30
China	18.50	31	2.70	24.90
Sri Lanka	6.60	16	3.00	45.40
UK	–	6	5.80	96.90
USA	–	7	13.70	44.10

Source: Health Policy of India, 2001

Total expenditure on health in India stands at 5.2 per cent of the GDP but only 20 per cent of it is spent on public health. Eighty per cent is spent on salaries, infrastructure etc. Only 1.3 per cent of the central budget is earmarked for health. The states allocate about 5.5 per cent of their total expenditure for health. Health being a state subject, the central government provides only additional funds to the states.

Health Delivery System

The new health policy assigns a key role to the central government in designing national programmes of health with the active participation of the state governments and local authorities. To make this cooperative endeavour a success, the policy envisages gradual convergence of all health programmes under a single field administration. To make a dent on the stability of diseases like malaria, T.B. and HIV/AIDS, all programmes should be carried out through autonomous bodies at state and district levels. This would limit the role of state departments of health to monitoring and technical support. These bodies would have management boards having representation from all sectors of the society.

The current state of health infrastructure at the primary level is highly un-satisfactory. The lower level facilities are dysfunctional over large parts of the country. Even the supply of essential drugs is grossly inadequate. Diagnostic services are rarely available. Patients have to consult private physicians, and purchase medicines. As such very few of the potential beneficiaries go to the primary health centres. This in turn encourages the medical professionals attached to the PHC to absent or to come late. For the outdoor medical facilities the present funding is insufficient. The presence of health personnel is often much less than required by the prescribed norms; the equipment is obsolete and the buildings are dilapidated. Indoor facilities are not much better. At best, they, are inadequate, essential drugs are not available, the equipments are old and unusable and the medical personnel are ill-prepared to handle complicated cases. As a result, only 20 per cent of the potential users avail of the OPD facilities and only 45 per cent of them avail of the indoor facilities. This is in spite of the fact that at least half of the people cannot afford to spend money on health.

The new policy gives priority to revival of the primary health system by investing in physical infrastructure, posting more medical personnel and providing essential drugs. These measures would attract the beneficiaries to the health centres in larger numbers.

The short fall of medical personnel in the backward areas is really serious. Physicians and nurses do not want to work in rural and tribal areas. The new policy calls for the posting of the practitioners of Indian System of Medicine and Homeopathy. The services of senior nurses and paramedical personnel with adequate experience and training can also be considered.

Health Administration

The new health policy emphasizes the implementation of public health programs through local government institutions. And hence it urges all state governments to decentralise the implementation of all public health programmes to these institutions by 2005. In order to achieve this, the financial incentives, over and above the resources allocated for disease control, will be provided by the central government.

The NHP-2002 recommends the involvement of the private sector in the provision of health facilities. For this, it suggests the enactment of suitable legislations to regulate minimum infrastructure and quality standards in clinical establishments and medical institutions; and also statutory guidelines for the conduct of clinical practices and delivery of medical services by 2003. It also encourages the private sector to enter the insurance field.

The policy encourages setting up medical institutions to cater to the needs of foreigners and NRIs on payment in foreign currency and such services to be treated as 'deemed export'. Use of telemedicine in tertiary sector and cooption of non-governmental practitioners in the national disease control are other important recommendations.

Access to Medical Education

Medical colleges are very unevenly distributed in the country. The states, which did not allow private sector to open medical colleges have lagged behind the states, which encouraged private initiative. Such states did not have adequate resources to establish new medical colleges to meet the growing demand for health personnel or to provide quality education in the existing institutions. The new policy suggests the setting up of Medical Grants Commission on the lines of University Grants Commission to fund the upgradation of the old colleges and the setting up of the new colleges.

It is commonly perceived that the current syllabus of undergraduate medical education is excessively theoretical, making it difficult for the fresh graduates to effectively meet even the primary healthcare needs of the population. This might be one of the reasons for the reluctance of the new graduate to go to remote areas. The new policy, therefore, envisages changes in the curriculum to make it need-based and skill oriented with adequate scope for practical training. This would prepare the medical graduates to fill the shortage of field staff currently being felt, especially in the primary health centres.

Certain medical disciplines, such as molecular biology, gene therapy, anesthesiology, radiology and forensic medicines have now acquired added importance. They are important not only for treatment of patients but also for advanced research. These disciplines, however, do not get their due place in the curriculum. The new policy aims at removing this shortcoming within the next few years.

Lack of research is one of the major weaknesses of the Indian medical education. In fact, very few of the medical graduates opt for research field because it has a long gestations period and not highly remunerative. Lack of adequate fund for research is another major hurdle. The new policy envisages increase in government funding for medical research to the tune of one per cent of total health spending by 2003 and two per cent by 2010. Domestic research will be focused on new therapeutic drugs and vaccines for tropical diseases such as TB, malaria and certain strains of HIV/AIDS and would be conducted in a mission mode to achieve early results. Emphasis would also be laid on time bound applied research for developing operational applications.

Health Intelligence

Absence of systematic and scientific information system is a major deficiency in the health scenario of India. It is almost impossible to get reliable morbidity and mortality data, let us say district-wise and disease-wise. Hospital data are unreliable because patients come from long distances also and no one collates data on their places of origin. Even with respect to diseases, the information available is not dependable. Many people die before they reach a hospital or consult a trained physician. Cause of death remains unknown and is often classified as fever or dysentery.

The paucity of information is not limited to morbidity and mortality alone. We do not have dependable information about the financial resources used in the health sector. Very little information is available about the private sector's role in the provision of health facilities in the country.

To get over this problem, the new policy aims at completing of baseline estimates of the incidence of common diseases like TB, malaria, blindness, etc. by 2005. It also wants that statistical methods to update the baseline data through random sampling be in place soon. It also aims at establishing a longer timeframe baseline estimates for other communicable diseases like hepatitis and Japanese Ensephalitis, and non-communicable diseases like CVD, cancer, diabetes, accidental injuries, etc. There is also a proposal to establish national health accounts, conforming to the 'source-to-users' matrix structure.

Standards for Food and Drugs

It is proposed to strengthen the food and drug administration, both in terms of laboratory facilities and technical expertise. The standards of food items would be progressively tightened so that they are close to codex specifications. Quality standards for drug are also proposed to be raised to the levels of those in developed parts of the world.

Other Components of Health Policy

Specialized Services: Given the size of population in the reproductive age group, there is acute shortage of medical personnel with specialization in 'public health' and 'family medicine' disciplines. The new policy envisages progressive increase in post-graduate seats in medical colleges in these disciplines to one-fourth of the total. This will apply to nursing and paramedical courses too.

Urban Health: About one third of the total population of India lives in cities. Half of the urban dwellers are really urban peasants and their economic and social situation is none better than that of the rural people. It is, therefore, proposed to reach these less privileged people living in cities through an urban primary health care structure. There would be one primary health centre for a population of one lakh. The funding of these primary health centres will be the joint responsibility of the local, state and central governments.

Mental Health: Mental health disorders are more prevalent than visible. This is a disease, which does not add much to mortality figures but it has serious adverse implications for the affected persons and their families. Serious cases of mental disorder require hospitalization and treatment under trained supervision. Unfortunately, most of the mental health institutions are woefully deficient in physical infrastructure and trained manpower.

The new policy envisages a decentralized mental health services, including diagnosis of common disorders by general duty medical staff and prescription of common therapeutic drugs, for ameliorating the more common categories of mental disorders. The mental health institutes would be upgraded by the central government to treat the more serious cases needing specialized attention.

Occupational Health: Working conditions in several sectors of our national economy in the country are sub-standard. The long-term risk of chronic morbidity is particularly marked in the case of child labour. The new policy envisages periodic screening of the health conditions of the workers, particularly for high risk health disorders associated with their occupation.

Women's Health: Women are exposed to a great variety of infections and other diseases, particularly during pregnancy, delivery and post-delivery months. They along with other under-privileged groups of people are significantly handicapped due to disproportionately low access to healthcare. The new policy envisages specific programmes targeted at women's health funded by the Central Government. It also provides for appointment of more specialists to meet the specific requirements of women.

Medical Ethics: The new policy urges the Medical Council of India to notify the current code of medical behaviour and remind the medical personnel of their duties towards the sick. It recognises the need to keep a vigilant eye on the ongoing research in the field of gene manipulation and stem cell with a view to frame appropriate guidelines and statutory provisions in the future.

NATIONAL POLICY FOR ISM & HOMEOPATHY–2002

The National Policy for Indian System of Medicine and Homeopathy-2002 has further strengthened the 1983 national policy goals and objectives. The growing disenchantment of people with allopathic system of medicine, the search for alternative systems, which do not produce long-and short-term side effects, has increased. Fortunately in India, we have Ayurveda, Unani Medicine, Naturopathy, Yoga, Homeopathy and several other systems, which are ready to supplement and compliment the modern allopathic system and in some cases even replace it.

In India too, the popularity alternative medicines is on the increase. India possesses an unmatched heritage of traditional medicines and healthcare. It is highly diverse, flexible and inexpensive and is readily accepted by the people because, despite the inroads of modern medicine, the traditional system continues to be popular. Ayurveda is spreading very fast all over the world. Even in developed countries, people have realized its potentialities and Ayurvedic medicines have become a major item of export. The Unani system is similar to Ayurveda. It is also spreading fast, especially among the Muslims. Same is the case with Naturopathy and Yoga. Both have acquired great reputation in recent years and Yoga teachers are in great demand all over the world.

The latest policy has reiterated that the above systems of medicine offer a wide range of preventive, promotive and curative treatments that are cost effective and efficacious and that there was need to integrate these systems in our health strategy. Budgetary support has been augmented and fiscal incentive available to the allopathic system has been extended to ISM&H too. The main objectives of the policy are:

1. to promote good health and expand the outreach of healthcare to all the people, particularly to those without health cover, through preventive, promoting, mitigating and curative intervention of the ISM&H;
2. to improve the quality of teachers and clinicians by revising curricula to contemporary relevance and to researchers by creating model institutions and centers of excellence and extending assistance for new infrastructural facilities;
3. to ensure affordable ISM&H services and drugs, which are safe and efficacious;
4. to facilitate availability of raw (basic) drugs, which are authentic and contain essential components as required under pharmacopeial standards to help improve quality of drugs both for domestic consumption and export;
5. to integrate the ISM&H in heathcare delivery system and national programmes and to ensure optimal use of the vast infrastructure of hospitals, dispensaries and physicians;
6. to reorient and priortise research in ISM&H to gradually validate therapy and drugs to address in particular the chronic and new lifestyle related emerging diseases;
7. to create awareness about the strengths of these systems in India and abroad and sensitize other stakeholders and providers of health; and
8. to provide full opportunity for the growth and development of these systems and the utilization of their potentiality, and strength revival for the of their glory.

In pursuance of the above, the Central Council for ISM & H has recommended that at least one physician from the Indian System of Medicine and Homeopathy be posted in each primary health centre. It has also recommended that in case the vacancy of allopathic doctor is not filled up because of the non-availability of suitable candidate, it should be allocated to doctors with ISM &H degree. It has also recommended that specialists from theses branches be posted in rural areas too.

Earlier, only 2 per cent of the central budget for health was allocated to ISM &H (98 per cent went to modern allopathic system). Attempts are being made to increase the share to 10 per cent. Over 400 medical colleges now offer graduate degrees and drug standards are now being strictly enforced. Over 8000 plants, which are stated to possess medicinal properties, are being protected and 500 of them grown in medicinal plant nurseries. Special attention is being paid to the North-eastern states which are very rich in medicinal plants.

Revitalization of local health traditions, protection of intellectual property rights of ISM, publication of ancient medical manuscripts, and medical tourism constitute the other elements of the policy. Yoga is being introduced in all systems of medicine as a therapy for systemic diseases.

HEALTH PLANNING

Health planning is a part of national planning process. The Planning Commission of India allocates funds for various sectors of national economy. Health and family planning jointly gets about 5 per cent of the total allocation. The Ministry of Health and Family Welfare gives its requirements to the Planning Commission. The schemes prepared by the ministry are partly national in coverage and partly regional and local. The state ministries of health and family welfare prepare their own state plans for health and family welfare and submit the same to the

Planning Commission for appropriate allocation of funds. The Planning Commission examines these proposals and tries to accommodate as many proposals as possible. Fortunately, in case of health and family welfare, the problems are almost common and hence the task of the Planning Commission is not so difficult.

Apart from the sectoral aspects of health planning, there is an equally important spatial aspect. Funds for health cannot and should not be allocated on the basis of population alone. There are states in the country; districts within the states; and villages and towns within the districts, which, for a variety of reasons, did not benefit from planned development equitably. They are very much behind. Then there are some states, districts, block and villages, which have moved up the ladder of health and family welfare. Funds should, therefore, not be allocated blindly on the basis of population number or administrative units. Equal distribution not only proves to be unequal but also counter-productive, although it is least controversial. What we, therefore, need is a plan that is sectoral-cum-spatial.

This is not the place to discuss in detail the process of health planning. It is not different from general planning process, except that it oriented to health and family welfare, and beeds to that be integrated in the overall plan of the country or area. It may, however, be noted, planning has three basic components: plan formulation, plan execution, and plan evaluation. The three dimensions form a cycle. Health plan must be based on needs and demands of the target group and constraints of resources; it must have goals, objectives and targets, it must priortize the projects and schemes, must have a planning and executing machinery, and must be monitored periodically.

Ministry of Health and Family Welfare prepares five-year as well as annual plans for implementation. The same thing is done at the state and district levels by respective authorities. The main objectives of the ninth five-year plan for health were:

1. spatial integration of sectoral plans;
2. development of speedy disease surveillance and response mechanism;
3. develop integrated non-communicable disease control mechanism;
4. include health as a part of environmental impact assessment;
5. handle disasters promptly and speedily;
6. reduction in population growth; and
7. implementation of reproductive and child health programme by effective maternal and child care.

At least six per cent of the annual national budgetary commitments should be spent on health. This should apply to the planned investment also. India has yet to reach this target. As given in Table 20.6, allocation for health and family planning in various five-year plans has remained less than six per cent, and the share has been declining.

PLANNING FOR THE FUTURE

It is clear that the New Health Policy is quite comprehensive and covered many grounds which were untouched in the 1983 policy. If implemented in right earnest, the health scenario in the country would undergo definite change for the better. We, however, know that making a document is one thing and to follow it up quite another.

Table 20.6: Five-Year Plan Allocation for Health, Family Welfare and Water Supply (in crores of rupees)

Plan Period (except annual plans)	*Total Plan Allocation*	*Allocation for Health*	*Allocated for Family Welfare*	*Allocation for Water Supply*
I Plan (1951–56)	1,960	55 (2.8)	0.1	–
II Plan (1956–61)	4,672	141 (3.0)	2.2 (0.05)	–
III Plan (1961–66)	8,576	225 (2.60)	25 (0.29)	11 (0.13)
IV Plan (1969–74)	15,779	335 (2.12)	284 (1.8)	459 (2.91)
V Plan (1974–79)	39,322	682 (1.73)	497 (1.26)	971 (2.47)
VI Plan (1980–85)	97,500	1821(1.87)	1010 (1.04)	3922 (4.02)
VII Plan (1985–90)	180,000	3393 (1.89)	3256 (1.81)	6522 (3.6)
VIII Plan (1992–97)	798,000	7576 (0.95)	6500	16711
IX Plan (1997–2002)	?	?	?	?
X Plan (2002–07)	?	?	?	??

Source: National Health Policy, India, 2001

Within the new policy framework, priority should be given to the following:

1. Better maintenance of existing hospitals and medical training institutions;
2. Qualitative change in primary health services particularly in rural areas;
3. Early detection and treatment of communicable diseases;
4. School health programme; and
5. Change in medical education programmes to turn out large number of trained personnel with two to three year training to handle general health problems and common diseases.

The existing hospitals, particularly those run by state governments, are in very bad condition from all angles: hygiene, medical attention, availability of drugs and infrastructure. First priority should go to their improvement. The primary health centres already functioning in rural parts of the country are in much worse conditions. They need urgent attention before new centres are started. Surveillance of communicable diseases is still very poor. Often cases are detected after it is too late. We need a more alert system. School health programmes suffer from many deficiencies. Children are the future citizens of the country. School health programmes not only help improve health of the children but also attract children to schools. They should get priority attention. And lastly, there is no denying the fact that 85 per cent of the sick suffer from most common diseases. If timely preventive and curative services are available, they will recover back to health. In the absence of health attention, the cases get complicated, and mortality rates increase. What is needed is a doctor who has just three years of theoretical and practical training, not a five year graduate or MD to handle such cases. It will be better if the old discarded 3-year programme of LMP (licentiate of medical practice) is reintroduced in our colleges. The new graduates should serve in some rural health centres for at least five years and then given an opportunity to go back to medical colleges to complete their bachelor degree programme, if they so wish. I think, such a programme will suit the current as well as future public-health and medical requirements of the common people of India better.

SPECIAL PROGRAMMES

Programming means translation of plans into activities, which could be executed to meet the objectives set in the plan within a given timeframe through a series of projects and schemes. Health programming, therefore, means far more than a discussion of various programmes in the health and family welfare sector. We would, however, not go into the larger issue of programming of the whole sector. We will confine ourselves to only programmes, which are being operated to prevent, control and eradicate diseases. Many others are discussed in relevant chapters elsewhere in the book.

In all, there are about twenty programmes to control diseases, improve environment and living conditions. A list of them is presented below. More details of these are given in chapters that deal with various diseases.

1. 20-Point Programme,
2. Basic Minimum Needs Programme,
3. Water Supply & Sanitation Programme,
4. National Family Welfare Programme,
5. Health-For-All-2000 (HFA-2000) Programme
6. National Malaria Eradication Programme,
6. National Filaria Control Programme,
9. National Leprosy Eradication Programme,
10. National Tuberculosis Programme,
11. National AIDS Control Programme,
12. National Programme for Control of Blindness,
13. Iodine Deficiency Disorder (IDD) Programme,
14. Universal Immunization Programme,
15. Reproductive and Child Health (RCH) Programme,
16. National Guineaworm Eradication Programme,
17. Japanese Encephalitis (JE) Control Programme,
18. Kala-Azar Control Programme,
19. Dengue Fever Control Programme,
20. National Cancer Control Programme,
21. National Mental Health Programme, and
22. National Diabetes Control Programme.

In this connection it would be pertinent to know the difference between control, prevention and eradication of diseases. Prevention means checking the spread of the disease; control means stopping its occurrence locally; and eradication means its complete elimination.

While implementing health programmes, two points need special attention: one, health should not be treated as a medical issue alone; it is a social and environmental issue to begin with. People must be convinced of the utility of a programme. Then alone it would take off smoothly and achieve its goals; two, spatial and perspective planning before a programme is launched is a must. In this regard, the area intensity of the disease should be marked and possible reasons for the same should be short-listed. Community leaders must be involved in the programme to mop up support and instil confidence.

EPILOGUE

Health is a vital aspect of human life; it has, however, not received the attention it deserves or the attention paid is based on certain fallacies, which have been given scientific rationale. Unless human body and mind are optimally healthy, man can neither achieve his full potentials nor can he contribute his optimum to the society. Good health is a prized possession; it must be maintained at all costs.

Good health depends on three factors: the outer environment (habitat); the style of life (habits), and healthcare. The environment consists of five gross elements: land, air, water, energy and space. All the five must be available in the quantity and quality human body needs. The style of life of each and every individual should be such that promotes good health. Over-eating, under-eating, over-sleeping, under-sleeping, over-working, under-working, negative thinking, anger, jealousy, desire for body welfare at the cost of inner peace and harmony, eating and drinking something that does not suit human biology and lack of balance in life and living are injurious to health. And finally, health depends on the quality and quantity of promotive and curative measures available to people. Everyone gets sick some times or the other. If prompt and appropriate attention is not given to the sickness, it may endanger life.

All the three aspects noted above can be effective only if the attitude of the people towards health is positive i.e. health is something that must be maintained through healthy habitat and habits. Only occasionally people should resort to curative measures. In other words, health is the responsibility of each and every individual. It is not the responsibility of doctors and hospitals. Healthy person is not one who gets sick often but gets cured by doctors; he is one who does not get sick and if he does get sick he is able to recover fast by change in his environment and lifestyle. It is rarely that a healthy person goes to a doctor for cure of diseases. The future health policy must direct its attention to this approach to good of health.

REFERENCES

1. Ministry of Health, Government of India, *Annual Report,* 2001.
2. ——, *Health Policy of India*, 1983 and 2001.
3. ——, *Health Information of India,* 1998.
4. Registrar General of India, *Census of India Publications*, 1991 and 2001 Censuses.
5. UNDP, *World Development Report*, 2000.

21

Management of Health Services

One of the very hopeful trends in the health scenario of India is the increasing capacity of the health services to control communicable diseases. When the health of the people has deteriorated to the level it has in India, the immediate task of the health services must be to check the high morbidity and mortality rates due to communicable diseases by whatever means available. India has tried to move in this direction during the last five decades of its independent existence. The strategy has worked fairly well and today the country has been able to reverse the trends at least in some respects. India has controlled many diseases and it has eradicated quite a few of them. But it has to go a long way before it can create a healthy society.

Many diseases are yet to be controlled; a few which appeared to have been controlled are on their comeback trail and several new diseases not known earlier have posed new threats and challenges. Whether India will succeed in controlling diseases depends much on a host of factors: health policy, access to health facilities, investment in health and international cooperation. In this chapter we would examine how India manages its health services and the quantity and quality of health services, it offers to people keeping in view the fact that the ultimate solution lies not in checking diseases through medicines but in making the body of the people so strong that the diseases are not able to make inroads easily. That means greater attention to health by the people themselves, food security and a healthy style of life.

We noted earlier that the expectancy of life in India has gone up and death rates have declined. More mothers live to see their babies and more children live beyond their infancy. Far less people become victims of communicable diseases. May be, the results are not as spectacular as we would like them to be, they are nevertheless good and satisfying to some extent. Much of these improvements are direct consequences of quantitative as well as qualitative improvements in public health facilities: primary health centres, physicians, nurses and paramedical personnel. Knowing that changes in the styles of life are slow to come, any perceptible improvement in the health of the people in the short-run can occur only through further improvements in public health facilities.

HEALTH ADMINISTRATION

Health services in India are organized at three territorial levels: national, state and local. They are public (government), semi-public or private. While public health is essentially a public affair, private initiative is quite prominent in specialized services rendered by hospitals, clinics, and individual physicians and surgeons. In this section emphasis is laid on public health services and their management.

National Level

The Central Ministry of Health and Family Welfare looks after Health and Family Walfare. Health is a state subject and hence the role of the central government is more facilitative than executive. The Ministry of Health is headed by a cabinet rank Minister and the secretariat by a senior Indian Administrative Service officer. The Ministry has two major departments: Department of Health and Department of Family Welfare; each being headed by a Secretary.

To render medical advice to the government and to manage the health services and programmes administered by the health department, there is a Director General of Health Services, who is a medical specialist. He formulates plans, organizes surveys, coordinates various activities carried out by specialized units, appraises the work in progress and helps the government in planning and policy making as and when required.

To be more precise, the D.G. Health advises the government on following matters:

1. international relations and quarantine,
2. control of drugs standards,
3. medical education,
4. post-graduate training,
5. medical store,
6. medical research,
7. health schemes operated by the central government,
8. national health programmes,
9. central health education bureau,
10. health intelligence (information), and
11. National Medical Library.

A large number of health issues fall in the concurrent list of the Constitution of India over which both the Central and State legislatures have the power to make laws. To make health services effective the cooperation and coordination among are the Central and State Governments is a must. Further, even the central government schemes can be implemented through the State health services alone. Central Government does not maintain field staff. To ensure positive and constructive cooperation between the Central and State authorities, a Central Council for Health was created as early as 1952. It is headed by the Minister for Health. Health ministers of various states are its members. The Council has played a very positive role in the promotion of health and family planning in the country.

The Council is entrusted with a number of functions, important among them are:

1. to evolove broad outlines of policy measures covering all aspects of health,
2. to suggest legislative measures to improve health services in the country,
3. to lay down health related development patterns for the whole country, and
4. to recommend distribution of funds, and to establish organisations and institutions to strengthen cooperation between the Central and State Governments.

State Level

The states known as provinces in pre-independence India, got autonomy in matters of Public Health under the Montague-Chemsford Reform of 1919. By 1921-22, the provinces set up their own organizations to take care of Public Health. The Government of India Act 1935 further strengthened the provincial autonomy in this respect. Health was put under all the threee lists: Central, Concurrent and Provincial. The provincial list included provision of medical care, preventive health services and pilgrimages within the respective provinces. The position of health has remained almost the same in the Indian Constitution enforced in 1950.

The States and Union Territories have their own health departments each header director of health services. There is a Minister for Health in the state cabinet. In between, the Health Minister and Health Directorate, there is the Secretary for Health and his administrative staff. Some states have more than one minister looking after different aspects of health. Such practices come in the way of coordinated functioning of the health services.

The Director of Health Services, is the chief medical officer and advisor to the state government. He organises and manages the health services of the State. Each health region and each functional unit is headed by a director who reports to the Director of Health Services of the state.

Local Level

The lowest unit of administration where the presence of the central government is strong is district. The District Magistrate or Collector who administers the district, belongs to central services. He represents the central government through the state government. Each district has several types of administrative and functional zones. For revenue purposes, there are taluks/ tahsils below the district. Each taluk is divided into revenue villages. For development purposes, the district is divided into development blocks and each block into gram panchayats. The police department has its own Circles and Thanas; and so has the postal department. The electoral constituencies can cut across even district boundaries.

The head of the district health administration is the Chief Medical Officer (CMO). He is supported by three deputy CMOs: Civil Surgeon, District Health Officer and District Family Welfare Officer. All of them are state government employees and hence transferable from one district to another. The district hospital functions as the distict health centre. Linked to the district hospital are the lower level hospitals, PHCs and sub-centres. The function of these officers and hospitals is to provide primary healthcare to people and to handle emergency cases.

The hospitals at the district and sub-district levels form an integral part of the health services. Some of them are specialized hospitals for tuberculosis, leprosy and other diseases; they are often classified as rural and district hospitals.

At the development block level are community health centres (CHC) or primary health centres (PHCs). Then for each group of ten villages, there is sub-center of the PHC. At the village level, there are health workers attached to the sub-centers or primary health centres.

CHCs are upgraded PHCs; they possess some additional facilities such as a 30-bed hospital, X-Ray machine and specialists in surgery, medicine, obstretics, pediatrics, and gynaecology. 2424 PHCs were upgraded into CHCs in 1996. Each CHC is headed by a Community Health Officer (CHO). The CHO can refer the patients directly to the state level hospitals. He also functions as the medical officer of the PHCs.

The main functions of the PHC are:

1. medical care in general;
2. maternal and child health (MCH) including family planning;
3. basic sanitation including provision of safe drinking water;
4. prevention and control of epidemics;
5. health education;
6. referral services;
7. training of health guides;
8. collection of health information;
9. basic laboratory services; and
10. participation in national health programmes.

Each PHC is supposed to have seven medical and paramedical personnel, in addition to general administrative functionaries: one medical officer, one compounder/pharmacist, one nurse mid-wife, one health worker (female), one block extension educator, and two health assistants (one female and one male).

Each sub-centre of the PHC serves ten villages. It is supposed to have one male and one female health workers (both salaried) and one voluntary worker.

HEALTH SERVICES

Health services in India not yet adequate. The problems are three-fold: inadequacy, urban bias and lack of service motivation among health workers. Inadequacy of health services arises from the fact that health has not received the attention it deserves in Indian planning and budgetary system. They are very thinly spread particularly in rural areas where majority of people in India live. Medical personnel tend to concentrate in urban centers; they are not willing to serve in rural areas. As a result, the quality of services available at the CHCs, PHCs and Health Sub-Centres needs much to be desired.

During the last fifty years, the improvement in health services has not kept pace with the improvement in other sectors of the Indian society and economy. It is clear from various health indicators for the year 2000 AD. The expectancy of life in India was 62 years; it was higher for men than women. Infant mortality rate (IMR), which is often taken as an indicator of health status of the people was 77 per 1000 live births; in the USA it was 6.9, in UK 5.9, Japan 3.5 and Canada 5.3. It is attributed to the lack of health education and poor access to health services. We would look at the condition of health services and management in this chapter in greater details.

Health Manpower

Medical personnel – the physicians, nurses and paramedical staff-constitute the backbone of health services. In 1943, there were only 47,400 registered medical practitioners, which meant that doctor-population ratio was 1:6300. Just one nurse was available for 43,000 persons; one health visitor for 400,000 persons; and one midwife for 60,000 persons. The dentist-population ratio was 1: 300,000; and pharmacist-population ratio stood at 1: 40,00,000. As against this, there was one physician for 1000 persons; one nurse for 300 persons; one health visitor for 4770 persons; and one midwife for 618 persons in UK.

These figures reveal that we started the development of health services in India with a very poor base. According to the Bhore Committee's very conservative estimates, India, for its population of 370 million in 1948, needed four times more doctors; a hundred times more nurses and health visitors; 20 times more midwives; 825 times more pharmacists; and about 90 times the number of dentists.

Almost fifty years later in 2000 AD, there were 4.07 physicians, 3.02 nurses, 1.63 midwives and 12 dentists per 10,000 populations. There were 2.56 in patient beds in urban areas and just 0.18 in rural areas. Compare these figures with that of other countries. Number of practicing physicians per 1000 population in the USA was 2.70. in UK 2.00, in Canada 2.1 and Japan 2.1. The number of nurse per 1000 population was 8.10 and 8.80 in UK. The number of acute care beds per 1000 population in the USA was 2.90 and in UK, 3.90. The average stay in hospital is considered to be an indicator of the efficiency of health services. It was 6.90 for UK and around 9.00 for Germany and Netherlands.

Similar is the case for life expectancy at birth. Again taking the figures for 2000 AD, it was 76.80 years for the USA, 77.80 for UK, 81.20 for Japan, 79.80 for Switzerland and 79.70 years for Sweden.

Allopathic Doctors

Soon after the independence of the country, a number of new educational and training institutions were set up by central as well as state governments to augment the existing stock of qualified doctors and dentists. The impacts of these measures were quite salutary. The physician-population ratio was 1:5880 in 1951; it improved to 1:3700 in 1971 and then on to 1:2080 in 1996. Currently, it stands at 1:2000. In 1998, there were 52 physicians per 100,000 population; in 1951, the number was just 7.

Laudable as these improvements may appear to be, compared to the developed countries of the world, the situation is not very commendable. It would be pertinent to compare the doctor-population ratio of India with that of other countries of the world. Table 21.1 and Fig. 21-1 give figures for 1958-59 and 1988-92. Similar is the case with regard to dentists.

Table 21.1: Doctor-Population Ratio in Select Countries

	Country	*Population per Doctor: 1958-59*	*Population per Doctor: 1988-92*
1.	Italy	691	213
2.	Germany	725	394
3.	Switzerland	749	590
4.	USA	805	420
5.	Canada	927	455
6.	Japan	943	610
7.	France	1,004	346
8.	UK	1,065	714
9.	Turkey	2,139	1,351
10.	Sri Lanka	4,701	1,143 ?
11.	India	6,157	2,080 (in 1996)
12.	China	8,700	730
13.	Pakistan	14,769	2,941
14.	Indonesia	94,654	7,143
	World		746

Source: WHO, World Health Report, 1998

The improvement in doctor population ratio noted above is not, however, uniform all over the country. There are wide differences among the urban and rural areas as also among the various states of the country. Public health is largely the responsibility of the government sector. In 1991, the population served by each government doctor was 6150 in Andhra Pradesh; it was higher than 15,000 in the states of TN and UP, and lower than 5000 in states like Goa, and most of the mini states of the country.

Fig. 21.2 gives the doctor/population ratio in different parts of the country. It is based on the registration of medical practitioners in state medical councils. This gives an indication of the relative access to health services. It must, however, be kept in view that these averages can often prove misleading.

Most of the medical personnel are city based and rural areas are very poorly served. In 1997, the number of medical specialists required in rural areas was 11,622. Only one-third of the positions (3,731) were filled. The shortage was as high as 67 per cent with respect to paediatricians, 62 per cent with respect to physicians, 56 per cent with respect to obstetricians and gynaeocologists and 55 per cent with respect to surgeons. The situation was far worse in some of the major states. Some states had no specialist in any field (Figure 21.3).

Rural-urban differences in the provision of health facilities are very wide in India. Special efforts have, therefore, been made to post more physicians and other health workers in rural areas but with only partial success. Two thirds of the posts of doctors remain vacant. The living conditions in rural areas do not attract educated people in general, and doctors in particular. Remotely located states, experience greater problems in this regard. Many of the primary health centres remain without doctors for years. As in 1996, over 5000 doctors were needed to fill up the vacancies in PHCs.

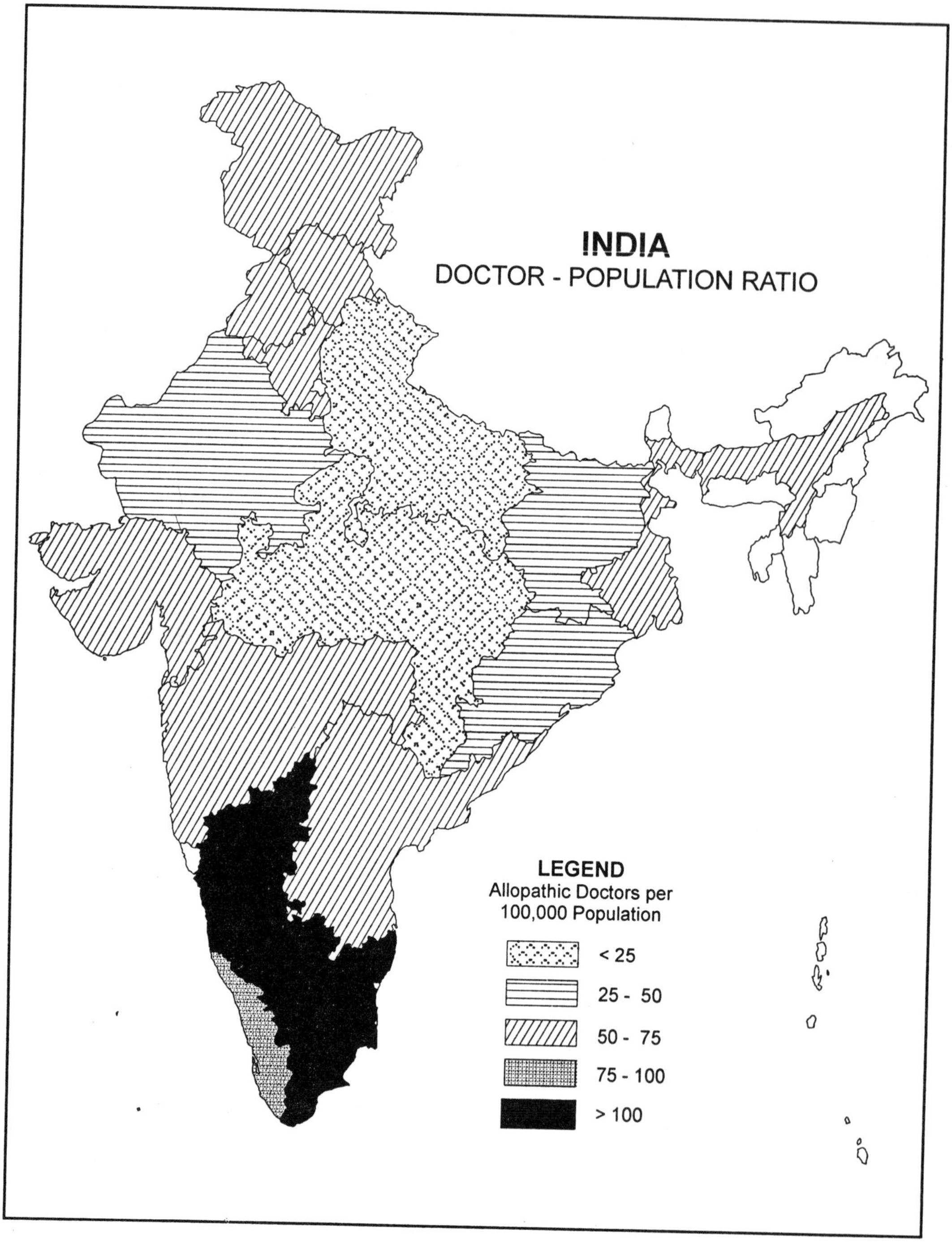

Fig. 21.1: World: Physician-population Ratio

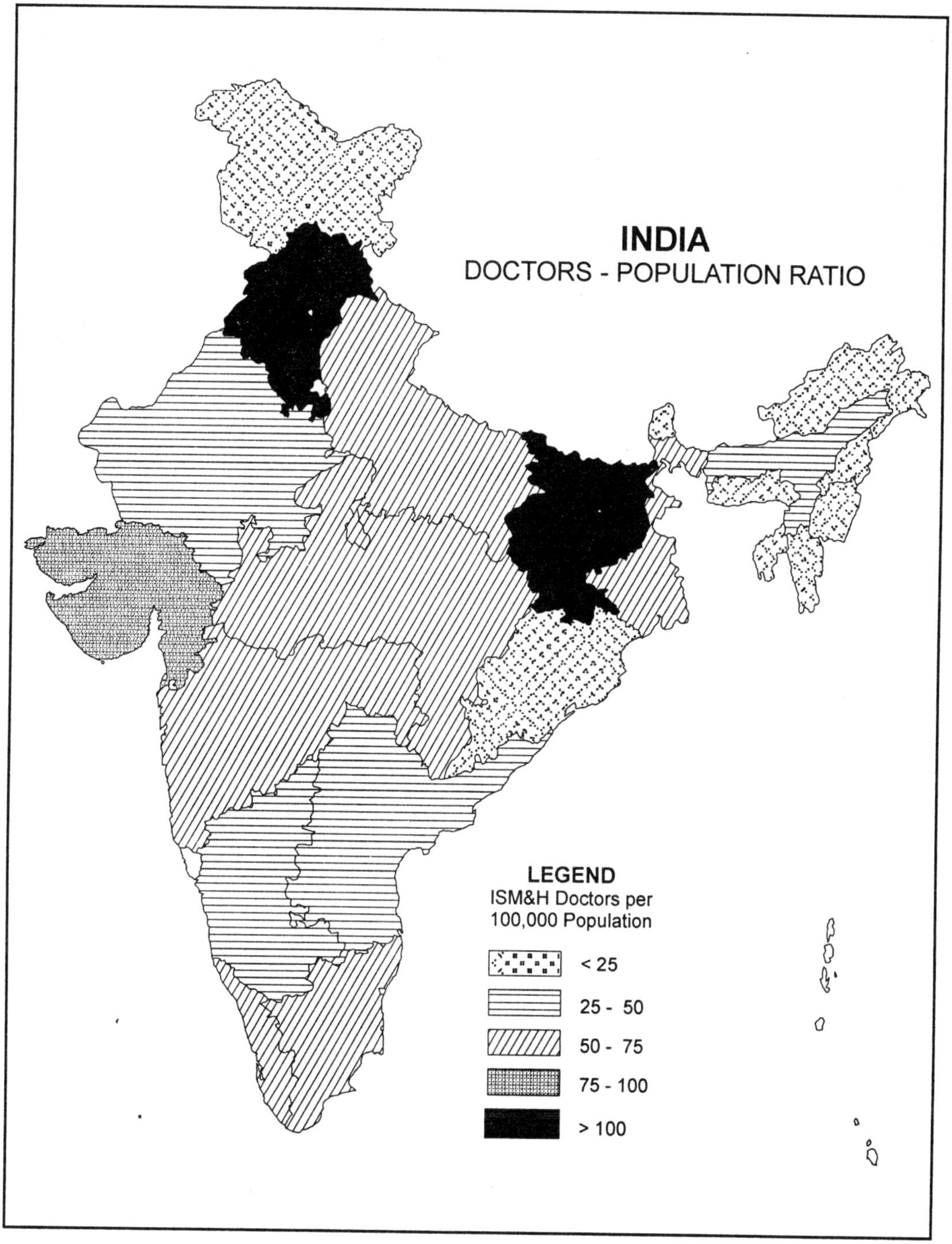

Fig. 21.2: India: Physician Population Ratio

Doctors Trained in ISM & H

Apart from the health personnel discussed above, over 375,000 physicians belonging to the Indian System of Medicine and Homeopathy provide health services to people. This category of physicians belong to one of the following systems: Ayurveda (350,416), Homeopathy (171,398), Unani (41,592), Siddha (12,528), and Naturopathy (267). The latter two systems are currently confined to Kerala, Tamil Nadu and Andhra Pradesh. But they have now spread all over the country, especially in urban areas. Further, there exist a large number of institutions and individuals who practise naturopathy but they do not have any recognized degree or diploma. Even Mahatma Gandhi practised Naturopathy and wrote a book on the subject. If a survey of practitioners of Indian system of medicine is conducted, one will find that naturopathy is quite popular in the country.

Table 21.2 and Figure 21.4 gives the state-wise distribution of registered Ayurvedic, Unani and Homeopathic physicians in the country.

Table 21.2: Number of Registered Ayurvdic, Unani, and Homeopathic Physicians in 1996 (state wise)

	States	*Ayurvedic*	*Unani*	*Homeo-pathic*	*Total*	*Doctor/lakh population*
1.	AP	21,261+259*	6,735	6,569	34,824	47.73
2.	Assam	250	–	11,518	11,774	46.30
3.	Bihar	75,711	3,250	25,050	104,011	109.85
4.	Gujarat	15,389	233	1,649	17,271	91.30
5.	Haryana	18,124	1,647	5,626	25,397	134.26
6.	HP	6,414	453	1,072	7,939	128.68
7.	J & K	343	162		505	5.50
8.	Karnataka	11,696+6*+1**	790	5,219	17,712	35.38
9.	Kerala	12,712+1329**	54	7,013	21,108	67.34
10.	MP	46,869	396	7,096	54,361	72.00
11.	Maharashtra	29,270	1,668	20,697	51,635	58.75
12.	Meghalaya	–	–	234	234	10.65
13.	Orissa	3,525	23	4,230	7,778	22.34
14.	Punjab	19,126	5,609	6,708	31,443	138.46
15.	Rajasthan	20,561	1,002	3,893	25,456	50.18
16.	TN	2,866+11198**	823	15,775	30,662	51.02
17.	UP	54,512	11,586	24,211	90,309	56.60
18.	WB	5,863	4,927	32,645	43,435	57.32
19.	Chandigarh	–	–	294	294	
20.	Delhi	5,924	2244	2,166	10,334	84.15
	India	350,416+12793	41,592	172,296	577,097	60.75

Note: * Naturopathy;
** Siddha. Many physicians practicing in a particular state may be registered elsewhere.

Source: Health Information of India

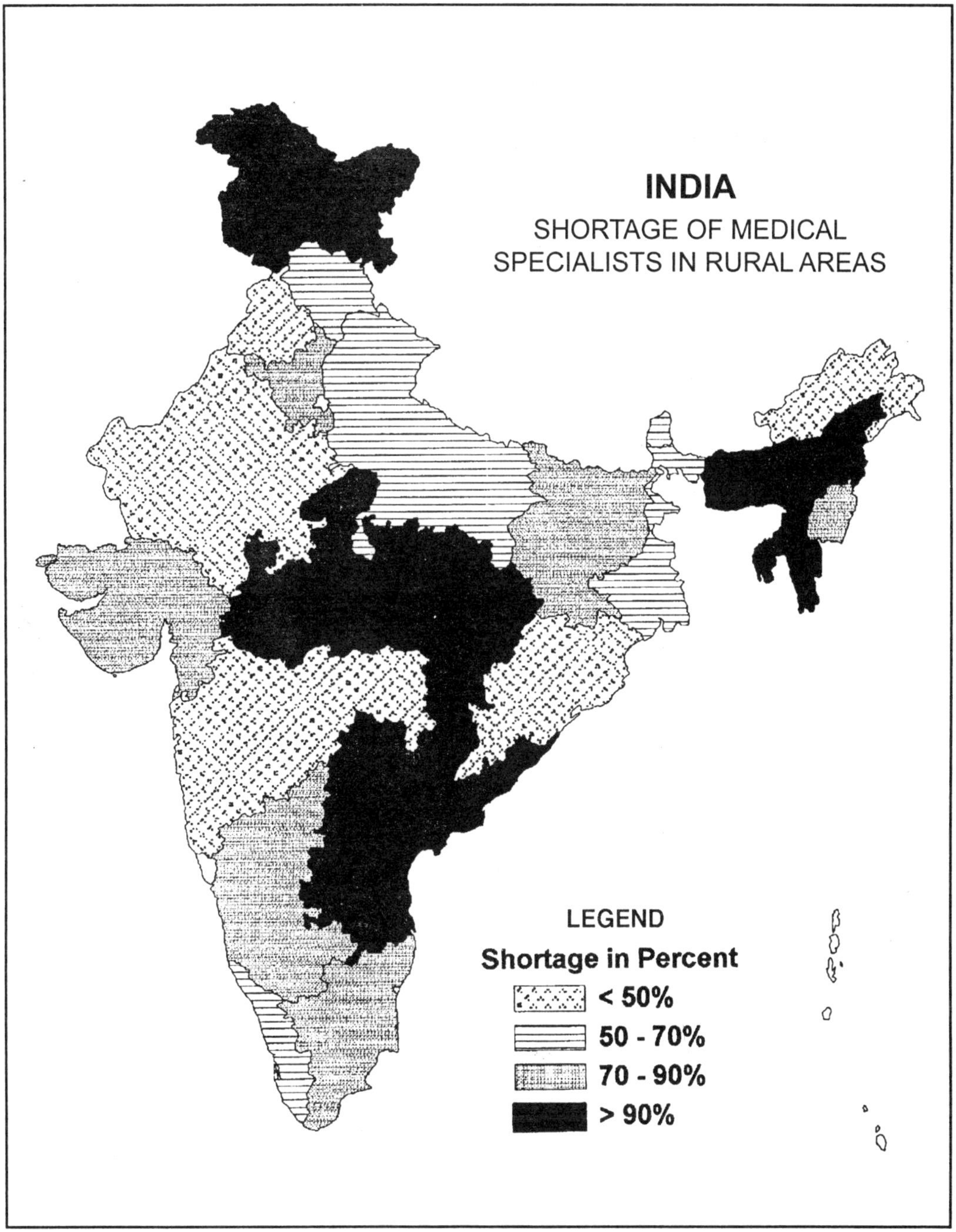

Fig. 21.3: Map of India showing State-wise shortage against required number of Medical specialists in rural India during 1995-98.

Source: Health Information of India, 1998.

Dentists

The situation with regard to the dentists is far worse. There are only 30,000 dentists in the country for a population of about 1000 million. That amounts to just 3 dentists per 100,000 population. In some states the situation is much worse.

Table 21.3: Distribution of Nursing and Paramedical Personnel-1996

	States	*General Nursing Midwifery*	*Aux. Nurse Midwives/ H. Workers*	*Health Visitor*	*Village Health Guide*	*Pharmacist*
1.	Andhra Pradesh	42,659	50,582	2480	34334	1112
2.	Assam	2,270	2,054	46	11001	950
3.	Bihar	8,883	7,501	1510	10431	1249
4.	Gujarat	68,045	17,087	1352	3004	882
5.	Haryana	4,344	5,663	326	270	517
6.	Himachal Pradesh	6,046	6,765	411	3450	292
7.	Karnataka	50,371	28,774	4926	15128	1165
8.	Kerala	24,914	7,758	748		847
9.	Madhya Pradesh	84,932	17,961	998	30619	2007
10.	Maharashtra	47,287	15,733	0	36506	1847
11.	Tamil Nadu	79,872	37,885	5851		1485
12.	Orissa	31,487	14,572	110	21017	1735
13.	Punjab	31,498	14,139	2574	9624	640
14.	Rajasthan	22,515	26,035	444	8982	2355
15.	Uttar Pradesh	15,199	13,158	2733	90111	927
16.	West Bengal	33,538	36,094	2983	39965	1231
17.	Mizoram	177	400	1	510	38
18.	Tripura	446	850	65	1834	87
	India	565696	283195	26578	320862	19749

Source: Health Information of India (1995-96)

Nursing and Paramedical Personnel

India had one general nurse for a population of 20,000 in 1951; it improved phenomenally to 1:1,612 in 1996. The ratio of auxiliary nurse-midwives and health visitors to population served was 1:3300; of health visitor, 1:35000; and of village health guides, 1:2900. The state-wise distribution of nurses and other paramedical personnel as in 1996 is given in Table 21.3.

The rural situation is not very satisfactory with regard to paramedical staff either. Sixty three per cent of the posts of nurse midwives have remained unfilled. And there are no takers for 15 per cent of posts of block extension educators, 40 per cent of those of health assistants and 30 per cent of health workers and those who are in position do not attend to their work. Of the 24,322 pharmacists and laboratory technicians needed in rural areas, only 25 and 40 per cent of them are in position. Despite the growing unemployment in the country, the tendency for the educated people to work in urban areas is on the increase. The shortage of nurses in rural areas in 1996 was 27,000, but 17,000 of them were unemployed. 2,088 positions of pharmacists were vacant and their overall shortage was 6,400, but 38,000 of the trained pharmacists were enrolled in the live registers of employment exchanges. Both the supply and demand are adequate and matching but place specificity is coming in the way.

Fig: 21.4 gives the state-wise distribution of nurses per 100,000 population as in 1997.

HOSPITALS AND DISPENSARIES

Number and Spatial Distribution

In 1947, there were only 6,669 hospitals (including all hospitals, dispensaries, primary health centers and sanatoriums) in the country: 4,617 in rural areas and 2,052 in urban areas. Uttar Pradesh, with one hospital for a population of 20,000 and one bed for 4,000 persons, was one of the best-served provinces. It is quite another matter that most of these hospitals, from today's standards, were very ill-equipped. In 1951, the year India launched its first five-year plan, there were just 8600 hospitals and 117,000 hospitals beds of all types in the country. Within a span of just 15 years, in 1965-66, the number of hospitals and dispensaries increased to14,097 and hospital beds to nearly 250,000 and by 1995 the number of hospitals went up to 43,322 (15,097 hospitals and the rest being dispensaries etc.) and the number of beds to 870,161 (623,819 of them being in hospitals). There was one hospital for a population of 61,881 persons in 1995 and if we take into account the dispensaries etc also, the population figure comes down to 22,000. The bed-population ratio stood at 1:1500. Added to the problem of overall shortage was the mal-distribution of the facilities. In 1961, when the hospital bed-population ratio in India was 1:1,570; it was 1:3,296 in MP, and 1:1,160 in J & K (Table 21.4; Fig. 21.5).

Public Health Facilities in Rural Areas

While 70 per cent of the population lives in rural areas, less than one third of the total hospitals and one-fourth of the hospital beds are located in cities. This urban bias in the provision of health services has been partly compensated by the establishment of 21,853 Primary Health Centres in rural areas as on April 1, 1996. These PHCs are supported by 132,778 sub-centres located in remote rural areas.

The situation in the tribal areas demands special attention. People living in the tribal communities are contracting the diseases, which were not there earlier. They are isolated to a great extent and are economically poor. According to the existing threshold norms, these areas in 1996 required 4,006 PHCs and 25,733 sub-centtrd. The states requiring more than 200 PHCs were MP (807), Bihar (489), Orissa (354), Gujarat (319), AP (315), Karnataka (317), Maharashtra (272), and Rajasthan (200). Eighty one per cent of the PHCs and 79 per cent of the sub-centres were already in position in 1996. Bihar and Assam are the two states, which were below the national average with respect to these facilities while the performance of Himachal Pradesh, Maharashtra, Sikkim and Tamil Nadu was far above the national average.

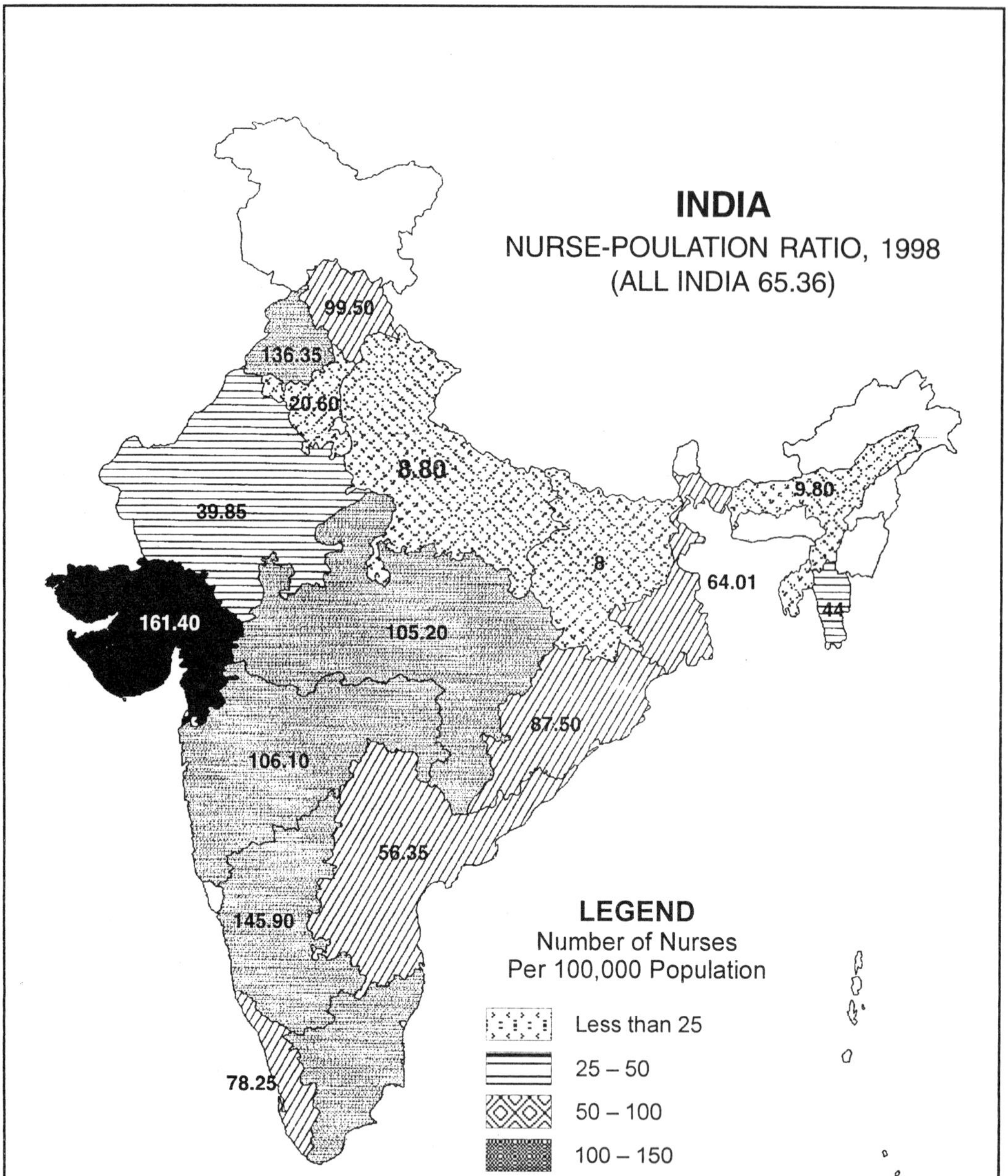

Fig. 21.4: Map showing state-wise distribution of Nurses and midwives per 1000,000 population.
Source: Statistical Abstract of India, 2001.

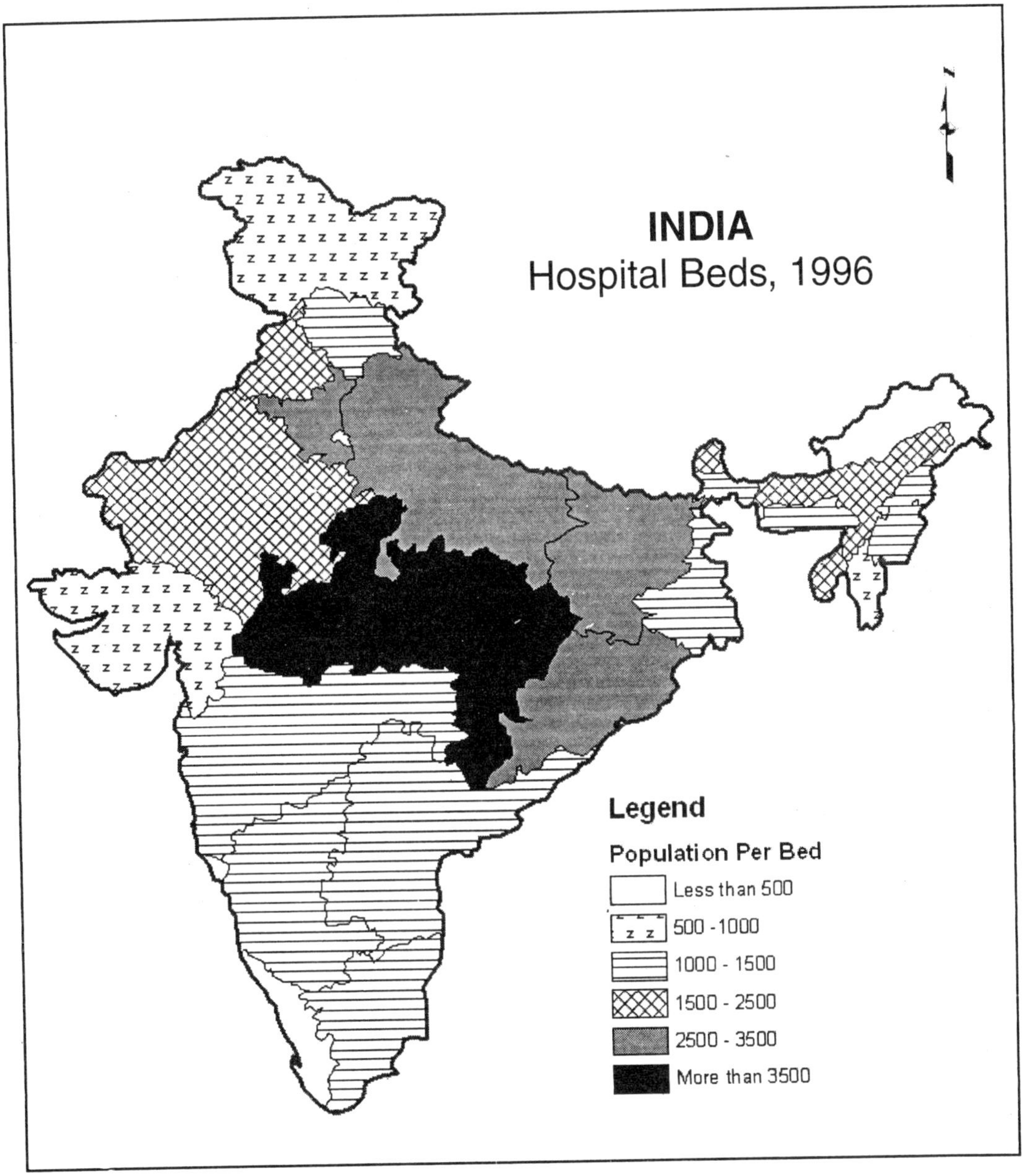

Fig. 21.5: Hospital Beds per 100,000 Population

Table 21.4: State-wise Distribution of Hospitals and Beds: 1996

	States	*Hospitals (Number)*	*Hospital Beds (Number)*	*Bed-Population Ratio*
1.	Andhra Pradesh	3133	69778	1:1057
2.	Arunachal Pradesh	262	2476	1:344
3.	Assam	268	12661	1:1968
4.	Bihar	328	29090	1:2969
5.	Goa	105	3848	1:358
6.	Gujarat	2528	63417	1:706
7.	Haryana	80	7230	1:2661
8.	Himachal PradeshP	63	5463	1:1165
9.	J & K	67	8202	1:868
10.	Karnataka	293	34469	1:1319
11.	Kerala	2107	97640	1:324
12.	Madhya Pradesh	363	18141	1:3770
13.	Maharashtra	3115	78920	1:1023
14.	Manipur	17	1626	1:1450
15.	Meghalaya	9	1828	1:1247
16.	Mizoram	12	1021	1:872
17.	Nagaland	29	1158	1:1358
18.	Orissa	273	11980	1:2937
19.	Punjab	220	14921	1:1542
20.	Rajasthan	219	21387	1:2417
21.	Skkim	1	300	1:1743
22.	Tamil Nadu	408	4878	1:1120
23.	Tripura	29	1866	1:1892
24.	Uttar Pradesh	735	47278	1:2593
25.	West Bengal	399	53732	1:1431
26.	A&N Isles	10	901	1:401
27.	Chandigarh	1	500	1:1540
28.	Dadra & N H	3	115	1:1448
29.	Daman & diu	3	150	1:680
30.	Delhi	77	19345	1:635
31.	Lakshadivi	2	70	1:943
32.	Pondicherry	29	3,136	1:332
	India	15,188	665,639	1:1451

Note: Bed-population ratio takes into account only hospital beds. Figures for some states pertain to years 1989-1993.

Source: Health Information of India, 1998

Health Economics

Health has remained a neglected item of government budgeting and expenditure. The health sector has a huge infrastructure but the funds allocated by the government, both central and State, are inadequate and hence are spread too thinly to be effective. The government has over the years allocated no more than 3.5 per cent of its resources to health sector. As a percentage of the GDP, it is around 1 per cent. WHO has recommended the member countries to allocate at least 5 per cent of the GDP for health. Health is a state subject but the central government gives annual grants for specific programmes and projects. Even this grant has declined from around 20 per cent in 1974-82 to 3.30 per cent in 1992-93. Naturally, the centrally sponsored schemes have suffered most.

Health and Family Welfare go together in government budgeting system. Over the years, the share of family welfare has increased while that of other health services declined. This has happened because population control has had a high priority in government policy. What is available to health is not only very thinly distributed but also mal-distributed. In fact the rural health services are so much geared to family welfare that other services remain neglected. Higher funding for family welfare, however, did not have proportional impact on population control.

This state of affairs in financing health services cannot go on for too long without very adversely affecting the quality of health services. The mushrooming growth of private hospitals and clinics is indicative of the deteriorating services in government run hospitals and primary health centers. In a way it is good that the private sector is entering the health sector in a big way; we cannot however forget the fact that these hospitals cater to health needs of the rich and upper middle class families. They are not accessible to at least half of the population of the country.

Health and development, no matter how we define the latter, go together. Poor health has serious implications for development. Control of population is important but the control and eradication of diseases that afflict the people equally are even more important. Health is an important element of human development; it cannot be neglected in a country which is moving fast on the road to development.

CONCLUDING REMARKS

Health is a major component of Human Development Index. According to the Human Development Report of the United Nations, India stands 124th among the nations in HDI. The major factors that give low HDI for India are low level of health and educational achievements.

India must develop new strategies for achieving Health-For-All targets within a decade or two. The following steps may help:

1. A three year medical diploma course should be introduced to train qualified youngmen and women in the basics of medicine. They should be posted in rural areas and opportunity be given to them to complete bachelor degree course in medicine after a few years of practice.
2. Housing facilities for the health personnel in rural areas should be improved on a priority basis to encourage health workers and specialists live there on a regular basis.
3. Each individual should be given a health passbook on which all details of his health should be noted down each year. Each time a passbook holder visits a doctor of PHC, it should be recorded.
4. Camps for health check up should be organised on regular basis in each PHC and its sub-centres.

5. Health and education should be integrated. The PHC doctor and health workers attached thereto should give regular lectures in the schools of the area. Schools should be used as centres of health education and general advice on sanitation, nutrition, water and health facilities available locally, at the district level or in neighbouring cities.

Health is as much a personal responsibility as a social responsibility. It is the job of the society to keep every one healthy by providing necessary knowledge and physical facilities. But if the individuals do not take care of their health and lead a style of life, which is injurious to health, then the society can do precious little. Injuring one's health deliberately and then asking the society to look after the sick would ultimately prove burdensome for all.

Social scientists have yet to give attention to health education, which makes people realize their own responsibilities towards their health. People who harm their health by indulging in unhealthy style of life are a great burden on the society. Time has come for a fresh thinking and action on this front. Health education must become a part of school curriculum. And over emphasis on curative measures must be brought down and preventive measures, specially those related to primordial medicine, must be encouraged.

REFERENCES

1. Ministry of Health, Government of India, *Health Information of India,* New Delhi. (An Annual Publication)
2. Annual Reports of the Indian Council for Medical Research, New Delhi.
3. WHO., *Regional Health Report*, Annual Publication
4. Registrar General of India, Census of India, 1991 and 2001. (See relevant Tables)
5. UNDP, *Human Development Report*, (annual publication)
6. Asian Development Bank, *Key Indicators of Developing Asian and Pacific Countries (Annual Piblication).*

22

Health Information

Availability of dependable and timely information is necessary for planning change and development in any field. It is more so in the case of health. Constant efforts have therefore been both at the national and global levels to improve collection and dissemination of information about diseases, medicines, health facilities, and ways and means of maintaining good health.

In medical terminology, four different terms are interchangeably used to denote health information: health data, health statistics, health intelligence, and health information. They connote slightly different meanings but in real practice they are not different from each other. Data consist of fact derived from the field surveys; they are raw and discrete. Health statistics means processed data presented in a generalized and concise form. It also includes the methods used in the collection and processing of data. Health information includes health data, information about other factors that influence health, medical data and data pertaining to diseases and their diffusion. Health intellegence is another term for health information with greater emphasis on collection and collation of data pertaining to different aspects of health.

HEALTH INFORMATION SYSTEM (HIS)

HIS includes collection, processing, retrieval and dissemination of health information. An ideal system of health information is one, which meets the needs of health planning and development, health education, health delivery system and which facilitates transmission of information speedily and without cluttering. Modern information technology has made it possible to meet all the above objectives at the same time. It is now possible to process information speedily through computers and transmit the same to long distances through internet using space technology.

The present system of health information in India is very unsatisfactory. Even the most basic information about the health of the people in different parts of the country is hard to come by. The birth and death data are yet to be perfected. Spatial information about diseases, epidemics, causes of mortality and morbidity, nutritional status of the people, environmental stresses, quality of health delivery system and spread of diseases are either not available or they are of poor quality.

Let us take the case of birth and death records. Only a small percentage of deaths take place in hospitals. The same is the case with the births. Further, fairly good number of those who are born and who die in hospitals belong to other places. Their births and deaths are often recorded twice at two different places. The hospital records are rarely used to locate the dead. Quite a large section of Indian population living in rural areas does not care to register births and deaths. Except for a few diseases, which are obvious, people do not know the cause of death. Most people, therefore, die of, 'fever' or 'stomach problem'.

Now there is plan to use modern information technology to link each village with the district head quarters, the district with the state capital and the state capital with the Delhi through a network of computers. This new development can be used by the health sector so that relevant health information becomes readily available. With the availability of satellite imageries, it should be possible to locate each health facility on maps. Global Positioning System (GPS) can be used to provide cost-effective mobile service to even remotest villages. GIS can be utilized to relate health information with environmental information, on the one hand, and socio-economic data, on the other.

A good information system would have the following ingredients and characteristics:

1. It should be people-oriented and people based;
2. It should be clear and uncluttered;
3. It should be presented in a form that is easily understood by the users;
4. It should present the information briefly and simply using tables, statistical tools, graphs, diagrams and maps;
5. It should be standardized to facilitate periodic revision;
6. It should have provision for to — and — fro feedback; and
7. It should be spatially interlinked from village or town level to the national level.

The health information should cover all relevant information. A short list of the areas that should ideally be covered is:

1. Relevant demographic data;
2. Relevant economic data such as income level, income distribution, occupational structure, etc.
3. Vital statistics;
4. Quality of environment;
5. Food security with special reference to nutrition;
6. Health status: morbidity, moratlity, disability, quality of life, access to health services, etc.:
7. Health resources: manpower, hospitals, beds, etc.;
8. Utilization of health services: occupancy rate in hospitals, admissions of patients, etc.;
9. Impact of medical care and disease control programmes on the health situation;

10. Spatial distribution of vital facts, health services and diseases marking areas that need special attention; and
11. Financial information: planned outlay on health, cost of health programmes and projects, and budgetary provisions, etc.

SOURCES OF HEALTH INFORMATION

The sources of health information are as varied as the data themselves. Health information, as noted earlier, is of two types: sectoral and spatial. The latter can be global, national, regional, or local. For international comparison, we need national level information; for understanding intra-national disparities, we need state and district level information and for understanding the reach of health services and programmes to remote areas of the country, we need village and city-ward level information.

The sectoral breadth is also very wide. Health is the cumulative product of a variety of medical, environmental, social, economic, cultural and psychological factors. One has to be conversant with all these aspects to understand health and related problems. Apart from these, we have the nuances of the biological processes of the human body on which various factors impact. Biological, anatomical, epidemiological, pharmaceutical, technological and other factors related to health have also to be taken into account. Information about all these factors and elements are crucial for health planning and development. Sources of health information are thus very wide. In this chapter we can give just a few of them.

UN Agencies

Chapter 23 gives some details of the international agencies, which are concerned with health and health related issues. Important among these are WHO, UNICEF, WOLD BANK, UNIDO, UNEP, ILO, UNESCO and UNDP. Each of these agencies publishes reports, both annual and periodical, which contain health information pertaining to various countries of the world. These data help in comparing the Indian situation with other countries of the world.

Registrar General of India

The office of the Registrar General India is responsible for the registration of births and deaths. The office is concerned with decadal population census. Records of births and deaths give the birth rate, death rate, fertility rate, etc. Age and sex composition of population gives information about the number of people in different age groups, the changes in the composition in terms of place of residence, occupation, religion and language through time and the projections for the future.

India has a Birth and Death Registration Act since 1873. In 1969, it was amended to make registration of births and deaths compulsory. It is the duty of the municipality or village panchayat, as the case may be, to register all births and deaths giving the name, date, day and time of birth and parent's name in case of births; and name of dead, his parent's name, date, day, time, age, and cause of death. The data so recorded are collated at the district and state levels and then forwarded to the Central Bureau of Health Intellegence, Government of India.

In addition to births and deaths several other vital details, are collected and published by the state governments and Central Bureau of Health Intellegence. Important among them are records of marriages, divorces, adoptions, legitimizations, recognitions, annulments, legal separations, etc.

Sample Surveys

National Sample Survey Organization conducts sample surveys on a variety of subjects. Many of these are relevant to health. National Institute of Nutrition, Hyderabad also conducts surveys on the nutritional status of children and women. All these data are published and made available to whoever needs them.

We have already discussed the survey of Causes of Death (Rural) conducted by office of the Registrar General each year (for details see chapter 20). This survey is being made more broad-based as time passes. The data derived from the survey are the only statistically reliable data on causes of death.

Five-Year Plans

The five-year plan documents are important sources of information on health. Before a plan is prepared, a large number of working groups are constituted on different subjects including health and family welfare. There were 6-8 working groups on health related subjects.

The Working Groups consist of senior officials and experts. The reports of the Groups contain lot of useful information. The health component of the plan is based on the recommendations of the Working Groups. The final plan document has a chapter on Health which gives the current situation, the achievements in the past and the proposed action in future.

Central Bureau of Health Intellegence

As mentioned earlier, the Government of India has set up a Central Bureau of Health Intellegence to collect, collate and publish health related information. The Bureau brings out an annual report-*Health Information of India*. It is a very valuable source of health information. It contains information on population, birth and death rates, social and economic indicators, medical and para-medical education, medical facilities, community health, public health, causes of death and health programmes.

The utility of the volume will increase if it is published timely. At present, it comes out 3-4 years behind schedule. The 1998 volume became available only in 2001. It should be brought out in a better format with appropriate charts and maps. It also needs to be made more comprehensive.

Hospitals and PHCs

One of the important sources of information are hospitals. Every patient who goes to a hospital has to register himself giving full details of his whereabouts. Once he is admitted in the hospital, information about his disease and the treatment given to him is also recorded. In most cases the history of the patient's health is also noted. All this information is, however, never collated and used for planning health services.

The only information that comes out of the hospitals and PHCs is the total number of patients treated. We are still quite unaware of the incidence of various health problems in different parts and regions of the country. As such there is a tendency to give equal attention to all regions.

This problem is particularly serious with respect to food security. India has so much buffer stock of foodgrains but anywhere between 5 to 10 per cent of people do not get enough to eat and at least 20 per cent people are malnourished. What is the degree of under-and malnourishment in different regions and districts of the country is not known. This is the reason why we hear of starvation deaths even in 21st century India.

Notification of Diseases

A minor source of information is the notification of certain diseases by the local and state governments. For example, the state government of UP has notified over 400 cases of polio during the first 9 months of 2002. Bihar has notified increase in kala azar cases. Newspaper reports are other important sources of information. Although these reports may not always be reliable, they are not baseless either. They, gives the base for further investigation and eventual authentication.

Private Medical Practitioners

Private medical practitioners are an important source of health information. Unfortunately, this source has not yet been tapped effectively. Same is the case with druggists. If one knows what drugs are sold most at what places or region, one can have a general idea of the prevalence of diseases. Further, it also gives an idea of the trends in drug intake and consumption.

Epidemiological Surveys

Epidemiological surveys are conducted before plans for the control and eradication of diseases are chalked out. Unfortunately, the data derived from such surveys are used only for programming purposes. It is never used to find out the causes underlying the spread and intensity of the disease in question.

Pollution Control Boards

Many diseases are caused by environmental factors. Pollution Control Boards of various states and ministries of environment, water resources, science and technology, and departments of meteorology, soil science, land resources and ocean development collect information on ecological degradation and environmental pollution. These data help in relating diseases to environmental factors. Unfortunately, health modelling for different ecological zones of the country has yet to be started.

Health Legislation

Laws are enacted by national, state and local governments to ensure compliance of measures, which protect and improve people's health and also make the health delivery system more effective. There are also laws or regulations regarding flood and draught relief; measure to help people affected by earthquakes and other natural calamities. All these legislative measures provide useful information about the health status of the people.

Health-manpower Statistics

Health manpower is of two types: general and special. General category of doctors and paramedical personnel is almost ubiquitously distributed to take of the general health of the people. The special type is related to specific diseases. Areas afflicted by leprosy, for example, have personnel specializing in leprosy. The same applies to many other diseases. The distribution of such specialists is indicative of the prevalence of particular diseases.

Master and Ph.D. Theses

Research work done in universities, medical colleges and medical research centres also provides valuable health information. Unfortunately, the information from these sources is not fully tapped and many of the useful findings are lost forever. Only that part of the information that gets published in magazines and journals reaches the people.

GEOGRAPHIC INFORMATION SYSTEM (GIS) FOR HEALTH

In the last quarter of the twentieth century, the space application technology in conjunction with electronics and computer technology has brought about a revolutionary change in information system. The earth observation technology, otherwise known as remote sensing, has become an important source of information and tool of analysis.

Remote sensing, coupled with mapping and map-making procedures, called Geographic Information System (GIS), represents the latest methodological and technological thrust in all sciences including medical. The computers have revolutionized the transfer and exchange of information; it is now possible to transmit real image of the sick organs of the body and consult a specialist thousands of kilometers away. Further, it is now possible to get day to day information about droughts, floods, diseases, medical and health facilities. With the help of Global Positioning System (GPS) technology, it is possible to extend prompt medical aid with minimum cost.

Synchronization of geoprocessing technology (GPS and Remote Sensing) with emerging computer and internet information technology standards based on 'open systems', 'distributed processing' and 'component ware-framework, provide open Geographic Information System (GIS) architecture to facilitate Information Systems and Solutions over internet/intranet for developing DSSs and GDSSs on sustainable health facilities and health delivery systems. The pluggable Computing Models (component wares) include GIS tools, Imaging tools, Expert tools and RDBMS tools.

What is where and why? How to minimize cost in delivering services? How to respond to patients/clients needs and demands at shortest possible time and lowest possible cost? These questions confront medical and paramedical personnel all over the world. Health is an essential services; it mediates between life and death. It has to be provided at the right time and right place. GIS helps immensely in meeting the health requirements of the people promptly and cheaply.

COMMUNICATION SYSTEM FOR HEALTH DELIVERY

One of the major challenges the health planners and workers face is gap between them and target group, which, in this case, is the patient. Speedy and uncluttered communication between the two is essential for efficient health delivery system. The cases where the outbreak of an epidemic reaches the concerned authorities after a week or so are not rare. At times, the patient is not able to see the gravity of the situation. Often an attempt is made to get relief through home remedies. The cases where the message does reach the medical officer in time but he does not take it seriously are also there. Delay can prove disastrous. Communicable diseases spread rather fast and a week's time is enough for a disease to take epidemic form.

How to convey right information through the most efficient channel of communication to the target individual or population is a question that has remained unanswered for centuries. This section of the chapter has attempted to give a model of communication system, which offers an approach to the solution.

Process of Communication

Communication means coveyance of information from source to the destination. The source may be a laboratory or a person; the destination may be an individual, group of people, common people or a place. The information generated at the source goes to the person whose job is to convey it to the final destination. He may be a scientist, researcher, newspaper representative, doctor, pharmaceutical company, government or the international agencies like the WHO. The form the information takes before it goes to the channel of communication depends upon the sender. If he so wishes, he can distort the information. Supposing that the medium of communication is the newspaper. The newsman presents the facts in a form that suits his paper's requirements and policy. News may be same but newspapers often give them in different forms and versions.

So, once the information is generated at the source, it may not necessarily be conveyed by the conveyer in the form it was given to him. People who transform information to suit the real or imaginary requirements of the channel play the role of encoder. He is the first source of distortion (noise) in the communication process. After the encoder puts the message in the channel in a particular format (language, waves, pulses), it need not reach the destination in the same form in which the encoder sent it. In case of the newspaper, the message may not get the place it deserves. Or it may be printed in a form and place, no one would ordinarily see. In the case of radio waves or satellite imageries, mechanical failure can become a cause for distortion. So the channel itself is the second major source of noise in the communication system.

Before the message reaches the destination, it has to pass through a decoder. Let us take the radio communication. The verbal message is encoded into radio waves and then decoded into verbal message. Suppose a postal letter reaches an illiterate person. That person has to go to a literate person to hear what the letter has to say. The person who reads the letter changes the contents and gives a different version. The encoder may be a person or a machine. The third source of noise in the communication system is the encoder.

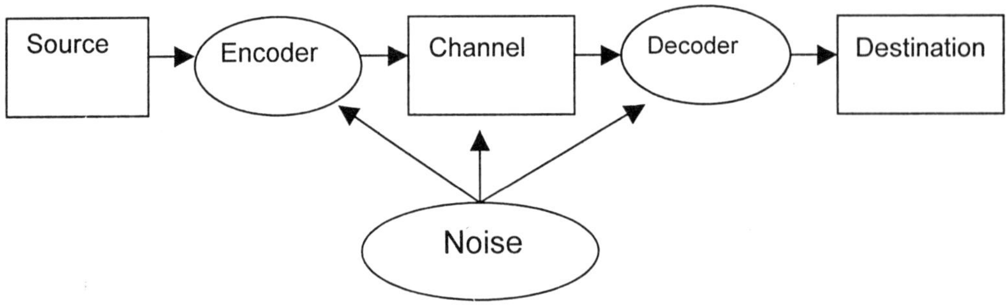

Fig. 22.1: Process of Information Transmission

When the message reaches the destination it is once again transformed by the target person or group before it is acted upon. Much depends on the psychology, attitude and inclination of the person. A good message coming from a 'bad person' is never relied upon; but even 'bad' information coming from a 'good' and reliable source is relied upon. A good and efficient communication system is one that is free from noise; it is uncluttered and it gives information in the form that is easily comprehended.

Health Education

There is difference between health education and medical education. The latter includes training of medical personnel for treatment of patients. Health education means equipping people with knowledge about how to maintain good health. Educating people about health involves communication.

As we saw in the model at Figure 22.1, the first requirement of a good communication system is usefulness of the information as people see it. And if there is useful information that people do not consider it useful, the people would have to be convinced about it. That again means good communication system. People use tobacco because they are not convinced about its bad effects on health. A good communication system can change the situation. All this comes under the purview of health education.

Health is an aspect of life in which all are interested. Everyone wants to know more about it. Many people go to astrologers to find out possible dangers to their health in the future. Unfortunately, people know very little about health and if they know they care little about their health either due to ignorance or just inertia. Most people break the rules of healthy living. Overeating, under-eating, consumption of poisonous things like tobacco, alcohol and toxic medicines has now become a common practice. Active living, exercise, good breathing habits, and regulated life to give the body and mind peace is becoming uncommon.

In traditional societies, people tend to believe in ghosts and gods as the source of disease. In modern societies people think that health can be maintained with the help of mulit-colour modern medicines. They treat human body as a mechanical device. Many people do not observe the rules of hygiene and sanitation. Even educated people are not able to resist the temptation of eating things sold on the footpaths of dusty cities.

Why does it all happen? One of the very important reasons is the failure or lack of health education from early childhood. Health education must be a part of primary education. Mahatma Gandhi defined primary education as moral education. Health education is part of moral education. Not much attention has been paid so far to devise an education system, which integrate health education.

All educational processes involve communication, health education included. Correct and effective communication to each and every individual about human body, its nutritional requirements, causes of diseases, prevention of diseases with the help of healthy style of life, etc. The chances of distortion of knowledge about health are greater because people tend to believe in what had been traditionally practised. Or what they have been watching from early childhood. Poverty and ignorance are two great enemies of good health. If life has to be saved and there is no money to pay for the doctors or medicines, people run to those who claim to possess special supernatural powers. If people are given health education from early childhood they would neither fall prey to medicine men, traditional or modern.

REFERENCES

1. Central Bureau of health Intelligence, Government of India, *Health Information of India (*Annual Publication).
2. Registrar General of India, *Census of India* publications.
3. ——, *Mortality Statistics of Causes of Death,* 1998.
4. ——, *Survey of Causes of Death (Rural),* 1998.
5. National Sample Survey Organization, Periodical Reports on health, disability etc.
6. For incidence of various diseases, data can be had from the Directorate General of Health Services, New Delhi.
7. Statistical Abstracts of various state governments published annually.

23

International Cooperation in Health

With increasing globalization of diseases, international cooperation in health became a necessity. Diseases do not follow national boundaries. They move from place to place with the people. In fact, the first attempt at international cooperation began in the wake of high mortality from cholera that overran Europe in 1830 and from other infectious diseases like yellow fever. The first International Sanitary Conference was held at Paris in 1851. Of the twelve European countries that participated in the conference, five of them signed an International Sanitary Regulation but could not agree to the mechanism for its enforcement. Practically, no progress was made until 1892, when an International Sanitary Convention on Cholera was signed by the participating states. Five years later another Convention dealing with the prevention of plague was adopted in 1897.

At their Rome meeting in 1907, the 12 participating states of the International Sanitary Convention signed an agreement to establish International Office of Public Hygiene (*Office international d'hygiene publique-OIHP*) at Paris. The main function of the OIHP was to provide general information on public health, especially infectious diseases, including yellow fever, cholera, malaria and tuberculosis to the participating countries. In 1909, its functions were broadened to include food safety, hospital building and administration, school health, and industrial hygiene. The OIHP had a permanent secretariat and a permanent committee of senior public health officials of the member governments to manage the office. The OIHP published a weekly epidemiological bulletin.

On the other side of the Atlantic, an International Sanitary Bureau was set up at Washington DC in 1902. Two decades later in 1923, this bureau was renamed as Pan American Sanitary Bureau and finally as Pan American Sanitary Organization. At the same time, a sanitary council was set up in Egypt to take care of the common health problems of the Middle East and North African countries.

When the League of Nations was formed in 1919, it was, among other things, called upon to take steps enhance international cooperation in the prevention and control of diseases. The OIHP at Paris, was proposed to be brought under the League but it did not materialize. The League set up its own Heath Organization at Geneva independent of the OIHP. The two bodies continued to function independent of each other until the end of the Second World War and formation of the UNO in 1945. The international sanitary convention was revised in 1926 to include two more diseases i.e. smallpox and typhus. The International Sanitary Convention for Aerial Navigation came into force in 1935.

WHO COMES INTO BEING

Realizing that health of all peoples was fundamental to the attainment of peace and security in the world, the 1945 Conference of the United Nations, held at San Francisco, USA considered the possibility of setting up an international health organization. A preparatory technical commission was set up for the purpose. The members of the commission were health experts; they did not represent the nations of their origin. The commission recommended the establishment of World Health Organization (WHO) and suggested that three separate bodies, the World Health Assembly, the Executive Board, and the Secretariat, should manage the organization.

The first International Health Conference under the aegis of the United Nations was held in 1946 in New York. Attended by the representatives of 51 members of the United Nations, and 13 non-member nations, specialized agencies, and NGOs, the conference drafted the constitution of the WHO together with a protocol to transfer the OIHP to the new organization. To ensure that the WHO did not interfere in the internal affairs of the member nations, it was requested to act as a directing and coordinating authority on international health work but its assistance to governments of the member states was subject to requests from and acceptance by them. All nation states were invited to be members of the World Health Assembly with no provision for the expulsion of a member. The constitution of the WHO came into force on April 7, 1948 (April 7 is observed as World Health Day each year).

The World Health Assembly is composed of all member states and meets once in a year in Palais de Nations, Geneva for 6-10 days. It has three main functions: appointment of the Director General, framing of the policies of the WHO, and nominating members entitled to designate a person to serve on the Executive Board. Each Assembly elects a President and five Vice-presidents who hold office till their successors are appointed. The work of the Assembly is entrusted to two committees: Committee A-Programme and Budget, and Committee B-Administration, Finance and Legal Matters. The Assembly makes its decisions through resolutions that can be tabled by any member for consideration. Resolutions on conventions and agreements must be passed by two-third of the members present, other resolutions can be passed by a simple majority.

The Executive Board consists of 32 members. Taking into account the regional representation, the Assembly elects the members entitled to designate a person technically qualified in the field of health to serve on the Board for a period of three years. The Board elects a chairman for a year and meets twice in a year. Its functions include giving effects to the decisions and policies of the Assembly, acting as its executive organ and taking emergency measures, for example, combating epidemics. The Secretariat is headed by the Director General of WHO and his staff, both technical and non-technical, are recruited internationally with due regard to regional representation, efficiency and integrity.

FIRST 30 YEARS OF THE WHO

The constitution of the WHO was adopted in 1948 by 26 member states of the United Nations. When the First World Health Assembly met in 1948, it had 48 members; when it closed a month later, the membership had gone up to 55. The membership on January 1, 1998 was 191. To make the services of the WHO more accessible to member states, its activities were decentralized and six regional offices were created: Brazzaville office for Africa, Washington DC office for Americas, Alexandria office for Eastern Mediterranean, Copenhagen office for Europe, New Delhi office for Southeast Asia, and Manila office for the Western Pacific (see Fig. 23.1).

The regional directors of the WHO are asked to be in close touch with the member states of the region and to prepare regional health plans and programmes in consultation with them. Assistance sought by the member states of the region are processed by regional offices keeping in view the policy guidelines of the WHO and regional/national needs. One of the most important tasks of the regional offices was and still is to provide effective contacts between WHO and the regional governments.

The World Health Assembly adopted a new International Sanitary Regulation in 1951, replacing the previous International Sanitary Conventions. These regulations were renamed as International Health Regulations covering cholera, plague, smallpox and yellow fever in 1969. A turning point in the activities of the WHO came in 1978 when a joint WHO/UNICEF international conference adopted a Declaration on Primary Health Care as the key to attaining the goal of Health For All by 2000 AD.

WHO provided technical assistance to the member states, promoted research, and set up formal laboratory networks for reference and exchange of information on various subjects related to health and medicine. Another activity of the WHO consisted of exchange of technical personnel and provision of essential supplies. It uses facilities created in various countries for research and development. Publications such as statistical and survey reports, region specific and disease specific commissioned reports, journals and other relevant publications are important means to diffuse information.

During the 1960s, cholera, plague and yellow fever continued to take major attention of the WHO but several other diseases like haemorrhoidic fever, malaria, yaws, yellow fever, tuberculosis, poliomyelitis, typhus, etc. too became its growing concern. It was also the period when measles was controlled with the help of a new vaccine and the new freeze-dried vaccine eradicated smallpox. The decade of 1970s was marked by a new awareness of the rights, status and role of the women and new meaning of development laying greater emphasis on non-monetary factors like health education and human rights. Life expectancy and infant mortality among the other social indicators were often selected for the construction of composite indices for development. The concept of health development, as distinct from the provision of medical care, and the rights of the people to participate in the development of their own health also emerged during this period.

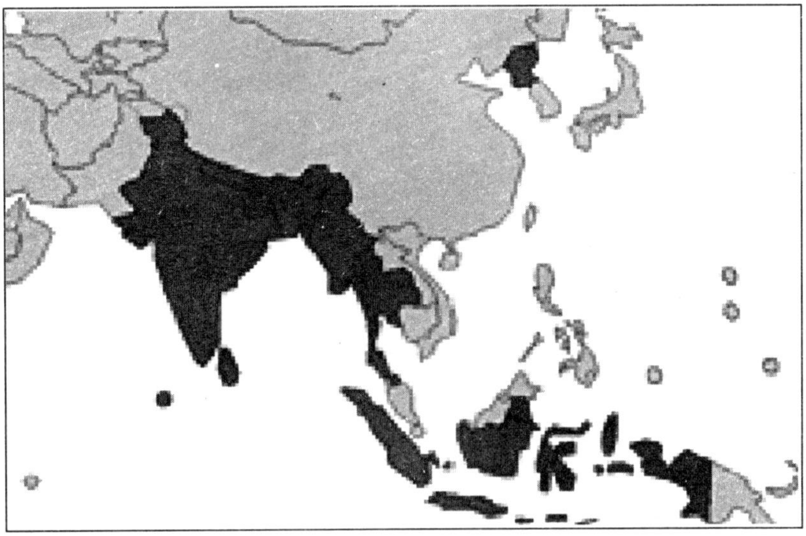

Countries in WHO South-East Asia Region

- Bangladesh
- Bhutan
- Democratic People's Republic of Korea
- India
- Indonesia
- Maldives
- Myanmar
- Nepal
- Sri Lanka
- Thailand
- Timor-Leste

Fig. 23.1: WHO Regions

Preventive rather than curative measures got a new boost and access to health services by the poorer sections of the society was recognized as necessary step in the provision of health for all. In response to these realizations, two special programme were set up: the Special Programme of Research and Development and Training in Human Reproduction was set up in 1972 and the Special Programme for Research and Training in Tropical Diseases was set up in 1975. Along with these steps, appropriate technology was applied in the health field too. It meant the adoption of technology that was scientifically sound, adapted to local needs, acceptable to the people and easily procured, maintained and applied on a mass scale to reach each and every individual in need of healthcare. The first WHO Model List of Essential Drugs was published in 1977: it contained 208 pharmaceutical products.

FROM ALMA-ATA TO 2000 AD

The International Conference on Primary Health Care at Alma-Ata in 1978 proved to be a turning point in the activities of the WHO. It declared that the existing health status of millions of people in the world was unacceptable and called for a new approach to health and healthcare to bridge the gap between the poor and rich sections of the society. It also gave primacy to primary healthcare and acknowledged that the resources of the world if used prudently were enough to meet the goals of health for all by the year 2000. The World Health Assembly and the United Nations General Assembly endorsed the declarations of the conference in 1979. A global strategy to provide 'Health-for-all (HFA) by 2000 AD' was adopted by the World Health Assembly in 1981, and the WHO called upon the member states to implement the same. To promote the development of national drug policies and further improve the essential drug list, an Action Plan on Essential Drugs was established in 1981. A 'common core of essential drugs' which satisfied the healthcare needs of the majority of the population and hence should be available at all the times in adequate quantities and at reasonable prices was added to the original list. The list contained 306 drugs in 1997.

The 1980s decade was the decade of epidemiological transition in the developing countries like India posing new health issues and problems. Rapid aging of the population and changing life styles led to the increase in the incidence of non-communicable diseases like cancer, hypertension, heart attacks, diabetes etc. While war against communicable diseases was still on, both morbidity and mortality resulting from modern life style (systemic diseases and accidents and injuries) shot to new heights. Cases of the most 'modern' of the modern diseases – the AIDS – increased rather dramatically. Realizing that Health for all by the Year 2000 was not attainable in literal sense, it's scope was narrowed down to the attainment of a basic minimum in respect of i.e. expectancy of life at birth = >60 years; infant mortality rate per 1000 live births = <50 years; and under-5 child mortality rate per 1000 live births = < 70 years. As seen from the data pertaining to various regions, as in 1997, many member states had not reached near this target. It may take another 25 years before almost all the member states would reach these modest targets. This does not mean that other programmes such as eradication of communicable diseases and control of systemic disorders etc. were relegated to the background. It only meant that they would continue to engage the resources and man-power in the twenty first century too.

FUNCTIONS OF THE WHO

As discussed earlier, the WHO has been playing a significant role in promoting the concept of the health for all at an affordable cost. The roles it plays as an international agency are international direction and coordination, and technical cooperation. Within the scope of these functions, its programmes have five-fold objectives: strengthening national health services, promoting and protecting health, preventing and controlling specific health problems, medical and health research, and management of its own work. A few of the main activities of the organization are detailed below.

ICD (International Classification of Diseases)

Health statistics offer data and analytical tools for research on causes and consequences of diseases apart, from being useful in policy formulation, decision making and prevention of diseases. The statistical study of diseases began with the work of John Graunt on the London Bills of mortality in the early seventeenth century. The attempt to classify diseases was made in the eighteenth century, published under the title *Nosologia Methodica.* At the beginning of the 19th century, the prevalent classification was published in *Synopsis Nosologiae methodicae* in 1785. The League of Nations appointed a commission to look into all aspects of health statistics and recommend a suitable classification. Based on the work of the commission the Health Organization of the League of Nations published a monograph in 1920 under the title International List of Causes of Death. Not much progress was made in this direction until the WHO stepped in and international cooperation became a reality. Nevertheless, it brought out the International List of Causes of Death in 1928.

The main purpose of the ICD is to permit the comparison of the causes of mortality and morbidity within and between the member states of WHO at the same point of time. The International List of Causes of Death was revised in 1948 and since then it is being periodically revised to incorporate new developments. The ninth revision in 1975 introduced the system of dual classification of diseases according to both etiology and manifestations. It also included the classification of morphology of tumors and also incorporated information about medical insurance, budgetary allocations for health, state of primary healthcare, etc. All this became possible because of the computerization of the information processing. The Tenth Revision (1993) introduced alphanumeric coding scheme of one letter followed by three numerals at the four-character numbering of diseases. This system facilitated incorporation of more detailed clinical information and almost doubling of the number of disease rubrics from 6700 in the Ninth Revision to 12,420 in the Tenth Revision.

WHO took up the work of unifying the separate international sanitation treaties in a single code. It brought out the first such code in 1969 as International Health Regulations (IHR). It is the only health regulation that is binding on all the states. The purpose of IHR is to help prevent international spread of diseases and in the context of international trade to do so with minimum of inconvenience to passengers. The WHO, however, cannot enforce IHR in case of diseases like AIDS which are not listed in the regulations.

Generic Names of Pharmaceuticals

As a result of the development of large number of synthetic drug substances, which become available internationally, it was found necessary to give a single internationally recognized name for an active drug substance for ease of prescribing, dispensing and communication among scientists and professionals. The WHO has listed such drugs with their names under the scheme of *International Nonproprietary Names for Pharmaceutical Substances (INNs).* To date some 6000 INNs have been listed. The very names of the drugs communicate to the medical and pharmaceutical professionals the therapeutic or pharmacological group to which the active drug substances belong. Newly selected INNs are published in the *WHO Drug Information.*

WHO also brings out international standards for drinking water quality since 1958 as an aid to improvement in water quality and treatment. The guidelines now cover three volumes and are published under the title *WHO Guidelines for Drinking Water Quality.* For food standards, the WHO has been working with the FAO to evolve *Codex Alimentarius* since 1962. It has established more than 200 food standards over 40 codes of hygiene and technological practices, more than 3000 maximum residue limits for pesticides and veterinary drugs in food, as well as 700 food additives and contaminants. It is aimed at protecting consumer interests.

The World Health Assembly adopted the International Code of Marketing of Breast-milk Substitutes (ICMBS) to contribute to safe and adequate nutrition for infants. It enjoins on the member states to stop advertising or other forms of promotion to the general public of breast milk substitutes or other products within the scope of the Code and to encourage mothers to breastfeed their babies. One hundred and fiftyeight member states of the WHO have subscribed to the Code. Biological standardization is another important concern of the WHO. In ensures the safety and efficacy of biological medicinal products including vaccines, plasma products and diagnostic agents.

Gathering of Vital Information

WHO inherited the activities related to health statistics and epidemiological surveillance from the Health Organization of the League of Nations, which published an annual epidemiological report from 1922 to 1938. It was restarted in 1951 as Annual Epidemiological and Vital Statistics of the WHO. It was converted into World Health Statistics Annual in 1962. With the development of the new fast track information technology, a new approach to health information was put into practice in 1994 and an annual report giving the status of health in the world with the title *The World Health Report* was brought out. Its objective was to expand the reach out of the WHO to the non-medical people and institutions interested and involved in health related activities, and to offer in a summary form the health scenario of the world pointing out the problems faced by the health system and the action required by the national governments as well as the international community.

Library service is a vital part of the activities of WHO. Its library acts as a central purchasing agent to obtain books, journals and information materials for libraries worldwide thereby helping the developing countries in procuring literature requiring foreign exchange. *Bulletin of the WHO* publishes articles from developing countries to ensure wide spread diffusion of the research results all over the world.

Assistance to Member Countries

WHO assists and works with member countries in combating diseases, specially the epidemic diseases. Its assistance takes variety of forms ranging from advisory services to direct financial assistance. Its most recent activity is geared to prevention of infectious diseases by mass immunization of people. In cooperation with the UNICEF, it has child and maternal health programmes running in many developing countries.

WHO has six regional offices to keep in close touch with the member nations and to respond to emergencies at short notice.

REGIONAL OFFICES OF THE WHO

As stated earlier, WHO functions through its regional offices that currently number six. Regional offices have regional committees composed of the representatives of the member states and associate members of the region. The head of the regional office is regional director appointed by the Executive Board in agreement with the regional committees. The regional office functions as the administrative organ of the regional committee and also carries out in respective regions the decision of the World Health Assembly.

Africa

As in 1997, there were 47member states in the region with a population of 612 million. Leaving aside Djibouti, Egypt, Sudan, Libya, Morocco, Somalia and Tunisia the whole of Africa is part of this region. The per capita GNP in 1955 was $564, ranging from $80 for Mozambique to $6620 for Seychelles. It is the most slowly growing economy. While Botswana, a tiny state in the midst of South Africa, recorded 6.1 per cent GDP growth, Gabon slid down to –8.2 per cent.

Almost all countries of the region have experienced colonial rule. Within a period of just eleven years (1960-70) as many as 36 colonies became independent countries. The region faced instabilities due to long drawn struggles for independence that often took violent turns. Power struggles among the cultural groups continue even today in several parts of the region. The instabilities have their own implications for the health and welfare of the people. Millions of people have been uprooted and become refugees. Health services, even if rudimentary, were dislocated and production of goods and services reduced.

This region is the home of sub-Saharan Africa that happens to be the poorest region of the world; where people die of hunger in large numbers. Despite some improvements in the literacy rates are 20 per cent or less and population growth as high as 2.5 per cent. The DGP growth rate in most of the countries of the region hovers around zero per cent. The health indicators for the region point to the tragic living conditions of the people. Life expectancy at birth is 53, infant mortality 89, and children under five mortality rate 239 per 1000. In all these respects, about 40 states have not met the HFA targets in 1997.

Efforts are on to develop health infrastructure by investing more in health, and train enough people to man the health services. Environmental improvements are being attempted with focus on safe water and sanitation improvement. This region suffers from food insecurity: undernutrition and malnutrition, the twin symptoms of food insecurity are widely seen in the region. National health system has been reorganized and strengthened with emphasis of district level services. Better integration and management of priority programme such as immunization, control of diarrhoeal diseases, provision of essential drugs and vaccines constitute important achievements of recent years.

The immunization coverage in the region is 68 per cent for the BCG, 58 per cent for the DPT, 60 per cent for the measles and around 38 per cent for tetanus toxoid among the childbearing age women. Epidemiological surveillance is still weak and hence morbidity and mortality attributable to communicable disease such as malaria, tuberculosis, leprosy and measles are still high. Yet at the same time, there are hopeful signs. The first priority of the people is health. It is recognized that reforms in the health sector are overdue, that the community involvement is necessary for progress, that international cooperation is a must for solving many health problems, and that biotechnology can contribute immensely to make the HFA programme a success. Given these perspectives, the region can now look forward to making further strides in years ahead. A synoptic view of the progress made by the African region in HFA is given in Table 23.1.

Table 23.1: HFA Targets and Achievements in African Region

S.N.	*HFA Indicators*	*1997 @*	*2025 target @*	*HFA targets 1997 @*
1.	L.E.	53	65	60
2.	I. M. R	89	47	50
3.	CMR	139	66	70

HFA = Health-for-all; E.L. = Expectation of life at birth in years;
IMR = Infant mortality per 1000 live births; CMR = Under-5 child mortality per 1000 live births; @ = Average for the whole region.
Source: WHO, World Health Report, 1998

Americas

This region consists of developed countries like USA, Canada and middle income countries of Latin America. In all, it has 35 member states and one associate member. The total population of the region amounts to 792 million (1997). Per capita GNP is $12,293 with a minimum of $250 for Haiti and a maximum of $26,980 for the United States. The annual average growth of GDP of the member states ranges from –5.4 per cent for Nicaragua to 6.1 per cent for Chile. In terms of quality of life, average life expectancy at birth is 73, infant mortality 28 and child mortality under 5-years 33 per 1000.

Economic trends indicate that with the globalization and liberalization processes set in motion during the 1990s, poverty, when seen in terms of the number of people below the poverty line, has deepened during the last ten years. No perceptible demographic changes have come to the notice during the 1990s. Fertility rates continues to decline and aging of the population had persisted. Its population is likely to reach one billion by 2025. 61.30 per cent of the population of the region is in Latin America. In 1950, it was 48.7 per cent. The birth rates declined from 40 to 19 within a decade (1970-80). The mortality rates are declining particularly of infants and life expectancy is on the increase. The difference between the high-and low-income countries of the region in these respects is obvious, however. The working population was about 400 million in 2000.

Violence in the region (in Central and South America) is responsible for large number of deaths. This is an area of major concern of the international community. The struggle against diseases is marked with successes: the region is free of poliovirus; enormous progress has been achieved in the eradication of measles, and neonatal tetanus. Diarrhea, intestinal and acute respiratory infections continue to take a heavy toll of life. Water supply and water quality together with solid waste disposal pose serious environmental problems. Only three quarter of the population has access to clean water.

As the communicable diseases decline in spread as well as intensity, non-communicable diseases have set in. Two-thirds of all deaths in the Americas are accounted by non-communicable diseases. The concerted and integrated approach to the control of these diseases is needed. Unfortunately, the institutional and financial support required for it is not forthcoming partly because of the economic slump and partly due to inadequate policy back up.

The HFA indicators are high for this region but there are several middle low income countries which have to go long way before they can catch up even their regional averages (Table 23.2).

Table 23.2: HFA Targets and Achievements in Americas

S.N.	*HFA Indicators*	*1997@*	*2025 targets @*	*HFA targets 1997 @*
1.	EL	73	77	60
2.	IMR	28	15	50
3.	CMR	33	18	70

HFA= health-for-all; EL = Expectations of life at birth; IMR= Infant mortality rate per 1000 live births; CMR = Under-5 child mortality rate per 1000 live births; @ average for the whole region.
Source: WHO, World Health Report, 1998.

Eastern Mediterranean

Consisting of 22 countries, the Eastern Mediterranean region extends from Morocco on the north-west coast of Africa to Pakistan bordering India. This region is highly volatile and torn by wars, internals struggles for power, terrorism and political instabilities. Modernization process sweeping across the region has loosened to some extent the hold of the age-old Islamic traditions. Different countries have, however, welcomed this trend differently. Israel, an odd boll in the region, has been a forerunner in modernization; it has developed a strong economy, even though not rich in petroleum resources. Egypt, the most secular of the Islamic countries, has also tried to modernize itself unhindered by the Islamic traditions. Other countries of the region, both oil rich and others, are still passing through a transition period: they are unable to see their potentials in full and are struggling to keep the country united.

The average per capita income of the region in 1997 stood at $ 1385 ranging from $ 17400 for UAE to $ 260 for Yemen. During the decade 1985-95, the growth rate of GDP ranged from –4.5 per cent for Jordan to 1.9 per cent for Tunisia. Life expectancy in 1997 was 64; infant mortality rate 69 per cent and under-5 mortality rate 94 per thousand. It is clear that the region needs tremendous amount of investment in health, apart from consistent policies to move towards the goal of health for all.

The pattern of illness is also changing in this region. The WHO has, therefore, changed its strategies in response to the changing health scenario in the region. Prior to 1970, emphasis as laid on communicable and infectious diseases, provision of essential supplies, experts and guidance. Despite good results, the national governments generally failed to continue the programmes after the WHO withdrew. Since 1980, the WHO decided to collaborate with the national governments to build public health infrastructure, train doctors and nurses and maintain supply of medicines. Allocation for communicable diseases was reduced but the resurgence of diseases like malaria forced the WHO as well as the national government to evolve double-edged policy: one directed at communicable diseases, and the other at non-communicable diseases.

In 1987, the WHO initiated a participatory process of integrated socio-economic development based on self-reliance, and self-management by organized communities and supported by external agencies including governments. It was termed basic needs approach. Religion being an all pervading factor in the region, involvement of the religious leaders was also sought in imparting health education. Teachers were trained for providing health education to children. To give further boost to these activities leadership development programme was launched in 1989.

As far as the HFA is concerned, this region is well ahead of other regions except Europe and Americas. It has already crossed the targets set by the WHO for the year 2000 AD. Some details of the prevailing HFA situation are provided in Table 23.3.

Table 23.3: HFA Targets and Achievements in Eastern Mediterranean Region

S.No.	*HFA Indicators*	*1997@*	*2025 targets @*	*HFA targets 1997 @*
1.	EL	64	72	60
2.	IMR	69	33	50
3.	CMR	94	41	70

HFA = Health-for-all; E.L. = Expectations of Life; IMR = Infant Mortality per 1000 live births; Child mortality per 1000 live births; @ =Average;
Source: WHO, World health Report, 1998

This region is marked by violence. Conflict among the states has taken a heavy toll of life. Arab-Israel conflict, Iran-Iraq war, Iraq-Kuwait war, and increasing internal disturbances in several states, particularly Afghanistan, have claimed many lives and rendered many more handicapped and homeless. Oil resources have made it possible to improve the health scenario in the region. Lot of progress has been made during the last two decades, but lot more is yet to be done to ensure health for all. The non-petroleum states are, however, disadvantaged. Attempts are afoot to eradicate measles and tuberculosis by 2010 and to provide safe drinking water as early as possible. Institutional arrangements to make health services and facilities reach the common man have become the cornerstone of health policy of the member states of the region.

Europe

The European region of the WHO consists of 51 member states having a population of 869 million in 1997. GNP per capita in the same year was \$ 11 126 with a minimum of \$340 for Tajikistan and a maximum of \$ 41 210 for Luxembourg. The annual average growth rate of the economy varied from –17.0 for Georgia to 5.2 per cent for Ireland. The average life expectancy at birth was 72, infant mortality 20 and mortality of children below the age of 5 was 27 per 1000.

The post-World War II efforts of the WHO included reconstruction of health services, maternal and child health, eradication of malaria, tuberculosis, STDs and promotion of environmental health. At the first European Conference on Public Health Administration in 1964, the growing menace of chronic diseases was highlighted. The 1984 European Conference on planning and management for health was a watershed in the development of health planning philosophy in Europe. It ushered in result-oriented multi-sectoral policies to be implemented at all relevant territorial levels. By 1987, ten countries of the region had a health policy document related to health for all.

To minimize the effect of economic recession the region on health services, the regional office of WHO created a new programme called 'Euro-Health–1990' to support the programme of health for all in Eastern and Central Europe including the central Asian republics. By 1995, the basic principles of health for all were widely accepted in the region. Noticeable improvements in pollution levels and further improvements in the access to drinking water, particularly in southern Europe, were the highlights of the 1990s.

With the population growth approaching less than one per cent in most of the European countries, the birth rate incessantly declining, and ageing of the population on the increase, the health situation in relatively less developed countries of Eastern and Central Europe has worsened during the last few years. Life expectancy too appears have reached its peak and in some countries has started showing downward trends. The countries on the western side of the region have, however, further improved the health situation and have almost reached all the targets of the HFA. They have failed to bring down smoking while alcohol consumption and drug abuse are declining, even if too slowly.

It is now clear that the European population will grow older as time passes. Its current share of 65+ population would increase from 13 per cent (1997) to 15 per cent by 2025. New problems are likely to further deepen. Europe has a problem of unemployment but at the same time it has a shortage of professionally trained manpower particularly the IT professionals. As such it would have to import these professionals from outside Europe. This would generate tension between the locals and the migrants. Imaginative migration policies are, therefore, urgently required. But the globalization process will gradually spread to services and manpower sectors too. The current policies of restricting movement of people across national boundaries will have to give way to free movement. But that is still a distant dream. Table 23.4 gives the state of HFA in the region.

Table 23.4: HFA Targets and Achievement in European Region

S.N.	*HFA Indicaors*	*1997 @*	*2025 target @*	*HFA target 1997*
1.	EL	72	77	60
2.	IMR	20	11	50
3.	CMR	27	14	70

HFA = Health-for-all; LE = Expectations of Life in years; IMR = Infant Mortality per 1000 live births; CMR = Under-5 child mortality per 1000 live births; @ = average for the whole region.

Source: WHO, World Health Report, 1998

South-east Asia

South-east Asia is a region with only 10 countries, but a huge population of 1457 million as in 1997. It is an economically developing region with per capita GNP ranging from a low of

$ 200 for Nepal to a high of $ 2740 for Thailand. The GDP growth rates range from 2.1 per cent for Bangladesh to 8.4 per cent for Thailand. Life expectancy is still low (63) and infant mortality high (68). It is a densely populated region: marked by poverty, illiteracy, and poor health-infrastructure. Death rates are declining, even though only slowly, and so are the birth rates. The region is in the midst of epidemiological transition. Communicable diseases are on the way out and the cases of chronic diseases and degenerative conditions are on the increase.

The decline in the cases of polio, measles, neonatal tetanus and other target diseases are the prime causes for the decline in morbidity and mortality. Near eradication of polio is perhaps the most spectacular achievement. It demonstrates that all communicable diseases can be wiped out if the people are convinced of the efficacy of the recommended health measures. Leprosy was one of the major debilitating diseases in the region having both health and social implications. It is now on the decline. But high rate of population growth, urbanization, overcrowding, increased mobility of the people, poverty, illiteracy, poor housing and sanitary conditions, malnutrition, impure drinking water, and environmental deterioration in general make it difficult to eliminate communicable diseases at a desired speed.

The problems related to epidemiological transition have further complicated the situation. While the classical communicable diseases still persist, the diseases of modern civilization, both communicable and others, are on the rise. Thus the region has to cope with a wider range of diseases than ever before. For instance, the HIV infection is spreading rather fast through the channels that the modern economy and society promote. Acute respiratory infections still kill millions of children below the age of five. Tuberculosis and malaria are yet to be eradicated: they together account for 6 to 7 million cases in the region.

Cardiovascular and cerebrovascular diseases are also on the increase, so are the cancers, congenital anomalies, endocrine disorders and accidents. True, the death rates from many of these diseases are still lower than what one finds in the industrialized countries, but it is only a matter of time before they get equalized if remedial steps are not taken promptly. The region is far behind the HFA targets (Table 23.5).

Table 23.5: HFA Target and Achievement in South-East Asian Region

SN	*HFA Indicators*	*1997 @*	*2025 target @*	*HFA target 1997*
1.	EL	63	72	60
2.	IMR	68	32	50
3.	CMR	85	38	70

HFR = Health-for –all; EL = Expectations of Life at birth; IMR = Infant mortality rate per 1000 live births; CMR = Under-5 child mortality rate per 1000 live births; @ average for the whole region.
Source: WHO, World Health Report, 1998.

Western Pacific

Covering a population of 1634 million, this region consists of 27 member states and one associate member. It has large countries like China, Indonesia and Australia and small island countries like Tonga. Wide variations in the GDP per capita reflect to a great extent the differences in the state of the health.

The regional office of the WHO was established at Manila in 1950. At this juncture very few cities had systematic water supply and sewage disposal facilities. War had its own effect. Health services were confined to curative medicine. Preventive measures were scarce. WHO concentrated on the control of T.B., yaws, malaria, diphtheria, and venereal diseases. Improvement in the environment was another priority. The same thrust was maintained in the 1960s with some success in the control of communicable diseases and improvement in the health delivery system.

1970s saw the emergence of cancers, cardiovascular diseases and accidental injuries as major killers along with a number of communicable diseases. Demand for medical services increased and the WHO responded by helping the member states of the region to augment their services by Infrastructure improvement and training of health personnel. In 1980s, special attention was paid to the strengthening of the primary healthcare facilities, particularly in the remote rural areas of the member states.

During the decade of 1990s, WHO policy became more focused and six priority concerns were identified for implementation. They were: development of human resources for health; eradication or control of selected diseases; health education; environmental health; exchange of information and experience; and strengthening management.

Since 1991, two primary trends have become visible in the region: the establishment of new health management system in the former centrally planned economies of former Indo-Chinese states, and encouragement to community participation in development. Programme of eradication of polio was continued during this period as a supplementary immunization activity and almost 100 million children were immunized by 1997. Substantial progress was recorded in the area of environmental health.

This region consists of states passing through different stages of health transition. Some states like Cambodia and Laos are still in the grips of communicable diseases. They are in the first stage of health transition. States like China, Malaysia, Philippines, and Vietnam are in the second stage. And then there are states like Australia, New Zealand, Republic of Korea, Japan and Cook Islands, which have entered the last stage of transition in which diseases of the modern civilization become the main health concerns. With such a mixed character of the states of the region some states will have to continue the strengthening the primary healthcare facilities and eradication of communicable diseases by environmental improvement and mass campaigns. Attention to new diseases like AIDS cannot be postponed, particularly because this region gets large number of visitors from outside. Health education targeting susceptible sections of the population with emphasis on life-style changes have become necessary.

In any case, health being a basic human right, all the member states should ensure that the relevant ervices are accessible to all; that they are of reasonable quality; and that they are available at affordable price. The state of HFA is given in Table 23.6.

INDIA AND THE WHO

India is one of the founder members of the WHO. The regional office of the Organization is located in New Delhi. WHO has a country budget of $ 1.4 million for India. This is in addition

Table 23.6: HFA Targets and Achievements in West Pacific Region

SN	HFA Indicators	1997 @	2025 target @	HFA target for 1997
1.	EL	70	75	60
2.	IMR	36	15	50
3.	CMR	40	17	70

HFA = Health for all; EL =Expectations of Life; IMR = Infant mortality rate per 1000 live births; CMR = Under-5 child mortality rate per 1000 live births; @= Average for the whole region.
Source: WHO, World Health Report, 1998.

to contributions made by other agencies like the World Bank and the member nations for specific health programmes and projects. The country budget can be used for contract services, fellowships, performance of work, local cost subsidy, and for supplies and equipment. About 600 activities in over 40 projects are being implemented under the aegis of the WHO in India. Important among them being: strengthening of primary health care of the tribal people, guineaworm eradication, control of communicable diseases, health education for empowerment of poor, promotion of health education for adolescents, malaria control, and vaccine preventable diseases.

OTHER UN AGENCIES

In addition to the WHO, India gets substantial amount of assistance from the UNICEF, UNDP, FAO, UNFP, ILO, and World Bank; and a number of non-governmental and other agencies such as CARE, Ford Foundation, Rockefeller Foundation, and International Red Cross. Bilateral agencies like USAID, Colombo Plan, SIDA and DANIDA, are also involved in specific health projects. World Bank has just offered 'State Health Systems Development Projects' to six states with a total outlay of Rs. 34, 200 million. More such projects are in the pipeline. The Japanese government has also assisted the country in improving health centres in the National Capital Region and for research in diarrhoeal diseases. The Department for International Development (DFID) is supporting programmes aimed at controlling malaria, vector control, tuberculosis, etc. The government of the Netherlands has helped Gujarat state in improving maternity and child health and French Government has assisted the S.G.P.G. Institute of Medical Sciences at Lucknow with FF 30 million.

UNICEF

United Nations International Children's Emergency Fund was established in 1946 by the United Nations to deal with the rehabilitation of children orphaned during the World War II. In 1953, when the rehabilitation work was completed, the General Assembly of the UN gave it a new name 'UN Children's Fund" but retained the original term 'UNICEF'. The South Asian regional office of the UNICEF is located in New Delhi. It serves Afghanistan, Nepal, Bhutan, Sri Lanka, Maldives and Mongolia, apart from India.

UNICEF works in close collaboration with the WHO and other agencies of the UN. Its assistance in such areas as nutrition, child health, maternal health, environmental sanitation, rural healthcare, health education, and other programmes which directly or indirectly benefit children, is substantial. Currently UNICEF is promoting a programme called GOBI, where G stands for growth charts to monitor child development; O for oral rehydration; B for breast-feeding; and I for immunization against measles, diphtheria, polio pertussis, tetanus, and tuberculosis. Since mid-1970s, it is also involved in Urban Basic Services (UBS) programme.

UNDP

Established in 1966, it is the main source of funding for technical assistance to the member countries of the United Nations. UNDP office in member countries functions as UN embassy in respective countries. Practically all UN activities are channeled through the UNDP offices.

FAO

Food and Agriculture Organization was established in 1945 with its head office in Rome, Italy. It has four main functions: (a) to help member countries raise the living standards of the people; (b) to improve the nutritional level of the people; (c) to improve the efficiency of agriculture and allied activities; and (d) to improve the condition of the rural people. During the 1960, it organized Freedom from Hunger Programme covering all countries of the world.

World Bank

World Bank was established to assist the developing countries in raising their standards of living of their citizens. The Bank gives loans at concensional rates for projects that can increase the growth rate of the national economy improve infrasture, such as transport, communication, public utilities and increase productivity of agriculture, industry and services.. It also serves as advisory body to member nations on economic reforms and policy alternatives necessary for removing the road blocks in economic development. The Bank in collaboration with the WHO and UNICEF also gives loans for building health infrastructure.

ILO

Established in 1919, International Labour Organization with head quarters in Geneva is responsible for raising the living standards of the labour. It prescribes minimum standards pertaining to health, welfare and working conditions of the labour. ILO assists national governments and NGO engaged in the promotion of above objectives.

USAID

United States Agency for International Development offers assistance to India in variety of fields. In the field of health, it has given assistance for the eradication of malaria, medical education, nursing education, health education, water supply and sanitation, control of communicable diseases, nutrition and family planning.

Colombo Plan

A select group of Commonwealth Countries met in 1950 at Colombo, Sri Lanka to chalk out a plan of action to increase cooperation among them for mutual benefit. The number of countries forming part of the Colombo Plan is currently 24: four developed countries: Australia, New Zealand, USA and Japan, and 20 developing countries of South and South-east Asia: India, Pakistan, Afghanistan, Iran, Nepal, Bhutan, Sri Lanka, Bangladesh, Maldives, Malaysia, Singapore, Mynamar, Thailand, Indonesia, Cambodia, Laos, Philippines, S. Korea, Fiji, Papua New Guinea. Canada and UK withdrew in 1991. Bulk of the Colombo Plan assistance has gone to agricultural and industrial development but some funds have also been given for health promotion. One of the outstanding achievements of the Plan in the health sector was the assistance New Zealand gave for the establishment of All India Institute of Medical Sciences in New Delhi.

SIDA and DANIDA

The Swedish International Development Agency was created in 1979 and Danish International Agency in 1978. The latter provides funds for the eradication of blindness in India and the former has assisted India in the programme for the eradication of TB.

CARE

Cooperative for Assistance and Relief Everywhere was established in 1945 in the USA. It is a non-profit and non-religious organization. In India, it has been engaged in programmes to provide food for the poor children. It also assists in improving health and nutrition. Its target groups are children, adolescent girls and mothers. It operates projects in collaboration with other agencies, particularly the government of India and state governments.

Rockefeller and Ford Foundations

These American foundation have been active in India and have provided assistance in various fields including health and nutrition. Established in 1013, the Rockefeller Foundation has been active in public health, medical education, and life sciences. The work of the Foundation started as early as 1920. All India Institute of Public Health and Hygiene in Kolkata was set up with the assistance of Rockefeller Foundation. It has provided grants-in-aid to a number of institutions including AIIMS, New Delhi and Nationals Institute of Virology, Pune. The current involvement of the Foundation is in the fields of agriculture, family planning, and rural training centres.

Ford Foundation has been active in the development of health services and family planning. Among the major health related projects for which the Foundation has given assistance are: pilot projects in rural health services; establishment of Nationals Institute of Health Administration and Education, at New Delhi; Kolkata Water Supply and Drainage Scheme; Family Planning Programme; and Research-cum-Action Programmes in the field of environmental sanitation.

International Red Cross

It is an international humanitarian organization having no sectarian or political affiliations. Established in 1864, it was the outcome of the effort of a single individual –Henry Dunant, a Swiss businessman, who, saddened by the sufferings of the people both combatants and commoners during the war, decided to launch an organization, which could have access to the battleground to assist those who needed medical help. A treaty was signed and an International Committee of Red Cross was set up. Currently, the Red Cross engages itself not only in helping the war-ravaged people but also others who need help to help themselves.

REFERENCES

1. WHO, *World Health Report,* 1998.
2. WHO, Regional health Report, 1997, South and South-East Asia.
3. Central Bureau of Health Information, *Health Information of India.*
4. Holstead, Scott B., *et al. Good Health at Lowest Cost, Proceedings of a Conference held at the Bellagio Conference Center, Bellagio, Italy.*
5. Vishwakarma, *R.K., Health Status of the Underprivilged, Indian Institute of Public Administration,* 1985.
6. Encyclopedia Britanica, Vol. 23, entry on WHO.

24

Medical Nemesis

Medicine is one of the oldest and most noble professions of man. To begin with, diseases were linked to external environment, and often ascribed to the displeasure of supernatural powers. The cures were also sought in the environment, particularly the plants and in the propitiation of the supernatural powers. While the role of supernatural powers in the treatment of diseases has secularly declined, plants continue to play a significant role as source of food and medicines. Even modern medicine has to rely heavily on plants for its pharmaceuticals. In recent years, plants, have entered the lexicon of modernity too; herbal means most modern Interestignly even sorcery and voodoo are no longer rejected as blind faiths. Faith healing is not too far removed from sorcery. The belief that there is something beyond science is growing all over the world even if slowly and imperceptively.

The experiential knowledge accumulated for several millennia by various ancient systems of medicine used to conduct further research on the efficacy of various plants and minerals in the restoration of health and treatment of diseases. Plants were classified and the efficacy of each in the treatment of specific health problems and diseases was standardized. Various parts of the plants: roots, stems, leaves, flowers, seeds, fruits, juices, etc. together with different minerals laid the foundation of various schools of medicine. The cumulative knowledge was codified in treatises to form *Materia Medica*. All ancient civilizations possessed such compendiums with the help of which medical professionals treated the sick.

It was believed that diseases were the outcome of some sort of imbalance in the internal functioning of the body. This could be caused by the supernatural powers or by such factors as unhealthy style of life, lack of nutritive food etc. Unless the balance was restored, a sick person would remain sick. The medicines were used to bring that balance back. Often medicines and sorcery went together. The basic cause of all diseases was just one: imbalance among the vital forces. The disease was cured the moment balance was restored. Thus medicine became a great boon to man: it was treated as goddess Danvantari in India.

Then began the era of modern medical science in Europe sometimes in the eighteenth century. The ancient theories of health and ill health were discarded and the old method of treating ailments was and given up. Modern science discovered the immediate and visible causes of ill health: the causes, which could be removed without bothering about balance and imbalance in vital forces. Later, diseases, specially the infectious ones, were defined as the malfunctioning of the whole or certain part of the body caused by germs which, when eliminated or subdued, brought the body back to normalcy. The germs can be eliminated by appropriate antigens or chemical formulations.

In the eyes of the modern science, human body is comparable to a machine. All machines need energy to work; so does human body. But now it is being realized, that it is not an ordinary machine. It is a live machine. Ordinary machines do not think, they are controlled from outside. Human body, however, has a mind of its own; it generates its own energy given the natural raw materials from outside; and it cannot just be repaired as a mechanical device can be. The current attempts to simulate the mind through artificial intelligence may lead to thinking machines too but there are definite limits. No machine would ever be able to function like human brain. Medical science, however, still persists in thinking that human body is a machine and can be repaired, if something goes wrong with it. To day man has in his possession terrific amount of modern medical knowledge to tinker with the human body.

Today curative medicine has become a huge business enterprise. Each day new and avowedly better medicines are released in the market. Scientists are confident of finding cures for diseases like AIDS too, even though we know that many diseases are incurable. Aggressive advertisement of medicines has further strengthened our faith in them. Today man has almost the same faith in modern medicine as our forefathers had in supernatural powers. It is because of this blind faith that we do not care for our health; we have left it entirely in the hands of the physicians and surgeons.

Health depends on two factors: how much attention we pay to our body and mind, and how accessible we are to health counseling and services. Modern man tends to neglect the first requirement; reliance on medicine has proportionately gone up. The situation has come to a pass that medicine has become a major cause of morbidity and mortality. While man's dependence on medicines and health services has gone up many-folds, his natural instinct to keep his body and mind healthy without medicines has almost disappeared. Added to this is the inaccessibility of medicines and medical services to all equitably. Medicines are overpriced and the service orientation of the medical profession has nose-dived; it has become a commercial proposition. More people die of medicines, directly or indirectly, than of any other single cause. It appears that medicine is no longer the goddess Dhanvantari; it has turned into Nemesis, the goddess of vengeance. It is clamouring to deliver retributive justice to human species.

Why is medicine, the goddess of health and vitality, has turned into nemesis, the goddess of retribution? We would try to seek the answer to this question in this chapter.

WHY HAS DHANVANTARI BECOME NEMESIS?

Cure-centred Mindset

The drug industry and the medical profession have jointly succeeded in changing the mindset of the people in favour of curative measures and drugs. People do not strive to be healthy, nor do they care for their health. They have been assured that there is cure for every disease; all that they have to do is to go to the doctor. They, therefore, invite diseases by leading an unhealthy lifestyle. Violation of the laws of nature and the biology of the human body initially produce temporary and short-term ailments. Suppression of these ailments with modern chemical medicines pollutes the body further and gives rise to systemic disorders, which cannot be cured by medicines. People are sick without diseases. The whole biological system of the body is degenerating. Medical Nemesis is on its job.

Health is largely the responsibility of the individuals. Most people are born healthy; very few are born with hereditary diseases even if they are born with certain disease promoting tendencies. Those who are born healthy must remain healthy all through their lives, if they do not abuse their body and the environment around them. In early childhood, the responsibility for health lies with the parents and the society at large. On parents depends the nutrition and hygiene of the child, and on society depends the external environment in which the child is brought up. Failure on one or both the fronts can render the child unhealthy and diseased.

When the child becomes an adult, he is himself responsible for the maintenance of his health. Health should be his first priority. He must take pride in his good physique, alert mind and stable emotions. He must not stress his body and mind beyond its threshold; he must follow the laws of nature. He must take nutritive foods and drinks and do adequate manual work to digest whatever he eats. But none of these things he learns from the parents or teachers any more. As such practically everyone tends to abuse his body and mind in a variety of ways, especially in youth.

Unhealthy Lifestyle

What is healthy and unhealthy style of life may be difficult to define for different environmental and cultural settings, but there do exist some common denominators, which apply to all human beings and all geographies. These common factors are derived from the fact that human body is an organic system and there are certain bio-cybernetic laws, which govern its functioning.

When we think of a system, our mind immediately goes to a mechanical engine; it does not go to our own body. We live in a world, which is presumed to be a mechanical world. We tend to think that everything from the universe to the solar system and then on to the living creatures and within them the tiny cells function like a machines. The truth, however, is that it is a false notion. There is a vast difference between a mechanical system and a biological system.

Unfortunately, this vast difference remains blurred in the eyes of the modern man. His worldview is mechanistic. He sees his own body also as a machine. If not functioning properly, it can be set right in the same way as a machine is set right. Its parts can be replaced or repaired; its blocked arteries can be cleared; and a new energy can be infused in it. He does things that are harmful to his body and mind and cares not because there are physicians and medicines, which can cure the diseases. The mindset is oriented to medicines, physicians and hospitals. Here lies a serious health problem.

Transgression of Professional Ethics

Ethics mean basic principles of right action, especially with reference to any particular person or profession. Medicine being one of the oldest professions of mankind, has evolved a code of conduct, which everyone engaged in it has to adhere to. These ethical standards were laid down from the very early times. Erosion of medical ethics is one of the main reasons for the Medical Nemesis to strike against man. Humanity cannot survive without ethics. Medicine is a profession that deals with the life and death of the people and it cannot play its role effectively unless it is imbued with certain ethical standards derived from the feeling of services, love, affection and compassion. During the last hundred years or so, these ethical norms have been relegated to tertiary status. Selfless service and dedication, that once constituted the guiding principles, have given way to greed all the way from medical education to manufacture and sale of medicines and to the treatment of the sick.

Is there a set and pre-determined medical ethics? Ethics is something that does not change with the change in the mood of the society. It has its roots in human values and was first codified by Hippocrates, the father of western medicine in sixth century BC. Charak, the father of Ayurvedic system of medicine, also suggested a similar code of medical conduct. Our physicians still swear by the Hippocratic ethics before they get their license to practise. The original form is reproduced below.

> *I will look upon him who shall have taught me this Art even as one of my parents. I will share my substance with him, I will supply his necessities, if he be in need. I will regard his offspring even as my own brethren, and I will teach them this Art, if they would learn it, without fee or covenant. I will impart this Art by precept, by lecture and by every mode of teaching, not only to my own sons but to the sons of him who has taught me, and to the disciples bound by covenant and oath, according to the Law of Medicine.*
>
> *The regimen I adopt shall be for the benefit of my patients according to my ability and judgment, and not for their hurt or any wrong. I will give no deadly drug any, though it be asked of me, nor will I counsel such, and especially I will not aid a woman to procure abortion. Whatsoever house I enter, there I will go for the benefit of the sick, refraining from all wrong doing or corruption, and especially from any act of seduction, of male or female, of bond or free. Whatsoever things I see or hear concerning the life of men in my attendance on the sick or even apart therefrom, which ought not to be noised about, I will keep silence thereon, counting such things as sacred secrets.*

In India each applicant at the time of registering as a medical practicener with the Medical Council of India has to submit a signed declaration as provided in the relevant statutes. These are very elaborate and cover every aspect of medical practice. The applicant has to agree to abide by the same. Unfortunately, the code of conduct prescribed is rarely followed in practice.

As one gleans through the ancient treatises, one gets hints of even more stringent ethical rules prescribed in eastern cultures for medical practitioners. The medical ethics in practice, however, negates much of it. And the oath taken by young physicians today is just a formality. The students of Hippocrates and Dhanvantari have become hypocritical.

The breach of trust begins from the very start of medical education. A substantial number of young men and women enter the medical colleges not because they love the profession but because it offers opportunities to extract money from people in distress. Medical education is very costly. All those who acquire it become medical professionals trying to extract as much as possible from the sick, both rich and poor. Money is the motive that drives people to go for medical profession. The exception are few.

No wonder their that despite huge investment in medical colleges, health centres, and hospitals, poor people do not have access to health services. They do not have money to pay for the doctors, medicines and hospitals. Even those who are admitted to government hospitals fail to get required health services on time and at a cost they can afford to pay. More people die because they could not afford to get medical aid than from all diseases combined.

Unethical Trade Practices in Medicine

Among the unethical methods adopted by pharmaceuticals, especially the Multi-National Corporations (MNCs), are:

1. price manipulation;
2. exaggerating the benefits of their products;
3. suppressing the side-effects of medicines;
4. hard selling by giving false and exaggerated information;
5. swindling of public institutions; and
6. influence peddling among governments, law makers, and medical professionals including professional journals.

Pricing of Medicines

Pharmaceutical industry is one of the most profitable industries today. It is possible to sell drugs whose manufacturing cost may be just Re. 0.10 per tablet, for twenty five rupees. The needy i.e. the sick in pain and fear of death pay it grudgingly. The poor, however, suffer and die for they do not have the money to buy costly medicines. The people who die because they could not afford to get appropriate medicines must run in millions the world over.

Most of the drug manufacturers are multi-national companies. They form cartels to control drug prices and earn profits higher than even banking and beverages companies. Recent attempt to regulate at least generic drugs have not met with great success. Very recently, the European Union Commission fined the Big Pharma, a cartel of MNCs, for unethically rigging the prices of vitamins and grossly overcharging unsuspecting consumers

A key factor in the profiteering is the existing patent rights under the WTO. The existing patent rights allow unconscionable mark up on medicines for 20 years. The patent is on the product; not on the process. It denies the other innovators to improve on the product or to produce the same product using a different, may be simpler, less expensive and better, process to produce it. It thus denies the rights of patients to have access to cheaper medicines.

When the fear of anthrax gripped America after September 11 attack on the WTC in New York, the demand for ciprofloxacin, the patented drug for the disease, shot up. The potential market demand for the drug was 1.2 billion pills. German Transnational Bayer A.G., one of the Big Pharma, which held the US patent for the drug valid until the end of 2003, could supply only one-sixth of the demand. Its wholesale price of the drug was \$4.63 per 500 mg pill. In panic buying each pill cost \$7.00 (two pills are recommended for 60 days).

The price of the drug really bears no relation to the cost or to the amortised 20 year old original investment in research. The company sells the same drug for \$1.51 in Canada and for just 13 cents in India. Indian companies retail an identical drug for just 6 cents a pill. Indian companies like Cipla, Reddy's and Ranboxy, which are in the business of producing high quality generic (non-patented) medicines, offered cipro at 6 cents or less a pill to US. But it was not accepted. Not wanting to rock the IPR boat, the US asked Bayer to reduce the price to approximately 30 times the price at which Indian companies were prepared to supply the drug.

In yet another case, 39 Big Pharma companies charged $10,000 to $15,000 for a year's supply of antiritrovirals for a single patient. South Africa has more than 4.7 million HIV/AIDS patients. Sub-Saharan Africa has still larger numbers. And the disease is spreading very fast in other countries of the world. This high price of the drug is not within the reach of majority of the people of the developing countries.

The Indian company Cipla signed up with Medicines sans Frontiers of South Africa to supply the same drug combination at $350 a year. The People of South Africa forced the government to go for Indian drug. The Big Pharma sued the government for not respecting the patent laws. The pressure of public opinion and outcry was so great that it finally dropped the case. The people won and many more lives were prolonged or saved.

Indian companies have succeeded in this venture because India does not allow product patent; it allows only process patent. It is permissible for a company to make the same drug using a different, more efficient and cheaper process and giving it a different name. But how long will India be able to do it?

False Claims

Profit depends on the sale. Drug industry, therefore, promotes the sale through a variety of means; one of them being advertisement through mass media often falsely claiming the efficacy of its drugs. More often than not, it is the name, which is sold, not the effectiveness of the drug. People are dazzled and mesmerized by patented names, attractive wrappers sexy print and TV advertizements and high prices. It unethical and fradulent for anyone in public life to earn money by recommending to others the medicines they have not experienced. But who cares for ethics any way? We have gone modern. Some of the life-saving drugs are indeed out of reach of the poor all over the world and practically every one in the developing parts of the world.

Not infrequently the method of testing the efficacy of new medicines is highly questionable. It is claimed to be scientific. Correlations are converted into causal relations and random sampling is converted into purposing sampling to get predetermined results. The needy consumers are looking for quick relief. They tend to believe in what the drug companies say. Who has the time and inclination to question the methodology used in testing. Moreover, people repose so much faith in modern science that anything that is claimed to be scientific or scientifically proved, is taken as true.

Not long ago, it was claimed that mother's milk was not so healthy for the baby. Orally given baby foods were essential to keep the baby healthy. Mothers, even in remote rural areas, bought baby foods to ensure the health of their babies. Within a few years, infant and child morbidity and mortality increased partly because the claim that baby foods were superior to mother's milk was patently false and partly because bottles used to feed liquid food to the babies were not sterilized enough to kill bacteria and germs. The baby food industry prospered while the babies died. Now the mother's milk has come to the center-stage again. Mothers are advised not to give baby foods until the baby is at least six months old.

They deliberately suppress the side effects their medicines can produce. They influence the professionals and medical institutions by presents and sponsorship of conferences and other activities to promote the sale of their products.

Sale of Fake, Prohibited and Outdated Medicines

Fake medicines constitute 15-20 per cent of the medicine business in India. There are factories to churn out these medicines. They look genuine as far as the wrapper is concerned, but consist of similar looking materials with lower or no medicinal value. They sell rather cheap and cater to a fairly huge Indian market covering the poorer sections of the society and undiscriminating individuals from other sections too. Patients in critical conditions, if administered with these diseases, die.

Apart from fake medicines, the sale of outdated medicines is quite common, especially in the rural parts of India. Even those who can read the expiry date printed on the wrapper ignore it. Many of such medicines are not effective in serious cases.

Sale of prohibited drugs is another big problem in India. Many drugs that contain harmful chemicals have been prohibited in the developed countries of the world. Drug manufacturing companies do not stop production of prohibited drugs. They continue production for the market of the developing countries as if people in developing countries are lesser creatures. The same applies to insecticides and pesticides. DDT has been prohibited since long but it is still available in the market in developing countries.

In our country, just 515 medicines, are sold by 3000 different names. These medicines are banned in other countries of the world and their production and sale are considered as crime. Doctors and scientists have said that these medicines are dangerous and can produce paralysis, cancer, blindness, and produce many other dangerous sicknesses. They make the immune system of the humans weak and can cause death. Here is a list (Table 24.1) of such internationally prohibited drugs, which are openly and legally sold in India (as on January 1, 2003).

Table 24.1: Banned Medicines and their Adverse Effects

Sr.No.	*Name of the medicine*	*Countries where it is banned*	*Effects*
1.	Oxyfin Botazon Oxypose Largestic Neurojesin Sungril Oxygen Parabutazon Kliocvinal Phynil Butazon Actimal Aljiril Aristopyrin Butacartidan Butaproxyvan	UK Japan Germany Sweden Finland USA Canada Italy Bangladesh Australia Malaysia Israel Jordan	By taking a small amount of this medicine the intestine gets small punctures and can cause blood cancer. These medicines have taken more than 15000 lives. It has been given B where it is banned.

(*Contd.*)

(*Contd.*)

Sr.No.	*Name of the medicine*	*Countries where it is banned*	*Effects*
2.	Ambkvinal Eliqueen Ambijayam Fort Emicure Emicleen Emigil Plus Choloropectiden Dyedoqueen Introgyem Aydojol Aydocyclin Metaqueen Neutrojyem Aydohydroxyqueen Queenijol Analgin	Japan Norway Sweden Germany Denmark Nepal Bangladesh Spain France Sri Lanka	Paralysis in legs, blindness. Because of these medicines 10,000 people got paralysed in Japan
3.	Beralgun Buskapan Butaljin Fargestic Marlajin Oxypose Sinaljestic Jimaljin Altrajin Finoljin Parajin	Australia Austria Belgium Canada Denmark France Greece Italy Japan South Korea Mexico Nepal Sweden USA UK Germany	It destroys the white blood cells in the human body. The structure of the bones and the muscles of the human beings get affected and cause death of a person.
4.	A.T. Fort Mayestrojanfort Orosekron fort Orgaalotin Ostron S.G. Fort Cholorastrap Satraptamycin Introstrap Intestrostrap Straptostrap	Australia Austria Belgium Canada Denmark Greece Italy New Zealand Norway South Africa Thailand UK Singapore USA Germany Bangladesh	If it is given to a pregnant women, the child gets handicapped. It also affects the production of the white blood Cells in the body of the human beings.

(*Contd.*)

(*Contd.*)

Sr.No.	*Name of the medicine*	*Countries where it is banned*	*Effects*
5.	Drooling Drooling Dekadyurabolin Brufen Ivabolin Novaljin Aspirin Kaimer Kaimoral Kaimoral Fort Alfapsin	Bangladesh UK and all other countries of the world	It affects the immune system of the body and the person soon dies.
6.	Acetophenetideen Fenacitin Acromycine Docabolin Histaprade Pericart Parydron Irgofen Mygril Mygrenil Stiptoment	Canada Cyprus Chile Denmark and many other countries	They affect the lever of human. The vitamin present in these medicines only increases the cost of medicine and nothing other than that.
7.	Tetracyclene Thoron Trynarjick Restil Kamaslop Plasidox 2 Plasidox 10 Plasidox 5	Bangladesh Denmark Italy Japan New Zealand Peru Greece Norway Spain Venezuela Bangladesh Nepal, etc.	The colour of the teeth of the children gets brown and gives severe damage to the body.

Source: Zee News Network, Inside Story, January 2003. Patenting of Natural Products

Patents Law

Here comes another setback to health of the common man. A large number of plants have been traditionally used as medicines. They have become part of the health culture of Indian society. Almost the whole of the Ayurvedic, Unani and Folk medicines use these plants in the treatment of various diseases. The other major medicinal components are minerals and salts. Now the American companies have started taking patent rights on formulations based on these plants. If this is allowed under the IPR regime, the common man in countries like India will be deprived of his own medicines.

CHEMICALS KILL MORE PEOPLE THAN SAVE

Self-medication

People have become so drug-friendly that they now indulge in self-medication on a vast scale. There are a large number of drugs in the market, which are claimed to cure headache, insomnia, common cold, fevers, indigestion, muscular pain, etc. almost instantaneously. Practically, all of them are toxic; they give instant relief but pollute the body and prepare the ground for more and new diseases.

And they all are recommended and promoted by one film stars and cricket players. What an unsportsmand like behaviours! About the film personalities less said the better they play with the lives or the very people who make them heroes and heroins.

Rural parts of India are full of fake doctors who know something about allopathic medicines used by qualified physicians. They are not trained physicians. Many of them resort to this practice when they fail to pass even their high school examination. They are very popular among the people partly because they prescribe medicines, which appear to give instant relief and partly because they are readily available. They know how to give injections and glucose. Their medicines work in cases where the patient would have recovered anyway, medicine or no medicine. But they damage the health of not a few by prescribing wrong medicines; they are responsible for many health complications and even deaths. They cannot diagnose diseases; they prescribe medicines on the basis of obvious symptoms.

Quite related to self-medication is the problem of over-and under-medication. Over-dosing leads to several health complications and under-dosing reduces the resistance of the body to diseases. Some people get addicted to medicines. They do not get sleep unless they take sleeping pills. Constipation is another common problem for which people take medicines on regular basis.

Under medication is also a serious problem. Very often patients of communicable diseases do not complete the full course of medicines. The moment they feel better, they stop taking medicines. The germs still in the blood stream get used to the medicines. When they attack next, a normal dose of medicine does not work. Soon a new medicine with much higher potency is needed. As the cycles continue, diseases become incurable. Such problems are common in cases of leprosy, tuberculosis, malaria kala-azar, etc. Antibiotics are being used like salt and sugar. When we get ordinary cold, physicians prescribe strong antibiotics to stop its onset or severity. We rarely realize that the resources we waste on such medicines do not add to our health. Common cold is essential to restore balance in the body. It is also a warning against too much indulgence to secure body welfare.

In India alone there are as may 60,000 antibiotic medicines in circulation. Many of them are not only costly but also hazardous for health. India is a land of medicines more the land of diseases. There are over 17,000 pharmaceutical companies churning out medicines for unsuspecting people, both literate and illiterate. UK has just 400 companies producing medicines. Aggressive marketing, misinformation and gullibility of the people really sick or made to feel sick helps these companies market their poisonous products on a wide scale.

Air, Water and Food Pollution

Drugs are used not only to save life but also to take away life. Hundreds of pesticides, fungicides, insecticides and poisons available in the market are meant to kill. And we produce and use these drugs to kill the organisms that are supposed to be harmful to us. Let us not get into a debate on violence and non-violence. Even if we justify the killing of harmful organism, are we not killing the harmless and beneficial organisms too at the same time. Our chemical pesticides and insecticides have made many birds and rodents endangered species; some have disappeared from the scene. We are not fully aware of the interdependence between the harmful organisms on the one the hand, and the harmless and health promoting organisms, on the other.

India is one of the most chemically polluted countries in the world. High level of toxic chemicals are found not only in foods but also in the air released by industrial units based on hazardous chemicals and also because of the reluctance of the knowledgeable people to raise their voices despite a host of laws banning their use and misuse. Medicines that contain mercury, benzene and formaldehydes can cause hazardous diseases.

Farmers use zinc-based compounds, recycled from lead, to get high yields, which can cause serious damage to lever. More hazardous is the use of asbestos, dye-based products, chemicals like chlorine, mercury and compounds used in electrical industry, and bonding materials used in electronics. There are around 100,000 known chemicals all of which are paraded as safe as their tests are often manipulated. A single toxic test done on animals would cost around six million dollars. Who will go for such a costly exercise?

Food adulteration is a common problem in India. It takes place at the time of harvesting, storing, distribution and cooking. Each year hundreds of people, children included, die of food poisoning. Many food preservatives are harmful and the drugs used in storage do have their adverse effects on health even if minutely.

Weapons of Mass Destruction (WMD): Chemical

From killing of microorganisms with the help of chemicals, we have now entered a new era of modern civilization of killing human beings by resorting to germ warfare. It means use of harmful and deadly chemicals or biological agents as weapons of war and mass killing. Chemical weapons are made up of poisonous chemical compounds, whereas biological weapons are living microorganisms. These weapons can cause injuries or death in many ways: inhalation, contact with skin, or ingestion of contaminated food.

A chemical attack usually involves dispersing agents into the air. This can be done in various ways, such as firing artillery cells that burst in the mid-air, or using airplanes to spray the agents over an area or to just mix it with ordinary powder and distribute the same through mail etc. Because chemical agents are considered to be random, dangerous and particularly cruel weapons, they have been rarely used.

Chemical warfare agents can be grouped into two general types: those that affect the body and those that damage the nervous system. The ones that affect the body are: phosgene gas, chlorine gas, hydrogen cyanide and mustard gas. These gases enter the body through inhalation. The nerve agents act as blocking the transmission of nerve messages throughout the body. These agents include sarin, soman, tabun, and VX. Whether inhaled or absorbed through the skin, a single drop of nerve agent can shut down the body's nervous system. They cause death within minutes after exposure.

Large-scale use of chemical and biological weapons is a relatively recent development although they have been used even in ancient times. The chemicals, which we use in agriculture, medicine, etc. to kill bacteria, viruses, germs and pests are harmful to human body. They have therefore been used in the past as weapons of mass destruction. During the First World War, the German forces released chlorine gas. In 1917, they used mustard gas too. By 1918, all major powers used chemical weapons to kill enemy forces.

Italy used chemical arms in a limited way in 1930; Egypt used them against Yemen in 1960; Iraq used in Iran-Iraq war in 1970s; in 1995 a Japanese cult called Aum Shinrikyo released sarin nerve agent in Tokyo subway killing 12 and injuring 5500 persons.

Biological WMDs

Biological weapons constitute a unique class of weapons; they are living organism. These biological agents represent a dangerous threat because they are alive, and are, therefore, unpredictable and uncontrollable once released. This is one important reason why biological weapons have been rarely used.

Biological warfare agents include bacteria, viruses, fungi and other living microorganisms that can kill or incapacitate. Since they can reproduce, these agents have the unique potential to spread rather fast. Some of the agents make their victims very sick without necessarily killing them. Examples include the microorganisms that cause tularemia, Q fever and yellow fever. Agents that can prove lethal are bubonic plague bacteria and smallpox virus. Anthrax bacteria are usually found under the soil surface and cause disease primarily in the cattle and other grazing animals. But if released into the air and inhaled, a few thousand spores can be fatal. Botulinum toxin is another lethal agent. It is not a biological agent as such; it is a product of bacterium *Clostridium botulinum*. The toxin is dangerous whether inhaled or ingested in food or drink. Just five liters of botulinum toxin could poison the source of untreated water supply.

The first recorded use of biological agents was by the Romans using dead animals to foul water supply of their enemies. Tartars infected the enemy by catapulting bodies infected with bubonic plague over the walls of Kaffa. Some historians believe that this even was the cause of plague epidemic in medieval Europe killing 25 million people.

In the fourteenth century, plague infected cadavers purportedly were catapulted into an enemy camp in the Russian Crimea. In colonial America, British delivered blankets from their smallpox infirmary to Native Americans hoping to infect them with the diseases. In 1918, Japanese formed a special unit in their army called Unit 731, which specialized in biological warfare. In 1931, Japan attacked Manchuria and used the prisoners of war for biological warfare experiments. In 1941, Japanese planes sprayed bubonic plague over parts of China. The Japanese released thousands of plague infected rats before their surrender in 1945.

U.S. biological weapons programme started in 1942 was meant to counter the Japanese and German advances in this field. It focused on anthrax spores when delivered with a conventional bomb. First tested in Guinard Island off the coast of Scotland, it provided adequate data to improve the delivery system. The infection however could not be contained to the Guinard Island; it spread to the coastal areas of Scotland. In 1956, the then USSR accused the USA of using biological weapons in Korean war. Several tests were conducted in the USA during 1960s, which demonstrated that biological agents could be dispersed in a variety of non-explosive ways from moving vehicles etc. The tests also proved that US was highly susceptible to a biological weapon attack. Similar tests were carried out in the Soviet Union also. In 1979, there was an explosion at a plant in Sverdlosk and an outbreak of anthrax followed. The most recent concern of biological warfare has come from the developing countries. During the Persian Gulf War, the US troops were immunized against harmful bacteria. And now, the technology of biological warfare appears to have fallen in the hands of terrorists. The cases of anthrax spores being sent out through letters have alarmed the world of the dangers ahead. There is a lurking fear that soon plague and smallpox would be spread around to kill millions of people.

From Conventional to Unconventional Chemical/Biological War to Terrorism

In general, the world is consistently moving towards humanitarianism. Killing of innocent men, women and children having nothing to do with wars has never been approved by the world community ever since man stepped on the path of civilization. Asoka after seeing the dead bodies of hundreds and thousands of Kalingans whom he subdued became an apostle of peace. Even during wars, the civil society was spared from the onslaught of the soldiers. But the creed of the terrorists is different; they try to terrorize the people and governments by mass killings.

Terrorism was earlier confined to a few pockets of the world and was identified with the struggle for self-determination and independence. Once the cause of the tension was eliminated, it disappeared from the scene. But now a group of religious fundamentalists has decided to use biological warfare as a means to impose its ideology. This group has declared itself the custodian of Islam. Islam is a religion of peace, compassion, and fellowship. But the group has interpreted it differently to suit its own mindset. It believes that by killing the people, it can frighten the world to accept its diktat.

Terrorists are no longer isolated groups. They are now a well-knit international organization. They are backed by financial contributions from a variety of sources including the gullible public and have billions of dollars at their command. They use riffles, bombs, even missiles to attack and kill people. On September 11, they used hijacked civilian aircrafts as bombs to destroy the twin towers of the WTC in New York and a part of the Pentagon building in Washington DC. They killed over 5000 people just in one go. As if it was not bad enough, they have now launched biological warfare against humanity by releasing in the air anthrax bacteria. Who knows which other diseases are going to be revived in years ahead?

While it is difficult to turn anthrax into a weapon of mass destruction, it is quite easy to grow the bacteria in the lab and distribute small quantities piecemeal even through mail. A few milligrams of anthrax contains millions of anthrax spores, enough to infect thousands of people, if dispersed in densely populated areas. Cases of anthrax spores containing letters have come to light in many countries of the world. It is still just a threat but the mentality behind its use is horrible. It may next try to spread plague or smallpox. How sad it is that medicine created to save people from the jaws of death is being used to carry people to the jaws of death. The world has changed indeed in more than one way. May be, the Medical Nemesis has descended on earth!

REFERENCES

1. Ellich, Evan, *Medical Nemesis.*
2. K.V. Sundaram and M. Moni (eds.), *Sustainable Development and Sustainable Life Styles*, New Delhi: Bhoovigyan Vikas Foundation, 2003.
3. Zee News Network, Inside Story on Medicines, January 2003.

25

Challenges Ahead

The desire to lead a healthy life is common to all human beings. Man has, therefore, from times immemorial tried to evolve life styles, food habits and medications to keep him, his family members and people in general physically, mentally and emotionally fit. Innumerable approaches and methods were developed in India: they ranged from *Mantra-tantra* and folk medicines to Ayurveda and Yoga therapy and several other variants of all these such as Unani system of medicine, until we came to the so-called modern medicine in eighteenth century.

Medicines and medicines men have multiplied since then, as diseases grew in number and complexity. Even the uncommon diseases became common; those that were rare became frequent; and those that were peculiar to specific ages and regions became universal. As we enter the twenty first century, we appear to have reached a turning point on our road to healthful life. We realize that our forefathers who linked health to the style of life (food we take, the work we do, the mental images of the world we create, and the feelings we have about others) were not wrong, most of the time, if not all the time.

Medicines are important, as they would always be, but they have their inherent limitations; they cannot ensure a healthful life. They can cure but cure does not solve the problems of health. We need a healthful life to enjoy it. Increased longevity of life would become a curse if much of the old age is spent in bed. Increased expectancy of life must be backed by increased expectancy of healthy life. Living alive with the help of medicines, hospitals, physicians and surgeons is no living at all. We, therefore, have to aim at a healthy society disease free society – an aim that may never be fulfilled, but is worth pursuing. In this case, as in all other aspects of human life, travelling itself is the destination.

Medical science has so far paid attention to curing diseases; only for the last few decades attempts have been made to nip the disease in the bud with the help of vaccines. Diseases have multiplied and their lethality increased to such an extent that medicines do not appear to be a panacea nor are even the vaccines. Attention has now to go to primordial approach to health: preparing the body through appropriate lifestyles for diseaseless living. But the change in the lifestyles alone would not guaranty a healthy life. The environment in which we live, the food we consume, the air we breathe and the water we drink, must be health promting. Even then the diseases will attack human beings but they would not be as widespread as they are today, nor would they be as numerous either. The hopeful part of the whole situation is that it is now possible to achieve this goal. Modern science and technology, which is competent to develop medicines and other methods of saving life, can also help us in creating healthy free society. We do not need more hospitals, more doctors, more nurses, more medicines and medical instruments; we need less of diseases. The twentyfirst century should, therefore, be declared as the Century of Disease Free Society.

PRESENT SCENARIO

The world has made much headway in the control of communicable diseases. We can now see the light through the tunnel, even if fuzzy. These diseases are now confined to only those parts of the world where development remained stunted for over a century: where modern medicine did not reach and the traditional approaches to curing diseases were thrown overboard. But even in these less developed parts of the world, international cooperation and national efforts are fast changing the disease scenario. True some of them are on their comeback trail but the day is not far off when the well known communicable diseases would become things of the past. As long as mass poverty and illiteracy continue and investments in public health remain puny, these diseases may continue. We can give another twenty years (2001-20) for this transition to pass off.

Absence of traditional communicable diseases would, however, take us only thus far. Even before the hold of these diseases started loosening, new communicable diseases and systemic diseases have taken roots. They are growing rather fast in intensity as well coverage. Not very long back, they were confined to the industrialised countries; now they have spread their tentacles to the countries too. Some of these diseases like AIDS and Hepatitis B spare no people: developed, developing or undeveloped. Heart ailments, diabetes and several other diseases of modern civilization discussed earlier in chapter 11 are on the increase.

Heroic efforts are on to change this dismal situation. We still hope that science and technology would solve the problems sooner than later. WHO at the global level and national government at the local levels are trying their level best to control and eradicate diseases. Each year new vaccines or medicines are discovered; and new knowledge is gained about the causes of diseases. But the progress we make on this front is followed and even accompanied by new ailments brought about by the so-called modern civilization. They result from the human failure to follow the laws of nature pertaining to food and drinks, exercise and rest, thinking and doing; and the norms of the society in matters sex, and social relations. AIDS, cancer, hypertension, diabetes, heart ailments, arthritis and several other diseases belong to this category. They have no cure; they are life-long degenerative diseases. In fact, many of them are not diseases in the conventional sense. They are disorders with which the patient has to live forever. They can be controlled but cannot be cured.

A review of the progress we have made in the field of medicines, medical research and health facilities shows that much of the credit for achievement must go to scientific progress and socio-economic development in general. New discoveries and inventions in medical sciences have enabled man to win over many diseases. But the benefits from these developments could reach the people only when incomes, educational levels, and overall living standards improved. This situation is not going to change in future either. Child mortality will further decline, mortality and morbidity attributable to communicable diseases will also decline, expectation of life will further improve, birth rates will decline, and so also the death rates. But the sufferings of the people due to poor health may not decrease commensurate with progress we make in the field of medicine. It may even increase if positive changes in the lifestyles of the people do not take place; if the quality of the environment does not improve; and if abject poverty is not banished from the face of the earth.

THE EMERGING FUTURE

The food production in the world has more than doubled in the last 40 years or so. Malthus was proved wrong. There is no reason for this trend not being continuing given the new biotechnological advances, particularly in the field of genetic engineering. Per capita GDP has increased by 2.5 times in the last 50 years. Literacy rates are increasing incessantly. The number of people who were chronically underfed and malnourished has declined.

The life expectancy is on the increase and fertility rates are steadily declining. Spectacular progress has been made in reducing under-5 years mortality. Twenty two million children below the age of five died in 1955; the number in 2000 AD was less than 10 million. Infant mortality rate per 1000 live births in 1955 was 148; it came down to 55 in 2000 AD. But overwhelming percentage (97 per cent) of children dying before they reach the fifth birth day are in the developing countries.

Many of the adolescents who are about to enter active life did not get the attention, affection and environment to develop healthy attitude towards life and living. In the developed parts of the world, the single parenthood and widespread disturbances in the married life have left children in the lurch. In the developing countries poverty tells upon the upbringing of the children adversely. When they get to the age of adolescence, they have a feeling of deprivation; they grow as angry, violent and crime-prone citizens. Neither the urban slums nor the poverty stricken villages provide the kind of environment, which is conducive to sanity in adolescents. Result is obvious: rash driving and accidents resulting therefrom, alcoholism, violence, delinquency, drug abuse and sexual escapades.

Sexuality is the sign of forth coming maturity. Today's adolescents are prone to go astray unless their upbringing in early childhood is up to the mark and they have adequate opportunities to release their latent energy creativity. Unsafe sex has landed many young men and women in deep trouble. The cost of their deviant behaviour to the society is enormous. The number of adolescents who contract HIV infection is on the increase. The girls aged 15-19 gave birth to 17 million babies in 1995. Pregnancy and childbirth in early age is risky for the mother as well as the baby.

As child mortality declines, more people are being added to adult population. Currently, just 50 per cent of the population is in the working age group of 20-64. The health of the adults is of vital importance for the society because it is this section of the society that takes care of the children and aged and generates wealth and service. Unfortunately, about 15 million adults die prematurely each year. It includes 1.8 million deaths due to HIV infection, 2-3 million due to tuberculosis, and over half a million due to pregnancy and childbirth. Most of these deaths are preventable.

A large number of adults in the developing parts of the world still succumb to conventional communicable diseases. Much progress has been made in the control of these diseases but the antibiotics that worked in the past have become blunt for the mutated viruses of today and tomorrow. Moreover, new diseases like HIV infection have added to the already a difficult situation. The non-communicable diseases like cancer, diabetes, coronary heart diseases and hypertension, do not spare the adults.

The population of the aged is on the increase. Maintaining the health of these people; taking care of them; and giving them the feeling of dignity, is the biggest challenge we face today. With the breaking of the joint family system and increase in longevity of life, on the one hand, and the inability of the governments to do all that is necessary for the aged, on the other, their position has become quite precarious. Even in the developed countries most of the old and disabled people cannot meet more than a fraction of the cost of the healthcare they need. The developing countries face even greater problem in this respect. They are still in the stage of minimizing infant mortality and child mortality. Not many persons live long enough to need support from the government and civil society. The impact of the shortage of resources for health is likely to be more seriously felt by the senior citizens of these countries.

Women are one of the most vulnerable sections of the society, particularly in the developing countries. Discrimination against women begins even before they are born. In many a developing country, female foetus abortion and female infanticide are not uncommon. The girls do not get the same attention by parents in matters of food, education, health and other basic needs that the boys get. The mothers who die of childbirth are in plenty. Women live longer than men; increasing longevity of life will favour them and they will be proportionately more than men among the aged. But this natural advantage will be offset by the discriminatory treatment they get in the society.

AGENDA: 2020

Looking at our achievements of the past few decades we can visualize the direction in which we are moving and the problems and prospects of the first quarter of twenty first century. It would be hazardous to attempt any prognosis for a more distant future. The issues that will dominate the next 25 years will be poverty, environment, child mortality, status of women, communicable diseases, cancer, systemic disorders, gerontology, style of development and style of life. These are the challenges humanity faces in twenty first century.

Health-for-All

It is clear that the road to healthful life and living is still a distant dream, the advances in science and technology notwithstanding. The hurdles and pitfalls are many, some are common to all countries while others are country, region and group specific. Among the hurdles that need attention are: environmental pollution, urbanization, poverty, stressful life, inadequate quantity and quality of food, overeating and consumption of junk food, increasing use of alcohol, drugs and tobacco, over-medication, insufficient medical facilities and lower priority people tend to give for health. All these do not apply to everyone and every part of the world. Some of them are specific to the industrialized countries, other to the developing counties and still others to both.

Apparently, there is no panacea for the health problems people face today. The attack on diseases and ill-health must be multi-pronged. Firstly, the imperatives for good health must be pursued with vigour and persistence. Man must change his style of life and living to conform to the biological needs of the body, and civil society must aim at and seriously work for a pollution free production process, less stressful social organization and more widespread and better managed health services. Earlier health was the responsibility of the individuals and families. It has now come in the purview of the government and private agencies. The health services have expanded fast during the last few decades. But this has not led to reduction in the number of people who get sick and number of diseases afflicting them. Secondly, the latest advances in bio-and information technologies must be brought to bear on the health scenario as speedily as possible. Vast areas of the world are still devoid of even the most rudimentary health services. These gaps must be filled fast enough to make a visible impact. And finally, the persistent poverty, on the one hand, and widening gap between the rich and the poor, on the other, must be recognized as great hindrances in the path of good health: the available resources must, therefore, be increasingly diverted to those who need them most.

So far one of the indices of good quality of life has been expectancy of life. Now the stage has reached when it should be coupled with expectancy of health. People should live for 125 years. But they should remain in sound health. If longevity of life means being bed-ridden for years and decades and surviving on medicines, then the very purpose of it gets defeated. As the non-communicable chronic diseases grow in number and intensity, the old strategy of attacking each disease separately must be replaced by a comprehensive chronic disease control package incorporating prevention, diagnosis, treatment, rehabilitation and improved training of health personnel.

Focus on Primordial Medicine

It is the time for India, nay the whole world, to focus attention on primordial medicine i.e. living according to the biological laws of nature and depending more on nature than on medicines for getting over diseases as and when they come. This does not, however, mean that scientific research related to health, diseases and medicine should be stopped. In fact, scientific research is a must and more and more resources should be allocated for this purpose. As health situation get more complicated, scientific research has become indispensable. What is being emphasized here is the need to lay emphasis on 'the science and art of good health'. Our objective should be good health, not absence of diseases.

As Gandhi said, more hospitals and doctors per unit of population do not mean a health society. Hospitals and doctors are responsible for poor healthy of the people for they make people less responsible towards themselves. Primordial medicine promotes self-responsibility and care of one's own health.

Access to Health Facilities

Access to health facilities is one of the major problems in rural India in particular. There is no shortage of PHCs and sub-centres to meet the primary health needs of the people, but the personnel required to run these health centres either are not there or they do not attend to their duties. Many of the PHCs remain deserted and infrastructure created goes waste. While at the same time, the quakes flourish. This means that there is demand for health services but this demand is not being met.

There is move now to stop the quakes (jholachhap doctors) from practising medicine. Many of them have been arrested in recent years. It is illegal to practise medicine without required qualifications. But in the absence of qualified doctors, where can people go? One great quality of the quakes is that they are driven by both immediate and long-term prospects of making money. They are, therefore, always at the beck and call of people. As against this, the primary health centres and hospitals are so negligent of the patients that poor people find it difficult to get service there. The private nursing homes are too expensive for them.

The suggestion made earlier that rural health centres need just half-baked doctors who can attend to minor ailments, who can visit the villages to inquire about the health of the people, who can give lectures on health and hygiene in village schools and who can refer cases to hospitals before the patient becomes serious.

Here is yet another suggestion, the very fact that the *jhola chap* doctors propser in the country indicates that people need such barefoot doctors. These why not formalize them as health assistants after a year-long training in basics of medical services? It would be easier to bring them into the formal sector than to stop them from practicing.

Food Security

Health of the people is very much dependent on the quality of life they lead. The first prerequisite of a tolerable quality of life is wholesome diet (includes water), clean house to live, access to good quality education and health services, adequate income, employment and clean environment. Our record of the last 25 years on this front is not very encouraging and the globalization, privatization and liberalization processes that have been set in motion are not likely to take us very far.

The problems involved are twofold: production and distribution. On the production front, there are hopeful signs but on the distribution front problems are really serious at the global as well as local level. The whole social system, legal included, is in favour of the well off. Technological changes do bring about new opportunities to increase production, but much of the increase is gobbled up by the rich nations and people: very little of it trickles down to the poor. It is doubtful if this situation would change in the near future unless there is a genuine effort to uplift the lot of the poor. No doubt, there will be very many conferences and seminars, many populist measures such as distribution of food grains at cheaper than market rates, but but the benefits of such measures are more likely to go to the rich than for the poor.

India in 2001 had 60 million tonnes of buffer stock of foodgrains. It needs only 25 million tonnes to meet any unexpected shortfall in the production. A substantial amount of this grain is kept in the open as covered warehouses to store such a huge amount of grains just do not exist. The granaries are really overflowing. Yet, cases of starvation deaths are not rare. Conditions in which the real poor of India live is shameful and society, which tolerates such inhuman conditions cannot be said to be really civilized.

The scope for increasing food production has increased with the introduction of GM plants. But nothing would change the situation if the attitude of the people does not change; if they fail to have love and compassion towards others. Even food thus acquires a spiritual context.

Controlling and Eradicating Diseases

Infectious Diseases

Many of the communicable and viral diseases, which were great killers in the past, have been eradicated but several others continue to be health hazards for millions in the developing countries. Three new developments have further complicated the situation. First, some of the communicable diseases like malaria are on their comeback trail. The time tested antibiotics just do not work. The vectors of the diseases have become resistant to antibiotics. Enhancing the power of the medicines gives only a temporary reprieve. Second, with the improvement in the means of transport and communication, movement of the people from place to place has increased. This promotes rapid spread of the diseases. And three, new diseases like AIDS having no known medicines are spreading fast with a vengeance.

According to the International Forum of Antibiotic Resistance, there are patients today in hospitals for whom there are no effective therapies. Until very recently, almost all drug resistant bacteria were confined to hospitals, whereas concentration of sick people and high antibiotic use contributed to the evolution of stains capable of evading antibiotic attack. Now it is not uncommon for patients to come with drug resistant microbes that are circulating in the community. Antibiotics wipe out bacteria that are susceptible to them. But when used improperly, they can encourage the growth of bacteria that had adapted to them. And because bacteria can swap genes under the right conditions, drug resistant germs can share their resistance mechanisms with other germs. Increasing drug resistance is frustrating treatment of common infections all over the world.

AIDS is not linked to environmental conditions to which most of the communicable diseases are: it is a product of social pollution and can be eradicated only if people adhere to the principles of responsible sex. In any case, the current situation in this regard is highly disturbing. The disease is spreading fast and taking away the adults whose contribution to the society has just begun. Despite campaigns and appeals, the HIV infection continues to increase. As moral standards decline, more of such problems are likely to emerge. While discussing the issue of availability of food, we cannot ignore quality. Today in India for more people suffer from malnourishment than under nourishment, overflowing graineries cannot ensure proper nourishment of the people.

Many of the conventional communicable diseases still pose problems. Some of them have been controlled; others are under attack. But as stated earlier, so long as poverty and environmental degradation remain, communicable diseases will pose health hazards. Unfortunately, both of them are in plenty in the developing countries. The situation as of today (2001 AD) is not a happy one and poses serious challenges for the next 25 years. If the world can get rid of the communicable diseases by 2025, it will have very favourable impact on health of the people all over the world.

Cancer

Among the non-communicable diseases, cancer is one of the most widespread fatal diseases. Some kinds of cancers can be cured, if detected early; for others there are no medicines. Unfortunately, it is still uncommon to detect cancer before it is too late. The disease is spreading fast in the developing countries whose medical resources are limited and expensive to use. Cancer cases are on the increase all over the world but more so in the developing countries where modernity in its most vulgar forms has just begun to creep in.

Systemic Disorders

Like cancer, the systemic disorders like diabetes, hypertension, arthritis, cardiovascular problems, etc. are on the increase, particularly in the developing countries. There are no medicines for these diseases; they can be controlled though by change in the lifestyle and some medications. Given the current urbanization and industrialization processes and the related pattern of life and living, these disorders cannot be avoided. The solution lies in rethinking about urbanization and industrialization processes, on the one hand, and the style of life they promote, on the other. The biological needs of the human body must be ensured: it must be stress free; it must have enough exercise, it must get clean and nutritive food; it must not be stuffed with toxins; and it must be emotionally blissful. Man must strive to move in that direction. That is the final medicine for such disorders. As long as man transgresses the norms of good life and living set by nature, these disorders will continue to increasingly haunt him. These problems will also multiply fast as the expectation of life goes further up. Older people are more prone to these disorders. And when they die they leave behind their legacy through the genes, which their children and grandchildren inadvertently inherit.

Mental Disorders

Mental disorders too are on the increase. As life becomes faster, ambitions fly high, and stresses increase, more and more people are likely to be mentally disoriented. The answer lie in more specialists appears to treat psychological and mental illnesses. But it is only a part answer to the problem. Prevention is certainly more important than cure. If life must be fast, there must be ways of slowing the mind for sometime to enable it to recoup and regain health. If stresses must increase, there must be compensatory ways to relax and release the tension. If ambitions must rise and rise, then there must be opportunities to feel small, to burst the balloon of our false ego. It all boils down to one simple formula: man must come down to earth and feel that he is like all other living entities products of the Mother Earth, that his greatness lies in service and simplicity, in creation and creativity, and in peace and harmony.

Bringing Mortality Rates Down

Child Mortality

One area where we are destined to make much headway is the area of child mortality. Most of the children die of diseases, which can be prevented. The success achieved in the eradication of plague, smallpox, cholera, guinea worm and several other diseases and the progress we have made in the eradication of malaria, dysentery and diarrhea give us a hope for a safer future. True, some of the diseases are coming back but ways and means would be found to control them.

But these hopeful signs are tempered by new problems in the offing. With increasing urbanization and accompanying social changes neglect and abuse of the children is emerging as a major problem. Then there are diseases, which children inherit from their parents. The health of the children thus gets linked with the health of the parents. Infantile HIV infection is a problem of great concern.

Maternal Mortality

Health of the females is important not only because they have equal right to good health but also because on their health depends, to a great extent, the health of the children. So long as the status of women in the society is lowly, their health will continue to get relatively less attention. Fortunately, the situation is changing fast in favour of the women. Two things that come in the way are illiteracy and poverty. In countries like India, literacy among the girls is spreading fast and far more of the girls are going to schools and colleges than ever before. Their performance in schools and colleges is far better than that of boys. They have started occupying important positions in all walks of life.

The trend that is set is likely to further deepen and widen so that by 2025 at least 50 per cent of women and 75 per cent of the girls below 19 years would be literate. The change that has set in is the result of sustained efforts by the relevant United Nations Agencies, national and state governments, and the women activists. This change will have a very favourable impact on the health of the women.

Care of the Aged

The number of elderly persons is on the increase. In the next few decades 6-8 per cent of the people would be in the age group 65+. These people need special attention in the same way as children need special attention. They are exposed to all the diseases that affect human beings in general plus very specific type of diseases very common to aged persons only.

The elderly need special doctors, hospitals and treatment. India is not yet prepared for this, nor is there willingness to face this challenge squarley. To some extent, the challenge is already there but our response is still lukewarm. The New Health Policy-2001 also does not pay adequate attention to gerontology and problems associated thereto.

With increasing longevity of life, the chances of more and more people living longer but being bed-ridden for years and decades are no longer remote. The problems are especially serious in developing countries as they are still at the crossroads of the first and second epidemical stages while the third stages is knocking at their doors. Child and maternal mortality is still very high and the communicable diseases are yet to be won over. Only during the last two decades, the signs of hope have become visible. Health problems associated with ageing population need to be tackled on a priority basis.

WOULD BIOTECHNOLOGY HELP?

Cloning of sheep was made a reality in late 1990s. With the arrival of the new century, the cloning of human beings may also become a reality. Advanced Cell Technology, a Massachusetts firm, has created a cloned embryo, a tiny cluster of cells that were the exact genetic replica of their female donor. This development has dismayed the whole world. Religious leaders have condemned it as unethical and others see a great danger to human destiny. Many governments have vowed to legally ban it. It may be mentioned here that there is no cloning in nature except in case of identical twins. Cloning entails extracting the nucleus from a donor's cell and injecting into a fertilized egg whose own genetic material has been removed.

The opposition emanates from the potential misuse of the techniques to create 'made-to-order' human beings and may be to set in motion a genetic chain reaction, which may wipe out the whole human race. People who are engaged in this activity have no understanding of all the processes that can occur in an embryo to make cloning a success on a perpetual basis. It is thus possible that many of the cloned humans would die soon or will remain in illhealth. Who will take care of them?

Research on cloning of animals shows that 95 per cents of the cloned embryos died during pregnancy and those which survived diet soon after birth. Among those, which survived suffered from serious deficiencies. Most of them had problems of heart and lungs not functioning properly. Only a very few are well like Dolly. We have enough load of the disabled; why should we then venture to create frankesteins and an unbearable load of disabled human animals? It is not only a moral question; it is also a practical question of research for what?

To suggest that further researches will reduce the dangers, which now appear to be inherent to cloning, is not valid. Nor is the suggestion that it would lead to creation of human beings who would be free from diseases, anger, bad habits etc. or it would enable childless couples to have children. Human destiny does not lie in all humans being saints and mahatmas; it does not lie in one type of human beings. It lies in diversity, in variety, and in disparities. Good and bad must remain together otherwise man will have nothing to aspire for, to work for and to die for. Nature has worked for millennia to create human beings and man now wants to multiply himself in minutes and seconds at his will. He is trying to do away with both Nature and God. There must be something fundamentally wrong with him!

We need a globally accepted and enforced bio-ethics that should guide our future research and action in such critical areas as biotechnology, molecular biology, human cloning, production and use of chemical and biological weapons, ecological balance and sustainable development. In fact, we need a convention against violence and for non-violence.

EPILOGUE

Finally, let me emphasize, even at the cost of repetition, three basic requirements for a healthy and happy society: environmental cleanliness, healthy style of life, and further and continuing developments in the field of medical sciences.

There is no possibility of creating a disease free society without improving the quality of our physical and social environment: the food we eat, the air we breathe, the water we drink and the house we live must be healthy. Taking into account the policies being pursued today at the global as well as local levels, it is not difficult to predict that the urban slums will continue unabated for another 25 years and rural poverty scenario would not change drastically. We still feel that there are technological solutions to environmental problems: in reality technology can play only a supportive role. Unless man finds a substitute for the fossil fuels (which does not appear to be feasible in the next 25 years), air pollution cannot be checked. It is difficult to get potable water even in rural areas. Industries, hte cities and the chemcials used in agriculture have polluted even the ground water.

The solution of the environmental problems lies in socio-economic policies more than in science and technology. The current race for national economic development presupposes greater use of fossil fuels and greater air pollution, especially in cities. The increasing use of fertilizers and pesticides and continuing discharge of urban effluent are polluting our rivers fast. And toxic drugs, alcohol, and other intoxicants are pouring toxins in our bodies fast enough to derail the metabolic system. Maybe, the environmental problems will be less acute than what they are today, but they would be felt more seriously as the knowledge about the harms they inflict becomes more widely known.

The second basic requirement is a change in the current style of life. We have discussed this issue in this volume elsewhere. Our lifestyle – food habits, work, approach to health, etc. – is essentially unhealthy. Unless we change over to balanced diet, less stressful life, slower speed, greater stress on peace and harmony, and medicine free health, we cannot lead a healthy life.

The need for continuing medical research cannot be over emphasized. Changes in the style of life do not come in a day. They take generations. In the period of transition, new diseases are emerging. There is urgent need to know more about the role of heredity in the creation and transmission of diseases from parents to children. Two millennia ago Sushruta described diabetes as a condition both passed through the seed (genetically) as well as influenced by environmental factors. But the genetic secrets are yet to be unraveled fully.

India must intensify its genetic research programme. It could not participate in the Genomic project because of excessive cost (Rs. 5 billion). It is, however, concentrating on the new human diversity programme to study genetic variations in the Indian population to know, which groups are susceptible or immune to diseases like tuberculosis, diabetes, cancer, thalassemia, sickle cell, anemia, etc. India should also initiate research on new degenerative diseases and new drug targets for common blood disorders.

With the successful decoding of human genome, it should be possible to map the genome of each individual. A genetic test is already being used for a variety of purposes, ranging from catching criminals to identifying the causes of many diseases. It is also being used to cure diseases by genetic manipulation. There are great possibilities in years ahead. But as noted earlier, the negative side of genetic research is equally great. How man uses this knowledge, depends on his spiritual state of mind. Let us hope that man will be wiser than what he has been so far.

REFERENCES

1. Ellich, Evan, *Medical Nemesis.*
2. Irwin, L.W., *Health for Better Living.*
3. Scott, B. Hallstead, *et al.* (eds.), *Good Health at Low Cost, Proceedings of a Conference Held at Bellagio Conference Center, Bellagio, Italy, April 29-May 3, 1985*, New York: Rockefeller Foundation, 1985.
4. Sundaram, K.V. and Moni, M. (eds), *Sustainable Development and Sustainable Life Styles*, New Delhi: Bhoovigyan Vikas Foundation, 12003.

Appendices

APPENDIX A

LIST OF MEDICAL COLLEGES (MODERN MEDICINE) AS IN EARLY 2003

Andhra Pradesh (20)

1. Andhra Medical College, Vishakhapatnam
2. Deccan College of Medical Sciences, Hyderabad
3. Gandhi Medical College, Hyderabad
4. Osmania Medical College, Hyderabad
5. Guntur Medical College, Guntur
6. Kakatiya Medical Collge, Warangal
7. Kurnool Medical College, Kurnool
8. Rangaraya Medical College, Kakinada
9. S.V. Medical College, Tirupati
10. Siddhartha Medical College, Gundala, Vijaiwada
11. Mamta Medical College, Khammam
12. Kamineni Medical College, Narketpalli, Nalgonda
13. SVS Medical College, Mahboobnagar
14. Narayan Medical College, Nellor
15. Government Medical College, Anantpur
16. ASRAM Medical College, Elluru
17. MNR Medical College, Sangareddy, Medak
18. Pratima Institute of Medical Sciences, Naganaur
19. PES Institute of Medical Sciences and Research, Kuppam
20. Ka'turi Medical College, Guntur

Assam (3)

21. Assam Medical College, Dibrugarh
22. Gauhati Medical College, Gauhati
23. Silcher Medical College, Silcher.

Bihar (8)

24. Patna Medical College, Patna
25. Nalanda Medical College, Patna
26. Katihar Medical College, Katihar
27. AN Magadh Medical College, Sherghati Road, Gaya

28. Darbhanga Medical College, Laheriasarae
29. Jawaharlal Medical College, Bhagalpur
30. Mata Gujri Medical College, Kishanganj
31. Sri Krishna Medical College, Muzaffarpur

Chandigarh (1)

32. Government Medical College, Chandigarh

Chhattisgarh (2)

33. Pt. J.N.M. Medical College, Raipur
34. Chattisgarh Institute of Medical Sciences, Bilaspur

Delhi (5)

35. Lady Harding Medical College (Delhi University), New Delhi
36. Maulana Azad Medical College (Delhi University), New Delhi
37. University College of Medical Sciences (Delhi University), Shahadra, Delhi
38. All India Institute of Medical Sciences, New Delhi
39. Vardhman Mahavir Medical College, Safdarjang Hospital, New Delhi

Goa (1)

40. Goa Medical College, Panji

Gujarat (11)

41. Smt. NHL Municipal Medical College, Ahmedabad
42. BJ Medical College, Ahmedabad
43. Government Medical College, Bhvnagar
44. Medical College, Vadodara
45. Government Medical College, Surat
46. Pramukh Swami Medical College, Kaira
47. Sri MP Shah Medical College, Jamnagar
48. Government Medical College, Rajkot
49. C.U. Shah Medical College, Surendranagar
50. Municipal Corporation Medical College, Surat
51. Swami Vivekananda Institute of Medical Sciences and Research, Valia, Bharuch

Haryana (2)

52. B.D. Sharma Post-graduate Medical College, Rohtak
53. Maharaja Agrasen Institute of Medical Research and Education, Agroha

Himachal Pradesh (2)

54. Indra Gandhi Medical College, Shimla
55. Dr. Rajinder Prasad Government Medical College, Kangra

Jammu & Kashmir (4)

56. Government Medical College, Jammu
57. Acharya Shrichander College of Medical Sciences, Jammu
57. Government Medical College, Srinagar
58. Sher-I-Kashmir Institute of Medical Sciences, Srinagar

Jharkhand (3)

59. Rajendra Medical College, Ranchi
60. MGM Medical College, Jamshedpur
61. Patliputra Medical College, Dhanbad

Karnataka (30)

62. Adichunchangiri Institute of Medical Sciences, Bellur
63. Al Ameen Medical College, Bijapur
64. AJ Institute of Medical Sciences, Mangalore
65. Bangalore Medical College, Bangalore
66. Basaveswara Medical College and Hospital, Chitradurga
67. Dr. BR Ambedkar Medical College, Bangalore
68. Father Muller's Medical College, Mangalore
69. Government Medical College, Mysore
70. Jayajagatguru Murugharajendra Medical College, Davangiri
71. Jagatguru Sri Shivarateshwara Medical College, Mysore
72. Jawaharlal Medical College, Belgaum
73. Karnataka Institute of Medical Sciences, Hubli
74. Kasturba Medical College, Manipal
75. Kasturba Medical College, Mangalore
76. Kempegowda Institute of Medical Sciences, Bangalore
77. Khaja Banda Nawas Institute of Medical Hospital, Bangalore
78. KS Hegde Medical College, Mangalore
79. KVJ Medical College and Research Hospital, Bangalore
80. KVJ Medical College, Sullia
81. Mahadevappa Rampure Medical College, Gulbarga
82. MS Ramaiah Medical College, Bangalore
83. Navodaya Medical College, Raichur
84. S. Nijlingappa Medical College, Bangalore
85. Sri B.M Patil Medical College Hospital Research Centre, Bijapur

86. Sri Devaraj Urs Medical College, Kolar
87. Sri Siddhartha Medical College, Tumkur
88. St. John's Academy of Health Sciences, Bangalore
89. Vijaynagar Institute of Medical Sciences, Bellary
90. Vydehi Institute of Medical Sciences, Managalore
91. Yenepoya Medical College and Hospital, Chitradurga

Kerala (11)

92. Academy of Medical Sciences, Kannur
93. Amrita Institute of Medical Sciences, Kochi
94. Cooperative Medical Collge, Kodhi
95. Dr. Sumervel Memorial CSI Hospital & Medical College, Karkonam, Thiruvananthapuram
96. Malankara Orthodox Syrian Church Medical Mission, Kolencherry
97. Medical College, Kottayam
98. Medical College, Khozikote
99. Medical College, Trissur
100. Medical College, Thiruvananthapuram
101. Pushpagiri Institute of Medical Sciences and Reseach Centre, Tiruvalla

Madhya Pradesh (6)

102. Gujra Raja Medical College, Gwalior
103. Gandhi Medical College, Bhopal
104. Netaji Subhash Chandra Bose Medical College, Jabalpur
105. MGM Medical College, Indore
106. R.D. Gardi Medical College, Ujjain
107. Shyam Shah Medical College, Rewa

Maharashtra (35)

108. Annasaheb Churaman Patil Memorial Medical College, Dhule
109. Armed Forces Medcal College, Pune
110. B.J. Medical College, Pune
111. Bharati Vidyapeeth's Medical College, Pune
112. Dr. V.M. Medical College, Sholapur
113. Dr.Panjabrao Deshmukh Memorial Medical College, Amravati
114. Government Medical College, Aurangabad
115. Government Medical College, Kolhapur
116. Government Medical College, Nagpur
117. Government Medical College, Nanded
118. Grant Medical College, Mumbai
119. Indira Gandhi Medical College, Nagpur

120. Jawaharlal Nehru Medical College, Swangi, Wardha.
121. KJ Somaiah Medical College, Sion, Mumbai
122. Krishna Institute of Medical Sciences, Karad, Satara
123. Lokmanya Tilak Medical College, Mumbai
124. Mahatma Gandhi Mission's Medical College, Navi Mumbai
125. Mahatma Gandhi Mission's Medical College, Aurangabad
126. Maharashtra Institute of Medical Education and Research, Pune
127. Maharashtra Institute of Medical Sciences and Research, Lathur
128. Mahatma Gandhi Institute of Medical Sciences, Wardha
129. Meeraj Medical College, Meeraj
130. NKP Salve Institute of Medical Science and Research Centre, Nagpur
131. Nasik District's Maratha Vidyaprasarak Samaj Medical College, Adgaon
132. Padmashree Dr. DY Patil Medical College for Women, Pimpri, Pune
133. Padamshree Dr. DY Patil Medical College, New Mumbai.
134. Padmashree Dr. DY Patil Medical College, Kolhapur
135. Rural Medical College, Loni, Ahmednagar
136. Rajiv Gandhi Medical College, Thane
137. SRTR Medical College, Ambajogai
138. Seth GS Medical College, Mumbai
139. Sri Bhausaheb Hire Government Medical College, Dhule
140. Sri Vasanta Rao Naik Government Medical College, Yavatmal
141. Topiwala National Medical College, Mumbai
142. Tarna Medical College, Navi Mumbai

Manipur (1)

143. Regional Institute of Medical Sciences, Imphal

Orissa (3)

144. MKC Medical College, Ganjam
145. SCB Medical College, Cuttack
146. VSS Medical College, Burla, Sambalpur

Pondicherry (5)

147. Aarupadai Veedu Medical College, Pondicherry
148. Jawaharlal Institute of Medical Education and Research, Pondicherry
149. Mahatma Gandhi Medical College, Pondicherry
150. Pondicherry Institute of Medical Sciences, Pondicherry
151. Vinayaka Mission's Medical College, Pondicherry

Punjab (6)

152. Christian Medical College, Ludhiana
153. Dayanand Medical College, Ludhiana

154. Government Medical College, Amritsar
155. Government Medical College, Patiala
156. Guru Govind Singh Medical College, Faridkot
157. Sree Guru Ram Das Institute of Medical Scineces and Research, Sri Amritsar

Rajasthan (7)

158. Dr. SN Medical College, Jodhpur
159. Jawaharlal Medical College, Ajmer
160. Government Medical College, Kota
161. Mahatma Gandhi Medical College, Jaipur
162. RNT Medical College, Udaipur
163. SMS Medical College, Jaipur
164. Sardar Patel Medical College, Bikaner

Sikkim (1)

165. New Medical College (Sikkim-Manipal University) at Gangtok

Tamil Nadu (17)

166. Chennai Medical College, Chennai
167. Chengalpattu Medical College, Chengalpattu
168. Christian Medical College, Vellore
169. Coimbatore Medical College, Coimbatore
170. Government Kilpauk Medical College, Chennai
171. KAP Vishwanathan Government Medical College, Trichy
172. Mohankumarmangalam Medical College, Salem
173. Madurai Medical College, Madurai
174. New Medical College, Toothukudi
175. PSG Institute of Medical Sciences and Research, Coimbatore
176. Perindurai Medical College and Research, Perindurai
177. Raja Muthiah Medical College, Annamalai Nagar
178. Sriramchandra Medical College and Research Institute, Chennai
179. Stanley Medical College, Chennai
180. Thanjavur Medical College, Thanjasvur
181. Tirunelveli Medical College, Tirunelveli
182. Vinayak Mission's Kirupananda Variyar Medical College, Salem

Uttar Pradesh (12)

183. BRD Medical College, Gorakhpur.
184. GAVM Medical College, Lucknow
185. GSVM Medical College, Kanpur

186. Institute of Medical Sciences, BHU, Varanasi.
187. Jawaharlal Medical College, Aligarh.
188. King George Medical College, Lucknow
189. LLRM Medical College, Meerut
190. Maharani Lakshmibai Medical College, Jhansi
191. Motilal Nehru Medical College, Allahabad
192. PV Narasimharao Medical College, Dehradun
193. SN Medical College, Agra
194. Santoshi Medical College, Ghaziabad

Uttaranchal (1)

195. Himalaya Institute of Medical Sciences, Dehradun

West Bengal (7)

196. Burdwan Medical College, Burdwan
197. Bankura Sammilani Medical College, Bankura
198. Calcutta National Medical College, Kolikata
199. Medical College, Calcutta
200. Nilratan Sirkar Medical College, Kolikata
201. North Bengal Medical College, Darjeeling
202. RG Kar Medical College, Kolkata

APPENDIX B

LIST OF AYURVEDIC COLLEGES AS IN EARLY 2003 AD

Andhra Pradesh

1. Dr. BRKR Government Ayurvedic College, Hyderabad
2. Dr. NR Shastri Government Ayurvedic College, Vijaiwada
3. SV Ayurvedic College, TT Devasthanam, Tirupati
4. Government Ayurvedic College, Warangal

Assam

5. Government Ayurvedic College, Guahati

Bihar

6. Government Ayurvedic College, Patna
7. Government Ayurvedic College, Bhagalpur
8. Dri Ravindranath Mukherjee Ayurvedic College, Champaran
9. Sri Dhanvantri Ayurvedic Mahavidyalaya, Ahirauli, Buxur
10. Rajkiya Ayodhya Shiv Kumari Ayurvedic Mahavidyalaya, Begusarai
11. Swami R.T. Ayurved Mahavidyalaya, Manjhol, Gaya
12. Motisingh Jogeswari Ayurvedic College, Chhapra
13. Nitishwar Institute of Medical Science, Kanholi, Muzaffarpur
14. Rajkiya Maharani Rameshwari Bharatiya Chikitsa Vigyan Sansthan, Mohanpur
15. Ayurved Medical College, Gaya
16. Dayanand Ayurved College & Hospital, Siwan

Chandigarh

17. Sri Dhanvantari Ayurvedic College & Hospital, Chandigarh

Chhattisgarh

18. Government Ayurvedic College, Raipur

Jharkhand

19. Suryamukhi Dinesh Ayurved Medical College & Hospital, Ranchi

Delhi

20. Ayurved & Unani Tibbiya College, Karol Bagh, New Delhi

Goa

21. Bharatiya Sanskrit Prabodhini Gomantak Ayurvedic Mahavidhyalaya & Research Centre, Vaje

Gujarat

22. Government Akhandananda Ayurvedic Mahavidyalaya, Bhadra, Ahmedabad
23. JS Ayurvedic Mahavidyalaya Nadiad
24. Government Ayurvedic Mahavidyalaya, Baroda
25. Aryakanya Suddh Ayurved Mahavidyalaya, Baroda
26. Seth JP Government Ayurvedic Mahavidyalay, Bhavnagar
27. Government Ayurved College, Junagarh
28. Sri Balhanuman Ayurved Mahavidyalaya, Lodhra
29. Sri OH Nazar Ayurvedic Mahavidyalaya, Surat
30. Sri Gulabkunverba Ayurvedic College, Jamnagar
31. Gujarat Ayurved University, Jamnagar

Haryana

32. Sri Mastanath Ayurved College, Rohtak
33. Sri Manusingh Memorial Ayurved Degree College, Sonepat
34. Gaur Brahmin Ayurvedic College & Hospital, Rohtak
35. DET Murarilal Rasiwaria Ayurved College, Charkhi Dadri
36. Sri Krishna Government Ayurvedic College, Kurukshetra

Himachal Pradesh

37. HP Govt. Institute of Post-graduate Education and Research in Ayurveda, Paprola

Jammu & Kashmir

38. Jammu Institute of Ayurved and Research, Jammu Tawi

Karnataka

39. Govt. Ayurved Medical College, Mysore
40. ALN Rao Memorial Ayurved Mahavidyalaya, Koppa, Chikamagalore
41. Government Ayurvedic College, Bangalore
42. Govt. Taranath Ayurvedic College, Bellary
43. AV Samiti Ayurvedic Mahavidyalaya, Mrankeri, Bijapur

44. Ayurvedic Mahavidyalaya, Old Hubli
45. Sri BM Kanaknadi Ayurvedic Mahavidyalaya, Shahpur, Belgaum
46. AEA's Ayurvedic College, Davangere
47. NKJ Ayurvedic College, Bidar
48. Dr. BNM Ayurved Medical College & Hospital, Bijapur
49. USS Ayurvedic Medical College, Mysore
50. SS Ayurvedic Medical College, Isarilakmapur, Haveri District
51. Sri Vijai Mahantesh Ayurvedic Medical College, Ilkal, Bagalkot district
52. Bapuji Ayurvedic College, Shimoga
53. TAME Society's Ayurvedic College, Hospet
54. TAME Society's Ayurvedic College, Bhadrawati
55. Amruta Ayurvedic College, Chitradurga
56. Bapuji Ayurvedic Medical College, Chitradurga
57. SDM College of Aurveda, Hassan
58. KVJ Ayurvedic Medical College, & Hospital, Sulliya, Dakshin Karnaaka
59. Sri JG Cooperative Hospital Ayurvedic Medical College, Ghataprabha, Belgaum
60. Sri Kalabhairaveshwara Swami Ayurved Medical College, Bangalore
61. Institute of Ayurvedic Medicine and Research, Bangalore Palace, Bangalore
62. Sri Guru Balmiki Maharshi Ayurvedic Medical College, Jaglur, Chitradurga
63. Alva's Ayurvedic Medical College, Moodbidri, Dakshin Kannada
64. SGV Ayurvedic Medical College, Bailhongal, Belgaum
65. Mahaganapati Ayurvedic Medical College, Hoysalnagar, Dharwad
66. Shivayogeswar Ayurvedic Medical College, Inchal, Belgaum
67. TSPS Mandal Ayurvedic College, Sindhagi, Bijapur
68. RET Ayurvedic Medical College, Raichur
69. Sri HES's Ayurvedic College, Bhawaninagar, Gulbarga
70. KPSVS Ayurvedic Medical College, Manvi, Raichur
71. SBVVS Ayurvedic College, Bagalkot
72. SBVMG Ayurvedic College, Jamkhandi, Bagalkot
73. Sri SBS Ayurvedic Medical College, Mundargi, Gadag
74. DGM Ayurvedic Medical College, Gadag
75. VVS Rural Ayurvedic Medical College & Research Centre, Badami, Bagalkot
76. KBS's Rural Ayurvedic Medical College, Ramnagar, Belgaum
77. BM Jain Ayurvedic Medical College & Research Centre, Badami, Bagalkot
78. Kalidas Ayurvedic Medical College, Badami, Bagalkot
79. RGES's Ayurvedic Medical College, Ron
80. Muniyal Institute of Ayurvedic Medical Sciences, Manipal
81. Dhanvatari Ayurvedic College & Hospital, Siddhpur, Uttar Kannada
82. Ramakrishna Ayurvedic Medical College, Bangalore
83. Sri DM College of Ayurved, Udupi

Kerala

84. Govt. Ayurvedic College, Dhanvatrinagar, Ernakulam

85. VPS Variar Ayurvedic College, Kottakkal, Malappuram
86. Vaidyaratnam Ayurvedic College, Ollur, Trichur
87. Govt. Ayurvedic College, Kannur
88. Govt. Ayurvedic College, Thiruvanathapura

Madhya Pradesh

89. Government Ayurvedic College & Hospital, Gwalior
90. Government Ayurvedic College, Jabalpur
91. Government Dhanvantari Ayurvedic College, Ujjain
92. Pt. Shivashakti Lal Sharma Ayurved Mahavidyalaya, Ratlam
93. Government Ayurvedic College & Hospital, Burhanpur
94. Government Ashtang Ayurvedic College & Hospital, Indore
95. Government Ayurvedic College & Hospital, Rewa
96. Pt. Khushilal Sharma Ayurvedic Mahavidyalaya, Bhopal
97. Rajiv Gandhi Ayurved Mahavidyalaya, Shahpur, Bhopal

Maharashtra

98. Tilak Ayurved Mahavidyalaya, Pune
99. Ashtnag Mahavidyalaya, Pune
100. Sri Gangadhar Shastri Gune Ayurvedic Mahavidyalaya, Ahmednagar
101. KVTR Ayurvedic College, Dhule
102. Vasant Dada Patil Ayurvedic College, Sangli
103. Ayurved Mahavidyalaya, Ahmednagar
104. MAMSBS Ayurvedic College, Pune
105. College of Ayurveda & Research Centre, Akurdi, Pune
106. SST Ayurveda Mahavidyalaya, Sangamner, Ahmednagar
107. VKRYoga & AS Siddhakala Ayurved Mahavidyalaya, Sangamner,

Ahmednagar

108. BSDT Ayurved Vishwashanti Dham, Wagholi, Pune
109. CSMSS Ayurved Mahavidhyalaya, Aurangabad
110. MSPM Ayurvedic College, Aurangabad
111. Govt. Ayurvdic College, Osmanabad
112. SCM Ayurvedic Vaidak Mahavidyalaya
113. SGR Ayurvedic Mahavidyalaya, Solapur
114. Yashvant Ayurved Mahavidyalaya, Kodoli, Kolhapur
115. Ayurved Mahavidyalaya, Peth, Basegaon, Kolhapur-
116. GES Ayurvedic Medical College, Ranklaves, Kolhapur
117. DCS Ayurvedic Mahavidyalaya, Deopur, Dhule
118. Dada SSN Ayurvedic Mahavidyalaya, Nandgaon, Dhule
119. Ayurved Medical College, Chalisgaon, Jalgaon

120. Chaitanya Ayurved Mahavidyalaya, Saketgaon, Bhusawal
121. RA Poddar Ayurvedic College, Worli, Mumbai
122. SKG Mittal Punarvasu Ayurvedic Mahavidyalaya, Mumbai
123. Ayurved Mahavidyalaya, Sion, Mumbai
124. YMT Ayurvedic Medical College, Navi Mumbai, Mumbai
125. RJVSBS Ayurved Mahavidyalaya Savanwadi, Sindhudurg
126. Nalsopara Ayurvedic Medical College, Nalsopara, Tahne
127. BSM Ayurvedic Mahavidyalaya, Nagpur
128. Government Ayurvedic Mahavidyalaya, Nagpur
129. Shri Ayurved Mahavidyalaya, Nagpur
130. Sri RK Tosniwal Qyurved Mahavidyalaya, Akola
131. Vidarbha Ayurved Mahavidyalaya, Amravati
132. Sri Gurudev Ayurved Mahavidyalaya, Amravati
133. DMM Ayurved Mahavidyalaya, Yeotmal
134. Sri GMS Ayurved Mahavidyalaya, Pushad, Yotmal
135. Gramin Ayurved Mahavidyalaya, Patur, Akola
136. Lt. SRC Ayurved College, Chikhili, Bildana
137. APESMS Ayurved Medical College, Kudwa, Gondia
138. SSSS Medical College, Yashwant Mandal, Nashik
139. LKR Ayurved Medical College, Khede, Kolhapur
140. VVPF Ayurvedic Medical College, Sevagaon, Ahmednagar
141. DY Patil College of Ayurved & Research Centre, Pimpri, Pune
142. Govt. Ayurved College, Wazirabad, Nanded
143. AD Ayurvedic Medical College, Islampur, Sangali
144. Manjara Ayurvedic College & Hospital, Latur
145. Dhanvantari Ayurved Medical College, Latur
146. EAR Ayurvedic Medical College, Manchi Hill, Ahmednagar
147. National Medical College of Ayurvedic Sciences, Sangamner
148. Chhatrapati Shivaji Ayurvedic Medical College & Hospital, Ashti, Beed
149. Sumananjali Pratisthan Ayurved Medical College, Aurangabad
150. NP Ayurved Medical College, Aurangabad
151. RP Ayurved mahavidyalaya & Rugnalaya, Puma, Prabhani
152. JJM Women's Ayurved Medical College, Jeysinghpur, Kolhapur
153. Jupiter Ayurved Medical College, Nagpur
154. BV College of Ayurveda, Shankarpur, Pune

Orissa

155. Gopalbandhu Ayurved Mahavidyalaya, Puri-
156. IGM Ayurvedic Medical College & Hospital, Jagamara,

Bhubaneswar

157. Mayurbhanj Ayurved Mahavidyalaya, Takhtapur, Mayurbhanj

158. KATS Ayurved Mahavidyalaya, Ankushpur, Ganjam
159. Govt. Ayurvedic College, Bolangir
160. Sri N. Ayurved College & Research Institute, Bargarh

Punjab

161. Government Ayurvedic Mahavidyalaya, Patiala
162. Desh Bhagat Ayurvedic College & Hospital, Amloh, Fatehgarh Saheb
163. Sri SSMD Ayurvedic College & Hospital, Moga, Faridkot
164. Mai Bhago Ayurvedic College for Women, Muktasar
165. SKSES Ayurvedic Medical College & Hospital, Sarabha, Ludhiana
166. Guru Nanak Ayurvedic Medical College& Hospital, Muktasar
167. Guru Nanak Ayurvedic College & Research Institute, Gopalpur, Ludhiana
168. LN Ayurvedic College, Amritsar
169. Dayananda Ayurvedic College, Jullundhar City

Rajasthan

170. Parashrampuria Rajasthan Ayurvedic Mahavidyalaya, Sikar
171. National Institute of Ayurveda, Jaipur
172. MMMM Government Ayurvedic college, Udaipur
173. Sri Bhanwarlal Dugar Ayurvedic Vishwabharati, Sardarshahr, Churu

Tamil Nadu

174. Sri Venkataramana Ayurvedic College, Chennai Ayurved College, Coimbatore
175. Dharma Ayurved College, Sriperumbudur, Kanchipuram
176. Sri Sankara College of Ayurveda, Tiruchrirapalli
177. Sri Sairam Ayurvedic Medical College & Research Centre, Poonthamdalam, Kanchpuram-
178. Sri Jayendra Saraswati Ayurvedic College, Thiruvallur, Nazarathpet

Uttaranchal

179. Uttaranchal Ayurvedic College, Dehradun
180. Government Gurukur Kangri Ayurvedic College & Hospital, Hardwar
181. Government Rishikul Ayurvedic College, Hardwar

Uttar Pradesh

182. Government Ayurvedic College & Hospital, Lucknow
183. Rajkiya Lalit Hari Ayurved College & Hospital, Pilibhit
184. Bundelkhand Government Ayurved College & Hospiotal, Jhansi
185. Government Ayurvedic College and Hospital. Atarra, Banda

186. SRM Government Ayurvedic College & Hospital, Bareilly
187. Swami Kalyandeo Government Ayurvedic College, Rampur, Muzaffarnagar
188. Sri L B Shastri Memorial Government Ayurvedic College & Hospital, Handia, Allahabad.
189. Sham-e-Ghausia Minority Ayurvedic Medical College & Hospital, Saheri, Ghazipur
190. Aligarh Ayurved and Unani Medical College & Hospital, Aligarh
191. Institute of Medical Sciences, Faculty of Ayurveda, BHU, Varanasi
192. Government Ayurvedic College & Hospital, Jagatganj, Varanasi West Bengal
193. JB Roy Government Ayurvedic Medical College & Hospital, Kolkata
194. Institute of Post-graduate Ayurvedic Education & Research, Kolkata

APPENDIX C

LIST OF UNANI COLLEGES AS IN EARLY 2003

Andhra Pradesh

1. Governemtn Nizamia Tibbia College, Charminar, Hyderabad
2. Dr. Abdul Haq Unani Medical College &Hospital, Kurnool

Bihar

3. Govt. Tibbia College, Kadam Kuan, Patna
4. Zulfiquar Haider Medical College and Hospital, Nawalpur, Siwan
5. Saifia Unani Medical College and Hospital. Leheriasarai, Darbhanga
6. Nizamia Unanai Medical College and Hospital, Gaya

Delhi

7. Ayurved and Ynani Tibbias College, New Delhi
8. Faculty of Medicine, Jamia Hamdard, New Delhi

Jammu & Kashmir

9. Unani Medical College, Institute of Mdical Sciences, Srinagar
10. Kashmir Tibbia College, Hospital & Research Centre, Srinagar

Karnataka

11. Government Unanai Medical College, Bangalore
12. Luqman Medical College & Hospital, Bijapur
13. Tipu Sultan Shaheed Educational Trust Unani Medical College, Mysore

Madhya Pradesh

14. Saifia Hamida Unani Medical College and Hospital, Burhanpur, Khandwa.
15. Al-Farooque Unani Tibbi College, Indore
16. Hakim syed Ziaul Hassan, govt. Unani Medical College, Bhopal

Maharashtra

17. Anjumane Islam Tibbi College and Hospital, Nagpada, Mumbai
18. Mohammadia Tibbi College and Hospital, Nasik
19. Unani Medical College and Hospital, Pune
20. Taj Tibbia College and Hospital, Nagpur
21. Ahmed Garib Medical College and Hospital, Akkalkuwa, Dhule
22. Iqra Society's Unani Medical College, Jalgaon

Rajasthan

23. Rajputan Ayurved and Tibbia Medical College, Jaipur

Tamil Nadu

24. Government Unani Medical College, Chennai

Uttaranchal

25. KGN Unani Medical College, Dehradun

Uttar Pradesh

26. Govt. Takmil-ul-Tib college and Hospital, Lucknow
27. Government Unani Medical College, Allahabad
28. Jamia Tibbia Deoband, Saharanpur
29. Ibne-Sina Tibbia College and Hospital, Azamgarh
30. Deoband Unani Medical College, Sharanpur
31. Allama Iqbal Unani Medical College, Muzaffar Nagar
32. Aligarh Unani Medical College and Hospital, AMU, Aligarh
33. Ajmal Khan Tibbia College, Aligarh
34. Sham-e-Ghausia Minority Unani Medical College, Ghazipur

West Bengal

35. Calcutta Unani Medical College and Hospital, Kalikata

APPENDIX D

LIST OF HOMEOPATHIC COLLEGES AS IN EARLY 2003

Andhra Pradesh

1. JSPS Govt. Homeopathic Medical College, Ramnathpur, Hyderabad
2. Dr. Gururaju Govt. Homeopathic Medical College, Gudiwada, Krishna Dist,
3. Govt. Homeopahic Medical College, Ravindranagar, Cudappah
4. Dr. A. Ramalingatha Govt. Homeopatheic Medical College, Rajmundry

Assam

5. Dr. JK Saikia govt. Homeopathic Medical College, Jorhat
6. Assam Government Homeopathic college, Haibergaon, Nagaon
7. SJN Government Homeopathic Medical College, Guwahati

Arunachal Pradesh

8. North-EastRegional Homeopathic Medical College and Hospital, Itanagar

Bihar

9. R.B.T.S. Govt. Homeopathic Medical College, Muzaffarpur
10. Gaya Homeopathic Medical College, Gaya
11. Bihar Homeopathic Medical College, Patna
12. Magadh Homeopathic Medical College, Biharsharif
13. Temple of Hanneman Homeopathic Medical College and Hospital, Katihar
14. MM Homeopathic Medical College and Hospital, Soranpuri, Patna
15. Kant Homeopathic Medical College and Hospital, Khilvat, Hajipur
16. Patna Homeopathic Medical College, Patna
17. Sinha Homeopathic Medical College and Hospital, Lahrisarai, Darbhanga
18. Dr. Halim Homeopathic Medical College and Hospital, Ekmighat, Laharia Sarai
19. Mangla Homeopathic medical College and Hospital, Srinagar, Siwan
20. BNM Homeopathic Medical College and Hospital, Saharsa
21. GDM Homeopathic Medical College and Hospital, East Ramakrishna nagar, Patna

Chandigarh

22. Homeopathic Medical College and Hospital, Chandigarh

Chhattisgarh

23. Raipur Homeopathic Medical College and Hospital, Raipur
24. C.C. Homeopahic Medical College, Bilaspur

Delhi

25. Nehru Homeopathic Medical College, Defence colony, New Delhi
26. Dr. B.R. Sur Homeopathic Medical College and Hospital, Motbagh II, New Delhi

Goa

1. Kamaxi Devi, Homeopathic medical College, Hill Tp Shiroda.

Gujarat

1. Anand Homeopathic Medical College and Research Institute, Anand
2. Dr, VH Dave Homeopathic Medical College, Anand
3. Smt. A.J. Savita Homeopathic medical College and Resarch Institute, Nagpara, Mehsana
4. Ahmedabad homeopathic Medical College, Ahmedabad
5. Sri Shamlaji Homeopathic Medical College and Research Institute, Godhra
6. Gujarat Homeopathic Medical College, Vadodara
7. Baroda Homeopathic Medical College, Varodara
8. Rajkot Homeopathic medical College, Rajkot
9. SCEMRT Homeopathic Medical College, Rajkot
10. CDP Homeopathic College, Surat
11. Sri C.N. Kothari Homeopathic Medical College and Research Centre, Surat
12. SM Mahila Homeopathic Medical College, Vadodara
13. Swami Vivekanand Homeopathic Medical College, Bhavnagar
14. Sri C.N. Homeopathic Medical College, Vyara, dist. Surat

Haryana

1. Navyug S.S. Brahmanand Homeopathic medical College and Hospital, Karnal

Himachal Pradesh

1. Solan Homeopathic Medical College and Hospital, Solan
2. Himalayan Homeopathic Medical College and Research Centre, Solan

Jharkhand

1. Homeopathic Medical College and Hospital, Mihijam, Dhumka Dist.
2. Singhbhum homeopathic medical College and Hospital, Jamshedpur

Kanataka

1. Government Homeopathic Medical College, Bangalore
2. Homeopathic Medical College and Hospital, Gulbarga
3. Father Myller's Homeopathic College, Kanakandy, S. Kanara
4. AM Sheikh Homeopathic Medical College, Belgaum
5. Bhartesh Homeopathic medical College, Belgaim
6. Shiv Basav Homeopathic Medical College, Belgaum
7. LEA's Homeopathic Medical College and Hospital, Dharwad
8. SB Srikolu Homeopathic medical College, Sankeshwar, Belgaum
9. Dakshin Bharat Hindi Prachar Sabha, d. B.D. Jatti Homeopathic Medical college and Hospital, Dharwad
10. Bhagwan Buddha Homeopathic Medical College and Hospital, Bnngalore
11. Al-Amaan Homeopathic Medical College, Bijapur

Kerala

1. ANSS Homeopathic Medical College, Kottayam
2. Dr. Padiyar Memorial Homeopathic Medical College, Ernaculam
3. Government Homeopathic Medical College, Iranimttom
4. Sri Vidya Dheeraj Homeopathic Medical College, Thruanantapuram
5. Government Homeopathic Medical College, Calicut

Madhya Pradesh

1. Government Homeopathic Medical College and Hospital, Bhopal
2. Hahnemann Homeopathic Medical College,, Bhopal
3. Lal Bhadur Shastry Homeopathic Medical College, Bhopal
4. Narayanshri Homeopathic Medical College, Bhopal
5. RKDF HomeopathicMmedical College and Hospital, Mandideep, Dist. Raisen
6. Shivang Homeopathic Medical College and Hospital, Bhopal
7. Pt. Ravishankar Shukla Memorial Homeopathic Medical College, Indore
8. District Homeopathic Medical College and Hospital, Ratlam
9. Vasundhara Raje Homeopathic Medical College and Hospital, Gwalior
10. SRSSPS Homeopathic Medical College, Gormi, Bhind
11. Rajiv Gandhi Homeopathic Medical College, Ondore
12. Sri Gujarati Samaj's Homeopathic Mrdicl College, Indore
13. Indira Gandhi Memorial Homeopathic Medical College, Prakashnagar, Dhar
14. Sendhwa Homeopathic Medical College, Sendhwa
15. Swami Pravanand Homeopathic Medical College and Hospital, Chhatarpur
16. SMT. S.M. Deo Homeopathic Medical College and Research Institute, Balaghat
17. Mahatmas Gandhi Homeopathic Medical College, Jabalpur
18. Sagar Homeopathic Medical College, Hospital and Research Centre, Sagar
19. Anushree Homeopathic College and Hospital, Jabalpur

20. Sophia Homeopathic medical College, Gwalior
21. Homeopathic Medical College, Akola
22. PHSPM's Homeopathic Medical college, Khamgaon
23. Sri janata Homeopathic medical College, Akola
24. Pt. J.L. Nehru Memorial Institute of Homeopathic Medical Sciences, Amravati

Maharashtra

1. Lokmanya medical Foundation's Homeopathic medical College, Pune
2. D.S. Homeopathic Medical College, Pune
3. KSM Homeiopathic Medical College, Nagapur, Dist. Pune
4. Smt. Kanchanbai Babulalji Abad Homeopathic Medical College, Chandwad, Dist. Nasik
5. Motwala Homeopathic Medical College and Hospital, Gangapur, Nasik
6. MHF's Homeopathic Medical College and Hospital, Sangamner, Ahmednagar
7. Ahmednagar Homeopathic Medical College, Ahmednagar
8. Anantrao Kanse Homeopathic Medical College, Jumnar, Pune district
9. Kisan D, M. homeopathic Medical College, Shirpur, Dhule Dist.
10. Smt. Chandaben Mohanbhai Patel Homeopathic Medical College, Mumbai
11. Venguria Homeopathic Medical College and Hospital, Bhalawad, dist. Sindhudurg
12. Yerala Homeopathic Medical College and Research Centre, Mumbai
13. VVSMD Homeopathic Medical College, Apati, Ratnagiru Dist.
14. VYC homeopathic Medical College, Kolhapur
15. Sri J.P.E. Society's Homeopathic College, Kolhapur
16. Samanth Education Trust's homeopathic Medical College, Satara
17. JJMT Homeopathic Medical College, Jayasinghpur, Dist. Kolhapur
18. DS &VK Homeopathic Medical College, Kolhapur
19. GNR Homeopathic Medical College, Sholapur
20. Sri Takhatmal Sriballabh Homeopathic Medical College, Rajapet, Amravati
21. Homeopathic Medical College, Akola
22. PHSPM Homeopathic Medical College, Khamgaon, dist. Buldana
23. Sri Janta Homeopathic Medical College, Akola
24. Pt. Jawaharlal Memorial Institute of Homeopathic Medical Sciences, Amravati.
25. Nagpur College of Homeopathy and Hospital, nagpur
26. Gondia Homeopathic medical College and Hospital, Gondia
27. P.B. Homeopathic medical College and Hospital, Chandrapur
28. Anantbharati Homeopathic Medical College, Nagpur
29. Sri Bhagwan Hoeopathic Medical College and Indira Gandhi Homeopathic Hospital, Aurangabad
30. S.K. Homeopathic Medical College, Beed
31. DKMM Homeopathic medical College, Aurangabad
32. Foster Development homeopathic Medical College, Aurangabad
33. KSPM's Latur Homeopathic Medical College, Latur
34. BSPMPSK Homeopathic Medical college, Hospital and Research, New Nanded

35. PRS's PD Jain Homeopathic Medical College, Parbhani
36. Dr, DY Patil Homeopathic Medical college, Pimpri
37. National Medical college of Homeo sciences, Sangamnerm Ahmednagar
38. Dhanvantary homeopathic medical College, hospital and Research Centre, Kamatwade, Nasik
39. PSPM's Mahila Homeopathic Medical College, Kilgiri nagar, Sholapur
40. Bhaati Vidyapeeth homeopathic Medical College, Pune
41. Sri CMEMM's homeopathic Medical CollegeBhusawal, Jalgaon
42. RMSS Homeopathic Medical College and Hospital, Gandhingaj, Kolhapur
43. CHKHomeopathic Medical College, Alibagh, Raigad
44. Virar homeopathic medical College, Virar, Thane
45. GP Homeopathic College, Miraj
46. Dr. M L Dhawale Memorial Homeopathic Institute, Chambur, Mumbai
47. Dr. Ulhas Patil Homeopathic Medical College, Jalgaon

Orissa

1. Dr. A.C. Chandra Homeopathic Medical College and Hospital, Bhubaneswar
2. Cuttack Homeopathic Medical college, Cuttack
3. Biju pattanayak Homeopathic Medical College, Brahmapur, Ganjam
4. Orissa College of Homeopathy and Research, Sambalpur
5. Utkalmani homeopathic Medical College, Rourkela
6. Mayurbhanj Homeopathic Medical College and Hospital, Baripada, Mayurbhanj

Punjab

1. Homeopathic Medical College, Abhore
2. Lord Mahavira Homeopathic Medical College, Ludhiana
3. Sri Guru Nanak Dev Homeopathic Medical College, Ludhiana
4. Institute of Homeopathic medical Education and Research, Chunnikalan, Fatehgarh
5. Kalyan Homeopathic Medical College, Taran Taran, Amritsar

Rajasthan

1. Dr. MP Khuteta RajasthanHomeopathic Medical college, jaipur
2. Yuvaraj Pratap singh Memorial Homeopathic medical College, Alar
3. Bharatiya Homeopathic Medical College and Hospital, Bharatpur
4. Rajasthan Vidyapeeth Homeopathic Medical College, Dabok
5. Swasthya kalyan homeopathic Medical College and Research Centre, Jaipur
6. MNS Homeopathic medical and Research Institute, Bikaner

Tamil Nadu

1. Govt. Homeopathic Medical College and Hospital, Thirumangalam, Madurai

2. White memorial Homeopathic Medical College, Attoor Vaayanur, Kanyakumari
3. Vinayak Mission Homeopathic Medical College, Salem
4. Dr. Hannemann Homeopathic Medical College, Salem
5. Nethra Homeopathic Medical College and Hospital, Coimbatore
6. Sharada Krishna Memorial Homeopathic Medical College, Kulasekharam, Kanya Kumari.
7. Venkateswara Homeopathic Medical College and Hospital, Chennai
8. Sri Sai Ram Homeopathic medical College and Research Centre, Poonthamdalam village, Kanchpuram District.
9. RVS medical Trust Homeopathic Medical College, Sulur, Coimbatore
10. Tamil nadu homeopathic Medical College, Salem
11. H. Homeopathic Medical College, Kaneripalli.

Uttar Pradesh

1. Bakson Homeopathic Medical College and Hospital, Noida
2. State national Homeopathic Medical College and Hospital, Lucknow
3. Pt. Jawaharlal Nehru State Homeopathic Medical College and Hospital, Kanpur
4. State Lal Bhahadur sashtri Homeopathic Medical College and Hospital, Allahabad
5. State Brij Kishore Homeopathic Medical College and Hospital, Faizabad
6. State KGKHomeopathic Medical College and Hospital, Moradabad
7. State Homeopathic medical College and Hospital, Ghazipur
8. State Shridurgaji Homeopathic medical College and Hospital, Azamgarh
9. Sri Sai Nath PG Institute of Homeopathy, Allahabad

West Bengal

1. Bengal Homeopathic Medical College and Hospital, Ismile, Asansol
2. Vivekanand Homeopathic medical College and hospital, Birbhum
3. D, N. De Homeopathic Medical College and Hospital, Kalikata
4. Homeopathic Medical College and Hospital, Kharagpur
5. Mahesh Bhattacharya Homeopathic Medical College and Hospital, Howrah
6. Metropolitan Homeopathic medical College and Hospital, Sodepur, Dist. 24-Pargana
7. Homeopathic Medical College and Hospital, Midnapur
8. West Bengal national Institute of Homeopathy, Kalikata
9. NC Chakravarty Homeopathic Medical College and Hospital, Howrah
10. P.C. Memorial Homeopathic Mdical College and Hospital, Kalikata
11. The Calcutta Homeopathic Medical College and Hospital, Kalkata

APPENDIX E

LIST OF DENTAL COLLEGES AS IN 2003 AD

Andhra Pradesh (13)

1. Army College of Dental Sciences, Secunderabad
2. CVS Krishnamurthy Teja Institute of Dental Sciences & Research, Tirupathi
3. Government Dental College and Hospital, Hyderabad
4. Geetam Dental College, Vishakhapatnam
5. Kamiyeni Institute of Dental Sciences, Narketpally, Nalgonda
6. Leonara Institute of Dental Sciences, Rajamundry
7. Mamata Dental College, Khammam
8. NTR UHS Dental College, Vijaiwada
9. Narayana Dental College, Nellore
10. Sibar Institute of Dental Sciences, Takelpaddu, Guntur
11. Sri Sai College of Dental Surgery, Vikarabad, Rangareddy
12. St. Joseph Dental College, Dugirala, Elluru
13. Vishnu Dental College, Kovvadu, Bhimavaram

Assam (1)

14. Regional Dental College, Gauhati

Bihar (7)

15. Dr. B.R. Ambedkar Institute of Dental Sciences and Hospital, Patna
16. Mithila Minority Dental College and Hospital, Loheriasarai, Darbhanga
17. Patna Dental college and Hospital, Patna
18. Buddha Institute of Dental Sciences, Patna
19. Sarjang Dental College, Darbhanga
20. Dr. SM Naqvi Imam Dental College, Behera
21. Darbhanga Dental College, Darbhanga

Chandigarh (1)

22. Oral Health Science Centre, Chandigarh

Delhi (2)

23. Maulana Azad Medical College (Dental Wing), New Delhi
24. AIMS Dental Surgery, New Delhi

Goa (1)

25. Government Dental College and Hospital, Goa

Gujarat (4)

26. Government Dental College and Hospital, Ahmedabad
27. Government Dental College and Hospital, Jamnagar
28. KM Shal Dental College, Baroda
29. Manubhai Patel Dental College, Baroda

Haryana (6)

30. BRS Institute of Medical Sciences, Panchkula
31. DAV Centenary Dental College, Yamuna Nagar
32. Dental College (Medical Campus), Rohtak
33. Maharshi Markandeshwar College of Dental Sciences & Research, Mulana, Ambala
34. Sri Baba Mastanath Dental College and Hospital, Rohtak
35. Sri Govind Tricentenary Dental College, Hospital and Research Centre, Budhera, Gurgaon

Himachal Pradesh (4)

36. Bhojia Dental College & Hospital, Budh
37. H.P. Government Dental College and Hospital, Shimla
38. Himachal Dental College, Sundar Nagar, Mandi
39. MNDAV Dental College & Hospital, Solan

Jammu and Kashmir (1)

40. Government Dental College, Srinagar

Karnataka (41)

41. AJ Institute of Dental Sciences, Mangalore
42. AME's Dental College, Raichur
43. Coorg Institute of Dental Sciences, Coorg
44. Government Dental College, Bangalore
45. RV Dental College, Bangalore

46. Dr. Shyamla Reddy Dental College, Bangalore
47. Dayanand Sagar College of Dental Sciences, Bangalore
48. HKDET's Dental College & Hospital, Humnabad
49. VS Dental college, Bangalore
50. KGF College of Dental Sciences, Bangalore
51. Bangalore institute of Dental Sciences and Hospital, Bangalore
52. MS Ramaiah Dental College, Bangalore
53. Maratha Mandal's Dental College and Research Centre, Belgaum
54. Raja Rajeshwari Dental College, Bangalore
55. KLE Society's Dental College, Bangalore
56. Maruti Dental College, Bangalore
57. Oxford Dental College, Bangalore
58. Rajiv Gandhi College of Dental Sciences, Bangalore
59. Babu jagjivan Ram Dental College, Bangalore
60. NSVK Dental College and Hospital, Bangalore
61. Krishnadevraya College of Dental Sciences, Bangalore
62. Sri Sevalal College, Bangalore
63. PMN Memorial Dental College and Hospital, Bagalkot
64. SB Patil Institute for Dental Sciences, Bidar
65. SJM Dental College, Chitradurga
66. Bapuji Dental College, Davangiri
67. College of Dental Sciences, Davangiri
68. SDM College of Dental Sciences, Dharwad
69. HKE Society's Dental College, Gulbarga
70. A.L.Badar Dental College, Gulbarga
71. Sri SN Institute of Dental Sciences, Hassan
72. Shravathi Dental College, Shimoga
73. Farookquia Dental College, Mysore
74. ABSM Institute of Dental Sciences, Mangalore
75. College of Dental Surgery, Mangalore
76. Venepoya Dental College, Mangalore
77. College of Dental Surgery, Manipal
78. JSS Dental College, Mysore
79. Sri Siddhartha Dental College, Tumkur
80. AL Ameem Dental College, Bijapur
81. KVG Dental College, Sulia

Kerala (5)

82. Dental College, Medical Campus, Trivandrum
83. Dental College, Medical College Campus, Calicut
84. Government Dental College, Kottayam
85. PMS College of Dental Sciences & Research, Vittapara, Thiruvananthapuram
86. Mar Baselios Dental College, Thankalam, Ernakulam

Madhya Pradesh (4)

87. College of Dentistry, Indore
88. School of Dental Sciences & Hospital, Indore
89. Modern Dental College and Research Centre, Nainod, Indore
90. People's College of Dental Sciences & Research Centre, Bhopal

Maharashtra (23)

91. Armed Forces Dental College, Pune
92. Government Dental College and Hospital, Aurangabad
93. Government Dental College, Mumbai
94. Nair Hospital Dental College, Mumbai
95. Government Dental College, Nagpur
96. D.Y. Patil Dental College, Navi Mumbai
97. Bhartiya Vidyapeeth Dental College and Hospital, Pune
98. Pravara Rural Dental College, Loni, Ahmednagar
99. Jamnalal Goenka Dental college, Akola
100. V.P. Dental College and Hospital, Sangli
101. C.S.M.S.S, Dental College, Aurangabad
102. VYW Society's Dental College, Amravati
103. Mahatma Gandhi Vidyama NDIR'S Dental College & Hospital, Navi Mumbai
104. Sharad Pawar Dental College & Hospital, Wardha
105. Vidya Shikshan Prasarak Mandal's Dental College & Research Centre, Nagpur
106. Yerela Medical Dental College, Navi Mumbai
107. DY Patil Dental College & Hospital, Pimpri
108. MA Rangoonwala College of Dental Sciences& Research Centre, Pune
109. Tatya Saheb Kore Dental College & Research Centre, New Paragaon
110. Taena Dental College, Navi Mumbai
111. Anna SahebChudaman Patil Memorial Dental College, Dhule
112. Pandit Deen Dayal Upadhyay Dental College, Solapur
113. SMBT Dental College, Amrutanagar

Orissa (2)

114. SCB Medical College (Dental Wing), Cuttack
115. VM Lord Jagannath Institute of Dental Sciences & Research, Bhubaneswar

Pondicherry (1)

116. Mahatma Gandhi Dental College, Pondicherry

Punjab (11)

117. Punjab Government Dental College and Hospital, Amritsar

118. Government Dental College and Hospital, Patiala
119. Christian Dental College, Ludhiana
120. SGRD Institute of Dental Sciences and Research, Amritsar
121. Dashnesh Institute of Reseach and Dental Sciences, Faridkot
122. Guru Nanakdeo Dental College & Research Institute, Sunam
123. Baba Jaswant Singh Dental College, Hospital and Research Institute, Ludhiana
124. Khalsa Dental College & Hospital, Nangal Kalan, Mansa
125. Desh Bhagat Dental College, Muktsar
126. National Dental College & Hospital, Gulabgarh, Derabasi
127. Laxmibai Institute of Dental Sciences & Hospital, Patiala

Rajasthan (4)

128. SMS Medical College (Dental Wing), Jaipur
129. Darshan Dental College, Udaipur
130. Pacific Dental College, Udaipur
131. Jaipur Dental College, Jaipur

Tamil Nadu (14)

132. JKK Nataraja Dental Hospital, Komarpalayam
133. Tamil Nadu Dental College, Chennai
134. Savita Dental College and Hospital, Chennai
135. Rajas Dental College, Chennai
136. Sri Balaji Dental College, Chennai
137. Meenakshi Ammal Dental College, Chennai
138. Sri Ramchandra Dental College, Chennai
139. SRM Dental College, Chennai
140. Thai Moogambigai Dental College & Hospital, Chennai
141. Rajah Muthiah Dental College and Hospital, Annamalainagar
142. VMS Dental College, Salem
143. Rajas Dental College, Vadakankulam
144. Shri Mookambika Institute of Dental Sciences, Nagarcoil
145. Shri Ramkrishnan Dental College & Hospital, Coimbatore

Uttar Pradesh (19)

146. Awadh Institute of Dental Sciences, Lucknow
147. KGMC Faculty of Dental Sciences, Lucknow
148. Sardar Patel Institute of Dental Sciences, Lucknow
149. BHU Institute of Medical Sciences (Dental Wing), Varanasi)
150. Rama Dental College and Hospital, Kanpur
151. Subharati Dental College, Meerut
152. Santosh Dental College, Ghaziabad

153. VMS Internationasl Dental College, Mau, Sitapur
154. Saraswati Dental College, Lucknow
155. Kothiwal Dental College & Research Centre, Moradabad
156. DJ College of Dental Science & Research, Modinagar
157. Dental College, AMU, Aligarh
158. UP College of Dental Sciences & Research, Lucknow
159. ITS Centre for Dental Studies & Research, Muradnagar, Ghaziabad
160. Harsharan Das Dental College, Ghaziabad
161. Career Institute of Dental Sciences & Hospital, Lucknow
162. Kantidevi Dental College, Mathura
163. Institute of Dental Studies and Technologies, Modinagar
164. Institute of Dental Sciences, Bareilly

West Bengal (2)

165. Dr. R. Ahmed Dental College, Kolkata
166. North Bengal Dental College, Darjeeling

APPENDIX F

LIST OF COLLEGES PHARMACY, AS IN 2003

Andhra Pradesh

1. Dept. of Pharmceytical Science, AP University, Waltair
2. University College of Pharmaceutical Sciences, Kaktiya Unversity, Warangal

Assam

There is only one school of Pharmacy offering two year diploma course.

Bihar and Jharkhand

3. Anisabad, RSL Yadav College of Pharmacy, Patna
4. Bihar College of Pharmacy, Patna
5. Dept. of Pharmaceutical Sciences, Mesra, Ranchi
6. Dept. of Pharmacy, Muzaffarpur Institute of Technology, Muzaffarpur
7. Indian Institute of Pharmacy, Jamshedpur

Chandigarh

8. Department of Pharmateucal Sciences, Punjab University.

Delhi

9. New Delhi college of Pharmacy, Pushpa Vihar, New Delhi
10. Faculty of Pharmacy, Hamdard University, New Delhi

Goa

11. Goa college of Pharmacy, Panji.

Gujarat

12. A R. College of Pharmacy and G.H. Patel Institute pf Pharmacy, Sardar Patel University, Vallabh Vidyasagar
13. B.K. Modi, Government Pharmacy College, Rajkot

14. Lallubhai. M. College of Pharmacy, Ahmedabad
15. Dept. of Pharmacy, MS University, Baroda

Haryana

There are ten Schools of Pharmacy, each offering only two-year diploma Course

Karnataka

16. College of Pharmacy, Bangalore
17. Bapuji Pharmacy College, Davangere
18. Bashveshwar School of Pharmacy, Bijapur
19. College of Pharmaceutical Sciences, Kasturba Gandhi Medical College, Manipal.
20. H.L.Thimme Gowda Pharmacy College, kengal, Bangalore
21. Farooqia college of Pharmacy, Mysore
22. Gautam College of Pharmacy, Bangalore
23. Golden College of Pharmacy, Kolar
24. Govt. College of Pharmacy, Bangalore
25. HKE Society's Institute of Pharmacy, Bangalore
26. JSS College of Pharmacy, Mysore
27. KLE Society's College of Pharmacy, Bangalore
28. KLE Society's College of Pharmacy, Belgaum
29. KRE Society's Karnataka B. Pharmacy College, Bidar
30. Kapanidhi College of Pharmacy, Bangalore
31. Luqman College of Pharmacy, Gulbarga
32. Maratha Mandal's college of Pharmacy, Belgaum
33. College of Pharmateucal Sciences, Manipal
34. MMU College of Pharmacy, Ramnagaram, Bangalore Distt.
35. National College of Pharmacy Shimoga
36. NGSM Institue of Phatmaceutical Sciences, Derlakette, near Mangalore
37. PRS College of Pharmacy, Hanumanth Nagar, Bangalore
38. RK Samiti's Kishanlal College of Pharmacy, Nawbad, Bidar
39. SAG Tilsi College of Pharmacy, Harpanhalli, Bellary Distt.
40. SJM College of Pharmacy, Chitradurga
41. Sri K. Venkatapatheppa College of Pharmacy, Chikmaglur
42. Sri Siddha Ganga College of Pharmacy, Tumkur
43. Sri Siddha Ganga College of Pharmacy, Bangalore
44. TVM College of Pharmacy, Gandhinagar, Bellary
45. Vishweshwarapura Institute of Pharmaceutical Sciences, Bangalore
46. V.L. College of Pharmacy, Raichur

Kerala

47. Trivandrum College of Pharmaceutical Sciences, Trivandrum

Madhya Pradesh

48. Dept. of Pharmaceutical Sciences, Dr. HS Gaur University, Sagar
49. College of Pharmacy, SGSITS Campus, Indore

Maharashta

50. A.B. College of Pharmacy, Sangli
51. B. V, Poona College of Pharmacy, Pune
52. Bombay College of Pharmacy, Kalina
53. College of Pharmacy, Nasik
54. GUS College of Pharmacy, SNDT Women's University, Sir Vithaldas Vidya Vihar, Santa Cruz, Mumbai
55. Division of Pharmacy, Dept of Chemical Technology, University of Bombay, Mumbai
56. Govt. College of Pharmacy, Satara
57. SN Institute of Pharmacy, Pisad, Dist.Yeotmal
58. Kamala Nehru College of Pharmacy, Aurangabad
59. Maharashtra college of Pharmacy, Nilanga, Latur Dist,
60. Nagpur College of Pharmacy, Nagpur
61. Dept. of Pharmaceutical Sciences, University of Nagpur, Nagpur
62. P.R. college of Pharmacy, Loni, Ahmednagar
63. PKMK College of Pharmacy, worli Sea Face, Mumbai
64. College of Pharmacy, Sholapur

Orissa

65. College of Pharmaceutical Sciences, Burhanpur
66. KM Institute of Pharmaceutical Sciences, Raurkela
67. Faculty of Panrmacy, Seemania Mahavidyalaya, Jharpokharia, Mayurbhanj
68. Sri Jaidev College of Pharmaceutical Sciences, Bhubaneswar

Punjab

There are 14 Schools of Pharmacy in Punjab all offering only teo-year diploma course.

Rajasthan

69. B.N. College of Pharmacy, Udaipur
70. Pharmacy Discipline, Birla Institute of Technology & Sciences, Pilani
71. Faculty of Pharmacy, LM College of Science and Technology, Jodhpur

Tamil Nadu

72. Institute of Pharmaceutical Technology, Annamali University, Annamalainagar

73. A.K.College of Phaemacy, Krihna Coil, Dist. Kamrasjar
74. CLBM College of Pharmacy, Jyotinagar, Chennai
75. Dr. Kartikeyan College of Pharmacy, Royapuram, Chennai
76. JKKN College f Pharmacy, Kamarajpalayam
77. JSS College of Pharmacy, Ooty
78. KM college of Pharmacy, Madurai
79. Pharmacy Dept., Madras Medical College, Chennai
80. Pharmacy Dept., Madurai Medical College, Madurai
81. Periar College of Pharmaceutical Sciences for Girls, Trichirrapalli
82. SB College of Pharmacy, Shivakashi
83. Ultra College of Pharmacy, Madural

Tripura

There only school offering two-year diploma course

Uttar Pradesh

84. Department of Pharmaceutics, BHU, Varanasi

West Bengal

85. Department of Pharmaceutical Technology, Jadavpur University, Kalikata

Index